RESTORING DEMOCRACY TO AMERICA

JOHN F. M. McDERMOTT

RESTORING DEMOCRACY TO AMERICA

How to Free Markets and Politics
from the
Corporate Culture of Business and Government

THE PENNSYLVANIA STATE UNIVERSITY PRESS
UNIVERSITY PARK, PENNSYLVANIA

Library of Congress Cataloging-in-Publication Data

McDermott, John F. M., 1932–
Restoring democracy to America : how to free markets and politics from the corporate culture of business and government / John F. M. McDermott.
    p. cm.
Includes bibliographical references and index.
Summary: "A narrative history of the gains in economic and political equality in the United States starting in the 1870s. Argues that many of these gains have been reversed since the 1960s, and proposes solutions for reversing this downward spiral"—Provided by publisher.
ISBN 978-0-271-03724-0 (cloth : alk. paper)
ISBN 978-0-271-03725-7 (pbk. : alk. paper)
    1. Business and politics—United States.
    2. Equality—United States.
    3. United States—Economic conditions—1945– .
    4. United States—Economic policy—2009– .
    I. Title.

JK467.M31 2010
320.51'30973—dc22
           2010021713

Copyright © 2010 The Pennsylvania State University
All rights reserved
Printed in the United States of America
Published by The Pennsylvania State University Press,
University Park, PA 16802–1003

The Pennsylvania State University Press is a member of the
Association of American University Presses.

It is the policy of The Pennsylvania State University Press to use acid-free paper. Publications on uncoated stock satisfy the minimum requirements of American National Standard for Information Sciences—Permanence of Paper for Printed Library Material, ANSI Z39.48–1992.

For the next generation

                                                       Alex Dembitzer

                                                      Amy Annette

                                          Eli McClintock-Shapiro

                                                  Emma Dwyer

                                                     Ian Kennedy

                                                       Jake Dwyer

                                      Leah McClintock-Shapiro

                                          Louisa Dembitzer

                                            Mac Chapwell

                                              Thea Rose

                                           Zak Annette

Contents

Preface: A Life of Thought in a Life of Politics ix
Acknowledgments xiii
Introduction 1

Part 1
THE HISTORIC ADVANCE, CA. 1870–1970

ONE The Historic Advance: Setting a Context 13
TWO Interpreting the "Sixties" 49
THREE The Modern Reaction 77

Part 2
RECAPPING AND BEYOND

FOUR Social Stratification and Social Dynamics 123
FIVE Institutional Elites and Social Action 151
SIX The Inner Government Within Liberal Democracy 185

Part 3
PROPOSALS FOR A RENEWED HISTORIC ADVANCE

SEVEN On Strategy and Organization 223
EIGHT The Reform of the Police Power 251
NINE Civilizing the Corporation 285
TEN A "Civilized" Employment System 319
ELEVEN International Government and International Chaos 357
TWELVE Political Reform 387

Notes 417
References 451
Index 467

Preface

A LIFE OF THOUGHT IN A LIFE OF POLITICS

I "got political" at roughly eleven o'clock in the morning on Friday, September 5, 1959. It had been arranged that I would teach mathematics at the Brooklyn campus of Long Island University, but the contract was delayed for several weeks while they determined how many sections they'd need. When it did finally arrive that Friday morning, it came with a twist: I was to swear that I was "not now nor ever have been a member of the Communist Party" and so on and so forth. To my own surprise I wouldn't sign such an outlandish thing. On the telephone the mathematics chairman was sympathetic but insistent. In short order I fired off a letter full of refusal, indignation, the Bill of Rights, J. S. Mill, and very likely, some mention of Kant and Spinoza.[1]

Feisty now, I applied for another mathematics job, though I learned that it too required a loyalty oath—at my alma mater, Brooklyn College. The hiring committee were very friendly, very enthusiastic, and offered me the job. Ashamed that I had led them on, I confessed I couldn't take their job because of the oath. Now their enthusiasm knew no bounds; I was to return in a few days to see their college president, and he would waive the requirement. I should have seen what was coming; that great man, Harry Gideonse, was a legendary foe of academic "reds" of every hue. The promised waiver was never mentioned. In filibuster mode he alternated coarse bullying with coarser bribes to get me to sign and when that failed, heave-hoed me out his office door.

As I literally staggered out into the hallway, it dawned on me that doing political sorts of things required joining forces with others. In the ensuing half-century I've done just that. I've been a campaign and primary worker, a "ward heeler"; an activist in organizations for peace, civil rights, and better living and working conditions; a political journalist; a war correspondent, sit-inner, and jailbird; a traveling agitator; a radio producer; a trade union official; a lobbyist at all levels of government; an author, editor, and publisher; an NGO director; and coming full circle, a scholar, an educator, and of all things, a professor emeritus. This book has a scholarly side, but it is equally shaped by that varied political experience.[2]

I grew up an Al Smith Democrat, but careerism had rendered me apolitical. I emerged from my encounter with the loyalty oath a liberal Democrat again. By the time of the Cuban Missile Crisis I was the state director of the New York chapter of Americans for Democratic Action and hobnobbed with people in and around the Kennedy administration. Two senators, Keating of New York and Smathers of Florida, were then leading the charge to have Cuba invaded and Castro overthrown.[3] That looked ominous, and it seemed clear, moreover, that support for such an adventure was growing dangerously. "Don't worry," soothed my Washington liberal colleagues, "JFK has the situation well in hand." Of course he didn't! The Russians read the omens as I did and reacted with their wretched scheme to put nuclear weapons into Cuba. We met their folly with our own; as we now know from the conferences and documents, the threat of those Russian missiles to the balance of power was equal to, or perhaps slightly less than, the threat to JFK's reelection chances.

I found the crisis a real eye-opener. It had been only too visibly coming; the administration at first temporized but then reacted by "going toe-to-toe with the Russkies," as the movie's grim humor put it. I came to see that the modern U.S. government, like so many others, acts too often in fundamentally irresponsible ways, takes too little account of the effects of its actions on the lives and well-being of others, and learns little if at all from its mistakes. These are faults in the system itself, not just errors on the part of "the great and the good." Add to that the duplicity and incompetence of the Bush II administration, the six-year slide into the Vietnam War (1955–61), the painfully slow recognition by the Establishment (1961–68) that we had no genuine interests at stake there, and then the prolongation of the war for five to seven more years (1968–1973 or 1975) to provide Kissinger "a decent interval." Add to that the tolerance of three administrations toward the pandemic of church-burning, kidnapping, and killing around the civil rights movement from the 1954 Supreme Court's school decision to the murders of Chaney, Goodman, and Schwerner in Mississippi in the summer of 1964. And add to that global warming and the burst credit bubble!

One can summarize the same facts but in more measured statement. During the span of my adult life, government has grown more shortsighted. It bases its policymaking on skewed calculations, fails to learn from its mistakes, and relies more and more heavily on the military abroad and police and market violence at home to force events to turn out as planned, with little or no career or other penalties for the authors. That at the least makes plausible the hypothesis that the contemporary U.S. political system, perhaps once marginally functional, has become even less able to cope with the problems that now beset us.

Having said that, I should add that I don't find politics all that easy to fathom. My first published piece, "Does the Goldwater Movement Have a Future?" (1965), managed to get it entirely wrong. I was very sure it didn't. I coined the term "crisis managers" (1967) to convey scorn about the national security elite, but the expression is now used to praise them. My "Technology: The Opiate of the Intellectuals" (1969) was much celebrated and remains in print. But from the beginning I understood it as if a narrow headlight on a dark road, good enough for what it revealed but giving no hint of what lay to the left or right, or even just beyond the beam. Too much of my other writing back then was of that same, limited character—forays and interventions but with insufficient depth or breadth of understanding.

In the mid-1970s I took that lesson to heart and switched priorities from activism (and journalism) to a sustained effort to study and think about modern politics, economy, and society and of how and to what ends they could be changed. Two earlier books of mine—*Corporate Society: Class, Property, and Contemporary Capitalism,* an analysis of the form of society specific to the corporate era, and *Economics in Real Time: A Theoretical Reconstruction,* a theoretical analysis of economic relationships in a corporatized world—helped to establish the intellectual foundations for the present effort.

My earlier work suffers from an excess of windy moralizing, which I have tried to rein in. In this book I point out the dysfunctional behavior of present institutions and propose how the institutions should be repaired or replaced. I am more knowledgeable than most about how difficult it is to bring about social and institutional reform, but at the same time I also have considerable experience of how political things happen and can be made to happen. Accordingly, the proposals are plausibly apt for our time, could eventually be adopted, and would be likely to effect the changes desired. It would be folly to claim that I've entirely succeeded in those aims, but the discussion will, I hope, press the discussion onward.

Acknowledgments

I am so much aware of the debt I owe to the many friends, colleagues, comrades, and even some quite casual acquaintances who, over a half century, have made a key contribution that found its way into this book. Sometimes it was a thought, or a line of argument, perhaps just a citation, or even a skeptical or counter response. I have tried to include all of their names. Many have since died, which is of course even more reason to call them to mind here. They include A. J. Muste, Andy Kopkind, Bill Passanante, Bob Browne, Bob Engler, Chuck Schwartz, David Baumgardt, David Houston, Eddie Kaye, Francis Mark, Hope Shapiro, Howard Zinn, I. F. Stone, Irving Shapiro, Jack Westoby, Joe Thomas, Ken Bridenthal, Lee Baxandall, Len DeCaux, Manny Granich, Margaret Nelson, Mary Kennedy, Megan McClintock, Mike Harrington, Peggy Duff, Peter Henig, Renate Staude, Roy Bennnett, Seymour Melman, Stanley Millet, Steve Nelson, Tiziano Terzani, Tom Stirton, and Willard Hutcheon.

These pages began with those 1959 loyalty oaths. I was then married to the late Kaye Gallagher McDermott. Kaye had no tolerance at all for McCarthyism; the decision to refuse the loyalty oaths was ours, not mine alone. Her courage, support, and good cheer as we faced a future that we knew we didn't understand are as green in my mind now as they were a half century ago.

And I also wish to thank those many still contributing to "the Democracy" and resisting its dismantling in word and deed: Abbie Record, Al Haber, Amy Kesselman, Andrea Peterson, Anthony Econom, Barbara Kessel, Bernard Rose, Beverly Thaver, Bezhad Yaghmaian, Bob Ross, Bob Wolfe, Carol Brightman, Carole Silver, Chris Gunn, Clair Chapwell, David Fasenfast, David Gullette, Dick Flacks, Don Goldstein, Don Gonson, Don Leka, Edward Greer, Ellen Rosen, Ellie MacGregor, Florence Howe, Frank Thompson, Gary Mongiovi, Geraldine Chapwell, Gil Skillman, Harry Lustig, Hazel Gunn, Heidi Gottfried, Holly Maguigan, Howard Turner, Hugh West, Jacques Bude, Jacques Wilmore, Jesse Lemisch, Jim O'Brien, John

Annette, Josephine Turner, Judy Coburn, Julie Shapiro, Katherine Stone, Lennie Gooding, Leonard Liggio, Linda Ditmar, Linda Friedman, Lionel Thaver, Margaret Gullette, Marion Ross, Matt Drennan, Michael Keaney, Michael Meeropol, Mike Brown, Myra Jehlen, Nicola Murray, Norman Levy, Paddy Quick, Peppe Viera, Raymond Gregory, Richard Rothstein, Rick Soto, Robb Burlage, Roberta Salper, Ros Baxandall, Ruby Jackson, Ruth Sherref, Saul Slapikoff, Seweryn Bialer, "Simp" Simpson, Stan Israel, Steve Bronner, Steve Max, Susie Peerce, "Terry Smith," Thelma Shorter, Tony Leiman, Uwe Bergman, Walter Goldstein, Warren Friedman, and Winston Langley.

I want also to thank Sanford Thatcher and his colleagues at Penn State Press for their many efforts and substantive contributions and, not less, the staffs of my main "research institution," the public libraries of Brookline, Cambridge, Newton, and Wellfleet, Massachusetts.

And for helping me so much and in so many ways, I thank my wife, Frances "Frinde" Maher.

John F. M. McDermott
Boston, April 2010

INTRODUCTION

Argument and Outline

Government can no longer govern. It must instead negotiate—on their terms—with the private banks, corporations, and industry associations.[1] This is not just about naked power. We now accept *co-sovereignty* as a proper right of private sector institutions. It is this which freezes a worsening divide between rich and poor; ever greater and longer unemployment; inadequate public investment in education, research, and infrastructure; harmful environmental practices; recurring speculative bubbles; destructive trade deficits; a bloated national security apparatus now turned inward; a too costly yet underperforming health system; and elections now further skewed to corporate influence by grace of the Supreme Court.

Of course, from their inception 130-odd years ago, the larger private firms have always challenged government's power to govern. But with the continuing growth in the size and economic importance of the larger private sector firms, the demise of the Progressive impulse, and the defeat of the reforming movements of the 1960s, their claim to at least *shared* sovereignty with government has won through.

This book analyzes that defeat and the consequent explosion of private sector power. It then probes our wider institutional arrangements to better understand the processes that have created this present. Most important of all, it offers proposals in six major areas that, together, are calculated to restore Constitutional supremacy and, with it, popular sovereignty both for the short term and in the future.

The study reflects over a third of a century of my thinking about politics. What has become manifest with time is that our political dysfunctions are not really traceable to "the usual suspects," such as too much money in politics or the religious Right, but to a "negotiation between government and a very few very large institutions." Avenues for sustained popular political action are few and weak. We still see this disjuncture between institutional perceptions of reality and the actual situation of the governed in the Obama administration's early response to the economic crisis. The distress of large numbers of our people is viewed as secondary, something to be dealt with more or less in passing, once the "more important" distress of a small number of institutions has been fixed.

This administration may ultimately respond better to popular need than its predecessor, but to date it remains within a universe in which the institutionalized entrepreneur or investor is the key player. In this universe economic recovery equals the recovery of these investor institutions. For all its twists and turns, this administration's strategy has been to transfer wealth directly to financial institutions in order to restore their fortunes more or less to what they were before the crisis of 2008.[2]

Well-founded estimates of the restoration range from $2 to $11 trillion, which is to say, to between one-seventh and four-fifths of the value of the entire GDP! It is a staggering transfer of wealth to a tiny fraction of our population when the net benefit to the public is uncertain even in the very long term.

It seems plausible that a smaller shift of wealth, by transfers to threatened and foreclosed homeowners, to laid-off workers with little or no present income, to threatened small business owners, and to students being forced out of school, would more immediately check the recession, lessen the hurt it presently inflicts, limit the number of further victims, and even more quickly restore the health of the financial sector. But that way of looking at things is alien to a world limited to institutional players.

Interestingly enough, the economics fraternity, both policy and academic, appears to have exchanged its belief in a "market" economy, not for "socialism," as some have witlessly claimed, but for an economics of investor primacy. The "market" is an interactive conception with many, many players, none more important than the others. Investor primacy is a purely linear conception; everything starts and then remains dependent on investor behavior. If those investors are few, as they are, investor primacy equals investor oligarchy. Naturally, economics orthodoxy holds that these big investment firms are creatures of and in the "market." This sustains their fantasy that the investment function in a modern economy has not been centralized in a few mega-institutions, even though they also—in a separate mental compartment—consider these institutions "too big to fail." But in a crisis one may be forced by events to disregard the purely cosmetic side of one's ideas and act on their operative dimensions. Thus the president's erstwhile devotees of the "free market"—such as Lawrence Summers, Paul Volcker, Ben Bernanke, and Timothy Geithner, like Bush's Henry Paulson—now act on that linear conception of investor primacy, which means investor oligarchy.

The Historic Advance

If the political system is blind to the mounting problems of our people and thus less capable of addressing them, then the path to repair demands more than a handful of reforms. It calls for the renewal of "the historic advance," whose blockage four decades ago signaled the ability of the institutional players to stave off the democratic polity. This conception of a "historic advance" is the essential counterpoint to the decline of the political process.

It refers to the cumulative changes in the situation of the urban laboring populations of Western Europe, North America, and later, Japan over the century ending in the 1970s. Circa 1870, urban laborers were typically only a minority of the population. They lived at the margins of subsistence and society, suffered high rates of illiteracy and disease, had only a minimal participation in the national polities, if any, and were largely viewed as foreigners by their own societies. One hundred years later that had changed. The urban laboring population had become a numerical majority, and their living standards had leapt upward, not least due to the expansion of schools, social insurance, and the rest of the modern welfare state. Illiteracy and epidemic diseases had been seemingly erased forever; the "lower" orders had gained an influential place in an increasingly democratic political process and participated more or less as equals in the cultural realm.

After the defeat of the tumultuous Sixties, this trend was reversed. Politics went from liberal to illiberal, from relatively open to firmly closed. Unemployment rose, upper income rose sharply, middle income stagnated, and lower income fell. Attacks on the welfare state and on its funding became both common and effective. Among the very poor, tuberculosis and venereal diseases made a comeback-by-neglect. The distribution of good health, like that of housing, education, and cultural opportunity, also tilted against middle- and especially lower-income groups. Unions came under sharp attack, and their weakening further undercut the role of the urban laboring population in the polity. Internationally, détente gave way to an even bigger arms race, arms exports rose dramatically, and the cold war was expanded in Africa and Latin America, to be succeeded in time by an endless "war on terror."

The historic advance is analyzed as a vector sum, on the one hand, of cumulative, popular, democratic demands and mobilizations that culminated in the mass, multiclass movements of the Sixties and, on the other, of the emergence of modern corporate forms, first of business organization, later of political and cultural institutions, which demanded and achieved a higher-quality labor force. The entry of the lower-class laboring populations, previously excluded and now wanted, into their national societies on an equitable basis took the form of a multiclass social, political, economic, and even cultural agent, here called by its nineteenth-century name, the Democracy.[3]

But within the improving situation of the urban laboring strata, a new social class was also born and rapidly developed. For the moment and as a first approximation, we can refer to the urban laborers as "the workers" and this new "middle" class as "the cadre." The latter was created and especially nurtured within the developing corporative institutions, becoming in time a relatively privileged class inclined to desert the advance, bring it to a close, and roll back some of its gains.[4]

To Follow

Part 1 of the book characterizes the advance itself, the emergence and maturation of "corporate society," and its novel social structure and social players. One cannot view the advance and subsequent halt in mechanical, historicist terms. The Democracy was an ensemble of morally related, mass, multiclass social movements acting over historic time in socially conflicted situations culminating in the Sixties. Then, from roughly 1958 to 1970, across the whole of the developed world, it attempted to continue the historic advance beyond limits imposed by its corporate partners in the historic vector. These movements for modernization were defeated, thus ushering in a period of reaction that continues to the present. The burden of Part 1 is to clarify this interpretation of late twentieth-century history and to show how it is plausibly rooted in the evidence.

Part 2 analyzes the corporation-shaped, or "Intersection," society created by and within the historic advance, that is, by an emerging collaboration among corporations, government, and the educational system. It contains a new sort of middle class, the cadre, whose advantages and privileges flow from its central productive role within corporate and corporately organized institutions.

Reflecting their work, corporate society is a "fabricated" society in which "spontaneous," or "natural," or "traditional" social forms such as the family, dynasty, individual property, and even patriarchy have been subordinated and then transformed. For the most part, "society" is now directly fabricated in the coordinate division of labor and hierarchy that first emerged within the modern corporation in the years between the two world wars—elite, cadre, and worker. That division of labor and its functional hierarchy have since spread to the other two cooperating institutions of the Intersection, namely, government and those cultural institutions that are capped by the modern university system. The leitmotif of "spontaneous and natural" society versus "fabricated" society will be qualified and modified as our analysis proceeds, but the contrast cannot and should not be entirely eliminated, as we will see.

Corporate or Intersection society features a distinct kind of social ordering, called "life courses," and these differ from the familiar classes. Weberian and Marxian classes are social forms that arise within networks of market relations and merely influence, no more, the identities and social action of individuals and groups. Life courses or courses develop within formal organizations as their constitutive elements. Like classes and other predecessor social orders, they are hierarchically structured but in and over time. A "course" is not primarily a term of static social classification: it connotes substantive, determinate change over time both for social ensembles and for individuals.

Social, economic, and even political advantages and privileges tend to be widely distributed to all of the life courses. Corporate or Intersection society is the child of the democratic impulses that fueled the historic advance. But, as befits a society organized around formally organized institutions, power-political initiatives tend to be centralized within the highest life courses, mainly among the strategic elites of the leading institutions.

Thus the paradox: corporate society is at once more egalitarian and democratic than its predecessor society, but its elites also have a greater capacity to induce or block social change potentially hostile to their institutions.

It is this last that undergirds the political problematic revealed in the defeat of the Sixties. Liberal, parliamentary democratic political forms are poorly suited to govern the relations among the highly centralized institutions such as inhabit the Intersection. We know from business history that the corporate form of organization was designed to minimize external influences on its behavior. Its strategic elites enjoy administrative and financial controls that enable them to guide and even to fine-tune the behavior of their organizations: the blunting of external influences is a corollary.

One outcome of growing corporate autonomy has been the decline of the influence of the democratic electorate over the private corporation and over the executive departments of government, which have, not incidentally, aped corporate forms of internal organization. In fact, as I'll show in chapter 6, the more democratic the political system, in the familiar meaning of the word, the less able it is to govern the institutions of the Intersection.

It is necessary to emphasize that no conspiracy theory of "elites against the democracy" is called for, such as dogged kindred theories of institutional modernization such as C. Wright Mills's *The Power Elite* (1956). A major undertaking of Part 2 is to propose a theory of elite institutional action that is empirically grounded within the specific nature of contemporary society. The analysis traces the outcomes of social transactions among persons and groups of equal and unequal power. The possession or de facto exercise of socially potent *institutional* assets is a key factor determining outcomes within corporate society.

Elite "subsocieties" are shown to emerge around the possession of various kinds of socially potent assets. In the logic of this analysis one does not assume that the antecedent recognition of joint *interests* gives rise to these subsocieties, that is, first the joint interest, then the subsociety as, say, cause to effect. A priori methods, such as employed in some contemporary sociological and economic studies, have been excluded as far as possible.

The analysis proceeds on the basis that in conflicts between individuals exercising assets of differing social potency, the resolution of the conflicts will tend to reflect that inequality. Very crudely, people with more power can impose greater costs in the resolution itself on those possessing less power. And where persons with assets of similar social potency come into conflict, there will be *at least some occasions* in which a mutual accommodation is reached, as perhaps in something so prosaic as a merchants' association. Subsocieties of elite persons emerge as the "precipitate" of actual and possible conflicts among themselves, which come to be seen to have zero-sum outcomes and where resolution costs can be imposed on other, weaker third parties. It is out of that analytical matrix, both its straightforward logic and its conformity to what we experience in social conflicts, that I construct the larger social theory of Part 2.

One can readily understand that in a society in which large, formal organizations play so great a part, the possession of or the exercise of institutional assets will have particularly strong effect. It is this effect that plays so great a part in the analysis of corporate or Intersection society and that serves to confirm the historical material of part 1.

Part 3 proposes a set of reforms that would, if successfully implemented, renew the historic advance. Because so much of what happens in modern society occurs between and within institutions, the major obstacle to be overcome is not mounting intended reforms but sustaining them to eventual adoption and fruition. Progressive reform faces a terrain notably more hostile today than it did in the past. The "semifabricated" society tends to erase elements alien to itself.

Accordingly, desired reforms must reinforce each other to ensure that none is defeated in isolation. Their mutually supportive advance must have sufficient weight, width, and depth to achieve potentially decisive results. Part 3 develops this idea in six areas, as follows.

First, there is need for an oppositional political organization that can sustain a renewed advance, not over a single campaign or even a generation but over an epoch. The organization proposed in chapter 7 is designed with that ambitious program in mind.

Our historical experience of the twentieth century warns us of the potent and toxic political role of the police power, that is, the so-called law enforcement community of police, courts, prosecutors, and prison officials. I make a number of proposals in chapter 8 to change the police themselves into an ally and not a foe of further social and other democratization.

The forces of late nineteenth-century progressivism and social democracy tried and were ultimately checked in their efforts to subordinate the emerging corporations to society's purposes. Our task today is more daunting, since they have over time perfected their own and supporting levers of power. Chapter 9 takes up this effort on a new basis that takes conscious account of the unsuccessful attempts of the past.

Fourth, if the Democracy was the popular agent of the historic advance, the urban laboring population was its single most powerful player. That population has today been politically demobilized. A historic achievement, though not, I think, intent, of the welfare state has been to undermine the societies and traditional cultures of the urban laboring population and thus alter its capacity for autonomous political activity. The problem is difficult to address, and addressing it is only hindered by explanations that invoke "consumerism," "the media," or any other sort of bread and circus. Chapter 10 does not take up the deeper problem of reviving an autonomous political culture in the urban laboring population, but it does address a necessary condition for such a renaissance, namely, the creation of effective institutional forms of lower-class economic and political resistance that go beyond traditional trade unionism.

There is already an international governing structure that imposes its economic design on most of the countries of the world but avoids taking responsibility for the political and social effects of that "globalization." There is also an emerging international middle class, advantaged by "globalization," which accordingly gives it a potent political "constituency." The burden of chapter 11 is to take the measure of these present political realities.

Sixth, if the reforms proposed in chapters 7–11 can be achieved, they will go a long way toward correcting our current political dysfunctions. In chapter 12, I argue that the modern state form, including that established by the U.S. Constitution, is undermined by the international state system, which emerged out of the Treaty of Westphalia and which has survived more or less intact over the ensuing three-and-a-half centuries. Now, because of the overwhelming, unrivaled power of the United States itself and of its democratic allies, there is a window of opportunity to begin to dismantle that state system and to sow the seeds of a less brutal, more consensual international political system. Proposals are offered to that end.

Our present intellectual and moral situation resembles the one our forebears faced a century and a quarter ago. It was already clear then that the world created by the Congress of Vienna, and later reimposed with such vengeance by the failures of the revolutions of 1848, was dying. It was not clear at all what was to come, but the women and men of that time managed to create a powerful and enduring political culture of change and reform, exerting just enough foresight and force to achieve over time a historic advance in the well-being of the average Western European and American. Then as now, no one could read the future, but the actual situation was then and now is such that no socially conscious person can refuse to act with whatever intelligence, foresight, and learning he or she can muster. The value of what follows in this book lies not, ultimately, in its truth or falsity, but in what it can contribute to our learning about what we should do tomorrow and the next day and the next after that to create a better universal society.

PART 1

THE HISTORIC ADVANCE, CA. 1870–1970

1

THE HISTORIC ADVANCE

Setting a Context

Beginning roughly around 1870, there was a leap forward in the conditions of the urban laboring classes in North America, Western Europe, and Japan. That "historic advance" terminated around 1970, and a distinct reaction set in that endures today. The advance itself was both the result of the efforts of the lower classes and their allies and the product of an evolving capitalism. What eventuated was a new *kind* or *species* of society and dynamic social structure. In the United States that society developed and matured across the years 1870–1970. After 1945, the Western European countries and Japan shed the "Bismarckian" restraints on their development and by around 1960 had caught up to the "Americanist" pattern.[1]

In 1870, urban workers and their families were a small minority of the national populations save only in Great Britain. But there too they had at best subsistence incomes and were crowded into slums or isolated mining districts. They had inadequate diets and were mostly without medical services, which made them vulnerable to periodic epidemics of smallpox, cholera, typhus, diphtheria, and tuberculosis. They were barely literate and, in general, neglected by their societies save for, perhaps, some churches and, only gradually, the primary school. They worked under harsh master-servant legal codes, were subject to corporal punishment at work, could be fired without notice, and were forbidden unions. There was little or no provision for the unemployed, the injured or handicapped, or the elderly. Universal suffrage was a thing of the future. Because of electoral intimidation of immigrants, this was also true in the United States.

Workers almost everywhere were viewed as "the dangerous classes," to be controlled by the police baton and the cavalry saber.[2]

Roughly a century later that had changed. Urban dwellers had vastly increased in number. Their wages were typically well above mere subsistence, and their housing reflected that. Medical and educational services were increasingly available. Their children were longer fated to follow their parent's footsteps, and there were legislative protections for lower-class health and dental needs. The employment relationships had changed from master-servant to employer-employee, which is less unequal and offers the worker some protection against arbitrary firing and workplace intimidation. For men, if not yet for women, physical harassment, even coercion at work, had largely ceased.[3] They had gained the vote and were beginning to play a major role in politics through their unions and political parties. In sum, the urban laboring classes were finally being admitted into the national society, polity, and culture. They weren't quite yet considered full equals, but at least they were no longer excluded as dangerous foreign elements.

These changes had not come all at once. Often important gains were followed by disastrous losses; the pace of change was uneven, its locus spotty. But this era saw a steady improvement in virtually every aspect of the lives of these city dwellers across Western Europe, North America, and Japan—an improvement that definitely was under way by 1870, and grinding to a halt by 1970.

We should read the advance as a vector sum of two, often opposed, sometimes cooperating historical developments. One was the effort of urban dwellers and their allies to win what they thought was their rightful place in their societies. The other was provided by that extraordinary institution, the modern diversified business corporation. Before turning to the role of modern corporate business, we should briefly look at the popular side of the advance.

Evolution of the Democracy

The historic advance began with the birth of the social-democratic movement in the last decades of the nineteenth century and ended when it faltered in the last decades of the twentieth.[4] But social democracy was not created ex nihilo in 1870, nor did it die in 1970. It is embedded in a more elusive, longer-lived social phenomenon, the "Democracy." The term is an old one but still useful. It comprises not only those laboring men and women who have struggled for political and trade union rights but also their many allies drawn from the middle, upper, and intellectual classes. The use of the term is justified, I think, by the intellectual and organizational continuity of democratic, populist, socialist, and other broadly humanist and secular ideas and values, including feminism, among identifiable groups of persons since the American and French revolutions. My argument is that the Democracy was not simply the intellectual heir of a literary tradition but its still-living, adaptive, social embodiment across time.

Minimally, we should entertain the hypothesis that from the eighteenth century to the present we can identify an intellectual and political tradition, maintained throughout the period by identifiable groups and organizations of men and women. It was this, I argue, which took the empirical form of the social-democratic moment during the period of the advance.

The Democracy has always been revolutionary in its inspiration and multiclass in its social material reality. But its multiclass dynamism has always depended on the lower, often lowest classes, who have provided both its moral impetus and its "big battalions."

To say that the Democracy is revolutionary is not to say that it is *necessarily* insurrectionist, though in Europe especially, insurrections in 1789, 1848, 1871, and 1943–45 were and are an integral, inspirational, and still-formative part of its history. Rather, its revolutionary character comes from its quest for social arrangements free of what it sees as the demonstrable wickedness of the past and the present. In *To the Finland Station*, Edmund Wilson expressed this particularly well; he credited to Giambattista Vico (1668–1744) the intrinsically revolutionary idea that society is a human creation, that *we* create social arrangements and can therefore reshape them when and to at least some degree how *we* choose. In this view, existing social arrangements do not reflect the wisdom of the past, as with Edmund Burke and his epigones, but mostly its irrationalities and injustices.

The revolutionary character of the Democracy is also underlined by its perennial tinge of Babeuvism. The influence of Gracchus Babeuf (1760–97) is, unfortunately, too little known in wider circles. Babeuf, not Marx, defined *the* uniquely modern conception of the relationship of wealth to poverty.[5] Aristotle had left a tradition in political thought that the division between rich and poor is "natural" to every society; it cannot be avoided, but has to be prevented from growing too extreme. The impetus to the

Democracy's social thought is not Rousseau's passive "Man is born free but is everywhere in chains," but Babeuf's revolutionary intervention that the rich are rich *because* the poor are poor.

Babeuvism also lives on in a third element of the revolutionary tradition of the Democracy—the *spectacle*, particularly the spectacle of the French Revolution. Increasingly reactionary as his political views emerged, Nietzsche was right to see that the historical imagery of a spontaneous mass revolt against "unbearable conditions" forced upon "the people" by "the rich and the powerful" remained extremely potent, intrinsically "popular," seemingly ineradicable, and possibly repeatable.

Nietzsche was reacting particularly to the revolutions of 1848, which he saw as the children of 1789. Despite over a half century of thoroughgoing repression of republican forces, especially, but not only, in France, when revolution erupted again in Paris, political ideas, groups, and even personalities that looked to *the* Revolution were at its center. Despite the efforts of the Directorate, Napoleon, the restored Bourbons, and then the Orleanists, the memory of the "Great Revolution" remained a potent political force in the popular consciousness. There were cognate links between "1848" and the Paris Commune, which Nietzsche also condemned, and it remained an animating force in the French Resistance of 1942–45 and on into 1968 as well.

The history of the Democracy in other countries is different, but, I would argue, not fundamentally so. In the United States, for example, there is some striking continuity in views among the Sons of Liberty, the Antifederalists, Shays's rebels, the antebellum Workingmen's and Locofoco parties, the post–Civil War Populists, the IWW, the early CIO, and the movements of the 1960s.

Like the Democracy's Vico-ism and Babeuvism, lively, widespread memories and images of popular revolution live on. Though often faint, they have emerged often enough and powerfully enough to rank them as elements of a modern, still-lively folk tradition.

Throughout its history men and women from many classes have played central roles in the Democracy. Among them are not only popular leaders like Robespierre, or Blanqui, or Debs, but others, like Jane Addams and those others who animated the Settlement House movement, and Helen Keller and Margaret Sanger, who devoted their lives to improving the lives of those whom the existing society ignored. We should also include among its ranks playwrights like Beaumarchais, Schiller, and Büchner and composers like Kurt Weill and Leonard Bernstein, who fused popular and democratic musical traditions with those of the classical composers. Much of the impetus for the development of modern social science, as with Lester Ward in this country, and even of science itself, as with Einstein, came from intellectuals who saw themselves as undermining social superstition and strengthening Enlightenment values.

By and large it is hard to find any modern movement for social amelioration that does not ground its legitimacy in this particular, activist tradition of the Enlightenment. In that sense at least, the historic advance can be viewed as "of a piece."

I do not mean to imply or even to insinuate that the Democracy and the social good are one and the same thing. As many will readily point out, the communism of the Third (Leninist/Stalinist) International was also born within the ranks of the Democracy, as was the anarchist "politics of the deed." Nevertheless, most of the liberating social changes that modern people enjoy and celebrate have been the projects at some point in time of some part of the Democracy—and opposed by its opponents.

The Nature of the Democracy?

The Democracy is not a "social movement" or a "political movement," and it doesn't correspond to what we conventionally mean by a "culture." The Democracy has contained within its historic ranks persons and ideas that contradict each other, sometimes in open conflict. Thus the difficulty of giving a definition that includes this and excludes that to the end of giving an unambiguous meaning to the term. "Culture" could be used since the word allows some leeway as to what is part of a given culture and what is not.

Unfortunately, in present usage the term "culture" has a museum quality about it, as in, say, "Black Culture" or even "the culture of poverty," where it refers to some past content, often idealized, enduring more or less intact and integral into the present and the future, desirably or not as the case may be. But if the Democracy is a culture, it is an adaptive one—which takes us back to square one. To say that something is adaptive is to say that it changes, possibly into something that is barely if at all recognizable as being the same thing as we move our gaze across time.

It is actually closer to what military commanders call an "axis of advance," that is, not a list of points to be attacked, but a set of broad movements that will achieve a desired strategic result. Hardly ideal, the term "axis of advance" will serve until a better one comes along.

Of course no single commander commands the Democracy, but many have served in it in leadership roles. The famous scene in Schiller's play *Don Carlos*, for example, in which Posa demands freedom of thought from the tyrannical King Philip II of Spain, has been an inspiration to modern movements dedicated to that very thing.[6] There is thus a palpable sense in which both Schiller and, say, Human Rights Watch can be placed within the Democracy. In fact, inspiration and emulation are frequently the glue that holds the Democracy together, not common views. Our civil rights demonstrators were inspired by Lexington and Concord, and the Soweto rising was inspired by the civil rights movement. In a very real sense the Democracy is an actual company of men and women of different classes and cultures who across time and in diverse ways have taught and inspired one another to further some aspect, however modified, of human liberation that first germinated in the visions of Vico and Babeuf.

A third identifying characteristic of the Democracy is that it includes the historic effort of the lower orders of European and North American society to improve their own situation. Solely for convenience of expression, I will refer to these lower orders as "workers," but with three caveats. First, the term "worker" usually connotes "male worker." This is a legacy of the obsolete ideology of the Third International. It lives on in our language about these matters and elides the role of women and whole families in the history of "the workers." Indeed, the assault on the Bastille was begun by Parisian women. The Knights of Labor, briefly at the center of U.S. labor history, had two kinds of local affiliates, called "lodges," workplace lodges and community lodges, and it was the latter that often took the lead.

Second, we also tend to view the evolution of worker consciousness as a product of workplace (thus generally male) experience and solidarity. David Montgomery's *Fall of the House of Labor* (1987), though otherwise gender nuanced, is one expression of this tendency. But even as women were being expelled from the paid labor force elsewhere, their role, as in the famous "Bread and Roses" strike in Lawrence, Massachusetts, in 1912 and in the textile and electrical industries, remained central. Old-time labor activists often cite family gardens, typically maintained by women and little heralded in the history books, as central to the fabric of lower-class resistance.

And third, Leninist ideology echoes still in the idea that workers depend upon a revolutionary intelligentsia for leadership. In fact, workers have long demonstrated not just job consciousness but a wider, flexible political and cultural consciousness. We see this in the annals of the revolutionary clubs in Paris during the Great Revolution—and almost a century later among the participants in the U.S. eight-hour movement, where a new kind of worker demanded that work be limited to eight hours, leaving eight hours for sleep and eight hours for education and self-improvement. Later we see a popular quest for self-improvement by self-education in the popularity of the Little Blue Books, cheap editions of the classics offered to a working-class readership.[7]

As far as I can discover, the very first tract championing the workers' right to leisure was written for a working-class readership, not a revolutionary cadre. This was Paul Lafargue's 1907 *Le Droit à la paresse* (*The Right to Be Lazy*). His argument is drawn from the Greek and Roman classics—a beast is fit only for labor, but to be human requires the leisure to pursue self-education and other forms of self-improvement. The "new theater" of Ibsen and Chekhov and, more surely, that of George Bernard Shaw also participated in this cultural project of universal liberation.[8]

Edward Thompson's *Making of the English Working Class* showed the influence of, especially, lower-class religious culture in the emergence of a distinct English *working* class with identifiable continuity to the (then) present. His stress on working-class culture was found liberating by younger historians in the United States, especially in contrast to the then dominant sociology of Talcott Parsons and the aridity of Marxism. But Thompson's "culture" is adaptive; that's the point of his argument, and in this quite unlike the "museum" conception of culture. At least then in his sense, the Democracy can be called a culture, a living, adaptive culture spanning multiple generations, interacting across many social, ethnic, and ideological borders.

Everyone's Exceptionalism

A social-democratic template seems apt if we restrict our gaze to Western Europe and, possibly, Japan. However, it seems a poor fit for explaining developments in the United States. From the time of Werner Sombart's

Why Is There No Socialism in America? (originally published in 1906), historians have declared that the U.S. experience departs from the social-democratic template. The United States has had no mass socialist party since prior to World War I, and even then it was never a threat to either of the two major political parties. Moreover, unlike France, Germany, and Italy, the United States has never had a mass communist party or a major Marxist influence in trade union circles. In this same vein, it is argued that U.S. workers lack "class consciousness" or at least the sort of class consciousness that characterizes workers in Britain and on the Continent.

There is also the well-known argument that since the United States never experienced feudalism (Harz 1955), there are affective republican bonds, lacking even in France, that bind U.S. workers with the other classes. It is gospel too that U.S. workers have realistically expected that they—or more likely their children—will rise to the privileges and advantages of the middle classes. Further arguments tumble out in support of this "exceptionalism." U.S. wages have traditionally been higher than those of their foreign counterparts. And, of course, there is the famous Turner thesis, which locates the source of this exceptionalism in the effects of the frontier.[9]

However widely held, the Turner thesis is remarkably fragile. The frontier closed more or less as the then U.S. Socialist Party was still approaching the peak of its influence. More, those hyphenated Americans who increasingly populated the post-1870 U.S. working class did not go to the frontier but to Fall River, New York, Philadelphia, Pittsburgh, Detroit, and Chicago, to cities where manufacture was burgeoning. Mining and logging in the West did draw migrants from the east, but the politics of the Western Federation of Miners and its offspring, the Industrial Workers of the World, was typically far to the left even of the European immigrants who replaced them back east. Turner simply doesn't hold.[10]

It should also be observed that the "socialisms" of the United Kingdom and of the Continent are really two different things. The Continental variety has had a distinctly Marxist tinge, the British version hardly any, its roots reaching back to traditional British reformism via the Fabian Society, and to the union chapels (locals), whose name betrays their religious foundations (Thompson 1966). The socialists of France and those of Germany also differed, the former ranging from stolidly republican to enthusiastically insurrectionist, the Germans more measured in their programs. And neither tried to transition from reform to revolution like the Marxists of Vienna (Sassoon 1996). If therefore the Italian communism of the

Romagna resembles the "sewer socialism" of Wisconsin, it seems fair to conclude that there are many, many "exceptional" varieties of worker ideology, the American no more so than that of the others. On this score, I find two further arguments persuasive.

Seymour Lipset's *Political Man* (1960) is now badly out of date, but the voting data he provides for the later years of the advance (in part 2 of *Political Man*) suggest a much closer correspondence between the political behavior of working-class Americans and Europeans than the "exceptionalism" thesis appears to allow. When we switch our view from ideology per se to workaday political projects, the differences between the Americans and the British, much less between the Americans and the French, seem almost to disappear. André Gorz argues this very point in *Farewell to the Working Class* (1982) when discussing the ostensibly revolutionary French Communist Party. On weekdays, so to speak, French communists pursued only a mild, quite cautious program of incremental welfare state reform; they reserved calls for bloody, hair-raising "proletarian revolution" for their Sunday sermons.[11] That was also the pattern for both the "evolutionist" British Labour Party and the "revolutionary" Communist Party of Italy; they called for the ultimate socialist future "on Sunday," and strove cautiously for welfare state reforms the rest of the week.

"Exceptionalist" writers tend to dwell on the demand for nationalization of industry on the part of overseas workers and socialist parties. But where nationalization did occur, as in prewar France and postwar Britain, there was typically not much socialism to it, that is, little or no increase in workplace democracy or worker decision making, no end to alienated labor, and little or no economic planning based on humanist priorities. In British coal mining and in steel, the industries were technologically backward and poorly managed. Nationalization was designed exclusively to inject new capital and livelier management. This priority is likely to be replicated in the current U.S. government "seminationalization" of the banking, automobile, and insurance industries. In France, Leon Blum's nationalization of the armaments industry was intended primarily to speed up the pace of rearmament against Hitler.[12] But the actual behavior of the U.S. New Deal government of the 1930s easily equaled, I think surpassed, the socialism of most Western socialist governments before and since. The National Recovery Act of the early New Deal legislated a quite planned economy; and even more socialist, the Tennessee Valley Authority planned and carried out the integral development of a multistate region. But these peaks of 1930s socialism were not worker inspired; they represented a conception of conservative planning put forward, like the later European coal and steel community, by technocrats, not workers. In short, considering the range and variety of socialisms in the countries we've discussed here, each was different, each to that extent exceptional, and the U.S. case hardly stands out from the others.

One last observation can be made here, and it does point to a U.S. "exceptionalism," though not with its traditional import. Beginning in the 1870s, the United States moved to a more advanced industrial stage in which middle-class managers, not skilled workers, provided a novel technological and managerial basis for its industry. This did substantially change the dynamics of the U.S. working class from the overseas variety.

David Montgomery (1987) shows that American socialism was a political expression of, mostly, skilled workers. These were workers who had actually managed the work of production before the corporate era, guiding it both through their own technical skills and by directing the work of their apprentices and unskilled laborers. Workers' self-management was the norm for them.

For example, during the famous "lockout" and ensuing strike of 1892, the Homestead, Pennsylvania, plant of Carnegie Steel was among the largest and most modern in the world. As was the custom in those days, it was managed by its workers and not, at least in the modern sense, by its managers. The roughly 3,800 workers at the Homestead plant were supervised by its 800 skilled workers. Carnegie paid the Amalgamated Association of Iron and Steel Workers as a subcontractor. There was a "tonnage rate," with the Association receiving a sliding scale of payments based on the market price for the steel produced. The union divided those monies between its members and apprentices and the "common laborers." The skilled workers of the Amalgamated doubled both as workers and middle managers, supervising their unskilled assistants and controlling the precise technological processes and standards, and the rewards, of steel production.[13]

But the steelmaking process was then being better and better understood by scientists and engineers, which of course undercut the indispensability of the Amalgamated's skilled workers. After breaking the union, the company produced better steel, more reliably, and with a more docile—and cheaper—labor force. We see at Homestead the germ of the modern industrial class system of manager-over-worker around which work is organized.

The point here is that in the United States, uniquely so,[14] the technological and managerial basis of industrial work shifted away from skilled workers who had learned their craft in an apprenticeship or on the job to school-trained managers early in the historic advance. There were two overwhelming advantages to using school-trained managers. It broke the restraints on productivity and profits imposed by skilled artisans like those of the old Amalgamated. The schools would henceforth provide as many loyal company managers as were needed. And it directly linked changes in industrial technology with the modern university as a center of research. Traditional ways of doing things would no longer restrain the scale and the variety of the things that could be produced by the emerging corporations.

At the same time, these changes introduced two radical departures into the Democracy. In the United States an older independent, propertied middle class was transmuted into new corporate employee class whose interests were less, not more, hostile to business and to technological values. And the "natural leadership" of the skilled workers, with their socialist traditions of workplace control and autonomy, was undermined.[15]

In sum, there were notable differences in the pace, details, and extent of the welfare states introduced throughout the developed world during the later stages of the advance. In that sense, each working class and its multiclass allies were different, were "exceptional." Save for differences in timing, all converged to use the state, not to nationalize industries but to moderate the business cycle, raise wages and living standards, extend the franchise, introduce social insurance and jobless benefits, and extend the reach of the schools and the health system.

In brief, through the agency of the Democracy, the urban laboring population, formerly excluded from "society," won its way to a newer, somewhat freer, somewhat more egalitarian polity, economy, society, and culture. This was a signal achievement. But it was not alone in this agency.

The Social Agency of the Modern Corporation

At least since Marx, capitalism's critics have viewed it as *disintegrative*, a force standing apart from other social forces, undermining them and replacing older social relationships with its "cash nexus." Apt in its time, that view is now out of date. Since their inception circa 1870, the developing modern corporations have, singly and together, been *integrative* institutions, creating a new, appropriately characterized "corporate society."[16]

One must raise one's sight a bit from the classic issues of corporate size and wealth. The modern corporation is really a world-historical institutional form, as influential in this time as the Roman Church and the Chinese civil service were in theirs. In truth, the *emerging* corporations contributed a powerfully liberating, and almost surely indispensable, effect during the period of the historic advance. Now we must first distinguish where the big firms still contribute to the commonweal from where they don't. Next, we must try to formulate such policies, proposals, and reforms as are needed by that commonweal. And we must try to figure out how to win their adoption. But the first step in this ambitious program is to free our outlook from the past and to take the actual measure of the modern corporate firms, both separately and in aggregate. In that vein we shift our standpoint to a more compelling and transparent conception, the *omnicapable corporation*.[17]

The diverse impacts of the modern corporation have to be viewed under at least seven headings. Each of these is integral with the others, but it will be useful to take them up separately. Thus we have to analyze the modern corporation

1. As an institution that has introduced and produces under its own aegis the virtually unlimited diversity and quantity of commodities and commodity services that have abetted and accompanied the historic advance, and
2. As the generator and multiplier of an ever larger part of the social surplus that makes the advance possible.

Beyond these directly economic aspects, modern corporations in the aggregate should also be seen as altering the social structure though which the advance was carried out, and then halted. Accordingly, we have to examine the corporation

3. As generating a threefold internal division of labor into workers, managers, and strategic managers.

That includes

4. Founding and nurturing to maturity a new kind of middle-managerial and technological class that is not an Aristotelian "balancing" class but that blocs socially and economically with

5. A fundamentally new kind of upper class of strategic managers and owners that has shed the dynastic form of earlier elites,
6. Helping to establish a unique and dynamic institutional relationship between itself, government, and a mass educational system, here called the Intersection, which, in turn,
7. Over time has extended the corporation's division of labor, authority, and reward into a broader, society-wide, class-like social hierarchy.

The Omnicapable Corporation

One of the most important trend lines in the history of the modern corporation has been its development from relatively simple commodity- and goods-producing firms to institutions that produce and distribute almost all the goods and provide almost all the services that make the social, material, and cultural life of modern society possible—thus the neologism, "omnicapable." Since I have written on these things elsewhere (most extensively in McDermott 1991), the present account can be reduced to bare essentials.

Modern corporations began in the United States, first as specialized commodity producers—the "Trusts"—in, for example, steel, kerosene and lubricants, meat packing, electric power generation, and later Ford's very elementary commodity cars, the Models T and A. Here we see a small handful of undifferentiated products, but mass produced and then sold under monopoly or near monopoly conditions.[18]

From the 1920s on, the major firms, acting through franchises and other satellites, extended their control over not just pricing but also product variation and consumer advertising.[19] They simultaneously branched out into multiple, diversified product lines. GM was the pioneer here, selling its cars through its own dealers. Departing from Ford's focus on a single commodity car, GM offered a group or "line" of differentiated cars priced to appeal to incomes from the modest to very rich. The firm simultaneously offered integrated servicing facilities for its autos, which, again, Ford and the others had not done, including the willingness to purchase the old, used car as part of a new sale. The firm also took up a major position in the production and distribution of, first, home refrigerators, and then later freezers and air conditioners. As part of this diversification, the firm pioneered modern consumer credit services through its financing satellite, the General Motors Acceptance Corporation. It also moved into the manufacture of diesel engines, railroad locomotives, trucks and farm equipment, aircraft engines and airframes, and a position in the ownership and operation of passenger airlines. And with the onset of World War II, GM became a major manufacturer of a wide assortment of weapons and weapons systems.

What is socially significant here is the corporation's development of centralized financial control systems, which expanded its ability to operate successfully in multiple lines of business. Product diversification and a direct intervention into consumer sales were outcomes of the growing managerial and financial capacity of the firm, that increased capacity regularly flowing over into new business endeavors as the latter became mature enough in the marketing and technological dimensions to be subject to centralized, orderly management. Integral to this growth was the rapid growth in the number of different business, engineering, and other technological specialists coming out of the nation's higher education system. GM's expansion was thus equally a matter of fitting uniformly qualified technological specialists and managers being produced by the business and engineering schools into its own centralized, rationalized business structure.

Until perhaps the late 1950s and early 1960s, the behavior of the larger firms was still mostly of this nature. A firm's endeavors had a "family" resemblance to one another. GM mostly cut, shaped, and sold metal; EXXON produced and distributed petroleum-based products; DuPont offered chemicals. Apropos of this, the big firms still organized themselves into "industries"—autos, electrical equipment, insurance, steel, aluminum, and so forth, each distinct "industry" consisting of a few really large firms surrounded by a handful of smaller ones, each engaged in a "family" of related businesses.

In this fashion the big firms created a society-wide change in all aspects of consumption. Corporations influenced popular taste and culture, from the indirect changes wrought by the automobile on, say, modern design and residence patterns, to the more immediate influence of advertising, film, and fashion. Almost all the major kinds and sorts of today's consumable commodities have actually been created within and brought to common use via the instrumentality of the big firms. It is thus true to say that virtually the entire texture of social-material life was becoming a corporate product.

From, say, the middle of the 1970s on, the growth in managerial and financial capacity continued but in a new direction. Aided substantially by the growth of information and communications technology, increased corporate managerial capacity was able to absorb hosts of brand-new, unrelated fields and specialized markets. GM, for example, did not "cut and shape" automated teller machines (ATMs), but it still became a major operator and servicer of ATM systems. General Electric (GE), formerly more or less limited to the electrical machinery industry, became a major power in the world of network and cable broadcasting; Time, Inc., became a major producer and distributor of films, novels, nonfiction, and poetry.

As a reflection of these changes, whole lines of business, once locally or regionally based in specialized firms—among them, fast food, frozen and other processed foods, baked goods, beer and soft drinks, fashion, sporting goods, insurance, real estate marketing, and banking—fell under the aegis of very large, diversified corporate firms.

More recently, the private firms have expanded into government, social services, and cultural businesses. Private hospitals and nursing homes are one part of this, HMOs another. Private firms have expanded substantially into the prison business and policing. They have made major inroads into the provision of food services and into maintenance, cleaning, and security services for elementary and high schools. The government's former monopoly of the postal service is now rivaled by the express delivery firms and the electronic communications firms. Much, perhaps most, of the electronic intelligence and the logistics for the U.S. military are now provided by private contractors, who also now directly sell military and police security services. As testimony to these latter, roughly one in seven of those Americans involved in Iraq (in early 2006), both in military logistics and in carrying out direct military security operations, were employees of private firms.[20]

From the wild and woolly 1990s there was a still-further development in the activities of the big corporations, all of which appear to have separated them further from production and involved them more and more in finance, often in outright gambling with their own firm's and others' securities. But we must not pass too quickly from the social and productive achievements of the big firms, however much our attention is now called to their financial overreaching.

Some business involvement in policymaking comes from an interest in selling some related good or service. The pharmaceutical firms want government to fund research that will lead to the development of new, profitable drugs. The textbook giants have an interest in selling to the school systems and major universities, and the cultural dimension of their wares is an unavoidable consequence. The big communications firms influence cultural agenda through periodicals, television programs, films, records, disks, and books, both fiction and nonfiction. More politically direct, corporate money pours into such think tanks and foundations as the Cato Institute, the Coors Foundation, the Heritage Foundation, the Hoover Institute, and the Manhattan Institute, which in return have cast favorable light on ideas that reflect a range of corporate interests and promulgate a corporate-centered worldview.

It is plausible to think that the historic advance could not have occurred, or at least gone so far, absent the evolution of the producing and distributing capacities of omnicapable corporations. But at the same time, the very texture of the advance took material and social-material form decisively influenced by a single, evolving institution. Subsequently we will look into further, more important reasons for thinking this, but at present suffice it to say that the expanding wealth of society made far-reaching social and social-material improvements in the life of the lower orders less ominous, less threatening, and less relatively costly to the more powerful, better-off sections of society.

Generating the Social Surplus

The future of a society is created out of the social surplus, that part of the wealth that it generates over and above what is needed to produce todays exactly like yesterdays, and tomorrows exactly like today. The vast increase in the social surplus in the corporate era helped make the historic advance possible, and our inability to keep the corporations to a socially equitable agenda instead of their own, often more narrowly defined one ensured at the same time that it would sooner or later come to an end.

Interesting enough, the Progressive movement in America, like Eduard Bernstein's wing of European social democracy (Bernstein 1961), appears to have underestimated the implications of a growing social surplus that was taking initial form as corporate revenue. These reformers were generally confident that the Trusts could be regulated by government and socialized to better behavior by the other institutions of a then-multifaceted society. At the time such a view was not at all implausible because the noncorporate parts of society seemed vast, diverse, politically powerful, and eternal.

These would-be corporate reformers, acting through the political process, initially won not a few victories over the big firms. But post–World

War I regulation weakened, and from not later than World War II the firms began to contest with government over who was to be the regulator and who the regulated. In short order the regulated firms came to capture the regulatory agencies and employ them for their own purposes; the (then) Federal Aviation Administration, the Securities and Exchange Commission, and the Food and Drug Administration provide good instances of this. As this contest over the surplus developed, the relation between elected government and corporation further shifted. By the 1970s and 1980s, the power of the firms had delegitimized regulation as a public policy, and in the years since corporate influence in and over government has only grown. The major 2004 tax legislation was written within industry associations, then shared with friends in Congress and the Treasury, and then made into law with very little change. The federal government was forbidden by law from negotiating the prices of the drugs it must purchase for the new Medicare drug benefit. The Defense Department has not infrequently adopted expensive weapons systems under pressure from Congress (which was under pressure from the interested industry) and then paid for them without benefit of competitive bidding. And as I write this (spring 2009), that autonomous power of the realm, the financial industry, has been given the keys to the public treasury.

These developments seem more or less inevitable. It should not come as a surprise that when confronted with the prospect of having their revenues taxed or regulated away the big private-sector firms would devote some of their surplus to blunting unwanted government and electoral intervention into their affairs or to steering it into more supportive, friendlier uses and directions.

Here we underline the wider conundrum posed for a society and its democratic government in trying to maintain corporate support for social and other agenda. The big corporations are not just one among the institutions of society. Both the web of social-material life and the social surplus are largely generated within the firms. Inevitably society has had to adapt itself to that.

From the Corporation to the Corporation's Social System

A distinct social universe has been created in and by the evolution of the corporate firm. The everyday experience of most Americans, their self-identity, the authority they exercise, their personal prestige, their economic functions, their income, and their broader cultural and educational formation stem from their place within the corporate economy or, for the young, from a current reading of their prospective place within it.

This was not always so. There was a time in the recent past in which at least five other major economic/occupational roles competed with the corporate-generated variety to complicate the national social structure. There were farmer/proprietors and their dependent labor force of hired and seasonal "hands." There was an enormous small business sector, accompanied by another distinct labor force.[21] To this we should add large numbers of medical doctors, dentists, lawyers, accountants, real estate brokers, and others who earned their living in the "free professions." At present, each of these realms is dominated, if not in raw numbers, then in raw influence, by employees and functionaries of large, corporate-organized agribusinesses; by satellited firms, often the franchises of big national companies; by hospitals and HMOs; and by corporate law and accounting departments. Even the mother in her home, nurturing infants and small children, is now within the corporate ambit. The views, principles, and expectations that guide her in having and rearing the children, the institutional aids and complements to her work, the products she relies upon, even the hopes she entertains for the children—all of these express one-sided corporate economic, social, and cultural influence. Although we can find important residues of pre- and noncorporate persons and influences, the trend line is also toward greater, not lesser corporate domination.

The modern corporation features its own distinctive division of labor, as we saw prefigured in the Homestead Lockout: upper management, manager/technologist, and worker. It is this division which has tended to replace the others, as in retailing, many of the professions, agriculture, even fisheries, and in both government and other large organizations. There is a higher managerial elite within whose ranks the strategic control of the institution is concentrated. Carefully marked off from them in role, authority, and reward is a vast middle echelon of corporate employees—the cadre—who are for the most part managers, administrators, or higher-level technologists. One of the keys to the industrial and accompanying social and political dominance of the corporatized form of business is, as already argued, that upper management has developed to a degree without precedent the ability to deploy, manage, and monitor an enormous range of human activities because they fall under the very specialized knowledge, techniques, and technologies embodied in a cadre of obedient corporate employees.

The cadre has the ability to deploy, manage, and monitor the work of the third corporate class, workers or, in more technical parlance, semi-skilled workers.[22] I stress again that while the triad—upper management, managers, workers—carries profound sociological and class structure implications, it must be understood as *fundamentally an institutional phenomenon, only derivatively a sociological one.* One's productive and social identity in contemporary Americanist society is determined in the first instance by one's place and function within and one's relation to the corporation.

The boundaries of this triad change, but not their interrelations. Many technologists and lower-level "straw bosses" were earlier located within the management echelon but have since been pressed down into the ranks of the workers. A post–high school education was once a ticket into the management echelon. At present, even a bachelor's degree, certainly one from a nonprestigious institution, may be only a ticket to the worker ranks, with characteristically lower pay, lesser security of employment, lowered chances and even expectations of advancement, and forced earlier retirement.

The functional triad here is strategy/administration/labor, and it corresponds by institutional design to the social productive triad of upper strategic manager/cadre/worker. That division of labor was first perfected within General Motors, General Electric, and Sears, Roebuck in the period between the world wars and has come since to be the characteristic *social-organizational* feature of virtually every major institution in the United States and the developed world. That is, governments, universities, research institutes, hospitals, publishers, farms, film studios, and even modest-sized businesses now typically ape the corporate division of labor and authority. This is so evidently the case that it appears entirely "natural" and extends into what were formerly such different milieus as real estate, farming, commercial fishing, higher education, and all levels of government. As people's roles and authority come to be more or less decisively attached to where they stand in that tripartite arrangement, no matter what the field of endeavor, so too has their prestige and, more striking, the size, kind, and surety of the rewards and privileges the society offers them.

Quite obviously, this triadic social-productive/institutional organization of affairs did not spring fully grown from the heads of its creators. One advantage of treating the century from 1870 to 1970 as a unified period is that it comprises the birth of the modern corporation and the emergence of its transformative effects on the class system as well as society, culture, and politics, especially the cadre's gradual maturation, and finally, during the 1970s, the beginning of discordant changes that portended a different industrial/social/political era.

A New Kind of Labor Force

Some background explains much about the unique character of the modern workforce. In the early corporate period, the United States could not match the United Kingdom and Germany, the then-dominant industrial powers, in the productivity of its labor force. Both had deep reservoirs of the sort of skilled workers who then dominated in metalworking and in most other manufacturing. Moreover, the German university and technical high school systems were then unmatched in the rest of the world.

By contrast, the United States drew its expanding labor force from immigrants mostly of agrarian, not industrial-cultural, backgrounds, from Italy, the Balkans, Syria and Lebanon, the Russo-Polish Pale, and other often backward regions of Eastern and Southern Europe and the Caribbean, Latin America, and the Far East, few of whom even spoke English. If the United States was to have an industrial workforce, it was not going to be imported ready-made but instead created on this seemingly inferior foundation. This required a special focus on the organization of work and on how technological knowledge was integrated into it. Its solution led to the "invention" of two historically new laboring classes.[23]

A new division of labor was needed, between employees trained in the nation's schools, universities, and institutes to manage the work and to shape its technological dimensions, and those who were to carry out that work under the direction of the others. We should note too that the cadre formed within the educational and scientific systems were usable only within the institutionalized division of labor developed within the nascent corporations. Their historic numbers suggest the social scale of the change, that is, why we must speak of a "class" and not merely of a new category of employees.[24]

There is an extensive literature on these changes, but in the United States, influenced initially by Frederic Taylor's *Principles of Scientific Management*, and more recently, by Harry Braverman's widely esteemed *Labor and Monopoly Capital*, it focuses on the change from worker self-management in the past to the modern system, in which virtually every motion and every second of the workers' effort is shaped, monitored, and measured by their managers. But two other developments are of equal interest and, for us, of greater importance.

The first we have seen is the vast expansion of the numbers of employees within modern, especially U.S., industry who are located within a special, privileged managerial echelon. These include both *line managers,* who have direct supervisory roles over subordinates, and *staff managers,* who gather, process, and disseminate information on behalf of the higher-level, strategic managers of the firm. In addition, in the United States, but less often overseas, *university-trained technical and technological specialists* are also located within the managerial echelon. This vast expansion of managers and technologists also ramifies into different specialties, a process either just preceded or shortly followed by an apposite university degree program and credential. At one time, for example, engineers could be conveniently divided into electrical, civil, chemical, and a few other types. At present, each of those generic varieties has itself spawned scores, sometimes even hundreds, of subspecialties, and this ramifying process continues apace. Managers—flow, quality assurance, financial, inventory control, personnel, recruiting, systems, advertising, facilities, and so on—now also come in increasing numbers of kinds. The lower kinds and strata of both managers and technical personnel have so multiplied that they are now being pushed downward out of the managerial echelon.

The aggregate finding is that if we look over the entire expanse and texture of the knowledge possessed by our civilization, that part of it which has industrial, and now overtly social, uses is a near monopoly of the cadre class. Worker skills and ingenuity still have major importance in industry and the wider society, and we still depend upon the kind of universal "common sense" so admired by our forebears. But most of the knowledge utilized for social outcomes, and the most important of it, and the most dynamic of it, does function increasingly as a cadre monopoly.

The other point is that the evolution of the employment relationship from the master-servant template, which was common even as late as the 1920s, to the modern employer-employee scheme is most developed with respect to cadre. The less draconian employment arrangements for other employees are a derivative of that and not vice versa. The employer-employee relationship differs from the master-servant variety in that the former is dynamic and adaptable, the latter static and weighed down by past practice, the former needfully abreast of the latest in reliable knowledge and technology, the latter repeating things more or less as they were done in the past—*and*—the former acutely susceptible to the influence of higher managers, the latter a historic center of resistance to their control. That this change is customarily discussed in legal-contractual terms is, I think, of less importance than the functional changes inherent in it, a quality clearly needed if the modern employment system is to function in an orderly manner and not a series of ad hoc adjustments.

Aristotle's Middle Class?

We should in passing mark the cadre class's social and political alliance with the elites that run the corporations. This demands a historic departure in social theory. From the days of Aristotle (see his *Politics*, bk. 4), it has been argued that the middle orders in a society play a needed balancing role between the other classes. Aristotle argued that there was a clash of interests between the few wealthy and the many poor, to borrow the classical terms for these things, that threatened to be socially destabilizing.

One does not have to be a Babeuvist to think the wealthy are wealthy at least in part because the poor are poor, and that even moderate solutions to the social instability caused by poverty require some forbearance on the part of the rich. Of course, social conflict can be over other matters than "who gets what," as Aristotle also well understood; but at least insofar as there are differences between the rich and the poor, those differences will give rise to a related degree of political and social clash between them. Moreover, by the very terms of disputes over wealth, there is not really likely to be an equilibrium where the wealthy will, in effect, freely agree, "We have enough," with the poor reciprocally answering, "Yes, we want no more than we have."

Aristotle's great insight is that this clash over wealth has been a factor in every society, awaiting only events to turn poisonous, as we saw in Europe, especially in Weimar Germany, in the period between the wars. Accordingly, there have also been powerful forces in every society that guarded against the wealthy pressing down too hard upon the poor, and the poor too ambitiously pursuing their grievances against the rich. Thus we come to the classic role assigned to the middle orders of society, those "both more numerous than the rich, and richer than the poor." As Aristotle saw it, the middle orders of society would tilt now this way and now that, now to the rich and now to the poor so as to maintain a balance between them and thus preempt any violent social changes. His account still seems eminently plausible and, in fact, remains a major postulate in mainstream political science.

But it does not describe the social and political role of the modern cadre. The differences between Aristotle's upper and middle classes were rooted in two antagonistic forms of property and the competing interests they gave rise to. Conflicts between great property owners and everyone else have filled more than one historical narrative, from Republican Rome to the present.

But modern cadre *share* a property interest with our elites. Their social institutional role is to manage the lower orders within arrangements designed to expand the wealth of corporate firms and their beneficiaries, in whose number they are included. This implies that modern society is defined by its property-based social "alliance" of the "rich" and the "middle" against the "poor." At the polls, modern cadre have sometimes played Aristotle's balancing role; but whatever their other roles, they have a property interest to act as allies and not foes of the interests of the elite-dominated institutions in which they serve.

Obviously, those old terms—rich, middle, and poor—are too stark. The main point of cadre control over the workers is not, as in the past, to defend attacks on property by the lower orders but to organize and equip the workers to maximize the expansion of corporate wealth. The link to the historic advance is that elite and, later, cadre were deeply involved in the expansion of the social productive powers of the workers. That expansion both increased the productive capabilities of the mass per se and provided a springboard for some elements of that mass to become part of the rapidly expanding cadre. And that in turn has, as we know, itself required the broadly shared, expanding standard of living and culture, which was a prime feature of the historic advance. If one was to create and recruit a cadre from among the workers, the latter themselves had to have a higher, not dire, standard of living and culture.

Class, Family, and Dynasty

The modern corporation has also given rise to a very different kind of "rich" or "elite," or "upper class"—to use some of the locutions for the very richest and most influential segment of the institutional structure. Indeed, this is so much the case that the term "class" as put forward both by Marx and Weber is no longer valid. But for the moment it will be less confusing if we use it when describing modern social stratification.

Class analysis of almost any sort in sociology is usually about collections of individuals, but class analysis in historical studies is subtly but crucially different. In historical studies, class analysis is about families. In European society, say from the seventeenth through the beginning of the twentieth centuries, the primary elements that constituted the classes, especially the propertied classes, were families, not individuals.

The link between family and class is so important and so often lost sight of that it deserves explanation. Historically speaking, great wealth or other property ownership of the sort whose power spills over into the political, cultural, and social realms was not really that of individuals. Normally, a single individual's life is insufficient to allow for this sort of spillover. But as the passage of time sanctifies the often dubious origins of the founder's personal fortune and as his heirs are socialized not in the humble village of his birth but in Grosse Point or the West End, and then go on to wed similarly situated children of the other wealthy or powerful, a true upper class emerges. Family structures and family linkages become the medium in which wealth and power are preserved in time, extended in space, and lifted above the rest of society.

We can say of this that wealth is *dynastically organized*, that is, held within distinct families and passed on over time via mainly marital arrangements with other, similar families. For example, one speaks of Rockefeller family wealth when in fact the group that held that wealth consisted of the Rockefeller, Rogers, Aldrich, Flagler, and several other families who were related to one another, variously, by marriage and historic business ties. *Dynastic* power, I would argue, has provided the glue of class systems based on private property ownership. It involves an interplay of private property, wealthy families, and dynastic linkages. Here, it is the logic of "family" that extends a time dimension, otherwise lacking, to the calculus of classes. Analytically speaking, "class" is only a static classification term unless and until the logic of family extendedness in society and time is appended.[25]

Thus "family" is the bridge to the social characteristics of wealth holding. It upholds the paramountcy of inheritance and paternity as a source of prestige and power and undergirds a patriarchy in which the life chances of women and children are subordinated to the dynastic exigencies of the family. A patriarchal ethos, which exaggerates male acquisitiveness or martial power or some other aspect of putative male supremacy, takes its life and significance from those dynastic property arrangements.

Intimate linkage between one's life chances and family identity held not only among the wealthy and powerful and not only for women and children. Nineteenth-century bourgeois novels revolve around the threats to men's, and women's, life chances stemming from their own family's rise or fall in fortunes, while the voices of Dickens and Hugo point to the devastating effect of the class and family life chances of the poor or otherwise deprived. It seems fair to say that the immediate precorporate upper and middle classes are aptly viewed as propertied, family-based dynasties in an emerging market system, and the inequities and the alleged iniquities of their poor are equally aptly viewed as stemming from their failure to achieve such advantageous social place in that emerging market system. Family, to repeat the central point, as the intermediate structure between generations, is the dynamic substructure of *class*.

A moment's reflection suggests the difference from today's increasingly corporative society. An institutional apparatus—the Intersection—intervenes to alter this class/family/life-chance nexus. This apparatus is the medium within which the most decisive modern intergenerational social processes occur. Schools and universities, government and foundation, corporation and army, trade union, profession, and industry association together form a more connected or integrated society than existed in the precorporate age. It is perhaps arguable that differences in privilege between the social strata are not particularly reduced in and by our society of organized institutions, but it is surely the case that all social strata are more integrated one to another within those institutions than anything we are likely to find in and between the segregated family structures of, say, Victorian society.

One can plausibly hypothesize that the rise of and the steady growth of modern feminism and its values are related to the weakening of family-based classes as they give way to an institutionally created and institutionally based social order. This is not to say that modern feminism was in some sense inevitable, or not importantly resisted, or not needful of its great and so often scorned pioneers. Nor should we overlook Barrington Moore's insight (Moore 1966) that obsolete social orders and values, such as patriarchy, don't disappear by themselves. They need to be pushed off the historical stage, else they linger and thereby poison the future. But feminism is incompatible with the patriarchal reproduction of a dynastic social order, of its stable because gendered hierarchy, and of security of property via inheritance according to the preferences of the patriarch. From a longer point of view, feminism is struggling with the rearguard of a retreating social system. Or, equivalently, that invidious gender differences, however difficult to overcome, are no longer central to a society that reproduces its social order, its hierarchies, its wealth, and other privileges primarily within institutions, and only secondarily through patriarchy, that is, via families and their dynastic linkages in space and time.

By "derating" the role of families in determining an individual's life chances, one also implicitly suggests that his or her social mobility is enhanced. But that seems to me to be among the lesser changes introduced both into social theory and society itself by the enhanced role of institutions in the social shaping of individuals and indeed of society itself. Contemporary society is not a version of nineteenth-century society in which individuals have more social mobility; it is a different creature.

Contemporary elites are institutionally, not dynastically, based. Even for a male, a fat inheritance, however helpful, needs supplementing by a high institutional post. Even the largest family fortunes can be maintained only from some member's access to the higher posts of or "insider" status within a major modern institution, especially the private corporation. This family scion will not spend his or her time "improving the estate," arranging an advantageous marriage for a child, or administering a family business. His or her tasks will be institutionally defined and will be carried out in the institution's prescribed manner. Contemporary wealth and power and other socially potent assets have an institutional, *not* a dynastic, basis.

As one would expect, the "modes and manners" of the wealthy and powerful pass over to those less so. Thus, for a middling sort of person, his or her station in life is also immediately determined by whatever institutional training and acculturation was required to gain or retain cadre status and reward. And the worker's career, for good or for bad, is also determined by his or her ability to negotiate the institutional network created by government, the education and health systems, and the private corporation.

Both the Weberian and Marxian conceptions of class are not quite adequate as terms of modern social analysis, that is, for the developed societies. "Class" theory is stretched hither and yon by different contending schools today, not because they are tendentious or witless, but because—for two reasons—the theoretical characteristics of the class calculus are too coarse to capture the different, more ramified, more integrated and dynamic social relationships of our own society. Institutions, not families or dynasties, supply the needed time dimension to social stratification. And the apparently greater social integration of the ranks and orders of a modern society argues that formal social organization has replaced the closed family and dynastic networks of the previous era.

The term "class" is unavoidable in contemporary social discussion unless one wants to engage in lengthy paraphrase. But wherever I employ class language, I am in fact referring to a more complex and more modern form of social stratification. My position is that as a term of analysis for modern Western, capitalist societies, the term "class" is out of focus. That is not such a startling conclusion. We would not expect to find a modern society comprised of lords, merchants, and serfs. After the immense qualitative change in European and American societies brought about with the historic advance, we should expect a different group of social formations in different relationships to one another. At the least, the reader should entertain that as a hypothesis that will be subsequently expanded and, hopefully, confirmed.

The Intersection

A contemporary, developed society is re-created at the intersection of cooperative relations between corporation, government, and the schooling/research system led by the universities. These relations evolved so quickly that one can find in them elements of social design and intentionality.[26] In that evolving relationship of this institutional network, hereinafter the Intersection, with the urban laboring classes we can already discern the lineaments of the historic advance.

One characteristic that distinguished early corporate leaders like Carnegie, Rockefeller, Morgan, and their colleagues from freebooters like Fisk and Gould was that they recognized that expanding the business was more profitable than having a monopoly. Moreover, they quickly learned that the initial barrier was their capacity to manage the increasingly large and diverse business opportunities that were visibly opening to them. Accordingly, the post-Trust period of corporate history is marked by the close attention of business leaders to management issues. In time they came to see that there were really three distinct managerial problems to overcome. There were inadequate numbers of lower- and middle-level managers, and those who did exist did not yet have the tools to get effective control over and expand the productive activities of the workers. Then too a handful of central managers had to be able to control those subordinates so that they pursued coordinated corporate aims and not discordant private priorities.[27]

And there was the problem posed by workers typically drawn from the rural poor, both domestic and foreign, who were poorly skilled, not yet acculturated to industrial rhythms, and often predisposed to some form of socialism. After a period of corporate-administered attempts to address these obstacles by loosely organized holding companies, by the shop management strategies put forward by Taylor, and a plethora of company towns like Pullman, it was recognized that they could not be solved within the confines of the firm itself.

We have already referred to the evolution of the corporation from holding company monopoly to diversified firm; the existing literature on these subjects is both good and extensive, which permits us to move on to the other problems. It was soon recognized not only that more middle-level employees were needed but also that they would require relatively uniform training and socialization. One had in effect to create professions in management and in engineering that had not heretofore existed. This need and, often, this desire met and corresponded to changes then occurring within U.S. higher education. The land-grant colleges had already been founded to provide agricultural and related scientific education and research in place of the gentlemanly and theological priorities of the older universities. Moreover, even the latter were then beginning to follow Johns Hopkins University in adopting the German model, which emphasized the university's major role in research and in the production of technically adept graduates.

Accordingly, one had to expand the base from which an emerging cadre was to be drawn. In the 1870s, thanks to our republican and Protestant traditions, there was already more or less universal primary schooling. Then from the latter part of the century, secondary schooling expanded while at the same time state departments of education imposed greater order on teacher training, curriculum, and performance standards. These reforms were extended into the primary schools, which now functioned as feeder institutions rather than, as before, terminal ones. By the 1920s a more or less uniform, more or less universal high school education had become the norm, and the first seeds of an expansion and standardization of college education began. A genuinely revolutionary step in this otherwise gradual evolution was the passage of the G.I. Bill in 1944.

College education became the virtual norm for young people by the 1960s, so much so that the bachelor's degree no longer guaranteed entry into the ranks of the cadre. As we know from our more recent experience, this expansion of higher-degree-holding continues and is itself closely linked both to the proliferation of the distinct forms and kinds of managerial and technical specialists and to the downward social mobility of their lower ranks.

I have perhaps unavoidably fallen into teleological language to describe the parallel trajectories of corporate employment practices and the expansion and proliferation of educational outcomes. It is hard to read the historical literature about corporations and educational institutions and believe that their coordinate development was entirely a matter of chance or accident. The corporate end users of degrees, from primary school diplomas to "post-docs," have always paid close interest to the way the school systems operated; and the latter, sensitive about their funding, have always acted with an acute awareness that their work and business interests should closely overlap.

The key coordinating institution has been government, especially the federal government, though some states, such as Wisconsin, New York, Massachusetts, and California, also contributed changes in the educational system that took on national importance. Government did not *direct* the coevolution of corporation and school, but it would be fair to say that it has acted as *herder* and *funder*. By encouraging cooperation between the corporate and the educational systems and through its often farsighted underwriting of both basic and applied research and by providing tuition support and promoting antidiscrimination measures to make education more available to a greater number, government has encouraged a greater farsightedness among educators and business leaders than they might of themselves have generated.

Several observations should be made here about the work of the Intersection taken as a whole. First, it establishes a sorting mechanism in which virtually every child is directed into different kinds of learning and acculturation and, as his or her life course takes shape, into the different kinds, levels, and "quality" of vocational posts that must eventually be filled.

Second, it gives priority to its higher, more advanced products, not its lower. Those young people who for one reason or other are deemed not fit to advance are culled out; the survivors of the process, as we say, move "up." The system resembles an orange-sorting machine with the smaller fruit disappearing in order through the increasingly larger holes until only the biggest remain. A crude image but not false.

Consistent with this, U.S. education, at least to the present, has disproportionately funded its higher, not lower ends. U.S. university education and research still leads the world, as it has for a half century now. That enviable situation coexists with significant pockets of illiteracy and, perhaps worse, mass semiliteracy. These too are the result ultimately of policy, not inattention.

Third, worker socialization and education is a by-product of the formation of the cadre, but withal a very successful by-product. The same educational and other cultural processes that form a cadre create as their residue workers with gradually improving social-productive characteristics.

This process of culling by the criterion of school success and failure has the additional advantage of creating not merely the consciousness but the lived reality of the cadre's social and industrial superiority over the workers, thus of the naturalness and rightness of the better rewards and privileges falling to that life course.

The U.S. Intersection probably rewards privilege almost as much as it encourages merit. The point is, however, that it brings the entire population into a functioning role within the main economy. Virtually every infant begins life as a consumer, is sent to preparatory work as a child and adolescent, and is then channeled on to be a producer/consumer in the economy. By contrast, the sort of, say, German primary school that was satisfied to teach the children of workers and peasants that the Kaiser loved all his subjects equally and that Luther was right about the Jews was simply inadequate to sort an entire population to the advantage of economy and state.

More on Gender

We can see the far-reaching effect of the modern Intersection in its transforming effect on gender relations. It confirms, I think, the world-historical significance of the shift from a dynastic to an institutional social system. Where traditional gender roles have interfered with the universal culling and directing work of the Intersection, they have been modified and adjusted; again, this is not part of the disintegrative effect of an older capitalism but the engendering of a new, more profoundly integrative social system. A modern society cannot and increasingly does not ignore the fact that one-half of its potential "manpower" and, more important, one-half of its potential cadre are female. Our society maintains many older, gendered prejudices in the culling, training, and deploying tasks of the modern Intersection, but pointedly, they are maintained much more powerfully in the lower, not the higher ranks of the labor force. Heavy manufacturing and construction work remain only a little gender altered, but the ranks of all the modern professions have been significantly opened to female advancement. A modern society organized by an institutionalized elite, at least to that progressive and humanist extent, has a totalizing, all-absorbing character.[28]

One can only hold up a weaker, more tentative argument about "totalizing" with respect to race questions. U.S. policy, especially during the Johnson administration, successfully created a "critical mass" of minority-group middle- and professional-class individuals and families. This is an "institutional" class, not a "dynastic" one, which has over time acquired the wherewithal to compete socially without government support. My sense is that these developments are obscured in part by the contemporary discourses on race, which, for different reasons on the part of different populations, seem stuck in yesterday's realities.[29]

The division of labor, authority, and reward associated with the remarkable success of the private business corporation has spread into nonbusiness institutions such as government agencies, universities, publishers, research laboratories, NGOs, and so forth. In some cases, the transfer has been total; in others, only partial. University administrations have adopted "corporate form," though their faculties typically retain considerable professional autonomy from direct management. However, the increasing use of non–tenure track part-timers who are simply employees—nothing more, in spite of their advanced degrees—clearly reflects the spread of corporate organizational practices. The growing role of management in medical and in psychiatric practice, through the influence of hospitals and HMOs, supported by the power of the insurance industry, also reflects the same sort of "corporatization" of work organization in the nonbusiness sector. The current trend in elementary and secondary schools is to increase the authority (and reward) of education managers. In short, the corporate form of work organization vastly expands the discretionary authority and control of institutional elites and the employment opportunities for cadre. It has become so widespread that it is now seen as the "natural" way of organizing institutional tasks in the society at large, no more, no less. It introduces a stronger because formal hierarchy in place of older, oftentimes looser kinds of hierarchy; and as observed earlier, jobs and education levels once sufficient to join the cadre are changing, with many at the lower levels being pushed down into ordinary "employees."

The Historic Advance: The Other Path

The historic advance was the result of the convergence of the actions of elite, cadre, and the Democracy; of conservatives and reformers; of capitalists and popular movements. From roughly 1870 to 1970, Americanist society threw resources into the creation of modern cadre, which modified the productive characteristics and thus the general social advantages of the laboring population, a consequence that was not entirely unintended. Here was the path of convergence with the Democracy's Vico-ism, its Babeuvism, the Left republican dynamics of its middle-class/worker political bloc. The convergence was predictably most pronounced and most successful in the Americanist setting, and less so in what I call a Bismarckian context. Given our national history of the universal common school, the need to Americanize the immigrant generations, and the opposition that would arise against any overt program to create a special, separate "aristocracy," it is hard to imagine any other result. But in Bismarckian societies with still lively quasi-feudal vestiges of rank and preference, an alternative trajectory of development was pursued; there incipient cadre were merged into the semifeudal gradations of the *Mittelstände,* while the transformation of workers from servant status to modern employees was accordingly slowed.[30]

Thus it is fair to say that when the American and Soviet armies met at the Elbe River in Germany in the spring of 1945, it was a species of European society and not merely a German army that had been utterly defeated. Across Europe, a Bismarckist compromise between the very old and the very new had historically found its rationale and justification in the promise it offered against social disintegration caused by restless, militant workers and on behalf of national security against aggression by the other, neighboring rival nations. At the core of those promises, serving as their guarantor, were the landed and military aristocracy, holdovers from the *ancien régime* of pre-1848 and the social codes they enforced. This Bismarckism was decisively discredited as well as defeated on the battlefield; in that defeat lay the ruins of its historic promises. Virtually every nation in Europe had been successfully invaded and conquered by foreign armies, some for the second time in a generation; everywhere resistance and other antifascist groups of pronounced worker and leftist tendency claimed the mantle of the victory and the mandate for social reconstruction. And at the center of the Bismarckist failure stood Germany, loser now of two major wars, occupied largely by "barbaric hordes from the east" and the "uncultivated" and "mongrel" Americans, her Prussian core about to be ceded to the inferior Slavs, and her Junker elite thoroughly discredited by their collaboration with Nazi expansionism and extermination policies. The truth, which was quickly accepted by all the dominant European political and social formations, was that purely industrial elites and their society had proved themselves more militarily and politically potent than the military/aristocratic variety.

Americanist Victory and Beyond

The sheer brutality, paranoia, and mendacity of Stalin's Soviet Union have made it easier for American apologists of cold war policies and their foreign friends to spin magical narratives about selfless America coming to Europe's rescue, American economic generosity, and America the democratically designated leader of the Free World. The more humble truth is that in the immediate postwar years both the United States and the Soviet Union quickly reorganized their zones of influence to reflect their own social systems. I think it is underappreciated still to what degree force was employed by "our side" as well as "theirs." In Belgium, regular British troops were used to intimidate resistance groups intent on governing. In Greece, the British, later the Americans, simply reimposed by military force the very figures and political parties that had governed Greece so brutally and badly for the Nazi occupiers (Mazower 1993).

All over Western Europe, something like the same process was repeated.[31] The middle and upper parts of those societies, variously collaborators or at least appeasers of the Nazis, were thoroughly discredited, while worker and other Left-political tendencies and groups had taken up the national banner and the Allied cause and now proposed a European social renaissance. In this they were thoroughly and effectively opposed by the power of the United States: the Resistance was forced to surrender its weapons; the more radical and demanding of them were edged out of government. The Allies sought out and propped up safe, centrist figures. Shadowy Allied intelligence operatives resuscitated the old parties of the Center and Center Right. A good deal of money passed under many tables, and Allied influence thus extended. Where needed, force was used, as in Greece (and in the Philippines), to discourage the recalcitrant. American *realpolitik*, hard-edged American determination, and American coercion succeeded so well that this redoubtable trio could be rendered historically in the sweeter accents of rescue, generosity, and democratic choice.[32]

But for all that the United States tried to restore prewar European political parties of the Right, it could not restore the discredited social system and the quasi-feudalized economic arrangements that had formerly given them life. Save in Greece and in Spain, the Americanist template was also enthusiastically adopted by Europeans and Japanese and not just imposed by the Marshall Planners or the Occupations. Accordingly, the 1945–60 period has to be accorded an immense American, Americanist, and even democratic humanist success story, very nearly as much so as the conventional narratives maintain. While many discredited figures from the interwar and war years presided over political circles, more important was the continual Americanization of the societies themselves under the twin impulses of an emboldened Democracy and a capitalism free from its self-imposed prewar constraints. School opportunities were vastly expanded, personal incomes rose, production soared, and a more egalitarian/meritocratic impulse ran through those societies. By 1960, give or take a few years, the previous social gap between European and Japanese societies and the North American variant had substantially closed up. Crucially important, in the rising rates of university attendance, the historic creation of the new, modernist cadre was in rapid process of completion.

The Historic Advance Halted

But circa 1970 the older economic alliance between elite, cadre, and the trade unions gave way to a zero-sum rivalry. The public sector, formerly considered the cradle of universal prosperity, became a contested terrain fought over by the better-off taxpayers on the one side and the less well-off, not yet "successful" classes, orders, races, and ethnic groups on the other. Rapid economic growth, formerly championed as an engine of equality, was condemned as an inflationary threat to property. High rates of unemployment, once thought the greatest of evils, were sought after in the policies of the main national central banks and the main international financial agencies. Trade relations between the developed and the nondeveloped world, never that equitable, worsened against the poorer parts of the globe. The contours of contemporary politics both national and international were altered by what were previously thought to be reactionary economic and political philosophies and by challenges to secular humanism mounted by fundamentalists among the world's main religions. One can go on and on citing the changes. In a nutshell, precisely those forces and alliances which until the 1960s appeared to guarantee not only the continuation of the historic advance but also its acceleration and its spread were undone. A less, not more, humanist world developed, and so steadily and so powerfully for the last third of a century that it is fair to read that as a new historical departure rather than a case of the familiar Left/Right pendulum we had experienced earlier during the twentieth century.

2

INTERPRETING THE "SIXTIES"

The hypothesis I want to explore in this chapter and the next is that the international movements of the "Sixties" attempted to push the historic advance beyond what was acceptable to their erstwhile bloc partners and in so doing they came up against the outer boundaries of permissibility for a liberal democratic society like ours. In the ensuing contest, these movements were defeated and, to avoid a repetition of the threat, several of the highest elite subsocieties acted to impose a genuine reaction, that is, a rolling back of the most important and threatening gains of the Democracy. While I don't consider this reaction an actual conspiracy, I think it is fair to conclude that the different elite groups were reacting to one another's behavior and thus *converging* into a new historic bloc with now a more conservative, even reactionary sort of politics. This is a complex thesis to argue, but there is sufficient evidence at least to establish its plausibility and its practical significance.

The civil rights movement of 1954–67 was part of the historic advance. The antiwar and other "protest" movements were too, though this is less well understood. The movements of the Sixties were attempts to continue the historic advance, but they took place at a time when the political bloc that had carried forward the advance for the previous century was being replaced by an essentially reactionary one.

By 1970, in the United States, in Western Europe, and in Japan, the creation of a modern workforce had been achieved. The cadre life course, previously in need of public-sector nurturing, had matured. From a class "on the make," it had become a class that had "made it." The normal preferences of privilege began to assert themselves, and they included growing opposition to the very public sector that had nurtured *them* and, more widely, a stance favoring lessened opportunities for those lower on the social ladder. In the United States, this was most clearly expressed in growing opposition to the aspirations of the then most aggressive, exposed group in the Democracy, the nation's black population; in other countries, immigrants and "guest" workers would be targeted.

The Nixon of the 1968 and 1972 U.S. presidential campaigns ran on a platform of slowing racial change. Even the dimmest, most distracted voter could see that the opposite of Nixon's Silent Majority had to consist of *a* or *the* "noisy minority." His Southern strategy had the transparent aim to bring into the Republican Party those conservative Southern whites opposed to further (or for that matter, any) racial change, but he also used racial appeals to defeat the national protest movements of the time. The inner documents of the Nixon presidency, now on the public record, strongly support this point.[1] This was part of a larger shift wherein both parties appealed to the suburbs, as well as to the Southern and the Western states, where middle-class voters were increasingly cool to social changes that advantaged both the Democracy and the Democratic Party.

Elites constituted the other breakaway from the former political bloc, and for closely related reasons. Social investments once aimed at raising the productivity of the entire workforce now seemed less efficient than more focused investments in cadre and some of the already more productive cohorts of workers. In addition, elite fears of "wage-led" inflation and a growing sense that the nation was becoming ungovernable led to a shift away from the conciliatory "moderate Republicanism" of the Eisenhower administration. Over the two decades after 1970, the nation's business elites would steadily reject their former toleration of and limited support for the New Deal, the Fair Deal, and the Great Society. This was integral to the broader shift among political and cultural elites toward what I call the modern reaction.

The Sixties as a Movement for Modernization

Too much of the existing literature about the Sixties is deeply flawed, guided too heavily by a few earlier student memoirs built on a special "generational" paradigm. My reasons for this dissent are particularly well founded.

Throughout 1965–72, I was an itinerant agitator against the Vietnam War and the cold war perspective that animated it. I was invited to visit and speak at 124 different U.S. college campuses, quite often more than once. Overall, I made about two hundred such visits over the eight-year period. I also had off-campus speaking engagements during several of my visits to universities in large cities.

I would typically arrive at a campus well prior to whatever public events were scheduled, in order to meet with the organizers. My minor celebrity usually didn't rate a motel or a hotel; the best I could hope for was the spare room of a faculty member. Sometimes I "crashed" on a student's sofa or a mattress on the floor. Once I even slept in an old sleeping bag in a tree house. Actually, "roughing it" put me on closer terms with the campus activists. We could examine as comrades what successes and problems there were, and I could put them in touch with other, kindred campuses or groups and, of course, bring in information both about the war policy and about doings elsewhere.

Their typical organization was a campus antiwar committee consisting of both students and faculty, with graduate students often playing a prominent role. A small, isolated campus typically had intimate links to adult groups in the town, county, or region. There were seldom chapters of Students for a Democratic Society (SDS), and most activists didn't belong to that organization. There might be one or two SDSers, and surely someone had and circulated the SDS news organ, *New Left Notes*. The latter was very important because activists wanted news of other campuses and often copied new organizing ideas and other tactics.

Too much of what I observed in the period has simply not found its way into the literature. There is too much emphasis on students, notably on the more privileged ones. Flacks (1972) and Keniston (1965 and 1968) are very good, but their coverage is still only partial. There should be far more material than there is about, among others, working-class students and working students, graduate students and high school students, young workers generally, serving soldiers, public-sector workers, church groups, the elderly, and the handicapped, all of whom played major roles in the movements of the period. Earlier women's activity was absent from the literature, though this has changed. At one campus I visited in 1968, a gay male student group was at the center of all civil rights and antiwar activity in the region, and gay students played a notable, if then low-key, role on several campuses.

Not only is the SDS given an exaggerated importance, but so too is its New Left rhetorical and ideological framework, one that I found was not widely shared by, and often opposed by, the antiwar students, including many in the SDS itself. For example, in spite of its very recent publication (and excellent bibliography), Horn (2007) remains mired in this very rut. I heartily recommend Marwick (1998) as the best of the literature I've seen. Some of my more detailed differences with Marwick and with Daniel Bell (1976) will also follow in the text.

Now almost a half century later, there should be a more detached literature that treats the Sixties as a historical phenomenon within modern U.S. and developed-country history, and not as an aberration. What we call the Sixties encompassed a phenomenon occurring in virtually every developed country by a great mass and diversity of social players. It is a serious scholarly failing that there is a dearth of critical, comparative monographs and interpretive studies bringing the period into contrast to "1848," or "1919," "1936," or "1946," that is to say, to other periods marked by popular risings that spread across national borders and arguably constituted political watersheds in modern political history.

What needs to be shown first is that the Sixties were an attempt to continue the historic advance, but in doing so posed a credible threat to the existing scope and authority of elite advantages and, of course, to the now-secure privileges of the matured cadre. They were not an attempt at "revolution," and they were not aimed to overthrow governments or even classes. But there was an attempt to radically recast the respective roles of elites, cadre, and the Democracy; and it was this that was thrown back.

Given the unusual scope of my experience of those times here and, somewhat less, internationally, I am comfortable in talking about the Sixties in a way that contradicts much of the now-burgeoning literature about that period. My analysis will often allude to overseas events but with less assurance than when the text refers to the United States. On that basis, then, my thesis is that the Sixties were primarily an attempt to continue the historic advance but under the changed social circumstances I have alluded to. Such a continuance now posed a threat to the interests of the former social partners of the Democracy. The threat took place on three different fronts. First and most obvious, there was the attempt to intervene directly in foreign policy formulation and execution, initially on the cold war nuclear front, later in demanding a popular veto over the waging of the Vietnam War and the policies that animated it. Second, the Sixties represented an attempt, however crude, to overcome the limits of liberal, representative democracy: this took the form of an attempt to overrule its *democratic* limits by extraparliamentary means. This effort began with "direct action" to force federal government intervention against segregationist violence in the U.S. South, but "direct action" was later extended to issues surrounding schools, the environment, industrial safety, and other areas. Finally, the Sixties rejected the Intersection shift in favor of the now matured cadre and tried to sustain and even broaden the open opportunity policies that had characterized the historic advance. This was, I believe, the deeper dynamic of the oft-cited "cultural revolution" of the period. Crudely, in opposition to a maturing Americanist social system whose template required the lower orders to fit themselves to a narrowing rewards system, the Sixties explored, proposed, and often acted out a more tolerant, egalitarian, less industrially driven conception of the good society. This attack on the Intersection, especially on the role of universities within it, underlies many of the harsher judgments made still about the "incivility," the "irrationality," and the propensity to "violence" of the Sixties protest movements.

Of the changes proposed during the period, some, such as the attack on legal segregation, ultimately gained the support of the relevant elites, but the other attempts to win a radically changed society and polity did not. Political elites and their allies fought back and were successful in forestalling further, less tolerable change, most critically in preventing dilution of their one-sided influence in both the elected and the inner or permanent government.[2] As a result, the defensive system surrounding elite privileges was strengthened and has subsequently been extended during the long reactionary period that followed.

The Historiographical Problem

The extraparliamentary character of so much Sixties political behavior has too often led historians to dismiss the period or to characterize it in terms of some of its later, often outlandish features, such as drug use, "dropping out," and revolutionary posturing.[3] But this is to take a too-unhistorical attitude to the past. Perhaps the way to see this is to call to mind the great *jours* of the French Revolution, those special days in which masses of Parisians took to the streets. Among the most important of these was the march of the revolutionary crowd to Versailles on October 6, 1789, which took the king into custody and contributed both to the end of the monarchy and the defeat of the royalist conspiracies. But these mass demonstrations were frequently provoked by or their demands capitalized upon by sympathetic forces within the National Assembly. The history of that great revolution is a history of how the popular demonstrators, on the one side, and first the National Assembly Orleanists, later the Jacobins and the Mountain, on the other, fed off each other. But the alienation of the Sixties from the mainstream political system, and the reciprocal unwillingness of mainstream political figures to identify with it, meant that its great *jours* produced only ephemeral results. They occurred, they cowed the authorities for a time, but they left no substantive political residue, so that when they ceased so too did their effect. This in turn helped demobilize the demonstrators, the cycle continuing until there were so few demonstrators and residues that both were swept away.[4]

Many of the events, tendencies, causes, and organizations of the Sixties placed themselves entirely outside the conventional political process because the civil rights experience had taught them that that was the only way to force the government to deal with the urgent problems of race. They applied that lesson to the problem of international conflict. It was at the time a reasonable position to take. The political system had waffled for the decade since *Brown* on whether, how, and how much to defend the civil rights of black citizens and their allies; by 1968 both the cold war and the Vietnam War were being waged at great human and financial cost but without prospect of "victory." Accordingly, distrust of the efficacy of "liberal Western democracy" became a defining political outlook of the activists and organizations of the period. The frequent mass street demonstrations should be recalled to mind or the physical seizure of contested sites ("sit-ins," "occupations"). These were typically accompanied by lists of "demands" that otherwise had no traction whatsoever among elected officials.

By thinking and acting in this manner, the Sixties activists were following the political science orthodoxy of the time. In the "pluralist theory" of, say, Seymour Lipset (see Lipset 1960), the direct, authoritative participation of the electorate in political policies and decisions was, it was argued, not desirable. The masses were too often afflicted by irrational tendencies such as "working-class authoritarianism" and "chiliastic" or "millennial" political ideologies. Lipset, like so many of his professional contemporaries, wanted to limit the role of popular elements in the polity, preferring to see politics as a negotiation process between elites. Even worse, the legitimacy of those elites to negotiate on behalf of the masses rested not on active, informed consent or even consensus but on a conception of shared "values" and "norms" reminiscent of the thought of Talcott Parsons.

Pluralist views of this nature were also widely shared among the nation's liberal spokespeople and media commentators, who at the time not infrequently lectured the demonstrators that by going outside normal political channels they would create a right-wing reaction, as in fact they did. It is perhaps arguable, however, that the timidity of the Center-Left guaranteed that when that reaction arose, it would only be tepidly resisted, as in fact it was.

Now, in retrospect, after our historic experience of elite sins of commission and omission related to Vietnam, the nuclear arms race, and civil rights, and today's financial "meltdown," Lipset's views no longer appear that reasonable, that responsible, or that prudent. But if this sort of "pluralism" was the reigning orthodoxy of the time, then democratic renewal had to come from outside "the system." My point here is not that we activists were right and the "Establishment" was wrong, but that the political roots of street demonstrations, sit-ins, and such cannot simply be dismissed as youthful excess guided by "chiliastic" or "millennial" fantasy. There was a core—at least that—of political realism in thinking that contemporary elites had to be pushed into addressing what clearly were pressing public policy problems and that that pushing could come only from "outside the system."

This reliance on "outsider pressure," however, poses a major problem in interpreting what these demonstrations were intended to achieve. If, by contrast, the era had been dominated by an organization (the CIO or the People's Party, for example) and left a finite imprint in the polity (such as industrial-type trade unions or a legislative legacy), it would be somewhat easier to interpret. The Sixties did give rise to a number of more or less conventional political campaigns, but these and related parliamentary-style actions should be viewed as more or less peripheral to its early and quite central trajectory. Basically, one must accept the evanescent quality of the organizations and "demands" that characterized the period and then try to tease out their meaning as best one can.

Complicating the matter further is the fact that so few figures in, say, the Western governments, parliaments, and political parties embraced the demonstrators or their various causes, and then—like Senators Fulbright, Eugene McCarthy, George McGovern, and Robert Kennedy—only partially and very late in the game. In Britain, the Labour Party, like the left-of-center parties in the rest of northwestern Europe, was captive to conventional trade union demands. As a result, Labour and other major Left parties, when they did not steadfastly support NATO, America, the Vietnam War, and nuclear weapons, at least remained discreet when it came to criticizing them. Both the mass Western communist parties, in France and Italy, openly espoused "revolution" but nonetheless, in summer 1968 and in "the Hot Autumn" of 1969, tried to sever workers from students and to rein in worker demands (Horn 2007). Most revealing, in 1972, forces in the Democratic Party in the United States that were favorable to much of the Sixties actually captured the party's nomination for the presidency. But immediately there were mass desertions among party leaders and elected officials in favor of the formerly despised Nixon. FDR's own son, Elliott, even headed the influential Democrats for Nixon national campaign organization. Deserted by much of his party, including its elite, presidential candidate George McGovern suffered the Democrats' most lopsided defeat in modern U.S. history. Meanwhile in the Senate and House, where great numbers of legislators finally came to oppose the war as an utter folly, no common front was joined with the extraparliamentary opposition. Thus, unlike in eighteenth-century France, where the victories won by the great *jours* were crystallized by and then secured by parliamentary forces, in the United States at least, the great movement of the 1960s in most of its respects remained in the streets and excluded from the halls of power.[5]

We cannot know what that Parisian "mob" thought and wanted when they marched out to Versailles to seize Louis XVI, but the National Assembly's subsequent actions fixed their imputed thoughts and intentions as comprising the destruction of the monarchy. That, at any rate, is how the march played out in the formal political process. All else shrinks more or less into historical unimportance and thus ultimately into oblivion. But this sort of historical oblivion is precisely the problem we face in interpreting or, better, unraveling the political meaning of the Sixties.

The interpretive situation is further complicated in that even now, nearly four decades after the Sixties ended, they excite considerable scholarly enmity and contempt. In the literature about the period, one rarely finds ideologically unfreighted accounts.[6] In learned circles no less than in the political realm, the period is still controversial.[7]

Finally, our reading of the Sixties is made even more complex because of events over which most activists, at least in the United States, had little influence. From mid-1965 on, the United States and the rest of the industrialized countries faced a surge in inflation so serious that it led to major structural changes in the international financial system, that is, the replacement of the Bretton Woods fixed exchange rates between the dollar and other currencies and the introduction of so-called floating rates. By and large, economic policymakers saw this inflation as wage-led, and the changes both in the international financial system and in domestic financial policies were as a rule calculated to rein in, first, wages and, second, the scope and generosity of social welfare benefits.[8] The prime targets of this ultimately effective assault were the trade unions, which—ironically—supported none of the interventions of the Sixties. In the United States the AFL-CIO leadership under George Meany opposed the Sixties root and branch.[9] Within elite circles, however, wage-push inflation was widely seen as further evidence of the social destabilization "caused" by the Sixties activists, on a continuum with drug use, campus disobedience, alleged "nihilism," opposition to nuclear weapons, and other departures from proper, civilized behavior. As a result, a drive to reduce trade union influence coincided and often overlapped with elite-sponsored attacks on the extraparliamentary demonstrators.

In retrospect, trade union support for the Vietnam War, which continued to and even beyond its actual ending, reflected badly on the stewardship of Meany and his successor, Lane Kirkland, since it was the least privileged young workers and not the better-off students who directly paid the war's blood price. This policy reflected the AFL-CIO's utterly unrealistic assessment of its own power. The following, often cited within trade union circles, is, I'm told, not apocryphal: once when charged by a critic for not trying to bring new unions and members into the organization, Meany is said to have snapped back that there was no point to the criticism because the AFL-CIO already had all the members it needed!

Rethinking the Sixties

We must answer, or at least attempt to answer, four questions if we are to have a more accurate understanding of the Sixties than current literature provides. First, do the Sixties actually *deserve* consideration as an unusually important and distinctive period or set of events? Second, what do current interpretations of the Sixties tell us about it as a period? Third, what issues were being contested, and by whom, during those obviously tumultuous years, and are they of sufficient social-political substance to justify our attention? And fourth, did they amount to anything? Did a substantially different long-term political dynamic arise in clear consequence of and of commensurate scale with the events and contestations of the Sixties?

I will take up the first three issues in this chapter, the fourth in the next.

The Significance of the Sixties

Upon what basis can the period be marked off as of particular historical significance?[10] The sheer international scope and scale of the tumult must be weighed. Dissident movements and protests of unusual size, ultimately embracing tens of millions of people, arose more or less simultaneously in virtually every developed country, and elsewhere as well. In Western Europe these occurred in Britain, Northern Ireland, Denmark, Sweden, Norway, Finland, Belgium, the Netherlands, Luxembourg, France, West Germany, Italy, Portugal, Austria, and even in Spain and Greece. In Eastern Europe, there were uprisings in both Poland and Czechoslovakia. In Asia, South Korea, Japan, the Philippines, and Indonesia also passed through periods of especially intense social and political turbulence.

In the Americas, the United States and Puerto Rico, Canada, Mexico, the Dominican Republic, Cuba, and Guyana were affected, as were most of the West Indies. In South America, Argentina, Brazil, Venezuela, Uruguay, Chile, Peru, and Bolivia all witnessed major, related political disturbances. Australia and New Zealand were also stirred in this period.

I am uncertain whether to include the anticolonial surge that passed through, especially, the French and British spheres of Africa at this time, but at least South Africa must be included because of the links between the demonstrations that led to the Sharpeville Massacre and the U.S. civil rights movement, and we should probably include the Lumumba interlude in the Republic of the Congo as well for the same reason Thus, prima facie and allowing that some countries on the list upon closer examination might subsequently have to be removed, the Sixties occurred in over three dozen different countries and, notable in itself, in every country of the developed world save perhaps Switzerland. In the Arab world, this is a period of pan-Arabist revival and of the growth particularly of the Palestine national movement, but I don't feel knowledgeable enough to link these things with the wider international movements save, perhaps, via the spread of anticolonial feeling. At any event, as I pointed out in an earlier essay (McDermott 1997), the scope of this tumult dwarfs even that of the epochal year 1848. On this basis alone, one must bring the historian's attention to what occurred, why, and with what effect.

There was also enormous variation among the individuals who took an active role in the mass demonstrations typical of the period. The Sixties clearly include the U.S. civil rights movement. One is also familiar with the news photos of those years of great masses of students from all of the Western countries. Less noticed though equally obvious from the photos was the mass role throughout Europe and North America of pensioners and other elderly. The students tended to focus on opposition at first to the nuclear arms race, later to the war in Vietnam, but the pensioners typically tried to link war and arms expenditures with the dearth of funding for social services. They were frequently accompanied by the first manifestation of the movements of the handicapped more or less around the same dichotomy. The modern feminist movement revived in this period, most frequently within the wider "Movement" context, although it was to significantly outlast the latter and to still-enduring positive effect. In the later part of the Sixties, large numbers of serving soldiers, especially Dutch and American, joined in the protests and demonstrations: as the U.S. commander in Vietnam later admitted, it was mass disaffection and even outright rebellion in the ranks that precluded a favorable military solution there for the United States.[11]

Workers played a significant role and not only in the mass demonstrations. In Britain, the Miners Union helped topple three governments over traditional employment issues (Brown 1986). In France for a brief period in 1968, there was fear that the students and the workers would together oust the government; there were press rumors in 1968—since confirmed—that DeGaulle visited France's NATO divisions across the Rhine to seek their pledges of military support to maintain the regime. All over Western Europe there was, as one economist describes it, a "hinge" in the rate of growth of worker remuneration, and this at the expense of both proprietary income and inflation.[12] In the United States this was the period of rapid growth of unions in the public service and, to a lesser extent, of hospital and elder-care workers. These unionists formed the backbone of many of the earlier demonstrations against the war in Vietnam. In Italy, northern workers of largely southern origin waged a series of strikes and other actions on behalf of syndicalist demands about workers' control; these workers were also openly influenced by the U.S. civil rights movement.[13]

There was considerable interconnectedness between the movements in the different countries. In Northern Ireland and South Africa, respectively, Catholic and African demonstrators against civic inequality tried to copy the nonviolent tactics of the U.S. civil rights movement. I have in the past credited the latter with having had incalculable international importance both as a rising of African peoples and as an exemplar of the potency of nonviolent philosophy and tactics. In Greece, the movement was against royal and other rightist domination of the government, but its flag and symbol was the distinctive cross-like emblem of the wider European Campaign for Nuclear Disarmament. In Poland and, especially, Czechoslovakia, the opposition looked to Western movements for their models but to Western governments for support.

In the United States, white activists passed back and forth between the civil rights and antiwar wings of overlapping movements; among younger blacks this was pronouncedly less so, but among the older people and especially black trade unionists there was the same easy transition from one movement wing to the other, as a matter of timeliness rather than of priority.

As in Greece, the movements in Latin and Central America had a strongly nationalist, anti-American tinge. But the considerable density of international contact between the movements in the different countries reflected a vibrant internationalism. I was at the time not particularly active in international contact work, but I nonetheless met and talked with activists from Argentina, Mexico, Japan, Sweden, Britain, France, West Germany, Greece, Cuba, Vietnam, the then Ukrainian SSR, Australia, and Puerto Rico. Always, the subject of these discussions was the state and prospects of "our" movement, that is, what we viewed as a single international movement against the world left us by our fathers and the cold war.[14] I recall both the sheer exuberance and the dark realism of these marvelous men and women. As it turned out, some were to know exile, prison, or even death in the defeat of their national movements over the following decade.

The Current Understanding of the Sixties

It is now widely held that the Sixties represented a purely or at least predominantly cultural movement, not really an attempt at social and political reform or to establish different foreign policy priorities. There are a number of different versions of this cultural theme, and it is useful to look at three of them.[15]

Some leading student memoirists of the period have argued that it was a cultural revolt based on the unique generational experiences of the young women and men who came of age during the 1960s. The concept of a "generation" here serves to mark off a mostly cultural response by one age grouping as opposed to those who came immediately before and after; I think the concept also avoids any claim that the Sixties should be judged by their success in changing government and social policy. I suppose one could say on this point that the Sixties were not ultimately political, though they were politically alienated. These memoirists typically emphasize the experience of growing up under the threat of nuclear annihilation; often they recall hiding under school desks during air raid drills (see Gitlin 1987). Drawn from prosperous families in a prosperous era, they discounted material striving and were contemptuous of materialist values. Influenced by popular Freudianism, they had little patience with the rigid sexual morality that dominated the schools and the media, especially film, in the 1950s. Almost all had grown up believing that the United States was egalitarian and democratic, and were affronted as they became more aware of the Jim Crow system of Southern racial segregation. As important, they had radically different tastes in interpersonal relations, lifestyles, film, literature, music, dress, and values generally than their immediate forebears. Overall, the memoirist literature alleges a deep divide between the college generation of the 1960s and their mentors and parents. Much—though not all—scholarly work has tended to follow that cultural/generational interpretation as well.

In a way, this was characteristic of the intellectual formation of the time in which cultural factors per se were central in explaining social matters; this fashion was a reaction against an unimaginative Marxist materialism and the structural/functional sociology of Talcott Parsons. Subsequent scholarly and intellectual tendencies in social history ("history from the bottom up"), postmodern and feminist theory, deconstructionism, critical legal theory, and queer theory have been partial to such culture- or ideology-based terms of explanation, and there the matter rests today. On these bases then, it is argued that the Sixties represented a significant cultural watershed, a departure by a singular generation toward a more modern, critically materialist, less nationalistic, less violent, less racialist, less sexist and sexually repressed, thus healthier culture and personality formation and yet toward a less individualistic, more socially and ecologically responsible ethos.

The most powerful argument for some sort of cultural interpretation observes that so-called Sixties cultural values, then held by an embattled minority, have become widespread today (see Marwick 1998). Conservative critics of the Sixties agree but point to a popular mass with too great a sense of entitlement, too little social discipline, a popular mass that is too tolerant of drugs and violence, sexually licentious, dismissive of the eternal verities, and contemptuous of the accomplishments of what they refer to as "dead white males."

But Gitlin's generational thesis suffers from the fact that his generation was not uniquely active during the formative period (1958–64) of what was later to grow to a mass movement. Massive numbers of students became active only after the escalation of the war in early 1965. That earlier movement period was diversely peopled by those who had been active earlier in the postwar surge of 1945–48, by those who had been drawn into the battles against (Joseph) McCarthyism in the middle and late 1950s, and, of course, with those engaged from the mid-1950s in the struggle for racial equality and against the nuclear terror. According to the photographic evidence, the earliest demonstrators against the Vietnam War, like the earlier nuclear marches, were past university age, including many elderly and retirees. Within Students for a Democratic Society (SDS), then minuscule, soon to be the most famous of the American student organizations of the 1960s, the reigning view was that opposition to what was still a small war was a distraction. I took an active part in the SDS national conferences at Pine Hill in New York in 1963 and 1964. The Vietnam War was not a big issue at either conference; indeed, at the former there was a lively opposition to proposals that the organization give more than pro forma attention to it. The focus was on interracial work with the Student Non-Violent Coordinating Committee in the South and cooperation within the National Student Association, a federation of college student governments, on expanding the rights of students. Even in early 1965, the war ranked only a distant third or fourth on the SDS's list of priorities. In short, a generational explanation tells us something important about the period of the High Sixties, 1965 to 1968, and the later phase, 1968–74, but little about how a dissident movement, as it were, sowed the seeds of its later growth.

What, then, triggered what was to become the mass U.S. movement? It is very hard to argue that it was triggered by a single event. But there was a pattern of significant events in the period, say, 1954–58. The Supreme Court's school desegregation decision of 1954 was obviously important, as were several other decisions against the apparatus of the "Red Hunt." The Army-McCarthy hearings of mid-1954 discredited not only that redoubtable senator but the whole anticommunist apparatus. The mid-1950s witnessed a rebirth of civil rights activity North and South. The 1956 congressional elections brought in a whole new "class" of liberal legislators. One of its first acts was the passage of the Civil Rights Bill of 1957, which further animated that campaign. Nuclear threats against "Red China" over Quemoy and Matsu and the Soviet Union's economic and foreign policy successes were broadly unsettling. When in 1957 it was the Soviets and not the Americans who successfully put the first artificial satellite in orbit—*Sputnik*—there was a national reaction that seems hard to credit now. That launch and the series of corresponding U.S. failures to accomplish the same task undermined the American Success Story, which had been dominant since the late 1940s. All of these developments created openings for multiple opposition groups, heretofore hemmed in by that success story, to begin the process of expansion that would lead to the massive movements of 1965–68. Later the Kennedy campaign in 1960 and his bellicose inaugural address also frightened many to greater action, as did the series of international crises culminating in the October 1962 Cuban debacle.

The cultural changes cited by Gitlin and others were crucial, but so were the critiques of U.S. policy and society advanced by increasingly confident and assertive dissidents.[16] The U.S. "Left," still safely in the hands of warring pro- and anticommunists, played a small role here. For the East Coast at any rate, the tiny pacifist groups had particularly creative effects. There was no "movement" awaiting me in 1959–60, but there was an optimism among scattered activists that their numbers, understanding, and influence were growing. The figure of A. J. Muste looms large in that experience, as well as that of his associates such as David McReynolds, Ralph De Gia, Bayard Rustin, and David Dellinger. They seemed to think and act on a continuum with various Quaker groups associated with the American Friends Service Committee, especially the Fellowship of Reconciliation. All were tied together by the incomparable journalism of I. F. Stone.[17]

The period from around 1957 to spring 1965 saw the steady growth of an organized, though still small opposition with an increasingly persuasive analysis of where the country was and where it was too recklessly chancing social, political, and international danger. An alternate worldview was being created in opposition to the official versions of reality.

But even in the North then it could be dangerous to play the critic. I can recall a small antinuclear march down Madison Avenue in 1961 or 1962 where we were pelted with garbage, some of it dangerous, thrown from high-rise apartments along the route. I then knew of only three locations in and around New York City where one could distribute antiwar or antiracism leaflets without offers to have one's nose punched. And it was easy to lose one's job, as I did. But like so many others drawn into organizations for social change, I took seriously what the existing activists said because whatever sense they made was multiplied by their moral example. In 1959 there were only a handful, and by 1962 and the Cuban Missile Crisis only a few thousand, but by 1965 we were at the edge of a movement of hundreds of thousands that was soon to grow to millions.

That's why I find Marwick's "culture but not politics" distinction inadequate. His book is really indispensable. It contains an enormous mass of detail, covering the United States, Britain, Italy, and France, about the cultural changes that led up to the "High Sixties"; I've found no other single volume on the Sixties nearly so interesting and informative. But it is flawed from the analytical point of view. He finds it sufficient to judge that the period's politics was not of great importance because, in his view, no revolution was possible and only a few people, often the most marginal, aimed at such a thing.

Against this argument we have to weigh in the fact that in almost all the cultural changes proposed and enacted by the emerging movement were oppositional in character, that is, were actively opposed to and by the existing structures not only of cultural but also of political authority. Those who wanted to see mature films in the 1950s had to overcome the influence of the Hays Office, the motion picture censorship agency. If one wanted to read Henry Miller, one had either to fight the Post Office or to break the law. To get or hold a job you might be asked to pledge support for the McCarthy witch hunt. If black and white socialized together in public, they might be assaulted by young toughs. A white woman accompanied by a black man would be openly called a slut or a whore. Gay men were routinely beaten up. Abortion was illegal, and birth control information difficult to come by save in the larger urban centers. Sexual activity among the young was busily frustrated by school and other authorities. McCarthyism had been wounded but was not yet dead. History and political science curricula and the mainstream book reviews were resolutely patriotic, more than ready to suggest moral turpitude on the part of those who questioned the Korean War, the perfection of our institutions, or the wisdom of deterrence.[18] The emerging culture, which Marwick describes so ably, had to have a political dimension, and it had to have people willing to fight on that political front. It was able to enact itself as a major cultural mode, often indifferent to politics, only after there was an effective, mass political movement and, I think, because of it.

In short, it is difficult to understand why Marwick insists on making a dichotomy between culture and politics. It is as if his template for deep political change was classic Leninism—there must be a revolutionary situation and a proletarian agent of historical revolutionary agency. But since these were lacking, this could not be a revolution, but since it was a sort of revolution, the only sort it could be was cultural. QED. (See, for example, Marwick 1998, 10.)

It is a strained thesis to think that cultural conflict can ever be entirely dissevered from politics, if for no other reason that when different cultural values are enacted, they entail changes in already stratified societies, thus altering the existing pattern of winners and losers. Of course, it is foolish to argue for the primacy of politics, or of economics for that matter. I think Marx is right here, not his *Marxisants* followers. "Politics," "culture," "history," "economics," and so on do not represent different realms; they are different, overlapping standpoints from which we try to understand the totality of our social experience. Invariably—or at least most of the time—changes in one of those ostensible "realms" corresponds to changes in all, or several, of the others as well. The Sixties were deeply and intrinsically political; given the values espoused and the degree to which they so deeply aroused existing elites, "they" had to be political; and in fact, their oppositional character was what marked them as a cultural departure then and ever since.

The Issues of the Day

In his book *The Cultural Contradictions of Capitalism* (1976), Daniel Bell is extraordinarily hostile to the student movements of the 1960s, even to the point of ignoring their contributions to the passage of the Voting Rights Act under Lyndon Johnson or the earlier achievement of a nuclear test ban treaty under Kennedy. To say that I was put off by this book the first time I read it would be a gross understatement. I've mellowed since, in part because over the years I have come to admire the rest of Bell's work.

Bell accepts that the Sixties were largely populated by Gitlin's generation. His insertion point in criticizing it is the idea that a capitalist economic system undermines its own social and cultural systems via its successes and not, in the classic Marxian account, through its failures. Crudely, by encouraging individualism and materialism while producing great wealth, it tends to undermine the discipline the economic system needs to create that very wealth. If Bell didn't originate this by-now-familiar argument (as I think he actually did), he has certainly given it the erudition, analytical quality, and prestige that encouraged some smaller minds to co-opt the idea.

Bell's attack on the New Left and the Sixties characterizes it as the last, finally bankrupt and destructive stage of "modernism"; for him it opposed immediate gratification to disciplined self-denial and impulse to reason, and asserted the primacy of the self over society. Thus, at one of its poles modernism represents a pointless disruption of social norms and destruction of the social peace. With little attempt at subtlety or polite indirection, it is there that Bell locates the New Left. A "pathetic celebration of the self," "vulgar," "empty of originality," and "craving for violence" are only a few of the charges he levels (Daniel Bell 1976, 132, 86, 123, 143).

There were parts of the New Left and the student movement for whom those slings and arrows are well directed. Such egotism, publicity hunting, Yahoo-ism, and other, related antics were not solely the work of the marginal persons found in every social movement. One whole stream of the Sixties, especially after 1965, emerged from the modernist roots of the Beats, from among ecstasy seekers, out of experimental theater, and out of the influence of the reigning novelists of the just-previous era; it is in his discussions about just such roots, by the way, that Marwick is incomparably informative.

Bell's picture of the Sixties and the New Left seems no more than his own angry fantasy: the innumerable student activists and audiences that I met tended to be intellectuals, patriotic in a way that Bell would undoubtedly favor, more pragmatist than ideologue, more earnest than a New Yorker like myself was used to, but casual and democratic in their manners. In the early days, many had risked their lives in the South; later many would defy, not evade, their draft boards. Student activists tended to be close to and not alienated from liberal and progressive faculty members, condescending about the legendary stupidities of their college administrations, and deeply disappointed at the government. Ironically, I found them remarkably similar to the U.S. Army officers of similar age and education that I met on the front lines in Vietnam. These people did not turn into Bell's Yahoos; they were displaced by an alternate leadership because they failed to change U.S. policy. Many went into the Eugene McCarthy (1968) and McGovern (1972) presidential campaigns as a last attempt to set the country straight and, once that failed, moved away from the student movement.

But for the most cogent response to Bell's views, which are still not without influence, we have to return to his characterization of modern society as "an uneasy amalgam of three distinct realms: the social structure [what he calls elsewhere the *techno-economic order*], the polity and the culture" (Daniel Bell 1976, xi). Immediately, he identifies the political system as dominant over the others. Then he adds, tellingly, "The three realms—the economy, the polity and the culture—are ruled by contrary axial principles: for the economy, efficiency; for the polity, equality; and for the culture, self-realization (or self-gratification)." "Culture," for Bell, following Ernst Cassirer, whom he cites (12), is the world of expressive symbolism. By contrast, "culture" for both Gitlin and Marwick takes not only symbolic but also behavioral and institutional form.

It is not clear what his distinction of the three realms rests on or why he makes it. Knowing Bell's other work, one would say that the so-called techno-economic order has its own imperatives for social priority. In Bell's view the imperative needs of this order are self-generated and neither assigned by nor wholly consistent with the values of the polity and the culture.

If the Sixties had been made up of the moral and cultural equivalent of louts, then they could simply be dismissed. But the young people in the civil rights and antiwar movements were the "best and brightest," not the ambitious technocrats of the Kennedy administration.[19] They were young men and women who under appropriate circumstances might have entered public life, reconstructed race relations in the country, and moved the nation out of an already stalemated cold war.

That suggests that we have to look more critically at the imperatives of the techno-economic order. Of course, to point out—truly—that the "techno-economic order" is built on privilege, property, and one-sided power is to take the easier than the harder argument. I would say instead that even the "purely technical" imperatives of that realm are utterly conditioned by political and social priorities. Those imperatives, for rapid technological change, for example, would not have been so pressing if they had not had military applications, or so economically compelling if those economic benefits had not flowed to those in the elite and cadre life courses. In short, the "purely technical" imperatives of the techno-economic order were a product of the political and social priorities of the elites and the cadre, who insisted on having first claim on socially generated resources and refused to be subjected to socially imposed values that contradicted their sense of privilege. Of course, this is precisely what both the politics and the culture of the Sixties wanted to debate and ultimately change. Many of the young women and men of the time saw the witlessness of continuing cold war and the shallowness of social and economic success based on faster rates of technological development and exploitation than the "other side" could muster.[20] By dismissing the activists of the Sixties as hooligans and worse, Bell slides around this objection. It would be interesting to see how Bell would handle the reverberations of the proposition that the young people who became so utterly alienated from "the system" were the best, not the worst, of their "generation."

The Sixties did have a vision of sorts of a different society and a different world. Like all such visions, it was a little a short on detail and a little hazy on process. Had the Sixties been more successful, that vision would have proved less glowing than it seemed at the time, but again that's true of visions generally.

The argument between Bell and the Sixties is actually quite straightforward. Bell argues that there was a disjuncture developing between the economic, the political, and the cultural realms *because the economic realm could not change its existing imperatives or permit them to be changed by others.* The Sixties movements adopted a conservative stance here, thinking the economy should serve the good society, not require the sacrifice of other, often traditional values! In the 1960s, these were serious issues seriously posed by serious people.

It is very, very odd that the Sixties are now alleged to be irrationalist. Consider the following propositions—all which were accepted by most of the Sixties and rejected by most of their mainstream opponents:

- The Vietnam War was foolishly entered into, poorly waged from the U.S. side, unnecessarily prolonged, and would continue to have corrosive effects on the U.S. and the world economy.
- The cold war was essentially stalemated, thus expanding military spending was pointless.
- President Kennedy brought the world to the brink of nuclear war in 1962 as much for domestic political reasons as for international power-political reasons.
- "Deterrence" was not merely a matter of deterring nuclear war but an active gambling game of threat and counter-threat.

- Toppling the Iranian government in 1953 and the Guatemalan government in 1954 left a legacy not to the advantage of the United States.
- The racial gains made in the 1960s would provoke a backlash among whites but were not sufficient to satisfy black citizens or make a real difference in their life chances.
- Society was sufficiently wealthy to better care for those at the lowest income levels.
- The existing social relationships between adults and youths and females and males, like those between blacks and whites, needed to be brought up to date to conform to changed circumstances, practices, and values.

But to accept that these were true, or even just plausible, argues, as did the Sixties, that the techno-economic order was at fault for being out of sync with an emerging culture (in Gitlin's sense, not Bell's) and that the political system wasn't able to harmonize the disjuncture. In fact, given the "axial principle" of the political order, equality, presumably translatable to "democratic representativeness," it should in principle have been able to. But we have already met the then favored doctrine of pluralism and its "interposition" between a large mass increasingly conscious of the need for change and institutionally resistant elites. That the actual political system didn't seem to work was what led people into the streets.

The point of the dialectical exercise just concluded is to show that Bell's triune scheme can as easily be used to defend as to condemn the Sixties. The condemnation doesn't rest on the logic of the scheme but on the, I think, highly special way in which Bell has interpreted the character and trajectory of the young people of that decade.

Resisting the Intersection

The limitations of Bell's conception of culture as essentially a symbolic order and the more anthropological conception of culture implicit in both Gitlin and Marwick suggest that we need a more comprehensive and, I think, more historically rooted account of the culture of the Sixties than is found in any of the three books cited. And, as a corollary, one that will make sense of the extraordinary hostility that much of the U.S. intellectual/university elite still directs at the young people of that era. The thesis

I want to argue is that the "cultural revolt" was a revolt against the changes in the Intersection that were brought about largely, though not solely, by the maturation of the cadre life course.

Recall that for roughly a century it had been consistent Intersection "policy" to invest heavily in improvements in the life situation of the urban laboring classes with a view to transforming their menu of productive skills. This transformation was ideologically portrayed as providing a rising standard of living for everyone and, as important, opening up new and previously unheard-of opportunities for each succeeding generation. As it turned out, both the funding and the ideology reached their apogee in the decade and a half after World War II. Accordingly, it was in that very period, in both the United States and other developed countries, that the convergence between this transformation and the values of the interests of the Democracy was most marked. But it was also the period in which the matured cadre life course began to cool to the open-ended opportunity society they had just managed to join.

The Intersection system, then as now, sorted out virtually the entire population of children and young people, directing them into different educational cum life-course channels, differentially acculturated, socialized, and credentialed them, and then passed most of them automatically into the labor force or, as was then preferred for women, away from the labor force.[21] Three things changed about this system as the 1950s turned into the 1960s. First, it was well into a significant quantitative and qualitative shift, most prominently in the educational system. It earlier had been a "small batch" operation offering a relatively small proportion of the age cohort the chance to "rise in the world," in short, a veritable font of tens of thousands of new opportunities for tens of thousands of new graduates. But by the 1960s the educational system, especially in higher education, was a "mass manufacturing" system in which several millions of young people were to be competing for a shrinking number of new opportunities. This opportunity process was also being increasingly viewed with a jaundiced eye by the existing, newly minted "haves." At any event, the increase in size of the system, and concomitant lessening of student prospects, was reflected back into educational institutions in the form of fewer choices in classes, increased class sizes, more crowded and shabbier dormitories, and more distant and more bureaucratic administrations and professors (or more likely, adjunct instructors or graduate students).

It was at just this point in time that the Selective Service System's channeling work came to widespread student attention through the SDS publication, *New Left Notes*. The report created a stir because the Intersection system had been "sold" to college students as a system for increasing their freedom and opportunities, while all along it had been cooperating with a hidden agenda, namely, to "channel" young men into those roles called for by "the national defense." The guiding principle of the System was that every young male without exception had as his primary duty the obligation to serve national security. That was true whether one was in college or not. For male students one had to be in the top half of one's freshman class, the top third of the sophomore class, the top quarter of the junior class. That failing, the student's national obligation was to serve instead in the military. Science majors more readily got deferments than literature students, and so forth. Then the draft board kept tabs for another handful of years on what you did after graduation to see that it accorded with the national security priority.[22] There was also increasing awareness of a gendered channeling function within the system; women and men were channeled differently, the men into national service, the women out of the "opportunity" workplace. In its culture, in its staffing, and in the day-to-day treatment of women students, the higher education system was denying to women the very sort of equality of opportunity it trumpeted in its own justification.

Bell, like some other important intellectuals of *his* generation, is not well placed to see this, although perhaps he and they should be. In their own youth, the U.S. educational system was the way out of the immigrant tenements; as with Bell, Irving Kristol, Irving Howe, and Norman Podhoretz, success at New York's then tuition-free City College was the portal to elite positions in U.S. intellectual life and its cultural institutions.[23] In fact, I think one should associate with Bell's generation of intellectuals the root idea that the modern American university represented a kind of perfect institution whose presence overcame what would otherwise be the sins of a stratified society. They saw it as engaged in the business of knowledge production by scientific and intellectually competitive means, institutionally directed against all forms of social superstition, and devoted to undoing purely partisan ideology. They saw it as a supremely meritocratic institution where success came only—or very, very largely—from personal intellectual accomplishment and not breeding or inherited wealth. Their "University" was the guardian, in Plato's sense, of the higher values of the society, in this case of the egalitarian and democratic values of the United States.[24]

I must confess to having long shared Bell's beliefs about the "University," my convictions only weakening as I saw how poorly even the most accomplished and prestigious American universities, like my own Columbia University, coped with McCarthyism and how avidly they looked for opportunities to make research money off the cold war. In any case, this very rosy view of the American university by Bell and his cohorts was an ideological construction rationalizing and justifying the presence of university elites among the national elite and of university cadre as among the most important and productive cadre in the country. And as we now appreciate in an age less dazzled by the University, prestige within the modern university system depends not a little on which university one works at, the identity of one's mentors, "insider" research grants, cronies in the department or at the publishing house, and ideological correctness of one stripe or another. I do still believe that the culture of the research university is socially invaluable, but one has to deal with cases, not a prettifying ideology.

In any case, it wasn't Bell's "University" that the student generation confronted in the 1960s; it was Clark Kerr's "multiversity," the knowledge factory, the impersonal channeler of life prospects, ally of the Selective Service System and the Pentagon, and sexist par excellence. In fact, we don't have to divine that. The earliest accounts of student rebellion in Marwick, covering Britain, Italy, and France, as well as the United States, focus on student discontents with mundane things like visitation rights for students of the opposite sex, complaints about housing, scholarship availability, and overcrowded classrooms. Undergraduates complained that they were taught mostly by graduate students, with the latter unhappy about being underpaid. Both complained that the curriculum was ossified, politically scrubbed, a reflection of faculty interests, and usually male ones at that. It is, I think, a sustainable thesis that the Sixties generation had expectations that they were going to enjoy the university experiences and career promises of Bell and his age cohort and instead ran, as they said, into a "system" that, in a popular image, sorted, folded, stapled, and mutilated them instead.[25]

Moreover, it was not a neutral system merely responding to the technical imperatives of Bell's techno-economic order. It necessarily reflected something at least of the existing order of stratification of wealth, opportunity, prestige, access to power, and so on of the country. Worse, the Intersection system came to fullest flower in a particularly repressive time in the United States. As earlier suggested, the schools and university curricula were skewed toward a rosy view of the United States, its behavior, and its institutions. In the era just previous to the period we are discussing, many professors and teachers with dissident views had been ousted from the system.[26] Meanwhile, adjunct cultural institutions like the broadcasting, film, periodical, and book publishing industries celebrated the Great American Success Story. In short, the culture of the era preceding the Sixties, though it directed veritable salvos of "freedom" at the other side of the cold war, was, to put it mildly, politically well disciplined.

For male students, as we have seen, the university system was partnered with the Selective Service System.[27] There are many accounts now of females being counseled away from the more prestigious courses and professors, and away from graduate studies or careers. And there was worse. I recall attending a retirement party in the mid-1990s at a university in New York City for a professor friend. In the course of the speeches, another professor bragged of a vulgarism he long used in the classroom to force female students to sit at the rear rather than the front of the room. Even in that late time and in that relatively sophisticated environment, his vulgarism was received by many with hearty laughter.

Why the Sixties Failed

A narrowly cultural conception of the Sixties doesn't really hold up. The evidence is fairly compelling that the Sixties should be likened instead to, say, the late 1840s, that is, conceived as a watershed political challenge to the existing structures of authority and privilege. It is on that basis that I want in the next chapter to examine why and how the Sixties failed to make the changes it evidently desired. That failure, of course, has been a major reason for mainstream history to color the period as essentially a cultural phenomenon, its "style" vastly outweighing its political substance.

It is not clear why the Sixties demobilized politically after 1968. The line of explanation that makes most sense to me is that the Sixties suffered a crisis around 1968 stemming from their inability to stop or limit the war. The crisis was also materially abetted by the increasing alienation between black and white political activists. Even by the fall of 1967, it was evident that its bursting growth was coming to an end, that the movement was already a player in national politics, and that, accordingly, one had to work out the programs, strategies, and organizational forms for this new stage. As one must expect when one has achieved a measure of potentially threatening political influence, elite political figures were already casting about for ways to counter and check the movement. Instead it took a sharp turn away from actual political tasks, becoming less instrumental in character and more purely expressive, seemingly more interested in displaying its existence than in representing the needs of the country. There was a radical shift of leadership in the movement. This shift took two forms, both destructive. Political failure discredited the older leadership, which gave way on the one hand to cultural radicals like the "Diggers," who celebrated an ethos of extroverted alienation (see Gitlin 1987 and Daniel Bell 1976).

On the other hand, failure encouraged a tendency within student ranks to view events in terms of ideology rather than programs and policies. This was evidently and, I think, destructively true among young black activists. "Black Power" animated very little in the way of political program; it was more often a substitute for political program. Within the SDS, two ideological streams arose, one more destructive than the other. The Weathermen, later Weatherpeople, have of course passed into legend (and the 2008 presidential election!).[28] Their alter ego was a breakaway from the U.S. Communist Party called the Progressive Labor Party. The latter claimed to represent the Chinese brand of revolutionary communism and not the "revisionist" Soviet brand. Chicken and egg are hard to separate here, but on some of the more elite campuses, most dramatically at Harvard and Columbia, a new student leadership arose that divided along these lines. Via their success in packing or intimidating SDS national and regional meetings, these groups came to share the dominant influence in SDS, which, embroiled by their angry, sterile, sometimes even armed rivalry, soon collapsed. Many students left the student movement, going on to participate in the McCarthy, McGovern, and some other campaigns; but there, too, their inability to change national policy ultimately demobilized the political wing of the movement. Somewhat later, many 1960s political activists gravitated into NGOs, the trade unions, social work, policy science, and other social change activities. A half century on, I run into such people all the time, mostly in and around economics-related issues, programs, and publications, in educational reform, and in the environmental movement.

The withering of the student movement took place more or less at the same time as, and partially because of, the splintering of the civil rights movement between integrationist and nationalist/separatist tendencies. The rise of feminism and feminist organizations also helped splinter much New Left and kindred movement activity; however, modern feminism could not, I think, have made the gains it has if it had remained saddled with a distinctly left-wing association. The slowing economy also played its part in demobilizing "the Movement," as did the success of the Nixon administration in appearing to wind down the Vietnam War when it was in fact covertly delaying its termination. And there was a new mobilization of conservative, even reactionary forces, such as the movement led by Governor George Wallace. In the last analysis, all this adds up to saying that the political wing of the Sixties was politically defeated.

3

THE MODERN REACTION

American historians tend to believe that the United States has not had a reaction on the classic European model because we lack a feudal past.[1] But the evidence indicates that we have to entertain the possibility that at least some of the categories of classic European politics transferred over to this formerly innocent republic.

Characterizing the Present

The most recent period of U.S. history is unusual to the point of novelty. The United States had experienced through November 2008 the longest conservative ascendancy of the past one hundred years. For example, the combination of the "Preparedness" drive when Woodrow Wilson's administration suppressed critics and opponents of the U.S. entry into World War I, followed by the infamous Palmer Raids against "radicals" and then their anti-immigrant sequel, stretched from 1917–18 to perhaps 1923–24, or about five to eight years. "McCarthyism," an amalgam of the Truman Loyalty Security Program and the witch hunts by the Senator Joe of that name, and including those of the House Un-American Activities and Senate Internal Security Committees, lasted from 1947–48 to perhaps 1954–57, or six to ten years. The modern period of conservative domination dates from the election of Richard Nixon in 1968, or perhaps his reelection in 1972, that is to say, *nearly four decades*.[2] The very length of this conservative domination does suggest that it is more than a normal phase in the alternating cycle between conservative and progressive periods in U.S. politics.

The cumulative changes over this era also carry the strong implication that the advance of the Democracy had been halted and even rolled back. The "mixed economy" earlier dominant in the United States is giving way to what is widely called "privatization." There has been a shift in the power-political relationship between government and big business; the former, once the (admittedly timid) watchdog over the latter, has become more or less its satellite. This was accompanied by extensive dismantling of the welfare state, not just "welfare" payments per se. There has been a weakening of the opportunity structure for the lower half to two-thirds of the population, with accompanying effects on income distribution and other social indicators, including the nullification of a once considerable trade union power. There has been a return to a bipartisan racial policy, which, though extending liberality to some parts of the black population, has blocked the possibility of significant change for its vast majority.

Closely related, there has been an evolution toward greater federal influence over domestic policing, a huge expansion in the size and influence of that police power (courts, prosecutors, police, prisons); and again a novelty in the United States, the police power has become a significant player in the political process. The presence of the police within the political process is one of the hallmarks of classic European reaction.

Changes in foreign policy since circa 1970 can also be included, though the case for a unique reaction is less clear here. Since the administration of Theodore Roosevelt, foreign policy had been the almost exclusive prerogative of the highest national security elites. This exclusivity, itself an alien import from the European state system, was challenged by the movements of the Sixties, but this was countered by the reaction that set in after 1970. After the great public storms over Vietnam and nuclear war policy in the 1960s, there was some return to major party collusion, or "bipartisanship," in foreign policy, that is, the parties agreeing not to intrude on the inner national security government here. The wars in Afghanistan and Iraq-2 were supported, if hesitantly, by congressional Democrats as well as Republicans. There was early congressional passivity over military interventions in Iraq-1, Granada, Libya, and Panama, and later in Colombia and Bolivia. But there is some change from the past. Bipartisanship in the era of Truman and Vandenberg and Eisenhower and Mansfield was in foreign diplomatic and political policy. At present, those are hesitantly marked by party differences, but the parties have colluded in U.S. trade and monetary policy and in the exclusion of the public from any significant input there. It is to the point that trade policy and international monetary policy, unlike other, more traditional diplomatic and "political" issues, have been prioritized by the most influential U.S. elites. Arguably, the current meltdown of the U.S. and world economies is one product of this bipartisan collusion.

Three distinct but interacting developments appear to explain how and why there was such a sharp and extended reaction to the Sixties. There was a heightened sense among business elites that the Sixties helped bring on, first, the economic upheavals of the early 1970s and, second, the social breakdown that accompanied them. Third, there was a mobilization against those changes on the part of the more conservative, less secular, "traditional" part of our society.[3] Each of these developments, potent in itself, was multiplied by its interaction with the other two. There were other changes too that will be integrated into the following narrative, but these three seem most central and powerful.

Mobilizing Against Economic Upheaval and Social Breakdown

Ronald Reagan's election in 1980 confirmed a radical change in the political dynamics that had marked the period after the New Deal of Franklin Delano Roosevelt. This in good part reflected a new political mobilization on the part of corporate elites (Phillips-Fein 2008). The mobilization was signaled in the first instance in the 1970s by the birth of many new, well-funded conservative foundations challenging the former influence over public affairs of the centrist Ford and Rockefeller Brothers foundations. The Heritage Foundation (founded in 1973), the Coors Foundation (1975), the Cato Institute (1977), and the Manhattan Institute (1979) joined with the older but now revivified Hoover Institution (1919) and the American Enterprise Institute (1943), for example, to provide research and informed advocacy for a much wider range of much more far-reaching proposals and initiatives than business-oriented conservatives had mounted earlier.

This mobilization altered the agenda for public debate and, consequently, legislative and executive action. It familiarly called for lower taxes, but added to that call an increasingly successful drive to use private-sector criteria to govern the size of government budgets and the spending of public monies, which entailed where possible the privatization of many traditional government functions. To that end there were several vain attempts to replace Social Security with private retirement accounts, and several successful attempts to turn military logistics functions over to private firms and to counter the exclusive mandate of the public elementary schools with charter schools and educational voucher schemes. Under the influence of business mobilization, taxes on upper incomes and private corporations were radically reduced, the airlines and interstate trucking industries were deregulated, the separation between savings banks and investment banks was erased, and government action on the economy was redirected from producing full employment to its Phillips curve opposite, maintaining significant unemployment in the interests of price stability.[4]

This long-term shift in the public/private balance was further empowered by the inflation of the early 1970s, which was characterized as "wage-led."[5] Accordingly, there was new pressure to marginalize previous trade union influence over economic policy and to hinder union expansion. "Privatizing" was particularly thought to weaken the public-sector unions, which had expanded considerably during the 1960s and which had shown a greater disposition to press for new social welfare programs than the (already) declining, more traditional unions in the private sector.

There was also a widespread public impression, not entirely ill-founded, that the unions had become merely one more among the participants in the institutional tête-à-tête, represented a relatively privileged segment of workers, and were a barrier to the further economic advance of black, female, and Latino workers. The diehard support of the AFL-CIO for the Vietnam War and, later, for U.S. interventions against political change in Latin America also served further to weaken the former labor-liberal political bloc that had played such a great part in Democratic Party domination of U.S. politics from 1933 to 1968.

Both cause and consequence of this weakening of the trade unions was the shift of Democratic party officeholders away from "bread-and-butter" issues of economic fairness, which are of particular concern to workers, and toward issues like abortion, affirmative action, the failed Equal Rights Amendment, environmental issues, and so forth, which are of concern primarily to middle-class, cadre Democrats. The result was a decline in party loyalty and electoral support among the workers.[6]

The business mobilization seems as inevitable as political matters can ever be. Governmental intervention into the economy was bound to draw its own reaction. New Dealers, Progressives before them, and later, Great Society adherents had assumed that government could by regulation make private corporations more socially responsible. But it should surprise no one to discover that governmental regulatory bodies are reflecting public interests less and less and industry interests more and more. Thus the National Labor Relations Board has become a hindrance to union organizing, the SEC gave its blessings to anarchy in the securities industry, and polluting firms hide behind the friendly decisions of the Environmental Protection Agency. As we saw, the modern social surplus is produced within the big corporate firms, and they enjoy the option to redirect it to their own, not society's, purposes. Corporate elites had always engaged in a bit of this redirection, but in the 1970s and 1980s they both expanded and focused the effort.

Economic Narratives

There are a number of "deep" explanations for the business mobilization that fairly represent what occurred, that is, explanations rooted in unforeseen and unplanned economic changes. The following, though severely condensed, is sufficient for our purposes.[7]

In the late 1960s, the recovery and expansion that followed World War II ended. Some authors also point to the end of the "long wave" technological environment at the time, namely to the decline of the "auto-industrial age" of heavy manufacturing industries and the emergence of a more service-oriented "postindustrial" economy (Rothschild 1973; Daniel Bell 1973). At any event, modern economies are dominated by firms that "engineer" the characteristics of their markets, hence can raise prices in the face of stable or declining demand and profitability, and many did.[8] This fed an inflation so severe that it threatened domestic securities values and weakened the dominant role of the dollar in international exchanges. This in turn led to a decline in the real price of petroleum, mostly paid for in dollars, which then led OPEC to administer the two "oil shocks" (shortages and price rises) of 1973 and 1979. In this same period too, corporate profit rates seriously declined, which was an effect of a lag in new investment that corporate profit-taking had caused.

One corollary of the "end of the long wave" was that firms based on heavy manufacturing and its related industries faced declining opportunities for new investment and for productivity growth, hence profit growth. Firms slow to cut wage costs would find their securities prices stagnant, even declining, and accordingly, were subject to takeover efforts by outsiders or, not infrequently, by upper management insiders. This encouraged a vigorous effort to relocate productive processes in low-wage countries and to substitute overseas for domestic suppliers. That "relocation" and "substitution" are what is normally emphasized when one speaks of "globalization," as in Thomas Friedman's facile work *The World Is Flat* (2005).

In spite of this unfavorable conjuncture of changes, the then still powerful trade unions responded to rank-and-file pressures by demanding pay raises sufficient to keep up with the rapid inflation, and in spite of stagnating productivity to continue to insist on rising standards of living. Brown (1986) shows there was a veritable leap upward (a "hinge") in the annual rates of wage increases in Italy, Japan, France, Belgium, Britain, the Netherlands, Sweden, (West) Germany, and the United States. In his analysis, this was cost-push, that is, wage-push inflation rooted in the changed attitudes of younger workers, who had not experienced either the prewar or wartime worker hardships and who consequently assumed as their birthright an ever-increasing income. In his view, as in mine, this period bears comparison with "1848" as a time in which old, established social values and social discipline were being sharply challenged.

It was in this period too that the Phillips curve, formulated earlier but ignored for almost a decade, began to win adherents among economists and economic policymakers, that is, that employment rates and inflation rates were inversely related.

As it turned out, the "hinge" further aggravated the problems the U.S. and other economies were facing. U.S. behavior was especially harmful here; both its domestic and international debts rose very rapidly, caused in part by the Johnson administration's unwillingness to sacrifice increasing domestic consumption even while fighting a ruinously expensive war in Vietnam.

This fear of raising taxes, in spite of the pressing need to do so, along with "excessive trade union demands" and the rebelliousness among the young, was seen by some observers as evidence of a general decline in social discipline. Bell's "cultural contradictions," no less than the worries of the Eisenhower Commission,[9] may be seen as further evidence that this alleged decline in social discipline formed part of the background for the economic and social reactions being pressed in some elite circles.

Parenthetically, there are some flaws in this apparently plausible narrative, at least about the effects of overseas competition. Until quite recently, 90 percent or more of international trade occurred between and even within the very large international firms, hence at administered, not competitive, prices. Most telling, the technology, the financing, and the markets for goods and services now produced in, say, Malaysia, Indonesia,

India, Mexico, and China were and still are Western, that is, "globalization" is largely a phenomenon occurring within and in relation to a handful of very large firms based in and selling in the traditional industrial countries. The claim that Western workers "have no choice" but to tighten their belts because of non-Western wage competition is thus fundamentally deceptive. Policy rules here, not necessity. That suggests that "globalization" has at least as much ideological content as it does economic reality.

Winners and Losers

We must also add to our narrative the changes introduced from 1968 onward into the international monetary and trading system. These were intended to slow economic growth, thereby fostering greater economic and social discipline across the board, and, in that, were largely successful.

Under the previous accords among the main trading nations in 1944 ("Bretton Woods"), the dollar served as a substitute for gold in international transactions by the simple device of the United States pledging to redeem dollars from any member nation at a fixed dollar/gold price. So long as dollars were in short supply in the world, and U.S. technical and economic aid essential, other nations wished to seek and hold dollars, not inclining to convert them into gold. But with the high U.S. inflation in the mid-to-late 1960s, there was a rush to convert dollars to gold and in response to this demand, the United States voided the dollar/gold link in mid-1968. Nevertheless, it tried to maintain fixed exchange rates between the dollar and other major currencies. But as both the U.S. debts and inflation continued, in 1971 the other nations allowed their currency/dollar exchange rates to "float," that is, vary in response to the relative scarcity or surplus of their currency with respect to dollars.

As many commentators have pointed out, this shift to floating rates was a step of exceptional importance, for it exposed each national economy to the same sort of often dampening economic pressures they had faced before the establishment of the Bretton Woods system. Prior to these agreements, each country's domestic prices, hence wages, had in the relatively short run to adjust to the flow of gold in and out of the country. Credit, hence economic activity, was stifled when gold fled because of high prices, high wages, or inflation; it was revivified when gold flowed back in response to low prices, low wages, and deflation. These golden tides could be abrupt and often unpredictable and, to that extent, inhibited economic activity and, especially, growth. Keynes and his followers, who had a major hand in crafting the Bretton Woods agreements, wanted an international economy in which each nation was protected from such international gold flows, which, by depressing popular incomes had both caused and then maintained the Great Depression. As long as other countries found it advantageous to accept and amass holdings in dollars, the fixed dollar/gold arrangement retained some of that Keynesian desire. Essentially then, these Keynesian constructions protected the level of employment, wages, investment, and economic activity within each industrial country from unwanted changes, including competition, originating outside its borders, thus giving employers and employees considerable "wiggle room" in setting national wage rates, minimizing unemployment, and using inflation to stimulate growth.[10]

In each of the European countries, Bretton Woods hastened the recovery from the devastation of World War II and helped raise living standards because its provisions allowed for cooperative agreements between national employer associations and trade union federations. In the United States this structure was replicated in the relationships of the AFL, the CIO (which merged with the AFL after 1955), and eastern financiers, which were brokered by the then dominant New Deal/Fair Deal/New Frontier Democratic Party. That amity was of course founded in Keynesian/Bretton Woods policies and would not survive their demise.

Even before the end of Bretton Woods and continuing after 1968–71, most Western economic elites had been trying to stem inflationary pressures via agreements with their respective trade union federations to institute an "incomes policy," that is, that wage increases and social services expansion would not exceed productivity gains. Under more straitened economic conditions, wage and income policies naturally became more conflicted and in some cases, notably in the United States in 1981 and in Britain in 1984–85, that led to conflict between the government and the trade unions, in both cases won handily by government.

In the United States the conflict was between the then brand-new Reagan administration and the air traffic controllers' union; by refusing to support the controllers, the AFL-CIO leadership accepted a "temporary" defeat—from which it has not recovered in the ensuing quarter-century. In Britain, the National Union of Miners, without support from the Trade Union Congress, tried in March 1984 to prevent the Thatcher government from closing down much of an obsolete coal mining industry. A veritable war followed in which roving bands of strikers and whole battalions of police were pitted against each other in mass physical altercations. Mrs. Thatcher, who earlier had had to bow to the miners' militant tactics, had used the ensuing period to expand the size of and improve the crowd-control capacities of the police; by March 1985 the NUM was thoroughly beaten and, in further consequence, the trade unions lost their influential place in the setting of economic policy.

From being partners in national rebuilding, the trade unions were now viewed as the most dangerous enemies of the overarching need to be or to become competitive and were, accordingly, either virtually ousted from government influence, as in the United States and Britain, or at the least, saw their political influence sharply reduced. This political power shift in turn served to direct government behavior away from welfare state expenditures and toward tax cuts for business; greater permissiveness for the latter to reduce their employment, environmental, and even fiduciary responsibilities;[11] new forms of assistance to the bigger corporate players; and a more hostile business environment for the smaller firms.[12] In the United States at least, the growth of large firms in industries such as trucking and banking at the expense of many smaller companies, and the rapid growth of franchises in lines of business also only recently dominated by smaller firms, such as fast food, real estate, financial services, and retailing generally, is not unrelated to this wider movement toward greater corporate influence over government policy. "Privatization" has many faces, but all of them reflect a major historical political power shift away from trade unions and small firms, with government the arbitrator, to an ingathering of power in a relatively small number of great corporations exercising more and more influence over government policies.[13]

The transformation of government from arbitrator between union, regional, urban, and corporate contenders and into the instrument of the last is a corollary to the demise of the other, noncorporate contenders. Basically, there are no or few forces now to countervail the power of "big business";[14] and accordingly, government has more and more become the agent of, and not the arbitrator over, business power.

The period 1968–71 also represents the rout of the century-old social-democratic/progressive strategy to check corporate power. Attempts to revive traditional liberalism must confront the fact that its core strategy, to use government to regulate the worst excesses of corporate power, has been historically overcome by the greater ability of big business to win and hold government support. Ironically, at the center of this historic liberal defeat is its expansion of inner government, that is, the expansion of regulatory bodies like the Federal Reserve, the FAA, the SEC, the EPA, the Labor Department, the Civil Rights Commission, and so on, which were generated by the liberal/progressive movement. Those agencies still regulate, but they rely on the expertise of the regulated industry, not the public and "critical social science." One can only successfully regulate big business before the fact, that is, if one can *prevent* its ingathering of one-sided political and, especially, economic power. Afterward is too late. I addressed this conundrum in chapter 1 and will return to it in chapter 9.

A Maturing Cadre

The maturation of the cadre class or life course also fed into this new medley of economic policies. In the United States from the late nineteenth century, and for the other capitalist powers from 1945, the public sector was an engine of investment in human capital with the emerging cadre life course its prime beneficiary. With that expansion more or less achieved around 1970, one would expect a shift in the politics of this life course away from support for the public sector.

There is a great deal of literature about the shift of one-time voters from the big cities, where they supported New Deal/Fair Deal policies of "big government," to the suburbs, where they now vote Republican, insist on lower taxes, and oppose "big government." But this is readily understandable as a simple reflex to the reality that the cadre, reared mostly by the public sector, had reached "critical mass" by the 1960s, hence was able to reproduce itself with family resources, and thus saw further government encouragement of educational opportunity for others as threatening to their own children's social and educational advantages.

This is a huge change. From the Progressive Era through the Great Society of LBJ, that is, from around 1900 to the 1960s, the dominant political bloc among the nation's emerging cadre class—not necessarily the majority but those who took the political lead—had offered support for more democratically shared economic and social opportunities. It especially embraced support for expanded public education, at first for the elementary and high schools, later for university education via the growth of publicly funded higher educational institutions, the G.I. Bill, and related interventions to expand access to private colleges and universities. Even more broadly, it was the public sector, both directly and via its effects on the private sector that gave birth to, nurtured, and expanded this cadre class. But as the cadre matured, it changed from a "class on the make" to a more "privileged class," and this inevitably undermined cadre support first for workers and later for nonwhites and immigrants.[15]

One cannot understand the tectonic shift of cadre politics save by interrupting our narrative to analyze two points that are tied together by conflicts over issues of social mobility. The slowdown in economic growth attendant on the end of the Bretton Woods system implied a slowdown in upward social mobility and, *pari passu,* greater competition over the social advantages previously won by the emerging cadre. These now had to be more tightly reserved for their children. To this must be added the (then) highly visible entry of black people into a competition over upward social mobility that had formerly excluded them, but an entry too slow to satisfy all and thus one that brought a police response.

"Social mobility," "equality of opportunity," and other, related expressions are so sacralized in our political discourse that one can easily lose sight of just what they mean, how they actually work, and what political and other consequences they bear in train. The following simple model has the virtue of directing some additional light on those three questions.

Modeling the Contradictions of Social Mobility

Let us imagine a population of 200 persons comprising the membership of two adjacent social strata, a higher and a lower. On the basis of the existing literature on social mobility, we can more or less realistically assume that 60 (or 30 percent) are now in the higher stratum, the other 140 (70 percent) in the lower. And with the same literature in mind, let us further more or less realistically assume that in a single generation 30 percent of the higher group, 18 persons, will fall to the lower, being replaced by 18 newcomers rising from that same lower group. On the same assumptions, (about) 42 of the lower group (30 percent of 140) will fall still lower over the same generation and be equivalently replaced. But I want to focus only on the initial interface.

For the moment, let us further assume no increase in the absolute size of either stratum and no increase in the relative size of the higher stratum. For the moment, we want to focus on the simple exchange of persons between the two adjacent strata over the course of one generation.

For the sake of historical relevance as well as simplicity (and whole numbers), let us assume that at a point only one of those rising eighteen is black, as is one of the falling, that this maintains the underrepresentation of black people in the higher group, and that one wants to take steps to change this.

Accordingly, some such steps are taken to ensure that, say, two of the ascending eighteen will be black, so that black persons will eventually be represented in the higher, more privileged stratum in proportions more akin to their proportion of the entire population.[16] The technical problems here are complex but not overwhelming. We really do know how to intervene in the processes of social mobility. One of the enduring achievements of the civil rights victories of the 1960s and subsequently was to expand the numbers of black people in the cadre life course and, to a somewhat lesser degree, among the ranks of the skilled, higher-paid, more secure workers.

But whatever the technical ease of inducing higher rates of upward social mobility for a targeted group, the political fallout is hard to obscure from those who are disadvantaged by it.

One of the pressing faults of public debates over social mobility is that they ignore the fact that as some climb, others must fall. Quite often, it is implicitly assumed that there will be economic growth, which will reduce the threat for those in danger of falling. Thus much of the liberal political and social theory I was raised on in college eagerly focused on this issue of growth and conveniently avoided having to discuss the unpleasant fact that in every generation a whole cohort of people do in fact drop from a more to a less advantaged stratum.

Or it may be that economic recession will help disguise the nature of the fall; it will make it appear that many others are in the same sinking boat and, again, disguise the unpleasant fact that downward social mobility is just as much built into the system as the sunnier, upward variety.

Upward Mobility or Lateral Mobility?

Upward social mobility has also been confused with the very different phenomenon of lateral social mobility. In the first, one rises in the same privilege hierarchy; in the latter, one passes without rising or falling from one privilege hierarchy to another, different one. This is a very substantive point, and to confuse them, as I think they were confused in the social science I learned in university, is to deceive oneself and to cripple one's reading of both past history and present public policy. The period of the historic advance in the United States was uniquely marked by very large-scale lateral mobility, that is, from rural/small town middle class to big city cadre/middle class. In a sense, a whole class moved laterally. The "middle class" in the United States circa 1870 was almost exclusively made up of members of the entrepreneurial professions (doctors, veterinarians, lawyers, dentists, architects, and so on), farmers, and small and medium business owners. The great bulk of them resided outside the main industrial cities. Over the next roughly one hundred years, many of this middle class were transformed into employees, joined the manager life course, and moved from small towns and the countryside to the cities and the suburbs. The bridge for this historic shift was the Intersection, most visibly its public sector in education and related areas.

In the social science I was taught, this transformation was almost always miscast as an example of upward and not lateral mobility. Its historical reality actually consisted of the shift of the son of the prosperous Moline manufacturer into a management job in a big Chicago firm, or the path of the well-off farmer's son into a successful career in high-tech engineering via Iowa State University. But my teachers, like myself, typically came out of families that had immigrated to the United States in the late nineteenth and early twentieth centuries and, perhaps forgivably, embellished the American success story by assuming that as the second- and third-generation hyphenated Americans went, so went the nation; immigrant children actually "moved up," but almost everyone else "moved over."

Lateral social mobility in an economy stepping from small business and agriculture to one predominantly organized by large corporate firms has entirely different political consequences than the upward social mobility that still tends to preoccupy much of the social science literature. There is normally a very great deal of upward and downward mobility in a society, but it is only in special eras that we can find its effects overlapped by massive lateral mobility. When lateral mobility was very high, upward mobility was both hidden and got a boost, as from expanding school opportunities, increased college enrollment, and expanding jobs in the cadre course. But when that era came to a close, upward social mobility became more squeezed. And, of course, voters willing to support measures enhancing lateral mobility may balk at the different ones required to abet the upward variety. It is, after all, one thing to fund the state university system on behalf of the sons of well-off rural and small-town bourgeoisie, quite another to bear the costs of raising the social standing of the sons and daughters of the urban working class. I think this historic phenomenon explains much, perhaps most, about the narrowing of the U.S. opportunity structure in the 1960s and thereafter. If anything, that narrowing was multiplied by the conundrums already implicit in the upward/downward mobility model and its social realizations.

Mobility Conundrums

Let us return to those conundrums. It is possible that the "ups" and "downs" in such mobility may be tied to growth in the relative size of the more privileged stratum. Again, in my college years this was often confused with economic growth, though clearly there may be discrepancies between the effects of a larger pie and those of changes in the distribution of the pieces of the same pie. If the latter, there can be very sharp economic consequences, as can be readily illustrated.

At the present writing, a reasonable approximation is that the upper 30 percent of employed persons earn about one-half the national personal income. On that basis, each such person enjoys roughly 1.666 units of the national income (50 divided by 30), while the lower 70 enjoy roughly 0.714 of the same units (50 divided by 70). The mean income ratio between individuals in the higher and the lower strata is then roughly 2.33/1. If for the sake of argument one expands the upper group by 10 percent, then the appropriate income will somehow be directed to them, for that is one of the main rewards of upward social mobility. Now 33 upper-stratum persons should enjoy roughly 55 percent of the national personal income (33 times 1.666), while the 67 persons remaining in the lower group share the other 45 percent or 0.67 units each. Note, however, the change in the ratio of mean personal income between the two strata: it rises from 2.33/1 to nearly 2.5/1. Of course these are only hypothetical figures, not real ones, but they make the point: expanding the relative size of the more privileged has a real impact on the income of the less privileged. Here a 10 percent expansion of the higher stratum is associated with a nearly 7 percent fall in the mean income of the lower. One can expand the relative numbers of the privileged in a society for a while, but at some point it seems to promise a sharper level of socioeconomic tension, possibly even actual conflict.[17]

Putting these unpleasant complications aside for the moment, we should go back to the simpler model—if there is no or insignificant economic growth, then the size ratio of the strata remains more or less constant. It is here that we want to increase the size of the rising black cohort from one to two, or whatever.

Focusing on the exchange of persons between the higher and the lower strata, the initial exchange was of 17 whites and 1 black rising to replace 17 whites and 1 black falling. The new situation will be 16 whites and 2 blacks rising, 17 whites and 1 black falling. These numbers serve to illustrate a potential political problem, namely that white downward mobility will be directly proportional to black upward mobility. The more of the latter, the more of the former.

The problem is that in the model and, more important, in reality, the process is as visible as any public process in our society. The model suggests that the parents of the initial upper 30 percent would realistically be aware that their children have a very high chance—almost 1 in 3—of falling from their privileged birth status and that consequently most of them will be attuned to those public policy choices that will help or threaten their children's chances. This, of course, is the very stuff of school board politics, the not-so-hidden issue behind so many debates about expanding or contracting the public sector, what's really being talked about when state university tuition is on the agenda, or affirmative action, or primary school enrichment programs, or charter schools and "public school reform."[18] Social fury may even come to surround the kind and frequency of tests that children are given; and as in the 1970s with "Jensenism," there may even be a revival of the idea that school opportunities should be based on the "superior" genes of the already advantaged (see Jensen 1969).

We actually know that the parents of the lower group are not as involved in these issues, but some surely will be. Those who have grander ambitions for their children will be looking quite as hard at this process of exchange between adjacent strata as it takes the visible form of tax breaks or loan guarantees for tuition, school board budgets, state university policies, or—wider—the hiring practices of firms and promotion policies within the office or plant.

Race, Corporate, and Social Mobility

Normally, the rises and falls in social mobility involve anonymous individuals. But such was not the case as the 1960s proceeded and as social mobility opportunities were shrinking, hence becoming more a center of potential social disputation. This was also the very same era in which black Americans *as a group* entered what some writers too casually refer to as the social mobility game.

As my own understanding of the U.S. racial situation has evolved, I've found that one can neither understand it nor cope with it entirely in the familiar terms of the social psychology of racism or in the cryptobiological way in which race so often enters contemporary discussions.[19] One useful, alternative way of thinking about race in the United States is to understand that black Americans have been viewed until the quite recent past, including the Civil Rights Era, as if they belonged to a premodern "order" or "rank" or "estate"—in the feudal way said to be lacking in this country. It is a historical distortion to view past black/white relations solely as a function of informal social attitudes and superstitions or a regional peculiarity or, even earlier, as is common, under the rubric of a history of special suffering and social deprivation in slavery.

One can and should question whether the experience of black Americans under slavery forms a radical disconnect from the social experience of other U.S. groups, or soon-to-be U.S. groups elsewhere in the same period. If, for example, we take 1850 as a base date, U.S. workers in the coal and metal mines, in the maritime trades, in domestic service, and in much factory work labored under systems that still had a heavy feudal overlay insofar as they granted to the "master" a one-sided authority to hire and fire at whim, to change work regimes and hours, to demand favors and kickbacks from his underlings, and even to physically chastise them. Six-day work weeks of ten or twelve or more hours per day were the norm. As we know from the textile and mining districts, everyone in the family had to work just to make ends meet in normal times; in poor times or during seasonal downturns, as in the mining districts, one ran up debts. One then had no alternative to the infamous "company store," since miners then were often paid in company scrip, not regular money. Soon-to-be Americans in southern Italy, Ireland, Poland, Greece, and other then socially primitive regions actually lived under conditions little different than serfs, in which the master had an authority over his laborers' daily lives in most ways as harsh and unconditioned as that enjoyed by the old slave masters of Georgia or Mississippi.[20]

Until quite late in the nineteenth century, the social-material and even moral conditions of so-called free-laborers and peasants were not radically different from those that held in the antebellum slave states of the upper

U.S. South.[21] The point, of course, is not who suffered more, an ultimately vain question, but that everywhere prior to the historic advance ordinary men, women, and children lived brutalized lives. Stretching back to ancient times, all the generations of every lower order are bound together historically by the shortness, the narrowness, the overwork, the poverty, the ever-present suffering, and the abasement of their lives.

On the other hand, it is significant that in "nonfeudal" America, black people were viewed as a distinct order or rank—a separate "body" and not a collection of persons. My use of the word "body" or "corporate" shouldn't be confusing in spite of its association with a form of business firm. It points instead to the fact that black people in the past functioned in our law and polity not as individuals but instead in terms of their membership within a formally or institutionally designated group, at various times black people, Negroes, African Americans, and so forth. Their various and distinct personal fates and fortunes have been in almost every case deeply influenced, for good or ill, by that political incorporation. One can add "law and polity" because until quite recently the "order" status of black people had a defining legal dimension.

The legal incorporation passed through four phases: slavery, Reconstruction, segregation, and the Civil Rights Era. Each points to a different, coherent, and continuous legal and political place for black people in the United States, a place not occupied by the whites. I doubt if anyone would disagree about slavery or Southern Reconstruction. Later, in the post-1890s or segregation era, some few blacks were able to sneak in under the radar to economic and professional success, though in the South the selfsame government policy looked the other way at the systematic violence that first established the Jim Crow segregation of the races and then subsequently maintained it from 1876 to 1965.

An "order" difference was also for a time operative at the inception of the civil rights legislation in the 1950s and 1960s. Under U.S. law and practice, black Americans were then given a special corporate legal status. The law and the practice realistically assumed that black people were discriminated against in hiring, promotion, firing, housing, access to credit and health care, voting, even driving. Accordingly, black people were for a period placed under special legal protections to which they could uniquely appeal for redress. Those alleged to offend against those protected rights of black people were not presumed to be guilty of committing discriminatory crimes, but at the same time neither were they "innocent until proven guilty." Typically, alleged offenders had to show that they hadn't participated in a pattern of discrimination, that is, prove that they hadn't broken the law.

The courts and political practices have since the 1970s minimized, though not entirely eradicated, that "corporate" status of black people (Ford 2005), but the memory of it remains politically potent—at least arguably until the presidential election of 2008. The concept of "reverse discrimination" may now be legally vacuous but remains politically potent.

In the past, conservative legal theorists and political commentators railed against incorporating black people as a group into a special and advantaged legal status, or at least they did so after the fall of legalized segregation. But in the debates of fifty-odd years ago that created the civil rights system, liberals and other racial reformers were in fact arguing not against the formal incorporation of blackness per se, but for a new, more apt form of incorporation. They typically argued that antidiscrimination legislation and, especially, the *diktat* of a civil rights administrative apparatus was a temporary expedient, justified by the omnipresence of Southern legal segregation and Northern, officially sanctioned discrimination. As one argument went, it was essential to create a "critical mass" of black managers, lawyers, teachers, police, fire fighters, plumbers, masons, carpenters, foremen, doctors, nurses, professors, scientists, and so on to break the patterns of discrimination, a mass large enough that it could in the ways customary for other groups protect and reproduce itself and thus, in good time, make antidiscrimination and related programs unnecessary. Hence, if the Constitution was stretched, occasionally even broken, it was broken in order to fix it by emergency measures that would serve this purpose and then pass away.[22]

This history is hardly arcane; it bears powerfully on the social visibility of black Americans even today. One hears it said that "they" are more socially visible than whites, but that idiom typically refers to skin color or other "obvious" African features. But of equal or perhaps greater importance today is that past history of social "incorporation" still makes black people uniquely visible in all the main venues in which political conflict over social mobility takes place, in hiring, firing, promoting, admitting to school, credentialing, and so forth. Though skin color and other "obvious" African features enter into this as markers, its importance is magnified a hundredfold by the black "incorporation," which has been so deeply embedded in the American historical consciousness.

This brings us to the nub of the visibility issue around social mobility and the poisonous racial conflict that it may, and often in fact does, engender. Insofar as black Americans are viewed as parts of a distinct "order" in the United States, that extra black person who is rising in the social mobility model we examined is thereby changed from a "him" or "her" to a "them." That is, if Arthur A. gets a coveted appointment to the fire department, or Elaine B. gets into the flagship state university, those who are disadvantaged or threatened by the step have a political target already created for them by the historic corporatization of our black population. Edward C., who is white and wanted that appointment but didn't get it, has been handed a ready-made "reality" that he failed not because of personal merit but because "they" have special privileges. This "reality" exists in our political discourse regardless of whether Arthur A. and Elaine B. made it entirely on their own or were aided by an acceptance procedure weighted to aid black applicants. Edward C. may not be a racist in any of the nastier connotations of that word; but unless he is an otherworldly philosopher, he's liable to conclude that "they" got the promotion because "they" don't have to rely on merit as he believes that he himself must.

The situation is further aggravated by the fact that in the United States social mobility was and still is cast in the language and value of personal achievement. The reader of course will readily recognize the rejoinder, Yes, because of racism/discrimination/the historical legacy black aspirants to desired posts in education and occupation were corporately made unequal so that, fighting fire with fire, the law gave them a corporative boost. That rejoinder so often falls on deaf ears because social questions are settled on the basis of ideology, not science, by power, not virtue.

Interestingly, the U.S. public has behaved far better than either my "incorporation" argument or the simple social mobility model would lead us to expect. Civil rights laws and procedures still have a very large, perhaps majority constituency among whites, and despite their halting slowness, they still hold black loyalty, despite considerable white and black agitation, much of it angry, against the functioning of the older civil rights system.

The early Civil Rights Era really had to continue the "incorporation" so as to enable black people to join the social mobility competition on something like equal terms. It was not then possible to enact equality per se, much less materially create it or even approximate it by directing massive resources into crash programs to end racially imposed disabilities and inequities in one swoop, say in a single generation or a Five-Year Plan.

The form that black equality had to take was limited to steps that would especially assist blacks to enter into the competition for social mobility under more or less equal playing conditions. Legislated and administered "extraequality" of opportunity would lead to equality for black people, at least to the degree that some would get ahead, and some wouldn't, just as some whites went up and others stayed still or fell off the social mobility ladder. But withal far too little opportunity was offered to some black people.

Enter the Police Power

If in 1965 many whites opposed the consequences of the new legislated "civil rights" advantages for blacks, the latter, at least vast numbers of them, felt that the process was too slow and their promise too scanty. Beginning in 1965 in Los Angeles, each of the next few summers was marked by an urban race riot. These led to a reversal in U.S. racial policy by 1968 and with it to a unique, even radical departure in national policing policy. The two are intimately connected.

By every measure the summer riots in Los Angeles, Newark, and, crucially, Detroit were the actions not of the despairing poor but of the disappointed better off. Portraits of arrested rioters showed them to be predominantly young people whose education and employment status placed them a rung up on the black, big city average for those things.[23] The lesson that was evidently drawn from these findings, both by "the public" and by officialdom, was that the nation's racial situation was so volatile that rapid racial reform was socially destabilizing and that the policy ought therefore to be to draw back; a period of "benign neglect" was called for to calm the riotous elements in the black inner city as well as George Wallace's supporters in the white suburbs.

"Benign neglect" would arguably calm down the suburbs, but because the black inner-city communities had been mobilized on behalf of civil rights changes for over a decade, there something additional was required. That something additional included such an unusual assignment to the nation's police and courts that its measure has yet to be fully taken. Building on the historical legal and political tradition of black "incorporation," the police and the courts were assigned to demobilize the existing protest movements. Black protest movements were especially targeted, for they were thought to encourage, if only tacitly, the more violent white students as well. The police and courts were also given a special brief to exercise some new degree of social control over the black population so as to inhibit the reemergence of a protest movement. Many of the dire consequences that have since flowed from this brief were not intended, so far as I understand, but at the same time could and should have been foreseen by a more responsible elite.

The public record supporting this view has been to date largely though not entirely circumstantial,[24] resting for the most part on an interpretation of official, elite, and police behavior. However, I believe the thesis can be established empirically without resorting to special findings or a conspiracy theory. The following narrative outlines the case.

We have to go back to the two commissions appointed by President Johnson in 1967, in the aftermath of the early urban riots, and in 1968, in the aftermath of the assassination of Robert Kennedy. Presidential commissions are quite extraordinary bodies. I think it fair to say that such commissions are often chosen and set to work when an elite policy consensus has to be reached and then a further effort made to convince the wider public about it. That was the case for the two commissions cited here. The first, the National Advisory Commission on Civil Disorders, was appointed in July 1967 and reported to the president during the following year. It is popularly referred to as the Kerner Commission, after its chairman, Otto Kerner, then governor of Illinois. The report issued by the Kerner Commission has a liberal and progressive ring to it, mainly, it appears, because of some clever, last-minute political maneuvering by its vice chairman, John Lindsay, a progressive Republican, then mayor of New York City. It was also a national best seller; the public bought over two million copies. Moreover, it is one of the highpoints of the old "War on Poverty," for it stresses the grievances the commission staff found among blacks about their situation and prospects. Complaints about the police play a major role in the report, both of their violence against and harassment of black people and of their ineffectiveness in dealing with crime. Similarly, the report underlines the need for better job and school opportunities, better housing, and better medical care if we were to avoid falling into "two Americas." Reading it today, one gets the impression of a realistic, perhaps slightly optimistic document.

Inside the commission there was, however, little unanimity, and among the staff there was considerable grumbling about the attempts by the White House to control the contents of the report. Whatever the case, President Johnson was unhappy with the result, most specifically over its stress on white "racism." Off the record, a leading White House staffer confessed to the *Washington Post* (Platt 1971, 42) that the report "over-dramatized the white racism theme" and was "counter-productive in terms of programs for the society as a whole." The staffer in question was Joseph A. Califano, LBJ's chief domestic adviser.

A new report with a vastly different emphasis was not long in coming. In the aftermath of the Robert Kennedy assassination in June 1968, the president appointed the National Commission on the Causes and Prevention of Violence, provided it with a moderate chairman, Milton Eisenhower, the ex-president's brother, but loaded it with "law and order" advocates. The incoming president, Nixon, extended the commission's lifetime for six months and then received its report during his first year in office.

This commission's nominal assignment was to deal with the outright criminal violence instanced by the assassinations of Robert Kennedy, Martin Luther King Jr., JFK, Malcolm X, and several other political figures, mostly black. Its report quickly disabuses one of that illusion, for the commission had another, special sort of political "violence" on its mind: it characterized as "violent" virtually all extraparliamentary efforts to achieve racial and even wider policy change in the United States. In short, it seemed to want to outlaw, and then take steps to demobilize, the very mode of popular action characteristic of the movements for social change in that era. No divination is necessary to reach this interpretation, for it is announced in the very first paragraph of the report itself: "Violence in the US has risen to alarmingly high levels," making "fortresses of portions of our cities," "dividing our people into armed camps," and "jeopardizing some of our most precious institutions, among them our schools and universities." Then, getting down to cases, the report announces its central point, "We solemnly declare our conviction that this nation is entering a period in which our people need to be as concerned by the internal dangers to a free society as by any probable combination of external threats" (Eisenhower Commission, xxv).

That's pretty strong stuff! Evidently in the year and a half since the appointment of the Kerner Commission, there had been a change in elite perceptions of the various social movements then agitating in the country. The Eisenhower Report is not even bashful about identifying "violence" with most of those agitations, however peaceful and however legal.

What is central is the report's own stress on police work as a major element in ending "violence." Much of the report is taken up with police issues, and its most significant recommendations deal with changes in police and court procedures, police training and financing, and an expanded federal role in assisting local and state police.

I do not want to exaggerate the role of the commission and its report. Perhaps we can only say that with this report a part of the national elite directed the police power to join the existing political structure for dealing in a formal collective way with the black population. In other words, the police, the courts, and the prisons merged their briefs with those of the various agencies of the War on Poverty and the antidiscrimination apparatus. But as over time the other agencies, notably the poverty and civil rights apparatuses, declined in importance and the liberal impulse weakened, the police and the ever more conservative courts came to assume the main institutional role in coping with racial problems in the United States. Further, such massive resources were soon poured into this police/court/prison assignment that the nation's police power eventually eclipsed older political controls. It has become a major player in elections and within the political calculations of the nation's elites. As I indicated earlier, this new power is a major component of the reaction.

Social Discipline

This alleged "breakdown in social discipline" in part underlay the actions of federal and local prosecutors against 1960s radicals. The authorities tied up the leaderships and the finances of various protest groups in lengthy trials, most dramatically around the riots during the Democratic Party Convention in Chicago in 1968.[25] There is also believable narrative evidence that to demobilize black protest police undercover agents managed to set some black militants into mortal quarrels with one another, especially in California, and at least one case where almost surely the police targeted and murdered a black militant leader, Fred Hampton of the Chicago branch of the Black Panther Party in December 1969 (Sullivan 2009). Through the Law Enforcement and Assistance Act (1994), federal funds and technical assistance were provided to local and state police departments, and there was an attempt to bring about greater uniformity in police training and orientation.[26] The police recommendations of the commission were being implemented by the time Nixon left office.

The brevity of this discussion should not obscure the importance of the changes in the power relations between the police and the policed since the 1960s. The recommendations of the Eisenhower Commission paralleled efforts in other countries to improve the ability of the police to control the sort of crowds and mass demonstrations that had proved so formidable during the Sixties. Throughout virtually the whole developed world, the police have vastly improved their communications and intelligence-gathering abilities on potential dissenters, while the police on the street have received new tools (batons, helmets, water cannon, plastic handcuffs), developed new techniques to compress the scope of demonstrators to make them easier to control, learned to steer marchers away from sensitive objectives (government leaders and offices, wealthy business districts, other sites of special political significance), and been retrained not to employ in front of the media the violence that inflamed both marchers and observers of yesteryear. At the same time, they have improved their ability to isolate and physically overcome selected groups formerly protected by the size of the crowd and to "snatch" targeted leaders out of crowds, and have learned to process large numbers of arrestees quickly so that it becomes impossible "to fill the jails," and so forth. To use a historical analogy, these changes in police control over crowds and demonstrations are as significant in weakening the possibilities of popular pressures as Napoleon's redesign of the streets of Paris was to afford rapid deployment of his cavalry and clear lanes of fire for his artillery.

And we have not even considered the vast increase in electronic surveillance by various police agencies before and since 2001.

The Ultraconservatives

But we must return to our main narrative. The elite counter to the alleged "breakdown in social discipline" also came in two other closely related forms, the appeal to the ultraconservatives and the war against drugs, ironically a war directed more against the relatively harmless marijuana than against so-called hard drugs.

We earlier met that category of persons whose views and values have remained relatively untouched even when otherwise immersed in the social material dimensions of modernization. An account of its mobilization as a political force in our era would single out Richard Nixon as its sponsor. In his successful 1968 presidential campaign, Nixon pursued what he called "a Southern strategy." If the strategy was Southern, it was only so in copying the way in which past Southern leaders mobilized racial resentments to keep blacks in their place. By all accounts, Nixon was not particularly racist—or at least no more hostile to African Americans than to Jews and other ethnics or indeed to any other groups or persons who opposed his ambitions and policies. But he seized the historic opportunity to make his party into the normal majority party against the racially divided Democrats.

The Democratic Party's majority status from 1933 to 1968 had rested on its ability to combine the most liberal and the most reactionary elements of our polity into one political bloc. To the very, very liberal cities of the North, it offered money and legislation, such as the Wagner Act and the G.I. Bill, which served to radically improve both the condition and the potential social mobility of big city ethnic voters, including no small number of black people. To the racially reactionary and otherwise conservative Southern voters, it poured in federal money for regional economic development projects like the TVA and military bases, and to support defense-related industries in places like Newport News, Charleston, Houston, and Marietta (Georgia). As Republicans in my younger years chronically complained, this Democratic "spend and spend, elect and elect" strategy was in equal parts principled, cynical, and successful. But the necessary condition to maintain it was that the Democrats go easy on racial change. The civil rights movement made that increasingly difficult with results now familiar to us.

American historians have not generally pursued the implications of the peculiar fact that the progressive aspects of New Deal/Fair Deal/New Frontier liberalism of the middle third of the twentieth century, though electorally supported by a majority, was ideologically congenial to only a minority. It was in that sense a political freak. The modern reaction has exploited that very difference. In fact, it promotes the opinion of many conservatives that twentieth-century liberalism was a minority view, antithetical to our traditions, and that all traces of it must be erased.

The success of this "Southern strategy" was such that it became routine for the GOP to rely for its electoral core on those who oppose further racial amelioration, who are hostile to women's rights, most notably around the issue of abortion, who fear gay people and to lose their children's obedience to "traditional values," and who would subject the law, the schools, and even science itself to their readings of scripture. The contemporary Republican Party still caters to those social groups who most resist and are most alien to modern conceptions of a secular, multiracial, gender-equal, scientific/rationalist, internationalist-oriented society or, more briefly, to a society based on tolerant humanism. Republican politicians and opinion makers, followed by some Democrats, have catered to and still encourage multiple forms of social resentment, fear, and superstition, including appeals to the most destructive forms of belligerent patriotism.[27]

The War on Drugs

The war on drugs has been an integral part of the elite/ultraconservative politics. As we now understand that Prohibition was ultimately aimed at forcing "un-American" immigrants to become socially obedient Americans, so too should we see the war on drugs as directed against the young, who are implicitly depicted in the antidrug literature as susceptible to become "ghetto" layabouts instead of "productive citizens" unless the police prevent it.[28]

There is a heavy police presence throughout our social life. This is a familiar case of the police industry tendency to conflate dissident or unusual social behavior of any kind with criminality. As we know, policing makes only a small impression, if any, in the scale of the drug trade. Indeed, it cannot, since the more effective the policing, the greater the shortage of the drug being policed, hence the higher its price, hence the greater willingness of both professional and amateur drug distributors to take their chances and of opportunities to "buy off" a cop or two. It appears that there is a hard core of hard drug users whose numbers do not radically change over time but who switch from heroin, to cocaine, to other hard drugs partly in response to what's available, or new, and partly in response to temporary police successes in checking the production or inflow of now this, now that substance. Much of the antidrug literature agrees with this view but goes on to argue, "Yes, hard drug use is more a medical and social problem, but policing is necessary to prevent the spread of the drug culture, in the form of marijuana, to the young."[29]

The checkered history of the war against drugs need not overly detain us. From the early part of the century, the old Federal Bureau of Narcotics carried on a campaign to demonize marijuana, but the issue rarely achieved more than local impact. That changed when, during his run for the 1968 Republican nomination, Nelson Rockefeller "made" the issue. He also set the pace for what was to follow, enacting antidrug laws in New York State that imposed long, mandatory sentences even for quite small offences. Only recently has Rockefeller's folly been recognized, and there is a move afoot to sharply reduce the severity of drug-related sentencing. In its earliest days the Nixon administration pursued an enlightened policy oriented to medical and psychological intervention, but the political possibilities of a war on drugs soon overwhelmed this. Under the Reagan administration, a national campaign was launched—a veritable war against drug users, but suspiciously focused on marijuana use.

The war on drugs is not only, perhaps not even mostly, elite engendered. I have already commented on the self-interested role of the police power. The extraordinary expansion of the size, budgets, and political influence of police departments rests heavily on their alleged protection of youth against the medical and social pollution "caused" by drug experimentation and use. The patently fraudulent nature of the antidrug literature suggests police self-interest, not selfless public policy.

To read the antidrug literature is truly depressing. In one volume I consulted, by a well-known, well-respected, well-connected researcher (Inciardi 1986), the body of his book freely admits, even documents, just about all the things that opponents of the drug war object to: that marijuana is not addictive in the short term and, unlike cocaine, has no immediate, dire medical consequences; that aggregate hard drug use varies only a little as a consequence of police activity; that medical and counseling intervention is just as effective; that the scale of imprisonment is more socially harmful than the scale of the drug trade; and that there is no correlation between experimenting or even habitually using marijuana and later hard drug use. Then, when the author turns at the end of a long book to a brief section on policy recommendations, he simply concludes that we should go on doing what we've been doing! It is very difficult to make sense of this somersault. In general, police industry self-interest outweighs professionalism; change will have to be imposed from outside.[30]

The war against drug use has also had quite enormous grassroots support, and not only from ultraconservatives. It is hard to imagine that the police industry could have reached its present pinnacle without popular support against drug use, or that the jails would be so full, or the public as fearful of "pushers" as they used to be of "subversion" or "foreigners."[31]

In trying to understand the public addiction to the war on drugs, we should return to Bell's contradiction between the axial principles of our economy and of the culture. Capitalism is a truly revolutionary economic system, forever changing itself, hence imposing adjustments, sometimes very difficult, on the rest of society. Urbanization offers a familiar but dramatic example. In the course of the century since 1870, the overwhelming majority of Western Europeans and North Americans moved from the countryside to the city, utterly changing their daily living and child-rearing habits. They learned new foods, clothing, technologies, tools, and techniques and unlearned those occupations that had previously done so much to define them.

It is implicit here that the ideas and the experiences of the previous generations will have only limited relevance to the world faced by their children, their children's children, and so forth. But the economic system crucially rests on beliefs and values reflecting the politically safe verities of yesterday. The other side of capitalism's economic dynamism is political and, especially, social conservatism. That contradiction favors a deeply irrational clinging to unadaptive, more backward forms of conservatism.

I think something like that is behind the reaction to so-called youth culture, which takes the form of the police war on marijuana. Drugs here are only the surface; the interior substance, I would argue, is an attempt by both privileged and ultraconservative families to halt and reverse the changes in values that capitalism has helped create in their children. As more than one observer has noted, in the United States we wage war against our own children.

The historical narrative supports this thesis. The culture and politics of the U.S. postwar world were carefully managed to keep dissidence and socially idiosyncratic behavior well away from young people. The film industry censored itself to avoid sex, violence, and other upsetting sorts of things. After a promising beginning, television went the same censored route. In fiction it was only slowly that the "filthy books" of, for example, D. H. Lawrence and James Joyce escaped the literary and officeholding custodians of "good" literature.[32] In politics, there was the period first of aggressive McCarthyism, then of "the American Century that *Time* magazine concocted to describe the Eisenhower years before Sputnik."[33] Neither the schools nor the universities wandered from the going orthodoxies.[34] The flight to the suburbs was sold to the public as a move into a promised land lacking the traditional city problems of noise and air pollution, unwanted neighbors, and disruptive temptations for the young.[35]

This suburban demi-paradise was shattered in a few short years, as was the "heartland" of small-town America. Prior to 1962 perhaps, young people seemed safely cocooned. In a world threatened by the poised ICBMs of the two superpowers and by so much disorder everywhere, suburban and small-town America supported the nuclear terror and pretended that the world was really "nice" and "wholesome" and would stay that way as long as they willed to believe it. The next handful of years changed that. Within the Elysian precincts there suddenly emerged alienated young people in their thousands, not merely rejecting the world of their forebears but also accusing them of being a font of racial, gendered, acquisitive, and warlike evils. Lacking the inclination to fashion constructive, measured reactions to change, especially racial and sexual change, their forebears embraced social and political reaction.

As I understand it, many of the more privileged social classes and orders in the United States, joining with ultraconservatives, have been locked in a refusal to face and react constructively to the contours of the present era. In foreign affairs, they've blustered and supported now this, now that war against an illusory and elusive enemy. They dread imagined enemies in their very midst, and they grapple blindly with them through policing strategies, occasional efforts to tame popular media culture (doomed to be overridden again by the "free market" they also espouse), and a generalized hostility to and rejection of the more cosmopolitan world bursting into life all around them. The suburbs have typically been peopled by men and women of greater than average formal education, but their politics has tended to merge with those of the ultraconservatives.

Given this past, the Obama election is at once both startling and so very hopeful. It is difficult, however, to assess its longer and deeper effects because much that is negative in our racial politics has been institutionally frozen into the behavior of our police institutions, which still enjoy considerable elite support.

Racial Policy, Social Control, and the Police

Since the late 1960s and early 1970s, the nation's elites, while well aware of the continuing inequalities, economic disabilities, even social pathologies of the lower perhaps one-tenth to one-fifth of the black population, have been unwilling to provide the leadership, the legislation, or the resources to correct even the correctable problems. The job market, the housing market, and the school system fail the black population in crucial but well-understood ways. Blacks also uniquely suffer from unequal access to medical, dental, and mental health care; to preschool; and to insurance coverage and banking, as well as other inequalities and social disabilities. Choosing not to address these problems but instead merely to contain their effects, the political elites have devoted enormous public resources to the police and the prisons. It is as if they accept that most U.S. institutions will fail to serve African Americans but believe that the police power will make them "good." Much the same should be said about the responses of the elite to the plight of our Hispanic and "legal" immigrant populations. If that seems unduly harsh, then perhaps it merits restating: our upper elites shirk "normal" elite responsibilities.

As for the Eisenhower Commission's brief to the police power discussed earlier, too many genuinely unfortunate consequences have flown from it. We have space to comment on only a few.

This is not the first or the last time the nation's police power has been assigned an important political role. Palmer's "Red Scare," Prohibition, and the "wars" on communist subversion, drugs, and terror come to mind. Moreover, as I'll further argue in chapter 8, since the institution of modern urban police forces in the early nineteenth century, they have always had a political role, although it was not until the historic advance began to falter that they were able to use that role as a path to political power.

The special genius of the modern urban police form (and a few state and federal agencies) is that it is a quasi-military body that quite literally "occupies" the policed area, that its members are selected and then further oriented to feel alien to the policed population, that it is constructed to be loyal to *whomever* is in power, which gives the police a generalized predilection for authoritarian figures and regimes, and that it has historically tended to consider political dissidence and criminality as more or less equivalent.

Modern German historians have singled out the German civil police of the Weimar era, who went on to serve the Nazis, even participating in significant numbers in the extermination of Europe's Jews (Browning 1992). But the Paris police broke the heads of leftists for the pre-1936 government, then the heads of rightists for the Popular Front in 1936–38; they arrested suspected Nazi sympathizers in 1939–40, then those opposed to Vichy's collaboration with the Nazis in 1940–44, then joined with anti-Nazi partisans fighting against the remnants of German and Vichy forces in the city in August 1944. By 1947–48, they were back to breaking leftist heads, but, true to form, broke rightist heads again in 1961–62, and so on.[36]

The twentieth century might well be called the century of the police, for it was then that the cited faults of modern police forces came to full, tragic fruition, that is, to serve whomever is in charge, though with a preference for more authoritarian regimes, while systematically conflating criminal with political behavior. In fact, for the police, political disorder is perhaps an even greater evil than the strictly criminal variety. Whatever the historical origins of this confusing of dissent with disorder, it has proven of enormous value to elites, and enormously harmful to society itself.

The Police-Industrial Complex

Given the role assigned to the police power, one should expect high levels of conflict between the minority communities and the police in their midst. Also, while it is true that some who volunteer for police work are apt to possess authoritarian and antiblack political attitudes, the position in which the police have been placed vis-à-vis the public is guaranteed to create such attitudes.[37] It was into this unpromising social mixture that the Nixon and subsequent administrations pumped vast new sums into first the police, and later the prisons. The sheer scale of the resources provided them have made the nation's police power a major contender within our domestic politics. The most innocent view sees the police power as if it were a giant industry with a commensurably powerful lobbying presence at every level of government and influential on virtually all domestic policy questions. If nothing else, police spending priorities have tended to preempt alternate uses of public funds, hence to have direct policy consequences.

This police "industry" is gargantuan. Its public-sector side consists of the nation's police forces and the corrections systems. As of 2004, the public sector of the police industry employed 1.86 million people, about a million of whom were police. Their collective budget (also 2004) was then $150.1 billion, or roughly 30 percent of the U.S. defense budget of the same year. In addition, the private-sector side of the police "industry" employed another 880,000 persons. All together, the "industry" was nearly twice as large as the armed forces and cost nearly half as much as the pre-Iraq defense budget.

If we take 1970 as a baseline, public-sector police employment alone had more than doubled by 1992, while public-sector police "industry" expenditure grew roughly seventeen-fold in the same period. No other industry save computers had growth rates like that.[38]

Ideology aside, the police role in racial and related matters has been strongly driven by individual and institutional self-interest. The police, the prisons, and more recently the drug enforcement and the immigration services have powerful lobbies in Washington, comparable to those of the pharmaceutical industry and the defense industry. All live on subventions from the public purse or other special public assistance, so that too often their policies are driven by the desire to increase that assistance regardless of the wisdom or usefulness of the policies they pursue. For example, in Texas, numerous local police forces are represented by a single union, which then bargains with city, county, and state authorities on their behalf. One of the union's vice presidents has coauthored a handbook for union officials. Each chapter is organized around a pithy saying or motto: the one for dealing with the legislature gives one a sense of their ethos. It reads, "If all else fails, we'll drop the bomb and live among the ruins!" Another reads, "If you're gonna make the power structure squirm, you've got to leave all of mama's childhood preachins outside the front door of the Association Hall." In all, the book is marked by the coarsest kind of cynicism.[39]

U.S. international health policy has been long tethered to the desires of the pharmaceutical industry to protect the patents, hence the extra-high profitability, of their products, which is especially embarrassing politically when it interferes with efforts to deal with the international HIV/AIDS pandemic. But a subordination of policy to gain is more characteristic of rogue industry behavior, not normal public service behavior; one can hardly imagine public health agencies trying to panic the public into supporting initiatives in alchemy or entrail reading.

The media treatment of the police falls in line with this inversion of service to self-serving. The omnipresent police dramas present a crime-soaked and violent world to their viewers, routinely mock Bill of Rights protections, lionize lawless police behavior toward suspects and arrestees, not infrequently approving of outright criminal violence toward them, and falsely suggest that the police will pursue and solve crimes when in fact most crimes, even quite serious ones, are neither "cleared" nor, often, even investigated.[40]

If these views about the police industry are approximately true, then we have built into our political system a continuing font of racial hostility and other rightward ideologies based not solely or perhaps even importantly on preexisting "prejudice" but instead resting in the institutional advantage of one of our largest, wealthiest, most powerful set of domestic institutions.

From the nature of the case, their racialism is then further transferred over into the public. In the conventional view, of course, the police industry merely reflects wider public attitudes about race. There's truth to that too, but the police power greatly magnifies those attitudes and can often be observed shaping them into a political force, as in New York City, Philadelphia, or Los Angeles. First, the police make socially manifest the inferiority of the, say, black and immigrant communities. In their systematic lawlessness and other ill treatments of minorities, they make racial/ethnic inequality a fact that is actually experienced by those who witness or hear about it, whether white or black. That is, one can experience—not merely think—that this or that group is inferior merely by experiencing how the city's police department or the immigration service behaves toward it. The inferiority of this race or that ethnic group comes to be "normal" and thus presumably "natural." Second, the police "industry" overtly presents itself as the protector of one part of the population against a shadowy, alien, nefarious, ostensibly violent "other." For conservative people generally, it is crystal clear who is protected by "law and order" and who "they" are on the other side. The police have been very successful in transferring this invidious distinction into the political arena, which is why it is a major growth industry, while medical research, education, and, until recently, defense have faced the budget cutters.

With the advent and spread of police collective bargaining since the 1960s, police unions have become players in electoral politics. Both at the local and the national levels, police union endorsement has come to be valued by candidates, and the normal price of that is support for increased police and prison appropriations, support for antidrug crackdowns, and support for measures that promote "law and order" and undermine constitutional protections that "coddle criminals." Because of the way we have enshrined the police, these police unions don't have to mimic conventional public-sector union behavior, that is, jump opportunistically around the political spectrum to avoid making enemies. They tend as a rule to support only, hence encourage only, a rightward swing in politics.

Returning specifically to police treatment of racial and ethnic minorities, I doubt, as I suggested earlier, whether the fathers and the framers of the Eisenhower Report intended that the nation's police power should now, more than a third of a century later, have assumed toward the black community (and other "minority" and immigrant populations) a social-control task somewhat analogous to that played by, say, Southern police forces a half century ago. And I doubt whether they intended to create a domestic institution with an associated political base that can barely be controlled by the civil authority.[41] But they ought to have foreseen and prevented such an obvious consequence of their recommendations.

Appealing to the Ultraconservatives

The spread of "Southern" police traditions brings us full circle. In this period of reaction, both characterizing it and pushing it forward is a new political bloc drawing upon both elite and cadre but also including in its ranks religious fundamentalists of the most extreme kind, many of the most socially superstitious on questions of race and sexuality, anti-evolution cultists, and our enduring hypernationalists. This bloc now exercises the sort of ideological and political influence over government policy and behavior once exercised by—at least some—children of the Enlightenment.

As we saw, ultraconservative elements were first mobilized around racial issues by the Nixon "Southern strategy" of 1968. But the mobilization has had other key components as well, most notably opposition to anything extending sexual permissiveness for young people, passing over to support for bans on federal money for family planning, a powerful anti-abortion drive,[42] support for the war against drugs, and, most recently, a deceitful opposition toward gay persons that takes the form of the "defense of traditional marriage."

A cautionary note: I have not seen a statistical breakdown of the fundamentalist and evangelical electorate by social class. But there seems fairly convincing narrative evidence that this part of the political spectrum is not populated solely, perhaps not even largely, by the poorly educated and socially marginal. The appeal of religious and political evangelicalism to educated, prosperous men and women of the cadre life course appears also to have been considerable. I would hypothesize that the narrowing of economic opportunity circa 1970 simultaneously with an increase in the numbers of black and other social-mobility seekers encouraged some atavism among the more conservative elements of the cadre. There is some warrant from the European past to argue that parts of the middle classes are frightened into religious and social superstitions during eras of social crisis.

If true, then we are witnessing something akin—I don't want to overstate—to the sort of political bloc of the elite, middle, and primitive that characterized the classic nineteenth- and early twentieth-century reactions in, say, tsarist Russia and Wilhelmine Germany. Then and there modernizing, corporate- and Intersection-based elites, themselves attuned to the modern scientific and technological world and their cadre, but fearful of the social forces awakened by that world, which in part they created, allied themselves in the political arena with the ultraconservatives, primitive individuals and groups that reacted to that same modern world with invincible ignorance, thus inchoate fear, resentment, and eventually punitive anger. In the United States, ultraconservatives have not historically had a really influential presence in politics; nor, save in the South, have they been catered to by the higher classes. In the present case, however, we do know that elite figures set out to mobilize it against their enemies. Nixon's "silent majority," clearly directed against "noisy minorities," comes especially to mind. The war on drugs has much the same function, as do "family values," pro-gun militancy, now "terrorism," and any number of those reactionary appeals that serve not to address problems but to keep them rubbed raw.

Modern Reaction

In any given period, the dominant political constellation emerges out of the selective compromises between, on the one hand, the main elite subsocieties and, on the other, the rest of the polity. If so, the relationships that hold between an elite subsociety and this or that nonelite group are both mutual and unequal, representing an accommodation between the preferences of the two as it emerged from their differences. I think it axiomatic that virtually every major group in a normal society enjoys quasi-advantageous relationships with some part of the dominant elite. To the degree that any such group is excluded from substantial advantages within the polity, hence society and economy, there is the danger that it will become a focus for fundamental change that threatens the privileges of the elite.

But even among these elite/nonelite relations, which I have characterized as normally both mutual and unequal, there are significant differences. There are many zero-sum conflicts built into a society, and hence no polity can resolve all its differences to everybody's equal satisfaction. Probably the best example is found in the modern historical relationships of labor and, say, middle management. Employer elites, even today, normally try to meet at least some of the interests of their workers, especially if the latter are organized by political party or trade union. The historical transformation of nineteenth-century master-servant relationships into the modern employer-employee paradigm is testimony to that.[43]

But managerial elites have even more important relationships to the middle-manager course, and so that where labor and middle management come into conflict, the former's interests are often sacrificed to the latter's.

If layoffs are required, or incomes must be cut, or job routines reorganized, or grievances settled, managerial elites will and do favor the middle managers over the workers.

Of course, in the political realm, where these things come to be acted out, every group is split to at least some degree. There are Democratic small businesspeople in this or that suburb, Republican black workers in the Deep South, gay conservatives, and fundamentalist liberals. Traditionally, where the local Democrats were Irish-American, the local Italian Americans supported the Republicans, as in New York, New Haven, and Boston for many years. At present, the GOP would like to create a similar counterpoint between black and Hispanic voters. Both major parties also have multiple ties and levels of ties to the dominant elite society: the aerospace and defense industries had long-standing links to the Democrats, testimony to the Democrat's longevity as the majority party. The medical and legal professions, long associated with the GOP, have lately tended to look more favorably on the Democrats. It is patently specious to say that all politics is local, but much of the color and confusion of U.S. politics comes from its infinite local variations of attachment and opposition, ideology and opportunism, sense and senselessness.

But the situation is not entirely chaotic, for at least since the late 1960s, the reaction has been animated and maintained by the political bloc that first formed around Nixon: the dominant elite subsociety embedded in the major diversified international firms, a great part of the cadre life course, and the ultraconservatives. What is so striking here is the acute political relevance that the ultraconservatives have offered to the bloc, not merely electoral power but moral and ideological relevance. Ultraconservatives, based in but not limited to a renewed Protestant fundamentalism, and stunned by the way in which modern commercial society has managed to influence—"subvert"—especially their young people, imagine that they can make a practical distinction between "liberal, permissive" manifestations of that commercialism and the rest; banal or even vulgar pop music is approved, but not "dirty" or otherwise offensive lyrics. The most violent, senseless sort of youth exploitation films are accepted, but not those that might seriously explore the moral dilemmas facing young people; anything that weakens an antidrug message is banned, but advertisements approving of wild parties are sponsored by the ultraconservative leadership of Coors Brewing. Sex can dominate the airwaves and the magazines for adolescents, but no support for birth control or abortion will be tolerated. In good part, ultraconservatism nurtures these denials and these contradictions.

However strained this distinction between the "good" and the "bad" effects of commercialism, the former to be deregulated, the latter expunged, it is precisely the distinction most advantageous to a still dynamic capitalist elite society and its allied manager course, which seek the benefits of unregulated economic change but want desperately to manage—often expunge—its social consequences. In short, there is substance to the elite/manager/ultraconservative bloc that has overwhelmed U.S. politics in the most recent three decades. It is not merely short-term expediency that leads such a large part of elite society to embrace ultraconservative personalities and issues. The Sixties really wanted to intrude into international policy formation. The trade unions then really were edging into a partner's role in the economy. The Intersection really was being challenged to be the bridge to a freer, more individualistic, less economistic future. The civil rights revolution did warn a maturing cadre that opportunity for others undercut the prospects of their own children. The alliance between the elites, the cadre, and the ultraconservatives has proven durable because these do fear, if for reasons of their own, the same sort of social, political, and economic change.

PART 2

RECAPPING AND BEYOND

The historic advance should be seen as the vector sum of, at first, two, later three historical trends. In the last part of the nineteenth century, the nascent corporate firms came to require a workforce with ever improving productive characteristics, and this was eventually seen to require not just a bit of training and education but an entire society made up of healthier, better-educated men and women, culturally subordinated to the rewards offered by paid work and motivated by the prospect of an improved future. One outcome of this was the emergence of a cadre class of managers and technologists, who now comprise the most important middle class of the economically advanced societies.

Over on the other side of the social divide of the Victorian Era, the Democracy had come very early to formulate a vision of a new society of abundance in which "the workers" or "the people" would develop themselves morally, culturally, and intellectually into a new, freer, higher species of humanity. The historic advance emerged out of the alternating conflict and cooperation of these trends and their bearers, and thus its long-term character is the child of both, its trajectory both foreseen and unforeseen, both intended and unintended.

This historic advance came to an end around 1970 in the defeat of the international upsurge popularly called the Sixties. There the Democracy was defeated by a bloc consisting of elite, cadre, and ultraconservatives. Most notably, by 1970, the middle or cadre class, itself a product and beneficiary of the historic advance, began increasingly, and realistically, to act as a privileged class and no longer one, so to speak, still "on the make." This class came to view the public sector that had nurtured it as a source of late-emerging social rivals; public statements of this belief have been and remain heavily racialized, although "race" also serves as a proxy for other, equally threatening but nonracial social challenges. In addition, unease among the elite about challenges to their authority over, especially, international security issues, social discipline, and domestic policing led to their shift away from the historic elite/cadre/Democracy bloc and toward closer elite/cadre relations with the ultraconservatives and other, essentially anti-Enlightenment, forces.

This alliance among the elite, the cadre, and the ultraconservatives has proved remarkably durable; however, it is not immediately clear why this is so. My hypothesis is that when the movements of the Sixties tried to expand the earlier advance, they collided with the boundaries of legitimacy and stability of the very society created by previous stages of the advance.

We've already seen that hypothesis, but in the next three chapters I want to explore some of its key elements.

In chapter 4, I will develop the differences, already cited, between dynastically stratified societies and those, like our own now, whose stratification is determined by and within formally organized institutions, and in which the population is divided, not into classes in the traditional sense, but into various *courses* or *life courses*.

A life course closely corresponds to a *career* but with two differences. While only the better off are said to have careers, every person has a life course, that is, a distinct path of change and development within the institutions of the Intersection over his or her lifetime. The second difference is that we normally see a career beginning with, say, one's first job, or perhaps choice of major in college, or type of graduate program. But virtually every person in a modern society passes through the institutions of the Intersection, starting at the earliest ages, where they are differentially equipped with further opportunities, industrial and social skills, and credentials. These differences mark off the different life paths or courses through the institutions of the Intersection. Borrowing from sociological theory, we can see a course as an ensemble of *roles* occupied by people and changing over time. As with a role, a course too has a socially prescriptive aspect.

That prescriptiveness carries as its corollary the thesis that contemporary, developed societies are not "spontaneous" or even "natural" in the senses given those terms by, say, Hayek, Popper, and the political science tradition drawn from Aristotle. *Within the Intersection a modern society continually and with intention alters the productive and social productive qualities of its labor force; to that same extent it is a "non-natural" or, better, a semifabricated society.* Understanding this difference requires a set of analytical tools that fill in the gap between social theories of strict historical determination—"the iron laws of history" or, perhaps, "the Dialectic"—and more purely voluntaristic accounts. A society that we characterize as semifabricated has to have elements of social intentionality and deliberation in it; the question is what they might be and how they interact.

The basic unit of the analysis I propose is the *socially potent asset*. Socially potent assets are merely the familiar assets we observe wielded (or endured) by each person, such as his or her access to wealth, educational advancement, social opportunity, level of culture, membership in different subsocieties, and so on. These, we can also observe, are more or less determined by the individual's trajectories within the Intersection. These trajectories themselves may change—there is social mobility both up and down—but we hypothesize that one's place in the social mobility and social advantages systems is determined within Intersection institutions, with one's initial family identity substantially less important than it was in the past. By definition, but also by observation, elites are persons who have more and/or more potent assets than others.

The courses themselves are analytically resolvable into parallel differences in *socially potent assets; this means that they are hierarchies in multiple social dimensions*—institutional place, status, income and wealth, education, level of culture, and so forth. Corporate society is exceptionally hierarchical, even by the standards of the past, because its hierarchies are an intended outcome of its larger processes of social fabrication. But these hierarchies are not relatively static, as in a familiar class system, and they are not sacralized in habit, tradition, rite, and superstition as they would be in a non-Vico world. They are ever being redirected to this purpose and that, thus changing, and thus are potentially (and often actually) contested. Thus, in corporate society the term "structure," as in *social structure*, should not connote an architecturally static sort of thing. Rather, an account of social structure marks the boundaries of tensions and possible conflicts between the courses and other groups and perhaps their only temporary resolution.

The institutions of the Intersection are formal organizations, and as such, they have managerial hierarchies that reflect the triadic corporate form we analyzed earlier—elite/cadre/worker. That in turn implies that their elites possess a power within their own institutions that is more extensive, finer-grained, and discretionary than elites enjoyed in the previous forms of society. For all that John D. Rockefeller Jr. owned the Standard Oil Trust, the control he could actually exert was relatively crude, for he lacked the financial and other managerial controls that have been developed within the corporate form of organization since his time.

If we are not just to rail against elites but instead accept that they now perform certain essential social functions, that still leaves the really key questions about them unanswered. We have hypothesized that elite power has a relatively high degree of selectivity and intentionality to it. Do the elites of the Intersection now exercise that power well or poorly? To what ends do they exercise that power? What effect does their exercise of power have on society itself? As part of the Democracy, we clearly want society to change in ways that will over time lower our dependency on elites, but do elite social actions now tend to stabilize, perhaps even increase our dependency on them?

Chapter 5 picks up the argument from this point. We need an empirically sensitive theory of elite social action, especially of their *intentional* social action. This discussion is about "power," but that category too often functions as "black box," that is, a source of analytically nontransparent explanations, or tautologically skips over substantive issues of fact. We need a more rigorously empirical and analytically scrupulous way of dealing with issues of power, especially of power exercised with a degree of intention. S*ocially potent assets* will function as the analytical elements out of which to construct the social logic that separates elites (collectively) from others and at the same time gives rise to the formation of *elite subsocieties*.

I am not interested in explaining elite behavior on the basis of some system of abstract *power* or ascribed *interests*. To do so is to appeal to a priori, deductive procedures. We must instead show how elite subsocieties emerge out of conflicts (and accommodations) within and between different kinds of elites and their assets and, of course, the nonelite groups in society. When elite subsocieties do act socially and intentionally, their actions will be viewed as a *precipitate* emerging out of some previously expressed preferences by their members. These must be empirically ascertainable. In the analysis to be presented, elite *power* and *interests* are always in principle and often in fact reducible to precipitates of elite preferences as winnowed out by preceding conflicts and accommodations within elite ranks and between elites and nonelites.[1]

We conceive of society as a whole as a network of dynamic, often contested relations between and among elites and with the other life courses and groups of the society. We should envision that network as if it were an engineering drawing of, say, a building in which we can identify not just each structural element but how each structural element is bolted, riveted, or welded to its neighbors. Unlike a building, however, a modern society is held in an only temporary equilibrium by relationships between the different courses and related hierarchies. That, essentially, is the burden of chapter 5.

Chapter 6 is about politics and operates at two levels, one historically generic, one specific to corporate society. I want first to show the historically affirmed weaknesses of liberal parliamentary democracy as a system of *representing*, that is, as a system for projecting the views and experiences of nongovernment individuals and groups into government.

I do not stress that liberal democracy is insufficiently "democratic" in the moral or ideological sense. That obviously is the case, but it is impossible, it seems to me, to have a representative *and democratic* system in any society and any economy that features strong differences in the distribution of socially potent assets; to the degree that *that* political process is truly representative, it will represent those inequalities! Liberal democratic systems have sometimes in the past been able to redress inequalities, but those efforts have been much more episodic and marginal than the steady, normally overwhelming pressure exerted by elites. What I want then to show first is that even under relatively ideal conditions, we of the Western polities have *agency government by assent* and not, as often trumpeted, *representative government by consent*.

Chapter 6 operates at a second level as well. It investigates how political institutions, designed to function within a "natural" society, function within the very different parameters of a semifabricated society. It made historical sense to say that the Sixties represented a revolt against the democratic and functional infirmities of agency government by assent, aiming, however blindly and erratically, to restore what was conceived to be traditional government by democratic consent or, as it was often called, participatory democracy. But if the Sixties did constitute such an extremely broad, powerful revolt of so many elements of society, then their defeat requires more than tactical or episodic explanations. It argues that the feedback mechanisms of the liberal democratic system of representing have become critically inefficacious. *The relationship between the democratic polity and the representing/governing apparatus of liberal democracy, marginally effective for precorporate society, has become acutely dysfunctional for a matured corporate society because of the latter's more powerful institutions and elites.*

If so, then the existing liberal, parliamentary political mechanism does not, at present, have the *capacity* to bring about its own reform. If that were the end of the story, I would find that extremely troubling; however, there are other *democratic* possibilities to explore.

Those three analyses will shape the proposals of Part 3. There the leading strategic idea is that modern political reform can only be accomplished and sustained within a wider *menu of institutional changes* whose general character is to strengthen the power of the Democracy while weakening that of the system of elites. I do not favor a demand for radical democracy or any kindred revolutionary break with the past. That task is the work of centuries, not only of today and even tomorrow, begun before us and continuing after us. But a severe imbalance between Intersection society and the Democracy is the key to the dysfunctional behavior of government and other major institutions that has so markedly developed since circa 1970. The task therefore is not "reform" in the customary mild sense of the word but rather to begin to redraw the power political relations between today's elites and cadre and the Democracy.

The burden of Part 3 is to identify those several "refabrications," if you will, of corporate society that *would* provide efficacious political channels and feedbacks between all of the governed and their government. A renewed historic advance will have to construct its own intellectual and political foundations, proverbially raising itself by its own bootstraps, but this time on the widest possible basis or, to use an older, powerfully moving expression, as the Party of Humanity.

4

SOCIAL STRATIFICATION AND SOCIAL DYNAMICS

I want to make transparent the present link between social stratification and social dynamics. I am particularly interested in elite social action that is marked by deliberation or intentionality. Some preliminary analysis will prove in aid of that.

An Abstract Stratification Matrix

Social stratification seems universal and entirely "natural," and to that extent we can fit almost all societies to some abstract matrix of the phenomenon. But over the course of human history it has also taken intricately diverse forms.

It is thus a useful exercise to take up the broader, possibly universal logic of how and why social stratification occurs, and then adopts the different forms that we can observe and the social outcomes peculiar to them. But there is an initial conceptual barrier to overcome.

Class theory is so vexed in contemporary social science that to use the term "class" is to join in discussion (and difference) with just about everybody on every social issue and all at once.[1] One could escape this quandary by avoiding the term entirely, but that would require too much paraphrase. A simpler procedure is available to us. Unless I specify otherwise, I will use the term "class" in its widest generic sense, that is, as "a," not "the" marker for social stratification in general and with no further assumptions about the relative importance of race and gender, or its economic or cultural content or lack of same, and so on.

At this level of analysis, we can give a very broad account of social stratification on the assumption that at some point in time a given society has or has had or will have an unequal distribution of any *socially potent assets*. Again I have in mind only such familiar assets as wealth, family position, insider influence, personal magnetism, superior information, institutional rank, level of culture and education, and so forth. I make no assumptions about why such inequalities have arisen, how general the phenomenon is, or which sorts of assets are more potent than others.

I only claim that if there are differences in a society in the possession or exercise of any socially potent assets, then certain other things will follow. It follows in the general case that that should lead "naturally" to the creation, preservation, or deepening of stratified clusters of other social assets and advantages. That is, if A has more of some socially potent asset than B, say wealth or political power, then A should in the normal course of events be able to direct that wealth (political power) to acquire other socially potent assets as well. And so on with the other socially potent assets. Wealth, for example, can aid in acquiring high social esteem, just as high social esteem can aid in acquiring wealth.

This claim explains what we know is widely true, namely, that persons in a society who possess one kind of socially potent asset commonly possess others as well, so that a chart depicting stratification by wealth would crudely overlay the one depicting political power, which would in turn crudely overlay one depicting esteem or prestige, which in turn would crudely overlay one that represented access to further economic opportunity, which would also crudely overlay the ability to pass social advantage on to one's children, and so on. Of course, the overlays wouldn't be exact and there would be exceptions, but one would generally expect to find nodes of clustered advantages as chart was superimposed on chart.

Thus, from a matrix assuming only an initial unequal distribution of socially potent assets, one can explain a great deal about social stratification, that is, why it takes the form of persons who enjoy clusters of such assets and enjoy them more securely and more securely across time than others. But this explanation doesn't account for at least two other major phenomena that widely accompany social stratification.

Unless we can formulate a principle that acts counter to this clustering phenomenon, we cannot explain why this process doesn't continue to the point where only a very few enjoy all the advantages of masters and the rest of the population is reduced to the abject state of slaves.

Why Are There So Few Classes?

This claim also fails to explain why societies tend to have only a small handful of strata, why there are more societies with three to eight classes than there are societies with thirty to eighty classes. Even the clustering of socially potent assets doesn't quite explain why there are typically only a few such clusters in any given society.

My preferred answer mixes some Marx with a bit of Aristotle. With Marx, I would point to the processes through which the social surplus is generated and then distributed. What is meant by the surplus includes all those goods and services not needed to re-create tomorrow in the image of today. I also share with Marx the idea that without a surplus everyone lives from hand to mouth, no one produces more than he or she needs to consume, there is little hierarchy, there are few or no strictly social processes, and in a very real way, society proper has not yet begun.[2]

Historically, and by definition, the highest elites are those who "own" a given society's most important kind or kinds of productive wealth. Here, *own* means to have priority of control, both de facto and de jure, over the main kinds of productive assets and the distribution of the surplus. If we wish to define property and ownership empirically, we need only turn to the legal or customary property system of the society in question and summarize it from the standpoint of the highest elite or elites. But such an empirical approach is no help if we want to use the terms analytically. We explain nothing about the special significance of property ownership in the antebellum U.S. South when we point to the ownership of land and slaves as an explanation for the wealth of the planter class. We're left only with the tautology that those who owned the main productive resources came to be the wealthiest, that is, they owned the main productive resources.

My earlier *Economics in Real Time* (2004) provides an economic or, better, a political economic conception and definition of property, not solely a legal one. It seizes upon the fact that property ownership typically gives "the owner" an effective claim over the use of a property in question and to its rewards, which at least in the first instance typically takes priority over the claims of others. These claims may be enacted by the law or, in more primitive societies, by threat of force or merely by custom. Accordingly, I defined owning property as enjoying a priority claim over the use and fruits of productive assets that is in principle independent of and normally greater than one's productive contributions. That is not to argue that owners don't ever make productive contributions, but it is to argue that their claims to authority and reward vis-à-vis their property are not limited by their actual productive contributions. Ownership is not identical to but is coextensive with nonproductive entitlement to part of the social surplus. This conception corresponds analytically to our root notions of what ownership and property appear to mean.

Turning again to historical experience, we know that more than one kind of property elite and productive property system may be found in a society, but that same experience also suggests that that makes for a politically unstable situation. The French revolutions of 1789, 1830, and even 1871 can be explained in part by conflicts between a landed and a financial aristocracy, overtly symbolized by the conflict between Bourbon and Orleanist claims to the French throne. Changes, some disruptive, in nineteenth-century Britain are as a rule partially explained by conflict between the older agrarian elite and the newer, rising elite of the factory and counting house. Our own Civil War employs a similar explanation as the Southern slave-owning class was losing its former political ascendancy to a new manufacturing elite and tried to recoup it by military rebellion. It seems to follow that in a stable society, there can be only one dominant property system and corresponding propertied elite.

In Marxist terms, the production of a social surplus requires a laboring population and commonly features a property system in which owners of productive assets claim and receive a share of the social surplus, which in principle and, normally, in fact goes somewhat beyond their actual productive contributions. That being the case, such a society requires some degree of social and related unity among the owners to guarantee their, by definition, extrafunctional advantages, and this in turn would seem to require the formation of an elite subsociety or subsocieties based (as will be explained in the next chapter) on *mutual discovered advantage,* which would function in the political, social, cultural, and moral realms to stabilize the conditions under which that surplus was produced and then secured to the owners.

It is consistent with this explanation to imagine that those who nominally own and deploy the productive mechanism might require a military society or order of some kind to protect them from their laborers, as in Sparta, or from foreign enemies, as in Hohenzollern Germany, and that the claims of that military element to the surplus might come to rival and even supersede those of the (nominal) property owners. Thus the importance of the nonlegalistic conception of property advanced earlier with its focus on ownership as a relationship between social groups keyed to the extra, in principle, nonproductive, dimension of the claims by one of them and the complementary confiscation of some at least of the outcome of the productive efforts of other strata.

I am not "reducing" all or even most social, cultural, and political activities to some sort of ostensibly more real, more fundamental "economic structure." I am merely asserting the thesis that one useful thread of the social analysis of stratification follows those social relations within the strata that actually control the social surplus. Such an apparently "economistic" approach has special relevance in an Americanist society such as ours, where one's job or profession, or lack of same, is material to one's place in the hierarchies of privilege.[3] But one doesn't have to universalize such an approach: as I already mentioned, in Sparta and Hohenzollern Germany nominal legal ownership of property was superseded by the need for a repressive police power or a military caste. In Tibet, as in parts of medieval Europe, nominal legal ownership of property was superseded by the presence of a religious-institutional elite. And that in turn suggests what I think is true, namely, that the central relationships between the highest, most powerful elite or elites and the laboring population will normally be of several, mutually supporting dimensions—economic, technological, social, cultural, dynastic, religious, military, and so on—with the relative importance of these dimensions varying from society to society.

The unequal relationship between elite and laborer is, as we well know from comparative historical studies, often unstable. On the one hand, there is a social formation more noted for the taking, not the making, of social wealth, and on the other, a social formation skilled in its making but clearly less so in its keeping. Aristotle, following Plato, assumes that in many societies, and of those, often the wealthiest, elites are few, and laborers many. Thus the intrinsic fragility of the social relations holding between the Few and the Many. Aristotle therefore stresses the key role of a middling social formation, more numerous than the Few and wealthier than the Many, that acts as a social balancer. In his view, this middle group shifts its loyalties back and forth between the mighty and the low to keep their conflict from destabilizing the society and polity and, of course, destroying their own modestly privileged position.

Aristotle's own social prejudices led him to assign too much weight to the balancing role of the middle social formation and not enough, I would think, to its normally closer, complementary ties to the elite. One must always remind oneself that in his discussion of Athenian society and polity he erases from his mind the fact that 80–95 percent of Athens's and Attica's inhabitants were slaves, and it was these who produced the bulk of its surplus. Unlike the slaves of the upper U.S. South, whose numbers after 1805 could not be replenished from the outside, and whose dietary and work conditions consequently had to maintain a more or less constant slave population, Athenians rapidly used up the lives of their slaves, for they could be replaced via the wars that Athens, like the other classical empires, waged for just that purpose. Under such a harsh slave regimen, no normal political processes would serve to control the slave population; slave revolts, small and large, would be common occurrences; and all the classes of the polity—that is, all those, rich or poor, who weren't slaves—would have to cooperate to muster the force to put them down. This social logic finds much confirmation in Athens and Sparta and, of course, in Roman accounts of the slave revolt led by Spartacus.

Aristotle's account of the balancing role of the middle group in society against the claims of elite and laborer assumes that we are dealing with issues other than those that concern slaves. Since slaves were the main productive element in the Athenian economy, his account loses some of its bite. A middling Athenian farmer, who probably owned a slave or two himself, played no balancing role where it came to slave issues. He would have to stand as militantly in defense of the slave codes as the grandest estate owner.

I would further observe that we often find that the middle orders of a society range themselves with the elites, typically acting as the latter's agents in maintaining unequal economic, political, cultural, and even moral relations between the Few and the Many. In turn, a modest part of the social surplus comes to be steered to them for both their particular social contribution to the creation of the surplus and their contributions to the stabilization and preservation of the social relations of surplus distribution. Again, this contribution may take many forms—religious, technological, military, and so forth—and the surplus that finds its way to them will normally include other perquisites than wealth alone.

Societies may have other classes or analogous social orders representing sometimes an old, dying social division of labor or an emerging one, sometimes a priestly or military order, sometimes an ethnic or linguistic division, or perhaps a peculiar regional or occupational division. But whatever those variations, there does seem to be an especially strong social logic acting to form at least three, if not main, then very common orders, to wit, elites who own the productive property, laborers, and an intermediate social formation who maintained, according to Aristotle, political stability. Historically, that middle group has also assumed other productive functions, one example being the monopoly exercised by the modern cadre over technology and administration.

This would explain the clustering effect we're trying to explain. A given system of producing a social surplus will feature a social division of labor in which there are at least three generalized, codified, multidimensioned social roles around which are maintained clusters of differential advantages and disadvantages. In the first instance, the relationship between elite and laborer is keyed to whatever technological, cultural, political, and other relations are apposite to producing the society's social surplus. With a view to assuring its one-sided portion of the surplus, plus social stability, the elite will, so to speak, share some part of the surplus with a middle element in society.

That of itself would seem, at least analytically, to account for the clustering we've been speaking of: the acquisition or denial of the various kinds and amounts of socially potent assets to each of the three main social formations should more or less correspond to the maintenance and reproduction over time of their different social contributions, but with the added proviso that productive contribution and productive reward are normally not fully coordinate.

Note that the same account also explains why the clustering of socially potent assets has a limit, why, that is, not every society tends toward a master-slave template. Clearly there are life situations for the laboring population that favor or do not favor their ability to contribute their labor to the creation of the social surplus. It is not, I think, an accident that slave societies tend to exhibit very, very crude, low-productivity labor processes.[4] As mentioned, in the ancient world slaves were used up to such extent that they were not able to reproduce their own numbers, and that can be accounted for by the fact that replacement slaves were easy to come by. But if one cannot readily replace "used up" slaves, then one has to treat them at least as well as, say, farm animals.[5] On the other hand, it is also true that slaves must be kept in a low social and cultural estate lest they rebel even more often than they actually do, and that in turn limits very sharply the productivity of enslaved laborers. It follows that there are imperatives imposed by the process of surplus generation itself that limit the degree to which any elite can monopolize socially potent assets, no matter how powerful they are in other respects. The ability to labor productively is in general a socially potent asset that can be, and historically has been, used, however feebly, by the lowest of the low to protect or even to improve their own condition.

With those final reflections, we have gone as far as we can with the schematized stratification matrix. The point has come to describe and analyze more closely the nature of stratification in our own modern societies. We start with the view that "class" is no longer analytically satisfactory, however much we must sometimes rely on it as a *generic* term in discussions of social stratification. No startling claim is being made here, merely that the social elements making up a social structure change as societies change. Thus, as castes, orders, and estates gave way to the nineteenth-century "class," my view is that the latter must give way to the contemporary "life course" or, more briefly, "course."

Courses and the Modern Division of Labor

The term "course" is an analytical development of the concept of a *career*, but with two differences.[6] First, as I remarked earlier, only the more privileged strata of our society have careers, that is, life courses that advance to significantly greater reward and privilege as one passes through the working years. For the lower parts of the workforce there is little scope for advancement of either income or responsibility. Yet their course of life also exhibits its own distinct patterns, as in earlier school leaving and earlier forced retirement. Second, we think of a career as starting when one is a young adult, as when someone enters medical school or takes that first, important job in the retail industry. But in present-day society that sort of major life-course step is partially prefigured in a person's earliest childhood and training, as in that *New Yorker* cartoon, and our theoretical apparatus ought to reflect that. Some, but only a few, slum children go on to medical school, whereas doctors' children are not expected to choose a life of factory work. There is no slight here of either the fact or the importance of social mobility. As I see it, there are well-understood switching points in each of the life courses where an individual, seemingly slated for, say, a worker life course, may be switched into a faster school track, encouraged to continue his or her education, possibly receive scholarship aid, and eventually end up with a professional career. All that is included in the concept of a life course.

There is some similarity between the concept of a life course and that of a *role*. In both, the individual's behavior is prescriptively guided. I suppose one could say that a life course is made up of a series of roles linked in time. There is some merit to that. I see a person's life course as "of a piece" but in time. One wants in the concept of the life course to capture the fact that each of the different life courses has its own more or less distinct pattern-in-time of socialization, education and training, credentialing, high culture, special knowledge and skill, "career" entry point and path, size, kind, reliability and regularity of income, and so forth. From the methodological standpoint, course analysis represents an attempt to overcome the time-neutrality of the concept of class. It is a way of capturing the fact that our society spends considerable resources to shape a usable and diversified labor force and one adaptable to changes over time. The concept of a life course, to some degree freely chosen by the individual but with important prescriptive elements, is, I think, reasonably apparent to us as we view what is both unique and important to present-day society over other societies, even its own predecessor.

What courses are there? The answer is to be found in the first instance by revisiting the dominant institution in our society, the modern, diversified private corporation and its division of labor. As I discussed more fully in chapter 1, the modern diversified corporate business firm was only "invented" about a century and a quarter ago, quickly perfected its form, and has since conquered the economic world. Its division of labor is clear enough, universal enough, and influential enough that it provides a warranted basis for identifying the social strata, the courses, which are to date specific to modern society.

The modern corporation is characterized by a three-way division of labor that is both social and technical in nature.[7] This division of labor is not an informal, tacit phenomenon. It is a formal feature of corporate organization; and as I have argued elsewhere (McDermott 1988, 1991), it is not incidental to corporate functioning and corporate success but itself *actually constitutes what it means to be a corporation*. The modern corporation as a unique social productive institution emerges from that division of labor. That it differs from proprietorships and partnerships in legal form of ownership is of far lesser import than the ensemble of social productive relationships embodied in its formalized division of labor.

Recapping some of our earlier discussion, at the very top of a corporation is a relatively small group of strategic managers who perform, essentially, the functions of the *entrepreneur* in conventional economic analysis.

They are the ones who decide what and how much to invest, select the labor and product policies to be followed, and perhaps conduct the relations with their very largest customers and suppliers and, of course, the government. Assisting them is a relatively large echelon of *staff* assistants charged with processing whatever information and intelligence is needed to enable the top management group to preside effectively over the *strategic* dimensions of the business. In the same second echelon are the larger ranks of middle and lower *line management*, who *administer* tasks and priorities as set by the strategic direction of the upper group. In the United States, though less so in other industrialized nations, *technical specialists*, such as engineers, designers, statisticians, and so on, are usually placed in the same echelon as line managers and staff. This middle and lower management, the *cadre* in our earlier discussion, are the direct interface both with the firm's employees and with its ordinary customers. At the bottom are the workers, who labor under a Taylorite regime in which the division of work, its organization and pacing, and its technical and other characteristics are one-sidedly dominated by their managers.

I have so far described the three-way division of labor only in its practical aspects, as a division of productive activity between three different groups of corporate employees. There are also three different career or life-course paths here. Thus the importance of the life course's time dimension. Workers are hired off the street from high school by the ordinary personnel office. When they reach age fifty, give or take a few years, the firms look for ways to separate them. Membership in the cadre usually requires some previous technical or professional training via the higher education system; such prospective employees aren't normally hired off the street but are recruited by the personnel office. Their promotion to greater responsibility and reward follows preestablished routes and channels. At age fifty they would normally be entering their peak earning and professional years. On the other hand, candidates for the highest echelon are, in the argot of the day, "head-hunted," at elite educational institutions, and in their career paths they are "groomed" for higher responsibilities and rewards, perhaps by a personal "mentor." At age fifty their careers should be at the point of takeoff into very substantial equity earnings in the firm.

The three-way corporate division of labor also has legal embodiment. In law, the board of directors have the property responsibility for the firm, subject only to the stockholders, who in practice tend to be somewhat passive; when stockholders are not passive, it makes the news. In law the upper management are the directors' legal agent in wielding the property of the firm, selling or keeping this branch as they see fit, dividing the firm's income among themselves, other stockholders, management, and the labor force; in fact, *inside directors,* that is, those who are active in upper management, normally dominate the board and thus the firm. They are normally paid in large part via proprietary income, in theory their income varying with the profitability and growth of the firm. As we have seen in the past several years, upper managers have vastly increased their own incomes even when their firms were floundering.

The division of labor and responsibility between middle and lower managers and workers is the main subject in U.S. labor law, a preoccupation that has also characterized most Western systems of labor law, which have tended to copy those of the United States (Taylor and Witney 1987). In the United States managers may not belong to unions, and workers who assume managerial responsibilities, even rather trivial ones, cannot remain represented by the union if management objects. Control over the work and the carrying out of the work are socially and, in this case, legally and institutionally separated.

This division of labor was first developed within the manufacturing sector of the economy but has subsequently spread to wholesaling and retailing, even to farming and fisheries, and throughout the services and government sectors as well. Educational institutions too have copied it. In fact, in the primary and secondary schools, and at less prestigious colleges and universities, the adoption of the three-way division of labor has already eroded the professional status of teachers and faculty members who are not "stars" while increasing the numbers, the scope, and the power of administrators.

There are further interesting and significant dimensions to the division between upper, strategic management, lower and middle administrative management, and the workers—the "bargaining unit" if there is a union—but they merely reinforce the same point. What does bear repeating is that the corporate division of social and technical labor is, in my view, correctly thought to have made possible the omnicapable corporation I discussed earlier. If there is a sharp *capitalist* distinction between the capitalism of the mid-Victorian era and of today, it rests on the social and material qualities of the modern firm. By astutely embodying a clear-cut distinction between strategy, administration, and labor in an actual organization, a handful of top managers have shown themselves able to supervise for well or ill an almost unlimited variety and scale of profit-oriented operations, having at their beck and call a full echelon of increasingly specialized administrators and technicians. Similarly, the technical and supervisory monopoly over the actual work of production by that managerial echelon means that the productive output of the workers ceases to be a function of worker skill and choice. That output is multiplied by systems of management supervision, technical control, machine routing, and so forth in which the managers' latitude to manage is expanded at the expense of the workers' own private inclinations (Edwards 1979; Zimbalist 1979).

Prior to World War II, this form of division of labor was limited mostly to the United States; elsewhere, the family or specialized firm was the norm, and production was carried on largely by skilled workers. However, the vastly superior productive and therefore capitalist qualities of the corporate form of organization led rapidly to its spread to every modern economy. In a real sense, the dominance of the corporate form of business *and* social organization has come to define what it means to be a modern society.[8]

On the Production of the Labor Force

When we turn our attention from the utilization to the production of this division of labor, we see primarily outcomes of an educational system funded by government. We can also point to the leading roles of government and the educational and research institutions in producing the knowledge needed by a modern, industrial society. Their employees are also increasingly organized in a division of labor closely borrowed from the corporate world.

But even when we take into account the productive effect of teachers, social workers, the medical workforce, and other social services providers, the picture is still incomplete. Much of the production of the future labor force goes on in the home, but in a way unique to modern society. The modern home is, increasingly, an appendage of the Intersection. All societies influence the way their own children are conceived, born, and reared; but in the past such modes were left to the teachings of the churches and the habits and customs of one's family and one's region. Class identity too, however important in other respects, was thought at most to *condition* modes of child rearing, but in modern society those modes take institutional, often administrative and prescriptive form, where they are directly shaped or determined.[9] Modern social institutions reach into the home to alter when we have children and determine how many we will have, to prescribe their prenatal care, decide the manner of their birthing, and virtually direct each subsequent stage of their lives. Again, one may disagree about the degree of intentional influence here. What is beyond argument is that the integration of family forms and behaviors within the Intersection social system is observably both necessary and complementary to the modern division of labor. Bestowing the course identity that will further emerge throughout the child's life begins with how a child is conceived, born, and raised. The modern mother, even if she stays at home, is subjected to a stream of social influences in the form of the baby and child-care industries, her mother, her own school experiences, the media, her doctor or other medical advisers, and so forth, including her social circle, who are, naturally, subject to the same influences.

These influences change over time, but in a single period they are observably convergent. The medical profession and the manufacturers of child-care products do interact, do borrow strategies from one another, imitate one another's products, and together interact with third parties such as government and the education industry. The private corporation is undoubtedly the starring institution of modern society, but its success comes in part from its complementary relations with the other two institutions of the Intersection.

One should speak also of a mentoring life course. However, mentoring in each of the main courses differs. A mother in posh Winnetka, Illinois, has and then imparts different social productive characteristics to her children than one in, say, an everyday lower-middle-class neighborhood in Brooklyn, New York. There are analogous differences for job and career mentors at the trade high school and at Harvard, and for later in one's course. As a life course, then, mentoring lies at right angles, so to speak, to the other courses, is differentiated considerably within them, and is further differentiated by the fact that some kinds of mentoring are paid jobs with their own career track and some are not. But if we are to grasp analytically the fact that modern society produces its social division of labor and privilege through formal, coordinate social mechanisms that reach even into the home, and span the stages of life, it is necessary to posit a range of mentoring courses all under the general rubric of mentor.

There are other life courses in today's society, but they will be treated only cursorily here. They are of some importance, but they present no additional special challenges to the issues of stratification and social action we are considering.

The Institutional Nature of the Main Life Courses

The basic three-way division of labor is roughly coordinate with—"clusters with"—stratification in the division of income and wealth, access to and the quality of medical and educational services, cultural outlooks, and the forms and frequency of political behavior. In the normal case, the boy or girl who will eventually occupy an elite, strategic post in the corporation, or analogous rank in government or the educational system, will have had an *institutional* path through childhood and early youth markedly different from that of the boy or girl who will do factory work and, at least after primary school, from that of the boy or girl who will end up as cadre. These, to repeat, are not "natural" but "semifabricated" divisions within the population; the different courses in a modern society are prescriptively patterned by institutional action. As we say so casually yet revealingly, a person with an Ivy League degree is "overqualified" for a run-of-the-mill office job, while that bright, ambitious young "boy" on the shipping floor lacks "credentials" for advancement into management.

As befits the shift from a dynastically based to an institutionally based social stratification system, there are definite *switching points* between the life courses. This locution is preferable to talking abstractly about social mobility. Especially in the school system and especially at its lower grades, some children from the lesser courses may be identified as candidates to move up in society, and there are hosts of switching points in the educational system that normally abet that. In both the secondary schools and the universities there are programs of study, teachers, advisers, and professors, even schoolmates, who identify "promising" young people and assist them to move laterally into programs, institutions, informal associations, and so on that lead to a higher life course. On the other hand, these switching points are more rare after the school years, thus giving further warrant to seeing the different life courses as time-structured and not as differential classificatory places in a relatively static, pyramidal social structure.

It follows that it is not enough merely to prioritize in the analysis the employment status of the members of the several courses.[10] One has to include both the preemployment and postemployment lives of people.

Accordingly, what I have been calling the corporate division of labor should more properly be called the *Intersection division of labor and life courses*.

Business, government, and the educational system have collaborated in altering the social productive characteristics of the U.S. population, the precipitate of that altering being the modern courses. In using "precipitate," I am reaching for a meaning that has elements of both historical design and historical accident. To repeat, it would be overstating the case to argue that that historical outcome was intended or foreseen by the agents of the Intersection. Yet it would also seriously understate the case to say that the modern U.S. life courses evolved, as it were, accidentally or unrelated to the expressed desires of the institutions of the Intersection. When one puts together accounts of the birth and development of the land-grant colleges; the rapid expansion of secondary education in the 1920s and of college education just after that; the evolution of state education department control over primary and secondary education; the union school movement; the settlement house movement; "Home Economics" and the Four-H Clubs; the Boy and Girl Scout movements; the Ford, Pullman, Rockefeller, U.S. Steel, and other experiments in "welfare capitalism"; the expansion of the management echelon; the spread of the Johns Hopkins university model; the G.I. Bill and federal educational loan guarantees; the development of uniform national testing procedures (SAT, GSAT, LSAT, and so on); and even the work of the Hays Office and other forms of control over the content of Hollywood films, one can see that the evolution of the social productive qualities of the workforce has an integral quality. In a historical process of conflict and accommodation among the various national and state elites of the Intersection institutions, various ways to fabricate the social productive characteristics of the U.S. population were more or less coherently tested out and then followed or rejected by the same Americanist template. I argue that this historical development was given crucial evolutionary direction by the instrumental social action of the relevant elites. If so, developments such as this can be seen as representing a third option, that is, as coming neither wholly of the intent of this or that coherent elite group nor as entirely independent of the intent of any elite groups. It is precisely this possibility of a third option—*intentional outcomes as vector residues of social and intra-elite collaboration and conflict*—which I will explore in the next chapter.

Multiple Hierarchies

Intersection institutions are hierarchically organized, and that has important implications for modern social structure. We can pass over the private corporation. Government, the main funding conduit for the educational and scientific/technical systems, has also adopted to a very great extent the three-way division of labor pioneered within industry.[11] In the U.S. system, and at least in theory, elected officials and their appointees make policy, and it is carried out by civil service echelons in which the distinction between the powers and responsibilities of higher managers, middle-level managers, and workers is strictly maintained.

The educational system features different but equally pronounced hierarchies. Within each teaching and research institution there are higher, strategic managers, a subordinate staff echelon, and a workforce. Because of the special knowledge and skills that some teachers and researchers possess, backed by their credentials from other influential educational and research institutions, they form a kind of fourth segment of the institution's labor. That's obviously less true of the elementary school, junior high, and high school teachers, who are increasingly treated as employees pure and simple, subject to almost Taylorite control by their department chairs and the principal. This is a main, I think unfortunate, thrust of present-day "educational reform."

In the colleges, universities, and research institutes, the pressure of the corporate division of labor also comes through. Many research assistants, lab technicians, and the like are treated simply as employees, rather than as full-fledged professionals. And of course, the proliferation of non–tenure track faculty, part-time faculty, and adjunct faculty further reinforces the divisions of task, role, and privileges of the corporate division of labor.

There are, however, two other dimensions of the educational and research system that further reinforce their hierarchical organization and, especially, the hierarchies of their outputs. The first of these is between the primary school and the junior and senior high school, on the one hand, and the university, on the other. In terms of the educational policies to be followed and their ripple effect throughout the whole educational system, the role of the university level is dominant. In spite of the fact that local funding is so much the rule in the United States, state education departments working in and through institutions of higher education have, in league with the federal government, tended over time to dominate in the field of education.

Within the educational system itself, there is another, reinforcing hierarchy of institutions, which range from elite universities like Yale or Stanford, to the less prestigious producers of the ranks of middle and lower management, and so on down to the sort of local junior colleges that costume things like "Hair Technology" or "Personal Skills" in the frippery of some sort of academic degree. The same sort of gradation can be found in the lower schools as well.

Those privileged young persons who enter elite primary schools, go on to elite preparatory academies, and then into very prestigious colleges or universities have a leg up on an elite course career. It is not a guarantee, however. A boy or girl from an elite family who fails to be identified by a mentor and, as it were, groomed by him or her has a somewhat reduced chance of entering an elite graduate or law school. Such mentors are also located throughout the more prestigious public high schools. Within the U.S. educational system, Americanist criteria dominate so that the school system produces outcomes congenial to the corporate division of labor. It is a mark of the aptness of that system that it reflects so strongly meritocratic imperatives, even as it preserves the social continuity of the upper elite course by tending somewhat to favor its children.

Taken in all its dimensions, then, the Intersection is intensely hierarchical in its organization; it follows, therefore, that it is equally so in its values and preferences and hence its outcomes. As I will develop later, this strongly hierarchical social material productive system sits uneasily with our nominally democratic political institutions and the populist traditions of the American people. I do not have as intimate knowledge bearing on the rest of the democratic capitalist world, but I believe a similar tension holds there as well.

"Raw" Power and Discriminating Power

By the terms of the three-way division of corporate—or Intersection—labor, the social actions of the several institutions are a reflection of the intentional or deliberate behavior of their strategic elites. This power is in several dimensions greater even than that wielded by the legendary "malefactors of great wealth" of the corporations' buccaneering years.

The legendary John D. Rockefeller Jr. of the Standard Oil trust again provides an illustration. Rockefeller was entirely the master of Standard Oil. There were few if any limits on the nature of the decisions he might consider. He defined his own authority. He could and did break the law; hire, fire, and blacklist almost at will; bribe or threaten public officials; and ruin the businesses of his rivals; he had no master. But having no master was deceptive because of the relatively undeveloped corporate division of labor at that time. Rockefeller presided over a relatively primitive management structure in a business context in which financial accounting and administrative controls were as yet relatively undeveloped and with a middle management that was by modern standards underqualified for its duties. A modern chief executive is not his or her own master; he or she is accountable to other members of the board, to the firm's bankers and major securities holders, to the firm's stock market performance, and so on. In that respect, our contemporary CEO is in a much weaker position than old John D. But the power to act of a modern CEO would be weakened if he or she were forced to rely on the primitive organizational tools available to Rockefeller. The power of the modern CEO is finer grained and can be more precisely aimed to more precise effect. He or she normally has or can routinely acquire intimate knowledge about this or that special market or this or that distinctive technology. Similarly, the modern CEO has greater choice about what region or even which country to carry out which of the firm's activities, even to choose which currency to employ. That implies that the highest reaches of the elite course have a kind, a scope, and a discriminating power denied even to the great John D.

But there is a further difference as well. As already argued, many corporate business firms are now deeply embedded in the creation and carrying out of public policies in health care, educational matters, national security, and environmental legislation, in virtually every significant field. The old Rockefeller was said to have owned the U.S. Senate for a time, but then too "his" Senate took up and legislated on a far narrower range of public policy issues and with less attention to detail than the present one does. A modern chief executive might, and often does, actually help write the legislation and rules that "regulate" his (or even her) firm or that keep other firms off his (or her) turf.

The hypothesis that comes of this admittedly crude contrast between the power of the old corporate moguls and that exercised by modern corporate and other Intersection elites can be formulated as follows: Rockefeller and his ilk intervened powerfully, sometimes irresistibly, into the American economy, polity, society, and culture of their day; but to use an earlier term, primarily in *disintegrative,* often purely destructive ways. The power of modern Intersection elites is *integrative,* often quite literally creating the defining features and the trajectories of change of our modern economy, society, and even cultures, not only here but worldwide.

Courses, Not Classes: A Critical Reflection

The analytical conception "class" is no longer adequate for the understanding of stratification in our modern societies, the instrumental social action of modern stratification nodes, or how those nodes interact to form an integral society.

Unfortunately, in its common usages today, "class" clumps together all kinds of stratification orders. For the sake of clarity, then, it is helpful to follow the lead of the great pioneers of class theory, Marx and Weber, and limit the primary application of the term "class" to societies in which stratification features are market generated. In Weber's case, one's "life chances" are in the first instance generated and separated by one's location in the market economy. Marx starts off in the same way by arguing that the great, significant divide in the emerging capitalist society of his day was between the propertied and the unpropertied, the significance of the distinction being that it determined the social fates of the two classes.[12] But in our own day, the influence of a vast educational system, which is the product of government enactment and not the market, operates to sharply modify one's life chances. This is not at all to deny the deeply stratified nature of most of the educational system's outcomes, but, as pointed out earlier, modern stratification does not rest on dynastic criteria interacting with a classic nineteenth-century market. Accordingly, it would introduce a note of excessive abstractness to say that mid-nineteenth and early twenty-first-century economic outcomes are "really" the same, with both purely and simply determined by the market.

Here not merely the descriptive but, more important, the analytical limitations of the concept of "class" fairly proclaim themselves. As I have suggested, in the logics of both the Weberian and Marxian class one looks to broad social relationships, especially with respect to private property ownership, as the key factor in *conditioning the secondary aspects of class,* as, for example, speech patterns, dress, place and kind of residence, political culture, and so forth. What is distinctive in the logic of *courses* is that one views institutional relations not merely as conditioning those other social and cultural aspects of the stratification system but as *directly embodying* them. They are part of the primary, not secondary, characteristics of stratification outcomes.

Second, social changes between generations and within one's lifespan that are directly created within the educational system are an important feature of modern societies, but "class" is prima facie a classification term and, to that extent, a term that lends itself better to static than to dynamic analysis. In Marx especially, there is little analytical room in the concept of class to allow for social mobility, nor does his analysis really permit the social and social productive qualities of the laboring population to improve very sharply over time.[13]

The extent as well as the character of social mobility is almost certainly exaggerated in mainstream social analysis. After all, most people don't change social class in their lifetimes; or if they do so, they do so only by a slight bit. And a good portion of these fall rather than rise. But that mainstream is surely correct when it points out that the political and economic ideas of the, say, worker's work experience may well not jibe with his or her hopes and expectations for his or her children. It is famously if unfortunately true that the prospect of opportunity for one's children tends to ameliorate worker grievances and make for a far less socially demanding, much more socially quiescent, working class.[14]

The second issue is more subtle but of perhaps even greater analytical importance. In mid-Victorian society the productive characteristics of the laboring population were both spontaneously generated and more or less static. One took one's workers as one found them, some literate, most not, some healthy, many not, some with developed, usable skills, most not. One's workers included prosperous, very literate printers as well as undernourished, illiterate children rescuing bits of coal from rock at the mine portal. It is an adequate summary of the broader situation, then, to say that it was the market that separated the different kinds of workers and workers' skills and brought their actual productive qualities, or the lack of them, into capitalist use. And thus it was the market as well that so sharply conditioned children's subsequent life chances.

One can and often does speak of the workers of today as if one were speaking of persons who in their social personae are the same as those that Marx and Weber observed in their times, in short, as members of a working class. But one badly deceives oneself in this. The laboring populations of today and of yesterday are so different that they demand separate treatment and even separate names. Unlike the workers of mid-Victorian times, the laboring population of a modern society and economy has been shaped by over a century of the historic advance, which, among other changes, both ramified and improved its productive characteristics.

I do not claim that the evolution of modern educational and health systems was guided solely or even primarily by someone's desire for a more productive workforce. Actually, there is some truth to that, but we need not rely on it. It is simply a fact that today's workers come to work with vastly different menus of institutionally produced productive skills than their great, great grandparents. Mid-Victorian and contemporary, say, factory or office or construction workers are as different as day from night. If one is analytically scrupulous, they should be distinguished by subscripts or prefixes, say V-workers and C-workers for Victorian and contemporary, respectively. Which is equivalent to saying that if some were of a certain social class, the others belong to a different one. I suppose we could then speak of V-classes and C-classes, but it seems more useful to simply employ a different word entirely and do away with the clumsy though accurate prefixes.

This further confirms that the market ideotype itself fits badly with today's economy. The market of mainstream economics is analytically conceived of as a simultaneous sale by auction for all goods and services, preceded by a universal bidding process, which eventuates in all those goods and services being sold at the same setting. I am both understanding of and, to a degree, modestly sympathetic to this strained conception. At the times and places that the conception was worked out, economic thinkers understood that there was some system and order to the emerging capitalist economy and the conception of an auction seemed as good a representation for such system and order as they could manage without stretching the observable facts too much. Every producer threw his or her goods into an abstract auction, every worker threw his or her body into the same auction, every consumer came there to satisfy his or her desires. If we accept that every ware was sold, therefore desired by someone or other, and that an orderly system of prices eventuated, then the auction model seems adequate.

But in our day, there are few if any such natural (technically called "Walrasian") markets.[15] Large firms examine their potential customers, their variety of tastes and incomes, their susceptibility to persuasion, and their reaction to style and color even of the packaging. Many firms sell only or largely through fully controlled franchises, and only at posted prices, though they may discount occasionally for tactical reasons. The firms are invariably producers of many lines of goods and services and thus may subsidize the prices of some at the expense of others, particularly for strategic purposes such as acquiring market share. This of course skews the price structure away from a one-to-one relationship between the price of a good and its unique economic value, which is how things have to be modeled in the auction paradigm. There is little blind throwing of goods today into an auction market; one accompanies one's goods through the entire marketing process from design through market assessment through the sale itself and, for many goods such as autos, through its useful life as well. Both directly and through the credit card issuers, firms infuse their markets with credit, that is, the money to buy their own goods. The company may even buy the car back via the trade-in with a view to ensuring the steady movement of goods over time.[16]

Similarly, modern labor "markets" are not Walrasian markets. They are engineered in the short run by employer collusion, custom, labor unions, government regulations, and more, and in the longer run by the actions of the educational system. Thus the menus of productive skills held by different men and women are changing over time. All in all then, both for the buying and selling of worker services and for the buying and selling of the consumer goods workers use, which in part determine the qualities of tomorrow's workforce, the economists' "market" is grossly inadequate from an empirical, must less an inferential, standpoint. It is too inapt a concept to be useful in this, the present society.

But if I am right to throw out "the market," then its offspring, the Marxian or Weberian "class," must be discarded as well.

There are especially insuperable difficulties when we try to explain possibly instrumental social action on the part of such Marxian or Weberian classes. There we can be unwarily propelled out of explanations that satisfy a scientific standard and into an essentially a priori deductive procedure. As I explained, one contemporary variant of class theory tries to explain things by first positing the existence of a class as an organic body that has "interests." Those "interests" are typically not derived from the observed behavior, say, of the capitalists or workers taken one by one, nor can they be directly observed from the ostensible behavior of the group as a whole. If those interests were so derived or observed and by that very fact validated, then neither the workers nor the capitalists could ever be said to misconstrue, or not understand, or not be aware of them. To escape this obvious difficulty in the analysis, one imputes a set of "real" or "basic" interests to the class as a whole and then deduces with their aid when the class acts on their behalf or, alternately, has "false consciousness" or errs. Moreover, when as in any group there are differences about its interests, it is by deductive leap, not observation, that the class analyst decides who understands and is acting in accordance with the group's "real" interests and who has fallen into "false consciousness" or some other erroneous understanding. This is a very strained way to go about social analysis. It looks like a way of shaping the analysis to yield predetermined results. I don't say that that is anyone's intention, but as in any deductive procedure, if it is not implicit in the premises, it won't validly be present in the conclusions.

Class theory was not always this difficult. If one follows social accounts of mid-nineteenth-century New York or London or Manchester or Parisian life, the phenomena one tried to grasp with the concept of "class" were not so elusive as today. In Britain, for example, even into the twentieth century, workers were visually distinguishable from the more favored classes: because of their poorer diet, they were almost universally of lesser stature than the higher classes. Bad teeth or early loss of teeth was apparently normal; and if their illustrators are to be trusted, the lower orders would visibly manifest symptoms of their untreated ailments like boils, abscesses, premature blindness, and so forth. Their costume was distinctive too, and, as in Shaw's *Pygmalion,* so was their speech. Walking on the street, one could as a rule distinguish the workers from the bourgeoisie from the aristocrats. The workers also lived in districts apart from the better-off classes, and one could tell at a glance which was worker housing and which not and which were sites for worker recreation and which were not.[17]

For the most part, individuals on the street today do not readily tell us their class identity. Very few people in a modern society dress in rags, and with few exceptions people appear adequately nourished. Sometimes, of course, one can tell people's social level by their speech, but that is as often a function of their grammar and subject as it is of their accents.

The best parallel to the social world of nineteenth-century New York, London, Manchester, or Paris is found in modern race relations. Just as one usually can tell now who is black and who white, one could as easily tell then who was and who wasn't a worker. Certainly, one can tell now almost at a glance the inner-city tenement from the suburban townhouse in the tailored, trash-collected, well-off white neighborhood. And that is the point. Unless we credit Marx and Weber, or Jane Addams and Jacob Riis, with being fools, they readily employed class analysis because they could readily observe the different classes. The sort of analytical acrobatics one has to go through now to validate the concept was a thing unknown to them.

This point hints at another which will become clearer as our exploration of modern social structure continues. As suggested by the distance between the physical appearance, speech, and mode of residence and recreation of the mid-Victorian classes, that society was not by our standards a particularly integrated one. The classes coexisted, but in their own domains, only brushing up against one another occasionally and not continuously.

This would be true too at the work site. The emergence of a social formation different from the workers *within the factory*, in the form of a professional management stratum, is a development that took place in the United States only toward the end of the nineteenth century (Stone 1975) and in Europe really only after the end of World War II. Before that, such few managers as there were remained, so to speak, in the office and did not come out onto the factory floor. The organization of production in a, say, steel factory was arranged between two kinds of workers, the skilled craftsmen and their apprentices/helpers/navvies. As earlier cited, in Carnegie's Homestead Steel mills, this was still the pattern at the time of the famous Homestead Strike and Lockout of 1892. Methodologically, these differences argue the paradox that one must be a historian in order to be a contemporary social analyst.

Now, as not then, there are a number of important institutions that bring the different social orders into more or less continuing social interaction. The doctor and the lower-class patient come into intimate contact, as do the teacher and the slum child, or the professor at the technical college and the ambitious worker. CEO and manager and manager and worker interact all the time. For better or worse, we all experience much the same electronic media. One gets a sense from the Victorian literature, and the complaints of the early socialist pamphleteers, that the different classes and orders were quite socially segregated from one another, as I suggested, even marginally more so than the racially segregated worlds of Europe's and America's big cities today.

Even this very brief tour of modern social relations strengthens our view that one cannot be satisfied with a static concept of social structure.[18]

Again, I suspect that such a concept of social structure was perfectly adequate to the relatively class-segregated society of the mid-Victorian era. But it is hard to apply a Euclidian metaphor to the relations between the different social orders today, some pacific and cooperative, some highly contested, bound together to form a whole. In fact, for a modern society the alterations needed to give a sufficiently dynamic dimension to "class" logic add up, I think, to the concept and analysis of "course" that we are presently employing.

Americanism—Its Methodology, Its Meritocracy, and Its Politics

My analysis to this point has stressed that modern, developed societies are "Americanist." An "Americanist" society is one in which economic institutions and economic elites play a one-sidedly determining role in its political, social, cultural, and economic lives.

Its methodology: I've sat in on endless discussions on the relative roles that should be played in our social theorizing by "raceclassandgender." I seem to remember that there were only two outcomes to those discussions. If on the one hand the participants were feeling feisty or—not seldom—angry, one or the other of the three alternatives was loudly championed and little agreement reached. On the other, if people were feeling friendly or perhaps just bored, one could count on an ultra-bland, utterly useless "all three are important" conclusion.

Americanism implies "none of the above." While it is true that how one gets a living is always important—for the individual or a whole society—it simply is the case that the modern, advanced capitalist societies have copied the American pattern in which economic institutions and economic elites are accorded a one-sided predominance that borders on the idolatrous. An Americanist society is both by observation and by definition one in which economic institutions and elites are deferred to, and they do not symmetrically defer to preexisting cultural, social, religious, and other imperatives. They more shape than they are shaped by how we understand and deal with the races, the classes, and the genders.

The change in the status of women in the developed countries represents a case in point. Those cumulative changes in women's legal status and in the career opportunities offered to them, their new and expanded place in public life and culture, the availability of choice in education and place of residence and in marriage and divorce, the availability of birth control and abortion, and greater latitude concerning the relations of men and women and of adults and children, all these and more bespeak a *world historical change* away from dynastically determined social arrangements and toward those that rest on corporate institutional bases. Equality of the genders is a struggle in progress, but that should not obscure the changes in historical circumstance that give rise to and empower that struggle.

This is not at all to say that "class = economic position" is the most important social category; in fact, one of the reasons I have rejected class analysis in the present study is that it is too narrow to incorporate both the Americanist character of the society and the evident influences of that kind of society on race and gender. There are other kinds of societies—the Bismarckian variety has played an appreciable role in our discussion—but one must refer back to the economic paradigm implicit in the Americanist conception if one is to adequately characterize Americanist society.

Americanism is also a morally and ideologically attractive concept since it implies a society in which each person's privileges and advantages are keyed to her or his contributions to the economy. At least in theory, and very often in practice, an Americanist society is a meritocratic one. We should not gainsay continuing inequalities in U.S. and, say, Western European societies linked to the good fortune of having, as we say, "chosen the right parents." But as argued, the shift from dynastic social arrangements to institutional ones, however incomplete, does imply a world-historic shift toward weighing every individual's economic contributions more heavily, his or her status at birth and gender less heavily, in the assignment of advantage and privilege, opportunity, social freedom, income, and the other graces of social living.

Meritocracy is ideologically attractive because it emphasizes one's efforts and achievements, not those of one's forebears or marriage partner. But it has a profoundly unattractive side as well. The ideology suggests that "losers" really deserve to be "losers" and thus deserve little, or surely less sympathy for "their own failure." Perhaps even worse, it conveys that depressing message to the "losers" themselves, even though, as we know, our actual meritocracy rewards previous entitlement at least as much as it does subsequent achievement.

Its politics embody still another "Catch-22." The very institutional networks—the Intersection—that create and sustain the meritocratic features of modern society also reinforce the very wide scope and legitimacy of the power of the highest elites of those institutions, as I just argued. This poses a genuine conundrum, both on the social side and, especially, on the political side. Socially speaking, the broad equality that is a feature of institutionally organized societies coexists with the greater and more intensive hierarchy that is also a feature of those societies.[19] I think our conceiving of the elites of our major institutions as—unlike traditional aristocrats—functionally legitimate disguises the existence of that contradiction.[20] At least through the years of the historic advance, the palpable reality of growing social, political, economic, and cultural equality tended to obscure, even blunt, the consequences of the parallel growth of institutional centralization and hierarchy in the emerging modern societies.

But this raises a key question that I will address in the next chapter and the one that follows. Has the functional performance of our major institutional elites kept pace with the growth of their power? Is it a responsible power, rooted in and legitimated by their social contributions? As I suggested earlier, the growth of the police power in the period of the reaction argues that it is not, that a disconnect has developed between elite advantage and elite contribution. But to argue such a thing requires a much more acute analysis of elite social action than we have thus far developed. We perforce need a better account of their power, the latitude of its exercise, and especially the degree and scope of its intentionality than we have so far clarified in this study. That is the burden of the chapter which immediately follows.

5

INSTITUTIONAL ELITES AND SOCIAL ACTION

There are a number of reasons to center the analysis of modern society on the actions of the highest institutional elites. The first is directly substantive in nature: the dominant contours of corporate or Intersection society are "semifabricated" within and between a relatively small number of quite large organized institutions. Moreover, as we know, the prototype of these institutions was historically designed to concentrate strategic decision making among their elites, and that appears to have been a prime factor in the rise to dominance of corporate forms of organization (Chandler 1962; McDermott 1981).

If we were to limit ourselves to the views and actions of this elite individual or that, or of this small coterie of elites or that, we would only have to read the record. The problem is to make plausible the purposive social behavior of social-scale groups of elites, and that raises substantial problems of theory and analysis.

The concept of the "social-scale group" is indispensable. In quite small groups, each member actually has or can have face-to-face contact with every other member, or is separated only by one or two intermediary persons. In social-scale groups it is in practice impossible for any member of the group to have personal relations with all or even much of the rest of the group. Hence the group is organized by social, not interpersonal relations. I will address that distinction below.

There is also a special methodological warrant to focus on elites. On the assumption that such elites directly preside over the disposition of the socially potent assets of their institutions, their own social behavior should in the general case be under less constraint than that of persons in the lower social orders, that is, of groups possessing, by definition, fewer or weaker socially potent assets. It follows that the actions of such lower orders of society would be expressed through a vector constituted by their own pursued interests *and* the constraints imposed upon them by the more influential, more powerful position we ascribe to elites. One has to assume that elites act within imposed social constraints too, but by the terms of the discussion these constraints will in the general case be weaker and more peripheral, and to that degree the preferences and/or interests of the elites will be less occluded, more apparent, more easily separated out by the investigator. I do not claim that we can analytically isolate the ostensibly pure and ultimate interests of elites, but the method proposed does seem the best calculated to discover the expressed empirical form and content of their preferences.

Can Any Social-Scale Ensemble Ever Act with Intent?

Historians not infrequently make social groups per se such as classes into historical actors with distinct ideologies or points of view, these groups *as groups* being said to pursue their interests in more or less intentional or deliberate ways. Many of these accounts, as, for example, of the role of "German capitalism" in undermining the Weimar Republic, seem eminently plausible, so much so and so well supported by historical evidence and analysis that they appear unexceptional. But kindred efforts, especially when we deal with the present, tend to bring the countercharge that the writer is proposing a conspiracy theory with the clear imputation that that sort of thing is always illicit. Individuals, it is said, can act with deliberation, and even a small group, like a club or a firm, can perhaps think as one, as on the model of an individual person, but the leap from those modest cases to ascribing intent (or belief) to social-scale groups, such as a class or a whole society, is at best chancy, if not downright illegitimate.

This was the problem C. Wright Mills faced in his book *The Power Elite* (1956). Although it seemed clear that he was hovering around the truth, it was also easy for critics to dismiss him, not always unfairly, as a conspiracy theorist. The problem then is to find a plausible way of ascribing intention and deliberation to elites and other social-scale groups without at the same time falling into anything tasting of conspiracy.

This is not really a matter of evidence. There is a great deal of information already in the public domain about the inner workings of this or that

U.S. institution, from the Federal Reserve to Fox News, from the energy giants to the farm federations, from those who participate in the very well publicized meetings of the World Economic Forum at Davos, Switzerland, to the somewhat more shadowy meetings held in Palm Springs where elites from different sectors of U.S. society meet to share information and discuss common interests. We need a plausible theoretical framework of elite action, sensitive to reliable evidence and intolerant of conspiracy mongering that will not at the same time scrub away a priori all possible inferences of unified or coordinated elite social action.

In the United States at present, it is generally writers outside the mainstream who try to bridge this gap, sometimes, as we saw, by positing that a large-scale group, even a whole class, has "objective interests" and pursues them with forethought and intent. Thus we find expressions like "the interests of the working class" or "the ruling class decided" or "the middle class was worried" used to explain events of social scale. During the first Gulf War, many journalists leaned to expressions like "The war came about because the ruling class wouldn't permit the world's oil supply to be cornered by Saddam Hussein." A common way to shape such explanations, as suggested, is to assert the distinct identity of, say, an upper elite (or class or analogous social formation), analyze out what one claims are their basic "interests" or shared "beliefs," and then to argue that what happened happened because "representatives" of that class successfully "pursued its "interests" or acted on those "beliefs."

Critics of such a procedure are quick to point out that it is not at all clear what it means for a "class" or "elite" to exist in any more concrete form than as a range of incomes in an income distribution table, or as a loose grouping of persons who seem partial to appearing in the society pages of the newspaper. How, then, does one go from a static income tabulation or ensembles of socialites in evening dress to imputing instrumental social action on the part of that ostensible "class." To clarify just what "the actor" consists of and to verify the claim that the "class," in analogy to a person or small group, pursued "its interests" instrumentally—with deliberation or intent—is a very big jump. And, of course, the claim that a social-scale group, even a whole class, has some relatively simple system of interests, and recognizes and acts with discipline to achieve them, would require overwhelming evidence and elaborate argument merely to establish a possibility, much less to come to a well-founded conclusion. Most social scientists today would admit that such claims are little more than metaphors describing events we cannot actually explain satisfactorily.

More than a few of those social scientists think that such explanations come to little more than facile conspiracy theories. But if so, then we must also accept its unpleasant corollary. If all theories ascribing intent or deliberation to elites depend upon conspiracy mongering, then clearly we cannot hold elites as a group or class responsible for what they do and how they behave. We can only suffer passively whatever depredations "they" seem to inflict and whatever errors "they" appear to make. This stark choice between conspiracy and fatalism is too coarse to fit not only our needs but also our experience. There must surely be another way of looking at the matter that avoids both horns of this dilemma.

Why Elites Are Still Necessary

In the radical democratic intellectual tradition, conceptions of an elite or a ruling class or kindred bear a heavy moral freight. Implicit is the idea that "the great and the good" are not only socially unnecessary but impose a wicked burden on society and their passing would be welcomed by all fair-minded people.

That is not my view. Elites of various kinds are and will remain necessary to modern society, and it seems to me a badly advised stance that—even just notionally—looks to their early historical demise. Our experience in politics underlines the extent to which the populations even of the advanced countries do not yet possess the political capacity to organize societies in their own interests and thus dispense entirely with their elites.

Lincoln's well-known aphorism about fooling some of the people all of the time and all of the people some of the time remains true. Unfortunately, all modern societies preserve large pockets of people who can be fooled all of the time; worse, the ultraconservatives make up only some of these persons and groups. In my years of politics I have regularly seen large groups of otherwise sophisticated people aroused to support what seemed then and now to me to be transparently foolish and shortsighted leaders and policies. The almost effortless transition from the cold war to the "war on terror," which we're still experiencing, testifies to that. So does the social hysteria aroused by public policy debates on any subject involving sex, whether abortion, gay marriage, or sex education for young people. Compounding the problem is the existence of persons, groups, and institutions—yesterday Hearst's empire, today Murdoch's—that, in their own interests, successfully encourage foolish, shortsighted, even hysterical behavior among the public.

Yet this represents only the negative side of the problem. We as a society and a polity have yet to develop institutions and institutionalized processes that would assuredly develop and maintain over time a more thoughtful, responsible political public and one that will be less open to self-interested manipulation by existing elites and others. And because of this insufficient development, the elites must perform the essential social tasks of organization and leadership. They may do these indispensable tasks well or badly, but for the present, no other group has the power to displace them and do what they do. It follows that, to some degree at least, elite privileges in wealth, esteem, authority, and so forth constitute a recompense. Of course, elite function and payment don't always and necessarily jibe. As we know, in the years leading up to the French Revolution, as in the United States today, elites often fall critically short in performing their social functions while nonetheless demanding heavy, perhaps even increasing rewards.[1] Property, as we saw, has its perquisites.

From this follows a further corollary: if there is a gap between what elites contribute and what they exact, that gap often has to be defended by different positive forms of coercion. Such coercion is commonly supplemented with the spreading of misinformation and even the encouragement of superstitions plausibly advantageous to the higher classes. In any case, I hypothesize that the kind and intensity of the coercion normal and institutionalized in a given society more or less measures the gap between elite social contribution and elite social exaction. Equivalently, the acceptance by a society's nonelite elements and orders of elite preponderance and their social tolerance of the different forms of coercion, on this view, give an accurate index of the level of political development so far achieved by that society, that is, of the lower orders' dependence on elites to construct and maintain an at least minimally tolerable society. It goes without saying that my view of elite/nonelite relationships is a Hobbesian, not a Lockean, one.

I don't take the preceding theses to constitute the last word in substantive political theorizing. But they do have a degree of historical warrant. As we'll develop the point shortly, it makes sense to understand that the trajectory of the historic advance hovered around the degree of political development of the Democracy; to put it in simple terms, one reason that Europe's and America's elites bowed to the gains of the great advance was that the Democracy was progressively shedding real dependencies on them, was evidencing increasing ability to partake of the political process; or to use an older locution, at least some among the lower orders had newly come to be part of the political classes.

My view of the role of elites is hardly novel. Marx's notion of a new society bursting through the integument of the old is one expression of it. Another is his observation that a society accomplishes all that it can and then must give way to the new (Marx 1968, 183).

In Marx, a ruling class, or their kindred in other kinds of social orders, expresses "the general interests of society." As I understand his meaning, it includes, first, the points I've already made about the necessity for elites to construct and maintain a society that the other classes and orders need but cannot create on their own and about the recompense that traditionally accompanies these elite contributions. Marx's position is that insofar as other institutions, orders, and strata can exert their political and other interests, those interests will normally be brought within, modified, and subordinated to a system of interests and social preferences in which those of the elites are paramount. My hypothesis is that it is the ability to organize a society accepted as tolerable by all other major social formations that is the unique contribution of elites and the reason why we tolerate them and their appreciable cost to the rest of us.

Only desperate societies make blind leaps into the future, and the profoundly tragic history of the Soviet Union is testimony to the cost that desperation can exact. But neither must one be satisfied by "reform" of the at best tatty, at worst barbarous societies we now endure. There is a "third way," not to leap into that revolutionary unknown but by trial and error to "learn our way forward" toward the creation of more humane, more egalitarian institutions. At present that especially means to spur the popular learning curve, to support those ideas, efforts, and institutions that tend to support long-term increases in the capacity of all the members of the Democracy to govern themselves and to more freely and critically create their own futures.

Much of the material to follow in this book will focus on elites, their identity, their origins, and the dynamics of their social organizations both formal and informal. If I am right so far, then to study elites is to study society in a particularly effective way. To trace out their uncontested social contributions is to trace out the current political incapacity of the rest of society. To examine their beliefs is to understand the accepted or at least operative "truths" of the rest of society. And, ultimately, to study why and how coercion is employed in a society is to have before one the template of elite incapacity and failure.

Ultimately, we want to be better able to understand how other, nonelite social strata and groups achieve and maintain social existence and advantage, how they act instrumentally, how they "intend" or "believe," all within the constraints imposed on them by the elite strata. Again, the extra complication here is that their beliefs and actions are arguably modified from what they might otherwise be if they were free of those constraints. It has accordingly seemed methodologically preferable first to look at the ostensibly simpler case provided by elites and, guided and cautioned by that, then extend the analysis to nonelites.

As I have used it up to now, the term "elites" is still theoretically ambiguous. It asserts the social marking-off of persons and groups on the basis that they possess particularly potent social assets but does not as yet identify the boundaries of that marking-off. It also implies, or at least still carries the innuendo, that elites are all equal, though I think we know that some indeed are more equal than others. And it carries the weak implication that some elite actors might act for the entire social group or a significant fraction of it, or at least that their actions will be assented to by the group, though we've not yet established in any analytical way how that might be.

Fundamentals of a General Theory of Elites: Advantages and Nodes

As I have already argued, social stratification along lines of wealth or income seems present in virtually all societies. Surely such a common phenomenon, whose variations we have experienced in so many social and historical situations, should not ultimately be that difficult to unravel. Accordingly, we can and should go back to basics and in an orderly way build up the conception of modern elites and their social action. By analytically reconstructing a stratified society we can clarify some of the salient features of our actual society and to that extent confirm the veracity of the initial analysis.

We begin, as before, with the sociological commonplace that our society is pronouncedly stratified and that that stratification takes the form of a differential distribution of *socially potent assets,* that is, assets the possession or exercise of which not only confer a private endowment but can also alter the behavior of others. It bears repeating that the "socially potent asset" is not an ideotype of the Weberian sort: I conceive that we can always identify such assets empirically and thus make plausible estimates of their potency in a given context. Such assets include wealth, income, access to the political process, status and esteem, access to and influence over the high culture, strategic positions within important institutions, and so forth. These are not evenly distributed across the society, and multiple kinds of these assets come to be held by some people in clusters. The link between the two points seems readily understandable.

As I have already argued, having a great deal of political influence is likely to correlate with higher, not lower, status, to be positively associated with higher, not lower, income, and so on. The case for analytically breaking down a society into several distinct, more or less discontinuous, hierarchical social strata comes from how the different assets interact with one another and create sets or nodes of persons enjoying differentially advantageous social potency.

We come now to a central problematic not only of this chapter but of the book as a whole. How does one link and qualify these nodes of clustered advantages into a conception of distinct social orders, as in life courses, or classes, or castes, or estates? How does one analyze and understand how these social orders come to have a degree of internal coherence such that they—or parts of them, or their "representatives"—become social actors? The key bridging idea here is that of the formation of distinct subsocieties within the elite course, or *elite* subsocieties.

Elite Subsocieties

We have assumed an unequal distribution of socially potent assets within a given population. Solely on that assumption, at least two further consequences follow. In a situation of social conflict between two persons, one of whose relevant assets are greater or more potent than the other's, there will be a tendency for the resolution of the conflict to reflect that very difference.[2] We need not assume a peaceful resolution; two shopkeepers may compete to the point where one or both are ruined. But there will also be cases where the conflict is brought to an end or a truce in which the weaker party accepts that he or she is outmatched and the stronger party can impose not an equal solution but instead a resolution that approximately reflects the relative difference in their powers. Equivalently, the costs or pains of a settlement here will tend to bear more heavily on the weaker party and less heavily, sometimes not at all, on the stronger.

There is also another possible outcome of such a conflict, namely, an equitable resolution based on the fact that the issue at dispute is between two or more parties of roughly equal social potency. This is the case where there are two scorpions in a bottle who either live or expire together.

Both as a logical model and as a social observation, this conception of the processes of social conflict between persons deploying socially potent assets like, say, wealth, place, or political influence is itself very powerful and is, I believe, the key to the theory we're reaching for.

If we make only the further assumption that the victors in such contests will *often* wish to stabilize their victories, that is, not fight them again and again, it follows that they will sometimes seek arrangements of accommodation with those as victorious and powerful as themselves, and against those who have lost out in these contests. I have nothing very esoteric in mind here; two restaurateurs who have had to coexist at the same mall might well cooperate to keep out new rivals. Politicians who won their primaries might seek to help each other in the next primary to their—as they say—"mutual advantage." Or at a wider level, people with inherited wealth or the prospect of the same are likely to agree that inheritance taxes should be low.

It seems plausible to see here the germ of the formation of elite subsocieties, that is, social ensembles of every size, in which those who have superior socially potent assets and have come into conflict with others similarly endowed join with those others to stabilize and protect the exercise of those assets. One need not assume that this always happens, merely that it sometimes, perhaps even often, happens. Thus, at this second level of analysis, the genesis and dynamic of elite subsocieties seems plausibly established. These elite subsocieties may take the form of actual organizations, like a corporate merger or a trade association, or merely have continuing informal or even cultural/ideological existence and effect.

Methodologically, I have not assumed anything about an initial commonality of interests between these owner/possessors. We merely assumed that there were outcomes to various conflicts and that some of the successful will *subsequently* exercise a preference to secure the outcome and *consequently* choose to cooperate with other like situated victors. Two points are crucial here.

Participation in a chamber of commerce or political cabal arises here as the outcome or *precipitate* of conflict, not a consequence of antecedent joint interests. Accordingly, when we say that the victors joined because they had joint *interests,* we are giving an after-the-fact account, not an account of the dynamic link between expressed preferences and the genesis and continuance of elite subsocieties. As I use the term, an *elite subsociety* of any kind is the residue of previously exercised preferences as I have just described them, and any statements about joint or opposed *interests* are nothing more than a way to reference that description succinctly.

Elite subsocieties embody outcomes reached by the previous preferential actions of their actors. To repeat, the existence of an elite subsociety does not assume an abstract joint *interest* of any kind; whatever linkages and alliances arise, they can be, in principle, fully accounted for as the product of familiar processes of conflict and accommodation around the possession and exercise of socially potent assets. It is only with the passage of time that the connection between these revealed preferences and the actual, empirical conflicts in which they were generated may become so attenuated that they take on a self-contained, habitual, rote form. The conception of *interests* is often used in the social sciences with something of that flavor. Again, that sort of attenuation is common, but it is theoretically dispensable, entirely so, in accounting for elite preferences and the formation of elite subsocieties.

Here I have given *a hypothetical generative account* of elite preferences and their expression in social action. When we look not to the abstract generation of elites but to an already existing society, very little in our account needs to be changed. Among existing elites there are all sorts of groupings that come together from time to time, whether to make a bit of money, or to influence the primary school curriculum, or to pass a tax law. Many of those sought-after preferences will run into opposition from other elite persons. *But because of their greater relative social potency, both as individuals and as subgroups, there will be a tendency among such existing elites to have settled on forms of resolution or solution that impose greater material, social, or other costs on nonelites than on themselves. Because this form of settlement of conflict is especially open to elites, conflict among elites of roughly equal potency is for this reason more likely to be so resolved; hence to that degree there will have emerged in the past subgroups and subsocieties that rest on joint or overlapping preferences that are greater than and more socially potent than, hence more likely to be socially enacted than, those emanating from outside elite ranks.*

That "greater than" is all that is needed for a theory of instrumental social action. From this simple, empirically rooted model, it follows that some socially significant features of modern society will represent—again not some imputed unitary interests of the elite—but the social precipitate of actual—or avoided—conflicts and accommodations, past or ongoing, both within their own ranks and with respect to the other courses and groups.

And it further follows that at least some statements of the form "The elite wanted . . . ," or "The elite thought . . . ," or "Elite interests were opposed to . . ." can in principle be analyzed into empirically ascertainable propositions. Such statements, however crude their metaphor, need not always be dismissed as conspiracy mongering.

Looking ahead, one can already see the special importance of these findings to a society organized predominantly by large institutions whose elites have considerable strategic resources at hand and considerable discretion to employ them in social action.

Social Relationships Differ from Interpersonal Relationships

I have deliberately cast elite and intra-elite social organization as *subsocieties*. Social relationships are different from interpersonal ones. Interaction in a society need not be and often is not face to face or direct but indirect. And, an apparent paradox, a society adds up to more than just the individuals who make it up.

The social theories of, for example, Hayek and Popper ignore this point because their arguments contain what used to be called, in traditional logic, the fallacy of reduction or decomposition (see Hayek 1944 and Popper 1967). A society is made up of individuals (true). Therefore, only individuals can decide what is best for the society (doesn't follow). Here, one has simply elided out of consideration the existence of specifically social relationships even though people's social relationships are typically powerful enough to modify their interpersonal ones. Correcting Hayek and Popper, one should say that a society consists of individuals and their relationships both interpersonal and social, but an even more accurate, nuanced statement would be that a society consists of the socially conditioned relationships among the individuals who make it up.

The following elementary exercise will enable us to see through the Hayek-Popper reduction. Two people by themselves can't normally constitute a social relationship, a minimal "society"; it takes at least three. Consider some relationships among three individuals, A, B, and C. Let A and

B be lovers and C a romantic rival of A. C has interpersonal relationships to both A and B of various kinds but in addition has another kind of relationship as well, that is, *to their, A and B's, relationship*. If C is jealous of A, that jealously is self-evidently predicated upon A's relationship to B; absent that relationship, C's jealously has no grounds and presumably would never have arisen or, should A and B split apart, might disappear. As a would-be lover of B, C has a relationship not solely to the other individuals but to their relationship per se. As human ensembles grow in size, they come to comprise many of these specifically social relationships, that is, relationships of which one term is an individual person and the other, not a person but a relationship among two or more other people. Analytically we cannot even stop there, for much of society consists of relationships between relationships, that is, relationships in which the primary terms are social relationships and not individuals. If we follow Aristotle, we will allow that these social relationships often dominate or at least sharply condition the kinds of individual relationships we ourselves do or will enter into.

Further Observations

Relationships within elite subsocieties will likely be more to the aggregate preferences of their members than will be the case for relationships among the nonelite, with that representative preferential character lessening as we traveled down toward lower, that is, less powerful individuals and social strata. Again, the logic of "more to the aggregate preferences" is all that is needed. That is, to predicate instrumental social action of an elite subsociety, we need not assume perfect unity of agreement within it, merely that, being made up of persons (or groups) able to displace conflict among themselves onto other, less-favored individuals and groups, it follows that the very existence and continuance of the elite subsociety carries a weak implication that it has embodied at least some significant degree of inner unity, or perhaps only passive assent, around any particular action. A subsociety, say, of merchants in a city may act together against incipient trade unionism without any meetings to plan a common strategy. Their informal subsociety will of itself often give rise to concerted action that is not organizationally coordinated, a matter of a group of persons "spontaneously" acting in parallel, or by "consensus," some aggressively acting together, others only "going along," which is to say, acting socially and not as a collection of disparate individuals.

A second observation is that not all elites are equal. This is not a theoretical statement but a simple observation. Sometimes that inequality is based on institutional position, where the secretary of the treasury has greater influence over economic policy than, say, the head of the local bank branch. Or it may be a function of someone's personal qualities or of habit or of some other factors. Clark Clifford, for example, exercised a powerful influence within the administrations of three U.S. presidents over a period of two decades. Most of that time he held no high office; his influence stemmed instead from the widely held belief, in elite circles at least, in the soundness of his judgment and of his influence with other elite figures and institutions (Clifford 1991). Only a thoroughgoing empirical study can unearth all the dimensions and subtleties of local, state, regional, and national elite relationships. But it is clear enough that there are protected domains for this or that elite group as well as overlapping hierarchies of influence.[3]

Third, at the very highest levels of a modern society, there does seem to exist a division of labor and responsibility among elites, and it is respected both within elite ranks and by "the public." The chairman of the Federal Reserve has immense, direct influence over banking, currency, and interest rates, less over other, one would think, related and equally important economic issues, like trade pacts or the pattern of wage settlements, and little if any over the investment plans of, say, the aerospace industry or the fiction list of a major publisher.

With this division of labor there is also deference among the elites in both the same and in different hierarchies. The local school board tends to go along with the state education department, whereas the leaders of veterans groups seem to look to conservative political leaders for their politics of the moment. Both the division of labor and the deference to different elite hierarchies are plausibly explained on the theory of instrumental social action that was earlier formulated. By definition, to be a member of some elite at any level is to be able to exercise at least some socially potent assets, and it will frequently, perhaps even normally, be the case that this exercise will be defended and possibly enhanced by other elites who are similarly or even just analogously situated. To the extent that this is true, other elites, alone or in other, differently based subsocieties, will to some extent at least seek to avoid conflict over that or those assets, or seek to resolve the conflict on a mutually acceptable basis. There will, of course, be zero-sum conflicts within and among elites that end with the ruin of one or both. But there will be at least some conflicts that will be mutually avoided or mutually resolved; and that, logically speaking, is enough to precipitate some division of labor and some hierarchy of deference at every level of elites. To repeat, the actual division of elite labor and of elite deference to other elites, which we can readily observe, need not be explained on the basis of (elusive) "shared interests" or denied *tout court* because it is readily explained on the same empirical/analytical basis that generates elites and elite subsocieties in the first place.[4]

To discover actual divisions of elite labor and of hierarchical deference is the work of the social investigator. Here it is enough to say that the plausible existence of such things is not precluded by an empirically warranted social theory.

It is this division of labor and the phenomenon of deferential hierarchy that gives rise to ideologies that rationalize and justify elite contributions and privileges. It seems plausible that ideologies of elite advantage arise integrally within the processes of conflict and subsequent accommodation among elites and then are further broadened and maintained to the degree that they continue to contribute to day-to-day conflict resolution among the elites or the protection of existing privileges against nonelite outsiders. In this view of things, the business leader who is zealous about the rights of private property is giving ideological form to his or her own concerns about the fragility of the business and the strength of labor, tax, and other threats to it. In generalizing "my property" to "our property" to "private property!" his or her private interest gains some further sheltering and protection by its social and ideological linkage to the protection of the property of others. Eventually, the ideological connection to the property of any particular individual will fade from view, and only the ideology will remain. What I want to argue via this commonplace observation is that the putative "interests" of the highest orders or classes of a society are a precipitate of this humble beginning, part of the process in which elites at different levels and of different kinds come by trial and error to practice and express their intra-elite relationships, and to exert pressures over time toward the development of a rough system of elite hierarchy, deference, and collaboration.

Fourth, it goes almost without saying that the processes of elite conflict, accommodation, and convergence will spill over into the political process per se. It will, of course, influence elections, sometimes decisively, sometimes not, but more important, it is the key to the expansion of "inner government." By the latter I refer to the modern increase of persons, agencies, and policies in that part of government that is relatively independent of the electoral process, such as the Federal Reserve, the National Security Agency, and the SEC. The phenomenon of "inner government," sometimes called "the permanent government," is intimately associated with the rise in the importance of and the scope of activity of large organizations organized in corporate form. I will take up this problem of inner or permanent government in its own right in the next chapter.

If we see this conflict model of individual, social, and institutional preferences as a continuing process, then at least two further points follow. Fifth, at least some macro-features of the society, economy, and polity will reflect and embody the preferences of some one or more elite subsocieties. One does not want or need or have any basis to say "all." And sixth, it is unlikely that there will be equivalently important or enduring social outcomes that at least some elite subsocieties do not support or at least tolerate. Conversely, the model establishes a presumption that at least some attempts to alter the social order in equivalently important ways will fail because they will run afoul of the preferences of one or more elite subsocieties, those preferences being deferred to, often even supported, by other such elite subsocieties. There are of course other reasons why this or that intended social "reform" might fail, but there is always the possibility that it did so because or in part because of opposition stemming from within the elite.

It follows, seventh, from our analysis that within elite ranks at every level there should be a greater degree of effective social capacity, including formal organization, than within the other life courses. The formation of elite subsocieties multiplies the potency of the already socially potent assets that give rise to them. And in fact we already know that to be a member of any elite is to be drawn into social interaction with other, like-situated elites, a kind of interaction that normally is enough to give rise to other kinds of power. A committee of any wealthy persons at all is not to be ignored by politicians. Analogously, even the most powerful persons seek to meet and to court influential politicians. It is not only a paradox but a fact that socially potent assets expand by feeding off one another.

In our kind of society, it is one's institutional position, not one's membership in some dynasty, that more often than not decides what kinds and amounts of socially potent assets one will exercise. The three-way corporate division of labor tends to multiply the effects of nodes of individual privilege and authority and imposes more formal or overt boundaries between them. These boundaries may simply take "natural form," as in establishing different residential areas based on wealth, or take cultural form stemming from different levels of formal education. Levels of institutional authority may bleed over into the imputation of broader social or political authority to their occupiers. And in some cases, as in the rights of management and of property, the law may superimpose its boundaries on those which seem institutionally imperative to some elites.

Thus, eighth, an institutionally organized or corporate society fundamentally changes the nature of the power wielded by elites. *It makes it less arbitrary, less capricious, even as it expands it exponentially.* Power less capricious but expanded? This is a combination that reaches, I think, beyond the political imagination of the Progressive Era and, equally, of the Weberian tradition in the social sciences. It is a combination historically emergent in its most acute form only in corporate or Intersection society.

The power wielded by elites is expanded in corporate society because membership within a large institution in a corporate society puts at one's disposal two whole other echelons of persons to carry out what one wants carried out. The point of organization by corporate form is to make action and outcome revolve around the persons, the intentions, and the knowledge of its highest elite, which is equivalent to making resistance from the bottom or the outside significantly less important, less efficacious, and even less visible. The exponentially expanded power of institutional elites, by being exercised through subordinates, is a highly insistent power that by design resists and thus often edits out "opposition" or friction" from the outside, that is to say, feedback from the outside.

The power wielded by elites is in corporate society less capricious because it is not typically the personal power of this or that elite. Even the CEO of a large firm most of the time acts within a role or roles, not out of his or her own unconditioned will and whim.

The Weberian orientation of so much Western social science paradigmatically views social processes in a tension between spontaneity and rationality. It implicitly conceives that the institutional channeling of elite power is weakened by that channeling. But one must see both sides of institutional elite power, both its exponential expansion and its narrowing or channeling by institutional interests. Both the expansion and the channeling pose novel problems for the Democracy.

Finally, the power exerted by institutional elites is multidimensional and intrinsically political in nature.[5] We normally associate the exercise of political power with governments and politics. But all modern Intersection institutions wield diverse and often fine-grained political power. I called corporate firms "omnicapable" in an earlier discussion, and later, "integrative." The actions of a corporation, government agency, or university, sometimes intended, sometimes not, modify political arrangements, change and even create cultural values, constantly alter social material life generally and social life itself. A decision by a corporation or government elite on some other matter entirely may cause a whole town to wither, or to be founded; it may of itself ruin or enhance an environment. It may wipe out a whole profession such as blacksmithing and create new ones out of whole cloth, such as electrical engineering. It may vastly expand the visibility and viability of an art form, such as classical music, and then, later, drive that same art form to the far fringes of commerce.

This sort of quasi-discretionary elite power differs at almost every point from the sort of thing we think of as a conspiracy. The latter is typically a one-off; the power of institutional elites is constant, not episodic. Conspirators almost by definition act in secret; the acts of institutions can rarely remain secret from an aggressive journalist or another offended institution. The need for secrecy and deception may limit the depth and width of the effects intended by the conspiracy; institutions are, as it were, poised and loaded to sustain the effects desired by their elites. Conspirators add their power arithmetically, so to speak, to gain their ends; the highest institutional elites typically have their power multiplied by the action of the subordinated, lower echelons of their institutions and by their relations with other elites.

It is increasingly evident that our current political system is not at all well constructed to deal with this sort of power, and, as we know independently of this analysis, contemporary government, the parties, and elected officials are loath to oppose the wishes of many institutions, and absolutely defer to the most powerful of them. Clearly, these observations should be analyzed for their possible relationship. But that would be to leap ahead before adding some further, necessary characterization to the broader social relations holding between elites and nonelites in our and other contemporary societies. As before in the discussion of conspiracy theories, I want to weaken or even eliminate purely voluntaristic explanations and even metaphors when we deal with the social action of modern elites.

Social Structure as a Dynamic System

One way of representing the real, that is to say, the efficacious, social structure is to conceive of the frontiers of conflict and accommodation among elites and between elites and nonelites. The analogy to a building or a bridge again comes usefully to mind.

In a simple steel bridge, each structural member—each rivet, bolt, weld, girder, strut, and truss—is subject to stresses from, literally, every direction. These stresses act variously to compress, to shear off, to bend, to twist, to stretch the structural elements. In an engineering drawing of the bridge, each of those stresses is identified and then calculated to see where and how the structure of the bridge will hold them in equilibrium. If a rivet must bear so many hundreds of pounds of shear, then the quality of its metal and the thickness of its neck must be strong enough to contain that shear under all eventualities. And, of course, one can't merely treat the bridge as a static structure of stresses. Wind, temperature, and the loads imposed by various kinds of traffic have to be brought into the system of counteracting stresses.

We can view a society in *somewhat* the same way. At every juncture between individuals and groups, there are multiple tensions and other stresses that the social structure must contain, and there must be a safety factor. However, unlike a bridge, a society is not an inert sort of thing. It must re-create itself from day to day and month to month, and it must adjust itself to changing social loads at all those moments.

Earlier I spoke of a society as exhibiting at so many points the handiwork of its elite. I use the bridge metaphor in search of the same point. Surely our model supports, and the narrative evidence suggests and plausibly could confirm, that contemporary society's inner structure is often the residue or at least shows evidence of elite action. We can imagine every person, group, and section of the elite, in their aggregate relations with nonelites, normally influencing the outcomes of both discord and accommodation. We can imagine too the multiple points of stress among nonelites. The latter are not so free in the ways they can settle matters on such frontiers of stress because their solutions must fit within the more powerful parameters of social arrangements that are the residue or handiwork of the elite. In general, the greater the contender's social assets, the more likely that the frontier of equilibrium will be shifted in its favor.

Some modern social theory, drawn after the influence of Gramsci, sees a one-sided cultural dominance of the elite—its "hegemony"—as the central phenomenon in shaping elite and nonelite social relationships and arrangements, and in maintaining them to the continuing advantage of the elites. Certainly one can point to many instances of this: the free market superstition comes to mind, or some of the more simple-minded versions of patriotism. But my preference in theoretical matters is to avoid as far as possible explanations that might act as black boxes or philosopher's stones, that is, explanations that provide solutions to social theoretical problems without making transparent their dynamic social processes. I find it more useful to treat modern U.S. society as an amalgam of differently endowed social strata—the main life courses—coexisting in tension with one another, vying to enact their social preferences in possible conflict with others. One sees cultural hegemony on the part of elites as an element arising out of and then stabilizing conflicts among and between elite preferences, and between elite and nonelite, but not in the general case the most important of such elements and, consistent with our earlier observations on the origins of ideological "interests," often giving only a cryptic, perhaps even distorted shorthand account of the full and actual dimensions of the conflicts.[6]

When some part of the elite engages in conflict with nonelites, say, management with a trade union, the resolution will normally reflect the relative power of the parties. But not to allow some accommodation on both sides is apt to preserve the conflict and, as is so often the case in social matters, to displace it onto other conflicts, as with the law, or to encourage anarchy or resentment that builds beyond the point of peaceful resolution. So I find it most plausible to imagine that the point or frontier of resolution of such a conflict will normally tend to be found more or less at the frontier of equilibrium of their relative power. That power takes many dimensions; in a dispute between management and labor, management usually has greater staying power, the law is generally on their side, as is the press, and so forth. A capitalist culture obviously plays a role here too in the form of both sides' acceptance of present-day property logic, of ideas of social and industrial deference, and so on. But management's advantages can carry them only so far. The union has its own power assets and can accordingly often fashion a more advantageous resolution for itself and its members than could a weaker or less well-led union or one made up of less united or less thoughtful or less determined members.

In conflict between nonelite social groupings, the frontier of settlement should have much the same character, that is, it should reflect the relative strength of the aggregate powers that are brought to bear on the conflict. But there is another, more or less equally decisive factor controlling conflicts between nonelite social formations and their subsocieties. These conflicts must be settled consonant with the more overarching frontiers of equilibrium established by elite enactment. In a conflict between labor and management, a small business owner cannot in the general case extend too generous a settlement to his or her employees; it will raise his or her prices too much, or upset various creditors or the trade association or the bank, or perhaps even fall afoul of state or federal labor policies. But in addition, it is also not unusual for the relevant elites to influence such conflicts by trying to maintain a balance between subordinate social orders to ensure that the elite itself has greater leeway of action. I think one can show that racial conflict in the United States is sometimes managed with a view to playing off white and black, but only just so, balancing the advantages that flow to the elite from such balancing with the dangers posed by provoking or prolonging racial differences too much.[7] It is a truism that the EU nations heavily subsidize their farmers with a view to maintaining the voting strength of the more conservative of the major parties.

As I see it, therefore, in a Weberian or Marxist class model the imputation of instrumental social action to such classes today may reverse the causal relationship between interests and action; group interests are not the source of social action. They are an outcome of it. To say as I did earlier about the Sixties that the national elite had an interest in "its" defeat is ultimately a retrospective editorial comment on those processes and the way they connected elite individual and institutional action to social outcome. Without the analysis of the process, the editorial comment is unsupported. With it, it becomes redundant. We only know what the "interests" of a class or other social formation are by investigation of outcomes of conflicts over time, not by a priori imputation.

I stress that this point has special weight for modern society because now, as not formerly, the relations between individuals and social orders have lost so much of the mystery and the sacralizing that was a common, stabilizing feature in past societies. We no longer believe that God will punish us if we go on strike, or that the dead husband will take offense if his widow remarries. Thus we have empirically to seek out the identity and outcome of interests, not assume them, or reason circularly to them, or draw our answers entirely from the past.

Nineteenth-century social investigators, dealing with easily discernible social formations that were not densely integrated to one another and that, throughout the century, waged conflict that seemed to them to follow divisions over property ownership, were hardly being unreasonable or unresponsive to the evidence before their eyes. To infer that French workers of the 1840s had an interest in reining in market capitalism, or that aristocratic English estate owners had an interest in high grain tariffs, demanded only that one accept the evidence of one's eyes. In that sense, Marx, Weber, and their contemporaries investigated, and theorized about, what was manifest to them. It is only when we pass to another, changed form of society that their reasonable procedures transmute themselves into the deductive logic of a certain kind of class theory. It is, I suppose, another warning that the sociologist must always also be a historian.

As we proceed, we will read a society as a system of frontiers of accord or accommodation within and between all major social and institutional groups around a hub formed by their cognate relationships to the elite. A good or bad elite, a functional or dysfunctional elite, or a far- or near-sighted one should all be evidenced by the nature of that hub. And, of course, in modern history we have seen each kind. If there is a difference specific to our society, it is that our society has denser nets of such relations than in the historic past, they tend to be both more stratified and more contested, and they play a more decisive role in social outcomes. Our different strata do not interact as minimally as their Victorian counterparts did; the very formation of each course is intimately involved at all stages of its development, in its institutions, in its culture and ideology, in how it views itself and others, in the social tools it can and does employ, as conditioned by its several relationships with elite subsocieties. The Intersection is the locus of the most influential of these relationships.

Elites and the Intersection

The institutions of the Intersection, hence their higher elites, play an unusually significant, perhaps historically unique, role in the construction of modern society. The school system, including here the universities, is of course at its center. Virtually every person enters that system and is sorted out there by formal education, acculturation, credentialing, and social networking into the different courses and stations of life. But the schools play more than a neutral service role. The school system itself is sensitive to the inputs of both government and corporation, and all of these Intersection institutions are hierarchically organized in the several dimensions already mentioned, their interaction reinforcing further that hierarchical quality in their educational and other social outcomes.

Obviously, there are also hierarchies among the universities, and these spread their stratification effects to the diverse high schools that feed them, and so on to the lower schools. Traditionally, too, more is spent per student per annum, and this obviously for more years as one goes up the educational hierarchy. Harking back to our discussion of the other kinds of hierarchy found in the Intersection, we can understand that present-day social life in, say, the United States is far less egalitarian than we normally imagine. Of course, there is still a lively, assertive air of equality that one can witness in the press, TV, and even in person-to-person encounters. It's a staple in all of those worlds that we like "to take 'em down a peg," that is, to deflate those who assume superior airs. Similarly, our national myths and a main thrust of the development of modern U.S. law assume the supreme worth of equality and try to extend its sway. But I think these things are not at all unrelated to the trend in social and other domains to place things under the hierarchies of the three institutions of the Intersection. We legislate equality because it is under threat. There is, for example, significant equality of opportunity within the school system, but how it works and for whom, when, and to what extent is not unlimited.

And that hardly bears on a different issue than equality or rough parity of opportunity. The victors in the social competition, no matter how narrow their margins of victory, step thereby into a rewards system that is skewed toward the top, even more so because we—the society—consider that the process of competition was fair. A just inched out B for the promotion, but A's income will henceforth dwarf B's. And so on. This comes of the fact that the distribution of reward and entitlement in our society is determined within and by institutions whose hierarchies, reinforcing one another, are not particularly susceptible to egalitarian values and popular influence, but are in fact often ideologically hostile to them.[8] Our society has much equality of opportunity, but a radically unequal system of subsequent reward and privilege. Equal opportunity corresponds to unequal result.

The Integration of Elites

Contemporary elites in the advanced countries are primarily formed and maintained within the institutional framework provided by the Intersection. As we saw, this represents a simply enormous historic change. The dynastic family or clan was in the recent past the social locus of wealth, as it was for most of the preceding eras. As wealth was then passed across the generations, it multiplied its social and political effects through cooperation between families to become a social force. Certain forms of wealth holding, maintained for a sufficient length of time, may even evolve into a society's defining social institution, as did landholding with its attendant tenantry during much of Europe's early modern history.

This dynastic form persisted even into the earlier phases of the industrial capitalist era. At one time it was, with reason, the intellectual fashion to identify a Rockefeller family grouping, a Harriman group, and a Mellon group among the great American fortunes, seeing them as distinct factions within a ruling class, sometimes cooperating against nonelite interests, but otherwise waging internecine warfare among themselves.[9] The model of dynastic conflict employed here is as old as the Guelphs against the Ghibellines or the Wars of the Roses in the late Middle Ages, and, from a reading of late nineteenth-century U.S. industrial history, not at all misplaced.

Friendship among grandparents or one's second cousins is a much less potent social glue for elite subsocieties than sharing institutional roles or blocks of shares in the same corporation or in a cooperating Intersection network. Persons who serve in the higher, strategic posts in those institutions together form a node of shared or overlapping, socially potent assets with which they can pursue both private and institutional preferences. From the nature of their institutional responsibilities each would often interact with other elites in the same institution and in other institutions of the Intersection. This interaction is the very substance of the formation and endurance of the elite course prefigured in the three-way corporate division of labor. It is then a well-supported inference to argue that in aggregate the national elite course per se forms a distinct elite subsociety that is a social aggregate whose degree of social and institutional interaction is marked off as both more asset-backed, more internally accommodating, and thus more efficacious than whatever social interactions emanate from the other courses. Empirically speaking, merely by virtue of their institutional positions, it follows that almost any subset of these elite individuals will have greater effect on social outcomes than most sets or subsets made up of nonelite persons. The emphasis here is *mostly, not always*. The former is more than enough for the logic we are pursuing.

A further effect of this change from dynastically based to institutionally based elites is that its greater division of labor affords a much greater and finer-grained efficacy to elite preferences. Boys are not limited to managing the family business, nor girls to nurturing the family's heirs. Both can and now do enter various business and other professional ranks where their influence, reflecting to a degree the values and preferences of their elite course, takes on a social, not merely a dynastic, scope. Thus it is now the case, as it was not formerly, that specialized elite input is present in virtually every social and political question. In the field of social work, for example, only a small handful of upper-class women helped form the turn-of-the-century children's aid societies, the settlement house movement, and the family court system. They had an enormous but diffuse influence over the values and objectives of the social system of their time.[10] That influence is now both expanded and ramified by the multiple institutions of the social system, each one of which is hierarchically organized and promulgates the results and values preferred by its own reigning elites. What is at issue here is not some imputed unity of what they promulgate but that so many social outcomes today, formerly perhaps chaotic and spontaneous, occur under institutional aegis, including, most crucial of all, the production of the productive characteristics and cultural traits of the entire labor force.

The narrative evidence about the higher national U.S. business elite today is that it does form a sort of integrated society, that it is integrated to a greater degree than whatever subsocieties might emerge from the other courses.[11] This world, once so prominently displayed in the social pages, is only now hinted at in the business pages. Yet it is more than evident there that the very highest business elites in the United States come into frequent contact with one another at venues like the Business Roundtable, or Bohemian Grove, or, regionally, the Vault, where, joined by some of the higher political elites, they confer about public policy questions. One does not have to suffer from political paranoia to conceive that these discussions have some effect on critical areas like inflation policy, levels of unemployment, rates of economic growth, issues of war and peace, educational reform, public works projects, and the like. In more recent years the World Economic Forum, among others, has brought together very high business and political elites from around the entire globe, to analogous but likely less decisive effect.

For elites to be "more integrated than" nonelites, not perfectly integrated, or integrated to some other specified degree is more than enough to carry the point. From the press, from memoirs, and from more formal studies, it does appear, for example, that among the highest elites there is a degree of division of labor. Within the institutional form of today's elite, this division of labor and the maintenance of stable hierarchies of influence are less inhibited by dynastic considerations; in a real sense the degree of integration and potential cooperation in that older "high society" was less than that among modern corporate and related elites. Because of either their personal qualities or their institutional positions, some individual members of the elite can become acknowledged authorities in this or that public policy area, as Andrew Mellon was on finance questions during the 1920s or the Achesons, McCloys, and Harrimans were on national security policy in the 1940s.[12]

What I propose is that some at least of the cooperativeness attributed to the highest U.S. elite appears to be well founded in the model we have been employing, namely, the enhanced ability of those with greater personal and social assets both to settle conflicts among themselves and to get around possible zero-sum effects, by shunting the terms and costs of conflict resolution onto the other, nonelite parts of the society—as mammothly and brazenly in the TARP process today. The existence of institutions like elite law firms, which make possible division of labor among elites, forms of conflict resolution, and alternative, noncompeting hierarchies, should be seen in aid of this.

Coming full circle, it is clear from the terms of the discussion that there are different levels and kinds of elites that shade off into the middling orders of society. Some of the elite groups are very powerful, others less so, and there are those whose power is marginal and shades off to nonelite ranks.

The model argues that elites enact their different, sometimes conflicting preferences, sometimes overwhelmingly, sometimes less so, and sometimes only in badly compromised form, or barely if at all.[13] In that sense, it is legitimate to ascribe intention or deliberateness to their actions, provided one is careful not to stray into the further metaphorical meanings of "intend" and its cognates instead of staying within the bounds of the logic of the residues of previous preferences and of preference vectors.

From the logic of elite division of labor and its consequences for deference within the elites, one need not assume that the entirety, say, of the national business elite are implicated in, say, a change in trade policy. It is enough that only some part of the elite can be observed to act on behalf of such a change, the deference of the others requiring little further explanation if we assume that normal intra-elite relationships hold. Thus again we appeal to the image of a vector sum, that is, that elite-induced policy or, especially, social change need not be the intended consequence of a specific group among the elite. Different elites, seeking different but not entirely opposed objectives and operating within a socially coherent elite, are likely to end up with the objectives of each only partially achieved. And, of course, once one allows that processes of conflict intervene between preference and outcome, it is always possible for there to be the unintended consequences of intended results. "Collateral damage" can be used to describe political and economic outcomes as well as the military variety. All of these observations flow easily from the model we have been developing; and, of course, all of them are readily instanced in recent U.S. history and politics.

Socially Irresponsible Elites

There is a last point about intra-elite integration that seems of special relevance in the present. It is plausible—sometimes all too apparent—that today's higher elites in the United States lack the *noblesse oblige* and display far less "disinterested public service" than was characteristic of, say, the U.S. elite in the 1940s. The recent looting of Enron and of so many saving and loans associations; the coarse, undisguised manner in which fat contracts have been awarded to the cronies of the administration of Bush II to, variously, rebuild Iraq or New Orleans or manage the extraction of Iraq's oil; the acceptance of burgeoning deficits; an extraordinarily bungled war; and elite tolerance of the sheer lawlessness of Bush II all suggest a shift to less socially responsible elites at the very top of our major institutions.[14]

The model points us toward a plausible, ultimately verifiable explanation of that shift, the explanation resting on the turmoil among U.S. business elites during the 1970s and 1980s. Because of various technological, global, financial, and even domestic political changes, there were major shifts in the relative power positions of the different corporate institutions. Great firms like RCA became the subsidiaries of new ones, like Time-Warner. Many others—one thinks of Pan-Am and TWA—simply failed. Within the upper ranks of business especially, these shifts weakened some elites and strengthened others, destroyed some and created others. The point is that many U.S. business elites were threatened by the turmoils of the post-Vietnam era. Because of intensified financial and intercorporate conflict, one would expect the center of gravity of elite energies to shift toward an advance of their own most material interests, a shorter-term time frame, a more ruthless imposition of the new costs or new risks on nonelites, and a greater presence of arrivistes. If it is true that the *noblesse oblige* of an FDR has given way to the rather more socially corrosive behavior of, say, the Bush family, it can be plausibly explained in that way.[15] FDR came along after several decades in which the national elite had been in process of stabilization through smooth growth of the modern, diversified corporation and its allied Intersection. That stability within the elite, one could argue, allowed, even encouraged, the state to take New Deal initiatives, which would not have been permissible during a period of higher intra-elite conflict. The existence of the Great Depression was important, obviously, but I think one must also credit the longevity and stability of that era's elite for the fact that they acted more or less collectively against the Depression, rather than pursuing a fragmented and individualistic policy of *sauve qui peut*.

Today's is a newer elite in which arguably a division of labor and of hierarchy is less settled and the outcomes of intra-elite conflicts are insufficiently stabilized. The narrative in support of this would of course point to the enhanced economic importance of firms in the South and West, and to the growth of the information industry at the expense of "Rust Belt" industries, to the greatly enhanced role of financial speculation in corporate affairs, and to ideological changes among Republican Party political elites seeking ultraconservative support. In retrospect, one should have forecast this. In the period immediately after the Civil War, somewhat the same pattern of elite change, intra-elite conflict, the imposition of social costs on the least powerful nonelite groups, a falloff of public service by elites, and an air of devil-take-the-hindmost also prevailed. If it seems less tolerable to us today, perhaps it is because now we know better.

Force and the Safety Factor

Force, sheer physical coercion, or the threat of it, is never not a factor in social stability.

I think that proposition sits ill with our customary way of viewing our own society as one with "limited government" and "government by consent." But if a semifabricated society is somewhat more conflicted, less inertial than the "natural society" of Hayek and company, then it follows that there need to be stronger mechanisms to assure stability. More fundamental, unless we assume, falsely, that there is a perfect harmony between the political incapacity of nonelites and the contributions and rewards of elites, a society needs and normally enacts safety factors to ensure the stability of advantages and privileges. In our society at least, this takes the form of a structure of defenses against unwanted, nonelite-induced change.[16] We can conceive of that defense structure as taking the form of multiple concentric rings or lines of defense that render each other mutual support. The following account is, I believe, less schematic than it would at first sight appear.

As in any society the first ring is inertia. Every society, even ours, is beset with social inertia, which is an important factor in its own right. Some of this inertia is buttressed by self-interested existing elites of various sorts, but the phenomenon of social and ideological inertia for the most part seems simply intrinsic to human social life.

Next is the ring or line of defense formed by the existing accommodation structures that tend to resolve conflict among the different strata. This ring represents the idea, earlier discussed, that a ruling class or higher elite does actually represent the general interests of society, maintaining arrangements that accommodate themselves to at least some of the more important preferences of each major group and institution in the society. Insofar as there is no significant threat of violence against the structures of accommodation, then it would follow that each group in a society has gotten some minimal menu of the things that it believes it needs and can obtain under present or normal circumstances. These menus can be vastly unequal and, to the outsider, appear unfair and inequitable. Nevertheless, I conceive that this ring operates under the principle of self-advantage. To the outsider, the feeling that this or that group has not got the best deal it could may be profoundly disturbing, as when we see the situation of slum dwellers in the inner city, or workers in a sweatshop, or the young women of the more conservative elements of the population. But if our social dynamic model is approximately right, then so too is the embrace by this or that group of what its leaders see, and its members accept, as its present advantageous arrangements vis-à-vis the elite. In order to accept this conclusion, one has to believe that people really do in some way understand their own situation, at least as far as their social experience permits, and are aware of some at least of its advantages and can thereby judge if there is too much risk to attempt change. Thus, in the Jim Crow South, especially during the earlier years of the civil rights movement, many older black people tried to hold back the militancy of their own children. This issue of when and under what circumstances a subordinated group should reject its current place and, in conflict mode, seek a changed one, is surely among the most trying, risky issues in politics.

The second ring is further buttressed by a third, that is, by formal ideology and by the hegemonic culture, which of course it reciprocally buttresses. I think ideology and culture in this third ring mostly function to say to the subordinate persons or groups that outside their current position, whose advantages they understand, is an indecipherable world of dangers and threats. This gives further symbolic but less calculated support to the system of mutual concrete advantage forming the second ring.

I vastly distrust the concept of "false consciousness," which is still routinely appealed to explain why this or that subordinate group is passive before its unfavorable circumstances. Those who accuse others of "false consciousness" routinely imagine that they themselves have a "true consciousness," which of course they want to impose, largely by ideological suasion, sometimes fantastical, on others.

This leads us to postulate a fourth ring of socially stabilizing defenses. Modern society suffers the generalized fear of anarchy and the unknown. That is, prior to the French Revolution it was common to think that one's own society was entirely "natural," so that there was little thought to alternative sets of social arrangements prior to the Second Coming. But along with Nietzsche we are all aware of the specter of the French Revolution, a fear reiterated by our media as they cover the "trouble spots" in the world with their daily atrocities. This not unrealistic fear that any social conflict at all might get out of hand constitutes a fourth ring in a modern society's defenses. It leads masses of people, of all the life courses, to positively fall backward toward existing arrangements even when they are amply aware of their faults.

There is a closely related fifth ring made up of socially induced superstitions enacted by societies to buttress their own stability. I think of this fifth ring as importantly different than the sort of hegemonic ideology and culture of the third ring and the ideological extrapolation of the fourth ring. Those I see as reasonably articulated, rationalizing, and justifying the routine details of the relations of the courses and of the institutions, of elites and nonelites. They conform to what might be called a mostly rational scheme of social difference and social preferment. What I have in mind for this fifth ring is the phenomenon of socially induced social superstition, that is, of the promulgation of very highly generalized ideas, often with barely discernible content, such as "revealed religion," "private property," "the market," "patriotism," and such like, which appeal not to the concrete advantages different persons gain from "going along" but to and beyond the outer limits of their imagination and experience. At bottom of these is the superstition, constantly reiterated by the existing structure of privilege and power, that ordinary people cannot and should not trust their own ideas, values, and beliefs but should instead defer to "their betters" or some mythical golden past or divine preference or whatever. So important is this phenomenon that it deserves to be singled out as a major ring within society's structure of defenses. The existence of this fifth ring also bridges over, in both social relationships and in ideological considerations, to the innermost defense of social difference and preferment.

The sixth and inner ring is simply coercion in the form of the police baton and the soldier's gun. It constitutes the ultimate safety factor in the defense of the stability of the social structure. One must be careful here to be simultaneously realistic and yet nonhysterical. Coercion is not the ultimate arbiter within societies, as I believe it often is between different human societies. Nor can the police be used willy-nilly by an elite against its opponents. In a modern society the police power is institutionalized, as are the conditions and details of its use. This is not to say that police behavior always follows the law. But even the lawlessness of the police is regularized, as in the United States today. Save in exceptional circumstances, elite use of the police for their own narrower advantages is contained by institutional rules and customs.

On the other hand, a modern society does not hold force solely in reserve; it employs it all the time, like the famous "deterrent" of our well-remembered nuclear war theorists.[17] I think we fail to appreciate this because force is the most stratification-sensitive of the rings of defense, much more likely to be used against the silent than the scribbling classes. The policeman at your door in the well-off suburb is perhaps soliciting for the Police Athletic League, but in the tenements he's likely to be looking for someone, and perhaps more ready to draw his pistol than his notebook.[18]

The police institution is a major element in every country's political system. In European societies, disposition over the police and other forces for domestic security has traditionally been both highly centralized and located within the inner, more or less permanent echelons of government. The United States has had an apparently more decentralized system. That appearance somewhat belies the reality. At least since the last part of the nineteenth century, there has been a tendency for police forces, formerly under local control, to be centralized under big city or statewide command. And since the "Red Scare" at the time of U.S. entry into World War I, there has been a steady expansion both of federal police agencies and of federal influence over the policies and even funding of local and state police departments. This double prong of centralization and of federalization has not to date created a unitary national police structure, though the provisions of post–September 11, 2001, legislation have gone a huge step in that direction. What we can see is a long-term expansion in Intersection society of elite authority over the uses and misuses of the domestic police power.

We should expect this. There seems a general tendency toward the expansion of the power and mandate of institutionally generated elites. And at a more abstract level, in modern society, organization normally replaces spontaneity: as in education, social work, and business, so too in domestic security. And, of course, one would expect that the inner ring of the society's structure of defenses should assuredly be under elite control.

There is also a less sanitary reading of the two prongs. They may express a growing divergence between the contributions and the privileges of our national elites. Within society, coercion is a philosopher's stone, able to turn the lead of elite dysfunction into the gold of assured and growing privileges. This is one of the topics we'll explore in subsequent chapters.

All of the rings interact; they support one another. No great attention or wisdom on the citizen's part is needed to see all of them at one glance. The social structure of differential advantage and asset, with its intensified outcomes of power and privilege, like a properly defended military position, is defended in depth by a system of mutually supporting lines of defense. Thus, even those rings not called actively into action in this or that situation do play a role all the time. In particular, coercion is never not a factor in social stability, however distant its prospect, but so too is the mutual advantage each major group enjoys within the system of the distribution of social reward and obligation. The structure doesn't rest solely in our heads either. Our habits and our fears work together to stabilize it.

To the six rings defending the social and political stability of what I have called "natural" societies, our semifabricated variety adds a seventh which is unique to it, and conceivably more powerful than all of the others: a preventive ring. One of the consequences, if not the aims, of the processes of social fabrication is to do away with social and political islands that have historically provided the birthplace for movements urging disruptive change. In the nineteenth century these were the mining districts and the worker tenements in the great manufacturing cities as well as special pockets in some of the agricultural regions.[19]

Intersection society tends to undermine social and other conflict ahead of time. I do not want to overstate the deliberateness or effectiveness of "preventive social engineering," but we can get a rough estimate of its latent power from the processes that Americanized the vast immigrant population that came here in the four decades preceding the 1920s. As soon as 1945, aided by the burst of national unity that accompanied our entry into World War II, potentially dangerous aliens were transmuted into "hyphenated Americans." This was, of course, a double-edged process whose historical complexity we do not have the space to analyze here. That is, on the one hand, those immigrant generations changed this country enormously. They and their supporters in the Democracy created unions where none had existed before; crucially abetted the Welfare State; created a more democratic and popular social and political ethos; laid the foundations of the modern civil liberties movement; demolished the power of anti-Catholicism and later of anti-Semitism; helped create a modern high culture in music, dance, literature, and film that freed itself from European models;[20] and, I would further argue, laid the deep foundations for the various movements of the 1960s, including the feminist and civil rights movements.

On the other hand, those same immigrants were deracinated by the processes of Americanization, and they themselves cooperated in obliterating their previous languages and cultures. Urban worker-immigrants particularly cooperated in marginalizing the socialist and other radical sympathies many had brought with them to the United States.[21] The success of this Americanization underlines the relative ease, extent, and rapidity with which a modern society can alter the deep culture and ethos of its own lower-class population. And that in turn implies that political dissidence, which arises more or less normally in a "natural" society, will be notably weaker where the foundations of social and cultural integration are subject to policy intervention by the authorities. Earlier, the schools were the prime though not the only vehicle for this integration of the social classes. Latterly, the media have played an important—though overrated—role. The irony, already remarked, is that the greater hierarchy of Intersection society is entirely compatible with declining sources of spontaneous social change from below. We will return to this problem.

Conservatives like Burke think the defense structures we have outlined are needed because mankind has base and savage instincts. Some of my anarchist acquaintances think they could be entirely dispensed with if only we had the proper cooperative social arrangements. But between those stark alternatives we can conceive of more discriminating possibilities. What sort of society would it be if each of the defense rings was altered or weakened? What would be the effect of altering Intersection influence to this end, or weakening the political behavior and influence of the police? Or of a secular advance in the political culture of the mass of the citizenry? Such things, I believe, would also shift the boundaries and the qualitative aspects of each of the other rings and, of course, of elite discretionary powers. Is there no way to alter the structure of social defenses, including the coercive ring, that would weaken the differences in privilege and power in society, rather than to buttress them?

It is useful to reemphasize that our focus on contemporary institutional elites has both a methodological/critical and pragmatic character. There is no implication here that all that happens must pass muster with elite "interests" or that elite social action comprises all, or even necessarily all the most important, social actions. An elite is elite because its preponderance of socially potent assets provide it with advantageous relationships to other, nonelite social formations; to study an elite, therefore, is to study both terms of those relationships, not just the elite term. Thus, my approach is not that this elite focus provides an intrinsically truer, "better" point of view. But *if* one has it in mind to try to alter the society, it is an intrinsically useful point of view. It marks out the special importance of those frontiers of conflict and accommodation that constitute what I earlier called the efficacious social structure, that is, the structure of the society's tensions. Beyond these claims, I would hesitate to go.

Coda

We are now, however, in a better position to respond to a question we earlier deferred. Is society created and maintained by the Intersection well or poorly governed by our contemporary political system? The society just described and analyzed is obviously very different not only from the dynastic society that immediately preceded it but, going back another century, from the society that gave birth to our form of national government. The oft-praised "Founding Fathers" conceived of a society of individuals and at best relatively small, local groups and institutions. Their political vision was of the relationships, essentially, of citizen to citizen, not all equal but all equally adult, male, white, and propertied. Our current politics is dominated by relationships between large, formally organized, intensely hierarchical institutions. That gives weight to the hypothesis that our modern political forms—comprising government, party, and media—are ill-suited to govern our present-day society. We can actually make that formulation more precise: they are very well suited to "represent" the institutions of the Intersection and their elites, less so to "represent" those outside those rarefied ranks. Again, this is not a moral/ideological critique. The word "democratic" shouldn't function with magical, moral overtones. When I propose that we need a radically different kind of democracy, what I want particularly to emphasize is that there is now an absence of feedback mechanisms between government and governed. This means that the many dysfunctional features of governmental and other institutional action remain invisible to the political system, and thus not only are not addressed, but cannot be addressed. Race would provide an excellent case in point, but hardly the only one. This lack of feedback is, as argued, a feature "engineered" into the institutions of the Intersection. In a contemporary Western society, systems of liberal, representative parliamentary government are supposed to provide that key feedback. My view is that they don't because, as they are presently constituted, they can't.

6

THE INNER GOVERNMENT WITHIN LIBERAL DEMOCRACY

In a modern liberal democratic system, individual citizens are represented "from the outside" and only episodically, and their divisions often cancel out their influence. Institutional "citizens" typically enjoy insider influence, which they exercise continuously, and typically not at cross-purposes with each other. On the face of it, the modern political contest between individuals and institutions is not an even match; however, there are problems with liberal democracy that cannot be blamed on institutional "citizens." We need to look at them again before we consider the changes brought by institutional "citizenship."

Theory or Experience?

One often hears that our political institutions would "really" be democratic save for alien intrusions of business propaganda, or voter inattention, or especially today, "big money." But in the United States we have had popular democratic institutions since at least the time of Andrew Jackson, and in France, Britain, Canada, Australia, and New Zealand for roughly 125 years. The rest of Western Europe and Japan add over another half century of experience. That cumulative experience casts doubt on the idea that our political dysfunctions are entirely due to "alien" influences; there is much nondemocratic, even antidemocratic, bias built into liberal parliamentary democracy, some of it by design.

My plan for the remainder of this chapter has a double edge. I intend to analyze how actual liberal democracy functions "in the long run," and then I intend to clarify how it functions in corporate or Intersection society, which is even more hostile to democracy. I want to solve a genuine conundrum, how to shape a democratic strategy that will make an uncertainly democratic political system work.

Our historic experience shows that representative government by democratic election favors and must always favor the preferences of elites and, to a lesser degree, the more favored levels of the cadre.[1] The institutional origin and resolution of so many modern political questions also favors the well educated over those less well educated, and the leisured over those who have less time to study the press and sometimes specialized media.

But the deeper flaw in such systems is that elected officials have an insecure tenure of office—they must face reelection. Attempts to make government more democratic serve to weaken that tenure. From the nature of the case, elected officials operate under the imperative to remove controversial—that is, tenure-threatening—issues into the realm of inner government and out of public notice. Thus the Hobson's choice offered by the present way of doing things: the less democracy and privilege runs amok, the more democracy and privilege multiplies!

Of course, the matter is not quite that simple, but it isn't impossibly complicated either. The discussion that follows will highlight only the political role of elites: we have already discussed both the methodological and substantive advantages of that preoccupation.

I have defined elites in terms of their possession and exercise of *socially potent assets*. By that very fact, political programs or measures that don't take the wishes and preferences of the elites into account are automatically "controversial." The political system, the actual political system, shows near genius in avoiding genuinely "controversial" issues. Invariably these ways favor powerful minorities, that is, elites and not the Democracy. Thus inner government, sometime called the permanent government, has more than a purely technical significance. To repeat, it is the main political form in which elite preferences are enacted and defended. Many, perhaps most, of the most important political measures fall under the sway of those parts of government where faces and policies are little, if at all, changed by the election returns.

All of the flaws in the system that we describe are worsened, not lessened, by the very centralized and hierarchical nature of the main institutions of corporate or Intersection society.

The Inner and the Popular Governments

A good way to establish both the importance and the limits of inner government is through the distinction between public publics and private publics.

Virtually every executive agency and congressional committee has private publics with which it has especially close relations. The Securities and Exchange Commission, for example, is in multilayered, intense daily contact with securities firms, with brokerage houses, with the different stock markets, and so forth. This group, taken together, is a private public. In the classic manner of any public, they observe their special part of the government, seek information about it, meet with its representatives, and try to influence it from the outside. But unlike the public public, private publics are not entirely on the outside looking in. Part of the career of a future brokerage lawyer might include a spell of working at the SEC in order to get to know its personalities, procedures, and other "insider" things. The leadership and cadre of the securities industry pay special attention to the Senate or House committees or subcommittees that deal with matters of interest to them, get to know the main players there, and establish working relationships with their key staff assistants. And, of course, the securities industry lobbies for bills and puts money into elections.

From the nature of the case, the information these private publics have on their targeted agency will normally be more complete, more detailed, and more up to date than anything available to the public public. That doesn't necessarily mean that private publics have access to secrets that the public can't learn. When modern government acts, it rarely does so with whispers. Letters and memos have to be written and calls made to a wider circle of people, perhaps to ensure that no one of importance is left out of "the loop" and interferes later. Thus each such person and his or her staff people are now "in the know." Any reporter who wants to find out what is going on can find out. He or she just has to be willing to dig for the information.[2] In fact, if the information is important to enough of a private public, it will find its way into one of the magazines, newsletters, or electronic reporting services that cluster at the interface between government and business.[3]

This notion of two publics also has a representational dimension. Almost all the citizens of a modern society are represented both in the public public, as citizens and voters, and in various private publics, such as for IRA holders, corporate employees, or owners of RVs. It is via the latter that we are most efficaciously represented in politics, not equally and directly but unequally and indirectly via our relationships to institutional hierarchies, professional societies, investment funds, consumer niches, and so forth. My savings may—and apparently do—encourage corporate environmental profligacy even though my voting tendency is "green."

Three useful points about the inner government can be drawn from this. All government agencies operate at some distance from "outsider" scrutiny; what they do isn't normally part of the daily round of news bulletins or on the tongues of TV's talking heads; but none of this can be kept from anyone who wants to know.

But there is more to the inner government than this. As I observed earlier, at least three areas of governmental activity are located within the deepest recesses of inner government and most removed from public scrutiny and, more important, public interference. These are the worlds of high financial policy, of (inter)national security, and of domestic security or the police power. These parts of inner government are not normally well covered, nor does there tend to be much analytical and critical depth in the reporting given to the public public about them. This is media deference, not incapacity.

The activities of this level of inner government are different in kind from the normal government agency. Here is where the most important dimensions of the social defense structure are most heavily secured. Thus what one really needs, wants, and rarely gets is the sort of politically sensitive reporting that made William Greider's study of the Federal Reserve at once so unique and so important (Greider 1987). Such news about the inner government is rare, and rarer still is coverage with a critical political perspective. By "critical" here, I don't mean "negative." One wants instead information and analysis that is aware of the importance to the public of what is being done by inner government and of how it might most effectively intervene. Instead, what we typically get is a brief story that the Fed has changed interest rates and that Wall Street is happy about it. The deeper and longer effects of that change on the rest of the country are rarely touched upon outside the business pages, and only barely so there.

I will continue to use the term "inner government" to refer to that part of government where elite advantages are institutionalized. But my stance is a not a populist one. There are many government activities that require expertise and experience, and it is entirely legitimate for these areas to be somewhat sheltered from the direct influence of public publics. But the inmost recesses of inner government are where government officials deal with the representatives of the highest, most exclusive, and most unified elite publics of them all. It is, after all, one thing for the aluminum industry to lose out over a proposed change in some import rule but quite another for a challenge to the National Security Council's latest "declaration" of covert war. The aluminum industry may be hurt in the first case, but the steel industry might be helped. When inner government deals with things that have the most important implications for the maintenance of elite advantage generally, that of itself is presumptive evidence of a higher elite consensus.

As if to underline the point, challenges to the most important strategic privileges of the most important elites are not defended solely by the normal social defense structure discussed in chapter 5. Sometimes the elite gears itself up to fight for what it wants. Two historic examples come readily to mind:

After much elite disagreement, and more than a little elite dithering, about what to do about Hitler, the fall of France in June 1940 galvanized an almost united front of elite U.S. spokespeople and institutions. Britain was now mortally threatened, and its fall to Hitler would represent a grievous, perhaps mortal blow to elite financial interests all over the world, deeply undermine the capacity of the United States to defend itself and its political and economic system, and no less important, place in deepest jeopardy the moral order favored by the widest, most influential parts of the then U.S. elite. My point is not that a Nazi victory was contrary solely to the interests of the elite; such a victory would have ushered in a more barbaric age. But it was the elite who organized the U.S. response and tailored it to their own advantage.

Various committees of the most prestigious were established to lobby Congress and the public about the need to support Britain. Laws and other rules were winked at by government and corporation in order to send military aid to the Churchill government. Beginning in January 1941 the U.S. Navy—entirely illegally—assisted the Royal Navy in tracking German submarines, and from late summer our navy was waging a full-scale but secret war in the Atlantic in all ways save the name (Morison 1984; Bailey 1979). Meanwhile, much of the press, not ruing this turn to arbitrary, even unconstitutional presidential behavior, were producing stories sympathetic to the Allies and hostile to the Axis, while Hollywood soon responded with over 150 pro-Allied, anti-Nazi movies.

What is also of note here is that opposition to U.S. support for Britain was demonized, almost semicriminalized both in name and sometimes in fact. That makes sense if we take the terms of dispute into account. When the highest elite circles have agreed something is in their vital interests, those who oppose it become a threat to the entire social defense structure. Those opposed to U.S. aid to Britain were accordingly painted as criminally foolish, disloyal, antidemocratic, anti-Semitic, and likely in the pay of Hitler. The term "isolationist" still retains that dishonorable connotation. A whole apparatus of snooping and spying was loosed on the opponents of war; and where possible, legal harassment and even prosecution were resorted to.

There is extraordinary irony to this bit of history. As more and more evidence of the criminality and barbarism of the Hitler regime became apparent, those who had been labeled as isolationists remained discredited after the war. But a route lay open to them to restore their credibility: vilification of their great antagonist, FDR. That continues even into the present in the form of charges that FDR had foreknowledge of the Japanese attack on Pearl Harbor but allowed it to occur. What is so interesting here is that the evidence is overwhelming that FDR and his advisers were hoping against hope that Japan would delay any aggressive move against the United States until spring 1942, when our defenses would be stronger. Meanwhile, FDR's thoroughly documented scheming to cause Germany to declare war on us (see particularly Bailey 1979) has passed into the historical shadows occupied mostly by scholars.

When, after World War II, U.S. elite figures and institutions felt we had to mount a major challenge to the Soviet Union's newfound power, a similar process of demonizing and criminalizing the opposition was engaged in. Senator McCarthy is still cited as its villain, but "McCarthyism" was a pillar of President Truman's 1948 campaign against the third party, "peace" candidate, Henry Wallace, two whole years before Senator McCarthy began his own crusade. "Trumanism" is a better name for the drive to make sure that no legitimate opposition to the cold war would be tolerated. It included an agreement between the two major parties to pursue what they called a "bipartisan" foreign policy, that is, to collude to keep public debate from occurring on the wisdom of the policy and the public public from interfering with it.

Both academic and journalistic circles tend still to blame an ignorant public for such things as "isolationism," the McCarthy witch hunt, the antiforeign hysteria of 1919–20, and the waves of superpatriotism that came over the United States in the aftermath of the destruction of the World Trade Center in 1991.[4] That's not entirely misplaced. Parts of the public are always poised to behave foolishly if given an excuse to do so. However, such outbursts cannot have major political consequences without elite action. Public hysteria in one place won't spread unless and until the media give it prominence. Sometimes the media do report an outburst of popular witlessness but then help dampen it by portraying it in a bad light, as with the homophobic crucifixion of a young gay man in Montana in 2000. But when the mainstream media fan an issue by intense coverage and one-sided treatment, one should suspect that parts of the elite are developing public support for some venture they consider important or calling down wrath on someone or some group they consider hostile.

If an obviously important issue is being ignored, or its opponents demonized, an elite hand in it is usually not hard to document, though the regular media will be loath to do the documenting.[5] As we now know, every interested member of the private public knew about the Enron scandal even as it developed. Only later and after the fact was the material exposed to the public public.

Modern institutions organized along corporate lines undertake to influence both the inner government and elected officials in a sustained, systematic way, and they devote such resources to the task as they think necessary. A company that pollutes, for example, will typically have better and more up-to-date information about its own polluting than, say, the EPA and can thus can often render its rulings and the relevant legislation technically ineffectual.

Paradoxes of "Representation"

Elite-induced scandals like the ones I just described are entirely normal and natural to our political system. It is important to understand why this is so rather than merely to be outraged when they occur. "The system" encourages no small degree of elite irresponsibility. This irresponsibility may take the classic and familiar forms of "accepting favors," winking at others' thievery, incompetent performance of the duties of one's elected or appointed office, the pursuit of policies at the behest of the few against the many, and so forth. But the precise point I want to emphasize is that the system of democratic representation lends itself to this. It is inherently faulty in two fundamental ways: it poorly transmits popular desires into government action, and has poor feedback to the public public about the success or failure of government action. That should not lead one to argue unreservedly against liberal, representative democratic government. But one must realistically assess exactly what we have, and that is a political system which is inadequate in both of the dimensions cited. Moreover, that failure rests in the very workings and procedures of the system. Of course, there are lots of foolish and avaricious people and groups who operate within the system, but their presence should not distract us from the deeper, more pragmatic truth: the system fails, not just its personnel, and very often the system abets or encourages those personal failures as well.

There are a number of salient dimensions to the weaknesses of the system. These dimensions are no mystery, but their cumulative effect is, I think, insufficiently appreciated.

First, the very fact that we elect someone as our "representative" makes him or her into a person who no longer mirrors our situation. He or she becomes fundamentally changed in relation to us from the moment of election. Second, it is often impossible for the system to express popular preferences that have even elementary degrees of complexity, such as a choice of more than two alternatives. Third, in a democratic system minorities have to rule; there is normally no alternative. In our system the most important minorities are the highest elites of the most powerful institutions. Fourth, the major political parties have at least as much interest in colluding as in competing. They do compete but normally only as long as it doesn't interfere with their more important business of colluding. Fifth, the least informed, most volatile, and even thoughtless voters are one-sidedly favored in the normal workings of the system. Sixth, and contra democratic "consensus" theory, there are major groups in every modern polity that are ideologically or tactically antidemocratic in their preferences and work consciously to frustrate the democratic dimensions and features of the system. The list could go on, but I'll stick to merely a baker's half-dozen. Seventh, the system of representation by election positively forces representatives to bow to insider minorities, especially institutional elites and their preferences. As I have argued, the more democratic the system, the more this will be the case, that is, there is no "democratic" solution to the problem. It was Churchill who once said that democracy was a terrible system, but it was better than any other we could devise. He was right on the first point, but the second assertion deserves another look.

Agency Government, Not Representative Government, by Assent, Not Consent

During one of the many, many "democratic" elections the United States staged in Vietnam during that war, a particularly sharp-witted peasant was quoted more or less as follows: "A candidate," he said, "is like a bird without feathers. Each vote represents a feather. When he gets enough of them, he flies away and is never seen again!"

Less colorfully, the moment a representative is elected, he or she now possesses 1/435 of the voting power of the House or 1 percent of that of the Senate or perhaps 1/12 of the city council, or nearly 100 percent of that of the governor's office. If before, he or she lived in our situation and experienced things as we do, now the representative has a different experience, and likely different thoughts and a new agenda, such as how to get reelected, how to gain influence in the legislature, how to become part of its elite, how to avoid enemies with long memories, how to avoid taking positions that might cost votes later, and how to impress important people and colleagues. Meanwhile, all sorts of persons and institutions who wouldn't talk to you or me want to talk to and persuade and reward this repository of "representational" power. In short, he or she is no longer a representative person, but a special one. There is a classic debate over whether a representative should mirror in his or her thoughts and actions what the electorate thinks or should instead take the responsibility for action on his or her own shoulders. The fact is that an elected representative now has a host of additional pressures, many of which can, and often do, separate the interests of voter and representative.

There is simply no way around the paradox that the very form of representation introduces distortion between the outlook and interests of representative and constituency. Upon election the nature of the representative's publics also changes very substantially. If before the election his or her fate was largely in the hands of the public public, now, in office, the larger influence is in the hands of the private publics. One is reminded of the old saying, "Poor Ireland, so near to England and so far from God!" Like God, the public public can be supremely powerful, but the different private publics are very near, have axes to grind, pay attention, and have the resources to help or hinder the legislator's career.

I'm not being cynical. As a lobbyist before both the New York State and New York City legislative bodies, I met some really horrible creatures, but also more than a few genuine people's representatives. The late assemblyman Bill Passanante from the Lower East Side comes to mind as a particularly smart, faithful, principled, progressive, hardworking man, and people's tribune. A more than decent guy personally, he also went out of his way to help lobbyists who shared his progressive principles. Among legislators with views as different from Bill's as night from day, there were also many good people, but they had to be hard-nosed to stay in office and have some influence. My memory of the New York State legislature is that it had mostly decent people in it, who did rather more good than bad under the unforgiving circumstances of electoral political life.

Orwell has argued how important it is to be scrupulous in the use of language in politics. If we apply his dictum here, then we of the Western democracies don't have *representative* government; our legislators, like our mayors and presidents, don't represent us, that is, replicate our experience and our interest profile in government. We don't want to beg the question of just how representative our elected agents are and can be. We have *agency* government. They are surely agents empowered by us; it is far less sure that they represent us.

Furthermore, we in the liberal democratic countries say that government governs with the consent of the governed. In Orwellian terms that's also not really accurate. Most voters most of the time have no way of consenting to this or that action of government; and in fact they can't, since government does so many different things, some of the most important of which are done away from the gaze and the knowledge of the vast majority of the governed. The distinction in English between "consent" and "assent" captures the distinction very well. We don't as a rule positively consent to the specifics of government action; we merely assent, that is, in a broader, more passive way, to the general tenor of government action. At best that is, and overlooking voter inattention, political sky-writing, and the other colorful sides of the relationship between the voter and government. Big institutions widely enjoy representative, consensual government; the public public usually get only agency government by assent.

Voting Can't Register Preferences

Voting procedures are profoundly deceptive when it comes to sorting or embodying the different, clashing preferences of the electorate (or the legislature). The principled nature of the difficulty was first clarified, I believe, by the distinguished Nobel economist Kenneth Arrow, as follows:

Imagine that three voters are offered the choice between three mutually exclusive, opposed courses of action or policies. Let the three voters be A, B, and C. A thinks that the United States should support Israel today in preference to the Palestinians. But A is so worried about turmoil in the Middle East that his or her secondary preference is that the United States support the Palestinians rather than do nothing.

B prefers U.S. support for the Palestinians over doing nothing. Militant on the subject, B also prefers the United States should do nothing rather than support Israel.

C's first preference is for doing nothing, but in the choice between Israel and the Palestinians, he goes with Israel.

Note that A's order of preference is Israel/Palestinians/stay neutral.

B's is Palestinians/neutrality/Israel.

C's is neutrality/Israel/Palestinians.

The paradox is that each alternative has a two-to-one voting majority in its favor. A and C prefer Israel over the Palestinians by two to one.

B and C, however, form a two-to-one majority for neutrality over support for Israel.

But then A and B give a two-to-one majority for the Palestinians over being neutral.

In short, each option has a majority, and it is the same majority, so there is no democratic method of eliminating one alternative as least favored in order to set up a runoff. Note that even though there are distinct preferences around each concrete alternative, all voter preferences cancel out.

With more voters and more choices, the same inability to sort preferences by voting, the same canceling would also be found, though it would be harder to decipher. Arrow's paradox is highly formal, but also of everyday, practical importance.

Let us now assume a big community meeting called to choose between the alternatives and with the same preference order and weight among the noisy attendees. If the chair is really capable and has his or her own preference, the order of the voting can be arranged to give the "right," that is, his or her decision.

The chair can propose that we should first clear the floor of too many alternatives. All those who prefer help to the Palestinians to doing nothing: a show of hands! OK, with so little support (one out of three) for a neutral stance, let's drop that alternative! Now, all who support Israel and who the Palestinians: it's Israel two to one. Democratically decided!

But if the order of the vote had been first to choose between helping Israel and staying neutral, the neutralists would have won the first round, and then lost by two to one to those who wanted to aid the Palestinians. Democratically decided!

As the reader can check to see, there is a similarly easy route to favoring neutrality in the final vote.

The paradox arises here because voting preferences are not automatically transitive in a group as they are in an individual. So and so prefers X to Y, and Y to Z. It follows that he or she has to prefer X to Z. But group behavior, contra the Hayek-Popper variant of the fallacy of reduction, isn't simply additive and transitive, as Arrow's paradox reveals. Practically speaking, a chair of a committee or a meeting, or one who steers bills to a vote of the entire body, or who drafts the bill itself or the proposition that will be put out to a referendum, can often decide the result by manipulating the procedure.

Two things follow here: first, our voting system can only dimly, if at all, take account of voter preferences, no matter how democratic the actual voting may be. Second and related, voting does not give an unambiguous decision procedure for dealing with public issues. As we just saw in a very elementary case, voting is in principle not a good guide to making democratic decisions; in too many cases, the procedure itself determines the decisions, not the voters.

There are ways of making decisions that are unambiguous and efficient and even reasonably fair. People who come first to the line get first choice of tickets; who gets to play on a pick-up softball team on a Sunday morning can be decided by lottery or by age or height. The chronic problems of who gets chosen, cronyism, quarrels and disputations, time-wasting consultations, and hurt feelings—all are avoided. Fine decision procedures for those situations, but voting isn't a good, unambiguous, even fair decision procedure—unless of course you and your friends are in the chair! It is a rare thing in politics when the chair is unoccupied, rarer still when institutions "chair" so much of the public policy process.

Representative Democracy = Minority Rule

Minorities almost always rule in agency or, if one insists still, representative democracy. This paradox is almost too easy to establish because minorities always have the advantage in our system. Voting by district, for example, which is the way we stock our legislatures and councils, has to favor minority rule. It can't be otherwise.

Assume that there are 99 voters who are divided evenly among 11 voting districts. That means that there are 9 voters in each district. To get a majority in the resulting committee or legislative chamber, one needs to elect 6 representatives and each of them needs only 5 votes to be elected. In short, under the stated conditions, 30 votes can bring about a majority even though it may rest on less than one-third of the 99 votes cast.

If, as in the real world, the voting districts have uneven populations, fewer votes will be required to have a democratic majority in the legislature. For example, if 3 of the districts have only 3 people in them, and 3 more have 11, then 21 votes out of 99 will suffice. That is, 3 of the districts can be won by margins of two to one, which requires only 6 total votes, and three more 9 persons districts at five to four each will provide 15 more.

The examples are interesting because they show that legislative (or Electoral College) majorities have little to do with aggregate voter preferences. When one elects by separate voting districts, what matters is where the popular votes are located, not how many one has in toto. The U.S. Senate and the upper houses of the state legislatures all provide extreme cases of this. In the Senate, the least populous twenty-five states elect the same number of senators, fifty, as the twenty-five most populous states.

Actually, we have already oversimplified this problem of minority rule. State legislatures and municipal councils are themselves normally controlled by even smaller minorities. As a rule, a legislature organizes itself into its own hierarchy: majority and minority leaders, whips, committee chairs, and so on.

Returning to our twenty-one-vote majority in the second example, a majority over the choice of leadership and program for the majority party requires only eleven votes. Thus, the votes of 88 of the 99 voters could in principle be ignored and the entire legislative body follow only the dictates of the majority of the majority representatives (11) drawn from the majority of the districts (6).[6]

Of course, we assumed that the majority caucus in the body was democratic, needing eleven out of twenty-one votes. But legislatures are notorious for other ways of favoring minorities in their procedures. Seniority often counts for who gets what committee chair, and the traditions or the rules of the body may make the committee chairs into tsars. Jesse Helms of North Carolina was just such a tsar as head of the Senate Foreign Relations Committee until he retired in 2002. Ambassadorial candidates who failed his hyperconservative litmus test simply couldn't be appointed because the rest of that "most distinguished legislative body in the world," as it calls itself, deferred to his cranky wishes.[7] The 435-member U.S. House of Representatives is normally run by a handful of people who together have been elected by but a minuscule fraction of the U.S. voting population.

All of the problems just discussed are multiplied in a corporate society. Of course, big institutions, say, the steel industry or the for-profit hospital systems or even the elite universities, do sometimes need positive government assistance. The steel industry normally wants import protections against foreign competitors, the hospital system more ample federal restitution fees for emergency room services. The elite universities are particularly interested in science and technology research grants. All of that sort of thing requires positive government action, and of course, as big, powerful institutions, they are reasonably well placed to win that positive, supportive government action.

But they are even better placed to block unwanted government action via the route of having key, well-placed people in this or that House committee or this or that industry-favoring appointee in a government agency. Unlike a private person of only limited resources who typically needs some positive assistance, big institutions often have as much interest in blocking unfavorable action by government as in winning its favorable action. An antipollution bill that gets stalled in committee is a pro-industry pro-pollution bill. An Immigration and Naturalization service that hinders government prosecution of employers that hire illegal workers is rendering a major service to employers generally, since it tends to drive wages and working conditions down everywhere else. The ability of minorities to block government action is itself a considerable, invaluable power within our political system; and as we saw, it is a sort of negative power particularly favored by that system and particularly available to big institutions.

The thoughtful reader will note that we've been discussing rule by minorities without at all bringing in major public controversies, the role of "big" personalities in one-sidedly influencing the processes of legislation, or in fact any other substantive "issues" issue. Rule by minorities in any system of district voting, such as for the House or the Senate, is procedurally guaranteed. And then it is customarily strengthened by procedural rules within the resulting body itself.[8] Perhaps the expression *agency democracy* also claims too much, since not all the agents get to rule. In any case, our system of nominal majority government does not and cannot empower majorities over strategically located minorities.[9]

Party Competition/Party Collusion

I said earlier that the major parties collude as much as they compete. As before, voter preferences are not of the first importance here.

This collusion starts at the state level. Every ten years the census forces a redrawing of the boundaries of national and state voting districts. This is no small matter. In the New York State legislature, the leaderships of the two major parties worked intimately on drawing those boundaries, first to help one another ensure that their own districts contained as few threatening blocs of voters as possible, next to make sure that something like the same was true for their chief colleagues and supporters. Then and only then did the collusion stop, and the competitive battles over boundaries of partisan advantage begin. Given the prizes at stake here, something very similar undoubtedly goes on in every state legislature where both parties have significant strength.[10]

Both major parties have an overriding interest in maintaining the "two-party" system, that is, their joint monopoly over mainstream U.S. politics, and they normally work together to maintain that monopoly. Areas whose populations might give rise to third parties or even just to party mavericks will typically be parsed out into several voting districts so the votes become dissipated, or bunched into one district, which is then written off by both parties.[11] Here again procedure transmutes itself into substance. Basically, the fewer the parties, the easier it is for their leaderships to exclude or minimize legislation they don't want.

If, for example, the U.S. House had a third-party representation, the majority could be decided by the shifting of votes, which in a two-party setup are nullified by the sanctions of party discipline and punishment. The House has 435 voting members. Let's assume it divides, say, 215 to 210 for the major parties but that the remaining members—only 10 of them—are from a third party. That 10-person minority has immense potential power by virtue solely of procedures; when the major parties can't agree, it alone can decide the majority. It can permanently attach itself to either major party or switch back and forth issue by issue. Worse for the party leaderships is the possibility that the third-party presence might draw unhappy major party backbenchers into alliances of convenience. Then the major party leadership would have to negotiate them back into the fold. One can extrapolate this into a legislature where each of the representatives must be dealt with separately in order to cobble together legislative or even procedural majorities. The main parties have a joint interest in preventing this that is so powerful that mavericks who switch party affiliation may be ostracized by both parties and their home bailiwicks stuffed with hostile voters at the next redistricting.

As a general rule, a two-party system minimizes the power of an individual representative and thus the influence of his or her voters back home. Which is to say, a two-party system acts almost always in support of minority rule. Although "the Founding Fathers" didn't want or anticipate political parties, they did favor elite oligarchic rule over democratic rule. As James Madison put it in *Federalist* no. 10: "To secure the public good and private rights against the danger of such a [majority] faction . . . is then the great object to which our inquiries are directed." In that ironic way, the system is working as they intended it to work.

There can be other, important reasons for the parties to collude. When I was active in New York State politics, the New York City Democratic leadership preferred to have a Republican governor in Albany. The reason is simple. There is federal patronage to be doled out when a Democrat is in the White House. Normally, Washington channels this patronage through the office of the mayor of New York City or the city's Democratic leadership, then still Tammany Hall. But if there is a Democratic governor, then he controls it. City Democrats didn't like that. Worse, the "upstate" Democrats tended to be more liberal than the Tammany Democrats and were also allied with their liberal friends in the City—who were legendarily anti-Tammany. The mere presence of a Republican governor helped the city leadership stay in power instead of aiding its real enemies, who were nominally of the same party. In exchange, the Tammany forces "went easy" in the gubernatorial race, which, naturally, was held in a different year than the mayoral race.

Another form of collusion often occurs where there is in effect one-party rule, as in the pre–civil rights South. Southern Democrats routinely helped their Republican counterparts, black as well as white, with some patronage and the odd favor. In that way, the small number of black voters, then overwhelmingly Republican, were blocked from using the GOP to achieve racial change. This sort of caged opposition also goes on in big cities, such as Chicago, where the dominant party also wants to prevent a real opposition from developing.

In short, whatever differences on issues may divide the two major parties, they have a very powerful shared *institutional* interest in keeping their own joint monopoly intact and unchallenged.

What I think is important to understand here is that minorities have the edge in U.S. representational politics. The party leaderships, themselves the creatures of minorities, are keenly aware of this and act forcefully to prevent other, opposed minorities from challenging their power. Again, New York State political history provides a warning example of the potential power of minorities to disrupt the power of the major parties.

In the FDR-Truman era there was a left-wing party in New York State; it was first called the American Labor Party, and later renamed itself the Liberal Party. Since the Democrats couldn't win statewide without their votes, the minority ALP/Liberal Party was able to shift the Democratic Party and its candidates, even in New York City, to the left. The Republican Party too was then forced toward the left. Later, as the Reagan Republicans came on the scene, a New York State Conservative Party effectively shifted first the GOP and subsequently the Democrats into the more conservative stance they now have.

To the extent that the major party leaderships count their own institutional power as more important than ideological stances, this sort of swing role for minority parties or groupings is best prevented. And in fact in only a few states, like New York and Minnesota, does the legal structure not positively inhibit the candidates of third or fourth parties from even getting on the ballot. A common way to do this is to set a very high quota of votes in the previous election to qualify a party's candidates for the next election and supplement this barrier by requiring a very large number of signatures for a nominating petition to place alternate candidates on the ballot. The final fallback position is to demand that some quota of those signatures be filed from each county or other subdivision. It is not impossible to collect signatures in New York City or Detroit to place someone on the ballot. Big-city voters, in my experience, will often sign the nominating petition even when they don't really support the candidate. Not so in rural western New York or, I imagine, in Michigan's Upper Peninsula, where people are cool to signing anything at all.

Ironically, the parties are most competitive not when they are governing or legislating but when they are raising money. For how that works we have to make a detour into the world of broadcast advertising.

At one point in the history of U.S. broadcasting, the networks and the stations produced their own programs and then sold advertising spots to sponsors. That world has been turned on its head, it is thought, by the deregulation of broadcasting started during the Reagan years and furthered in the Clinton years. In the contemporary broadcast world, the stations and the networks conceive that they have different blocs of listeners whom they sell to the sponsors. They program deliberately to catch and keep these different groups of viewers. Accordingly, it is the sponsor, not the broadcaster, who decides whether to continue or to cancel a show, depending on whether it "delivers" desired blocs. Basically, the shift is that the broadcasters don't produce entertainment; they produce viewers. The sponsors don't buy air spots; they buy viewers via the purchase of shows. The broadcasters sell news programs to the sponsors under the very same system. The uniformly high-quality, copious quantity, and critical, detached judgment that are so much a feature of U.S. broadcast news undoubtedly come of this system of sponsorship.[12]

This is very similar to what the major parties do: they deliver blocs of votes (organized interest groups) to this or that sponsor. Each party has blocs of traditional voters, including significant numbers who are disposed to vote for a particular party because they always have. Voter loyalty is a factor all by itself. One of the surest ways to tell how a person will vote is to look at his or her parents' past voting pattern or, even better, how the person has voted in the past few elections.

Because, as we saw, voter preferences are also so poorly, obscurely, and paradoxically expressed through the party system, it is not that hard for the parties to hold onto these voters. One can then deliver liberal voters to polluters and conservative voters to companies that produce liquor or racy movies. Since the two parties are increasingly needful of that sponsoring money, they compete very hard to get it. Here it is the sponsors who collude; no matter who wins an election, it is important to have given money to the winning party!

I think, by the way, that the importance of the issue of money in politics has been inflated. As we've seen, money has little to do with the institutional features of our political electoral system, which guarantee minority rule. Before there was such big money in U.S. politics, the parties and their leaders coped very well with controlling things, and without it they would similarly cope again. I do think that the current debate on money in politics ignores the way the system functions and underestimates the considerable ability of political leaders to prosper in just about any environment.

What is perhaps obscured most in that debate over money in politics is the stance of the broadcast industry. Most of the money in politics goes to the broadcasters to pay for political commercials. That material interest is reflected in the way broadcasters treat the issue of money in politics. They support campaign financing reform in public in a very polite way, but lobby intensely as insiders against proposals that might require them to give free air-time for electoral advertisements, or equal time for such ads, or ban certain kinds of issue advertising—which is among the biggest broadcast revenue sources. When all else fails, the broadcast industry stands up for "free" speech, which means in practice exactly the sort of speech they charge so much to broadcast.

In simple truth, the broadcast industry is part of the two-party system, usually acting with it to preserve the status quo, that is, minority, unrepresentative two-party rule.

On the Importance of the Especially Ignorant Voter

It is bad enough that the least informed, most volatile (that is to say, *foolish*) voters can undermine the functioning of the political system. But our electoral system also magnifies their influence. Paradoxically, party-line voters are among the more, not less, thoughtful voters. It is among the so-called independents that we find most of the most foolish. Basically, the thoughtless voter has the power to cancel out the influence of the more numerous thoughtful ones.

Both major parties are designed to have a realistic chance to win, say, national elections and thus rule the country. But that implies that they must cobble together many minority interests to form a majority or, more usually, a near majority. That in turn implies that at least the elites of those minority interests find some material advantage in supporting the party and in turn can offer more or less convincing reasons for their followers or clients to vote for it. For the GOP, small business leaders needn't get all they really want, but they must be given some legislative and, when possible, executive support against raising the minimum wage and the incursions of the trade unions. Black voters need not be extended equality on the spot, but the leaders of the various black communities and organizations must have access to the Democrats in Congress and, when possible, in the White House.

Representative democratic systems are reliable systems for serving minorities, and as a result both parties have a core of minority blocks, who with some realism stick with their party. Of course not all trade unionists vote Democratic, but if about 60 percent of them do, then the GOP too must have some equivalently large group or groups of voters who can be counted upon, election after election, to vote Republican whose numbers and bias add up to counter those blue-collar, or black, or whatever voters. In the past in the northeastern part of the United States, there was a tradition that Italian American voters went to the Republicans because the Irish excluded them from influence and rewards in the Democratic Party. For many years now, with the same logic but less success, the Republicans have been trying to garner Hispanic votes as a counterweight to the one-sided black voting for the Democrats. In the logic of politics that requires a few real concessions to the Hispanic communities or, to be more accurate, to their leaders and other elites; it can't be done entirely with smoke and mirrors.

Reflecting this dynamic, party-line voters tend to be the most informed voters. To be a regular Republican or Democratic supporter, contra ill-informed arguments to the contrary, means to know a bit more about the issues and the candidates, to see a bit better through the fog of a campaign, to be a little less swayed by the sillier stuff politicians say to get elected, and to be more likely to get out and vote on election day, regardless of the weather. Using a ballpark figure for national elections, these voters form the hard core of the 40 percent of the vote, give or take a few percentage points, that each major party can count on. Thus when a losing party approaches that 40 percent mark, they've suffered a "sweep" and a disaster. If, as happened to the Democratic presidential candidate in 1972, they fall below that mark, something very, very big has disturbed their traditional voter base, and the matter deserves really extensive analysis and fixing.

On those figures there are still 20 percent of the voters to be accounted for. These "Independent" voters tend to be less informed, more easily swayable, as likely to flood to the polls as to be too busy to vote, and so on. In the rhythm of a U.S. presidential campaign, these voters tend to be left alone in the beginning as the parties try to remind and round up their traditional votes. Up to the time of the national nominating conventions, Democrats tend to trot out the sacred memory of FDR and JFK, remind the elderly about who invented Social Security, and get photographed with black, trade union, and feminist leaders. Over on the GOP side similar shenanigans are going on.

After the conventions, however, both usually go after "the middle of the road," precisely the part of the electorate whose voting patterns are weighted to emotional pulls (God, godlessness, morality, the noisier varieties of patriotism, motherhood—provided it's neither planned nor spontaneous—wicked overseas enemies, wicked domestic enemies, other wicked people, and just to make sure, wickedness itself), impressions, prejudices, and often just plain silliness. Much of the dysfunctional character of U.S. electoral politics—and much of its entertainment value—comes from this phase of campaigning.[13]

The ignorant voter serves another political function as well. Because of his thoughtless, often unpredictable behavior, elites, especially around very important public policy issues such as national security, feel duty bound to arrange things so that all voter influence is nullified. This is not just self-interest at work; elites may be genuinely concerned lest a jingoistic public propel the government into an international crisis. In any case, the existence of the ignorant voter, whether being mobilized to support some elite program or sidelined to protect some good, bad, or indifferent policy, helps provide to the elite in a democratic polity part of the justification for their own politically privileged role.

Bread and Circuses, and Federalist Doctrine

In all the modern democracies there are major political forces, institutions, and other organized groups that don't accept democratic ground rules. There are many variations here, but basically these are individuals and groups who want to keep news from the voters, or to provide them with false information, to split them along quasi-superstitious lines, to equip them with idiotic political ideas and ideologies, and, in general, who work to lower the political capacity of the electorate. Some of this behavior is merely tactical on their part; that is, they have some sort of special interest which they think is best served by keeping the public public ignorant or confused or distracted.

At a somewhat deeper level, conservative parties in all the modern democracies tend to ride on noneconomic issues, often of a sensational or emotional nature. The current favorite is defending marriage against a group of people who seem to value it too much. Conservative parties need issues like this because, by definition, they are organized to serve the "haves" against the "have-nots." This is an old, even classic problem for them because have-nots tend to outnumber haves; hence ways must be found to finesse a few votes from the have-nots by smoke and mirrors, or by trying to keep lower-class voters away from the polls. In the past, poll taxes were often imposed to this end, but they have been ruled unconstitutional. Complex voter registration procedures were invented to do this, and they still serve, or arcane ballots—as famously in Florida in 2000. Police can intimidate the lower-class districts, as we saw.

Some of my Labour Party friends in Britain think that Margaret Thatcher perfected the use of issues not to win Labour votes but to keep the number of Labour Party voters low. That seems also to have been the case with Ronald Reagan and, later, with Bush I.[14]

There are also industries one of whose major product lines is voter distraction. In the period in which I cut my eyeteeth on U.S. politics, Sunday afternoons and early evenings were devoted to news and opinion programs, such as *Face the Nation* and *Meet the Press*. But since the mid-1950s, if I recall correctly, those time slots have been devoted to professional football and golf, men's tennis, women's tennis, professional basketball, college basketball, women's basketball both professional and college, baseball both professional and college, bowling, softball, soccer, volleyball, horse racing, boxing and "wrestling," auto racing, lacrosse, billiards, and even the "sport" of poker! The news and opinion programs have been for the most part relegated to Sunday mornings, where they face the weaker competition of God. This seems to have been motivated by commercial considerations, the advertisers being presumptively richer than God! This probably explains the general decline in broadcast network support of news and public affairs programs culminating in the broadcast deregulation steps in 1984 and 1996. Here it seems that the networks have an "innocent" interest in making money, and not a nefarious one in keeping the public poorly informed.

But the befuddlement work of the Hearst press of yesteryear and, say, Fox News of today is deliberate. They as a matter of course omit news that sits ill with their editorial opinions. They sponsor ferocious, highly sensational attacks on persons and policies they don't like by such prizefighters as Westbrook Pegler yesterday or Fox News's notably less literate commentators today. If the attacks are unscrupulous, it's only a small matter because they are driven by political principles that rank national chauvinism, "private property," racial "integrity," or what have you as much more important than rule of the majority. In saying this, I am not in the first instance making a condemnation. In a democratic system a citizen has the right not to believe in the rule of the majority. To put this in historical context, from the Federalists onward there have always been important political forces that rank property, or the rule of a well-born elite, or of the "better class of people" as more important than, as some might want to put it, the rule of "the mob," or "the yahoos," or "the ignorant." None of the so-called Founding Fathers were democrats in the twenty-first-century meaning of the word, and the political system they envisioned, witness *Federalist* no. 10, established what 1930s and 1940s conservatives called a *republic* and not at all a *democracy*, that is, a form of government in which the majority participate but do not really rule.

Democracy and the International State System

Another but more dangerous source of un- and antidemocratic forces in the political process is the modern form of the state itself. The modern *state* is a borrowing from the world before the French and American revolutions. It has yet to be purged of many of its predemocratic traditions and features. In Europe the forms and contents of state politics still reflect the compromises between "republican rule" and the *ancien régime* that came out of the unsuccessful, hence incomplete revolutions of 1848, 1945–48, and 1958–70; those failures left in place *within the state apparatus* the political power of older, prerevolutionary elites, especially the financial ones, the military, and "the advocates of order." Not even the collaboration of so many of these in the rise and rule of Hitler did away with a political form within which their power still flourishes.

In the United States those who pushed through the Constitution were a minority, oligarchs by nature and preference, and distrustful of the ordinary people; this distrust was only reinforced when, in the decade after the adoption of the Constitution, they witnessed "the excesses of the Revolution in France." That old reactionary, Edmund Burke, still has many followers today, and the rights of the modern state have for them a higher claim to legitimacy, loyalty, and obedience than the voice of the people. In every modern country, including our own, there are persons and forces that would readily overturn the rule of the majority if in their view the majority threatened the rights of the state itself. It is only because our conceptions of democracy have become so jaded and uncritical that we overlook the enduring primacy of *state interest per se* in the workings of the political system, which is to say, the enduring preferences of the highest elites who are embedded in the inmost parts of inner government.

These elites are so placed and so linked with one another that they are a political power in themselves. Our experience tells us that elites can panic this country into supporting a war with *anyone* and that that war will have overwhelming public support for perhaps one to three years, only after which other, critical views will gain a foothold in the media and mainstream. This has been the pattern regarding, among others, the Vietnam and Iraq wars and the several nuclear crises with the Soviet Union and China.

Both major parties in the United States can go into tactical antidemocratic modes, but the more conservative of the two is likelier to do so.[15] Here we brush up against a troubling problem in U.S. politics, namely, the emergence of a major wing of a mainstream party, the Republicans, which is positively anticonstitutional and antilegal in its outlooks and actions. This is a development that we haven't had before, or at least haven't had since the defeat of the Southern oligarchs in our Civil War, and which in principle shouldn't even be possible. It appears to reek of a feudal past, of kings who scorn parliament, or of jackbooted generals who offer opponents and critics "a whiff of grapeshot."

The problem has been apparent since the Iran-Contra scandal of President Reagan's second term. Some of the president's aides sold arms—illegally—to Iran in order to funnel most of the proceeds (while pocketing the rest)—illegally—to the right-wing contras, who were trying to overthrow—illegally—the Nicaraguan government. Congress had cut off contra funding, in effect forbidding further U.S. government military assistance to them.

A congressional investigation finally exposed and ended these machinations, and several important officials were convicted in connection with them. But they were convicted of the relatively petty charge of lying to Congress, and I think it fair to say that both then and now, the Iran-Contra affair was treated as a small crime, its seriousness mitigated by its support for the always sacred "anticommunist cause." The sentences handed down were slight; and the next president, Bush I, who himself was in on the scheme, pardoned several of the offenders.

But the congressional investigation actually revealed a much more serious level of criminality. The head of the CIA at the time, William Casey, was trying to establish secret funding sources for an illegal and unauthorized intelligence service within the intelligence agency. He and his associates were trying to set up "a government within the government," a secret branch of government that would be outside the bounds of the Constitution, the courts, the Congress, and the electorate. I understand this as treason, for in our system one owes ultimate political fealty not to "the country" but to the Constitution. All of this was public knowledge, but little was done about it, and that is the point.

Casey fell sick and died in the midst of these exposures, and his fellow criminals—Caspar Weinberger, then secretary of defense; Elliott Abrams in the State Department; an admiral, John Poindexter; and the better-known Colonel Oliver North of the marines—were forced to resign, were prosecuted, and were convicted of lying to Congress. But all then escaped punishment either by procedural appeals in the courts or by presidential pardon. One has to be troubled by these modest outcomes. But it gets worse.

Both Abrams and Poindexter were brought back into influential positions in the administration of Bush II. North was not, probably because his grandstanding before the congressional hearings had raised his profile too much. But the political system's lack of seriousness about undermining constitutional government is shown in the fact that he was nominated and then made a strong run for the U.S. Senate in Virginia and today still frequently appears on the sort of mainstream television that, as it says, shuns "controversy."

That these men had violated their oaths of office was serious enough, but that they had acted to undermine constitutional government goes to a whole new level of seriousness. I think the acts and the fate of these men suggests a deeper tendency within today's Republican Party to act outside the constitutional and legal framework, not as old-fashioned crooks, but as a matter of positive political preference and ideology. As they see it, the country "went wrong" when it voted in New Deal liberalism for a half century, that wrong turn must be corrected and its effects erased to "restore" constitutional government; until then constitutional violations are not only justified, they are requisite.

That would be a troubling ideology even on the political fringe; within the mainstream it is genuinely dangerous. It is, I think, within this larger political context that the Reagan, Bush I, and Bush II administrations have acted extraconstitutionally as a matter of course, whether it is a matter of selective obedience to our treaties and other laws,[16] trying to prejudge court outcomes via the appointment process, spurious calls to war, and the not so covert authorization of torture against prisoners held without sanction of law.

To put the best possible face on this wing of the Republican Party, two factors have to be weighed. The first is nominally the more innocent. It has to do with those "state interests" we've already talked of. While they have no sanction whatsoever within the Constitution, that document was framed against the memory of a willful King George III, who employed arbitrary force against the colonies. As a result, the Constitution is biased against a strong Executive. But history doesn't stand still. A century later, during the McKinley and, especially, Theodore Roosevelt administrations, the United States joined the blessings-of-empire game and accordingly reorganized its internal state organs in aid of that. Our navy, previously only a coastal defense force, was developed into the "blue water navy" called for by the "navalism" theorist Admiral Mahan. That is, it began to acquire so-called capital ships, which could operate in distant seas and which would enable it to snatch colonies from the similarly armed and armored capital ships of Britain, imperial Germany, Spain, and the other international naval powers. Our army, previously organized into light cavalry battalions and regiments for the Indian wars, acquired the classic organization of divisions, corps, field armies, and even the equivalent of a general staff organization, along with, of course, heavy artillery and the related accoutrements needed for war against the other major powers. Analogous changes occurred within our diplomatic service, and the first seeds of a national federal police agency were sown, eventually to become the FBI. The Wilson administration, even before our entry into World War I, completed the trinity of inner government with its formation of the Federal Reserve System after 1912.

These changes altered the organic character of the U.S. state, heretofore an elementary organization with very limited (or as, during Lincoln's presidency, temporary) powers, into a form which aped that of the other international players and whose moral and political roots through them reached back to Europe's *ancien régime*.[17] Naturally it had some similar effects, the most important of which was that it established a body of men within government who formally embodied a "state interest," an "interest" that coexisted with and not seldom competed with whatever "interests" were put forward by the voters and the constitutional order. We have already commented on this aspect of inner government.

The felons earlier cited from the Reagan days are not in the first instance a different species than such as Admiral Mahan, John Hay, Elihu Root, Henry Stimson, the later Dean Acheson, John McCloy, and the Dulles brothers.[18] They would cite in their own defense that they were acting in the interests of "the state" because the Congress, intimidated by the public outcry over the failed Vietnam War, was unable to pursue those interests. There is even something to what they say, since the national security apparatus, like the national financial apparatus often and almost by definition, operates beyond the bounds of constitutional mandate. That's the legacy of the European/great power state, and it was what was intended by Theodore Roosevelt and others of that generation, or, for that matter, by FDR when he was conducting his secret war against Nazi Germany. Much of the cold war too was waged out of sight of the electorate.[19]

Casey, Weinberger, Poindexter, Abrams, North, and their unindicted co-conspirators, however, represented only a cabal within the government that wasn't supported by the wider national elite. Political and other elites normally have at least some functional legitimacy; beyond their willfulness and their privileges, they conceivably serve constructive roles in the formation and maintenance of society. Casey and his ilk could claim no such real linkage. They were rogues, pure and simple.

At that time, the major U.S. elites had shifted to the view that the military interventions of the height of the cold war were no longer "in the national interest." Different policies and stances were called for. Casey and the others were to that extent a cabal acting against not only the formal constitutional order but also against the more important informal order that animates and preserves it. They were ultimately adventurers attempting to form a secret government of political criminals like themselves. Again, that they were not more severely punished points to a decline in the sense of responsibility we have a right to expect of our highest elites. Historical parallels are always strained, but it is cautionary to recall another political criminal and adventurer who, for attempting a coup against the Bavarian government, was only slapped on the wrist and to that degree encouraged to continue the attempt, eventually successful, to overthrow the Weimar Republic. Political criminality, when it involves national security elites and institutions, is always extremely dangerous, no matter how small, distant, and improbable the actual threat appears.

There is another dimension to this decline in the sense of responsibility on the part of our highest elites. As already mentioned, it appears that since the vast economic changes of the 1970s onward, U.S. corporate elites have attended more to the narrower interests of their institutions than to the broader political tasks of an elite governing class. Into that vacuum have crept political adventurers, many of whom were found at high-level posts in the Bush II administration, who were ideologically driven to destroy at almost any constitutional cost the welfare and civil liberties state stemming from New Deal liberalism and any limitations and all limitations on the international security state installed over the course of the now defunct cold war.

I grant that the linkage between the Casey gang and the Bush II administration needs much further argument and evidence to be really convincing, but I submit that that linkage is not entirely absent, and that even to the degree we suffered it, it was destructive in our overseas dealings and of the highest risk at home.

Summing up, one has a reasonable choice between viewing today's "state" and its inner-government-embedded "state interests" as a dire, immediate threat to our constitutional legacy or merely as a continuation of the "state's" normal anticonstitutional and antipopular tendencies. I think there is truth to both accounts and don't see a third, less threatening interpretation.

Inner Government Again

I have argued that the more democratic a system, the more the elected official will be inclined to push issues out of public contention and into the political shadows. As soon as one takes office, various groups both inside and outside the government will socialize the newcomer to the existence of other, but private publics whose rewards and retribution are much surer and closer to hand than those of the public back home. Our "representative" will see too that by favoring one voter preference one is pretty likely to offend others. Even preferring what the voters say they prefer is, as we saw in the Arrow paradox, a chancy thing to do. Politicians chronically think the public remembers better what it doesn't like than what it does. The idea that political majorities consist of fractious volatile minorities is not learned only by political figures who have short careers or who are stupendously favored in their personal qualities, including rare skills in double-talk.

Meanwhile, within one's own party there is every suasion "to get along, go along." Outside the comfortable confines of party orthodoxy, one is too exposed to the vagaries of the most ignorant, even foolish part of the public. There is, in short, every reason to go along with the political structure as it is, and to tread very warily when proposing even minor change.

This is not to say that a democratic political system is entirely useless. Its apparent promise attracts many good people into government who often do good things through it, such as a Passanante, a La Follette, a Harry Hopkins, or a Frances Perkins. And normally frustrated, from time to time a powerful public public rises up, as in 1964–65 over civil rights or in the election of 2008, and directly demands change. One doesn't want to undervalue those possibilities, but they represent exceptions, attractive and liberating to be sure, but rare, to the normal operations of agency government by assent. To be satisfied with that is to live very dangerously.

The most important elite preferences have several immense advantages in this system of fragile officeholders. They tend to be normal and natural. To challenge them is to step out of the "mainstream," to be "controversial," perhaps "radical," to threaten "free enterprise," to be a "dove" on military affairs or "soft on crime." Of course, all of these are loaded expressions and camouflage for very real, often very socially harmful elite interests. Those who wanted "more regulation" of the financial sector in the 1990s weren't being radical, and those who wanted to see the military power of the United States scaled back when the cold war ended weren't lacking patriotism; but elite interests are so deeply embedded in the political structure that they appear natural and normal, and those who challenge them have to overcome the presumption that they are against "the American way" or some other sacred cow.

Second, because the social structure of elite relationships to other non-elite groups and institutions is so dense and so self-interested on both sides, to challenge the elite on some issue is often equivalent to challenging some wide swath of other groups and institutions that, naturally, will rise to the defense. National-defense elites usually have the support of veteran's groups, the National Rifle Association, many of the more thoughtless sports fans, and those religious fundamentalists who are certain, against all recent evidence, one must add, that God is on our side.

If, as in the 1940s or 1960s, one threatens the structure of elite privilege, one may draw the same response, namely, an attempt to delegitimate or quasi-criminalize the very attempt. Then one is branded not merely as a maverick but as a danger to society; instead of being part of "the silent majority," one is now part of the noisy minority, with "kooky" morals, with a tendency toward "violence," and perhaps "disloyal."

In the extreme case, especially if one is a mainstream politician or officeholder, one can be redistricted out of office, or a particularly well-heeled challenger can appear in your district, or perhaps some agency or another will begin a politically inspired investigation of your life or finances. It need not actually find peculation; much of the public is inclined to believe that with government, where there's smoke, there's fire. Or, as in both the 1940s and the 1960s, there may be prosecution of this or that opposition figure or organization for real or imagined crimes, which also tend to discredit opposition itself.[20] For an officeholder or an elected politician to threaten elite preferences or privileges is to put his or her own career in jeopardy.

To make the system more democratic deepens, not solves, these problems; for the more democratic a representative is, the less secure his or her tenure of office. Thus, it cannot be otherwise that in a system of agency government, many of the most important policies and decisions will gravitate to the inner government; and from the nature of the case, the most important elite preferences and privileges will rest most deeply and securely within it.

The Institutional Multiplier

I've singled out the extra advantages that liberal, democratic political systems historically offer to minorities-in-general over majorities. Our problems run even deeper than that, for our political system is embedded within an integrative capitalism whose institutions comprise corporations as well as hospitals, foundations, media companies, school systems, universities, research labs, and so forth. All of the kinds of socially potent assets of the national elite are multiplied in their potency by the normal functioning of these institutions—resources, information, institutional memory, insider status, esteem, legitimacy, "connections," potential scope of action, potential duration of action, administrative assistance and expertise, and so forth. There is, I think, no mystery at all to the fact that the changing agenda of U.S. politics is now pretty much established by the actions, the influence, the needs, the expressed desires, and perhaps most important, the priorities of these institutions.

But these are institutions that have been historically fabricated to minimize the influence of outsiders over their deliberations and to maximize the discretion, the instruments, and the resources available to their strategic elites to carry out their institutionally prescribed priorities. It is here then that we find an additional barrier, here a designed-in institutional barrier further inhibiting the democratic feedback processes of our political system. It would be too much to say that today's liberal democratic political systems are exclusively preoccupied by institutional agenda, but it would be simply incorrect to say that, in the contest for influence between the public public and the elite private publics, the playing field is anywhere near to being level. Of course, as we know from the Civil Rights Era and perhaps now as opposition rises up against the second Iraq War and the financial crisis, the public public can from time to time formulate and try to enforce its own will. But that is—quite literally—the abnormal case. Overall, we now have a political system that is hyperdysfunctional. The institutions that fabricate social life resist interference by the public public, that is, the very persons these institutions act upon. Essential feedback channels are missing or blocked, and this in turn helps isolate the electoral-political system from the social and related problems created by the rest of our institutional system. We are at present victims of a profound crisis in our politics, a crisis resting not in wicked men or the power of money in politics or the machinations of the media or even of the spread of superstition among segments of the public public, but instead in an institutional system whose elements no longer mesh.

This, in the last analysis, helps explain the political system's inability to address civil rights from 1954 to 1964, and the Vietnam War from 1960 to 1975, or drugs for three decades, health care since 1946, and not least, Iraq and, especially, Afghanistan today. It was the political system, too, that against both historical precedent and elementary common sense collaborated by omission and commission with the securities industry to produce the present economic crisis. Deep-seated, clearly very difficult institutional change in our political arrangements is critically overdue.

Coming to Cases

One of the dominant American popular political traditions combines extreme individualism with notions of the free, spontaneous community of equals. Let us pass over the paradox involved in trying to commingle the two. This commingling was evident within the 1960s New Left and, earlier, within the ranks of the Industrial Workers of the World (IWW), and in fact goes back to the Antifederalists. But if I am right in identifying this as a popular political tradition, then there will always be powerful voices in reform circles to make this or that "more democratic." "Democratic" functions as a magic black box among many, many Americans. Take any problem, put it in the box, problem solved!

Clearly, our liberal democracy is double-edged. On the one hand, the gaining of the franchise by the Democracy during the historic advance was a material factor in its success. In those countries we characterized as Bismarckian, where premodern social formations variously blocked, slowed, and weakened the extent and power of the popular franchise, the advance itself was blocked, slowed, and weakened. Some sort of liberal representative democracy clearly was necessary to carry the advance as far as it went. But, as our previous analysis implies, that same political form also functions now to protect elite preferences and privileges; in short, *to try to limit or minimize those preferences and privileges by the democratic means familiar to us serves only to strengthen, not weaken, the phenomenon of inner government and with it, the powers of the elite.* Or to put it another way, the muted truth of liberal, democratic arrangements like those in Western Europe, North America, and a few other places is that really significant social change can only rarely cross the boundaries of today's elite power and privilege because this power and these privileges are embedded in it. Our system is much more open to institutional representations than to the democratic kind.

To achieve serious change, one therefore cannot, like proverbial generals, fight the next political war on the last war's political terrain and with the last war's political weapons. In order to alter significantly the democratic boundaries of the political system, one must at the same time weaken the present institutional system of elite and cadre advantages and privileges. There is a long historical record, both here and overseas, which indicates, first, how limited are the reforms that can otherwise be achieved and, second, that elites under very serious challenge will bend the law to strike back, and, if necessary or even just convenient, will seek the aid of the authoritarian Right. It follows then that one must change in the same processes the fundamental form both of modern society and the modern state itself. That last will require an alteration in the modalities of representation so as to achieve a tectonic shift, so to speak, in institutionalized, mutual feedback between government and governed.

To put the matter in still another way, society and the state in their present forms cannot accommodate the changes needed by the Democracy. Both broad social/institutional reform and specifically political reforms are required: we must sharply restrict the potential and the scope for inner government; substantially reduce the power of all higher institutional elites, especially of the private business corporations; exclude the police power from playing its traditional political roles; find ways to remobilize the popular side of the Democracy; and more effectively insulate domestic government from the imposed imperatives of the international state system. Only in these ways can we bring about a renewal of the historic advance.

PART 3

PROPOSALS FOR A RENEWED HISTORIC ADVANCE

We face a situation analogous to that faced by our forebears a century and a quarter ago. Then as now the ideas that had guided efforts at reform had been outstripped by events, and this required a fundamental recasting of the strategies and even of the institutional forms dedicated to social and economic liberation. Our predecessors indeed took much the measure of that new world.[1] But after a century and a quarter the advance has been checked, and even partially rolled back, by the modern reaction.

The gains of the past have made the Democracy far more capable than it was 125 years ago, but, on the other hand, there is now no emerging cadre working alongside it. More formidable, a semifabricated Intersection society is different from the late nineteenth-century variety. It is more integrated, more hierarchical, and its lower life courses are subject to powerful administrative, ideological, and other influences by Intersection institutions. Yet the obstacles blocking an advance, as then, are now formidable but not insurmountable, and the forces for beneficial change stronger now but by no means assured of success. With Vico, I think we have to see the creation of the future as a closely run contest between half-blind human endeavor and utterly blind, often very harsh fate.

I want to offer some proposals on behalf of a renewed historical advance. These comprise the major areas where change is especially needed. Some of the proposals are surely utopian for the short run, but, I believe, feasible if we look to longer time spans; what is needed are institutional changes, and these are the work of years, if not of generations, of a political culture that continuously generates alternatives, not just this or that moment of political inspiration. We begin in chapter 7 with a concept of a political strategy as embodied in a specific organizational form. The strategy and organization are calculated to cope with the characteristics, previously discussed, that are unique to Intersection society and, equally, to be sustainable over a span of years if not generations. The chapter offers proposals to this end.

Heeding the importance of coercion in a modern society, chapter 8 sketches a modern policing system. Chapter 9 takes up the central problem of civilizing modern economic institutions. Chapter 10 develops proposals to mobilize "the lowest of the low" to join in a renewed historic advance. Chapter 11 explores the international side of a renewed advance. It too contains programmatic proposals. Chapter 12 looks to create a political system more democratically representative than agency government by assent of the governed.

The scope of these chapters is exceptionally broad, and their aims are perhaps unachievable—even in the long run. That possibility has been implicit throughout our previous analyses: the deeper the institutional change needed, the less likely its achievement. But there is no other alternative. The special "fabricated" dimension of corporate or Intersection society requires a long-term, integrated political response. If, as I have argued, the historic advance has been turned back by the maturation of that sort of society, then piecemeal and ad hoc responses are in principle inadequate. One must take up as a single ensemble and for the long term the problems, opportunities, and difficulties we face.

The ultimate test of the ideas and the proposals put forward here is not that they constitute the last word of the discussion. Their test is that they press the discussion forward and do so with the requisite scope, consciousness of the past, and some thoughtful foresight about the future, if not for ourselves, then for those who will come after us.

7

ON STRATEGY AND ORGANIZATION

Our Present Situation

An identifiable political bloc has launched and until now has maintained the widest range of reactionary policies and ideologies. It includes the most influential elite subsocieties, themselves caught in a disorienting phase of their own history, a defensively postured cadre, and the ultraconservatives.

Elite subsocieties lead here. Business elites especially are still caught up in the technological, financial, and global changes that accelerated about three decades ago. Those shifted both the makeup and the outlook of corporate leaders. Famous firms, many with distinguished lineages, either failed or were gobbled up by others led not by members of the old Eastern Establishment but by newcomers "on the make." These latter, preoccupied with a volatile business environment that threatens their incomes and careers, and not yet secure in their elite status, have repudiated the *noblesse oblige* of their predecessors, turning to more bottom-line social philosophies. The social conscience of the business leaders of the 1940s, 1950s, and 1960s was not impressive. Nevertheless, compared to the behavior of so much of today's business leadership, those years look like a Golden Age of corporate responsibility.

In an older literature about "the responsible corporation," much was made of the thesis of Adolf A. Berle and Gardiner Means's *Modern Corporation and Private Property* (1933) that the shift from owner-controlled businesses to those controlled by professional managers meant that the corporate agenda was becoming more socially responsible, to wit, owners had had an interest solely to augment their own power and wealth, but as trustees for others professional managers had to act with greater social responsibility and from a wider sense of the needs of society.

Unhappily, experience trumps theory on this point. Professional managers have made their firms more antisocial, not less. High-minded, delphic corporate utterances at the top about socially responsibility give way at the operational level to narrow, single-minded obsessions by their subordinates. These are rewarded by how effectively they carry out imposed mandates to "contain costs," "increase labor productivity," "expand market share," or "improve the regulatory environment." Workers, consumers, the environment, and so on, encounter not the high-minded corporate "statesman" but his lesser manager on the make, for whom environmental safety or stable worker incomes get in the way of the performance he or she will be rewarded for and promoted for.

Modern firms led by professional managers are like the maximizers called for by neoclassical economic theory. Their guiding imperatives are their own interests, whatever the consequences to society, workers, safety, and the environment. We see this in the push to make SUVs, continued tobacco advertising to young people, the winking at securities industry fraud, and the denial of global warming. Berle's thesis about the top managers was always a bit of wishful thinking, but is now even further undermined by the antisocial actions of a newer, aggressive, unstable corporate leadership *sans noblesse oblige*. In this they are abetted, not checked, by the matured cadre. Even "bottom line" hardly does justice to the attitudes that today govern so much business behavior.[1]

The wicked paradox here is that even as we endure a business leadership and cadre with a reduced sense of social responsibility, their corporations have entered so powerfully into so many new social arenas. They have brought their commercial ethos into the political process and the education and health systems, into military matters, and the world of culture and communication. Pharmaceutical executives are now the most important players in medical insurance legislation, the weight of coal executives is not inconsiderable in air pollution regulations, textbook publishers directly influence curriculum decisions, and news to the public is weighed and edited by media conglomerates that also operate hosts of other lines of business, many of which require public ignorance or misperception about the candidates and policies that favor their interests. We have called modern capitalism "integrative," but it is integration on its, not other, terms.

Corporate misbehavior is not, ultimately, the work of bad people, although the executives of the major banks might sneak in under that wire. The modern corporation was designed by Alfred P. Sloan and his peers to maximize the firm's advantage in every area in which it acted. A corporate leader who wanted to act in a balanced, socially responsible way would have to be a genuine saint and, like such a holy figure, could hope for little more than martyrdom. Bad institutions have greater capacity for harm than bad men.

Moreover, by now we have learned that we cannot regulate such institutions. By giving this or that agency the authority to regulate business behavior, we create the imperative for business elites to draw the agency into their orbit as part of the inner government and, as we now know, that has actually been the historical tendency.

The cadre, in the form of the emerging manager course, was formerly a champion of the modern welfare state. Today it contains the most resolute champions for its reduction. One of the most potent political facts of the present era is the historical maturation of the modern cadre, hence of its social interest in denying to others the opportunities that allowed it to replace in wealth and importance the prior—let us call it—entrepreneurial middle class. Given the way we select, orient, train, and deploy the modern workforce in a modern technology and social organization, it is the cadre who are the main producing class for our social and social material life; and for them, now, progress in its broadest humanist dimensions is too often threatening. It is to the misfortune of society that this is the main modern producing class.

Finally, there are the ultraconservatives; called out by the business and political elites of the 1970s and 1980s, they are now mobilized as a major political force. One would expect the residents of formerly self-contained towns and rural areas to recoil when, via TV, film, and the higher education system, the more vivid varieties of sin are propelled so attractively into their and their children's midst. We reasonably expect as much from the traditional foes of the Social Gospel, abortion, sex education, evolution, ecumenicism, critical Bible studies, equal rights for women, rights of any kind for children, and the rest of the unfamiliar and hated modern secular canon.[2]

What adds so much to this witches' brew is that elements of both elite and cadre have adopted so many ultraconservative superstitions. As already suggested, the wars against gay marriage and drugs, now rivaled by the war on terror, also rest on the fears, some realistic, many not, of much of the most modern, accomplished elites and educated middle-class people.

Two other points should be mentioned in this brief recap. Agency government by assent is unable to prevail against the private sector, and this encourages the public's declining belief in the efficacy of democratic political action. This is ultimately rooted in how modern politics gives an increasing advantage to minority rule as political issues become more "technical," which often is just a synonym for "involve issues which are defined and resolved within an institutional tête-à-tête."

We must also not lose sight of the changed balance of forces between the Democracy and the modern state due to the greater size, efficiency, and tactical capability of a police power that is steadily drifting to the right in ideological orientation. From the nineteenth century through the middle of the twentieth, the threat of "the mob," of the crippling strike, the sit-in, or the "occupation" could almost always influence government behavior. Now, save in rare circumstances, the authorities can contain threats emanating from the streets, especially democratic threats to minority government. Not only can the police control the streets, but they also have an increasing electronic capacity for political surveillance.[3] No strategic conception for political and social amelioration can evade this double bind, namely, that the weakening of the power of direct popular action goes hand in hand with the expansion in the police powers of the inner government.

The limited successes of international counterterrorism policing seem to undermine this observation. But where "civilian" movements have successfully resisted government repression, as in Iraq and among the Palestinians, they have had ready access to arms, either from outside as among the Palestinians or just lying around in unsecured arms dumps. And, of course, a terrorist is so often an apolitical actor, engaging in nihilist, spasmodic reactions to conditions that seem utterly beyond changing.

Creating the Future

There will continue to arise tendencies in aid of the Democracy. *The problem is to give them expression in all their variety, and to lend them a continuous learning curve that will extend past our present lives, horizons, and imaginations.* And we must do this under the special conditions of a semifabricated society whose very fabric inhibits "unauthorized" social change. Is it possible to design an organization calculated to overcome the unique problems posed by corporate or Intersection society?

The historical record argues that no person or group of the Democracy saw the entire sweep of the advance in either its historical or its political richness. But very nearly all of them did see some part of that future and did help create some aspect of it. Paul Lafargue, who opposed the eighteen-hour work day with an argument for the "right to be lazy," did not foresee the rise of popular hobbies like travel or music collecting or the expansion of university attendance. High-powered corporate lawyers and highly stressed corporate executives were not part of Cady Stanton's vision for the future of women, nor did Keir Hardie blueprint the accomplishments of the Labour government of 1945–51. Yet Lafargue, Cady Stanton, Hardie, and countless others added a piece to the better world that made up the historic advance. Many of these people and groups knew nothing about the others, but their contributions merged into a coherent result.

Is it possible to re-create organizationally today an analogous ensemble of political relations among contemporary and future men and women who are animated by their attachment to the Democracy? Because of the unique nature of corporate society, it would have to be an unusual sort of political organization, very different than those we are familiar with. We have to grasp these differences in their useful dimensions.

Peggy's Law

Too often too little thought is given to organizational questions per se. The relationships between the purposes one wants to further organizationally, the circumstances blocking those ends, the people one wants within the organization, the people outside it that one wants to affect, and the form of the organization itself are subjects deserving of the most careful thought. Not every organizational form is apt to every purpose, nor is every group of organizational activists suitable to every form of organization.

My own views on this subject have ripened over the years, but many hark back to a special mentor and friend, the late Peggy Duff, one of the founders of Britain's Aldermaston Marches, which helped revive the European peace movement after the Korean War, and later the long-time secretary of the U.K. Campaign for Nuclear Disarmament (CND). In my view, Peggy stood well above others in her organizational understanding.

When the Aldermaston Marches began in 1958, peace and antinuclear activities were harmfully associated with fellow travelers and other apologists for the Soviet Union. Then, too, the cold war was in a particularly frigid state, so that it appeared pointless in practical terms to protest the way things were going. As Peggy explained, these two considerations determined who would and wouldn't be willing to march eighty miles in the rain and cold to Aldermaston to protest against nuclear weapons. The earliest marchers tended to be the most utopian, most moralistic, least political cohort of peaceniks, along with a sprinkling of other supporters of lost and often odd causes. Perhaps their "moral purity" helped, but whatever the reason, the marches created some stir in Britain, and others began to join them.

As the marches grew in size, they gave rise to the hope that the antinuclear movement might yet change public opinion. That brought in new people who wanted to present a more reasonable, less utopian message to the public. Some of the earlier types didn't like what seemed an unprincipled compromise and, *as a result,* took their departure. Over time, the marches generated new peace organizations, the most prominent of which was the CND. Success bred further success as new people flowed into the peace movement, eventually in such numbers (notwithstanding those who were exiting) that it appeared possible that, with suitable adjustment of the CND message, a peace faction could play a role in the mainstream Labour Party. As before, this attracted "more practical" people and drove some of the "more idealistic" people out. The peace campaign continued to grow to such a degree that some eventually thought it could gain a majority in the Labour Party, but again, that required even more political compromise; and again, some further recruits came in whose presence drove others out, and so on. As Peggy explained it, not many people lasted through the whole process; the "organization" had more or less entirely changed membership and outlook in a continuous, barely perceptible process lasting perhaps a decade.

Peggy thought that we should view an organization as if it were a pipeline, with some members entering at one end and others exiting at the other; the identity of each and the reasons for the entering and exiting are a crucial, perhaps *the* crucial, factor controlling the longevity, the direction, and the success of the organization. Obviously, such a process involves much more than a dialectic of the idealistic and the practical. Organizations are ensembles of individuals, and those who join do so for whole hosts of reasons, some private, some even idiosyncratic, some for this part of the program, some for that, some to meet girls (or boys), some who just like to be "different," some who are genuinely wacky, even some who have a touch of social pathology. Peggy believed that organizational leadership required thoughtful attention to all of these things.

Peggy's Law or, if you will, laws were and are routinely and foolishly ignored. Not every kind of organization is suitable for every person, as not every organizational form is suitable for all purposes. Conversely, not all purposes are suitable for a given organization. Many good people have incompatible aims—many of which should be pursued. "Participatory democracy" and the conventional "committee" are not universal panaceas. Sometimes expertise is irreplaceable, sometimes it is misplaced. There can be too much democracy, or too little. "Bureaucracy" isn't always bad. Leadership ability isn't one thing; it comes in many forms, and a given person may exhibit only one or two of them.[4] *Robert's Rules of Order* is more harm than help.[5] The list is endless. If there is to be an organization able to contribute to a renewed advance, it will have to be designed and then continuously monitored and adjusted with many contradictory purposes in mind, not preoccupied with some special purpose that is in particular favor at the moment. Heeding Peggy's Law, it must appeal to a wide range of different types of people, over considerable time, and clashing political ideas should be at home within it.

Instrumental and Expressive Organizations

Political organization is instrumental in nature. It is a tool or instrument ideally designed around a set of purposes and methods that are entirely or at least one-sidedly agreed to by its members. As indeed we know from experience, instrumental organizations function best when they exhibit enough unity of opinion to support unity of action. But this doesn't fit the requirement for an organization capable of sustaining the advance of the Democracy into an unknown future, which would have to accommodate vast differences of opinion, priority, and mode of political activity over the course of a historical era.

At the opposite end of the organizational spectrum are the expressive organizations, that is, organizations that do not unite their members in a definite, guiding course of action but that instead embody socially a shared idea or trait; a congregationally organized church is a good example of a (nearly) pure expressive organization. To belong to the church furthers no plan of action bearing on outsiders or on the future or on the social environment; it is a matter of joining with others to share in the worship; the expression "Christian fellowship" is often used in this context, but the human relationships comprised in a chamber music group that plays only for itself or perhaps a hobby club are much the same. To belong and to participate are to express engagement and comradeship with others in which instrumental ends are very much secondary to nonexistent.

The women and men who across history and geography initiated, aided, and so often sacrificed for some aspect of the historic advance were in an expressive relation to one another even though one element of that sort of relationship was missing: the palpable, face-to-face "fellowship" that embodies the sentiments of oneness or solidarity. If those of us from the 1960s may occasionally bore younger people with our memories of this feeling, we should (sometimes) be forgiven; life doesn't ordinarily allow a person the direct experience of such human solidarity.

Can the circle be squared? Is it possible to design a form of political organization that is instrumental in the sense that it furthers sets of human purposes, even among people who disagree on ideas and priorities, those disagreements being subordinated to *but not replaced* by larger bonds of expressive solidarity? It might be possible. To discover what shape it might take we have to look more closely into some of the more familiar forms of modern voluntary political organizations, looking for ideas that might aid in the creation of a new political-organizational form.

Conventional Democratic Task Organizations

Many people will be familiar with conventional democratic task organizations, and such organizations are not difficult to create.[6] A group of persons comes together over a desired objective, perhaps to nominate a candidate, to pressure an official, to educate the public on an issue, to help pass a bill, to appear before a government agency. The group adopts a constitution, elects some officers, and sets forth to carry out a program, that is, a blueprint of writings and actions on behalf of its objectives.

Assuming it is not just to remain confined to a tiny handful of people who agree on everything, the organization will in all cases but one need to foster a strong internal debate on the issues it is concerned with, both to educate members or would-be members who aren't familiar with the relevant information, issues, and sides, and also to be able to fine-tune and then pursue the organization's objectives. The life of an organization is in its program, and the life of its program is a lively, engaged, well-informed, opinionated membership. But the contentious debate that enlivens most organizations dedicated to specific tasks is antithetical to the stability of an organization whose specific task it is to serve as an umbrella organization for other, more narrowly focused task organizations.

When differences come up, a democratic organization will settle them via majority vote. Almost invariably, each such issue and each such vote will lead to the exodus from the organization of some cohort of people, or their retreat into inaction and silence. If one tries to avoid these differences, or fudge their result, that saps the democratic vitality of the organization in a different way, that is, by gradually weakening its programmatic focus.

An umbrella organization of conventional democratic task organizations must therefore be conceived and organized to bring together persons with sharply opposed opinions and priorities. When people disagree about the aims and modes of an organization, they are, as it were, making predictions about the future based on their present conceptions of what is true, possible, and pressing. The test of those predictions lies only in that future, and it would contribute to the learning process of a renewed advance if those predictions could be assessed rather than evaluated a priori. If one faction wants to launch a campaign for public funding for abortion and another feels that prudence demands emphasis on the private nature of choice, it would be better if each faction had the opportunity to test out its "forecast" on its own terms but still shared an organizational terrain where each could in comradeship and, without prejudice to either faction, assess the outcomes of the different strategies over time.

That common terrain would not be a venue where ideas would be merged or prioritized. New ideas, new projects, and new priorities will always arise, and it would be a fool's task to prevent or inhibit that redynamizing process. It would be a place where that redynamizing, and the disputes necessarily attendant upon it, could be continually subjected to critical, comradely intelligence with the goal, not of eventual agreement, but of *constant mutual learning.* The end in view here is to make conflict within the Democracy an engine of progress, and differences of opinion an engine of learning, hence both to quicken and to broaden the multiple paths of the advance.

Participatory Democracy

In an organization where participatory democracy is the rule, there are no dissenting, alienated minorities. The group strives instead for consensus and acts only on that basis. Ideally, in such an organization, the leader/follower distinction is played down as much as possible. Everyone is a leader, and discussions in search of consensus should elicit the views of the less voluble. In the 1960s in the United States, the method of participatory democracy was heralded as a solution to some of the classic problems of democratic organization. Over time, it was thought, this sort of intense democratic engagement among the members would "educate" everyone so that the leader/follower distinction would actually wither away.

To some extent these organizational ideas are part of our national political heritage and will inevitably arise again. As suggested earlier, there is a cultural tradition in the United States that emphasizes in the same breath both radical individualism and radical communitarianism. It was manifested as early as the dispute between those who wanted only a volunteer militia with elected officers and those, like Washington, who wanted a regular army with a military hierarchy. Later, the Constitution gave us a civil and political hierarchy, while the Bill of Rights was appended to satisfy those for whom hierarchy was anathema.[7] Clearly, there is some tension in that dual way of looking at the world, and the idea of participatory democracy took much of its appeal insofar as it appeared to reconcile the two poles.

The form, however, sacrifices too much of the instrumental side of organization to its expressive side. Participatory democratic modes are time-consuming and too blunt an instrument to carry out any but the simplest political tasks; one can use them to organize and run a rally, but they are out of place in a political action caucus, where difficult, not always clearly defined choices have to be made in timely fashion. Then, too, most groups do in fact have leaders, and it is the worst possible situation, from a democratic point of view and from the standpoint of organizational effectiveness when that fact is hidden or muted by ritual adoption of a participatory ethos. Some leaders are leaders by virtue of their greater foresight, their ability to inspire others, the intensity of their dedication, and the pleasure others take in working with them. The ethos of participatory democracy tends to lump all leaders into those who just like the limelight, or to "operate" behind closed doors, or enjoy power. It is a classic stereotype that all power seekers are male, but in fact some women have learned to employ the traditional manipulative tactics of ideological one-up(wo)manship, aggressive eloquence, personal magnetism, and the subtler techniques of putting others on the defensive.

Though very difficult, it is desirable for any political organization to have an ethos that singles out leaders with recognizably good traits and drives out posers, schemers, the domineering, and others of that ilk. Finally, if we are to conceive of an organizational form in which, over time, different, disagreeing elements of the Democracy will learn from success and failure, then *consensus* is just the opposite of the clash of ideas and programs that, as we know from history, is the very warp and woof of the advance.

Weak programs and *consensus* go together. The politics of the big national demonstrations against the Vietnam War, which set the pace for much local and regional activity, became frozen in a consensus set by the two factions then dominating the national organizing committee, pacifist groups and a political sect then called the Socialist Worker's Party. Both were organizationally and ideologically satisfied by a simple against-the-war message and opposed to "divisive" attempts to make the demonstrations more sensitive to changes in public attitudes. The departure of one whole cohort of antiwar protesters to the Eugene McCarthy political campaign, and another into violent "revolutionary" activity, was, I think, testimony to the sterility of that particular consensus. Perhaps among small face-to-face groups reaching consensus can be creative, but as the group gets larger and more diverse, trying for it can be stultifying.

Some years ago, I was for a time part of an organization that used the participatory mode. It met every week for about three hours of consensus seeking, even on issues like how to pay for the coffee. Extended discussion in search of consensus on questions like that meant that substantive programmatic and related differences had to be evaded, and they were.

I soon discovered that there was an inner leadership that took up the substantive matters that couldn't be decided at the meetings. That was fine with me, since I didn't want to be on the "inside" and the existing inner leadership seemed dedicated and competent. But experience points up the drawbacks to "participatory democracy." Leaders are inevitable in most contexts. It's best to recognize that and to have an organizational ethos that makes explicit the characteristics of good and bad leaders, and which holds them to responsible, effective behavior. It should go without saying that one of the first responsibilities of organizational leadership is not to be indispensable, and right after that, to ensure a steady supply of new leaders who embrace a strong organizational/democratic ethos.

On the other hand, the ideal of an organization of equals is extremely attractive from so many standpoints, mainly as embodying the comradeship of shared hopes, shared work, and the shared personal costs of working against resistance for a better world. The contradiction between the expressive and instrumental dimensions of organization might be overcome by emphasizing the former, and then by restricting the organization's instrumental functions to the purely generic realm. Here the consensus aimed at by the participatory ethos and mechanism would not be a matter of choosing priorities but of encouraging critically informed discussion of different priorities in a setting in which people share long-term values and hopes.

A Political Party

Many Americans believe in electoral means of inducing change, and some of them believe that inducing change by electoral means will require the "right" political party. Since both of the major parties are part of the problem, many reason that a new political party of the right sort will be the key to the "right" sort of change. Does the Democracy need such a new party?

First and most important, a political party must make choices: to favor or to oppose, to run a candidate or not, to support this legislation or that. Such choice making is clearly antithetical to the concept of an umbrella organization. Political parties have their role to play, but not as umbrella organizations for another historic advance.

There is classic danger to placing all or at least too much of the Democracy's efforts into creating the "right" political party. There is a very large cohort of progressive Americans for whom the "right" political party acts like alcohol to an alcoholic, a one-shot—no pun intended—solution to all sorts of really knotty political problems. Over the years that I've been politically active, there seems to have been a pattern to when and why that cohort decides to have another political party, why the party seems so attractive at the moment, and why its lifespan is so short.

There is a significant minority of Democratic Party voters and activists who believe, or hope, that the Democrats could be more ideological and progressive than they are. When, as so often, the Democrats behave badly, this cohort is wide open to the appeal of a third party. These we can call the Wanderable Democrats.

Pressing right up against this cohort on the political spectrum is another that believes in the potential efficacy of the electoral system to bring about serious changes but who are for that very reason put off by the Democrats. Many of these actually vote Democratic but do so grudgingly, not really identifying with the Party as it actually is, identifying instead with a mythical construction of how perhaps it was during, say, the FDR administration, or the New Frontier of JFK, or some other imagined golden age in the past.

Periodically, the march of events causes elements of the Wanderable Democrats and the Golden Age Democrats to merge, as in the Progressive Party in 1948 or, more recently, in Jesse Jackson's personal vehicle, the Rainbow Coalition. In my political lifetime there have been a number of similar mergers to form national, political third parties, but all founder on the same fact.

The relationship of these two groups is clearly fragile. If too many Wanderable Democrats threaten to wander, Democratic Party leaders are usually ready to make just sufficient concession—real or apparent—to bring the wanderers back to where they really want to be—safely within party ranks. The Golden Age types will then have no choice but to join them there. End of third party!

Typically, this process occurs when it comes time for a newly minted third party to consider running candidates. Wanderable Democrats are much more susceptible to the appeal for what is called voting-for-the lesser-evil, Golden Age Democrats less so. It is more or less what divided them in the first place. Accordingly, the wanderers tend to wander back to the party if given any excuse to do so. This is partly why in 1948 Henry Wallace's support declined so abruptly as the election neared. Much the same thing happened to the Ralph Nader candidacy in the 2000 election. As long as third-party politics rests on unity between Wanderable Democrats and Golden Age Democrats, I see no way to overcome the legendary fragility of their relationship.

On the other hand, however, people of both persuasions who seek electoral means for changing things make up a key part of the Democracy; and however skewed the present democratic mechanisms in favor of powerful minorities, they can also from time to time allow significant victories for majority interests. In short, an umbrella organization has to contain those who are committed to democratic electoral change, both within and outside the major parties, and those who prefer to work in the extraparliamentary area.

My third point is that long before an election and long before candidates are selected, something like 80 percent of the voters are utterly likely to vote for their party's designated candidate; nationally, the two parties more or less split this predictable voter group. For all their faults, the major parties enjoy a very tight loyalty from their supporters. The idea, chronic among third-party advocates, that the new party will grow because it will attract regular voters dissatisfied with the regular parties gets things backward. It seems nearer to the truth to argue that unless there is ahead of time a body of voters who have already left a traditional party, the new party will go nowhere. It will wither when the historic parties counter it with appeals to party loyalty.

At some point the Democracy will have its own political party—or its ethos will deeply alter all political parties. But that will come from the interaction of extraparliamentary and electoral activity, not from the latter alone. Again, we perforce need an organization in which that fruitful interaction can be forwarded, not inhibited, where those interested in the one but not the other will get out of each other's way even as they learn from each other.

My last point concerns the elaborate structures of the major parties and how those structures are rooted in local and regional life, rooted in such a way as to be impervious to most of "the issues" that typically animate third-party advocates. Two very different components—one very, very local, one not at all so—together comprise each of the major parties. I've had some experience of the local component in the midsized city of Yonkers, New York, as a "ward heeler" in the regular Democratic Party. Yonkers then had an elaborate party apparatus reaching down into each street of each neighborhood.

The men and women, mostly volunteers, who staffed it were not particularly ideological. "The issues" didn't move them save in a very general way. Some acted from a sense of civic responsibility; others found comradeship within the local party organization. A few had patronage jobs or members of their families had them. For reasons I still don't fully understand, the civic types and the comradeship types were as loyal to their local leaders as the patronage types.

The leaders tended to be lawyers, but they were also deeply embedded in local real estate, construction, and related fields. Their chief interests were in zoning issues; real estate taxes; construction contracts; city, county, and state purchasing contracts; legal fees; and kindred such things. Or they were themselves planning to run for office but would settle for a judgeship after many years of party service. In brief, the politics of the local Democratic organization was conventionally liberal and "civic," that is, interested in reasonable taxes in exchange for decent schools and well-run services—but also very sharply skewed to real estate, construction, and other career issues by the lawyer component in charge. Clearly, this whole agenda of interests has more to do with who's in and who's out than with the sort of national and international issues that traditionally call forth third parties.[8]

This apparatus arising from the bottom eventually bumps into those figures, sometimes officeholders, sometimes not, who supply or raise the immense sums now needed for elections. When I was active, both in Yonkers and later in New York City and statewide, there was a palpable boundary where the influence of the one gave way to the other. House seats and their state and local equivalents usually lay within the territory of the locals, while statewide offices, such as governorships, U.S. Senate seats, elected higher court judgeships, and big-city mayoralties, fell to those with access to elites and elite money. Because of the increased importance of television, hence the greater need for large amounts of cash, the boundary seems to have shifted downward, so that House elections and many state legislative seats are now more susceptible to the money raisers.

That boundary was brought home to me at the Democratic Party state nominating convention of, I think, 1962. Although the Yonkers "boss," Tom Brogan, was a considerable power in the state party, he, like the rest of us, waited on the convention floor to be told who the candidate for U.S. Senate was to be. That was a matter not vouchsafed even to such an important "pol" as the Yonkers city leader. Later I watched the former Democratic governor of New York State, Averill Harriman, as he made his way across the floor of the convention—and was greeted by absolutely no one and, on his part, greeted no one. Normally an important political figure can go nowhere at a party conclave without an endless series of embraces, backslaps, whispered intimacies, and all the rest of the greeting rituals of U.S. politics. Like our as-yet-unknown candidate for the Senate, Harriman came from a different dimension of the New York State Democratic Party—notwithstanding his having led that party as governor for four years.

The aphorism of former House Speaker Tip O'Neill that "all politics is local" is nonsense, as I'm sure Congressman O'Neill well knew. I think he was just being "colorful" for the media pundits (who still regularly repeat it) and was perhaps pulling their collective leg. He was, of course, a very effective fundraiser.

The importance of the party apparatus rests on two very powerful factors. First, the apparatus "represents" different groups of insistent local interests, as I noted, most heavily around local real estate and other property issues. And second, it has the inside track on nominating candidates. Colluding in the state legislatures, the two major parties make it easy for themselves to put their candidates on the ballot, difficult for everybody else. Many policy intellectuals impute wisdom to this structure, ignoring its roots in inflated paving and sewage contracts. The party apparatus has bargaining power against the money people, and vice versa. Thus, it is only when one major party in the state, or major subdivision of the state, has let the apparatus slip into ruin that there is realistic opportunity for a third party to "capture" a major party or its voters. That comes of the fact that the big money too will have disappeared when the party's nomination wasn't worth very much. The money will shift to the other party, and there will be much less of the hedging of bets between the parties that is customary when election outcomes are in doubt. But a successful third party cannot rest on air; it too must embed itself into the real interest structure of local politics.[9]

The Vanguard Party

There is a small, ever-present, sometimes influential, endlessly destructive tendency within the historical Democracy consisting of those attracted to Lenin's conception of a vanguard party, that is, a group organized around a "far-seeing" ideology that allegedly confers a unique authority to lead "the masses." Their actual leadership most of the time is tightly centered on a small, authoritarian inner group, and then delegated downward. On areas or issues thought by the group to be important, all of its members are expected without lessening of zeal to carry out of the leadership's "line" in their political and even personal lives.[10]

Such parties believe that "the masses"—everyone outside their own ranks—have insufficient political understanding and therefore need the tutelage of the vanguard, the party, themselves. Groups that refuse to accept that tutelage are deemed "enemies" ("of the Revolution!") and will become subject to the party's disruptive, "colonizing" efforts. Party activists will insist, in every setting, that everyone first settle the issue of the "correct" political line. The tactic is intended both to paralyze the effectiveness of the "mass" organization and to identify recruitable individuals. Vanguardists traditionally try to discredit the existing organizational leadership for their lack of a "correct political line" and because—in a self-fulfilling prophecy—the organization is too much devoted to talk only!

These groups are hardy perennials. The Socialist Labor Party has existed in its minuscule way since 1900 or so, the U.S. Communist Party for almost a century, the Socialist Workers Party for about three-quarters of a century, and the Progressive Labor Party for half a century. One can hardly imagine that, communists all, they will all go away or much change their ideas no matter what happens to communism anywhere else. That sought-after "correct line" is also a source of endless contention within and among them. The original Trotsky group split from the Stalin-dominated Communist Party and has itself generated numerous, mutually acrimonious split-off parties, each of which claims to be the true inheritor of Trotsky's mantle. Kindred splits in the 1960s gave rise to a handful of further "revolutionary" grouplets that continue today.

Each communist vanguard party offers itself, in Lenin's expression, as "the general staff" of the revolution. In fact, however, communist parties don't seem to be very good at revolution. No communist party has ever achieved a revolution in a developed country. Gorz (1982) provides a scathing critique of the gap between the French Communist Party's Sunday School revolutionary preaching and its weekday reformism. In France in 1968 and in Italy in 1969, when there was perhaps a genuine "revolutionary situation," their respective communist parties were quick to cool things down (see Marwick 1998). In each case the parties pleaded that the "bourgeois revolution" had to come first, and only after that could they pursue "proletarian" revolution. Both the French and the Italian communist parties have long been in that bind, as has the South African Communist Party after 1989. This intellectual somersault is the particular legacy of Lenin but also seems rooted in Marx's and Engel's notion that they could grasp the "(transcendent) laws of history."

Each vanguard group claims to be the singly superior agent to lead "the masses," but in fact they tend to flourish only when a mass movement arises, their fortunes rising and falling with it. In this country at least, they have tended to follow whatever groups seem most successful at the moment and have shown little political inventiveness of their own. This is just the opposite of the vanguard image they cultivate about themselves, but I think the point is supported in the historical record with perhaps a single exception.[11]

In general it is imprudent to work too closely with a vanguard group or party because they are irresponsible toward the work itself and ideologically committed to favor their own advancement or survival at the expense of the "ignorant" or "misled" masses. In their view one can always replace a mass movement, but the continued existence of "the Party" is an absolute imperative.[12]

On the basis of their own histories, and belying their insistent claims, the vanguard form is singularly ill-fitted for any role in the renewal of the Democracy, much less an umbrella role. The distinction between the mass and the vanguard is especially pernicious.

Because of their historical flirtation with the idea of armed revolution, and because of their sometimes close associations with the policies and interests of foreign powers, like the old Soviet Union, vanguard parties have been subject to massive police penetration.[13] It is common for undercover agents to try to provoke their unwitting radical comrades into illegal acts. I am told by Chicago friends that the person shown burning an American flag in a famous photograph in Chicago in 1968 was a police agent. Whatever the truth of that, it is simply an unhappy fact that the police play a major role in every vanguard organization—*and* that the typical member of such an organization tends to be a person who at least in that period of his or her life has a particularly intense devotion to the cause of the Democracy.

There have always been men and women of unusual zeal and dedication who want to join with others whose zeal is as intense as their own. Often these are young people who postpone career and personal goals for as long as they can, but there are also many who accept the burdens of a lifetime of service. It would in truth be invaluable if there were within the Democracy an organization that eschewed any and all "vanguard" authority over anything but was nonetheless a center for mutual moral and practical support, for exchange of views, and perhaps too for lifetime, comradely association.

Line and Staff

In modern organizations the distinction between *line* personnel, who exercise the powers of command, and *staff* personnel, who *only help those who command,* is fundamental. A business or military organization has two different but parallel echelons. Command authority is usually vested at the very top, and then simultaneously delegated and divided as it proceeds downward from the CEO to the division managers, to the regional managers, and so forth down to the workers at the bottom. The expression *line,* as in so much organizational theory, is drawn from the military, here those who command the battle line.

By the Napoleonic Wars, military organizations had grown larger and more complex, and commanders needed specialized subordinates who would provide simple things like regular supplies of munitions or as complex as coded communications. These were staff officers. As very large business firms developed in the United States, this line/staff arrangement was adapted at first to the railroads and later to large business organizations generally.[14] Thus any manager who has reasonably extensive command responsibilities will have a group of specialist managers to whom he or she can turn for reliable information combined with a professional assessment of the dangers and opportunities of different courses of action, and who can ensure that information flows reliably, securely, and swiftly between headquarters and the subordinate divisions, departments, and persons who implement the decisions made at the top. There is often bad staff work in industry and the military, but this does not negate the fact that one cannot command complex organizations or activities without the aid of an extensive staff. With good staff support, a military or a sales campaign is not a blind march into an unknown future but a process of assessing and adjusting in real time the actual results of the clash of the commander's/executive's aims and intentions with the sometime chaos of real events.

The development of a similarly extensive staff capacity would be of help to the many organizations of the Democracy and thus to a renewed and extended advance of the Democracy itself.

Organizing for a Renewed Advance

What follows is a sketch for an organization containing those features that would be most efficacious and most needed in aid of a renewed advance. It is conceived to carry forward that advance over a lengthy period in which the Democracy itself will undergo ideological, programmatic, and even generational changes. The proposal embodies an organizational form apt for what must be accomplished under always unfavorable but as yet unknowable circumstances. I believe the proposal is actually timely and practical.

But the perfect can be the enemy of the good. All of the features of what I'll call the "Staff for the Advance" (SFTA) are really needed, but any steps toward realizing any of those features would be useful. Highly idealized schemes are worth less here than concrete achievements. In that sense, the proposal can be seen as merely illustrative of a set of related organizational and programmatic issues whose resolution is needed for a renewed historic advance.

The leading idea of the SFTA is that it is a formally organized *staff* for a renewed advance. It is conceived as a mutual support network made up of men and women whose primary activity consists of work on behalf of some organization or project of the Democracy. Potential members need not be leaders of such organizations or paid staff people, but the SFTA should comprise those people who, within whatever income or time constraints they may have, conceive that their foremost priority is the work of the Democracy. That priority is very much like what Catholics call "a vocation" or Protestants "a call." Those actually are good analogies, for the SFTA should constitute, in the first instance, not just another instrumental organization but an expressive embodiment of the deepest sort of political and social commitment.

Membership should eventually be formalized in two steps: candidates should be nominated by the organization or program they are active in, and the latter should attest to both their commitment and their character. People who have no "home organization" in the work of the Democracy have no place in the SFTA. Subsequent to such a nomination, an ad hoc group from the Staff should vet the candidate's character and qualifications and, if concurring, then admit the man or woman into the Staff. These two steps would tend to make SFTA membership a coveted honor and confer upon the nominee a special moral prestige—again not unlike that which attaches to clergy or to lay preachers in some religious denominations. That prestige should, of course, have a double character, attesting that the SFTA member is recognized as a highly dedicated person who has already performed with skill and accomplishment in the ongoing work of some part of the Democracy.

At present, young people attracted to the movements for humanitarian social change tend to be drawn from the ranks of the better-educated, vaguely "upper-middle" classes. This is not at all unrelated to the demobilization of working-class activism that seems intrinsic to corporate society and about which we've already commented. It would be self-defeating for the SFTA to accept the class-skewing that comes from this. The historical Democracy was filled by persons drawn from every class but especially—in numbers and importance—from the lower and working classes. This will have to be true of the SFTA as well, even though it will pose an especially difficult hurdle at the beginning.[15]

The SFTA itself should have few or no regular meetings, for it has few or no instrumental functions. It is conceived as an organization that, as strongly as possible, embodies the distinction between line and staff responsibilities and between the expressive and instrumental dimensions; it is to be the organization of those men and women who, strictly obeying the mandates of the instrumental organizations with which they are affiliated, attempt in the best way possible to carry out those mandates. Being faithful to this principle is of the highest importance. The SFTA in no way should resemble a vanguard organization save that it consists of people whose highest priority is the advance of the Democratic movement—but it is an advance commanded by others. At the present time there are many such people actually working within the Democracy but who are separated by time, place, and difference of ideology and opinion. The SFTA is meant to bridge those gaps, not erase them.

There should be regional offices, each with only a traveling secretary or two. The duties of the latter should be to keep regular, face-to-face contact with SFTA members in the region, with a view to bringing some together from time to time as called for by their work. Such meetings might include some SFTA members to help one of their number who is physically or even morally exhausted—"burnt out"—and in need of support. It might only be that an SFTA person feels he or she needs advice or other assistance in his or her organizational or even personal life. It might be that a group of members see the need for some program or organization they are not in a position to mount, thus employing the traveling secretary possibly to use his or her other contacts to encourage such a new project. Or it might even be a full regional meeting to grapple with some common problem that a wide section of the SFTA membership has identified.

Whatever the nature of the meetings, they have as their object only to assist others' purposes. Consistent with the role of a "staff," the SFTA should take no political or other positions, formally sponsor no projects or organizations. If, for example, a project should form from the initiative of a regional SFTA, the project should immediately become autonomous of it, fully under the authority of its own members and governing structure.

Its origin was a service to the Democracy by the SFTA, but its activities are outside its remit.

The SFTA should mount only one continuing program, the sponsoring of internships for young persons who wish to contribute to the growth of the Democracy. Such a young person would ideally be initially nominated by his or her home organization or project, and the latter would perhaps underwrite some sort of stipend. Meanwhile, organizations and projects of the Democracy would, through the SFTA, identify staffing or project needs and on their basis issue invitations for interns. As I envision the scheme, it would, of course, provide a vehicle for young people who want to serve for a time in "the movement," but it should have other good effects as well. By means of a brief training and orientation course, the SFTA would try both to improve the organizational skills of the interns and allow them to experience something of the character and the diversity of the wider Democratic movement. In addition, the intern's sponsoring organization and the organization he or she subsequently works within would ideally monitor both the progress of the intern's work and his or her well-being, perhaps proposing recommendations for his or her future course of work. The internship scheme would create a network of relationships among widely different, perhaps distant, projects embodying different priorities and in that way serve the SFTA's aim to knit the Democratic movement together and to quicken its advance.

An ultimate test of the staff nature of the SFTA is that it should contain within its ranks persons of widely different, even clashing views and priorities—in their own persons and in the organizations they serve. The SFTA itself does not prioritize this or that principle or goal but instead looks to the longer run of the Democratic advance. As I argued, political and ideological fights are typically fights about anticipated futures and how best to cope with them. Those anticipations can be dealt with doggedly and dogmatically and in fact often have to be. And once a particular organization has set out on a course, it should pursue it in an integral and focused way. But in so doing that organization is in fact predicting what the future is or can be like on the basis of present knowledge and intent. It is important that such predictions be worked out in practice, but under observation by other, differing eyes. In this context, the SFTA itself is meant always to embody the full breadth of opinion of the Democracy in a setting of nonantagonistic exchange, a clash of view and experience where the Democracy's advance is the point of contact and agreement.

Political Differences

Can the SFTA have a legitimate basis for excluding any person or view at all? The question deserves more searching inquiry than can be given here, but my initial reaction would be to use as a guideline some widely disseminated statement of broad democratic and other humane goals that is at the same time neither too partisan nor too woolly. Perhaps the UN's *Universal Declaration of Human Rights* would serve here. If a person or a project falls reasonably within its terms, then there is the possibility of SFTA association. It bears repeating that the SFTA is intended to be an umbrella group not only for the here and now but into an indefinite future. It should be understood ahead of time that it is therefore necessary and desirable that there always be ideological tension and unease within its ranks; however, there must be a limit to what can be tolerated.

The following story raises the point in a particularly acute way: some forty years ago I sat in on a discussion in Georgia led by Miles Horton. Miles was one of the legendary fighters for racial equality in the South. At some point in the discussion he opined that it was important to keep up friendly contacts with Klan members as well as civil rights workers. Tellingly, the Southerners in the discussion, both black and white, went along with him on this point, while the Northerners, black and white, were appalled. Miles argued that many Klan members were really motivated by an attempt to preserve a familiar world and prevent what seemed to them a hostile future. Again, the Southerners tended to go along with Miles on this, while the Northerners, somewhat mollified, still thought he was being too far out. Would he remain friendly with a cross-burner or a dynamiter? Of course, where Klansmen were clearly thugs and brutes, Miles agreed, but there were other kinds of Klansmen too. The discussion was hot and heavy.

The problem is that many good people fight well for bad causes, or for what others believe are bad causes. One can write those people off or accept that both sides are capable of learning how better to cope with their differences. All of us at one time or another have believed false or unjust things and acted wrongly or, at least shortsightedly. Granted, Miles was arguing an extreme case, especially during a time and in a place where the Klan was on the rampage, but I think that was "the method to his madness." He could point to many examples of people whose life course took them from being fighters for segregation to being fighters for a new, racially integrated South; the late Supreme Court Justice Hugo Black was the best-known example of someone who had made that difficult transition. In any case, the episode stays in my mind as underlining how difficult it can be to separate political good and bad, and how important it is not to close political doors too soon or too tightly. With that in mind, Miles might serve as the ultimate godfather of the SFTA proposal. The later history of the South largely supports his outlook.

Politics of the SFTA

The SFTA represents an attempt to design an organization that over time can alter Intersection society. As we saw, that form of society is in the first instance particularly well defended by what in military terminology is called *a mutually supporting system of defense in depth*.[16] The elements of this system include the population's habitual acceptance that what is, is "naturally" what ought to be, the society's structures of interclass but unequal accommodation, its hegemonic ideologies and culture, the modern world's characteristic inchoate fear that change must give rise to destructive conflict, its particular Baconian "idylls of the marketplace," that is to say, the social superstitions that are generated by a given society, and, of course, the formal, skewed political process itself. The SFTA is not conceived as an organization that aims at this or that specific change but offers a deep social/organizational infrastructure capable of carrying forward a range of political and cultural interventions that will bring that defensive system under pressures of sufficient depth, extent, and longevity that can alter it in the interests of the Democracy. The design assumes that in short-term, head-to-head conflict with Intersection society, the Democracy is generally outweighed by those defensive rings and by the weight of Intersection institutions embedded in inner government, but that, over historical time, the trajectory of society can be changed from below by the forces and values of the Democracy.

As I have emphasized, modern Intersection society is very different from earlier societies, and the SFTA is designed to take those differences into account. Prior to the corporate era, one could reasonably conceive of society as the *social all*, that is, a boundless, many-dimensional, forever changing something-or-other within which everything of a social, economic, cultural, political, historical, personal, and spiritual nature was located. Such a conception has no borders, hence spontaneous occurrences appear not only possible but normal. This view of society as a meta-phenomenon, a something that always reaches beyond our intellectual and moral vision, was implicitly held by thinkers as diverse as Marx and Hayek, and each did appeal to "society" as the ultimate arbiter of their moral and political preferences. For Marx, the development of capitalism was ultimately antagonistic to "society" and would therefore have to give way. In Hayek more or less, the converse was argued to be the case, save for the presence of capitalist individualism, "society," the manifold, spontaneous "all," would be destroyed in the name of (organized) "collectivism." In short, both were reaching into the same bag of analytical/historical tools, but events have passed both by.

We now live in a semifabricated society whose contours are increasingly shaped by the institutions of the Intersection. This shaping touches every aspect of our personal and social experience. It has destroyed whole classes—such as peasants—and created others, such as the cadre. It now winnows out entire populations, selecting this cohort for privilege and that for deprivation through its educational and allied social activities. It has demobilized the political movements of the lower classes, and its schools inhibit their renewal by blocking the transmission of traditional lower- and working-class values. Its institutions create the main news—and then report and evaluate it. It creates, sustains, and gives expression to its own intellectuals both at the trivial level—the news readers on television, the columnists in the press—and the profound, that is, through the effect its foundations, book and journal publishers, and elite universities have on research agenda and the fabric of intellectual life.

It would be too much to say that the world created by the modern corporation is totalitarian. In fact, as we learned from so many post-Nazi and post-Soviet memoirs,[17] that concept overreaches, mainly, I think, because it was coined with polemical, not analytical, purposes in mind. But it is fair to say that modern Americanist corporate society has a totalizing character; it acts on every dimension of society, not from a narrow ideology-driven agenda but from its own open-ended profit-seeking/technologizing/institution-growing imperatives. But this means that it tends to forestall opposition to itself more powerfully than previous forms of society. There are no or few isolated corners in a modern society where opposition can develop and grow, as it were, at its own pace.

One can overreach when analyzing this totalizing effect, but it is both empirically warranted and prudent to accept that the social bases for anti-corporate/anti-Intersection oppositional groups or classes have shrunk since the maturation of Intersection society. Such groups arose and even progressed in that era, but I suggest that the defeat of the Sixties and the success and longevity of the reaction forces us to consider my point that the social bases of opposition themselves have significantly diminished.

The conception of the SFTA is in the final analysis "engineered" to deal with the world made by the modern corporation and the other modern Intersection institutions. It assumes, on the one hand, that there will continue to arise forces of opposition to that society, but on the other that they will face greater difficulties in maintaining and expanding themselves than was the case in precorporate society. It assumes that the learning curve of the Democracy will be more interrupted than in the past. If what we now think of as the "normal course of events" continues, corporate social and cultural systems will make it likely that the curve will be more stretched out in time, with less continuity between the generations, hence less ability to accumulate historical experience—if any at all. Our organizational argument is that without a conscious effort to avoid it, shortsighted opposition and conflict, which tend to divide the Democracy, will be more pronounced than in the past and have longer-lasting effects. It assumes that the police power will become better and better at hindering and even preventing opposition from achieving sustained social form and, when necessary, better and better at eliminating it.

It assumes that we can count less and less on the spontaneous healing and restorative powers of "society." It assumes that the "free market" for ideas has been to a critical degree replaced by an intellectual life modified by criteria of corporate acceptability. Intersection society is needfully quite tolerant of dissident opinions, but at the same time it places the heavy weight of its influence and action behind views that it itself generates and approves. In the "clash of ideas," theirs is the side with the larger battalions.

In the last analysis, that is the point of the SFTA conception. "Man makes his own history but not under the conditions of his own choosing." Those very conditions, I maintain, have changed to the deep disadvantage of the Democracy. If we are to make our own history today and tomorrow, we should apply the best wisdom and resolution that our limited vision can conjure and afford. That, ultimately, is the leading idea and justification to bring into being something like the SFTA.

In the next five chapters I will offer proposals that will, at least on their surface, appear more practical than the creation of an SFTA. That is illusory. If we do not address the novel historical and political problems raised by Intersection society, more practical, down-to-earth proposals will have,

I think, only a smaller chance of being enacted, however much they are needed, even in the very long future.

The staff association proposed here is an ideal construction. Its merit, however, lies not in its ideal conformation but in that it is a reasoned attempt to address in a practical vision the very new, generally unfavorable strategic terrain that the Democracy must operate on in the present world and in the face of the powerful, still vital modern reaction. If nothing else, I hope it will encourage the reader to thoroughly rethink the organizational dimensions necessary to support a renewed advance, that is to say, to conceive anew the kind of historical wit and tenacity necessary to burst the bonds of present-day society on behalf of an unknown but deeply needed future.

8

THE REFORM OF THE POLICE POWER

The Police as a Political Power

I want to treat the police power, that is, modern police institutions, as a part of the social defense structure. By "modern police institution," I refer in the first instance to police organized in military-like units in primarily our big cities. Uniformed state police departments have a similar orientation, training, and culture, as to a lesser but still critical degree do the federal immigration and drug agencies and the regular Secret Service and FBI agents. In the United States the police are mostly under nominal state or local control, whereas in Britain and on the Continent they tend to be organized nationally, as, for example, the quasi-military Carabinieri in Italy. What is remarkable about the police institution, as here defined, is how similarly it behaves in different times and countries.[1]

As before, my view is that the importance of the police power in any given society may serve as a crude index of the degree to which the privileged have not paid for their privileges. If this is indeed the case, then we should find that the actual role of the police is typically disguised in other garbs. And that too is the case.

The genius of the modern police is that they are designed to obscure the differences between crime and political dissidence. It is this institutionalized confusing of two such different species of social behavior that makes the police so reliable to the authority of the authorities. It underlies their tendency to support "authority" almost unreservedly and to employ violence against challenges to it. As I see it, then, one of the central problems of police reform is to rupture that link, that is, to erect institutional, legal, and moral walls between the police and political activity that are as high and secure and honored as that fabled wall between church and state. Without such a wall, it is difficult to see how a renewed historical advance can be sustained.[2]

There is another way to approach the same conclusion. The twentieth century, and the fragment of its successor that we've so far experienced, might be called the Century of the Police. We speak, for example, of the monumental crimes of Hitler and Stalin, but the murderers and the torturers in both the Jewish Catastrophe (Hilberg 1996) and the Great Purges were policemen or police auxiliaries, and it was police who committed the Armenian genocide and ran East Germany, and it is police who are running North Korea today. Similarly, it was police, with assistance from the military intelligence services, who saw to the "disappearance" of so many men and women in Indonesia, Chile, Argentina, Uruguay, Paraguay, Mexico, Guatemala, Colombia, and El Salvador in the years 1965–80, in some cases into the present. And, not to see only the mote in others' eyes, there is the sorry role of the police in the history of Jim Crow, in the repression of the U.S. labor movement before the New Deal, in the "red scares" beginning in 1917 and again in 1947; and it is the police who today, especially in the form of the immigration service, are being urged to abuses under the so-called Patriot Act.

I am not arguing that the individual cop on the beat, or even his or her chief, should bear the moral onus for historical police crimes; that would be a calumny. But at the same time, one is not wrong to see *institutional continuity* between the beating and sodomizing of a Haitian immigrant with a broomstick in a New York police station a few years ago and, say, the torture chambers of the Gestapo. Again, I'm aware of the vast differences in the two cases, but our twentieth-century police experience argues very strongly that, different as they were, there is an "institutional continuity." The modern police have been perennially hostile to the poor; to those of low status; to ethnic, linguistic, and racial minorities; and to political dissidents—in short, to any and all who suffer the antipathy of those in power. Accordingly, under moderate governments the police commit erratic "abuses," normally quite a lot of them, but under rightist governments, which have historically been somewhat more to their taste, they are prone to carry out the sort of political crimes that marked so much of the twentieth century. It is insufficiently appreciated, for example, how loyally the regular French and Czech police cooperated with the Gestapo during the Nazi occupation of their countries. Only slightly better known is the extent to which ordinary German policemen were employed in the *Einsatz* killing operations in Poland in 1939 and then again in western Russia in mid- to late 1941. There, ordinary policemen, aided and abetted by the operatives of the SS and Gestapo, took part in the always brutal roundups of Poles, Jews, Communists, and other "enemies"; presided over the digging of the vast pits that were to contain the bodies; and then directly carried out the face-to-face, one-by-one shooting of men, women, children, and even infants.[3]

I do want to repeat and to emphasize the differences between the helpful cop on the corner and a Gestapo or NKVD beast, but wish to add that anyone who cannot see that so much of the customary institutional behavior of the modern police is inimical to a democratic society—from beating black heads downtown to intimidating left-wingers, from disrupting peaceful protests to wholesale jailings at street demonstrations, from breaking strikes to looking the other way at right-wing goon behavior—lacks ordinary prudence. There is obviously continuity between the Weimar police absenting themselves when Nazi thugs beat up Jews or ransacked Socialist Party offices and the customary relationship between the police and the Ku Klux Klan, later the White Citizens' Councils, in the old U.S. South. It is in fact usual, not rare, for police departments to use right-wing groups to carry out violent activities the police want to occur but to also to be distanced from.[4]

It would misread history to argue that these are just glitches in police behavior, exceptions to the normal workings of police institutions, traceable to a few "bad apples," and therefore relatively easy to fix. As a social institution, the modern police have been designed and perfected to overcome the inability of their predecessors to control the urban masses. If the French Revolution is the symbol of modern liberty, equality, and fraternity, the modern police institution is the counter symbol of elite resistance to the rise of the Democracy.

The Military Form of Modern Policing

This same police dynamic, absent earlier, soon characterized the allegedly "exceptional" United States too. In the early part of the nineteenth century, urban U.S. policing was typically carried out by nonuniformed watchmen, locally recruited and locally controlled. Legend has it they tended to be in the pay of the local political bosses, the saloon keeper, and the brothel owner.[5] But at the same time, the local neighborhood character of these "police" inhibited the political repressiveness we associate with big-city police, state troopers, and federal immigration agents today; if the neighborhood was dominated by the Locofocos or the Knights of Labor, the local constables would normally have to go along or look the other way.[6] At present, the situation is not very different in the more prosperous small towns and upscale suburbs, where the police are hypersensitive to how they deal with the policed, to whom they have to justify their behavior and—obviously important—their budgets.

In this country low-quality, corruption-ridden, ideologically apolitical policing ended with the arrival of great numbers of immigrants to our shores as part of the process of industrialization. This brought the rise of mass political activities, including especially labor organizations. Earlier, the New York Draft Riots of 1863 made it evident that local constables were unwilling and unable to support the authorities during such crises. But it was probably the first national U.S. strike, among railroad workers in 1877, that brought the point home. Local constables were unwilling to risk themselves to "the mob," and many actually supported the strikers. As a temporary expedient, militia were brought in from the outside, for example, from Philadelphia to Pittsburgh, the latter a center of the strike, and they succeeded in quelling the "riots," although not before there was considerable property destruction.

The great rail strike of 1877 underlined the first of the new policing problems to be solved. Constables with local roots were too much influenced by their neighbors, hence unreliable in a political or industrial disturbance. In addition, they lacked the training, the discipline, and the concentrated numbers either to prevent the formation of "mobs" or to beat them back or disperse them subsequently. The general lines of a solution to this problem were not mysterious; as was well known from the European experience, such policing functions could only be carried out by forces that were deeply alienated from those who were to be policed. Thus the importance of the Cossacks in tsarist Russia, or soldiers recruited from a hostile, fearful Sicilian peasantry to control restive workers in Turin and Genoa. But those were stopgap solutions. One needed a permanent, serving organization able to not just beat back the urban mob but to prevent it from forming in the first place.

One can use soldiers to police "the mob," but unless there is underlying social alienation between the soldiers and "the mob," over time the soldiers are likely to sympathize with it, since "those people are just like ourselves." The antiwar movement during the Vietnam era provides a case in point, where ordinary soldiers, both here and in Vietnam, came eventually to adopt the antiwar, anti-authoritarian views of the protestors. I still recall several street demonstrations where young women went up to the line of soldiers to place flowers in the barrels of their rifles. One had to feel sorry for these young men to have to stand there like manikins while being flirted with in this sexually charged way.

The solution to this problem proved to be the quasi-militarization of the police. The military form of organization permitted a technical advance in crowd control, which continues even to the present writing, allowed for a wider variety of policing functions, and at the same time created alienating social and cultural barriers between the police and what they call "civilians." As we know today, police training, socialization, and discipline emphasize the difference between "officers" and "civilians." A police culture is fostered in which the police see themselves as misunderstood by and undervalued by "civilians," and hence believe that police must "stick together." The power of police culture is shown by the common police practice of providing alibis for each others' misbehavior, including, importantly, illegal behavior.[7]

This point needs to be stressed over and over again, especially in the current context of police reform via so-called community policing. The latter is at best a police strategy to limit the alienation between the police and the policed so that the community and the police are not actively warring against one another. But the idea that the police precinct and the local police officers should be as one with a socially diverse community is generally anathema; it flies against the much higher imperative that the police serve Authority per se, that is, those who wield the symbols of legitimacy, property, and stability. The events of 1877 may be forgotten, but their enduring lesson is not.

With the organization of urban police departments from the mid-nineteenth century on, the authorities finally had a reliable weapon against mass disturbances and strikes. But these early urban and state-level police departments were still not very proficient at collecting and using evidence in criminal cases and or at gathering useful intelligence about budding trade union or other socially dissident behavior. That incapacity would later be addressed by a movement stemming from the Progressive Era to professionalize, centralize, and give greater technical support to police work, increasingly aided by various federal agencies such as the later FBI.[8]

Meantime, to fill this lacuna, private detective forces such as the Pinkerton Agency, the Baldwin-Felts Detective Agency, the Rockefeller's Coal and Iron Police,[9] the Ford Motor Company's Special Police under Harry Bennett, and a whole host of railroad-sponsored police forces were formed. These had the technical capacity to maintain and share intelligence files and to conduct surveillance, especially of budding trade union threats, and had sufficient legal distance from the public authorities to provide cover for the odd kidnapping, beating, or even lynching of offending militants.

The Pinkertons made their mark in the prosecutions that led to the hanging of the Molly Maguires in Pennsylvania in the 1870s; they would continue to lead the way in industrial policing until the La Follette hearings in the late 1930s, which brought out the extent and the frequency of the criminal behavior of these private police (see Auerbach 1964). Since then, both the improvement of city and state police intelligence agencies and the intervention of federal police agencies have consigned the Pinkertons and their like to tasks like keeping order at the local mall (Morn 1982). But reminiscent of their heyday, a recent spate of stories about the poor security, brutality, poor food, and nonexistent medical care of privately owned and operated prisons, now a major industry in their own right, confirms what we should have known from earlier experience: farming out police and related work to the private sector is always wrongheaded.

Illegal Police Behavior

It is hard to follow the national press for more than a few days without reading of major illegal behavior on the part of the police. In Boston a few years ago, the police burst into the apartment of an elderly, innocent black citizen and roughed him up sufficiently that he died on the spot. They had gone to the wrong address. In New York at about the same time, the police fired several dozen bullets into a man "who reached for a weapon" while standing in the lobby of his own building. He was reaching for his wallet to establish his identity. Both the New York and Pennsylvania state police were caught falsifying evidence against defendants as a matter of course, abetted in this by their respective state police crime labs; these labs prove to be unthinkably unreliable (Moore 2009a). For over thirty years the city of Cincinnati has suffered repeated race riots brought about by police shootings of innocent black people; at the current writing the problems remain unresolved.

The New York City Police Department is often thought an exemplar of a modern police force. But in 1992 the City Council considered a Civilian Review Bill (of police behavior). There ensued a mass police riot around City Hall, several legislators were roughed up, there were the usual "nigger" epithets, and no arrests. In several cities, including New York and Detroit, rogue police officers have robbed drugs from dealers at gunpoint so they themselves could sell them and take the profit. The travails of the Los Angeles Police Department are familiar to all. One could go on about Miami or Philadelphia, or speed traps in Oklahoma or Georgia, or drug protection rackets in several other cities. Whatever the advantages of modern, professionally trained, militarily organized urban and state police may be, long experience has shown that they are chronically prone to illegal behavior and are proverbially cool to "outsider" efforts to prevent or limit it. The actual record displays the priorities of the modern police institution: it is much better at their central function, dissident control, and fair-to-awful on what is really a secondary task, crime fighting, even within their own ranks.

Chronic illegal behavior among the modern police is widely acknowledged among "criminal justice" professionals in both the universities and among police leaderships. There are at present two proposed strategies, which, if they could be enacted, are thought likely to prevent this. I remain unconvinced.[10]

The older of the two is the drive to "professionalize" the ordinary police officer. This continues the long-time strategy pursued by the main organization of police leaders, the International Association of Chiefs of Police (IACP),[11] which has been chronicled by Robert Fogelson. "Professionalization" was also seen as a major pillar of the police reforms promised by the Kerner Commission, appointed by President Johnson in 1967. Reading between the lines of, for example, the Kerner Commission's report, it is not difficult to see what they mean by "professionalization." The prototypical police officer the commission wanted to be rid of was the "good ole boy," the type identified with civil rights violations in the American South in the 1960s, people like Cecil Price, the sheriff's deputy who steered Chaney, Goodman, and Schwerner to their deaths. The Kerner Commission wanted a better-educated and better-trained policeman or policewoman, recruited not from the ranks of semirural toughs and courthouse hangers-on but from the striving lower middle classes, that is, one who would be socially alienated from the "good ole boys." But by the same token, such recruits have proved no less likely to be alienated from the poorer classes of blacks and to react to them with perhaps more ferocity and less empathy than their less sophisticated predecessors.

Overall, the results of these reform efforts have not been impressive. The best that one can say of "professionalization" initiatives is that they can reduce petty, day-to-day police corruption to a more tolerable level for a period of time. However, this sort of "professionalization" has not brought excessive shootings, street beatings, big-time drug-related corruption, racial profiling, racism, and the like down into the range of the tolerable.

The other contender is the effort, mostly by civil libertarians, to establish police review boards. This is a good idea whose time has not yet come. The police see this as an attempt by "bleeding hearts" and "liberals" to undermine "law and order." Much of the public, mesmerized by pro-police propaganda in the media, is actually on the side of the police. Thus if one could enact a strong police review procedure, the police themselves would stonewall it, and the public would support them.

The media treatment of the police is a positive scandal. There the police almost always pursue extended investigations of the crimes depicted. In police practice such investigations are reserved for the higher-profile cases. For many serious crimes little or no action is taken to investigate them. Cop-show investigations are typically conducted at the very edges of advanced forensic science; real police investigations are often botched by contamination of the crime scene; failure to contact witnesses; wrongful arrests, which then must be defended while good leads grow stale; and as we've seen, the use of manufactured evidence and "testilying." Media cops usually get their man, but in fact the real-world "clearance rate," that is, crime reports that lead to an arrest, is quite low, even for murder and rape.[12] Media police routinely violate the law—of search, of entry into private premises, with much abusive, threatening, often violent behavior toward suspects and arrested persons. This behavior is presented favorably, which is a subtle way of supporting the police propaganda that "their hands are tied" by the constitutional protections of our legal system and suggesting, contrary to the evidence, that the law is biased in favor of the villain, not the police or the victim. Too much of what is broadcast or screened is a paean to authoritarian, anticonstitutional, crudely illegal behavior by police institutions, which in the real world are only marginally successful in preventing and solving even the most serious and violent crimes and basically hopeless at controlling petty criminality.

In short, further police "professionalization" of the sort intended by IACP and the Kerner Commission will leave us with the unsatisfactory situation we've been in all along. And while one doesn't want to dismiss out of hand the possibly ameliorating effects of police review procedures on race relations, one can predict that, absent deeper, more radical changes in the modern police institution, they will leave untouched the long-term inclination of modern police forces to ally themselves with right-wing political forces and, at worst, to monitor, contain, and if necessary help beat back substantive political and economic change.

The Roots and Consequences of Illegal Police Behavior

A more effective, less corruptible police and a police inclined to champion, not subvert, constitutional standards are very closely related. Both require that we do away with militarized police institutions, which are now the norm. After over a century of experience we have learned the hard way that they are not really reformable. The problem in both cases—technically effective policing of crime and constitutionally friendly policing—is rooted in the military form of the police institution itself. There is a profound design fault here, not a reparable failure in a viable institution.

The initial and continuing rationale for the military form of the police institution is that it alienates the police from the policed and thus ensures that the former's loyalty will be to the authorities and against the urban mob—almost no matter what. Other chronic police problems flow from that same matrix.

As we know vividly from the police shows and films, police intelligence about crimes is crucially dependent on informants, that is, petty criminals who learn about one another's crimes "through the grapevine" and in other informal ways. The police get this information by threatening (illegal) violence on the petty criminal and by "looking the other way" at his or her crimes. Informants are essential to crime control, for without them the police would usually not know where to look or whom to look for. In fact, this simple acknowledgment of what seems an elementary fact of policing contains not one but four major faults of the modern police institution. It is a devastating admission.

First, police dependence on petty criminal informants stems from the fact that normal communications channels that ought to exist between police and policed have been blocked by the designed-in alienation of the police from the communities of law-abiding citizens they ostensibly serve. As we know, this blockage is acute and even dangerous in the relations between big-city police and the minority and immigrant districts, but it is present in almost all urban police/community relations. I repeat the obvious: this is a design feature of the modern police institution, not an unfortunate side effect. By heroic efforts and under ideal circumstances, one can limit the harmful effects of such alienation, but by definition heroic efforts and ideal circumstances will be relatively rare. What it means is that the police can have only a marginal effectiveness in policing ordinary crime. That is the price we pay for the relatively unconditioned loyalty of the police to abstract "authority" and not to actual citizens, to "law and order" and not to the actual laws on the books.

There is more: the informant system requires that the police look the other way at whole classes of petty criminals and their crimes. The leverage that a police officer has against a potential informant is that the latter has broken the law and that this can be "winked at" in exchange for information. Accordingly, much burglary, mugging, low-level drug trafficking, pimping, prostitution, gambling, car theft, pocket-picking, labor-and immigration-law violations and such are permitted by the police as a normal condition of policing. The police and the petty criminal are in a complementary or symbiotic relationship: each is necessary to the other, and each gains an advantage from the other that could not otherwise be gained. This relationship is both normal and essential to the sort of police institution we now have. The police must actually permit a great deal of crime in exchange for a limited ability to attack a minority of crimes and criminals. This devil's bargain is unavoidable for the modern police institution.

The third fault stemming from the matrix is that alienation from "civilians" of itself encourages corruption and other criminality on the part of the police. In the conventional wisdom there is the realm of law and a realm of lawlessness, and the police occupy the former and protect it against the chaos of the latter. Nothing could be more obviously false. In reality, the police occupy a third realm, a border region between criminals and "civilians," between law and lawlessness, in which they observe and permit a great deal of (we hope only) petty crime. For any police officer, not only the honest one, this is an awful position to be in and has further harmful consequences.

It is this conflicted reality, I am persuaded, that underlies violent police reactions in defense of their own legitimacy and authority. Most police are quite well aware of how much criminal behavior they and their colleagues wink at and, being human, are likely to be uneasy about it. This straddling of the worlds of legal and criminal behavior is arguably behind the police officer's typically violent reaction to those who challenge his (not usually her) authority. I surmise that the challenged cop knows only too well how little his real role resembles the fictive virtue assumed by police propaganda, and he is angry because the challenge to his moral authority comes too close to home.

The truth here is that the policeman or policewoman exists with one foot in each realm and must accept that there is no place else to stand. That anomalous position is often the bridge to further criminal behavior on the police officer's part. Alienated from the public, rubbing elbows with criminals and their enterprises, modern police officers grow used to rationalizing illegal behavior on their own part, or on the part of their police comrades. From there it is only a small step to accepting favors, taking bribes, seeking bribes, demanding a cut in a criminal's profits, ignoring the rights of the arrested, and indulging in physical brutality.

Again, I intend no slander against the rank-and-file policeman or policewoman. Given their situation, it is a wonder that more are not corrupt and lawless and that so many serve so selflessly and well. But no amount of private integrity can in the last analysis correct the faults designed into a bad institution.

Finally, the intimacy with lawlessness that is the normal lot of the police officer and police department tends to strengthen their typical ideology of obedience to abstract authority, what they call "the Law" but which, as we've seen, has only a passing relationship with actual legality. Only such an abstract, transcendent, and ultimately inscrutable deity could obscure from the thoughtful policeman and policewoman the moral and legal compromises that present-day policing is immersed in. Again, this is a feature designed into the police institution, and only with heroic effort and blessed circumstance can it sometimes be kept within almost tolerable bounds.

Imperatives for Police Reform

There are two overriding imperatives for fundamental police reform, and it is relatively easy to describe them, to see why they are imperative, and to understand how they would make policing more effective against crime and friendlier to the Constitution. Neither imperative is utopian, and both are sufficiently grounded in the realities of police work that they could gain some initial support from what is now called "the law enforcement community," that is, professional police, the courts, prosecutors, and others who are intimately involved in crime prevention and criminal apprehension. First, there should be *civilian operational control* over all phases of police work, from the selection, training, and orientation of police recruits to positive guidance over everyday police behavior and priorities on the street. Insofar as this leads to better relations between the police and the "civilian" population, this should be an aid to and not a limitation on the ability of the police to prevent and control crime.

But civilian operational control will not be adequate without police professionals in a complementary role. The sort of professionalization I am calling for, however, is not the truncated form suggested by the IACP reformers and the Kerner Commission, but professionalization in the same sense in which we use the term when we are speaking of other socially important professions such as medicine, architecture, teaching, and the law. We can take the points up in that order, first civilian control and then professionalization.

Civilian operational control of the police is needed to overcome the internal contradiction built into all previous police review proposals, which have left the front line of police policy and operations under the control of professional police commanders, and then placed over them a review board with an adversarial relationship to the police. Review boards are no better than irritating outsiders, critics after the fact and, in the view of working police, without all the facts. An aggressive review commission would threaten what present-day commanders feel is their necessary authority and what present-day rank-and-file police officers feel is their safety on the streets and will be tenaciously resisted. They'll have every motive to rouse public opinion against such boards, as they have done in New York City and other places. On the other hand, a timid commission would have insufficient effect. In both cases the public is left with insufficient control over the considerable police misbehavior we now suffer and which the board proposal is supposed to correct.

Furthermore, review proposals don't address the tradition that the police find dissident and criminal behaviors equally objectionable and equally in need of their attention. A review board doesn't address the police power's ambivalent position vis-à-vis petty crime and criminals, their straddling of the line between law and crime. And it leaves the police as a destructive force in the wider political arena, as in Mississippi in 1964, and since then in the reaction to drugs and crime in the 1970s and 1980s, a reaction self-interestedly embraced by the police. It has filled our jails to record levels, renewed a reckless death penalty, and yet allowed criminality, especially drug-related criminality, to continue to prosper.

It is testimony to how backward our ideas are on the subject that civilian control over the police is not more widely understood and accepted. If the Constitution had been written, say, only fifty to seventy-five years later, this very point would very likely have been embodied in it. The issue is the same as for civilian control over the military.

Police review proposals leave intact the culture of alienation between the police and the policed at the root of the faults in the police institution that I've just described. In fact, given the legendary strength of that culture and the way it is rooted in the very design of the police institution, it is probably more utopian to seek limited police reforms such as civilian review procedures than to work for a police institution fitted to present-day society, not the society of a century and a quarter ago.

It is also difficult to see how a historic advance can be renewed without altering the political role of the police. History doesn't stand still. The police have learned to cope with the nonviolent tactics that for a time baffled Southern police in the 1950s and 1960s, when such tactics were used to overwhelm the police ability to arrest protestors. Police had to take their arrestees "downtown" to the courts, which tended to weaken policing capacity at the scene of the demonstrations. Protestors would try to "fill the jails," wreaking havoc on correctional budgets and correctional discipline.[13] Prosecutors would be overwhelmed by paperwork and unable to proceed with charges against the demonstrators save in a few selected cases.

"Filling the jails" was once an effective tactic, but the police have learned to counter it. Modern police can operate mobile vans equipped as courtrooms so that demonstrators can be processed immediately and the police officers returned quickly to the street. They use temporary holding pens, which, since they are "temporary," can be designed to give the arrestees a harsh twelve, or twenty-four, or thirty-six or more hours. They issue summonses to individual demonstrators, thus stretching out both the threat to the demonstrator and the workload on the courts. Court procedures too have been streamlined.

The police have also learned more about crowd behavior and have adjusted their tactics and weapons of crowd control accordingly. They guide crowds away from sensitive points, often breaking the crowd into more manageable bits by driving parts of it into cul-de-sacs. Often these are constructed ahead of time as convenient, controllable crowd-collection points. There the police herd demonstrators into tightly packed, thus unsafe throngs so that the elderly and the handicapped, and families with children will want to leave and go home; this leaves smaller numbers of demonstrators, who then can be dealt with more harshly if the police so choose. Helicopters, prepositioned television cameras, and radio-equipped commanders give them greater tactical flexibility and allow them to gather visual evidence of lawbreaking or just to identify leaders. "Snatch squads" have been trained to break into crowds and selectively arrest key leaders or just randomly single out individuals for a roughing up and arrest. The police now carry new batons, large, transparent plastic shields, and plastic handcuffs and are equipped with water cannon and stun weapons, all to more effectively police crowds.

The police have learned from the military to control the locations and movements of reporters. "Embedded" reporters have privileged access to police commanders—and to preselected "innocent" sites—so that the story about the demonstration will favor the authorities and minimize if not positively undercut the legitimacy of the demonstrators—and any subsequent complaints about police violence. If there is to be illegal or questionable police violence, it can now be carried out away from journalists and cameras.

It is legendary that Napoleon redesigned the streets of Paris to create wide boulevards with clear fields of fire for his artillery and broad lateral avenues to permit the unimpeded movement of his cavalry to threatening trouble spots. The cumulative changes in police numbers, training, intelligence and surveillance capacities, and "riot control" tactics and equipment have a similar historical significance today.

In passing, there is one further police failing that I have not seen raised before. The normal defense of overzealous shooting by the police is that not to shoot as they did is to put themselves in some jeopardy. Forget for the moment the disingenuousness of this defense in so many actual cases. But a firefighter who refused to place his or her life at some risk to rescue an innocent person would be considered derelict in his or her duty. That risk is part of the job: the would-be firefighter knows that before the event, and we come to expect that both professional firefighters and even amateur, volunteer firefighters accept some real chance of injury, or even worse, to rescue fire victims.

It is stunning that the police do not subscribe to an analogous sense of duty. An acceptance of extra risk as a normal, expected part of one's duty would prevent a large fraction of the police shootings, which take innocent lives and sometimes those of other officers.[14]

It doesn't matter whether one attributes this failure to an alienated police culture, which risks civilian casualties for police safety or attributes it to the low skill levels of so many police and their commanders. Unfortunately, police professionals do have a high tolerance for abysmal skill levels in the ranks, and this has come to be accepted by the public and the courts. The frequent acts of heroism by the ordinary police officer on behalf of civilians exceeds what is institutionally asked of him or of her. But that points directly to the discredit of the institution as it now functions.

A new type of police institution would also demand a very different police officer. The realities and dangers of police work demand a far, far higher level of performance and judgment than we have had from the ordinary big-city police.[15] The principle here is that the life-and-death decisions that fall to the police officer on the street should be made by only the most judicious, thoughtful, almost Solomon-like sort of person. By contrast, the present-day police institution produces someone trained for only the crudest sort of police tasks, which results in low clearance rates and police misbehavior in the black districts. The inescapable conclusion is that we are accepting relatively unskilled amateurs when in fact we need highly skilled professionals. It is as if we recruited surgeons directly out of high school or junior college, gave them a smattering of training, fixed in their minds that the doctor is always right, and then sent them out to operate on patients. That the public discourse doesn't see how policing is akin to medicine, education, psychiatry, and the like is further testimony to its injudicious, imprudent, uncritical character.

The problem here stems not, I think, from the human material qualities of the average cop. The universal tale we hear now is that young women and men join the police with a very high sense of commitment to public service and an above-average education but are soon acculturated to behave like their elders.

A main and continuing source of low-quality policing is that within his or her department, the ordinary cop is too often a creature without influence in setting the very policies and priorities he or she must later carry out. The individual policeman or policewoman is at the very bottom of a very authoritarian hierarchy—which must be turned on its head. One wants a system in which the realities of street policing have direct feedback into street behavior, staffing, policy setting, training, and orientation. Now the average big-city cop is placed in a position little different from that of a raw recruit in the army, routinely told where to stand and when and how to act by his or her superiors. He or she has no real role in the conscious, critical formation of the policing he or she must actually carry out. This of itself creates an inadequate police officer. Because of the military form, the ordinary cop functions essentially as an automaton within the department. But this same person then goes out on the street, where he or she has the widest possible latitude to make life or death decisions in a split second within a world he or she has been already socialized to mistrust and even fear. It is a wonder that there is not more killing of civilians by police guns than there is.

The situation fairly cries out for a new type of police officer, who from his or her first day in the police academy is nurtured to grow into a self-supervising, responsible agent of the profession—again on the model of the other professions. Clearly the military form is a barrier to this. What one imagines is most desirable is a police officer who joins collegially with other officers and with competent, well-informed civilians in order to analyze, set, and continually adjust the standards that he or she will apply to such things as gun use, arrests, staffing issues, crime prevention and control priorities, and so on—not, I emphasize, in general but in the actual times and places where the policing is to take effect.

Obviously, one of the consequences of creating such a new, professional police officer would be to break the older police ideology, which makes the police institution into the unthinking creature of an abstract Authority.

The following set of proposals attempts to embody that sort of cooperative police/civilian policing.

The Policing Unit

To construct a more efficient and constitutionally friendly police institution, one should start at the level of actual day-to-day police operations. The opposite course is to start with the command-and-control system, but that would simply re-create the police as the obedient creatures of an authoritative hierarchy. Here, instead, the leading idea is to develop mutually informed, collegial police/policed relations. That seems likelier to break the old police culture and at the same time make for a greater capacity to deter, investigate, and catch out criminal activities.

Thus, one has to start at the operating police unit; in a big city that would be at precinct (i.e., neighborhood) level. Later we can consider how to integrate that operational unit into larger police structures.

The central design idea is that all policy, budget, training, and operational police matters *at the precinct or equivalent level* should fall under the control of a "police operations board." This board should comprise every party with a vital interest in police operations, to include first and foremost, the policed—the public—*acting through representatives chosen as we now choose juries*. Like jurors, they should be furloughed from their regular employments and activities, but unlike present juries, they should be properly paid. Authority over the police is centered on these public representatives; other board members are advisory only. These lay representatives, as I'll henceforth refer to them, should be of a number small enough to form a cohesive working group but large enough so that their internal relations still preserve a dominantly formal, not informal character. That calls for lay panels of eight to twelve persons, surely no fewer and I estimate not much larger.

Their term of service should be long enough that they can learn to control police operations and policy but not so long that their work becomes too rote and routinized. A term of three to five years seems appropriate, but experience with the new system might dictate otherwise. Lay representatives may serve more than a single term, but not consecutively. Board member terms should overlap to ensure continuity and institutional memory. Ample professional staffing has to be provided them, for I envision these lay representatives not as skating on the surface of police and criminal problems but as actually commanding and monitoring all police operations.

Next, the board should also include representatives of rank-and-file police officers from the precinct and, of course, a representative from the police command, the precinct captain or his or her designated representative. The possibly intimidating influence of the police commander can be offset somewhat by having no fewer than, say, three rank-and-file cops on the board.

The board should also include a judicial officer, that is, a representative of the court system. This is part of my larger conception, which envisions bringing the police institution into the court system and away from the influence of the legislative and executive branches of government. Borrowing a term from the past, we can refer to this court officer as a magistrate, and he or she should have judicial rank.

It is essential that the board operate under a legally enacted charter that lays out in sufficient detail its authority and the aims it is appointed to serve. An appropriate oath should be administered to each member.

I am not sure whether the district attorney's or prosecutor's office should have a representative on the board. My inclination is to incorporate such a representative, since one wants policing policy in a given time and place to have the support of all these interested parties—public, police, police command, courts, and prosecutors. It would be counterproductive if the board prioritized a certain type of crime and the DA's office prioritized another. Also, I think it a good thing to bring decisions as to what and when to prosecute more closely under the law and leave less to the discretion of district attorneys.

I envision all strategic and operational authority of these boards as resting in their lay members. The representatives of the police command, the rank and file, the magistrate, and the prosecutor's office should have only staff functions, not line authority; their function will be to advise, analyze, and inform. Their power must be important but indirect, as fits the distinction between line authority and staff support. Since this point can give rise to misapprehension, some discussion is in order.

For a start, the police command representative will normally have enormous influence over the actions of the board. If he or she is a competent, experienced, or even just forceful person, that alone will give him or her an influential voice. The problem is that he or she will have too much influence, not too little. Frankly, therefore, I see no loss to policing effectiveness for such a command representative to have only a staff role. If, on the other hand, he or she retains executive authority, that of itself both robs the rank-and-file cops of their autonomous voice and puts the board in the advisory, not operational, role I envision for it.

The autonomous role of the representatives of the rank-and-file police officers is crucial to effective policing, in two complementary ways. They are an immediate source of knowledge about the actual policing problems in the precinct, and about the continuing effects of this or that policy or operational behavior. It will be within the board that this exchange of information and viewpoint between police and policed will take place and its implications formulated into operational orders. It is here that the process of professionalizing or, better, reprofessionalizing, the rank-and-file police officer will first take place. If, as I propose, the representatives of the rank and file are also chosen by a jury panel method, we can envision a situation where each officer several times in his or her career will be forced to actively shape law enforcement, police/civilian relationships, the whole gamut of police work, as a responsible agent and not, as now, merely an automaton. Like others on the board, police representatives should be administered an appropriate oath of office, which obligates them to their board responsibilities and, not incidentally, should inhibit retaliation against them by unhappy police commanders or comrades.

Parenthetically, I do not see that this new police institution requires a wholesale turnover of existing police officers. The essence of the jury system is the fact that one can place ordinary people in deeply responsible posts and most will grow to fit the requirements. Of course, the faults of present-day policing are not entirely independent of the sort of men and women in the police ranks. From the nature of the case, at least some who are attracted to today's police institution are attracted because they like its faults, its authoritarian qualities, perhaps, and many policemen and women are already deeply immersed in illegal and other misbehavior. Some will change to meet the new situation, and some will not. The latter shouldn't even be on the police payroll now, and the former should be given every opportunity and even assistance to enable them to function well in the new police institution.

At the same time that one doesn't want rank-and-file police to be overawed or intimidated by their commander, one also doesn't want the lay members to "pass the buck" to the professionals. Lay people must take responsibility; since they will be in intimate working contact with police professionals, it is hard to imagine that they will not often defer to them and, in time, learn when to defer and when not. The point is that there is little chance in this police institution for lay members simply to police in ignorance of the dangers and opportunities faced by their professional colleagues on the Board with whom they will be conferring face-to-face. Here too the ethos of the juror places responsibility squarely on the lay person, and our experience of juries is that many if not most will take that responsibility very seriously.

It is obviously essential that the board have authority over personnel and budget decisions. As I envision the matter, the current police command-and-control system would more or less remain in place, but it would serve only technical and advisory staff functions and not, as now, command ones. In an effective working board, the police hierarchy could propose budgets, recommend personnel for promotions and assignments, and so on, subject to the approval of the lay members. One important interface here would be the person of the board's chief of staff, who in the spirit of the new police institutions should not be a police professional.

As I think must already be clear, these are not police review boards; they are operational control boards whose authority includes the formulation of policies, priorities, and even the actual orders that govern the everyday behavior of each officer on the street today and tomorrow. There are many laws on the books, and there is always a question of which will have priority of enforcement. In one precinct it may be that pickpockets and muggers should receive priority now, in another bank, robbery or domestic violence. The matter under review might be as elementary as to how to quiet young people on the street on a summer's night or how to police and protect against an increase in sexual assaults. The idea is that the board must aggressively follow policing problems and give positive, decisive guidance as to how they are to be addressed.

Implicit in this scheme is the idea that the board will positively control how and when shooting and other forms of force will be employed, and with what safeguards both for the policed and the police themselves. One of the reasons for choosing a jury panel selection system and incorporating a court officer on the panel is to make sure that these difficult decisions are made in a considered way within a positive legal framework.

A board should not just be what old-time union people called a "talking shop." Each member should be rotated to each shift in the precinct, or to one of its special squads, such as robbery or homicide, meeting as frequently with the police officers concerned as the situation calls for, both formally and informally, with groups and with individual police officers, so as to serve as a conduit for a reliable, up-to-date, relevant information flow to the rest of the board. I think, too, that such hands-on contact should both sober and embolden board members so that they will be less likely either to act like gods legislating from far above or, alternatively, timid creatures led by the professionals.

Larger police structures should be built up from these elements. This new form of police organization will of course require the devolution of many police functions and authority out into the precincts and the neighborhoods. This would be a positive gain, since the long effort to centralize police departments under their chiefs has not really achieved what earlier reformers promised. My initial proposal would be to replace the entire present police command-and-control structure with "operational police boards," dividing authority between center and periphery as is functionally called for and within the larger ethos of the new police system. Thus, wherever one sees a pressing need for, say, a uniform citywide policy or priority, that would fall to a citywide board. Of course, center/periphery conflicts would constantly emerge, but it does not seem organizationally impossible to imagine that solutions can be found, adjusted, readjusted, and even readjusted again and again until, as they say, "one gets it right." But the overriding priority is to place operational and policy control over day-to-day policing as close as possible to the policing itself.

Civic Obligations

A colleague has commented that it is impractical to ask lay members to give the time commitment to board affairs that the proposal requires. Experience argues otherwise. Thousands of Americans now serve on local school and library boards, and in volunteer fire departments and voluntary emergency service units, all of which require heavy time obligations. In the latter cases it is readily accepted that the volunteer will undergo periodic, sometimes even arduous technical and physical training sessions and will keep her- or himself up to date on changes in doctrine and technique. It is also understood by volunteers, employers, and the public that when the bell sounds, the firefighter or emergency service worker will respond immediately and for as long as necessary.

On the other hand, police board membership would take up more time, say, than is required of a captain of volunteer firefighters or chief of emergency service workers. Perhaps on the model of the National Guard and the Reserve forces, board members would be required to serve, say, one day per week, perhaps even full time. They should be reimbursed more rather than less generously, the amount corresponding to the important responsibilities falling to them and not to what they earn in civilian life. Similarly, their jobs/careers/seniority outside the board would have to be protected, as well as such things as pension and other benefit plans. None of these things are particularly arcane or even, considering the importance of the boards, very expensive.

It may be that board service will have to fully occupy a span of years, but if we understand the necessity sometimes of drafting young people for national security purposes, the same reasoning should apply to drafting all adult age groups for security on our streets and in our homes.

Board service should not be a career in and of itself. As with juries, the member is called to serve, serves, and then like Cincinnatus returns to private life. One wants board service to be considered an exceptionally important and prestigious task, a civic obligation that the normal citizen would be proud to assume, as traditional jury service should be, or military service, even if it does get in the way of other things both personal and professional. A positive civic effort should be made to ensure that those who have served a term on a board are recognized as having given an especially valuable and often difficult service to the community.

We accord that recognition to veterans of the armed services, even offering them special civic awards and rewards, sometimes a special tax status, educational assistance, and so forth. It might be that immediately at the end of board service a paid sabbatical leave would allow the member to "brush up" in his or her professional field or even just to catch up with family and, especially, other civic life.

All in all, it is desirable that the board member be placed in a personal, financial, and civic position to give his or her best attention to police board duties, and then to follow that up with a system of appropriate civic honors and even some material advantages.

It is hard to foresee precisely the civic and other structures necessary to complement board service, but it is evident that we as a society have a wide range of nonutopian options to explore and the prospect of learning over time which are apt and which are not.

The Jury Panel Method for Selecting Police Board Members

There are good reasons why members of a police board should be selected by the jury panel method and not elected or appointed. Direct election to the police boards is among the worst ways to fill such important posts, for reasons we have already discussed. Among them are the following: Elections often turn on the votes of the least informed voters and lead to rule by minorities. Once elected, representatives are no longer representative. The more competitive the elections, the more elected officials are inclined to shunt their responsibilities off into inner government, here the police professionals, and attend to the problem of getting reelected.

Very often elections are little more than a form of power struggle between opposed factions. That's hardly a good formula for the control of police work.

Electing the boards would be ignoring the lessons of the previous generation of reformers, who found that the local election of police officials was tantamount to placing power in the hands of those who had a pecuniary interest in how the police operate. On the basis of experience, local elections for police board members would often lead to undue influence over the police by those interested in using the police for political purposes and those profiting from illegal activity.

There is another possible danger to the electoral route. In the late 1960s New York City wanted to expand the influence of parents over the schools. To that end they introduced direct elections for local school boards. Some of these elected boards came to be controlled by people who wanted an inside route to the busing contract, or to sell paint or school supplies, or wanted the cleaning contract or even to control the jobs of the security staff. All sorts of people who didn't even have children in the system ran for the school boards either because, as above, they wanted to make some money off the post or because they wanted to get a leg up on plans for higher public office.

More instructive from our point of view was that in many districts the teachers union combined its own special interests and its money to win control of the local board. But this made a mockery of the initial impulse for locally elected school boards, namely, to give parents an equal voice with teachers and other education professionals in educational policy. On this model, too many local police boards would fall to the group with the most intense practical stake in their makeup and policies, who have lots of interested activists, and a union war chest—the police themselves.

Police unions have had an ambivalent effect on policing. Police unions were prohibited in my grandfather's days on the New York City force, and his pay kept him a poor man and limited his ability, among other things, to help in his children's education. Police trade unions, which really only came into their own in the 1960s, have succeeded in making police work a well-paid, at least materially attractive profession. But, with some notable exceptions, they have also served to deepen the defensive police culture, have been too ready to defend both criminal police officers and criminally bad policing, and have too frequently thrown their support to the most authoritarian, militaristic, right-wing political candidates.

Thus, it is hard to see that an electoral model would lead to either more efficient policing of crime or a more constitutionally friendly police institution. We would likely have all of the faults and few of the virtues of the present system. I anticipate that police control of the police boards would be the most likely outcome of direct elections. For that reason alone, "democratic means" are almost certainly the least desirable way to choose the boards.

But there is also a genuine quandary here. Existing police unions are perhaps likely at first to block the full professionalization of the police, on more or less the same conventional trade-unionist grounds that led some teacher unions to resist rather than advance the professional formation of their members. On the other hand, eventual union support would be requisite for the full flowering of the police professionalization here proposed. In the last analysis, the prospect of greater professional autonomy, higher status, higher salaries, and more effective policing should tend to weaken, though not erase, the opposition of even the most narrow-minded police union.

Direct appointment of board members would be no better. In a big city that would mean appointment by the mayor, the city council, or some other citywide authority. But this of itself would go some considerable way toward replicating the present overcentralized control of the police, hence a continuation of and not an end to their alienation from the policed and a preservation of defensive police culture. In addition, given the intrinsic importance of policing, there would undoubtedly be calls to appoint "not just anyone" to the board. The business community and other notables would insist on a "blue ribbon" board, which is to say, direct control by existing elites on the familiar model of how, at the national level, we select members of the Federal Reserve or directors of Central Intelligence.

Or perhaps the mayor or someone else with appointment authority would be inclined to use the police boards for patronage, to appoint his (or her) friends and supporters—a scheme redolent of official corruption, favoritism, and, since the police so often organize and help supervise balloting, even election fraud. In short, offered only the alternatives of control of the police by elected officials or direct election of the board, I'd be inclined to stick to the present system.

But, more important, there are positive arguments for the jury panel selection method of filling police operational control boards. A jury panel selection system would be far more representative of the policed community than a system of direct election. Persons of every walk of life, of every ethnic and religious group, of every educational attainment, rich and poor, young and old, would come to serve a term or two on the boards. Over time the boards would mirror the diversity of views and interests of the policed community and in that literal sense be representative of them.

Furthermore, the boards would not be composed of members forced to bow to the whims of public opinion. One of the strongest attractions of the jury panel system of selection is that the boards, like judges and juries in criminal or civil trials, would be free of the need to bow to outside pressures and thus able, as they have sworn, to turn their own best judgment to the most serious of duties. Of course, both fools and knaves would get to serve on the boards, a condition not absent from the other possible ways of selecting boards, which we've already rejected. But part of the genius of the jury system as we've experienced it is that even the fools and knaves have to persuade the rest of the jury panel, most of whom will in the normal course of events be trying to act judiciously. Of course, no human institution is infallible, but our experience with the jury panel system is that it has proven the most reliable way for citizens to protect each other's rights both from government and from one another. I think that those who have been privileged to serve on juries generally—not always—praise not only the seriousness with which jurors undertake their duties but also their judiciousness in deciding such profound matters as jailing the possibly innocent, freeing the possibly guilty, or even taking another's life.

The finite term of the police board, three to five years, gives the members time to grow into their duties, but not enough time to become permanent powers in the community. One does one's duty and then simply returns to private life—at least as far as influence over the police is concerned. Over time, of course, as the number of people who have served on these boards grows—both police and civilians—they will serve as a leaven within the community for more knowledgeable, less conflicted relations between the police and policed. That, of course, is in line with the primary intent of the whole scheme, to create a policing institution that is at one with its community and the Constitution and not, as so often now, an occupying authority.

First, jurors almost universally take their duties extremely seriously. In postverdict interviews one frequently hears jurors say things like "I believed he was guilty but there was not enough evidence to convict him." Or, as in a recent capital case in Massachusetts, "I really wanted to find him insane [so as to avoid imposing a death penalty—JM] but the testimony for that finding just wasn't strong enough." Statements like these, which, as I say, are typical of postverdict juries, don't show that juries are infallible, or always wise, But they do show that jurors are thoughtful, aware of their legal and moral obligations, and try to minimize the influence of their own private values and feelings in order to reach genuinely responsible judgments. These are precisely the qualities that should be embedded in the police operations boards.

The other two traits are equally apposite. As many have pointed out, during the late 1960s and early 1970s the federal government pursued a campaign of harassing indictments against many of the activists of the political movements of the time. Some considerable government effort and expense and a great deal of newspaper and politician comment supported this campaign. Yet the prevailing view among those attorneys I've talked with who defended in this sort of case was that in almost every instance juries refused to convict, and the postverdict statements by the jurors were very much of the tenor of the criminal-case jurors just cited, save one in particular: the jurors tended to mistrust and disapprove on constitutional grounds the government's campaign to silence its critics, and that fact materially affected their verdicts. This is a doubly impressive record, since the government tried to locate trials in jurisdictions likely to yield juries socially and politically alienated from those on trial.

The third point I'd make seems prima facie to argue against the whole scheme: American juries have been notoriously disinclined to bring in guilty verdicts against police officers, as in the Rodney King case in Los Angeles in 1992, when there was a videotape showing the police both kicking and clubbing a prone, nonresisting King. One can actually sharpen this point somewhat. For about a decade now, I've been particularly following police stories in the press. One great feature stands out: jurors are disinclined to convict police officers charged with shooting violations against civilians or with other kinds of violence against civilians—if by any stretch of the imagination that police behavior can be seen as a matter of legitimate self-defense or an expression of legitimate police authority. As we know, the abuses that follow from this reluctance to convict police officers are legend, especially in police dealing with minorities, the poor, young people, and dissidents.

Without being Pollyannaish, one can also see a positive side to this tendency, namely, that the public, as expressed through its juries, understands that police work is dangerous, that many who run afoul of the police are themselves dangerous, and that one has therefore to give the benefit of the doubt to the police officer on the street. That's a commendable realism, and one often exercised by juries drawn from communities that are most often mistreated by the police. The misfortune here comes not from citizen attitudes but from the organization, orientation, ideology, and culture of the contemporary police institution, which forces juries to make the stark, abstract choice between second-guessing the police officer after the fact or giving a relatively blanket endorsement of whatever he or she does. A police system organized under the operating boards here proposed would not only in the first instance lessen unwonted police violence, shootings, and the like, but also over time make for a citizenry and criminal juries willing and able to make more informed, more judicious, less starkly abstract decisions about police officers charged with misuse of their authority.

In the final analysis, a jury panel system offers a way of dealing with both the need for and the threat offered by the police. The workings and rationale of juries are already understood by the Democracy. The jury is an institution that is almost sacralized by its longevity and its historic effectiveness in checking government misbehavior. Very large numbers of our people have served on juries, so that a jury panel proposal for police boards is something that lies within their experience and will have at least an initial understanding, perhaps even sympathetic reception. The jury panel method of selecting police board members seems to me to be not only superior to all of the alternatives we've discussed so far but also a reasoned response to the many civic, criminal, and constitutional faults of each of those alternatives.

Legislative Priorities

In this country one often hears the expression "A government of laws, not of men," and yet the latitude given both the police and the districts attorney seems too little constrained by actual legal control. In my view, the policing institution here proposed should be supplemented by legislation more closely defining both the duties and the limits of both police officers and district attorneys.[16]

The police should be a branch of the courts, their rights and duties stemming from that and not, as at present, with the courts running to catch up with what they actually do and the ways they actually behave. In most states the police are ultimately an arm of the legislature, although they may more directly fall under local jurisdictions. But, as we have argued, this implies that the police are normally a creature of minorities. I've long thought it an anomaly that the police, in the last instance charged with enforcement of our laws, are not considered to be part of the courts. The police tendency to interpret "law and order" in an abstract, authoritarian way is not unrelated to this separation from the courts. It is highly desirable that the average police officer should view her- or himself as a judicial official charged not only with enforcing "the law" but also with advising about which laws should be on the books. Legislators are too prone to passing laws that are barely if at all enforceable—prohibition, once of alcohol and now of drugs, comes especially to mind—with the result that the police officer on the streets is too often made to police the unpoliceable.

The tension between enacted law and the assent of those who fall under it is a classic problem for the legislator and one that, if ignored, extracts a heavy price from the polity and society. To lessen that tension one wants to encourage a judicially conscious law enforcement and do away with the abstract authoritarianism the present arrangements encourage in the police. In that same vein, it is always an important issue how sternly a given law, even a good one, should be enforced; one cannot arrest every speeder and doesn't want to. Speed laws are basically enforced by drivers themselves in that by their restraint they separate out the reckless speeders for police attention. All in all, my argument is that a better policing institution would at the same time help make for better laws and, in the long run, a more law-abiding citizenry.

Similarly, it seems extraordinary that district attorneys, in practice if not in law, have so much leeway in choosing which cases they will prosecute and which they will ignore. In both cases, there should be closer legislative prescription, not only to correct this hole in our "government of laws, not of men" but also to create a barrier between the police and prosecutorial practices of the discredited past and those of a reformed future.

The final point I would make is that we need to break the near identification, traditional in the present police institution, between criminal behavior and dissident political behavior. That step would, I believe, inhibit the police from helping to prop up whatever "authority" currently claims legitimacy. The analogy I have in mind is that famous wall between church and state. What one wants to see develop is a body of law, an institutional culture, and a changed police practice that would give the benefit of the doubt to political behavior that *might* lead to the breaking of the criminal law. At present, the police, district attorneys, and other authorities use that possibility to justify monitoring dissident and other reform groups. On the wide-open proposition that government "has the right to self-defense," it is not unusual for police of local, state, and federal jurisdictions to break into the offices of such groups, taking membership lists, stealing office equipment, and disrupting their internal functioning through penetration agents, informers, and such like. In addition, the police are inclined to make harassing arrests, as of leaders at demonstrations. Governments, especially the federal government, have often in the past pursued a strategy of neutralizing dissident groups through nuisance indictments, thus compelling them to redirect their funds into legal-defense expenditures. What one wants to do is to make such tactics both intolerable and illegal.

This discussion now takes on added weight. Under the misnamed Patriot Act, the opportunities and the inclination for the federal government to do more political policing have been expanded.

There should be legislation offering special and unique protection to every sort of political activity. From a technical point of view that does not seem such a large order, since one can tie the whole matter to the legal protections currently in place for voting. A body of legislation presumptively barring both the police and prosecutors from interfering with activities *by individuals* linked to persuading voters on virtually any question likely to appear on a ballot would accomplish most of what is needed here. Note that there is no protection here for any activity that is de facto criminal or fraudulent; what one wants specifically to block is the self-serving assumption on the part of "the authorities" that because one is critical of this or that public policy, one is thereby more likely to break the law and therefore must be monitored by the police. I lack the legal knowledge to formulate the desired changes, but the legislative aim is clear enough: to make an effective distinction between crimes actually planned or committed in a political context and a political context in which crimes *might* be committed.

But More Is Needed

No legislative, or even constitutional, "wall" in aid of a transformed police power can be sufficient by itself. It must be supplemented by direct civilian control over the police. Long experience shows that, left to its own devices, the police power will chip away, if not definitely sweep away, both law and Constitution when it feels that "law and order"—the abstraction, not the statutes—are under threat from either the left side of society or "the dangerous classes." Recent experience should etch that into our consciousness—and include in its scope the behavior of the several federal intelligence and security agencies.

A "war on terror," like the old wars against communist subversion, is a diabolical conception because, by its very nature, it muddies criminal behavior with dissident political behavior in ways that the courts cannot well distinguish. The old war against "subversion" nominally targeted communists as agents of a foreign power, but the communist activities that Trumanism/McCarthyism mostly prevented were the legal ones, as well as a great deal of legitimate citizen opposition to the cold war policies and nuclear gambling of the U.S. government.[17]

It also led to serious constitutional abuses by the FBI and the Justice Department as a whole, and even by prosecutors and judges, most notoriously in the trial of Ethel and Julius Rosenberg. Excluding the defense attorneys, the judge met secretly with the prosecution team to discuss the case. Though believing Ethel Rosenberg innocent, they allowed a guilty verdict to be brought in against her and stood by as she was later executed. They had hoped that her death sentence would pressure Julius Rosenberg to identify his associates. Fearful that a gallant President Eisenhower would reduce a death sentence against a woman, the prosecution misinformed the president that she was no bystander, as they actually believed, but was the actual leader of the spy ring (Adams 1961). *Then they allowed her execution to go ahead after her husband Julius had already died in the electric chair.*

We are still paying for the political demobilization of workers and others on the lower end of the economy brought about by the anti-red campaign. The plain truth is that the police power used the war against subversion to pursue other, illicit ends and, moreover, prioritized those other ends over the hunt for actual spies. In retrospect, the anti-red crusade seemed to function mostly as an excuse for bigger budgets and patriotic posturing, and an expansion of the police power with a lessening of control by "outsiders."

Something like the same effects are being played out today in the war on terrorism. Persons with Arab-sounding names are now often stopped and interrogated when they board airplane flights, and occasionally even when they board a train. Nominally illegal immigrants are routinely swept up and detained, often for lengthy periods, or deported before they can muster legal counsel, this arbitrariness justified as a way of protecting the rest of us against the "threat of terrorism." On the other hand, the domestic war against actual terrorism features bumbling similar to what we saw in the anti-red crusade. Airport security personnel are regularly tested on their ability to detect and prevent guns or explosives from being smuggled aboard airplane flights; as we know from the press, detection fails as often as it succeeds. Happily, the antiterrorism boondoggle is so large, so vast, and so well, if wastefully, funded that the odds favor some degree of effectiveness against a terrorist bomb or a terrorist gun. But its major successes to date have been in its effects on domestic politics—encouraging anti-Arab, anti-Muslim, and anti-immigrant sentiments; encouraging vigilante behavior at the U.S.-Mexican border; expanding the immigration and security police; spending vast sums on testing equipment; expanding federal holding facilities; funding a major private prison industry devoted to holding ostensibly illegal immigrants in typically poor, sometimes life-threatening conditions; and last but not least, undermining the right of habeas corpus.

This "war against terror" has also given birth to legal findings that put many presidential activities beyond the reach of *any* law. It has extended electronic snooping and photographing and encouraged a geometrical expansion of covert government criminal activities such as "rendition," kidnappings, maintenance of secret prisons around the world, and administratively sanctioned killings of suspected terrorists overseas by "smart bombs" and drone aircraft.

From the nature of the case, this illegal "spillage" has proven virtually impossible for legislators and the courts to limit, much less prevent. Even well-written laws and well-reasoned court decisions have been stretched to provide cover for activity that eventually goes beyond the bounds of legality.

Controlling the misbehavior of federal agencies like the CIA, the Defense Intelligence Agency, and the National Security Agency poses special problems. It does not seem either practical or of pressing importance to have board-like management at the lower, that is, operative levels, save perhaps for the Immigration and Naturalization Service, which seems currently out of control. There we do seem to find common instances of rogue and other kinds of misbehavior, as by overzealous agents out in the field and, especially, by poorly trained, poorly supervised prison guards.

But in the CIA, DIA, NSA, and the like, the problems lie further up the chain of command, at the policy level and among the higher managers. There, at the uppermost levels, an operations board chosen by the jury panel method is wildly overdue. The safeguards that have been installed in the past, such as congressional oversight committees on intelligence matters and a special court to limit electronic eavesdropping have not kept those "secret" agencies within the bounds of law. Here I think the problem is threefold. It is undoubtedly the case that Congress has wanted only enough supervision to keep the worst-case intelligence agency abuses from embarrassing them politically. It really wants to wink at most even illegal snooping.

Then, too, there are political persons and forces in the United States, now including one whole wing of the Republican Party, for whom "national security," or some other such Baal, ranks well above constitutionality and legality. It is also in the nature of the case that such persons and forces will tend to cluster within the police, security, and intelligence services, or be socialized by them, where, justified by their own ideology, protected by the generally secret nature of their work, and covered by their political party and journalistic allies, they will continue to subvert our institutions. One must keep this constantly in mind. It is normal for there to be large numbers of persons in the intelligence and related services whose bizarre conception of patriotic "duty" *demands* that they not allow the Congress to limit or even to know about what they do. The secret, sometimes clandestine nature of the work they do serves as an invitation to go their own way, and the record is that they often do precisely that.

Finally, those officials who serve on congressional oversight committees and the special intelligence courts must come to understand the special nature of intelligence work, where not "going by the books," "wide latitude," in short, soft control, seems requisite. That means that the restraints that are periodically reimposed by Congress become looser and looser over time, so that eventually the policies and practices of the intelligence agencies—like, for example, Bush II's open-ended surveillance of telephone and Internet traffic, both international and domestic—escape all control. The regular courts have proved too tardy and too permissive in their rulings on this sort of thing, and the members of Congress have learned that interfering with these agencies can backfire. The old Church committee exposed a whole raft of illegal intelligence agency activities. It was no coincidence that Senator Frank Church was defeated at the next election by a very well funded challenger. The "intelligence community," like the police institution, has powerful friends that make them power players in our politics too.[18]

The problem that has to be mastered is that no court can precisely and imperatively distinguish legal from illegal behavior without inhibiting some needed administrative flexibility by the intelligence and security services. But that same flexibility is an invitation to abuses, and, as we have seen, such abuses regularly grow into threats to the constitutional order. The efficacious remedy is direct civilian restraint on these federal agencies through oversight boards staffed via the jury panel method. That would of itself limit the "socializing" that over time reduces congressional oversight to a rubber stamp. In this case, as perhaps more than in other uses of the board modality, its members would be especially sworn to defend the integrity of our constitutional and legal provisions, especially sworn to guard against the "creep" that congressional oversight and court reviews have proved unable to prevent. It is, of course, unlikely that such boards could entirely rein in the intelligence and security services, but they could make sure that the most dangerous abuses and those stemming from upper management are sooner and better curbed. The larger, remaining problem, to be addressed in a later chapter, is to limit ahead of time the ability, particularly of the executive, to get us into unnecessary international security scrapes in the first place.

The issues raised by the evolution of the modern police power, including here also the intelligence and security services, are of the gravest possible nature. It is a plausible thesis that there has been an accumulated growth in the power-political relations of the police over the policed and of the security services over the polity at least as dramatic as, again, that brought about by Napoleon's redesign of Paris. The modern police per se are an institutional legacy left us by the regimes of old Europe, as much a product of the infamous spirit of the Congress of Vienna as the restoration of the Bourbons. Then and still, the foremost duty of the police—not their everyday duty but foremost duty—is to serve authority and check the aspirations of what they used to call the *canaille* and we call the Democracy. Moreover, as we have shown, they have been and are far more effective at that than at checking and rolling back criminal activity—or communist spies or international terrorists.

I believe that there is a relatively broad public that wants a radically different and more effective institution directed against, especially, criminal activities. This public includes not only civil libertarians and the black and other minority communities but many in the FBI itself, in the legal profession,[19] and in the other professions dealing with public policy. And it includes many police professionals who are only too aware of alienation between the police and the policed and the corrosive effect this has on the ability of the police to fight crime effectively. The material conditions exist for major policing reforms; if not the reforms proposed here, then others perhaps equally far-reaching. In that sense, to want to introduce radical changes in the institution of the police is neither utopian nor "idealistic." Such changes are feasible and, given the long-term trend in the power-political relations between the police and the policed, of the very highest priority.

9

CIVILIZING THE CORPORATION

If there is to be renewal of the historic advance, the vast social and other powers of the modern corporation must be channeled to ends supportive of the Democracy and not, as at present, so often opposed to them. We need to free society from excessive, centralized institutional power. In economics especially, we need to be rid of the conception of "the market" that irresponsibly confuses General Everything Everywhere, Inc., with Gus the neighborhood grocer. In short, we need to civilize the corporation.

All of the reform proposals being put forward are needed to achieve a more tolerable society. But the modern corporation is at the center of the institutional alliance I have been calling the Intersection, and unless it can be tamed, none of the other reforms will have their desired effect. Some of that urgency will already be familiar to the reader, some perhaps less so. Let me begin by saying that we need to go beyond the triad of familiar alternatives—the free market, government regulation, and government ownership. I think that by now we should be well aware of the defects of each.

People in this country are, if anything, hyperaware of the defects of government ownership, undoubtedly fearing even more defects than there actually are. For kindred reasons, the electorate has been cool to expanded government regulation over corporate behavior, although this attitude is currently (early 2009) changing under the threat of a collapsing economy.

Actually, there is a long history of government regulation of the modern corporation on behalf of the public good, and until the 1960s it was widely thought successful. With the revival of free-market ideology from the 1970s onward, government regulatory schemes have come under a cloud.

This public skepticism was justified, but not for the reasons that then came into favor. As government regulatory agencies get older, they become the servants not of the public but of the businesses they were supposed to regulate. This is why today the EPA covers for the biggest polluters, and the Federal Reserve for the most reckless lenders. The more one examines the dynamics of this process in which government stops being the gamekeeper and starts helping the poachers, the more one is convinced that a program of long-term, effective government regulation of the corporations can't be sustained.[1]

As for the free market option, corporate villainies have been frequent enough and their social harm serious enough that it makes no sense to still believe in the virtues of a "free, competitive market" that in fact consists of one to three hundred collaborating firms acting in the interests of perhaps 5 percent of the U.S. population and perhaps 0.005 percent of the world's.

There is another, fourth option that will bring the behavior of all significant-sized corporations into a law-like framework. It envisions a novel economic government of laws, not men, an economy subordinate to positive legal enactments and not those evanescent "laws of the market." It would lead to an economy considerably freer and more democratically decentralized than is now permitted by our elites, and one more responsive to a wider range of values and needs than is permitted by the insiders and free riders who currently govern our economic life.

Our initial focus is on matters internal to the United States and the other developed countries; this material should be "under our belt" before we examine and make proposals for some changes in the international economic and political order.

The Corporation as Society Maker

An older, now classic literature about regulating the corporation assumed that it was simply one more institution *within* society, more powerful than most but with *disintegrative* effects on it. Accordingly, the strategic conception was prevention. But as we examine the modern history of the relationship between society and the corporation, the idea that corporations exist *within* society seems less and less cogent. The corporations have created a new society in which they themselves are the pivotal and paradigmatic institutions.

Consider that at the beginning of the corporate era in the 1870s, most of the U.S. population lived in rural areas and small towns, not in cities. By 1920, that had been reversed, not least through the growth of an urban, corporatized economy. Then, as if to underline the social power of the corporations, urbanization was reversed again as masses of people followed the big employers from the cities to the suburbs. Corporate behavior was not the only causative factor here, but it surely was among the most important.

Most of the things we now buy and use were actually created and brought to mass use by corporate firms. Gasoline, autos of course, electronic devices of every sort, artificial fabrics, frozen foods, almost all pharmaceuticals, modern paints and dyes, disposable diapers, plastics generally, telecommunications, credit cards, and so on and so on. These have fundamentally reshaped everyday social material life. Meanwhile, in the worlds of high culture, of books, periodicals, architecture, art, design, dance, and music, corporate influence is, if not everywhere dominant, then certainly everywhere significant.

The expansion of government has also been influenced by the corporations, sometimes to contain them, more often—conservative dogma notwithstanding—at their behest. Big government is the natural partner of big corporations, whether to fund technological change, subsidize major industries through "corporate welfare," deter the formation of unions and hold down wages, develop forests and other natural resources for private exploitation, or simply "assist" firms, such as the oil giants, overseas.

Corporations have absorbed so many occupations that most of us are now their employees and not free artisans or professionals. A century and a half ago most of us would have been in occupations that used traditional technologies and skills. These technologies and skills have largely disappeared from the public realm. Largely because of corporate influences, too, the percentage of women in the workforce has climbed from about 15 percent to over 50 percent, and whereas in the past they were predominantly young women awaiting marriage, they now include a cross-section of age groups, including a large cohort of mothers of school-age and even preschool children.

The division of labor between master and servant in, say, agriculture, industry, forestry, and fishing seemed at one time eternal and universal. All of these realms now utilize more or less the same three-way corporate division of labor. Before, say, 1890, there was no extensive managerial class and the corporate division of labor hardly existed. Now that division of labor governs the class structure of every modern society. It defines what we mean by a modern, developed society.[2] And of course, the number of the professions has had a quantum leap.

The modern corporation is not really a thing-maker, it is a society-maker. Soon after it came into existence, it became the vanguard of technological, demographic, and social changes that have created a new historical type of society. For the most part what we do, consume, know about, think; how we love; where we reside; how we dress, eat, entertain ourselves, travel; the social esteem we receive or are denied; and the mix of our obligations and our privileges are for most of us linked to our role or prospective role in a corporatized economy. One cannot exaggerate the extent of this or the radical nature of the change from the way things were before the development of corporate economy. Even the old warrior ethos built upon notions of honor was, as we saw, overcome by the corporate-produced armaments of, chiefly, the United States.

But there is even more. A few big media corporations determine what topics are covered by the news, how deeply they are covered, how the news is "spun" or slanted, and to whom it is addressed. These things are now determined by a few corporate media executives acting not as journalistic professionals but as providers of potential audiences to corporate marketers. This is actually a more serious problem than overt political slanting by the news media. Political slanting still treats the worlds of politics and public policy as serious, integral subjects in their own right. But presently the news has to compete with other "entertainment shows" for space on the tube or the dial. News programs have to justify themselves commercially by drawing more listeners than, say, sporting events or game shows. It is thus that auto accidents, particularly bloody crimes and petty sex scandals, none of which help the voting public govern itself, crowd out information and opinion about public policy.

The reversal of the relationship between business firm and society emphasizes the importance of civilizing the corporations. It is no longer enough to conceive of "reforming the corporations" in the older sense that society should prevent some of their behavior, to wit, whatever behavior is hostile to other social institutions or to other social values. In a strategic and longer historical sense, a modest conception of *reform* simply misses the point. We must *refound* our key institutions, especially the corporate firms, placing them on new and different moral, political, and legal foundations.

Progressivism and Liberalism Miscalculate

The progressive surge of the late nineteenth and early twentieth centuries, which later took the form of the New Deal/Fair Deal liberalism of FDR and Harry Truman, tried to reform "the Trusts," "Monopoly," "Big Business," "the Moguls," "Malefactors of Great Wealth," and so on. It is useful to take a closer look at that attempt.

The Progressives eventually deployed a three-pronged strategy of reforms; in retrospect, we can see not only that the strategy failed but why it did so. The first prong was to bring the corporations under government regulation. Initiated by the Bureau of Corporations under Theodore Roosevelt, it later came to include the antitrust efforts of the Department of Justice, the creation of the Federal Reserve System, and so on, all later supplemented by the "alphabet-soup" agencies of FDR's New Deal. Among the most important of these was the Security and Exchange Commission (SEC), founded in 1933, and, two years later, the National Labor Relations Board (NLRB).

A second, though later prong was to encourage what John Kenneth Galbraith called "countervailing institutions," of which the most important were labor unions (Galbraith 1952). The leading idea here was that the unions would counterbalance the corporations and thereby extend to the employee, hence the consumer too, economic equality.

The reformers had great hopes for the then-new social sciences, notably professional economics research, social statics, later sociology, and the new social science–based professions such as social work, urban planning, public health, and so on. Scientific objectivity, based on competent, unbiased research, would provide reliable information and a critical spirit in the public's dealing with corporate behavior and its near and distant social effects.[3] It was thought that the SEC would keep track of corporate misbehavior, study objectively just what remedies were needed, and then apply them with scientific detachment. Alternatively, the Department of Labor offered labor a voice within government but not merely the voice of biased trade union officials. Armed by the results of objective industrial investigation, it would have a power sufficient to ensure a more equitable and yet peaceful relationship between labor and management, with the public being the net beneficiary.

There is a very complex history to why these and other progressive/liberal reforms became undone. That they have been undone is a certainty. The SEC, as we know from the headlines, simply withdrew, prior to 2008, from regulating securities markets, which, with its encouragement, fell into reckless gambling. Kindred shifts in loyalty and advocacy have marked the other federal regulatory agencies, signaling, I believe, the broader strategic failure of the effort to regulate big business.

Moreover, the effort to regulate big business failed in part because knowledge became allied to power and not its challenger. The corporations have developed the expertise to win out over the progressives and their experts within the SEC and over the labor partisans within the Labor Department. There are other factors in corporate influence over government, such as providing campaign funds, threats to depart to other locales, the large army of corporate cadre who reliably vote corporate interests, and so forth. But my stress on social science and technological expertise links our discussion to earlier, ultimately unsuccessful efforts at reform.

The unbiased social science expected by the progressives has been transmogrified into the well-funded social science pleading of the corporate sector. Most professional economists are ideologically sympathetic to big business, and a very large cohort of them, including many of the most distinguished, work within industry or within the industry-leaning "think tanks." That's also true of sociologists, urban planners, in fact of the whole range of disciplines that the progressive/liberal movements thought would check, not abet, corporate social misbehavior.

It is important to understand the rich history that turned knowledge into a servant of power. But here we can sum up that history by reiterating what I think is the central and guiding point: in our society most wealth is created within corporate firms. That wealth is the font not only of economic change but, as we saw, of profound and continuing social and cultural changes as well. The reformers didn't fully anticipate the effect of this. Progressives and their first cousins, Europe's social democrats, accepted as "natural" the idea that how and where that wealth was created was a matter of economics, technology, and private property, processes best left to the businessman. Only when that wealth was obviously misused were they willing to intervene—not sooner—with regulations, even the (rare) substitution of state ownership for private enterprise.[4]

But once wealth is created, it becomes a force in its own right, as easily employed to buy up the media as to pioneer new technologies, as likely to induce changes in where people live as to produce cloth more cheaply. Wealth can be diverted from investor dividends to political uses so as to protect and extend those investor interests. Then, too, government itself is utterly dependent on the taxes that corporations and corporate employees pay. Thus, interference with corporate prosperity, no matter how gained, is itself a threat to the government's own interests.

Meanwhile, corporate-induced social changes have made government need even more in the way of tax dollars than it did before the corporate era. The unions are similarly compromised. When both the nation's jobs and its retirement funds rest on corporate prosperity, a threat to the corporations is a threat to those workers and those retirees as well. One could go on, but the central point is very powerful and sweeping. Once wealth has been created within the ambit of the private corporation, it locates the potential for overwhelming political, economic, social, cultural, informational, and even "scientific" *initiative* there as well. Looking over the past century and a quarter, we can see that when such great wealth is from the outset at the disposition of private corporate managers, it enables them to become so socially influential and so politically powerful that they will dominate government, dismiss, if not unravel, the trade unions, and arrange for their professional and professorial experts to tell the rest of us that what is happening is all for the best. There is a crucially important, historic lesson here: if wealth generally and the social surplus in particular emerge within the exclusive ambit of corporate leaders, it will make them too powerful for anyone else to contest their use of it.

The corporate economic mechanism in our society and culture is so powerful that all of our other institutions must adapt themselves to "the facts on the ground" already determined by corporate or, at least, Intersection behavior. Are teenagers a problem? The corporations didn't set out to create "teenager" as a distinct social category. It came rather as a by-product of other things. But very early on they learned to influence it in ways that radically advantage themselves at the expense both of teenagers and the wider society.

Perhaps it will suffice to use that "teenage" phenomenon as a paradigm for corporate-Intersection social influence generally. Corporations create material conditions, like the availability of mass-market consumer products. They shape the cultural and social meaning of those products. And then they help shape how the society and culture adapt themselves to them. It is within that context that corporate executives, conscious of their centrality in our economy, polity, and cultural system, and to the creation of the future, feel so very entitled to their lavish rewards and feel they have a right, sometimes even the obligation, to act with imperial disregard for the opinions of others. We see that arrogant and disproportionate power especially clearly today when the failures of a few have brought the entire U.S. economy perilously close to collapse.[5]

The need for a strategic alternative to the free market, government regulation, and government ownership therefore seems both obvious and pressing. It is necessary to reengineer the internal control of corporate firms so that as the social surplus is created and deployed, it will be contested then and there by representatives of society. In other words, if "society" doesn't have a share of power *within the corporation,* it will as now be its servant and not its master.

Many groups in our society have a vital interest in the social surplus and in consequent economic and other change. Their interests should be represented directly within corporate decision-making bodies. These groups include the workers (obviously), government, consumers, investors (small as well as large), public interest groups such as environmental and antipollution organizations, and the firm's bankers, suppliers, and wholesale customers. A proper scheme of corporate governance would place representatives of each social group with a legitimate interest in that firm's behavior in a position to help steer that behavior, not just react to it. Of course, one doesn't want a situation where each faction tries to nullify the others, nor one in which the "new insiders" collude with "old insiders" to the public's disadvantage. Accordingly, the first priority is to create an explicit law-like framework spelling out the duties and mutual obligations of these society-creating firms and their managements.

The Legitimacy of the Corporation as a Civic Institution

Before turning to the constructive tasks of this chapter, two prior issues should be resolved. Both concern corporate legitimacy, one from a civic point of view and the other emphasizing the political and social contributions of a private property system to individual freedom and autonomy. We can begin with the issues bearing on the legitimacy of the corporation as a civic institution. A large body of procorporate thought has argued that the modern corporations fit so well with the civic requirements of a republic based on "natural liberty" that it would be wrong to alter their present place within the scheme of things.

When the corporate era began with the early trusts and cartels of around 1870, some conservative social theorists were concerned that such great agglomerations of wealth and of power in the hands of a few were a threat to civic institutions. Traditional republican thought preferred a rough equality of condition between citizens and relatively weak institutional centers of power. As one can see from the popular expressions that came to be used then, such as "Moguls" and "Malefactors," one of the dominant motifs of criticism of the new corporations was that too much power was falling into the hands of fewer and fewer, more and more powerful individuals. Republican (small "r") fears on this point seemed more than justified as they observed John D. Rockefeller's ruthless competitive practices, Jim Fisk's corruption, George Pullman's dictatorial rule over the company town bearing his name, William Randolph Hearst's warmongering, and Henry Clay Frick's violence toward his own workers.

To these American conservatives, with their traditional fear of powerful institutions, the development of firms owned by men able by virtue of their wealth and power to stand outside the law was profoundly troubling. As a result, many people of quite conservative bent, such as Theodore Roosevelt, were part of the Progressive movement and supported its attempts to reform the corporations.

As time passed, it seemed that the maturing corporations were behaving with greater civic and social responsibility.[6] This became a factor in conservative acceptance of the corporate form of business organization. Among the most influential American voices in this reinterpretation of corporate behavior was that of the legal theorist, later high government official, Adolf A. Berle. In a book that became a virtual bible on the topic during the New Deal and after, Berle argued that as the first generation of corporate moguls passed from the scene they would be replaced by professional managers with a different ethos. This is the famous thesis of "the separation of ownership from control" (Berle and Means 1933) that I mentioned earlier.

As Berle saw it, the early moguls had only a narrow property owner's interest in their firms; their firms were their private possessions, period. That encouraged their resistance both to control and to reform from the outside. It encouraged them "to do with their own property as they wished," and as some added, God Himself directed.[7] But eventually these moguls died out and were replaced by teams of hired corporate managers. This "separation of ownership from control," it was argued, beneficially resolved the problem of corporate power. According to this view, also referred to as the "managerial thesis," corporate managers were more cosmopolitan than their owner predecessors, owed responsibility to their stockholders and their banks, were aware by virtue of their professional training of the wider economic effects of their firms, were used to working with government, and as professionals had a heightened sense of responsibility to their communities and employees. In short, professional managers made for a corporate leadership that acted not from a narrow property interest but from a more socially responsible ethos. Berle himself was only one of the many voices spinning out this "managerial thesis" from the 1930s onward, and its widening influence weakened further regulation of the big firms on the grounds that it had become unnecessary. Professional managers would act as trustees for the public.

The effects of this managerial thesis were further abetted by a theory of a "people's capitalism." Berle himself argued this in a series of later, less distinguished books, as did his son, Peter. Milton Friedman has also supported a variant of it (Friedman and Friedman 1962). Not surprisingly, the New York Stock Exchange has been one of its foremost champions. Pointing to a number of obvious facts, stock market publicists—and Friedman—drew from them what they imagined to be an equally obvious conclusion. Very large numbers of Americans owned stock in corporate firms, sometimes directly and, more important, through their pension plans, insurance policies, and mutual funds. Ownership of securities was democratized so that the big firms were now the property of the American majority and not, as before, that of a small wealthy elite.

The managerial thesis and the "people's capitalism" argument had enormous effect in rehabilitating the legitimacy of the corporate form of big business and weakened the progressive impulse to regulate business from the outside. During, say, the 1950s and 1960s there seemed much to recommend the idea that big business was safely in the hands of responsible trustees for the public interest. This idea reverberated in other forms too. One of the more influential was Galbraith's conception of the role of a professional/managerial "technostructure" within the corporation (Galbraith 1967). It was conceived to act both as a countervailing force to the pure property interests of owners and also as a part of the shift to manager-controlled firms. I have to confess that I myself for many years held the view that professional managers muted the greedier, more shortsighted species of corporate behavior. But time has shown that Berle's and Galbraith's views cannot be sustained.

Until very recently, the behavior of the tobacco industry was the most dramatic challenge to the Berle view,[8] and in two distinct respects. We now understand that the big tobacco managers have known for perhaps seventy-five or more years that smoking was lethal. No trustee-like behavior was or has yet been forthcoming. It was tobacco's Berlesian managers, not the owners, who developed the strategies to muddy or hide the science, harass tobacco victims with unending counterlitigation, target the young as customers, and in general act in ways that would bring tears of approval from such genuine villains as Henry Clay Frick and John D. Rockefeller. In this offensive against the public health, the industry's "technostructure" has been a willing accomplice. With the exception of a few "rogue" whistle-blowers, whole legions of tobacco industry chemists, biologists, doctors, lawyers, statisticians, public health researchers, and so on have kept scientific information dangerous to their companies away from the public and have tried to overawe, drown out, and "scientifically" discredit findings and researchers adverse to tobacco company interests.

We can point to many tobacco imitators, other big firms that are quite ruthless in creating and dispensing false information about the effects their products have on society and health and who enlist every politician and scientist money can buy in campaigns to protect and extend their harmful ways. How are we to explain this ostensible change among those former "trustees for the public interest"?

At the analytical level, Berle's managerial control thesis was sometimes accurate and at least plausible in an earlier phase of corporate development. On the other hand, there is a certain irony in the fact that it was also outdated by the time Berle wrote it down. In their founding days, the great "trusts" had weak internal management controls. Organizers like Morgan or Rockefeller simply took over the higher direction of scores of different firms, uniting their finances and, of course, their marketing and their pricing policies within the Oil Trust or the Steel Trust but intervening little in the details of everyday management. This sort of made sense. Because they had gained a near-monopoly position in the industry, issues like inefficiency and public distrust didn't seem to matter. If you wanted oil or steel, you had to do business with Rockefeller or Morgan at their prices and on their terms.

As a result of this primitive level of management, much of the early promise of the trusts as profit makers was not fulfilled. U.S. Steel, organized by Morgan in 1901 from a multitude of smaller firms, furnishes the classic example. It rapidly lost market share to other, lesser firms that had more effective internal managements. Some of these firms, like Bethlehem Steel, challenged the U.S. Steel monopoly by investing in techniques that made for better product more precisely attuned to user need.[9]

But the historic counter to mere agglomeration of firms on behalf of monopoly came about in the DuPont Corporation and General Motors, where the problem of proprietary control over middle and lower management was dealt with in a realistic and systematic way. Not to repeat what others (and I) have already said of this, GM assigned policymaking to its upper elite but delegated the execution of that policy to its cadre. The glue that held policy and operations together was a system of management compensation that gave middle and lower managers a share of company profits, thus tying their personal interests to those of the owners.[10] Berle's "natural" differences between the outlook of the owners of a firm and that of its hired managers were addressed and overcome at DuPont and GM, the differences erased by keying managerial reward to the firm's growth and the firm's profitability. These management and compensation systems came in time to be the industry norm: at present, few firms of more than modest size exclude their managerial echelons from proprietary rewards.

The results have made manager-operated firms more efficient profit and growth maximizers than yesteryear's owner-operated firms. This point really deserves more attention than it has been given in the legal, economics, and management literature. As I've already suggested, the point here is that lower- and middle-level managers must and do act to maximize the growth and profits of the areas under their own responsibility. Preoccupied with the performance of their own little domains as compared with their rivals' elsewhere in the corporation, they must act with a narrower vision and a shorter time line. It is this devolution of profit and advantage maximizing out into every corporate activity that has so mightily helped to "uncivilize" corporate behavior. The designer will be rewarded for making an SUV that sells well and has no material interest in the fact that it uses more fuel and rolls over; those questions are dealt with, if at all, in another department. The chemist undoubtedly has a clearer personal knowledge of nicotine's addictive effects than a higher manager could possibly have, but also a powerful motivation to take a more rather than a less rosy view of the problem and, if asked to testify in public, either to hide unpleasant results or to emphasize the uncertainty that surrounds all scientific research. (Of course, many have just out and out lied.) The Wall Street dealer in iffy securities has an interest in not seeing their value threatened by adverse publicity. Even the very lowest "strawboss" has some palpable interest in not blowing the whistle on what might be his or her own job.

Thus, one of the plausible effects of the shift to manager-operated firms is that every manager is in theory acting to maximize the firm's advantage in his or her narrow, specialized bailiwick *so that in the net of the firm's relations with the outside world, the firm's detailed, fine-tuned maximal interests are pursued in comprehensive detail.* Accordingly, what emerges is that the corporate firm's "big picture" tends to decompose into the sum of the miserly, shortsighted, society-minimizing pictures of its managers and technostructure. This is a "normal" development from modern managers and not an aberration based on "a few bad apples."

This seems a cogent explanation for what actually happened in the tobacco industry, in the automobile industry's dealing with vehicle safety and environmental pollution, in the asbestos industry, and of course, in the now-collapsing securities industry. In politics, it implies that the big corporations now have a "technostructure" of lawyers, public relations specialists, and lobbyists capable of going through possible or threatening legislation or regulatory action with a fine-tooth comb, designing strategies tailored to create, delay, or defeat the government action as it suits them, and able, should they choose, to generate "grassroots" support for their goals. The original John D. Rockefeller could buy the U.S. Senate, as apparently he did for a while, but he did not have the time, the technical expertise, or the imagination and the wealth to make sure that every bill entertained by the Senate and bearing on some minor corner of his empire wholly favored his interests. That requires a corps of professional managers and compliant lawyers. In a sense, Morgan and Rockefeller gave omnipotence to the corporate form of business, but it took Pierre DuPont and GM's Alfred P. Sloan to give it omniscience.

The good civic effects claimed by Adolf Berle's "separation of ownership from management" have been reversed. His managerial thesis should be understood now to imply a veritable leap in the corporations' pursuit of their detailed, short-term, narrow-focused interests in every area they touch upon and, supporting that, a major increment in their ability to block or use government action to their own ends.

The thesis of a "people's capitalism" is also pretty tattered these days. It became apparent in the financial pages as early as 2001–3 that, paraphrasing Orwell, while all investors are equal, some are more equal than others. There are now at least two different classes of investors within the securities industry who also have opposed interests: the "people's capitalists," who often own the securities, and those few others who manage them within the big securities firms, banks, and insurance companies. The several "insider" trading scandals that occurred at Merrill Lynch, Putnam, Adelphia, WorldCom, and elsewhere show that it is more or less common for the managers of the big investment firms to work against the "people's capitalists." They typically trade in and out of securities at the expense of these firm's smaller investors.[11] The financial press and media have naturally focused on possible violations of law, but the political economic aspect is more interesting and more significant. Berle saw the interests of corporate managers as beneficially diverging from the narrower interests of the firm's owners because of the scattering of stock ownership. Ironically, in the securities industry big securities managers reverse the terms of that equation. They now harmfully pursue their own interests, which are often opposed to those of the scattered small investors, whose pensions and savings are at risk. Virtually no one who has studied these things imagines for a moment that the actual stockholders have more than a fleeting, peripheral ability to impose their will on the big securities managers—unless of course they hold or themselves manage vast blocks of stock. The system of one man/one vote/little effect is the norm there.

Worse, securities managers constitute another layer of managers between the nominal owners of the firm and the direction of the business. But if this is the case, then the quality of civic responsibility that Berle and his colleagues wanted to attribute to corporate managers is without basis. That is why I think the criminal swindles of the Putnam and Merrill Lynch executives are not of the first importance. One can always pass laws and as a result obtain, at least for awhile, less crooked behavior in the securities industry, but no law can overcome the way the "managerial thesis" works today and its negative implications for a theory not only of corporate responsibility to its stockholders but of corporate social responsibility. *Pari passu* the same argument holds against a people's capitalism; if anything, securities managers have now an enhanced power, not least but not only via instantaneous electronic trading, to shave values from securities for their own and their allies' gain at the expense of the nonmanagers who own those securities. This behavior is possibly still more the exception than the norm; but however well or responsibly this or that corporation may behave, the deeper truth is that modern corporations are self-governing institutions over which the public, stockholders, and government have only a peripheral and usually fleeting authority. How one views this is of course a function of one's political views, but it is in any case a situation deeply at variance with the civic tradition of classic republicanism.

The Legitimacy of the Corporation as a Social and Political Institution

At the core of republican theory is the institution of private property and the idea that those who do not have personal, direct control of the physical requirements of life such as food and shelter cannot function as autonomous individuals or be responsible for their own behavior, in short, they cannot be true "citizens," only "subjects." Aristotle thought that to be without property was equivalent to being a slave and that idea has been maintained in conservative thought to the present. Karl Popper and Friedrich Hayek are recognized as the great modern proponents of this conservative fundamental, but we inherited the same idea from John Locke and Enlightenment orthodoxy via Jefferson's declaration of the importance of "Life, Liberty and The Pursuit of Happiness," the latter a cosmetic substitute for "Property."

Clearly, "the separation of ownership from management" within the dominant modern property form puts stress on the identification of "private property" with "natural liberty." It has further, negative implications for the character of society.

To begin: a modern or so-called developed economy can be distinguished from a premodern economy by its educated labor force and developed infrastructure. A modern economy needs a veritable host of specialists in its labor force; engineers of many kinds, experts in architecture and design, skilled machinists and construction workers, physicians and physicists, in short, every sort of expert from accountant to zoologist. And it needs whole legions of Berlesian workers who will act diligently and responsibly on behalf of the property of others but within a wider, controlling social ethos.

Further, without an infrastructure of telecommunications networks, roads, railroads, and dredged rivers and harbors and without access to pure water and the ability to dispose of massive amounts of industrial and other wastes, without research science and up-to-date medical professions, without a comprehensive school system and a supporting social welfare system, there is no modern economy; there is only "underdevelopment." In modern parlance, we would say that without a developed public sector one cannot have a developed private sector. This statement is true, but it conceals an important property issue.

To do what they do and to profit and grow as they also do, modern corporations must operate in societies with modern educational systems and modern physical infrastructures, the creation and maintenance of which require substantial investment. In short, if there is to be profit in the private sector, there must be investment in the public sector, two realms that are not that easy to tell apart. The distinction between a putative "private sector" and a "public sector" is a legal and cultural one, but economically speaking the two "sectors" are so complementary that one often cannot analytically distinguish them. To put it another way, the distinction between the two is a matter of law, not economics.

Some years ago, I looked into the question of public investment in infrastructure to get some idea of its scale relative to private-sector investment.[12] In the period I studied, the government had invested a little over a dollar for every dollar of private investment. This rough comparison, however, does not reflect the true scale of government investment. An investment in a new commercial product might return its worth to the private firm in a few years; an investment in a film can return its worth the first weekend after its release. But the public invests in educating potential employees for fifteen or more years before they begin to return that investment in taxes, and in bridges, tunnels, water and sewage systems, and the basic and applied scientific research that is central to long-time corporate profitability for far longer.

Thus, through government, we—the public—match private investment at least dollar for dollar, but the increased "earnings" that come out of this "developed economy" are viewed as the "private property" of the corporations, and their subsequent deployment is seen as among the "rights of property" of the private firms. Not a joint public/private sort of earnings, but purely private ones that, again quite ironically, the modern epigoni of Hayek and Popper insist are and must remain purely private under the Lockean/Jeffersonian doctrine of natural rights. What is wrong with this picture?[13]

What this suggests is that the common distinction between the public sector and the private one now serves among other things to camouflage the confiscation of the return on public-sector investment by private firms.

"Confiscation" is a strong word, and I foresee two objections to it. One could argue that the public in fact gets a return on, say, its investments in basic science, a return in the form of new products and economic growth. In fact, that isn't a terribly plausible argument, since the public has both to pay for those products and to work to create that economic growth. The firm's private investors also share in the advantages of new products and economic growth. But the investors get a second, additional return in the form of dividends and the growth in their share values—without additional labor or investment on their part. The public directly invests in the causal chain that brings about these extra dividends and higher share prices, but it gets no corresponding return. That return falls entirely to the private investor. On that basis, "confiscation" is a mild way to characterize what actually happens.

The other argument against the term "confiscation" revolves around the public's direct investments in education. Here, the argument is that that same public gets the advantage of this education in terms of higher wages later down the line, greater career opportunities, and so on and so forth. I've long wondered why this conception of the returns to "investment in education" has had such currency, since it is deeply confused.[14] The private investor gets the economic advantage from a more elaborate, successful education system via dividends and higher share prices that follow from, say, that creative chemist in the lab, and this economic advantage just falls to him or her without further effort, like ripe fruit from a tree. But for a member of the general public, an "investment in education" means at least twelve to twenty-five years of hard work at school—and the return on that investment requires at least forty hours of work per week for fifty weeks a year. Here again, that private investor is getting a free ride. He or she gets a return from a better-educated populace—plus the stockholder gains already described. The public investor only gets the first and, if the subject is education, must not merely "invest" his or her savings but must first get that education and then go to work in a job where he or she can use it.

The modern heirs of Hayek and Popper really don't have the natural rights tradition on their side, for in the natural rights tradition control over property is the key variable for a free society made up of individuals whose property, resting in their own hands, guarantees their autonomy as members of a republic of peers. However, the modern corporation is controlled not by its owners, but by its managers. Furthermore, the development of a class-like stratification within the world of financial securities directly creates inequalities in the control over and in the claims to the earnings of that property per se. You and I are both shareholders, but our returns are not proportional to our investment, for if I am an insider and you are not, then I will have regular access to information that will add an increment to my returns by lessening yours. Again, this disproportionality flies in the face of traditional property lore.

Finally, the public really does sacrifice present enjoyments in order to pay taxes that are devoted to straight-out economic investments. But at least some of the returns on that investment are entirely confiscated by the corporate players. If we were consistent Popperians and Hayekians, we would have to argue for a changed corporate system in which managers would have to (1) obey the expressed interests of all the stockholders; (2) ensure that shareholders returns were strictly proportional to the size of their investments; and (3) return to the public value for value received in educational, infrastructural, scientific, and other investments. And if they failed to do these things, we could charge them with grand larceny.

By no stretch of the imagination can we make today's corporate managers understand, much less obey, points 1, 2, and 3. But then, the philosophic/economic alternative to those points is not to wish them away. We should recognize that modern property forms require equally novel institutional adaptations in order to satisfy the complex equity claims of all the kinds, quantities, and qualities of the different sorts of "owners" and "investors," including those of society itself.

Unfortunately, our root ideas of property still depend on images of the farmer on his own land or "a man in his castle," that is, property forms in which a (male) owner is in immediate, direct, present control of a property of some sort and in a position to enjoy its fruits. But this is specious. Within a modern economy, property is already largely *social,* not *private.* In our economy, savings for investment are mostly generated via social mechanisms such as pension plans and IRAs and, of course, the public purse via so-called corporate welfare, and via fructifying investments in education, science, and infrastructure. The apportionment of the earnings of investment to various individuals is conditioned by still other social mechanisms such as profits for securities firms, rewards for their managers, and wages for their staff, by the tax code, and so forth. In our society, if we are to talk of a private property, we have to conceive of it as ownership not of distinct "things," like a house or a field, but of partial, fractional claims against institutional, social property forms. In a modern developed society the most economically significant and rewarding private property exists within and because of social property forms. That point guides the proposals that follow.

Proposals for Civilizing the Corporation

There are four main areas for corporate reform. First, if the public provides through its taxes half or more of the capital invested in our economy, then it should get a proportional return on that capital, not just some investment "externalities," as economists call such things, such as the benefits of having a more educated populace. Second, if corporate disposition of the social surplus affects so profoundly the fate of so many different kinds of people, then those same people should have a hand in directing the further uses of that surplus. This point has both a principled dimension and a practical one. The first follows from the idea of citizen autonomy, the second from the need for social institutions to have feedback mechanisms so that their real as supposed to ascribed effects can be assessed. Third, if the corporations are now civically autonomous, they lack republican legitimacy; this means that we need a new legal framework to reintegrate them. And fourth, if the higher managers and the middle/lower levels of the "technostructure" have been collaborating in corporate civic irresponsibility, downright mischief, and even some felonies, then we need to create efficacious legal and ethical standards for better behavior.

Of the areas for corporate reform, the second is really the least interesting and the easiest to conceive. As I suggested, the policy-setting and chief managerial organs of the big corporations should have memberships designed to represent each of the kinds of people affected by them. That would potentially include their shareholders, the securities firms who manage those shares, their bankers and other financial agents, and their auditors and insurers. It should also include their current employees and their retirees. Although I would like to see the differences between managers and workers weakened, at least at the present juncture the interests of those two groups are not the same and each accordingly should be represented. The top management team should also be represented. Those who purchase a firm's product have an interest and should be represented, both their wholesalers and franchisees and their final consumers. If both government and the public have an interest, as they do, those interests should also be represented, as should the major suppliers. At present, firms that have especially important suppliers often maintain board or other intimate links with them, as between automakers and their steel suppliers. That linkage should be maintained.

One can see why this is the least interesting and easiest of the corporate reforms to conceive. Moreover, such a reform would in fact be counterproductive. We've just sketched a board consisting of representatives of at least fifteen different interests, some of which are sharply opposed to one another. Even those who are partial to "worker control" will have to recognize that sharp contradictions *among the workers* might well emerge in such a board. Long-time employees might react differently to a proposed change, say, in product lines, consequently in work routines, than would relative newcomers. Or consider a firm in a failing industry that wanted to fight falling sales by making especially big advertising outlays, which it would pay for by lowering its dividends for an extended period. The firm's retirees have quite a different set of interests at stake here than those of the current employees. Or, with equal realism, say a firm once heavily dependent on steel products wishes to shift to greater reliance on aluminum and plastics. Here the steel supplier's interests may be at variance with the firm's need to stay abreast of new industry technologies.

One can also foresee perhaps irreconcilable disputes within such a board on many other issues, especially, I would imagine, on pay policies. One of the chronic faults of the present system is that it overpays those toward the top of the corporation and underpays those toward the bottom. This is not solely about greed. Managers and certain skilled workers are paid more largely because they are harder to replace. How does a truly representative board calibrate such differences when so many on the Board have self-interests in the outcomes?

At the same time, the positive rationale for having different, even irreconcilable interests represented within corporate governance structures is that, first, each of the different groups really does have a stake in the way the firm is governed, and, second, those interests often have zero-sum outcomes. Current corporate governance structures now resolve such differences by the simple expedient of championing the interests of those who work their way into the governance structure and ignoring or derating those of outsiders. Managers feel they deserve to be paid very, very well for an often difficult job. But workers feel that the difficulty and, possibly, danger of their jobs also deserves much higher pay than they are presently receiving. Rights are equal here, but force decides! It would be better to design corporate governance structures where, when rights are equal or at least in conflict, the final judgment will be based on more than force and be marked by extra care that all parties gain some advantage.

One also wants and needs more diversity within corporate governance, but not a board consisting of fifteen or more special pleaders. Berle's notion of trustees for the public interest wasn't a bad one; it is just that we want real trustees and not the ersatz ones created by the "natural" difference between an owner and a manager. However, before we can address the mechanics of representation within corporate governance structures, we need to restore civic legitimacy to the corporation. That should give us some better idea of the sorts of interests that should be represented in a reformed board of corporate directors.

The Corporate Charter: *Pour Encourager les Autres*

We in the United States have historically constructed a corporate legal person in the image and likeness of a one-sidedly privileged private person, a citizen with very few obligations and very many rights.[15] But I think we've now had enough experience of that unbalanced conception and are in a position to begin the reconstruction of a civically legitimate corporate legal person. To that end we should consider some features of the charter a civically legitimate corporation would have to have. I envision *a legal charter enacted by the national government, not one of the states, whose articles would lay out in a general way the multiple obligations of a corporation to its owners, employees, and the public; enjoin its board to pursue them; and establish an efficacious system of rewards and punishments to assure compliance.*

But is such a step not utopian? Given the depth of corporate propaganda in this country, its strength in all the media, including the academic ones, and the (now debased) republican tradition that private property is sacrosanct, how is it conceivable that the public, much less the courts, would ever be brought to take major steps to rein in the corporations? Even now, with the auto industry run into the ground by its leaders, and a securities industry still headed by witless horse players, it isn't clear that there is the political will to impose fundamental changes.

As always in the politics of the Democracy, high principle and low strategy have to be seamlessly merged.[16] The key power-political dimension of a program of corporate reform is the dependence the corporations have had on public-sector investments and other aids, a dependence that has exploded during the recent (2008–9) crisis. At present, as I've indicated, the economic growth and the higher earnings that those public-sector outlays make possible are given to the firms gratis. My proposal is that the public insist that there be value given for value received.

Imagine for a moment that a charter was drafted and enacted that laid out the social and other obligations of a corporate firm. Consistent with the republican tradition, the charter would not be imposed on any firm. Every firm, through its present governance structure, would be free to adhere to or reject it. But there would be a price for rejecting it, a very steep one in fact. Firms that did not accept the new charter as binding on their internal governance structure and their behavior would by that fact become ineligible for any special government favor whatsoever. It is when one reviews the details of that "price" that one sees to what degree the corporations have become dependent on a public and government forbearance that permits the confiscation of their investment by the "private sector." The firms, for a start, would lose patent and copyright protections and become ineligible to participate in government contracts, subcontracts, and licensing arrangements. Here we draw upon the model (and legal precedent) of antidiscrimination legislation where, for example, schools and colleges that reject antidiscrimination laws and procedures perforce are ineligible for federal aid. Traditionally, this has turned out to be a powerful suasion even on the most recalcitrant colleges and school districts.

Firms that choose not to enter the charter system would be ineligible for any and all provisions in the tax laws that grant special exemptions, investment credits, credits for taxes paid overseas, and so on. They would have to forgo all subsidies and participation in various assistance schemes, such as insurance against overseas nationalization. The firm's executives would lose their seats on those insider government boards that play such a great role now in formulating national security and international financial and trade policy and that thus contribute to corporate profits. It goes without saying that their products would be excluded from tariff protections. The firms that rejected the charter would also lose consular assistance for their overseas commercial activities.

Their workers would not be bound by any of the laws and rulings of the National Labor Relations Board, thus at a stroke relegalizing wildcat strikes, secondary strikes, boycotts and secondary boycotts; erasing the union's obligations to allow "cooling off" periods; and allowing the workers to conduct "job actions" over any management decision they disagreed with.[17]

In short, it would be unlikely that any firm could long refuse to accept the stipulations of the corporate charter.

The charter proposal has many desirable and realistic features. While it is unlikely that such a charter could be enacted in any foreseeable future, it lays out *an axis of advance* for the Democracy to begin the task of civilizing the great firms. It opens a path of legitimate challenge to every aspect of a corporation's behavior, from its product and copyright policy, through its labor relations, to its international activities. The U.S. subsidiaries of foreign-owned firms operating in the United States would be required to make the same choice about committing to the charter. Those that didn't would thus face the same denials as domestically owned firms. As for the latter's international activities, including "runaway" behavior, that too would fall under the net of obligations specified by the charter.

The charter makes concrete a program to push the big firms to be socially responsible. The strategic lever of withholding government favor from a given firm, absent a concrete reciprocal "payment" for that assistance, is powerful enough to be imposed, or try to have imposed, in detail.

What's more, the charter proposal is centrally within the republican tradition. The proposal is a way of making concrete and actionable the idea that modern property forms, socialized property as I've called it, merge private properties within them in extremely complex social ways. If taxpayer-funded research helped to create the modern electronic industry, as it did, helped (via the space program) to miniaturize computer components, and even funded much of the basic mathematics behind the PC revolution, then some substantial part of Bill Gate's net worth actually belongs to the taxpayers. Mr. Gates is claiming as his private property and "earnings" some of the returns of others' investments via government. By raising these socialized property/private property claims in a political setting, one takes a concrete first step toward removing the social superstition that currently surrounds "private property." One is not asking for private property to be confiscated by the nationalizing state, as in traditional social-democratic thought, or raising questions of high moral principle about corporate behavior that have a questionable philosophical basis and no immediate practical outcome; one is asserting practical, entirely legitimate, intuitively conventional property claims on behalf of their owners. But to do so is also to begin to enact a historical trajectory whose terminus would be—can be—a more civilized, socially responsible corporate firm.

Undoing the contemporary view of "private property" is really an attack on irrational and harmful social superstition. It is thought a violation of the Bill of Rights, for example, when a great media conglomerate is asked to offer balanced appraisals of the news, but not so when the views of all but a small handful of citizens are excluded from the airways. Not to understand and act on the changed forms and dynamics of private property is truly to betray the Enlightenment spirit, which correctly saw private property as an element in civilization's advance, and not, as is too often the case in our radically changed circumstances, a font of superstition and reaction.

The Form of the Charter

What one wants in the new corporate charter is a broad statement of a corporation's obligations to the different parts of society itself. One wants to assert that the first duty of a corporation's governance structure is to balance the competing claims of, essentially, three main constituents: owners and their coclaimants; employees of all levels and kinds, including retirees with fiduciary or other claims on the company; and the public. It is very difficult to formulate today an all-controlling principle to guide the corporate governance structure in all things today and tomorrow. My preference is that the charter should confirm the corporation as a special legal entity with some but not all the legal rights of a person, but also lay down that the corporation's rights come in tandem with and as a result of its continuing to accept an overriding social responsibility. This principle alone, if properly enforced, would go a long way to restoring civic legitimacy to the corporate form of business.

I will not here assay more than a rough sketch of the written form of the charter, partly for reasons of prudence but mostly because of the lawlike corporate environment I would like to see the charter initiate. I envision the charter as a statement of broad principles to be applied, challenged, and worked out much as present-day constitutional law is worked out. To that end, the charter should be a relatively brief document asserting that the corporate form of business organization is a creation by society in pursuit of broad social purposes. It should assert that the firm must serve equitably three different main constituents—owner, employee, and public. It should also include future generations as among those whose interests are especially affected. In fact, the ethos of environmental law and of laws protecting and conserving certain species of flora and fauna is more primarily relevant to founding a body of corporate charter law than current thinking about economics and business allows.

My present preference is for the charter to be enforceable by the regular federal courts. It may be that in the future that branch of the law would require special courts, but it would try the limits of plausibility to imagine that special courts set up at the outset would not lean too heavily on the existing business ethos of profits, "efficiency" (i.e., profits), and managerial "competence" (measured in terms of profits)—in other words, profits, profits, and profits.

There also need to be some changes in the way we grant legal "standing" to persons and groups to bring action against the firms. Here one wants on the one hand to avoid giving standing to groups or persons who are not directly affected by the actions of a given firm, and, on the other, not to place barriers in the standing of those who are. To complicate matters, on some environmental issues, for example, virtually every member of the public is affected, but one doesn't at the same time want to encourage cranks and eccentrics to bring nuisance suits. I do not have the expertise to sort out this nest of problems; and in fact, it is probably fair to say that the issue of "standing" before the courts is evolving within them. By and large, however, there seems to be a current tendency to narrow such standing, whereas to be consistent with the spirit and legal logic of the charter the reverse should be the case.

Just as with today's environmental impact statements, corporations that elect to accept the charter would file statements binding on their behavior that filled out the details of their compliance, as, for example, information about the nature of their governing structures and their operating priorities. These statements would not and should not be uniform across the corporate landscape. For example, firms in polluting industries would address their special obligations there. Firms in growth industries using cutting-edge technologies could and should allow for somewhat greater leeway for managerial freedom of action than firms in more economically and technologically stable industries. Service-providing and mercantile firms would normally require stronger inputs from their retail customers. Even within the same diversified firm, different charter compliance statements might have to be filed for different operating subsidiaries. The aim of the charter is not to impose a single rule on all companies but to bring all of their activities within an evolving, flexible, equitable legal framework.

A corporation's impact statement would have to include a justification for its size. There is no hard and fast rule here. Some firms now already big perhaps need to be bigger in order to cope with, say, global markets. But at the same time, some of the mergers we've seen in the past, like the classic case of U.S. Steel, created firms whose size was justified only by monopolistic considerations and the prospect of lucrative stock swapping for the founders and their cronies. Actually, I don't think this is a real issue. Boards with diverse directors serving only fixed, limited terms would lack that often all-consuming motivation that insiders now have to enlarge their firms. Moreover, the technical analysis of the business size best able to cope with different technological and marketing conditions is already reasonably well developed.

My thought is to exclude direct government participation in corporate governance. That is both a matter of principle and a practical safeguard. Because of the charter and the change in corporate governance structures that it brings, government's primary role shifts to judicial watchdog. Both the executive and the legislative branches would be largely displaced by the courts as the final judge of what was and was not permissible corporate behavior. As indicated, I think that is a desirable principle to pursue.

Prudentially speaking, the government-corporate relationship at present has, I think, many negative features that we would be wise to suppress. To take an extreme example, many governments, especially the U.S. government, use private security firms to carry out activities that in some sense need to be hidden from the public. Sometimes this is just a question of hiding how much money is being spent; in Iraq at present, for example (early 2009), direct Pentagon expenditures cover only about two-thirds of the money being spent there. That other third is being paid to private security firms guarding oil wells, training Iraqi policeman, and for mischief we don't yet know about. Much of the "dirty work" of counterinsurgency in Colombia at present falls to private security firms, thus casting a veil over U.S. government responsibility. In general, the now-huge international security industry, consisting of private firms using government monies, is testimony to the size and importance of a phenomenon to be suppressed as soon and as thoroughly as possible.[18]

Accordingly, there is too much risk, I believe, in encouraging further intimacy between government and industry and that argues against having government representatives on corporate boards. With the change in government's role from administrative regulator to judicial sentry, it is a change that brings no unavoidable disadvantage.

Corporate Boards

My sense is that at least half the members of a controlling corporate board ought to be public representatives. That way, any disagreements among owner and employer representatives would create a public majority. Following our earlier critique of various schemes for electoral representation, here too I see a jury panel method of selection of the public representatives as indispensable. I would apply the same principle to stockholder and employee members. Perhaps at some future time, after a period of resocialization, stockholder and employee representatives would be able to adopt less self-interested views, but at present I see no harm and much gain from adopting a jury panel method. That would create a range of the voices within the board, from stockholders, upper management, middle management, rank-and-file employees, and union members. In the nature of the case, a responsible board will be inclined to listen to that "insider" input, and that is what one wants, not more. At all costs one wants to avoid making the board a rubber stamp for owners, managers, workers, trade union officials, or bankers. By virtue of their indispensable role within corporate operations and their command over the details of policy outcomes, competent upper managers should be more than able to hold their own in such a setting.

At present, one of the main factors in corporate financial scandals, the overpayment of high executives and illegal corporate behavior generally, comes from the fact that outside directors, that is, those not directly active in the firm's management, have been in equal parts unwilling and insufficiently informed to overrule the directors drawn from the firm itself. My proposal that all board members be selected by jury panel method is obviously a reaction to this history of weak, ill-informed board members being dominated by the representatives of top management, who were too often interested solely in improving their own portfolios. That same history underlines the importance of providing to the board a full, competent staff formally separate from regular corporate staff. That could be accomplished by placing board staff in an echelon outside all other firm echelons, making them employees of the board per se and with their own obligations to the charter spelled out within it. Again, this is an area where more expertise than I claim must be married to the overriding strategic objective of creating corporate boards that effectively govern the firms and yet act as the responsible trustees of society's interests as laid down in the charter and elaborated in the body of law that would develop from it.

Trade Associations and Trade Unions

The charter would also be applicable to trade associations. These typically don't directly receive all that much government financial aid that could be withheld, but where a firm or its industry association has not accepted the charter, the firm's contributions toward the association's work could be made taxable or otherwise penalized. More significant, a business association that stood outside the charter would not be eligible to appear before

Congress, and its committees would be barred from lobbying on behalf of legislation and appropriations and could have no role in raising or steering money to election campaigns, either for candidates or for referenda on "issues."

It is particularly important to bring these trade associations under the legal framework established by the charter. Much of the political clout exercised by corporate firms is exercised through their trade associations: the American Petroleum Institute is the bedrock of the drilling lobby, and the insurance companies' trade associations who took the lead in defeating the Clinton health-care initiative are back at it at the present writing.

In addition, on the model of the lower-level corporate employee who is rewarded for his or her narrow-minded pursuit of the firm's interests, come what may, so too in the trade association. With an occasional exception, trade associations are rewarded by their institutional members to the degree that they succeed in advancing "the interests of the industry," a formula that has historically meant the absolutely narrowest and most shortsighted interests of the industry. The National Rifle Association may stand here as a case in point, not only for its dogmatic conception of hunters' and related interests but its pseudo-patriotic fanaticism on behalf of weapon manufacturers.[19]

Trade unions pose a quite different problem, for two reasons. For the most part only the more privileged workers have been able historically to win and to maintain trade unions. Unions are virtually absent among the lowest-paid, lowest-status classes of workers and, of course, among the unemployed and all but a few part-time workers. The unions have been faithful "in their fashion" to the interests of those toward the bottom of society, but more is needed, ideally from new kinds of organizations representing workers presently denied unions. I will address this issue in chapter 10.

The existing unions have also been special-interest groups, and not only on issues of gender and ethnic/racial discrimination. A writer as sympathetic to trade unions and their members as Henry Phelps Brown (1986) has argued, persuasively, I think, that when they were particularly powerful, the unions acted irresponsibly in their wage demands, in their insistence on overstaffing, and with sometimes legendary shortsightedness.[20] Given the present weaknesses of the trade unions, it seems mean-spirited to recall this sort of thing now, but a serious program of economic reform should not re-create some of the well-known mistakes of the past.

Furthermore, as I'll argue more fully later, the institutional form of trade union created by the U.S. National Labor Relations Board (NLRB) system locates too much authority at the top and confers far too little by way of worker rights, against both employer and union, at the bottom. By and large a thorough rethinking is needed of how workers are represented within our industrial system. There is no question that workers of all kinds need more power in the economy and polity, but how they are to get that power must be carefully thought out in the light both of past experience and the new sort of more democratic industrial regime being proposed here.

Creating a Management Profession

In his 1992 book *Who Will Tell the People?* William Greider recounts that a business association asked several hundred corporate executives about what they would do if some of the activities of their own companies seriously jeopardized the public health. About one in five of them said that they would do nothing at all. About half would fire any whistle-blowers; a further one in four said they would transfer a whistle-blower to another job! Only 6 percent claimed that they would take steps to correct the problem (Greider 1992, 353).

What this story implies is that the management profession is as yet only half a profession. It is surely an institution with a highly specialized, highly developed technique; and as currently trained and acculturated, its members, like the members of other professions, can do what they are asked to do without direct supervision by others. A financial manager, say, or a routing manager can be assumed to have ample ability to perform his or her tasks in a proficient way without someone else monitoring the details. But more is needed. A hallmark of a modern profession is that *in both the technical and the ethical realms,* the professional can and will perform the work *autonomously and responsibly.*

Managers too often see their ethical obligations to the firm as primary or, equivalently, that the ethos of the profession requires servility to the employer. However one formulates it, this is not the ethos of a complete profession. In architecture, the law, teaching, medicine, and accounting, we impose on the professional person a responsibility to the profession itself; that is, though the client or employer wants something done, the professional will not lower his standards to do it. In theory and, happily, most often in practice, a professional will not knowingly design an unsafe building, knowingly break the law, knowingly "cook" the books, knowingly misinform a student, or knowingly prescribe improper medication to a patient.

Of course, there are shoddy architects, crooked lawyers and accountants, irresponsible teachers, and medical charlatans out there. Also, as a colleague correctly points out, all of the modern professions are now under increasing pressure to serve the "bottom line," which degrades the quality of performance in fields as diverse as medicine and urban planning. Nevertheless, the professional organization and the professional ethos in architecture, the law, education, and medicine has had a largely beneficial social effect in motivating their members to keep to "professional behavior" and in providing effective sanctions against many and often the worst offenders. With the usual exceptions, the role of architects within the environmental movement, of lawyers in the ACLU, public defender's offices, and the military justice system, of teachers within all levels of schools, and of doctors within public health debates has justified society in yielding special rights and privileges to the several professional organizations, with government in some cases even correctly giving up its oversight role as such areas as the professional certification of physicians. It is in this context that the deformation of the management profession stands out.

The management profession (or, if one insists, professions) needs to be radically reformed. We need to place formal, binding standards of management behavior within the charter. We have to embody in law and practice that the first responsibility of every manager is "to the profession and its high standards," that is, to obey its ethos to serve the public, not the employer, not the owners. Like the medical and other professions, the management profession(s) should be licensed, and only a licensee would be allowed to undertake management responsibilities. Thanks to U.S. labor law, which reserves all management functions to the management echelon and forbids poaching by any and all outsiders, especially the workers, the full catalogue of management responsibilities is already very well and thoroughly defined in the law.

Managers should serve under an explicit legal obligation to report to the board, or, if necessary, to the press and public, anything that in their *professional judgment* is illegal or dangerous to the public; and when they do this, they should have the same sort of protected legal status against retaliation now provided to workers who blow the whistle on discrimination and occupational health hazards.[21]

If one is serious about professionalizing the management profession, then Greider's 20 percent who would do nothing at all would go on managerial license probation; a second offense would cancel the license. The 50 percent who would fire the alerting employee would be possibly subject, depending on the situation, to permanent exclusion from management positions; that 25 percent who said they would assign the offending employee to another job would be subject to fines. It is that 6 percent who would take steps to correct the problem that would form the core of the profession's future.

In truth, Greider's example reflects a situation in which business higher education, plus Sloan's managerial reward schemes, socializes cadre to think it is right and good to act as flunkies for "the investors"; the firms insist upon such servile behavior, and the law overlooks the social importance of surely the most influential modern profession of them all. My sense here is that many, probably most, of the men and women who now serve in management would welcome a well-thought-out strengthening of their professional autonomy.[22]

The Economy Beyond the Firm

An economy consists of much more than semiautonomous firms. If I have stressed the inner governance of the single corporation, it is because I wanted to emphasize that one must socially control the surplus where it is in process of being formed. To come in afterward and from the outside is merely to repeat what we now can see is the historic inability of the free market, government regulation, and government ownership to tame the corporation. Galbraith's optimism about the social responsibility of the technostructure has also come up short.

Society's influence must dominate within the corporate firm. It is an influence that for the most part will interfere with business success only occasionally and mostly rightly. Most conventional corporate priorities would in the normal course of events be ranked as highly by the new form of corporate governance as by the old: the generation of funds for innovation and growth, technical efficiency, entrepreneurship, and care in dealing with financial matters. But those are only some of the values that the economic mechanism must serve, and the function of the dominant public members of the board and of the charter itself is to balance those specifically business values against other equally necessary, equally desirable corporate performance measures, both for the short term and, now more and more important, from long-term social and environmentalist points of view.

I think that the trio of institutional innovations presented here would go a long way to civilizing the corporation—that is, the development of a new body of law governing corporate behavior based on the charter, abetted by boards of directors dominated by public representatives, and a management profession radically reprofessionalized on the model of the best features of the legal, accounting, and medical professions. These changes would make the corporation into a more responsible citizen in the republican body politic. And they would inhibit the firms from exercising the overwhelming but also one-sided political, social, economic, and cultural power that now makes the private corporation such a threat to the environment and the democratic political order.

Those last observations point to another whole dimension of business behavior that must be at least briefly addressed. As I have pointed out elsewhere, the U.S. economy is really much more cooperative than competitive (McDermott 2004). To understand this, one must put to the side the special pleading about free enterprise and the free market that has become the staple of so much of the economics and business education professions. In an economy like that of the United States, there has to be, and is, an immense amount of consultation and cooperation between firms, between industries, and with public agencies. I have in the past described this web of relations between firms, industries, and government as "coarse planning," and I'll continue that usage here. Coarse planning is everywhere in the U.S. economy, and in truth there is no alternative to it.

For a start, in normal times government undertakes to maintain a stable currency, act against inflation, ride herd on the trade unions, invest in research and development whose results fall to industry's benefit, and endlessly train and retrain the labor force. Here, government is trying to create an economic pasture as it were, a stable, predictable business environment well endowed with the sort of economic nutrients needed by modern corporate firms. It is an environment in which even the most ordinary corporate executives cannot normally fail to prosper.[23]

Government agencies collect and analyze a vast array of statistical information about the size and intent of different firms' investment plans. That information about, say, the aircraft industry's plans for the next fiscal year is the very fodder of the aluminum and electronics firms' own internal investment plans. And to think about it is to realize it could be no other way. Free-market theory has firms investing with a vacuum of information about the future: profit follows risk! But if one is interested in risk management, as, of course, modern firms are (or at least were before the Volcker/Greenspan years), then it is necessary to go the next step. Risk management requires a firm to establish liaison relationships with its suppliers and customers to learn what their plans are. The firm must anticipate levels of consumer income, try to gauge consumer preferences, keep abreast of relevant technologies in other firms, and so on. It would be foolish for, say, the petroleum industry to expand output if the travel, auto, and chemical industries were planning big decreases, or vice versa. And it would be insane for, say, the recording tape manufacturers not to take into account the marketing plans of the DVD makers. So common is this liaison between firms in interdependent lines of business that it is often carried out by middle-rank "technical representatives" and not even by higher-ranking policymaking executives.

In an economy like ours, most firms are technologically and economically interdependent, a point simply erased out of awareness by the superstitions of the economics theorists about contemporary "competition." Firms must cooperate, and that cooperation goes much wider and deeper than issues of price collusion. When the plans of each are uncertain to the others, as in the present economic panic, the plans of all spiral out of control.

The economics and business literature, inexcusably friendly to big business, tends to obscure the extent of corporate and industry cooperation lest it be seen as evidence of monopolistic price-rigging behavior and thereby draw political fire. As a result, too much discussion of a modern economy like that of the United States goes on within an otherworldly framework of "competition" and "free, unregulated markets." Forgetting entirely about ideology, one simply cannot give an adequate description of the U.S. economy if one depicts it as at bottom made up of firms perpetually at competitive war with one another.

Save in crisis times, as now, there exists an efficacious national corporate governance system. That it has been shortsighted and self-interested is why we have a crisis and why the crisis will be prolonged. The system is not centralized, and it does not have legal sanction, but it has often been reasonably effective for all that. In places like the Federal Reserve,[24] the Business Advisory Council, and the other numerous, sometimes quasi-secret organizations—some local, like the Vault mentioned earlier, some regional, some national—business leaders meet with one another in endless conferences. "Coarse planning" means that these high business leaders, along with the appropriate government officials, become acquainted, share information about and adjust their future plans, address troubling problems, including specifically political ones, identify areas where government should change its policies, and so forth. This is an elite subsociety, and not a cabal, a truly social phenomenon and not a set of interpersonal relations. Such collaboration and information sharing is in fact essential and entirely legitimate—save that a wider, more representative range of voices is excluded. Greater public participation in this world would also go a long way to erasing the worst social superstitions about the economy and the harm they cause.

10

A "CIVILIZED" EMPLOYMENT SYSTEM

In 1907, an Australian court ruled that the basic wage should meet "the normal needs of an average employee regarded as a human being in a civilized society." The author who cites this ruling adds, "This basic wage [Judge Higgins] held sacrosanct; no lack of profitability and no pressure of competition could justify reducing it by a penny" (Brown 1986, 281). I agree completely, but acknowledge that many will wonder whether there are realistic arguments to support a "Higgins wage" today, and what the effect of introducing such a wage might be.

I insist that "civilized society" today, a full century after Higgins's ruling, actually demands more than a "Higgins wage." It demands as well a discrimination-free workplace, occupational safety, job security, the opportunity to advance in earnings and responsibilities, and career flexibility. It demands that no person who wants a job be denied one, and that abusive treatment by employers be a thing of the past. It demands that employees have a say in the future of their jobs and thus a voice in the direction of the enterprise, and that the work of hand as well as brain be equally esteemed. None of these things will come to pass unless and until workers and others on the lower end of the social scale mobilize themselves anew to bring them about.

The burden of this chapter is to characterize the present employment system, to sketch a more "civilized" system, and to propose some ways that those most affected by the system can win the desired changes. A remobilization of the working classes generally, including the "lowest of the low," is indispensable to a renewal of the historic advance, and this will require a radical improvement in the quality and scope of worker representation.

This discussion has to proceed under two headings, one dealing with the better-off workers and the other with the "lowest of the low," that is, respectively, one about trade unions and their members and one about those for whom there are now no steady work, good work, livable wages, "normal" benefits, nor any real chance of "getting ahead." I begin by examining the basic U.S. labor system where these things play out, but with enough reference to other nations' systems to provide additional breadth and depth.

Employment at Will and the Rights of Management

The U.S. labor system is terra incognita for most otherwise informed people, even many social scientists. One of its basic principles is the doctrine of "employment at will." Sometimes called "free labor," it means that both the employer and the employee may terminate the employment relationship at any time and for any reason. Things are obviously a bit freer for the employer than for the employees. At any event, save where restricted by legal enactment or by a lawful contract, all the rest is "employment at will." But even those restrictions are narrower in scope and weaker in operation than most people understand, for they bump up against another basic principle of the U.S. labor system, the legal doctrine and customary precedents of "the rights of management."

Until perhaps the 1890s, even in big industry, work was customarily directed and carried out by skilled workers and their assistants and apprentices, as we saw at Homestead Steel. But with the rise of modern science- and university-based technologies of production, the (middle) management profession or cadre was born and with it an orientation to seize all those aspects of the production process that had formerly been controlled by skilled workers. In this sense, "the rights of management" are an extension of the "employment at will" doctrine to include not only employment per se but how the work is actually performed, by whom, at what speed, where, using what equipment and technologies, and within what disciplinary and administrative settings. These "rights" of managers had been evolving in law and practice since the "scientific management" movement at the turn of the nineteenth century, but were codified in the Taft-Hartley Labor Relations Act of 1947 and have since been confirmed and extended by state and federal court decisions. Management's opposition to trade unions, while fierce, pales in comparison to its defense of its managerial "rights."

In the modern U.S. system there are only three broad exclusions to the authority of the managers to manage as they will. There are state-enacted labor standards acts that limit the work week, guarantee overtime pay for overtime work, prohibit child labor, and ban involuntary labor. Too often these labor standards acts are simply ignored. A second exclusion prohibits employer discrimination against certain categories of people. The third imposes restrictions and obligations on management under the Occupational Safety and Health Act and its supplements. Otherwise, management retains the right to manage as it pleases, absent explicit concessions to unions made as part of a contract negotiation. A statement to that effect appears in every contract between management and a union.

The question remains, if managers have such broad authority, what do unions do, and just what member interests can unions represent?[1]

Thinking About Union "Representation": Industrial Unions

It is not enough that workers can vote like the rest of the citizenry. Equity demands that they, like the more influential classes and groups, have that second entryway into the political process afforded by institutions and organizations, traditionally unions. At present, U.S. unions, once so powerful, have fallen on dire straits.[2] This decline is not solely a result of the actions, however well-financed, powerful, and determined, of their enemies. Many unions, like those fabled generals of yesteryear, are still fighting the last war and, from a purely institutional standpoint, are ill-fashioned to fight today's. The self-satisfaction of labor "chieftains" and "bureaucrats" explains some of this, as perhaps does the workers' lack of "class consciousness." However, arguments like these are staples of discussions about trade unions—even when they are growing in size and militancy—as in 1919, 1936, and 1946. It is clear that further thought about the cause of union decline and how to arrest, and possibly reverse it, is definitely needed. Accordingly, I want to develop some ideas about the present, inadequate representational character of unions and later, in that light, propose some changes in modern union practice.

It is not enough to know that workers have occupational representation. One must also understand *what is represented and how it is represented.* In the conventional account, workers in the United States are represented in two very different ways. There are *industrial unions*, which typically represent all or most of the employees of a given firm or industry, as for Ford or the auto industry as a whole, and *craft unions*, which represent workers practicing a particular trade, such as carpentry or plumbing. The two differ in other respects as well.

Industrial unions in the United States are relatively new. They were organized at first in the auto industry, in 1936–37, during an illegal seizure by the workers of several key General Motors plants in Flint, Michigan. The then governor of Michigan, Frank Murphy, was both sympathetic to the workers and fearful of bloodshed; he refused to send in state troopers to clear the plants, so GM had to negotiate with the union. FDR's labor secretary, Frances Perkins, also played a key role here. The drama of the strike and the evident willingness of at least some public officials to lean toward the workers had a galvanizing effect (Kraus 1947). Even before the year 1937 was out, several million workers had won industrial union representation in the major manufacturing industries.

In theory, an industrial union brings every worker in a given industry into its ranks, skilled or not. Generally, the union has a separate contract with each company in the industry covering wages, hours, benefits, and work rules, but by playing the companies off against one another it tries to establish uniform conditions throughout the industry.[3]

Most members of an industrial union are not, as they say, "skilled," as are pattern makers, for example. They are called "semiskilled" or some such expression, and typically serve or operate some sort of machine. That machine may be as elaborate as a "space age" welding machine in an auto plant, or as simple as a conveyer belt that moves soft drink bottles to a capping machine. Commonly, the machine (or system) is programmed to do the job; the workers are needed to observe that it is working properly and perhaps feed it materials or snatch out obviously faulty product. These are not unskilled workers, a term that in the United States mostly covers people who do simple lifting, hauling, shoveling, or raking. Semiskilled workers need to be alert, watchful, responsible; and in a boring, repetitive, often noisy, and otherwise stressful setting, they have to monitor the workings of the machines and intervene responsibly and intelligently if something goes wrong.

The main industrial unions in the United States are affiliated with the Congress of Industrial Organizations (CIO), which is part of the larger organization, the AFL-CIO. The CIO, now Industrial Union Department, is really more than a federation of unions, just as the United Auto Workers is more than a federation of the Ford, GM, and Chrysler unions. In this part of the labor movement, authority has gravitated upward, mostly because of their original and continuing dependence on government. Without the help of sympathetic officials like Frank Murphy and Frances Perkins, the big companies might well have defeated the nascent industrial unions back in the 1930s, as they had defeated them in the textile industry in the 1920s, in the steel industry in 1919, and in other industries many times before that. It is this continuing need for close ties with the Democratic Party, particularly at the national level, that has located so much authority at the national union level and, as during the anticommunist hysteria of the 1950s, within the central CIO leadership itself.

How is a worker represented by an industrial union? And how does that square with "the rights of management"? The surprising answer is that an industrial union doesn't really represent the individual worker; it represents his or her job. This is not an obvious distinction, but it is one of very great practical import. Under "the rights of management," management cedes only a limited "right" to the union. In a precise legal sense the union thereby comes to "own" the right to represent the workers' job before company and government, and the workers are represented only as the temporary occupiers of those jobs. If the jobs disappear, to Asia or obsolescence, the union's rights and obligations cease. The union, for example, has no legal obligation to help workers do the job better; that remains a "right" of management.

It is important to understand that the union does *not* represent the worker's person, as, for example, his or her lawyer might. The union has a right only to negotiate rates and conditions for a job category and only for whoever fills that job and only insofar as they act within that category.[4]

Industrial unions establish "grievance procedures" with the employer as well, but this is an entirely different area than we just spoke of and has an entirely different legal and therefore representational character. When the union has a contract that a certain job gets such and such hourly rate, and such and such benefits, and so on, the company has given up only its normal, unilateral right to change those. But the rest of management's rights remain untouched. Accordingly, when workers have a "grievance," that is, when they claim that the company has in some sense wronged them, the union will represent them in the grievance process. But because of the rights of management, the union has no authority to force an equitable settlement of the grievance; as the worker's "representative" it has only an advisory role before the company. In sum, the union fully represents the worker's job, but it only partially and more weakly represents the worker's individual person.

Some of these grievances are about important matters, as when someone is fired or a supervisor expects sexual favors from his female, or even male, workers. Or the issue may be as small, though important to the person involved, as, for example, who gets first pick of vacation time. Typically, the aggrieved worker will go to his or her "shop steward" or "grievance committee," usually unpaid volunteer posts occupied by fellow union members, and that representative will take up the matter with someone from the company's personnel office. Informal settlements are common here, but when such aren't forthcoming, the "grievance," now in written form, will be "sent up" to a higher level for resolution. My experience as a shop steward was that the lower the level at which the grievance could be settled, the better for the worker, since higher union officials and company managers have other, they feel "weightier," concerns than whether, say, a bathroom is too distant from one's job site. Of course, my experience may not hold in other settings.

Workers have little or no individual juridical standing within the labor relations laws and regulations in the U.S. labor system and therefore few and weak individual rights; the system only recognizes the rights of worker types and job-category-occupiers such as "employee," "secretary," "lathe operator," "assembler."[5] The category is recognized and represented, not the person. It is within the grievance machinery that the worker becomes a name, a personality, somebody who is angry, upset, or even hysterical, and who is or can be dealt with as an identifiable and distinct individual. But as we saw, the worker's standing is very weak there.

Thus, it is not unusual that when negotiators bargain over a contract renewal, they will both agree to wipe the slate clean of existing grievances so they don't "spoil the goodwill" between company and union. Unions do this in part because it is cheaper to represent the workers as a group, more expensive to take up their individual complaints and desires. There is also an unspoken tradition in the industrial union side of the labor movement, inherited from the heroic days of union militancy, in which one represents "the workers" or "the working class," "the masses in solidarity," all speaking with but a single voice, and that tends to create a union culture in which the individual worker is somehow of lesser importance.

The steady decline of trade union membership in the private sector in the United States is undoubtedly linked to this fact that everyday quality-of-work issues can only be weakly, really inadequately, defended. In addition, younger workers don't rate job stability as highly as their parents did. Many will take and leave jobs to accommodate schooling, travel, or other interests. Or they may wander about the occupational map seeking work that they will find rewarding. And if and when they do find *that* job, they expect to enjoy advancement over the years.[6] These changes among younger workers are widely understood, but the unions have not found a way to respond to them. Unions, as we saw, represent the jobs, not the persons. But to the younger worker the job, hence the union, is of lesser importance. Some think union dues are an unnecessary expense, since they will be moving on, perhaps to another union job with another set of dues or, more likely, to a nonunion job where they will not have to pay "overhead."

Fitting Unions to the Rights of Management

There are now proposals before Congress for labor system "reform."[7] It confirms the narrowness of the AFL-CIO that none of the proposed reforms touch either of the issues I've raised here. Basically, the proposals want to make it easier for today's unions to win new members. That of itself would undoubtedly be a gain but not a very great one or very long-lived. The new members are likely over time to grow as disappointed with their unions as the older ones have. The long-term decline in the membership and influence of the unions is likely to be only marginally affected.

No reform is worthy of the name if it leaves the situation substantially as it is now. Ill-informed people imagine that unions (in industry, not the crafts) are representative organizations pure and simple. Not so. Government, not the members, governs the relationship of the union to the members. If we are to be literal about it, unions are quasi-governmental intermediaries between management and workers, somewhat more in the nature of labor subcontractors than representative organizations.

Unions do not constitute an alternative to or a substantive limitation on management rights, nor do they add much to the rights of the workers themselves. Basically, what we have had to date are trade unions that have been squeezed and distorted in their powers to fit them within and under the doctrine of the "rights of management." That point is absolutely basic. The fundamental fault in the present system is that management has many rights; if there is a union, it has some, subordinated rights; and individual workers, hardly any rights at all. We retain much of the legacy of the old master-servant system, where rights end at the employer's door.

The present form of industrial union is dysfunctional in other ways as well. Suppose present conceptions of labor system "reform" won through and it came about that the unions reversed the fifty-year decline in their membership and power. I agree that that would be a gain. But for whom, and for how long? *The sort of union we are familiar with, bargaining with the employers in a labor system like ours, has historically lent itself to one of three different outcomes, and all are undesirable.* This has been the international experience as well.

We think of unions as representing the "underdogs" of society. Half true! To have a union is to enjoy a considerable privilege over those other workers who don't have them. The very bottom strata of workers have historically not been able to maintain stable unions. And then there are those, lower on the scale, who can't even get work. At a time when the power of the unions reached and sometimes even exceeded that of the corporate elites, they imposed wage settlements that, through inflation, penalized those other workers who didn't have unions, and, of course, the public generally

As earlier cited, a labor commentator generally sympathetic to working people and their unions points to that "hinge,"[8] the sudden change upward in the rate of wage increases that occurred in the late 1960s. In roughly that same period in Britain, the governments of the Tory Edward Heath and the Labourite James Callaghan were turned out of office through inability to control trade union leaderships acting "as powers in the realm," that is, as if sharing equal power with the government. Here the price of union success was a degree of political anarchy accompanied by positive economic harm, often to the most vulnerable parts of the public.

This brings us to the second scenario. In the last analysis, unions cannot resist the combined power of government and the business interest. That was nowhere better illustrated than in the reaction to the "hinge." Under intensified business pressures, most Western governments imposed what is called an "incomes policy," also called "wage and price controls." That is conventionally thought to mean to restrain wage increases that go beyond labor productivity gains. But the same strength that can restrain union power is also enough to strangle union growth and power, and that is what has been occurring since circa 1970. We've had a regime not of wage and price controls but of wage controls only, stagnant and even declining incomes, and the ejection of trade unions from major influence over their national economies. Curbs on unions have been one of the key components in the end of the historic advance and, since then, in the excessive role of corporate elites in the political process. In this second scenario, union overreaching eventuated in their defeat, leading to declining worker well-being, a redistribution of income upward to the cadre and elite, and cuts in public services.

But what of the third scenario, where the power of the unions and the firms is more or less equal? That's the situation that current schemes of labor law reform want to create or restore. But that scenario is also undesirable. When, for example, in the 1950s there was rough power parity between the unions and the big firms in the United States, the two collaborated against the public. That classic format, as described in the auto industry in Serrin (1970), featured, first, a public show of militancy on the part of labor and of management, both swearing not to give in to the other. That was just play-acting. Fearful of a crippling strike or lockout, both government and public breathed a sigh of relief when the parties sat down to "craft an agreement"—which had been all but written from the beginning! Labor got increases beyond productivity and the firms covered that with price rises exceeding their new labor costs. The long-term decline of U.S. manufacturing is not unrelated to this historic collaboration, where the costs of inefficient methods, antiquated equipment, and both union and corporate monopoly were so easily off-loaded to the public. Not incidentally, this pattern was pioneered in the steel industry, which, naturally, has led the U.S. manufacturing decline.

These three outcomes are not the only problems with the sort of unions we have. The present form of the unions positively encourages the "bureaucratic," "top-down" unionism that labor reformers and labor's friends so often complain of. A modern industrial union has one overriding function, to obtain and then administer a contract with the employer, that is, to exercise "ownership" rights over some jobs. As before, it is as much a labor subcontractor as it is an organization that serves its members. Indeed, it places higher value on its relationship with management than it does on its representational relations with its own members. This is more or less unavoidable. The more insistent the voice of the membership, the harder for the leadership to negotiate and administer the contract. A union leadership that can't or won't control its members will also have troubles with the employers, who may as a result encourage a rival leadership faction or a rival union—as did General Electric and the rest of the electrical manufacturing industry in the 1940s and 1950s, when employer, church, and government joined forces to defeat a very good, quite representative union, the United Electrical Workers (UE), and to aid its less representative, anticommunist rival, the International Union of Electrical Workers (IUE).[9] Government will and in fact has reacted much the same way. Thus, the present system equally encourages labor leaders, the firms, and government to create and maintain a form of undemocratic, bureaucratic unionism—which over time has rendered the unions ineffectual. If we seek an explanation for the traditional nonideological brand of politics practiced by these unions, this legally imposed dominance of the labor subcontractor aspect explains more than any accusations of "lack of class consciousness" or "worker greed." The present form of U.S. industrial unions and their historic decline in members and power are two sides of the same coin. The form itself, a blessing to workers in its beginning, has proven decreasingly useful to its members and to other workers since 1955.

The quality of union representation of its members' interests has also been declining, in some cases radically. Unions are imagined to represent equally all of their members. But there has been an emerging tendency, as in autos, for the union to agree to a "two-tier" wage-and-benefit system. In a two-tier arrangement, new workers start at lower wage rates and benefits than the existing members. The arrangement is structured in such a way that *the newer and younger members will never catch up!* In other words, these agreements defend the older members' jobs and other benefits by sacrificing those of the younger ones.

A two-tier system is obviously unfair—"Some members are more equal than others," to borrow once more from Orwell. But there is a deeper significance to this. As many have pointed out, in accepting a two-tier system against the young, the union is actually confessing, "We have no future in this industry, but we will try to stave off defeat long enough to protect our present members. Those who come after them will have to fend for themselves." That is no more or less than an admission by union leaderships that the present institutional form of industrial unions is obsolete.

Workers need to be represented on the job. There is absolutely no substitute for that. Even a bad union is usually better than none at all. For all the faults I've ascribed to U.S. unions, the AFL-CIO and its member unions constitute the major barrier against further employer aggression against workers. They are among the champions in Congress and the statehouse for the poor, the old, the ill, for minorities and immigrants, for those who suffer discrimination, for the underpaid and the unemployed; in short, unions remain among the main voices of the Democracy in the political process. As before, the problem here is a bad institution; good people—in my experience, many wonderful people—try to do the best they can with it.

Nevertheless, all the outcomes of the present system are equally unacceptable. Carefully thought-out proposals for change are very badly overdue. But before entertaining proposals, we might look at another, different system of worker representation, namely, that of skilled workers through their craft-based unions.

Thinking About Union "Representation": Craft Unions

A crafts-based union such as the International Brotherhood of Electrical Workers (IBEW) arranges with, say, the local builders' association that the latter will use only unionized electricians, at union rates, and according to union rules and procedures. The builders' association might also agree to pay some monies into the union welfare or retirement fund. There are national unions of electricians and the other trades, but they are federations of local and regional unions; here power gravitates downward toward local and regional councils of cooperating crafts unions, not upward toward the national American Federation of Labor, now the AFL part of AFL-CIO.

U.S. craft unions are older than the industrial union; many date back to the first half of the nineteenth century, and the form reaches back to the medieval guilds and even back to classical Roman and Greek times (Glotz 1967).[10] Their members try to maintain a monopoly over an indispensable set of craft skills. Where changes in technology have not threatened the craft, these unions can extract a good price for the labors of their members, hence their persistence in the building trades. Craft unions typically band together in local building trades councils, where they cultivate local political connections. Their power is said to be such in a few trades that they can impose wasteful overstaffing or low output quotas. On the other hand, the skills of craft workers make them more efficient and reliable, thus cheaper to employ than unskilled workers, for, say, bricklaying or structural iron work on a building site.

Craft unions represent their members insofar as their skills are an inseparable personal possession and, of course, exercised.[11] Typically, the novice will enroll in a union-approved apprenticeship (training) program; advance, with the union's help, to journeyman's status; and, with further learning, time, luck, skill, and perhaps some "connections," rise to be a master electrician or master carpenter, where he (usually!) can supervise journeymen on complex jobs. Meanwhile, the union business agent arranges the details of the apprenticeship, now often in conjunction with a trade high school or community college, and assigns the worker to jobs as they come available. The "rights of management" are narrower here since union people typically manage the work on the job site. In an honest, well-run crafts local, more the rule than the exception, the individual worker's interests and concerns can and will be represented.

On the negative side, the crafts unions are sometimes family associations or otherwise too exclusivist, and, notably in the building trades, they have often resisted racial, gender, and even ethnic integration. There has also been some recurring pattern of union corruption. For example, when Big Bill Hutcheson, long-time president of the Carpenters' Union, died, he passed the union, like the rest of his estate, to his son and heir![12] But these issues aside, most crafts unions offer a stronger, somewhat more personal kind of representation to their members, actually following them as they advance in their careers from beginner to honored retiree.

The weakness of this somewhat better form of representation is that traditional crafts skills are eroded by technological change. Many years ago, the famous labor theorist Selig Perlman held up the (American) International Typographical Union as the very paragon of stable, powerful, bread-and-butter/no-ideological-nonsense trade unionism (Perlman 1949, chap. 7). And it was—until automatic typesetting machines and the personal computer more or less demolished the trade. In fact, while Perlman despised the old labor radicals with their talk of the "OBU" (One Big [industrial] Union), they were right that only a minority of workers of the crafts variety ever would be needed in modern industry. And that is the point about crafts union representation. Forgetting the labor wars between the partisans of the OBU and the "American Separation of Labor," crafts-type representation can at best benefit only a minority. Workers possessed of an indispensable craft, however hard they must work, are in an enviable position. But where the workers, like the vast and increasing majority, don't own a craft, employers can hire whom they want and too often pay them less than a Higgins wage.

We come here to the point in our analysis where we have to go off in two separate directions. On the one hand, we should examine how unions

A "CIVILIZED" EMPLOYMENT SYSTEM — 331

would function in a hypothetical future within the corporate charter system earlier proposed. And on the other, we should take up some of the useful things to be done by and for workers today and tomorrow within the present industrial system.

Unions and the Corporate Charter

Assuming the corporate charter program was enacted, bargaining over wages and other conditions would cease to be the wide-open, threat-against-threat sort of encounter we call "free collective bargaining," where someone generally takes a beating, often third-party outsiders like the public. The charter envisions the process of bargaining as taking place *within the firm's highest management* among representatives of different constituencies, each with rights over the firm, where each is obliged to temper one-sided claims as a condition of his or her office, where each is possessed of reliable knowledge about the entire economic situation of the firm and the industry, set within an evolving legal system calibrated to seek equitable outcomes among these competing, often incompatible interests. The corporate charter empowers every major constituency of the firm to participate equally in the distribution of the firms' assets and opportunities to reinvestment, workers, managers, suppliers, owners, creditors, and the public. No system can put an end to industrial conflict, but it can see that that conflict is conducted in a law-like setting where the power of each party and each interest is roughly on a par, and where wider social concerns are protected. My claim is that over time such a system would avoid the three negative outcomes associated with "free collective bargaining."

Assuming the charter system is in operation, the union would no longer "own" people's jobs and couldn't narrowly focus on the pay going to each job category of workers. Instead, it would function on the model of a European "works council," not engaging in conventional collective bargaining but representing the workers on all the issues that are presently left to management's "rights."

Where they exist, works councils and their authority are established by law.[13] The organic legislation initiating and governing a works council would need several different things. First and foremost, it should spell out an employee "bill of rights" in the workplace analogous to those a citizen enjoys in the polity—freedom of speech and assembly and the right to distribute newspapers and literature on the premises. Employees should also have the right not to be intimidated and, especially, to tenure of employment. Works councils would meet regularly and take up any and all issues of concern to any worker, seeking in the first instance to settle them amicably. Where this was not successful, workers (as well as management) would have the right to present their case to an industrial tribunal, a court with the statutory authority to impose settlements. In most present-day disputes between a worker and management, the burden of proof falls on the worker. The tribunals shift the burden of proof to management, which tends to make for a safer, more democratic, less stressful, less dictatorial work environment and, over time, a less conflict-ridden one as well.

Among the rights of workers in such a system is the right not to be fired save for cause. When the worker first enters the job, a document is negotiated between the worker, the council, and management laying out what the duties of the job are and what constitutes a proper level of performance. If then the worker is fired and the firing is challenged at a tribunal, management has to prove that the worker did not perform to the agreed standard. This both repudiates the doctrine of "employment at will" and embodies a substantive, defendable right on the part of the employee to his or her job. It also undoes the doctrine of the "rights of management." In such a system both parties have rights, so that disputes between them must be settled before a neutral third party but in a setting substantively weighed to the defense of the individual.

Come what may, corporate charter or not, the U.S. labor system badly needs to shed both "employment at will" and the "rights of management." It is an anomaly that in democratic societies in the twenty-first century, where citizens have substantive rights guaranteed to them and positively defended by other, powerful institutions, every shop and workplace can be run as a petty tyranny. Of course, not all workplaces are like that. Generally, and especially for the better-educated workers, the actual workplace tends to be run on a modestly consensual, "civilized" basis. That is decidedly not the case for the less educated, or for the factory and mill worker, or often for the young worker, or for *any* worker, even the better educated, when, as they say, push comes to shove.[14]

Proposal: Vocational Representation

Unions need to be more representative of their members' interests; the bond between member and union needs to be strengthened; and unions need to attract those workers who are today outside union ranks. Nowadays many working people shop around first before settling into a "career" job. They are as concerned about the future of their careers as they are about their pay and working conditions in the present. And many workers continue to acquire new skills and credentials over the course of their working lives in order to remain competitive and employable. These are desires and interests that unions ought to represent. Such unions would be, not industrial or craft unions, but vocational unions; that is, they would represent the worker's wider career and vocational interests from his or her first job through to retirement. As a labor educator and activist, I've had some small experience of this idea and believe that it is broadly applicable.

Over the last twenty-plus years of my teaching career, my students were for the most part older, part-time and evening students returning to college. Contrary to Leo Rosten's all-too-earnest fictional character in *The Education of H*y*m*a*n K*a*p*l*a*n*, they were not only the best but also the most intellectual students that I encountered over my entire career. They had different agendas among themselves. Some, the fifty- to seventy-year-olds, for example, felt cheated because they had not had university educations and simply wanted to learn, to be educated. Many of the others had worked a considerable length of time at their present jobs, had family responsibilities, and, as a result, could not contemplate leaving those jobs, but wanted either to upgrade their standing in the field they were in or, not infrequently, to seek more influential roles in their unions. And of course, there were a few, mostly younger, who were in a position to go on to law school, graduate school, or other professional training. The motivation of all these students was and had to be very strong. They worked their normal work weeks and at least three nights per week attended classes until late in the evening. When I myself was a part-time, evening (graduate) student, I managed two to three hours a day of study on the subway, but in the suburb where I was teaching, the students had to drive. That added at least another four to five hours per week when they couldn't study, or relax, or be with their families. Going to school only part-time, they faced this regimen for seven years or more, not the four years of the day student. I admired them then and still do.

Now, a different situation. For several years I worked alongside the training and upgrading fund of a union of health and nursing care workers. By agreement between the union and the industry, a percentage of the payroll was automatically placed in the fund. Any union member who was accepted into a recognized health-care training program automatically got his, or usually her, tuition and books paid for. For full-time study, there was a stipend, and the worker's seniority and benefits were maintained.

Those who work in health care are often at the bottom of the workforce, poorly educated, poorly paid, poorly treated, and have limited or accented English. Many are illiterate in their native languages, much less in English. Accordingly, the union ran classes for high school equivalency diplomas and others for college entry. These programs were strongly subscribed. More, they were a point of pride throughout the union among workers who had experienced how hard it is, both morally and economically, to be at the bottom of the heap.

Then, and, I think, still, the industry was chronically short of personnel in various medical and other health specialties. In spite of the usual fits of cost cutting that every industry goes through, it was by and large persuadable to keep the program. There was no "waste" for them. They had to approve the actual training and credentialing courses and got the benefit of a steady supply of needed, newly qualified, obviously well-motivated workers.

If vocational representation is to characterize tomorrow's unions, the AFL-CIO itself will have to take the lead. There will have to be agreements among participating unions on the following:

First, to join any union at all will qualify the member automatically to transfer at a later point, without fuss or additional cost, to any other union on his or her next job and to have his or her union seniority and any pension contributions carried forward on the books. If the worker's next job is nonunion, then union seniority and benefit contributions should be carried on the books until either one returns to a union job or retired.

Second, on joining the union the worker will have continual vocational counseling available, and as with the training fund, there will be material assistance and remedial training, if necessary, to enable the worker to take advantage of the educational opportunity and coordinate its demands with his or her private and work-related obligations. In my experience, schools and community colleges sometimes don't realize that small steps on their part to make their offerings "worker friendly"—such as negotiating with employers over class locations and flexible work schedules—can have a really major effect on enrollments. A union is ideally positioned to interface with the school authorities to effect this.

Third, the union should also be prepared to advise and assist the member in getting that next job when and as he or she is qualified or eligible.

These things cost money, but as with the hospital and nursing home industries, some employers or employer associations might invest in the upgrading of their own and potential workers. Big national employers might not find this cost effective, although many employers of my own students assisted them in furthering their education by releasing them from work and providing them with tuition assistance. Others directly rewarded their employees with pay increases for different certificates and degrees. Employers who are, by the nature of their businesses, wedded to a region could perhaps be induced to contribute to a well-thought-out regional training and upgrading scheme. Local government and school systems, including the community colleges, are often willing, sometimes anxious, to see their facilities used to upgrade the skills of the local workforce.

Where the union's members are convinced of the value of upgrading and credentialing programs, a small union payroll tax might gain support. Such programs could be a source of pride and old-fashioned solidarity around the idea that workers are raising themselves up by helping each other. As before, a union is uniquely positioned to manage, even coordinate education and upgrading schemes because union people really do have insight into what arrangements are needed to make things "friendly" and nonalienating for workers.

Fourth, there has to be counseling that reaches out to workers and helps them to understand that however poor students they might have been as teenagers, they are different now and are likely to find much, much more success, even pleasure, in study. There are too many workers who do not go on past high school, or who drop out at age sixteen because they've been counseled by a school official that they are not "college material." I was put into a non-college track in high school, and if I recall correctly, *all* of my later honor students had been told that they were not "college material" when they were younger. Some teachers and guidance counselors are biased against working-class people or people who speak or dress differently or are racially or ethnically different. Workers who were convinced by an "authority figure" that they had little or no potential for self-improvement should be reassured that authority figures are often wrong.

Fifth, workers in general need continuing counseling on job and other prospects, on how to seek jobs effectively, on how to respond in an interview, and so on. One of the advantages almost automatically falling to professional and other middle-class people is that they learn about wider job and opportunity prospects. They just pick it up in their everyday encounters. Working-class people are not normally well placed to pick up that knowledge.

Sixth, vocational representation should extend to advising and assisting workers in planning their children's education. These days some privileged children have "education coaches" or some such who seek out the most suitable colleges for them, unearth all the scholarship assistance possibilities, counsel them on their interviews, and show them how to get into the more desirable high schools or colleges. Workers don't have the resources or knowledge to do this for their children, which unfairly penalizes their families. This is another service that could be provided by their unions.

To repeat, no single union can undertake vocational counseling like this, but the AFL-CIO or a union consortium could manage it.

As soon as one shifts from "wages and hours" issues, which are complicated enough, and tries to represent workers in wider, much more complex ways, one needs infinitely more expertise that I can muster. Nevertheless, my sense is that the concept of vocational representation is overdue for the labor movement; it rests on the idea that higher wages on this or that job are insufficient to give workers and their families a fair chance at the social and other advantages assumed now as a birthright by other classes and life courses. A person's place in an Americanist social system is no longer determined just by one's wages here and now, but by one's path over time in a complicated system yielding different advantages to different people over the course of their vocational lives. As unions once broke the barriers of dire poverty and frequent unemployment for workers, now they should be trying to break through the "glass ceiling" that the system still imposes on its lower ranks. Like their parents before them, today's workers can win by mutual effort what is, as a matter of course, now reserved for others and denied to them.

Proposal: Representing Workers by Town, City, or County

In the post–Civil War United States, a major laboring person's organization, called the Knights of Labor, had a brief flowering. The Knights organized on the job but also in the community: they had area-wide "district councils" because so many of the things used by the workers of that era were produced locally, often in the same neighborhood. The baker baked bread, the butcher processed animals, and the cobbler made shoes on the premises. They were neighbors and were potentially subject to community pressure. Thus, when the Knights promoted wage and quality "codes" for different lines of work, their leverage rested less on strikes by the workers directly involved and more on community pressure and selective boycotting. People refused to buy the products of the offending employer and could put further social pressures on him and his family. The idea was that the whole community should unite to make sure that everyone was treated equitably.

Three things appear to have destroyed the Knights of Labor. They encouraged a strike in Chicago that turned particularly violent—the famous Haymarket Massacre.[15] That brought the wrath of the respectable classes down on their heads. Second, because boycotting really was effective, laws were enacted to make most of it illegal, and violations were prosecuted aggressively. Probably most important, neighborhood production of workers' consumer goods changed. The better manufacturing jobs moved downtown or out of the city. The workers' shoes came increasingly from Lynn, Massachusetts, their clothing from Manhattan or Chicago, and national producers arose to offer meats, cooking and heating fuel, fruit and vegetables, even dairy products. The neighborhood economic base of the Knights simply eroded, and with it the Knights as well.

It is striking and suggestive that so many of the lowest-wage employers today depend on carefully defined regional markets, as in a single town, city, or county. This is true of franchised retailers in groceries, fast food, sporting goods, pharmacies; the list grows all the time. If such franchised retailers were under local pressure to pay better wages and offer better conditions, they would have great incentive to yield to that pressure, since they would not be able to simply "run away" to another region.

What this suggests is that there should be area-defined unions, attempting to represent every worker in every franchise in a region, much like the Knights of Labor. One single union would try to represent every worker in the area who works for any franchised retailer. The area is the key, not differences of industry or skill. Such a union could enlist very powerful allies. The workers who staff Arby's and the CVS pharmacy are local women and young people who use local services, pay local taxes, and, with their families, vote in local elections. Local government would also have some interest in better wages, for that would improve the tax base.[16] Local parent and school officials have an interest in better wages; teen workers now work too many hours, at the expense of their schoolwork and valuable extracurricular activities. Higher wages could translate into fewer hours.

Parents and school officials could be energized to support a higher community wage scale, and local government, prodded by its own self-interested carrot and a parent/school stick, might well go along. The basis for this sort of thing already exists in alliances pressing for locally imposed higher minimum wages.

The Knights included small merchants in their ranks, on the simple proposition that if one merchant paid less, that gave the miscreant a competitive advantage. Local merchants today base their opposition to Wal-Mart and other outside retailers on very similar reasoning. They too might be enlisted in the community/regional "union."

However, there are strong reasons not to call it a union. Many hackles are raised by the very word. In addition, a union is very, very closely regulated in what it can and can't do in, especially, federal law. As we saw, U.S. unions are shaped (and restricted) more by a government agency, the NLRB, than by their members. Businesses often change the names of what they do in order to escape regulation. In some regions, local newspapers no longer consider those who deliver their papers "employees." They call them "subcontractors" in order to keep unions out, wages low, and benefits nonexistent; however, they still control all the normal management functions of the actual work. We can learn from this.

The community/regional "union" might try to negotiate a contract with the regional employers following the model of the skilled-worker construction unions. On the other hand, like the Knights, a regional "union" of retail workers might only draft a code of pay and work standards, engage parent and other community organizations to join in the effort, seek support for the code from local officials and school authorities, and then work to pressure—one by one—individual franchises to abide by the code. The pressure might take several forms, including informal community boycotts of the offending chain. Such boycotts need not be total (and illegal) to be effective. The sales targets and profit margins of the big national franchises are very high, and they dislike even small dips. One is not trying to "make them an offer they can't refuse" but instead to make them an offer they can live with comfortably.

Poorly paid franchise workers, both adults and teens, differ sharply in their work qualities. A local campaign to inform workers about who are the better, higher-paying, higher-standard, community-supporting employers would lead better workers away from an offending chain, leaving it with the less desirable, less productive, less profitable, less responsible remainder.

The key thing here is to identify the boundaries of the firms' markets. The "union's" membership boundaries should correspond to them. That way the firm is under maximum pressure, and the community/region has the maximum leverage.

There are existing unions that have small beachheads in the national franchises. They might oppose these community-based or regional "unions." In the history of the U.S. labor movement, that would not be unusual. But the existing unions could find that their best interests are served by this new—or reborn—type of "union." It is in the interest of every union that local officials, school authorities, and even merchants assume a favorable attitude to worker activities to improve their own situation. If this is the price of giving up a few dues payers, it will often be worth it. Second, many if not most of the workers that this proposal is aimed at are female, young, or part-time. They will later enter full-time, adult, career work, and it would be to the advantage of the local unions if these potential members had a favorable experience of collective action and could transfer their membership automatically to whatever union had jurisdiction over their next job. Given that unions in the private sector are now at nearly a hundred-year low, some ought to be willing to suffer some temporary membership losses in the interest of a growing labor movement that should in the not too distant future benefit them as well. Actually, given the resistance of the big franchisees to unions, few unions would be asked to give up any actual members, only potential members whom they cannot at present enroll anyway. There is room here for give-and-take and a reinforced understanding that unions are not just business operations; they have a broader solidaristic, humane, and civic function.

We have come by degrees to the situation of the "lowest of the low," that is, those who are now at the bottom of the labor system—and those even lower who are not even allowed into it.

Work as a "Natural Right"

In the United States the phrase "the right to work" has a bizarre meaning. It does not mean that everyone who wants a job has a right to a job. What it means is that workers have a right not to be forced into a union and that *employers* have the right to persuade them of that. Since this persuading is often done on the employer's premises and during business hours, employer *persuasion* often turns into employer *coercion*. This "odd couple" of employee and employer legal rights was enshrined in the Taft-Hartley Act of 1947 and has played a major role in the reduction of union membership to the minuscule levels of today.

I agree that people shouldn't be forced to belong to trade unions. But it leads to the unfortunate result that gains by the union also fall to those who work in the same shop but aren't members. It seems wrong that "free riders" should be rewarded by the sacrifices, financial and otherwise, of their coworkers. Practically speaking, "the right to work" undoes much of the rationale for joining the union and paying the dues. I don't have a solution to this conundrum about the "right to work," but I do want to talk about a different right to work, that is, as a "natural right" and not a pro-employer/anti-union slogan.

In the natural rights tradition of such as John Locke and his colonial American heirs, the basic natural, inalienable rights were three in number—life, liberty, and property, the last gussied up as the "pursuit of happiness." Life and liberty don't exist in a social vacuum; one must have material means, *firmly under one's own control,* to support a dignified and worthy life and, closely related, to prevent one from falling into dependence. One cannot really be an individual—a "free person" and not a "subject" of somebody—if one's life can be forfeit at the whim of king or Gestapo, or one's liberty arbitrarily taken away by the press gang. Or if one's living is at the whim of another.

Of course, in Lockean England, and later in Madisonian America, "natural and inalienable" as they might be, the rights to life, liberty, and property didn't belong to women, to servants, to slaves, to apprentices, to agricultural laborers, to maritime sailors, to young people, in fact to any of "the lower" orders, which is to say, to the vast majority of the people of the time. Only merchants and artisans, landowners, and, in Britain, aristocrats—one must appreciate that irony—actually enjoyed these natural rights, and they, for the most part, actively opposed their extension to the majority. But over time the contradiction between the natural origin of the rights, as they were thought of, and the unnatural denial of them to so many worked its effect. The lower orders and their friends seized upon this contradiction, and over more than a century and a half of often bloody struggle, they became the patrimony of the people of North America, Western Europe, Japan, South Korea, and a too small handful of others.

Our notions of property have also changed. Life and liberty are undermined, really nullified, if there is no economic security. We're no longer a nation of shopkeepers, independent craftspeople, and yeoman farmers, each secure in his own little property; we mostly work in and are dependent for our livelihood on corporations, government agencies, and other organizations, many of which are quite large and impersonal. Nowadays most of us accept the idea that the living standard of the population *as a whole* must be such that people can act as free people, enjoy the fruits of liberty, and be secure in their livelihoods.

That "as a whole" is no longer enough; we should be trying to make sure that every man, woman, and young person enjoys the rights of life, liberty, and property, not just de jure, but de facto, not just in our good intentions about the future but in the present fabric of our society, not just when times are good, but all the time.

If we take the natural rights tradition seriously, several things follow. There should be *at hand* to every man, woman, and young person a job at a wage that would enable the person to enjoy the full range of opportunities and privileges that the well-off enjoy. This does not imply absolute social and economic equality, but our notion of what constitutes a livable wage does have to reach the standard laid down by Judge Higgins in 1907. In a moment I want to spell out some proposals to make that into a reality. But first we have to clear away some ideological clutter.

Friendly Smiles of the Dismal Science

The idea that every working person could, in principle, earn a livable, "Higgins" wage finds its most resolute ideological opponents among professional economists. There is a long tradition in economics that warns workers against efforts to improve their wages, other than by, of course, greater obedience, harder work, longer hours, and, one imagines, "pluck." Such efforts, it is held, are ill-advised and, in fact, go against their own self-interest. This tradition is so long-lived and has assumed so many guises that it must be considered a bedrock of mainstream economic theory. One of its earliest variants was pressed as far back as 1836 by an English economist named Nassau W. Senior.[17] He argued that most of the working day of the manufacturing laborer was needed to make up the costs of raw material, machines, energy, and so forth, and it was only in the very last hours of the day that a "profit" was generated that could be shared between the manufacturer and his workers. One must appreciate the beauty of this analysis. Those "last hours" of the day were not hours seven and eight, but hours fifteen and sixteen. And it is not beside the point that Senior was also inveighing against legislation that would limit the hours of female and child workers!

His better-known successor, John Stuart Mill, offered the same advice but in a different manner. According to Mill's doctrine of the "wages fund," the iron laws of economics fixed a definite pot of money in an economy for workers' wages. If some workers, possibly by strikes, succeeded in getting more wages for themselves, it followed that there was less in the fund for others, who would have to earn less or, more likely, would be unemployed, there being insufficient wages left to pay them.

In the twentieth century, two new variants of Mill's reasoning emerged. The Phillips curve argues that the higher the worker's wages, the more likely there is to be inflation; in other words, if the workers' "pot" expands in dollars, each dollar must become worth a bit less, that is, prices will automatically rise. Hence, the battle to hold down wages isn't really anti-worker, for it is in their interest too to hold down inflation. And there is Milton Friedman's "natural rate of unemployment," so natural that to reduce unemployment further is automatically to cause inflation. One has to appreciate the irony here. Economists are absolutely sure that capitalists must in their own—and our—interests pursue higher profits, but it is tragically wrong for workers to pursue higher wages. That is, to pursue them other than, as I pointed out before, via greater obedience, harder work, longer hours, genuine "pluck," and with due deference to the friendly advice of the masters of the science of economics.

This set of ideas is rooted in fundamental economics doctrine. The theory is that employers have almost no control "in the market" over their costs in materials, energy, machinery and technology, rents, or the prices of their product. Within that price-taking prison a capitalist can hire and pay workers if and only to the extent that they create through their work value equal to their own wages. If they can create more than they are paid, the workers, it is argued, will go out and take jobs that pay those higher wages. And if they create less than their wages, they will have to be fired or their wages lowered. Pursuing this analysis further, as economists do with great skill and greater enthusiasm, it follows that workers' wages will be precisely set by their *marginal net product,* that is, at the tip-over point or "margin" where they produce no more and no less than the amount of their wages.

This is the very soul of modern wages doctrine, and it is adhered to by the most distinguished and accomplished professional economists. It is also pure Alice in Wonderland.

First, empirical studies of actual wages show that they vary enormously by region. Nonunionized sewing machine operators in New York City are presumably no more or less skillful than those of up-country North Carolina; nor do production carpenters in Florida produce less than those in suburban Boston. But there are large—often huge—differences in the wages paid in New York and North Carolina, in Florida and Boston. The regional situation, not "marginal net product," plays the major role here. Are there any unions? Are local officials supportive of or hostile to workers? Are local employers used to sharing their good fortune with their workers? What's the local unemployment rate? Are there immigrants or part-time women or other "cheap labor" available?

Second, the big firms and franchisers that make up most of the U.S. economy are price setters, not price takers. They do have to respond to various market pressures, but we know for a fact that they have considerable leeway in setting their prices. Accordingly, the fixed sum of money available for wages, as assumed in Senior, Mill, Phillips, and Friedman, and in marginal analysis in general, is just beside the point. Just as employers have wiggle room to set their prices, their workers have wiggle room to contest over the amount of the wages. Truth be told, "the iron laws of economics" are really made of taffy.

There is also a deep divide between economics as a prescriptive ideology and economics as a description-based science. The first is now dominant. It assumes that how much the workers can produce depends on their own intrinsic productive abilities; some workers have greater productive abilities than others, and in marginal net product analysis, this difference will be automatically reflected in higher wages for the one and lower for the other. That is why, in this orthodoxy, unemployment and low wages exist: some workers cannot produce enough to keep a job, others enough to earn a living wage. Ergo, if by union or political pressure they keep those jobs in existence or win those higher wages, Phillips's inflation or Friedman's "natural rate of unemployment" will kick in and erase the jobs and the increases.

But if we look at actual industry employment practices, we see that from one in four to one in six employees serve in the managerial echelon, where they bend their efforts to multiply the output of the others. Some of these cadre employees design new technology that produces more product at less net cost. Others reorganize productive systems to produce more product for less wages. We actually know that worker productivity in the United States has been steadily increasing over the past thirty years, while real wages have stagnated or fallen. Thus, while the "science" of economics treats worker productivity as essentially a fixed trait of the worker, like height or weight, management understands that worker productivity depends on investment, technology, education, and better management. The difference between the two approaches is that one is ideological and prescriptive, the other scientific and descriptive. Like Nassau Senior, today's economics orthodoxy has a "political" point of view.[18]

Where does that leave us? In the first instance, we know that productivity varies with better work organization and improved technologies. The shares of net product steered to worker, management, and investor claimants are a function of choice and policy, not immutable economic laws. Naturally, workers with only the simplest and elementary skills are not as productive as those with greater, more adaptable skills, but those differences are not immutable, which means that the present-day low-wage, high-unemployment economy is not inevitable.

The U.S. experience of World War II shows how genuinely hollow these orthodox notions of worker skill and adaptability are. In 1940, the entire U.S. workforce consisted of about 55.5 million persons, including the unemployed. Everyone else, in the orthodoxy, was viewed as not wanting a job or having insufficient skill to hold a job. But over the next few years the armed forces drew 10 million people out of the workforce and into the military. They were replaced by another, different 10 million people—the ones who "didn't want a job and weren't equipped to hold a job"![19] These workers then outproduced the rest of the world, equipped the armed forces of several countries besides our own, and, as an added fillip (certainly not Phillips), raised the U.S. standard of living a notch.[20] Note especially that that these "unemployables" were trained on the job and usually at full pay. They were not told, "First train, and then we *may* be able to find you a job!" They were already filling the jobs they were training for, and at the same time earning good money. This proved the strongest practical motivation to learn the needed job skills quickly, to be reliable, to accept direction, in short, to exhibit the very qualities orthodox theory claimed—and still claims—that they lacked.

We don't really know ahead of time who wants and will take a job, or who can produce and who can't. Of course there was a war on, and people wanted to help the country. But we also know now that many more people would seek work if they knew it was available, that they could earn decent money, and that they could learn the job by working at the job. Many women would like to work, but the wages they can earn aren't enough to cover child care, transportation, and work clothing. Of course, there are men and women among us who won't seek work even if it is available, who will "dog it" on the job, prove hard to supervise, come late, be absent, and so forth. But those people can't be discovered via the route of "pure" theory or even conventional social investigation. As our experience of the 1940s indicates, we have to create the circumstances that separate the wheat from the chaff. If we create those circumstances, then we'll isolate those who are vocationally pathological from those who only appear to be so because of our sins of omission. Until we actually create those circumstances, we are denying too many good people their right to life, liberty, and property.

Proposal: Eliminate Parasitical Employers and Jobs

There are too many jobs in the U.S. economy now that do not pay a Higgins wage, that is, do not pay enough for an adult working person and one or two dependents to live a properly civilized life. Worse, many of these jobs don't even pay enough for the jobholder to get by on. As a matter of principle, we should erase this low-wage economy completely. We shouldn't even distinguish between jobs that pay less than a poverty wage and those that pay less than a Higgins wage. Both are socially undesirable and for the most part economically dispensable. Such jobs and the employers who offer them should fall under a special legal category within which policies can be mounted, in time, either to raise the wages to the Higgins standard or ultimately to phase out those businesses and lines of work.

Here the rationale for social and legal intervention is overwhelming. If an employer pays less than a living wage, then the rest of society has to make up the difference. People who don't earn enough to live on have to have part of their living paid for by others; it may be through food stamps, or rent subsidies or the negative income tax, or Aid to Families with Dependent Children, or any of the other ways in which the society steers goods or income to the working poor.

An employer who pays less than a living wage is a parasite who depends on the rest of society to make up for it. That alone justifies social intervention. We should recognize only two legal kinds of wage: livable wages and "nonlivable wages." The category "nonlivable wage" would replace the "minimum wage."[21] Furthermore, it should be *illegal*. Paying a worker a nonlivable wage should trigger governmental intervention into the wage-setting process and the productive characteristics of the labor processes involved. This last intervention is central to the proposal.

The first step is to legislate a livable wage standard; as before, we can call it a Higgins wage. It's the present-day Bureau of Labor Standards cost-of-living modified to add at least a taste of financial security, luxury, pleasure, savings, and the other good things that the rest of us enjoy as a birthright. It should be enacted as the lowest wage one may pay. Once one determines what that monetary standard ought to be for a "typical" family head, it can be fine-tuned for other kinds of workers, for nonadults, and for those without dependents, and for regional variations as well as the differential impacts of inflation. The relevant legislation being in place, we can leave the details to the statisticians and other social investigators to work out the dollars and cents.

But we can't stop there; there are too many such jobs just to wipe them out at a stroke of the pen, and it would be grossly unfair both to the workers and their employers. Accordingly, such employers would apply for a license or permit to pay less than the Higgins standard. There would be two conditions attached to the permit. First of all, the employer would have to open his books and accounts to, let's call it, the Higgins Wage Authority (HWA). We know as a fact that there are many businesses that pay a nonlivable wage and that, because of that, rivers of profit flow to their upper managers and investors. This is often true in fast food, in retailing, very likely in meat and poultry processing, and so forth. Where this was the case, the license would be refused, and if a company continued to flout the wage standard, it would face criminal penalties. On the natural rights position we have adopted, they would be guilty of depriving their employees of a fundamental and inalienable right to earn a human living. The penalties should be substantial: fines a high multiple of the denied wages, removal of company officers for substantial lengths of time, possibly even a lifetime ban on holding any future management position, serious jail sentences where warranted, and the enforced dissolution of particularly offending firms with confiscation of their assets. Here the point is to put an end to inadequate wages, once and for all.

Some companies, for example, would not be able to pay more than they are presently paying because their productive processes just don't create enough net product to pay more. Here I see the HWA working with the employers through technological assistance, loans at very favorable terms, help in improving the quality of management and of sales, on the job retraining, the organization of purchaser or sales co-ops, whatever, to enable the employer in good time to meet the Higgins standard. It goes without saying that the employees themselves would have a right to organize themselves to participate together with the HWA and the employer to bring about a fair and favorable result as soon and as securely as possible.

Expenditures on this entire operation really should be seen not as costs but as investments. One is trying to end the sublivable wages of the employees, the parasitical state of the employers, and the legendary fragility of such jobs and businesses. The three are bound together, and to achieve that result, or even to approach that result, is to create a net economic and social gain. Thus, government loans and other outlays should in future weigh lightly on the firms. It is undesirable on the face of it to have small businesses permanently involved with the rules and officials of the authority or bearing substantial long-term debts. Perhaps, as the firms succeeded year after year in maintaining the Higgins standard, that would automatically amortize their debts in a reasonable space of time. Here the bottom line is that a healthier, higher-paying, more profitable, more secure small business sector would not only help improve U.S. society immeasurably but also, like education subsidies in the past, generate far more in new tax revenues than was spent on the loans. Basically, one wants an economically prosperous small business and entrepreneurial sector of the economy paying a civilized wage. That is worth the investment.

Inevitably, there will be firms and productive processes that will not improve enough to pay the Higgins standard. Here, one could help the employers and the workers shift into new lines of business. This sounds utopian (or draconian) but really is not. The gap between improving productive routines or sales routines and shifting to entirely new kinds of products, their productive processes, and their sales is not infinite. Shifting employers and workers to new lines of business would of course be more expensive and take longer. Inevitably there would be failures. But failure is the rule, not the exception, for small firms with primitive productive routines; under the present scheme those rates of failure should fall, and the opportunities to explore new lines of business would expand. Of course, one cannot turn every job and every productive process into a silk purse. Some will resist every effort; the task then is to reduce that sort of job and that sort of productive process to the barest minimum so that the present-day supports we give to the working poor will themselves be reduced to the barest minimum and become marginal to the economy rather than, as today, so central and important.

Proposal: Work on Demand

Years ago I heard the famous urban renewer (also "urban remover") Robert Moses propose that there should be work on demand for every person and at a decent wage. Moses' scheme was simplicity itself; on any given day, a person who wanted work could go to a convenient location, be assigned a day's work, and be paid for it at the end of the same day. The federal government, most state governments, and not a few country governments could mount such a scheme. I favor Moses' idea, although it needs filling out in a few respects.

Day labor of the sort Moses imagined should be available at a central location via what he called a "shape-up." Because all these jobs would be paid at the same rate, save perhaps for transportation and safety (risk) differences, by the end of the shape-up every person in the hall should be assigned a job. Some of these jobs would have to be makework. Since we now provide relief, AFDC, negative income tax, and food stamps to those in need, what we'd be doing here is no longer giving those to the working poor for free but having them earn those monies. I'm skipping over some serious issues about coercion here and ignoring the fact that some people are simply unable to work. One can modify the scheme to seem and to be less harsh and more understanding of people's weaknesses and incapacities. Nevertheless, one really wants people to work, to earn, to have money for a good life, to have a productive, therefore full place in an Americanist society.

Some "makework" of course isn't that at all. Our environment has grown fairly shabby. There are piles of trash that need to be raked, flowers that need to be planted, weeds that need to be pulled, and graffiti that needs to be cleaned off or painted over. There are home visits to the elderly, ill, and handicapped that need to be made.

Integrating unions into this system might be a problem. One does not want to use casual laborers to replace their members. Unions should be part of the directing boards of the work scheme, where they can defend their respective turfs. The day worker should become a member of some sort of the most relevant union and pay a reduced dues. Here the idea is to create a community of material self-interest among the unions to engage their support, not arouse their opposition. Given the radically weakened state of the unions at present, it really would be in their interest to develop new relationships of mutual advantage with governmental bodies and NGOs.

One can extend Moses's idea by providing the would-be workers with the opportunity to sign up for a week's or a month's work. Or even a year or more. There might even be a wage premium attached to this since it allows the job-offering authority to propose more complex jobs on more complex projects and to provide on-the-job skills training. Here we move away from simple makework and jobs requiring minimal skills. Our historical experience suggests the good effects of this sort of scheme. Virtually every national park still shows the handiwork of the old-time New Deal Civilian Conservation Corps (CCC) and Works Progress Administration (WPA), which built and improved so many of them.

Workers would have the option to ask that their work be closely evaluated and that those evaluations go into a permanent employment file. Those files would over time identify men, women, and young people who showed unusual promise as employees and who therefore would be sought after by the wider job market. Now, of course, people without work history, or an erratic work history, have little to show an employer and less motivation to perform to high standards. The files themselves would be a positive asset for the worker in transitioning from the public works scheme into the wider job market. Access to these files would be entirely up to the individual worker.

It might be good to allow high school students to qualify for the shape-up and to reduce their school time accordingly. Many boys and girls consider school a waste of time, and some of them extract a price from their classmates and teachers. The opportunity to earn money while pausing (or continuing only part-time) in school would point up the importance of the schooling. And, in the longer run, as I can testify personally and from my teaching experience, it should encourage them to complete their high school diplomas and even, for many, college degrees.

These school leavers should be given a "rain check" that allows them, after some suitable period of time has elapsed, automatic readmission into the school they left or its equivalent. Young people especially should never be made to feel that the school system has deserted them.

It is important that women with dependent children be able to join in this work scheme. During World War II, employers were so anxious to get women to work that they provided crèches, child care, and even community feeding services. These aids are readily duplicated, and the increased earnings of the women will amortize some of the expenditure through increased tax revenues to the sponsoring government.[22]

Finally, there is a need for transportation to bring the potential workers to the job center, to get them out to the job sites, and then to bring them home again. Many are jobless or underpaid because they can't get from the central city to the suburbs where the jobs are located or from one suburb to another. Solving the transportation problem would be relatively easy and inexpensive.

Immigrants

I am chary about moves to vastly strengthen discrimination laws, especially those keyed to race, since that tends to provoke the most atavistic of our citizenry.[23] Further, I am under the impression that the existing rates of change in law, regulation, political attitudes, and social practices increasingly protect the better-off people of the relevant categories—black people, women, the elderly, the handicapped, and gays and lesbians—from most job and other discrimination. Because all sorts of disadvantaged people and their relatives and friends have emulated the strategies worked out by African Americans, there now seems steady support for a more and more discrimination-free society.

At the same time, we know that antidiscrimination laws themselves discriminate—against the poorest of the poor and the lowest of the low. One has to have a job to be protected against employment discrimination, and have a Higgins income to take advantage of the housing laws. (That, of course, was part of the rationale for our earlier proposals.)

We particularly need wider and more generous protections for immigrants and their children, especially in matters of employment, education, and health. The greatest obstacle to decent policies for immigrants, however, is our national hypocrisy on the issue: too often the same persons, parties, and institutions covertly encourage illegal immigration and illegal employment on the one hand, while publicly championing draconian measures against illegal immigrants on the other, measures that they, and we, know will harm legal immigrants as well.

For example, in March 2007 the Immigration and Naturalization Service conducted a surprise raid on a leather goods firm in New Bedford,

Massachusetts. Three hundred and sixty-one people, mostly women, were immediately packed off to jails as far away as Texas. Massachusetts's governor had prior knowledge of the raid and had asked that it be coordinated with the State's Bureau of Social Services; the INS didn't. The governor's fears were realized. Many of the women had young children at home; others were caring for ailing relatives, facts that the INS ignored. The firm itself was subsidized by the state and was manufacturing leather goods for the U.S. Department of Defense. As the workers were being shipped off to their cells, the owners made their modest bail and immediately went off to a holiday or business trip to Puerto Rico: it wasn't clear which.

It subsequently emerged that two different firms, owned by the same people, were operating on the same premises. The workers worked for one firm for their eight hours but were then compelled to work another shift for the other firm! Since the two firms were nominally different, the owners "legally" avoided paying time-and-a-half for the overtime. They paid the straight rate for a compulsory work week of over sixty hours.

We see here so much of what is wrong about the current situation. People were arrested and sent out of state because they didn't have documents on their persons proving they were American citizens; basically, they were "typed" as Latin American and thus fair game. Who of us carries documents on our person attesting to our citizenship?

Second, they were treated as criminals, and their families and dependents, including children born in the United States—thus citizens—were also victimized. Third, the owners but not the workers were allowed bail, although it was they in the first instance who committed a crime. They claimed that they didn't know about the illegals, but of course they did. That's why they could pay them so poorly and force them to work long hours at low wages. Fourth, the state gave a capital grant and the Defense Department a contract to a firm that *they* knew or could easily have known was hiring illegal aliens. This story is all too typical of the sort of problems associated with illegal immigrants.

Immigrants, legal or illegal, leave their mother country for a multitude of reasons, usually compelling ones—there is no work, they live under a vicious regime, they can see no prospects for their children. One can hardly be angry at them for violating our laws. But the employers violate the law for gain, not to escape desperate circumstances. If the state grant and the federal contract were automatically revocable when the owners were lax in their hiring procedures, that would indeed have an effect on would-be employers. Then, too, all those INS agents and their airplanes and jails cost money, as do the hours of the state social workers who have to iron out the mess. The offending employer, if convicted, should be forced to make good all those governmental expenses. But by focusing on the illegals, one makes sure illegal immigration will continue and even prosper. Our public policy is hypocritical on this point; officials storm on about the dangers of illegal immigration, but as we see, they both financed and looked the other way until they had the chance to make a headline-grabbing raid or to make a buck.[24]

It is reasonable to insist that the immigration laws be enforced and, if faulty, changed, but the current climate is that the greater the enforcement, the greater the injustices likely to be inflicted on immigrants of every kind, with even harsher measures waiting in the legislative wings.

Most illegal immigrants come to the United States to work, period. A Higgins wage would itself go a long way to deterring employers from winking at illegal immigrants and thus help to keep the number of immigrants consistent with our ability to absorb them in a humane way.

Sometimes we ourselves create the conditions that trigger massive immigration. U.S.-subsidized corn undersells Latin American farmers, many of whom, thus ruined, come here to be further abused by people like the owners of that New Bedford leather factory. Policies aimed at balanced development between the United States and its southern neighbors would ease the problem of illegal immigration. Of particular note is the hypocrisy of our trade policy where we pressure our neighbors not to subsidize their farmers, while, of course, we subsidize our own and then help them to export those subsidized crops.[25]

It would reflect the most irresponsible kind of statecraft to take the position that existing laws and regulations should simply be flouted. Civil disobedience is for citizens, not government. By and large, I think that the adoption of the legal, economic, and institutional proposals put forward in this book would have a substantially beneficial effect on immigrants, but I am uncertain of how to shape realistic proposals aimed on immigration that would overcome the contradictions between justice and law expressed in the quandary just cited.[26]

Proposal: Protect Ex-convicts from Job Discrimination

There is a major group of people who need but don't have protection against discrimination, especially job discrimination. These are our ex-convicts.[27] Thanks mostly to our drug laws, U.S. prisons hold just over two million men and women, and there are between six and seven million people who have served time in prison, past and present. All of these people face crippling job discrimination when they get out of prison.

It would be too glib to propose a simple, blanket antidiscrimination statute if for no other reason that just under half the persons released from prison are within months convicted of another crime. Accordingly, it is reasonable for employers not to hire ex-cons, or to hire them for the most menial jobs, at the lowest pay, and with the least prospects. Given those high recidivism rates, it is inconceivable that any legislature would entertain such antidiscrimination laws in the first place. An end to, even a substantial diminution of, bias against ex-cons is inseparable from radical change in imprisonment and release policies.[28] Accordingly, to lay the foundation for laws and regulations barring job discrimination against ex-cons, there have to be ex-cons for whom such protections are transparently apt.

One scheme is to allow inmates to volunteer for a program that ties the length of their sentences to their progress in acquiring job and other social skills likely to prevent recidivism. I don't have in mind the strict-to-brutal "boot camps" of a few years ago, as they were called, which featured violent, sometimes lethal misbehavior on the part of their staffs and had, as it turned out, minimal if any success in reforming the young people placed within them.

I envision that the inmates in volunteering for the program would one by one agree to meet a number of high personal achievement standards as condition for an earlier release. They would be expected to complete their education to the highest level indicated by their relative abilities. They would be required to develop a high level of skills appropriate to working on the outside, possibly as artisans, possibly in clerical work, possibly in professional posts, as their ability and aptitude profiles indicate. Over time they should be closely evaluated as both students and "employees," those evaluations making up a career file that would have to be made available to potential post-prison employers.

With a view to separating the convicts from their old ways and old habits, their early days in prison should include a regimen to radically improve their general fitness; we can learn from the military's experience in separating recruits from former civilian habits and identities. The convict/volunteers should be housed apart from the rest of the prison population and progressively placed in situations in which their behavior has to be self-governing. Here as elsewhere the leading idea is that the inmate will be released as and when his or her progress in the system establishes a high likelihood that there will be no regress in civilian life.

It is desirable that inmates maintain "normal" relations with their spouses, children, parents, and so on. Conjugal visits should be encouraged and inmate earnings increased so that they remain integral contributors to their family's well-being. Some will howl against the idea, but inmates' wages should be high enough to make a substantial contribution to their family's income while they are in prison. Most inmates at some point leave prison, and one wants them to return to supportive social, cultural, and family settings, not jump into a post-prison world where they have had no useful place for a number of years.

When the convict has demonstrated that unusual effort, motivation, and actual achievement, he or she should be released. Then and only then, and as a further guard against recidivism, the released inmate would come under the special protections of antidiscrimination law.[29]

Rates of recidivism are key here. We should target a rate of conviction and imprisonment for the released inmates that is as low as that of the population at large. If that level of success could be attained, then both the public and the politicians could be convinced that the program represented a successful investment of tax dollars, a boost to law enforcement, and a boon to the security of life and safety of the average citizen.

Of course, many of those in prison are there for good and sound reasons. Whatever the original reason for their falling afoul of the law, such people often incorporate violent and other antisocial inclinations that the law-abiding population reasonably fear. On the other hand, most convicts do get out, and it is itself criminal that these are not fully prepared to live a predictably law-abiding, successful post-prison life. My thought, therefore, is that the initial program for early earned release from prison might with experience be expanded to cover eventually all those prisoners whose terms are such that they will eventually leave prison. Here the standard is not, as before, to shrink the incidence of recidivism to the levels of crime and conviction normal for the general population, but simply to cut it as much as one can. Any expansion of early release earned by achievement would be as successful as the fall in recidivism rates it achieved.

This proposal has the same core as the earlier one on livable wages. A person who is willing to learn and to work has an "inalienable" right to a Higgins wage, to be able to live as a human being does in a civilized society. Drug laws aimed at the poor, like the current casual public and official attitude to jailing offenders who commit little social harm, willy-nilly merge potentially law-abiding, productive citizens and potentially good parents and neighbors with those who really do suffer forms of social pathology.

One does not have to be "a bleeding-heart liberal" to understand that most crime is committed in a collusion between faulty social arrangements and those who cannot or will not make the extra effort to overcome them. In a liberal and enlightened society, Judge Higgins's "civilized society," every effort has to be exerted to make sure that social arrangements do not contribute to producing criminal behavior. Sometimes, as with the marijuana laws, the law itself needs changing, and sometimes our social practices need changing, as with less-than-civilized-wages. It is only to the degree that society itself is free of collusion in creating the conditions for crime that it is justified in depriving some of its members of their liberty.

The Inalienable Rights of the Managed

We are a society of employees—but as employees we have few rights. Inalienable employee rights need to be embodied in an enactment of constitutional scope and authority. We have listed some of those inalienable rights: the right not only to have work in general but to have tenure in one's present job, at a Higgins wage, in safety, with dignity, and without discrimination; the right to freedom of speech, press, and assembly on the job; the right to participate in shaping the future of one's job; the right to opportunities to change jobs and to learning and career training leading to advancement; and the right to genuine individual opportunities to rise from "the lowest of the low" within a political and economic setting that in time erase entirely that very status. It is not at all out of our power as a society, or beyond our pocketbooks, to go beyond mere equality of opportunity—which is really nothing more than *providing an arena for some to beat out others for the good life*. We want instead to approach Judge Higgins's "civilized society." An early key to that is, first, to end the positive social harm embodied in "employment at will" and the "rights of management" associated with it, and second, and more important, to pursue all promising opportunities to remobilize workers and their families to take their honored, traditional place within the Democracy.

11

INTERNATIONAL GOVERNMENT AND INTERNATIONAL CHAOS

Modern international capitalism is both a functioning government and a font of anarchy. The government is the consortium that presides over the international economy. It includes the Group of Eight (G-8),[1] the International Monetary Fund (IMF), the World Bank, the World Trade Organization (WTO), the World Economic Forum, and some other, related groups and meetings. Its membership is drawn mostly from the financial elites of the main capitalist governments and the leaders of the main international firms and industry associations. One may estimate the influence of this "government" from the scope of the international financial panic of 2008 and evaluate its competence from their fumbling, contradictory responses to it.

Today's inter- or transnational capitalism also harks back to the disintegrative variant we spoke of earlier. By exacerbating poverty and political instability, it positively contributes to expanding international lawlessness, on the part both of governments and private organizations. The West's attention is focused on private groups, like Al Qaeda or the Basque ETA. But the governments of Russia, Ukraine, Israel, Syria, North Korea, the Sudan, and, not to be outdone, the United States, among others, are leading the descent into disorder and barbarism.[2] Governments now regularly carry out both individual assassinations and mass murders, kidnappings followed by detention across international borders ("rendition"), torture, indefinite imprisonment without charges, *Nacht und Nebel* disappearances,[3] collective roundups that normally include innocent people, and collective forms of punishment, all as a matter of policy and not of rogue behavior. In this shadowy world, decisions on whom to strike and how are made not within any judicial oversight, but rather as a matter of administrative fiat by functionaries operating under a cloak of "security." No apologies are offered when, as so often, innocent bystanders die from a guided missile exploding in a market ("collateral damage') or from a nail bomb exploding in a mosque, or when the wrong person is assassinated or made to disappear, or when entire apartment blocks are dynamited or bulldozed because some "suspected terrorist," or perhaps his or her family, lived there.

For the present I want to focus on the growth of international government and its international constituency, not because they are more important but because they are less understood. At the same time, we should recognize that the reign of international lawlessness is intimately related both to what this quasi-government does and to what it fails to do. I will return to the issue of international lawlessness by national governments in the next chapter.

What we call "globalization" is an ideologized term for an overarching international economy that is characterized by two seemingly contrary though in fact mutually supporting tendencies: there is, first, the well-heralded dispersion of production facilities out of the older industrialized economies and into the periphery. But this is complemented by the centralization of financial governance and economic policies through the semiformalized consortium that functions as an international government for the few. This easily coexists with the few most powerful national governments, the United States, obviously, China, the EU, Japan, India, and so on, and on this reading it is murky at best whether it will come of its own rhythms to supersede them.

Corresponding to this economic government, there has already emerged a common international social structure in the developed countries that is partially but dangerously shared within the less developed world. This structure of hierarchy and privilege has been generated within and by the big corporate firms and, over time, more and more reflects its industrial division of labor as we have described it: elite, cadre/manager, and worker. There are other, holdover social formations in the less developed world, such as peasants, aristocrats, castes, clans, tribes, and such, but they are dominated, if not quite defeated, in virtually every economic, social, political, and even cultural dimension by the "modernizing classes." Backward social formations exist and often provide the social and ideological foundations for terrorism, but they do not dominate in the world economy or in most of the world's polities.

There is as yet no common international polity guiding or at least balancing out the international inner government, although fragmentary elements of such a polity already exist. It is the contradiction between rapidly changing economic and social development, on the one side, and political underdevelopment, on the other, that forms the matrix of the most serious international problems of lawlessness and brutality. Two points are implied here. First, the present international chaos, which is so life- and society-threatening, is largely a product of this unbalanced development. And that in turn implies that the Democracy's task of building effective, responsible, international government is by no means utopian; it is simply overdue. A socially responsible, democratically sensitive international government is very badly, I would say desperately, needed at present, but at the same time the underdevelopment of the international polity precludes having such government now and even well into the foreseeable future. It is this strategic quandary that I want to address here and in the next chapter. Upon what strategic political axis should the Democracy now try to advance? What should be done now to ripen the conditions for a Democracy-influenced polity and a less brutal world to emerge in the nearest possible future?

If from the point of view of positive, constructive programs that prospect seems distant from us now and so positively utopian, the negative is present and dire. Radical, disruptive economic and social changes occur in a context in which traditional political elites and ideologies, especially in the less developed world, though still intact, are ignored and overridden; they are weakened but retain reservoirs of local obedience and support. This is a main source of the several kinds of the political violence the world has witnessed in recent decades, from ethnic slaughter in central Africa and the Balkans to the rise of a highly politicized Islamic fundamentalism committed to the practices of terror, and, not less, the equally terrorist military and police responses to them by the powers of the developed world. Actually, this war has been prefigured for many years by the West's suppression of secular reform movements in the less developed world.[4] If it has intensified in the most recent era, that can be explained by the growing intensity and pervasiveness of the economic and social influence of the global firms. What may come to pass if the current economic downturn changes into a worldwide depression of the intensity of 1930–39 is frightening to contemplate.

International Inner Government

We already have world government, or, to be more precise, the economic essentials of world government and at least those political corollaries that are to the short-term advantage of the highest elites. Though typically overlooked, this is among the most important facts of the present era. One should not imagine a conspiracy here or consider this interpretation strained. The net effect of the actions of the IMF, the WTO, the G-8, the World Economic Forum, and the others, whose executive arm is often the United States, is to impose fundamental economic decisions on the other countries of the world, which used to be made by their own governments and which used to be thought "normal" for a government to make. The change is fairly recent. The building blocks of the Keynesian world that emerged after World War II were integral, individual sovereign states, each with a national economy that it had an acknowledged right and duty to protect.[5] Such key matters as interest rates, the money supply, and the rate of inflation as well as the size and role of their public sectors, their rates of economic growth and of wages, unemployment levels, the place of trade unions, and the pursuit or not of Keynesian deficit spending targets were accepted as lying within the competence of the national government on the spot. They chose their own social welfare policies and set their own tariffs and import subsidies. Clearly these are not small matters. They are the very warp and weft of what we think of as among the normal duties of the government of a sovereign state. Granted, for the smaller and economically more parlous nations, heavy-handed "advice" was offered by the richer and supposedly wiser countries. But at least in the formal sense, each country chose its mix of economic policies, and the material reality was such that all but a few had at least some range of freedom to do so.

As we see virtually every day in the news now, almost all of these economic parameters are now prescribed to the several governments, and the sanctions that lie to hand for the IMF/WTO/G-8 oligarchs to do so are more than sufficient to force their adoption. More, since the purse remains mightier than the pen, the shift from a Keynesian view back to Manchester liberalism has also changed the conventional view of what is legitimate. Accordingly, the international agencies that make up world government are almost universally accorded the right and indeed the obligation to impose on other peoples and governments what the internationals judge to be the *correct* policies that are uniquely required.

There has been simply immense interest in and ostensibly exhaustive discussion about the phenomenon of globalization, including its impact on the sovereignty and, indeed, the contemporary relevance of the nation-state. It is as if the nation-state is in the process of being superseded by this economic oligarchy. Some writers, such as Donald Sassoon, contrast what they see as the chaos of the present with the orderly Keynesian state system. Many, many others, more by implication than by statement, present us with a pluralist view of the world; in fact that is one of the main connotations of "globalization" as a contemporary term of description and analysis (see Friedman 2005).[6] Yet, as I have just suggested, the obvious facts about the supplanting of nation-state sovereignty by the international inner government are not hidden or mysterious, and are frequently talked about *in other—usually economic—terms*. But the political dimension is equally clear and compelling. One of the characteristics of this world governing structure is that it creates new political realities but does not take responsibility for their political consequences.[7]

World government has familiar elite preferences and effects: it favors the Right over the Left, the "private" sector over the public sector, management over labor, investor over consumer, big lender over small borrower, speculator over investor. By its actions it weakens trade unions, and its authority often cancels out the wishes of the electorate of this or that country. All of these things lie within what we are accustomed to think of as belonging to the political realm. But three of the peculiar characteristics of the present world economic government help to obscure this. First, its leaders and publicists see the economic realm as the decisive terrain, far more important than politics, culture, or national differences, which they do not deign to respect. They are economic determinists to a degree that would embarrass even the most naïve Marxist and do not meddle in politics—*unless* that politics threatens their immediate interests and preferences.

Second, it has the form of an inner government, a government directly of, by, for, and among institutional elites. It creates political messes but leaves the cleanup to the national politicians, whom it conceives to be no better than refuse removers. This makes for an intrinsically irresponsible international political order. Those who have the power to create political outcomes via economic policies won't do so, and those who are left to cope with the problems can't. This thoughtlessness is reflected in the current discourse on trade, tariffs, and protectionism.

It is enough for globalization's champions to reiterate the hoary principles of Ricardo on the advantages of international trade (if you can cure two beaver pelts an hour and I only one, and I can produce three quill pens an hour and you only two . . .) and let the effects fall as they may.

The actual effect of the globalization regime on the economies of Latin America and sub-Saharan Africa has been an almost immeasurable human disaster that UN agencies have been chronicling for many years. International reports routinely show that roughly one in six people on the planet stand perpetually on the edge of outright starvation; many tip over it.

Both the popular and the professional accounts of globalization emphasize the dispersion of producing facilities out of Europe, North America, and Japan and into the less developed world, as if this were a kind of spontaneous, "free-market" anarchy. This is the pluralist picture of globalization we've met before. It has helped create centers of modernization in what were such formerly benighted places as different as the Irish Republic and Malaysia and has threatened the wages and the jobs of workers in Manchester, Detroit, Tokyo, and the Ruhr. I don't deny the intrinsic importance of this dispersion of producing facilities, but it is only part of the story. One can produce shirts in Honduras and shoes in China today *because* the international financial system is organized to facilitate just that. There is now an ease to transferring capital, debts, credits, sales returns, currencies, and financial instruments of every other kind across international borders that enables the widest dispersion of the production facilities, makes irrelevant the distance a product will travel from where it is made to where it is sold and used, and bridges the many currencies these transactions will pass through. There is of course a narrowly technical side to this—in the improvement of electronic communications and in the container revolution in ocean shipping, for example. However, one must not allow this dispersion to obscure the fact that that manufacturing relies almost wholly on developed-country technology, often on patents, copyrights, and licenses from firms in the developed world, and sells very predominantly to developed world markets via a financial system rooted in the developed world. The term "globalization" as connoting a world economic environment of plural centers of power, influence, and contribution is deeply deceptive. The term is more ideological than descriptive.

Its political side is at least of equal importance, namely, that the pervasiveness and the effectiveness of the unitary international financial system turns workers everywhere into competitors. This of itself is a factor in the slowness of international political development, indeed in its regress in so many places.

One cannot really speak of *the* world government because that government does not take up the political responsibilities that we traditionally associate with a government. Nor does "it" have juridical standing to enforce its will, although to be sure it often imposes that will by economic *diktat*. Some of those political responsibilities fall to other elements of world governance, and many are just left hanging. We live in an incoherent international political order in which supranational authority and state sovereignty are mixed together in a hodgepodge. The UN Security Council has exhibited a selective degree of authority in overriding only some national sovereignties, as in the first Gulf War and its subsequent system of sanctions against Iraq. There has been similar Security Council overriding of national state sovereignty in the Balkans and in Africa. One can cite the reasons for Security Council intervention or, as with U.S. military aggression against Nicaragua in the 1980s and 1990s, the Council's refusal to intervene. Those concrete reasons, important in themselves, confirm that we live in a world in which international government exists, yet acts only selectively, its power overwhelming but politically irresponsible, the principles of its action opportunistically overriding or bowing to considerations of national sovereignty, erratically for good, erratically for harm. Weighing against that, one can observe the increasing role of the International Court, the hoped-for development of the International Criminal Court, and the greater willingness of a number of states to allow those courts a limited jurisdiction over the domestic and international behavior of their own nationals. I suppose one could sum up the situation by saying that there is not as yet a single world government but rather several fragmentary ones, the whole making up a deeply dysfunctional political system.

Terrorist interventions against the inequities and injustices of this system in turn encourage counterterrorist interventions by the national states. The causal train that follows is only slightly oversimplified: international economic order breeds national economic disorder, which breeds international nongovernmental terrorism, which breeds national government terrorism.

A Transnational Social Structure

There has also emerged an international or, better, transnational upper middle class of managers and other cadre. Again there is little mystery about this. We can observe in each country of the world a modernized, middle social formation that shares with its fellows in other nations (1) convergent educational tracks and occupations, (2) similar consumption patterns, and (3) kindred cultural and political preferences. This group (4) also tends to invest its savings in the developed world, particularly the United States, rather than at home. They (5) commonly share immediate institutional affiliations with their class fellows in other countries, as in having the same or related employers; and (6) they enjoy overlapping frequency and kinds of international travel and tourism, and often (7) have other direct personal or institutional connections, as through educational background or international intermarriage.

For convenience and consistent with course theory, I will typically refer here to this social formation sometimes as managers, sometimes as cadre, terms intended to express that their life courses characteristically center around their preparation for and later service within the hierarchies of corporate firms or with government. There they administer workers either directly or indirectly through the design of machinery or business or technological systems, which themselves control the activity of workers. Not all or probably even most managers are employees of the big, recognizable corporate firms, but the division of labor they work within and its hierarchy of authority and reward have been historically a product of those big firms and assiduously copied by other institutions; and, of course, all function within a corporate ambit.

The familiar corporate division of labor, authority, and reward has also reached into the more modernized parts of the less developed world. This comes partly of the employment policies of the big international firms, partly a matter of local infrastructures conforming to a modern mode of production, partly just a matter of copying the most prestigious forms of business organization.

Obviously related to this convergent division of labor within each national economy, managers tend to have had quite similar educational tracks. This is surely true at the university level, where the changing business technologies are directly absorbed into the curriculum. This in turn has altered the curricula of secondary and primary schools, where, except perhaps for stress on the national language, conventional patriotic sentiment, and, more typical than not, the locally dominant religious preferences, it too has created an international educational system with dominantly convergent tendencies. The related homogenization of primary and, more important, secondary education has also enabled masses of students to enroll in overseas universities. Thus occupationally and educationally we see the very definite marks of a managerial class or *course* emerging all over the world and with far fewer internal differences than are found between, say, peasants or workers from different countries.

This is reflected in the lifestyle and consumption patterns of the international managerial class. They wear similar clothing, use similar electronic equipment, drive similar cars, and even drink similar beverages. To travel internationally now, provided one has a bit of money, is to be in a position to use the same sort of credit card everywhere to buy the same sort of goods and appliances, to stay at the same sort of hotels, to dine on a convergent if not yet quite uniform international cuisine of U.S. beef, French wine, and Thai prawns, and to wash it all down with the same Scotch whiskey.

This lifestyle is frequently interpreted by critics within a theory of capitalist commodification, which stresses the mass production of similar goods and the advertising effort used to push their sale. But the more significant finding is that there is a transnational class of managers that share a social and material transnational culture.

There is also an emergent transnational *symbolic* culture. There remain significant differences between the managers working in Kuala Lumpur and in New York City, or in Seoul and Cape Town. But most of these persons can and do speak the same Americanized English. They hear or see the same news slanted the same way by the same big international communications giants. They see many of the same films and read many of the same books, and, as far as I can tell from my own travels in Europe, Asia, and Africa, except for a bow to some national sensibilities, they listen to much of the same music all over the world.[8] Theirs is a culture of the modern world, and one often at variance, even in deadly conflict, with the forces of the traditional national cultures.[9]

It is common for this cadre class or course to have the same or related institutional affiliations and use the same or similar communications equipment. Frequently, they even move in the same social circles. This is the class of persons who make up such a great part of the expanded international travel and tourism we've witnessed over the past third of a century. In the less developed countries, the very poor may travel once or twice in a lifetime to another country to seek work or avoid desperate straits. But in Europe and North America, not only cadre but all classes of persons participate in international travel and tourism. Many European and North American managers travel often from country to country on business. This increasingly dense net of contacts and affinities among managers in all the countries creates other links, as between graduates of the same universities, or the common experience of living in Paris or London for many years on overseas assignment, international friendships, intimate and otherwise, and—inevitably—international intermarriage.

The Globalization Constituency

It is important to understand the politics of this transnational middle class. Their way of life and even their symbolic culture place them ideologically closer to their class fellows in other countries than to the workers or squatters who live perhaps a mile or less away. One sees this in every city one visits. There are middle-class enclaves of people all over the world dressing alike, living in houses that look alike, and driving cars made by the same companies, "just up the road," especially in the less developed world, from people living in shacks or packing-crate townships. In the middle-class enclaves, people are not often on the street, but their late-model Hondas and Fords are, while in the other districts the streets teem with people and one sees smaller numbers of often banged-up, older rusty cars, vans, pickups, and hand and animal carts. The gulf between middle class and poor is not quite as obvious in the developed world, but it is still present.

Social and material differences of this magnitude suggest differences in political loyalties and behavior. There is good reason to argue that that manager in Manila has political preferences and interests more in common with his or her counterpart in Hamburg than with his or her co-nationals living a short walk away in the slums. The modernized middle classes in the less developed world tend to support a similar generic politics in favor of measures, principles, and international forces that buttress their different, very privileged, therefore politically exposed position within their own countries. Globalization, such as we know it, has not in the last analysis just been imposed on the less developed countries. There is a *globalization constituency* in each of them whose material and even spiritual interests simultaneously alienate them from their fellow countrymen and identify them with similar middle-class cadre everywhere.

I first saw this phenomenon while reporting from South Vietnam over forty years ago; "our" Vietnamese, for all their protestations to the contrary, modified their patriotic sentiment to fit their interests as clients of the United States and its cultural and material ways. But perhaps, I thought, the uncertainties of the war had caused this exaggerated clientism. But a Chilean upper-middle class with a long history of national pride and democratic politics welcomed the United States's barely disguised intervention to overthrow Allende, even encouraged it before the fact. Like similar Venezuelans today, these people saw that modernization had set them apart from their fellow countrymen and made them into a very visible, relatively small minority, too privileged and too few in numbers to stand alone in the domestic political arena. In wanting U.S. intervention, they—realistically I think—were saying in effect, "We need outside political support against our own people."

That of course had been true in Vietnam, where those who supported us were alienated from the rest by their Roman Catholicism and their typically privileged, urban lives. Today, the rapid pace but selective consequences of modernization have created a transnational middle class or cadre course essentially reliant on international support and far too weak and compromised to play the mediating role in their own countries between the few and the many that classic political science assigns to the middle levels of a society.

Political instability in a less developed country, whose sources we have just touched upon, discourages this relatively quite well-off middle class from investing their savings at home; they seek instead more stable securities, sites, and currencies, and this is one of the factors that made the United States, of all places, the largest contemporary importer of investment capital.[10] This outflow of potential investments from a less developed country tends naturally to slow economic development and thus creates conflicts between the higher and the lower part of those societies. And it sustains a material interest in the continued international economic, hence political, domination of the developed countries, especially the United States.

The putatively modernizing middle classes are, I would argue, a force maintaining the underdevelopment of their own countries because of their relatively rich lifestyles. This further strengthens their political loyalties to the global system, most particularly to the policies and even personalities of the U.S. government. In the United States, where the distribution of income is unusually unequal for a developed country, at least two-fifths of all national personal income goes to the upper fifth of income units.[11] That 40/20 formula already reflects therefore an extreme case of income maldistribution, but for the wealthy Americans at least, national personal income is so large that most people earning in the lower 80 percent are not in dire straits (or weren't before 2008). In a poorer country the income share to the higher classes is perhaps 50/15 or even worse; that is a smaller percentage of the population (15 percent is a crude estimate) taking home perhaps half (50 percent) of a much smaller national personal income. Add to this that the middle-class social material lifestyle approximates a European or U.S. one. For a Colombian or Kenyan manager, that implies a heavy dependence on imports from the West, and this in a poorly performing economy with very limited exports, and at international prices and exchange rates skewed by the "free market" in favor of the developed economies. All in all, we can see here not just major impediments to economic growth in the less developed countries, but actual barriers to economic growth that virtually guarantee their continuing national poverty.

If my analysis holds, it points to important political conclusions. Writers in the Marxist tradition tend to lay the world's impoverishment squarely at the door of international capitalists, who, they correctly assume, preside over the bigger firms at the center of globalization. The analysis just sketched argues that stagnation and impoverishment in the less developed world also have another major source. Paradoxically enough, it is precisely the so-called modernizing classes in the less developed countries who ensure their impoverishment under almost all the economic scenarios one can report or imagine. They consume more than can be produced for them at home and import the rest, thereby beggaring their lower classes and running up the country's overseas debt. With their higher living standard, their savings should be an important source of domestic investment, but, true to their antinational orientation, they send these savings out of the country. Thus, already socially and economically alienated from their less fortunate fellow citizens, they pursue a politics that places them, in effect, under the protection of, usually, the United States, thus deepening this alienation yet further.

The old communist nations—China, North Vietnam, Cuba, and North Korea—suppressed the consuming proclivities of *their* managers. This seems to have been key to their then considerable economic, medical, and educational achievements; they imposed a consumption discipline on cadre, hence on the country. This required the very primitive political features that characterized communism, that is, excessive centralization, denial of personal liberty, lock-step social discipline, free rein for the security services, and so forth. Of course, as these regimes age, that discipline has given way. Their present-day managers are suspiciously similar to those we find in the noncommunist world. I don't mean to overemphasize these similarities, but it is important to point to the consuming ways of middle-class persons throughout the less developed world as a factor in their countries' continued economic backwardness.

Collaborators

The political relationship of local cadre to the international economic elites is not the same everywhere. Variation is introduced by the positions of the traditional elites. In Africa, nouveau riche military officers tend to rule, while in Latin America those same ruling officers have links to the great landed aristocracies, which trace their origins to the Spanish or Portuguese empires of four centuries ago. Throughout the Middle East, there are oil-rich sheiks, victors in the tribal wars of three-quarters of a century ago or given a leg up by the then colonial authorities. Mostly, however, these elites carry on friendly political relations with the United States and look to it for support, sometimes against their middle and almost always against their lower classes.

These relations seem securely in place save in the Arab world. In the past the Western powers tended to ally themselves with Middle Eastern royals. Revelations in the past few years about sub rosa Saudi assistance to terrorist groups have weakened this particular constellation. It appears the Saudi were "paying off" groups like Al Qaeda so that it would attack only Western or at least non-Saudi targets. In 2006, the U.S. administration announced a new policy intending to accelerate modernization and even secularization in the Middle East. If that policy change is maintained, it will converge with the long-standing U.S. stance in Latin America and the Philippines. There the United States has supported two putatively modernizing classes: managers/cadre and the military. We've already discussed the modernizing conundrum associated with the former.

U.S. policy has over the years assumed that professional military men have an intrinsic interest in modernization. The leading idea is that they want modern weapons systems, thus the educated people to operate them, and therefore will serve as a force for social, therefore political modernization. By "political modernization," U.S. policymakers mean some form of liberal democracy. The hypothesis has not tested well, the great counterexample being the Argentine Air Force. The latter did modernize, often with French help, and did become an effective modern arm, as Britain unhappily discovered in the Falklands War. But the Argentine Air Force was also the most reactionary of the military partners who seized power in 1976 and set about exterminating oppositionists. In the accounts about the thousands of the "disappeared," the Air Force is most often prominent. Especially memorable are the accounts of drugged political prisoners being flown out over the Atlantic and cast, one hopes still unconscious, into the sea.

We have poured a great deal of military assistance into the Americas since the 1950s, but the Latin military still shows distaste for democratic progress, preferring their traditional cuisine of the military *putsch*. The thesis of the military-as-modernizer founders on two not at all obscure facts. The Latin (and Philippine) officer class is heavily drawn from the older landowning families or, with certain parallels to interwar Japan, from the ruined rural middle classes. The ideologies historically associated with such social formations tend to be ferociously antimodernist, typically scapegoating as communist any domestic foes seeking political liberalization or social modernization. Second, as shown in the Argentine Army's abysmal performance in the Falklands War or the Panamanian resistance to the U.S. invasion, Latin armies are not designed to fight other armies; regardless of the modernity of their munitions, they're usually low-morale, militarily incompetent, corrupt forces useful mainly for brutalizing civilians. A half century of expensive U.S. effort, materiel support, intelligence cooperation, and officer retraining has never succeeded in changing that, if indeed that was ever really the intent.

Another case refuting the military-as-modernizer concept is provided in South Korea, where the army clung to power and repression as long as it could. As in Greece, a great deal of effort, much of it truly heroic, was required on the part of liberal-minded politicians, trade unionists and socialists, students, artists, lawyers, and others to overcome the military and establish tolerable government. The South Korean case is especially heartening, for there was no EU, as in Spain and Greece, to aid the democratic forces, and the United States, protestations aside, gave one-sided support to the military dictators as long as they could cling to power.

The African continent was torn apart by U.S.-Soviet rivalry for many years, each power changing its favored gangsters from time to time as convenient. The French, the Belgians, and the British too have played destructive roles in Chad, the Congo, and Kenya. The term "gangsters" is perhaps not the best one could come up with, but it is clear that such as Mobutu in the Congo, Charles Taylor in Liberia, and Jonas Savimbi in Angola were individualist entrepreneurial adventurers, not responsibly linked to any actual social formations, even tribal groupings, lawless to a degree it is hard to fathom, ruling with a brutality that exceeded any rational purpose, at best plunderers of the body social, economic, and political. In the special case of South Africa, the United States lagged behind the other powers in deserting the sinking ship of apartheid.[12]

History as Tragedy

On their side, the G-8/IMF/WTO countries, especially the United States, have been replicating their domestic political alliances with the cadre course beyond their borders, that is, embracing the manager/cadre of the less developed world on a basis essentially similar to their embrace of the domestic cadre. That undermines their former, pre-1970s political linkages to the working classes and trade union federations of their own countries, an implication widely understood but usually discussed in narrower job and employment terms. I think the terms of discussion have to include an international political bloc linking the inner international economic government to an increasingly internationalized course of managers/cadre while at the same time trying not to disrupt too peremptorily older alliances with traditionalist national elites.

There is a combination of stupidity and canniness in U.S. "democracy-building" efforts overseas. Much of that assistance strengthens the police forces of the U.S. client. Some of this is well motivated to introduce conceptions of civil liberties and due process and to diminish police corruption. But to strengthen the police is to create greater potential for political repression, especially when these expanded police capacities are funded not out of local tax revenues, over which the populace has some control, but by an outsider, the United States. Thus, *regardless of their intentions,* U.S. development efforts have—almost everywhere they've appeared—contributed to the antidemocratic forces in the less developed world, not the democratic ones. Some U.S. policymakers possibly mean well here, but their lack of critical political perspective makes them responsible for the evils that have flowed from their policies, intended or not.

Alliances between capitalist forces of dynamic economic and even social change and a weaker, dependent middle class in states that are simultaneously trying to maintain the political privileges and pretensions of premodern, rural-based elites are something we have seen before. This was the stuff of what we called Bismarckism. Its almost inevitable failure was manifest between the wars (1918 to 1939), when restive, impoverished, disillusioned lower classes, often socialist, could no longer be contained by the older elites, thus forcing the industrial elites and the modern middle classes to seek the protection of the Far Right. Today, in the less developed world, the United States and other capitalist powers are resurrecting a kind of Bismarckian polity and with many of its familiar weaknesses. The potentially progressive political and social role of the managers/cadre is compromised by its junior partnership with the traditional aristocratic, theocratic, military, and agricultural elites. The latter, as we saw in Latin America in the 1970s and 1980s, prefer to destroy, not compromise with, the forces of political modernization and liberalism. In this pinch between Left and Right, the middle classes, as in central Europe between the world wars, tend to fear the lower class in the voting booth more than they do the generals on horseback.

Historical parallels are often deceptive, but alliances between elites and emergent cadre classes have to date shown a propensity toward rightist politics. The overblown size and consumption proclivities of the cadre in economically underdeveloped countries retard or even prevent economic growth. That lessens the stability of their nations' political structures and puts an increasing reliance on the military and security forces traditionally dominated by the older, backward elites. Marx wrote that when history repeats itself, it occurs first as tragedy and later as farce. I fear here that when history repeats itself, it is tragic every time.

Between the two world wars the circumstances we have been recalling to memory fed the emergence of fascist regimes in Italy and Germany, with kindred authoritarian, ultranationalist regimes taking power in Poland, Hungary, Yugoslavia, Romania, Finland, Portugal, Spain, Greece, China, and Japan.[13] None of the current underdeveloped states, save possibly India and Brazil, have the potential to threaten their neighbors and the world as Germany and Japan did then, but there are other kinds of threat. Contemporary threats to the rest of the world do not come from the governmental ambitions of the dependent smaller countries but from the failures of their societies. Overseas mentors help them to resist the changes needed to create societies able to stand on their own.

China is a special case, for it is already a superpower or nearly so. Unfortunately, one already sees intimations of a dialectic of fear between the United States and China being stoked by their respective military-industrial complexes. U.S.-Russian relations are similarly fraught. There really is now a pressing need to work cooperatively with both these countries in order to head off a new cold war.

I linked a specific political constellation to the phenomenon of international terrorism, and I believe I was correct to do so. Granted, such a complex historical phenomenon has multiple roots,[14] but I would argue that one of the most important of them is the international political constellation we have been discussing. The inability of the modernizing classes in less developed countries to maintain themselves without outside political, military, and security assistance creates a peculiarly destructive political situation. The values and the power structures of the traditional society are steadily eroded, but the replacement structures are too narrowly based, develop only slowly and erratically, harm so many both materially and spiritually, and are so obviously dependent on foreigners that the resulting chaos fairly invites just the sort of political response we find among the fundamentalist religious and ethnic brands of international terrorism.

The Marxist guerrilla of yesterday has been replaced by the religious or nationalist terrorist as the main opposition to developed country domination and its lopsided "modernization." Taking the larger historical view, the U.S. "victory" in the cold war was a Pyrrhic one. Communism and capitalism, whatever their other faults, foresaw that economic and social modernization went hand in hand; they were both part of the Enlightenment tradition that looked, however distortedly, toward human liberation. But in defeating that Marxist guerrilla, the United States and its allies have loosed upon us the suicide bomber animated by the starkest antihumanist superstitions.[15]

Traditional local and regional power structures don't just exit the historical stage. They remain in place but are unable to check by conventional political means their own decline. Hence the war of the shadows, the war of the chronically weaker party, resisting change with an ethos that permits no compromise with modernization and its supporting international political constellation. In a real sense the forces of terrorism are nihilistic in their outlook and aims. But this nihilism does not stem from some putatively Islamic desire for death and salvation; it takes its character from the actual terms of the international conflict, where one side judges, realistically to be sure, that it is too weak to win classic victories, and therefore stakes its all at every point of conflict to annihilate bit by little its otherwise omnipotent enemies.

If this is the case, then the war on terror is in the last analysis a war between two reactions. Elites in the developed countries, most particularly the United States, have rejected the community of interests they formerly enjoyed with their own working and lower middle classes. At the same time, they now ally themselves with elites and cadre classes overseas, who themselves have an even narrower community of interests with their own people.

"Globalization," of which this rightward alliance is constitutive, is cast in attractive ideologies of progress and modernization, but events have reversed the character of these terms. Economic and social modernization in the period of the historical advance brought the masses into the process, if not on equal terms, then on continually improving terms. As we've argued, the Democracy's gains in the historic advance received much of their impetus from the modernizing processes that were sometimes a condition, sometimes a secondary effect, of that. But economic and social modernization in the international capitalism that emerged during the historic reaction rests in part on a matured cadre course whose advantages are now more often in conflict with than complementary to the interests of the Democracy. Yesterday's still emerging American and European cadre had a world to win and sought and welcomed the aid of the Democracy to win it; today's cadre has already won its world and seeks allies to defend and maintain it. It is this shared defensive, even embattled, posture that in the last analysis permits one to talk of an international manager/cadre course as a political entity.

Specialists in the study of the many differently situated less developed countries will surely challenge as erroneous this or that point of my analysis or show how much I have omitted. Many of those challenges will be justified, since few formulae can fit a world as diverse as our own and no person is an expert on every country. But I suggest that the argument just presented about the development, character, and effect of the modernizing middle classes in the less developed world follows a thread of truth, and moreover, to the extent that it follows that thread, constitutes among the most important truths we can utter on behalf of a realistic, useful analysis of the world's present difficulties.

An Emergent International Polity

There is as yet only a rudimentary and fragmented international polity, but it has already scored some successes and is still growing. However, as measured by its ability to bring to heel the depredations of international inner government, the social formations it allies itself with, and the dark forces it arouses, the current international polity wields far too little power and exerts far too little influence.

Where one finds the greatest hope for the future is in the work of the NGOs in international aid and other humanitarian efforts. These range from the interventions of Doctors Without Borders to those of the international aid groups. The mass movements in several countries against sweatshops should be counted, as should the private efforts of small numbers of professional economists like Amartya Sen to urge more humanitarian policies upon the World Bank.

Trade union support for humane and peaceful international change has not been absent and today is still growing. The positive role played by trade unions today is unfortunately still obscured by their earlier depredations. From the end of World War II through the George Meany and Lane Kirkland presidencies, the international efforts of the American AFL-CIO were devoted to destroying unions they regarded as "soft on communism." In the heated cold war politics of the time, this policy too often replaced genuinely representative trade unions in, say, Italy or Guatemala, with organizations more interested in maintaining international battle lines than resolving industrial inequities. It was a sorry record whose effects have yet to be entirely overcome by the more progressive leadership the AFL-CIO has enjoyed since 1995.

The efforts of secular groups like PEN, Amnesty International, the Center for Constitutional Rights, and Human Rights Watch on behalf of prisoners of conscience are in a real sense complemented by the broader charitable undertakings of organizations like the International Catholic Relief Services. The work of the Red Cross and Red Crescent societies spans cultural and political divides often thought unbridgeable. Many of these efforts occur below the radar of the international news-gathering organizations, often for good reason: like a modern-day Underground Railway, the Sanctuary movement in the United States in the 1980s provided "safe houses" for political refugees from Latin America who were forced to hide from the American authorities as well as their own. Such work undoubtedly continues in the United States and elsewhere.

Signs of international political development are not entirely of a private character. Several Scandinavian governments have long cooperated with NGOs and UN agencies to provide food and shelter to hundreds of thousands of Sudanese and other Africans displaced by civil and sectarian warfare. Scandinavian and other foreign governments also finance the preservation of historical sites and monuments. Greece, for example, would be unable to preserve much of the classical heritage without this overseas assistance.

The Canadian government helped win the treaty banning the manufacture and use of land mines. The steps taken by the Spanish government and others, as in the Pinochet case, to prosecute politically inspired crimes against their own nationals, even when committed on foreign soil, point to a subtle but potent spread of enforceable international legal norms. The intervention by NATO and the EC to stop ethnic cleansing in the Balkans represents a crucial departure from the traditional doctrine that governments are morally omnipotent within their own borders. Earlier, Europe's social democratic parties acted in concert to support democratic rule in Spain and Greece. The Helsinki Treaty on human rights in 1975 was a joint product of several European governments and such private organizations as the British-inspired Campaign for Nuclear Disarmament (CND) and the international European Nuclear Disarmament (END). The treaty had a significant role in undermining the Soviet satellite system. We would be remiss in not mentioning the work of the UN Secretariat and of many of its affiliated activities.

My understanding of this new international polity is that it first emerged as a force after World War II as a result of international insistence that the crimes of the Nazi period should be documented and the worst of the offenders brought to justice. In Europe, the political impetus was often given by the former resistance groups, whereas for the United States the discovery in early 1945 of the bestial conditions in such concentration camps as Dachau (only followed much later by a full awareness of the Nazi's "Final Solution")[16] created a public opinion that could only be satisfied by what came to be the Nuremberg trials of, first, the major Nazi leaders, and subsequently of many of the minor ones as well. Whatever the cynicism that may now exist about those legal processes, for many Europeans and Americans, within government and outside it, some steps had to be taken to mark the crimes that the Nazis had committed and to try to prevent their repetition.[17] Credit here should also go to the international scientific community, especially to physicists, for its efforts to build a world public opinion against the spread, testing, and use of nuclear weapons.

Much of this early international community of opinion was swamped by the onset of Soviet-U.S. rivalry in the cold war. The earliest peace demonstrations against the cold war and the prospective use of nuclear weapons were led by persons and organizations overly sympathetic to the Soviet

Union and, to that extent, a repudiation of the internationalist sentiment that had been so important in 1946–48. It was only in the mid-1950s that the more genuine article was revived, primarily, as I understand that history, by the resolute political independence of the various pacifist-led movements against war and nuclear weapons. Here I think the Aldermaston Marches, which began in 1958, enjoy a place of honor, not only because they helped break the political uniformity of European opinion about the cold war but also because they eventually gathered under their umbrella other important, liberating causes, such as Greek resistance to the monarchy and, later, the "Colonels." Other international campaigners also deserve to be cited for the nuclear test ban treaty, for the opposition to the Vietnam War, and, of course, for the international campaign against apartheid.[18]

Several things make me think that this international polity will have increasing political influence. First, it is a political expression of the transnational cadre class. It is unfortunately not its major political "representative" but is sufficiently representative that it must perforce exercise over time some considerable influence. It is, I think, the genuine voice of what we may call "international civil society," that is, the voice that counterbalances to at least some degree the acquisitive and aggressive tendencies of the rest of the international middle class, giving voice instead to the minimal requirements for international civil peace and order.

The expression "civil society" unfortunately separates voluntary citizen activities and organizations, on the one hand, from the formal, political system on the other. It also implies that government in principle cannot, should not, and thus will not serve generalized social and humanitarian interests. Two aspects of that implication should be underlined. The conception appears to accept the idea that governments themselves do not and cannot under any circumstances represent considered, humanistic, critical popular sentiment, and therefore have no business trying to ameliorate the conditions of the less well-off. "The market" or "private initiatives" will do that rather than "big government" and "bureaucracy." Thus, in pressing the claims of "civil society," one can find oneself advocating a tendentious dialectic: government activity equals feckless compulsion, but individual initiative and community activity equals creative freedom. This is a logic that accepts the existing incapacities of the liberal democratic political systems, the common depredations of "free market" outcomes, and abjures altering the power of inner government and the private publics it serves.

I don't accept a logic that calls for the Democracy to operate only "within society" rather than, as in the past, to try to alter the forms and policies of the Western, developed-country governments. It is not always possible to avoid the expression "civil society" or, thus, the innuendo it carries and still be readily understood. The reader should be alert that in my usage "civil society" incorporates within it the idea and the determination that the persons and organizations now contained within the term will come to be ranged among the active political forces of the Democracy—if they are not there already. In the last analysis, the existence of power-wielding, legal, formal governmental structures that are free of the sentiments and preferences of "civil society," and not acutely responsible to that "civil society," are the very warp and weft of the harmful political world it must be our priority to change.

This still small and fractured progressive polity is also a child of the Enlightenment. It is not only a political movement but also a deeper moral and intellectual tendency, widely shared among the most articulate segments in both the developed and less developed world, conscious of its historical international character and of its value to the current world, enrolling in its ranks a one-sided plurality of the world's most distinguished scientists, authors, artists, and other cultural workers. Here I would especially cite its ability to transcend the cold war, in freeing itself from Soviet-inspired influence during the 1950s, then later helping to restrain the war-making proclivities of the U.S. government, and still later extending its influence into the Soviet bloc countries with progressive effect.

Forces drawn from international civil society undermined the power of Eastern Europe's communist parties. That undermining influence was delayed, frustrated, and often nullified by the aggressive cold war policies of the Western powers, most notably the United States. It is simply bad history to credit "victory" in that contest to the cold warriors, who, had they had their way, would still be waging it with nuclear threats; the encouragement of war and brutality in Africa, Asia, the Middle East, and Latin America; coups against elected governments; and all the other paraphernalia of that destructive period of modern history.

Finally, many of the groups ranged within international civil society are similar to those that made up the historical Democracy, while the values and goals it espouses seem also broadly similar to those that came to be embodied in the achievements of the historic advance.

Acting on the Reality

The very harmfulness of international economic and political developments and the lack of strong countervailing political institutions and forces compel us to plan and act now for a better world, not turn away from the prospect. It is not clear how much can be accomplished at the present juncture, but there are some opportunities that we should grasp. For a start, "globalization" should and can be turned on its head. That word is now employed as a code for a set of changes that ordinary people will suffer from and that—it is said—they can do nothing to alleviate. In this usage, "globalization" implies dire necessity, fatedness, the iron laws of economics. That's why I earlier described the term as being so heavily ideologized. But there is a palpable degree of control exercised over international economic trajectories by the international inner government. Even if the orthodox economists are right and influence over economic events by the G-8/IMF/WTO forces is far less than I believe it in fact to be, one is still right to emphasize the search for such controls as we can discover. Where our future is in the hands of fate, we can do nothing, but where human artifice is already at work, then the forces of the international Democracy should be developed so as to intervene on behalf of a less destructive, more humane international order.

The very real nature of the international inner government provides a focus for the critique of the fatedness of "globalization." That critique can be made both concrete and, eventually, a matter of practical outcomes. The very shadowiness, the institutional and rhetorical camouflage surrounding the international inner government, is the portal for the Democracy to reopen on a new basis the needed political discussion. But all that deals only with the ideological environment. What else should and can be done?

There are a number of efforts currently under way to give international civil society a greater effect in international affairs, that is, the NGOs active in international relief, medical, human rights, economic development, and cognate work. Many of these center on the United Nations, where there are attempts to upgrade the consultative status of NGOs with both the General Assembly and the UN Secretariat. In addition, former secretary-general Kofi Annan and his successor, Ban Ki-moon, as well as many of the UN Secretariat's agencies, have tried both to speak and to act for that international majority of the less powerful, the less influential, and the less well-off. All of this work ought to receive even more political attention and support from the forces of the Democracy than it does.

On the other hand, if we anticipate that the effort to counter, even reverse the harmful policies of the international inner government will be resisted, as it will likely be, then the UN, its leaders, and its agencies provide an uncertain platform. The UN's governing apparatus represents the member states, not their peoples. Within the General Assembly there is of course awareness and resentment of the way in which the less developed countries are beggared and humbled by the more powerful. Sometimes, as in its pressure on the World Bank, this leads to positive outcomes, but the General Assembly is as a rule more rebellious than constructive, its majorities too often swayed by evanescent events, or the suasion of the more powerful, to imagine that a long-term effort to construct democratic international institutions can be accomplished there. Even the secretary-general's tenure of office is too fragile for its occupant to oppose the wishes of more powerful countries, particularly the United States, as we saw with Secretary Annan's predecessor.

A main axis of advance on this international political front is over time to moderate, then constrain, and ultimately contain the policies of the international inner government. The intermediate goal is to develop a political environment in which the more urgent social, economic, and political needs of the world's majority can be pressed upon that inner government in such a way that, over time, it will be forced to take some greater cognizance of them.

One way to approach this problem is to use the model of the World Economic Forum. In the WEF, the movers and shakers of the private sector from both the developed and less developed countries meet annually, where they in effect both confirm and create the political environment in which the present inner government acts.

It would be worth the effort to establish a World Democratic Forum, a counter-WEF, which would be based upon the NGOs active in international service work, to have it meet simultaneously with or just before or after the WEF meeting, and for it to assess the several dimensions of the activities of the international inner government while promulgating an alternative set of priorities and policies.[19]

It is inessential and, I think, probably harmful at this time for the WDF to have a mass character, that is, to incorporate individuals per se. One doesn't want excellent resolutions that from the nature of the case will not be acted upon. Nor can one be satisfied with unruly street demonstrations. Rather, I see a greater formalization, visibility, and coordination of efforts by those organizations actually dealing with the effects of internecine war, international diseases and malnutrition, refugees, agricultural underdevelopment, human rights abuses, pressing environmental issues, and so on. The WDF would have to have a small secretariat through which invitations to its meetings would be issued and within which agenda would be hammered out. A WDF could be a fulcrum for concrete alternative discussion, proposals and policies, and some action, contra those of the WEF elites.

It is difficult to establish the democratic legitimacy of any body in a world so politically fractured. But I estimate that a World Democratic Forum would enjoy such a legitimacy on account of the esteem in which these NGOs are now held. This could be further buttressed by systematically locating the work, the statements, and the priorities of the WDF within the overt terms of the Universal Declaration of Human Rights. The Forum could and should be conceived as an action arm by international civil society on behalf of that document, which, now however ignored, has a political legitimacy stemming from its adoption by the majority of nations a half century ago. More important, it is a document that well expresses the thwarted hopes of the post–World War II years and, in many, many ways, the values that came to be embodied earlier in the historic advance.

The WDF would have a working relationship to the UN, but in light of the limitations placed on the General Assembly and the UN Secretariat, it should almost certainly not be constituted as an arm of that organization.

Whatever the merit, or lack of merit, of this suggestion for a World Democratic Forum, its political dynamic is pressing enough. One wants initially to create political "facts-on-the-ground" that will influence the international inner government toward more beneficial, less harmful policies. At present there are too few such facts-on-the-ground, or they can be too easily ignored. In that sense the work of the Forum would complement the effects of, say, the secretary-general's annual report and of the more progressive elements within the World Bank and other international governmental agencies. In time, of course, one wants to win formal consultative status for representatives of the Democracy with the G-8/IMG/WTO bloc and, eventually, to gain juridical sway over an increasing range of their activities.

Another point of entry to win influence over the international inner government and its clients might be to take up in a serious way the current tendency of some warring political groups and some governments to employ arms and explosives against third-party civilians as a kind of violent blackmail against the other side. Here I believe the international religious organizations might be able to exert particular sway both over international public opinion and, not least, within their own ranks.

It would be important to target particularly the logic or doctrine of "collective guilt" such as, for example, Israel imposes in the Occupied Territories and Gaza today. Israel is hardly alone in this. In modern civil conflicts, both sides hold the other side responsible for warlike actions, and governments then "retaliate only against terrorists," which actually means "indiscriminately." Given their greater resources, governments should bear the greater onus and the greater obligation to alter their military and police rules of engagement. The alternative is to continue the barbarism we now see spreading into so many conflicts. An international conference to formulate and then lead a movement to win binding international agreements strengthening the distinction between legitimate military targets and illegitimate civilian targets, whether persons, organizations, buildings, or other sites, would be particularly valuable. Such a call upon all governments, political organizations, and international courts to take steps to adopt and enforce such a distinction might also go some way to reduce the incidence of nonstate terrorism.

I reiterate that it is particularly important that such a document not focus solely on nongovernmental "terrorists"; the practice of targeted assassinations by several countries; of the United States in seizing and holding persons without recourse to the courts; and of seizing hostages, demolishing buildings, directing artillery fire, and so on, against civilians for purposes of "collective punishment" by other countries are now part of the de facto "rules of warfare" between governments and their opponents.

To the extent that such a document and the practices it championed would have effect on the wars of terror, it would also have some spillover effect in the international economic environment, which could then perhaps be further developed by the forces of international civil society. The larger point is that the decline of so much of the world into poverty, while a minority prosper and develop, is an integral element in the acceptance and spread of terrorism and of the persons, ideologies, and groups that employ it. And it bears in train the international lawlessness long practiced by the United States, emulated now by both its friends and enemies.

One could also envisage in some realistic time frame the creation of a transnational economic parliament, directly elected by voters in the G-8 countries and paralleling the G-8/IMF/WTO economic executive. It would not, of course, exercise sovereign powers. The model here instead is the manner in which the European Parliament monitors and attempts to sway the Brussels secretariat of the European Union. The rationale for such a parliament seems both pressing and direct: to monitor closely and to publicize on behalf of its electors the work of the world's faulty "government," to modify its more harmful actions, and to gain over time a degree of authority over it.

In making this proposal, I don't retreat from the earlier critiques of government by elected representative. Elections in the richer, more advanced, more democratically spirited countries result only in semirepresentative bodies, which can at best work around the edges of the interests embedded within the various inner governments, modifying them, making them just a bit less socially toxic. In the present international political situation, to achieve that minimal influence is still out of the question, but even a small modicum of electoral/parliamentary influence would be to the good.

I envision such a transnational parliament being elected only by voters from the existing democratic countries. One wants a pole of democratic attraction here, not one whose esteem would be compromised by members arriving via the sham elections we are familiar with in so much of the world. There is another potential advantage to this proposal as well. There is at present a unique (and perhaps closing) window of creative opportunity for the existing democratic forces in the world in that most of the richest and most powerful countries have, such as they are, the most efficacious democratic political systems. Few countries in the world today fail to identify themselves as democratic, but the fraud is transparent; most of the world's countries and peoples are ruled by oligarchs of one sort or another. That very fact, as much as any other, militates against any attempt now or in the foreseeable future to build a fully international political authority.

But by seizing upon the present overlap between the most powerful and the most democratic nations, one could envisage a transnational parliament that would be somewhat responsive to its voters. Simply because the locus of world economic power is in those countries, that provides a rationale in the first instance to parallel it with a democratically elected political institution. A further value follows: on the model of the way in which the attractiveness of membership in the European Union operated to undermine antidemocratic forces in Greece, Spain, and Turkey, such a democratic parliament might provide a pole of attraction for other peoples and countries to modify their own antidemocratic political systems with a view to becoming members. Certainly, in a world in which the word and value "democratic" has become so debased, the existence of an internationally elected body that upheld reasonable standards of popular representativeness and responsiveness would constitute a new advantage and possibly even a focal point for the forces of the Democracy in every country.

Proposals like these for a World Democratic Forum and a transnational consultative parliament for the G-8 and a few other countries must appear very thin and unrealistic when measured against the powers of the international inner government and its action executive, the U.S. government. It may even be that the Forum and the transnational parliament would represent misconceived efforts at the present time, though I don't think so.

There are two overriding facts in today's world, and there is no higher priority than to bring them into a better, more life- and society-serving relationship. They are what I have identified as an international inner government whose act and intent is to maintain economic conditions almost wholly of advantage to the rich and powerful and with too often catastrophic effect on the world's poor and ignored. And there are the glimmerings of an international civil society. At present the latter has too little influence over the planet's movers and shakers. The simple priority is to decrease the influence of the one and increase that of the other. At some point the world will take concrete steps to achieve that reversal between the inner government and the Democracy; inevitably, those steps will grow out of discussions very much like those we've just engaged in. At any rate, given the reality that the international system is extensively subject to deliberate governance today, it would be utopian to ignore the situation rather than try, in spite of the odds, to engage with it.

An International SFTA

It was implicit in our earlier discussion of the proposal for the Staff for the Advance (SFTA) that national borders were basically irrelevant to it. Like the Enlightenment, whose heirs and reformers constitute the modern Democracy, those who were earlier identified as potential members of the SFTA were conceived to represent a transnational as well as transhistorical intellectual, moral, and political force. Moreover, I would venture the judgment that among those men and women an internationalist sentiment is already dominant.

As before, one does not envisage the SFTA as a conventional political organization choosing from among sets of contested priorities and policies. The barriers against the emergence internationally of such an organization are in any case even more formidable (and possibly premature) than at the national level. One wants instead an organization where differing priorities and even principles are not hammered out in fractious debate but instead where continuing differences, including national prejudices, contribute to a longer-run learning curve, where agreement and consensus are neither the precondition nor the goal at some point in the future of political cooperation among differing persons and organizations. Instead, as in our previous discussion of the topic, the SFTA should be a site for the processes of learning and discarding that took place within the Democracy during the long historical advance. The SFTA is conceived both to accelerate those learning and discarding processes and, equally important, to do so in a contemporary political environment that is not as supportive of the Democracy as the period circa 1870 to 1970 was. As I argued earlier, the SFTA is an attempt to compensate by organizational means for the unfavorable historical environment faced in the present era by the forces of the Democracy. In the last analysis, its logic is that of an adaptive, progressive social intelligence overcoming the belief promoted by the international inner government that globalization is natural and inevitable.

12

POLITICAL REFORM

Here we take up the strategic political barriers blocking a renewed historic advance. Since it is institutional change that is particularly needed, some of the proposals will seem utopian. The U.S. political system is embedded in federal and state constitutions that are proverbially difficult to alter. And there is as yet no significant public that recognizes the necessity of fundamental institutional reform, as opposed to the reform of this or that policy, or the nature of the needed changes.

I think it is in any case helpful to offer proposals that, at least in the first instance, embody the changes that are needed. With further experience it may be that these will prove misguided. But the strategic aim is critical in the discussion that follows, and even misguided proposals can illustrate the problems to be addressed and clarify the sort of solutions that will, or will not, address them. The key thing is to push the discussion forward.

Agency Government

Chapter 6 included an analysis of the endemic weaknesses of liberal parliamentary democracy, such as we find it in Europe, East Asia, and North America. We focused on its failure to serve as a symmetrical two-way communication system between government and the governed. We observed too that the hierarchical design of the other institutions of the Intersection did not counter but rather intensified the already endemic weakness of the electoral system. The basic argument was that we misconceive our present political system as *representative* government. Our system and those of the other modern democracies rarely if ever yield governments that are *embodied majorities* in the sense of representing majority opinions. We elect people to government, but as our agents, not our representatives. The difference, at least in the first instance, turns on the asymmetry of those communication mechanisms. We speak of elected representatives acting "with the consent of the governed." To imagine that that "consent" is more than a highly formal, abstract, largely ritualistic sort of thing is to befuddle ourselves. Accordingly, we should speak of *agency government*, not representative government, and government by relatively passive *assent*, not informed active consent.

These earlier arguments did not rest on moral objections to government doing things that perhaps its citizens might not know about or like done or that break some moral or political principle. That's a different set of issues. I wanted to underline the functional incapacity of liberal parliamentary democracy, not its moral lapses. Government only suffers low, largely ineffective voter retribution when, as so frequently is the case, it acts for the few against the many, the insiders against the outsiders, the wealthy against those not so materially favored, or merely shortsightedly or downright foolishly.[1] In their defense, voters are too often blocked from learning over time which of their officials do represent their interests and thus are prevented from learning to distinguish the consequences from the appearance of important policies. As a result, they too often fail to discern failure, incompetence, and charlatanry, and are too frequently unable to recognize which political leaders might assist them in those things. The failures are complementary; government is not held accountable by the governed, and this itself aggravates the wider problem of its shortsighted, shallowly partisan, often profoundly irresponsible behavior. And the public, partly by its lethargy and inaction, partly by its institutionalized powerlessness, too often favors policies and proposals equally shortsighted and equally likely to eventuate in its own material and spiritual harm.

In our era, two further contributions have weakened the political system. Contemporary liberalism comes first to mind. Conservatives have been right to argue against a political culture in which, in the citizen-to-government relationship, obligation lies one-sidedly on government's side. The exclusive stress on "rights," like the similar stress on citizen "entitlement," weakens our sense of duty and obligation toward both society and government.

Of greater importance were the government-mounted drives in the 1950s, in and after the Nixon presidency and since, to discredit and demobilize those citizen forces most critical of its policies.² These were and still are enthusiastically supported by the conservative mainstream. The polity has yet, I think, to fully recover from the Truman and Nixon administrations. At any event, a greatly strengthened, intellectually critical sense of citizen responsibility for government behavior is badly needed and, not by chance, would be an outcome of a flourishing SFTA, especially if a revived mobilization of ordinary working people flourished alongside it.

To theorize the failure of democratic, representative government to embody majorities either of opinion or of interests, I marked out seven different system faults, six of which are malfunctions inherent in our current political forms of "representation": (1) that elected representatives become nonrepresentative by virtue of the very fact that they now hold office; (2) that voter preferences are nontransitive, hence that contradictory options may each be supported by majorities; (3) that democracy, as we know it, is normally a rule of the minority; (4) that the major parties collude as much as or more than they compete; (5) that the most ignorant voters normally decide elections; and (6) that there are powerful forces within all the modern polities that work to undercut the ability of the governed to govern themselves, who are in principle opposed to or fear "mobocracy" (or some other less polemical synonym) and to that end spare little effort to demobilize popular political activity, misinform voters, or induce in them ideologies and attitudes that neuter popular influence.

The "System" Just Doesn't Work

In that earlier exposition, I especially pointed to the racial problems the United States faced in the years following World War II. As I read the record, for all the vaunted genius of the "Founding Fathers" and the reforms of the Progressive Era, the U.S. political system was simply unable to deal with a pressing problem where it was clear that the failure would have harmful effects on the wider polity. The World War II experience had made the continuation of prewar institutionalized racial prejudice in the North and segregation in the South an untenable proposition. First, there was the earlier experience after World War I, when a somewhat similar situation had held. In order then to repress a reinvigorated movement for racial change by black Americans, the Ku Klux Klan reemerged with a rash of lynchings and other of their trademark contributions to the commonweal. Klan influence over major party politics also helped to undercut wider efforts to continue the integration of immigrants, add needed social welfare arrangements, expand civil liberties, and revivify the polity. In short, for the failure to take up the issue of racial amelioration in the 1920s, the entire U.S. polity had paid a steep price. But the 1945 black population was even more restive than that of 1919 and in an improved economic, cultural, and political position to do something about it.

Among the highest elites and other well-informed citizens in the 1940s, there was an awareness that there had to be significant racial change. The Ford Foundation's encyclopedic study of U.S. race relations by Gunnar Myrdal already signaled that awareness, and the subsequent report was greeted in many quarters as wise and overdue (Myrdal 1944). Nevertheless, through the years 1946 to 1954, attempts to pass fair voting, fair housing, fair employment, and fair schooling measures simply failed. We should remind ourselves that these were issues supported not just by a liberal minority.

U.S. racial practices also hurt U.S. interests overseas, although the army had signaled as early as the war itself that the exclusion of black soldiers from combat units, another child of continuing segregation, was a military liability. For much of World War II, black soldiers and sailors were routinely assigned to labor units as stevedores, unskilled construction workers, and so forth. When in mid-1944 there were unexpectedly high losses in the Army's fighting units, infantry and armor especially, the pool of black military manpower really couldn't be tapped. Even a conservative Southerner, the army chief of staff, George Marshall, was brought to see the price in military ineffectiveness that this represented.

For the record, in World War I there were "colored" U.S. fighting units, but they were placed within French colonial units—Senegalese and other North African—so that there would no racial "mixing" in U.S. regiments and divisions. It is probably fair to say that the initial exclusion of black soldiers from combat in World War II was a legacy of attempting to avoid the racial militancy that resulted from allowing black men to experience combat and its casualties in World War I. In any case, when an essentially conservative institution like the U.S. military takes the lead in racial progress, as it still so often does, it is a clear signal that the political process is critically and insufficiently adaptive.

The watershed event in the U.S. civil rights "revolution" was the Supreme Court decision *Brown v. Board of Education,* in May 1954, which struck down segregated schools. This is the date from which we can view the incapacity of the U.S. political system to address real-world problems. For the next ten years, almost without exception, the executive and legislative branches of the federal government simply refused to enforce a series of court decisions dismantling segregation in interstate commerce, employment, and other areas.[3] Even the courts waffled in enforcing *Brown*. Congress could not pass and the president's office would not enforce those laws necessary to protect black voters, integrated travel groups, black churches, and black activists in the South, all of whom were at daily risk to life and limb from the Klan and its more vigorous successor, the White Citizens' Councils. Under the legal doctrine of "interposition," Southern municipal and state leaders undertook a campaign of "massive resistance" to, especially, the court's school decision. "Interposition" was first cousin to "nullification," already politically discredited and refuted by the outcome of the Civil War. It held that state law interposed itself between federal law and state behavior, effectively blocking the authority of the former. Aside from outright refusal to obey the court's mandate to integrate schools, states such as Virginia redirected funds from the public schools into all-white private ones. This and other lawless behavior was championed by Southern political leaders and received more than a modicum of support and even practical assistance from many non-Southern politicians.

The wider public tended at best to be a passive spectator to this ugly circus. It was only when the wave of kidnappings, murders, and bombing grew out of hand, by the summer of 1964, that the Johnson administration finally acted, both directly and by proposing and supporting major civil rights bills in the Congress—and finally seeing to their enforcement. In any case, what we see here is a full decade of failure by the formal political system to ameliorate an acute racial problem, the failure comprising an inability or refusal by government to obey the law, the toleration of widespread criminal activities, the unpunished encouragement of those activities by otherwise prestigious political elites, and a passive public—until the extraparliamentary intervention of the civil rights activists built a program and a constituency that imposed action on the federal government.

If we drop entirely the tone of moralizing disapproval in the previous paragraph, we can see the period 1954 to 1964 as a decade in which the political system of the United States was unable to deal with an open racial crisis, even when that inability encouraged a breakdown of the rule of law. Both Eisenhower, in 1958 in Arkansas, and Kennedy, in 1962 in Alabama, had used federal troops to enforce the laws. But Eisenhower, who had criticized the Supreme Court decision from the beginning as unwise, was acting only to address the one instance of lawlessness at Little Rock High School, and Kennedy only the problem at the University of Alabama. Both administrations were widely understood to be trying their best to stay out of the civil rights struggles in the South.

Whatever may have been the personal faults of presidents Eisenhower and Kennedy and their associates, this has to be viewed as an institutional failure. The political system, taken as a whole, dealt with the Southern racial crisis in the "normal" way it deals with such political problems—until it was forced from the outside, "by the streets," to depart from its inaction. It is normal for federal officials to stay clear of local and state disputes. The application of federal laws there always raises jurisdictional nettles that are prudently avoided. Local and state officials have as allies influential businesspeople, U.S. senators, and party leaders whom one is wise not to offend. But even at the time, it was clear that segregation in Virginia schools or in the interstate bus terminals wasn't really like those other, traditional local and state matters. The issue wasn't kin to whether this county or another county got that federal funding for a bridge. There was an organized epidemic of criminal behavior. Citizens were being assaulted for voting and going to school. Worshippers were being killed in their churches. Sheriffs and their deputies were conspiring with the White Citizens' Councils to kidnap and murder people. Government officials were proclaiming that come what may they were going to break the law. In other words, entirely apart from the rightness or wrongness of segregation or integration, there was substantial lawbreaking going on, but political leaders North and South wouldn't intervene in that "local situation." The rule of law, tenuous in any society, was being flouted, and even governors and U.S. senators were urging people to participate in the flouting.

The highest U.S. elites deserve some praise, but more blame here too. While they one-sidedly supported desegregation, they were unwilling to expend their political capital by too openly siding with the civil rights people. Contrast that behavior with their very, very active, open support now for international free-trade arrangements. It's a matter of priorities.

We must not overlook the fact that much of the American public was long complicit in this too; only gradually did it cease to view civil rights activists as "reds," troublemakers, and oddballs. Even as late as the spring of 1964, the "public" didn't recognize that the country was caught in a political crisis that demanded political resolution.[4]

And "the system" doesn't even learn. Historical and political understanding of these events has since been obscured by high-sounding but empty rhetoric. Civil rights activists are praised for acting on the "moral imperative" of integration, and their opponents are accused of ignoring "the traditional American values" of equality and so forth. This is all well and good, but this smugness disguises the deeper incapacity of the political system. Now, of course, we at least call integration a moral imperative, but then, at the time, most respectable voices thought the tactic of "civil disobedience" was itself lawless,[5] embraced an attitude of "a plague on both your houses," or, like Eisenhower, thought the attempt "to bring social change through the law" was itself wrong, and those who resisted it therefore not quite so wicked as now we see them. It is, for example, credibly believed that there was collusion between the Eisenhower and Stevenson camps not to raise and not to differ about the *Brown* decision during their presidential campaign in 1956. We should not leap to moral outrage over this; as explained in chapter 6, the two parties collude quite as much as they compete. The principle appears to be that they will collude when they can't figure out which way their own political winds will blow tomorrow. It is a fair reading of the events to say that the political system simply failed for that decade.

Bipartisan collusion accounts, as well, for the long process of falling into and then being unable to exit the Vietnam War, the prolongation of the cold war after the 1954 Geneva Conferences, and possibly the Cuban Missile Crisis of 1962.[6] Nor should one lose sight of the present failure of the U.S. political system, not solely that of Bush II, to take steps to slow global warming. In all of these cases, the political relationships holding between the parties, the public, the media, and the government, both inner and elected, have failed to recognize or ignored genuine crises, have even acted to worsen crises, and have retained nothing of what they learned from the consequences. That sort of thing, if I am right, defines a dysfunctional political system and, barring a bit of exaggeration on my part, argues at least that our current political system is only marginally and occasionally functional. If that is the scope of the empirical critique, it is a devastating one.

The Democratic Dilemma, or the Functional Interdependence of Elected and Inner Government

In chapter 6, I also raised a further, seventh critique of elected, democratic government that is both different from and more fundamental than those we just reviewed. To think of elected government and what I called inner government as polar opposites betrays a lack of understanding of the "democratic dilemma." By that I refer to a functional relationship of interdependence between the representational efficiency of an electoral system and the consequences that has for the security of tenure of office of elected officials, hence on their determination to shift controversial and potentially controversial issues into the inner government.

For many people, the more democracy the better. The way to get rid of or to minimize the scope of the power of the permanent, inner, unelected government is to make the system more democratic, to allow "the people" to intervene in government more forcefully and more selectively in order to compel their elected officials to bow to their will. But like so many political truisms, this one isn't true either. The reverse is the case. The more democratic the system, that is, the more sensitive it is to voter intervention, the greater the fragility of holding elected office, the more powerful the imperative on elected officials to shift controversial issues out of the public's view and into the inner government. This intimacy between the democratic sensitivity of an electoral system and the boost it gives to the inner government is well confirmed in our historical experience and, of course, further intensified by the centralization of strategic authority in the main institutions of corporate or Intersection society.

Thus the dilemma for the sort of democratically elected, representational government now featured in the developed world and so highly recommended for the rest. When the system is very democratic, the inner government prospers. Of course, inner government also prospers when the system is undemocratic, for then the elites can simply go their own way. If we take the logic of the dilemma seriously, there will be an intermediate point on the scale of democratic-to-nondemocratic where the power of the inner government is least. Or so argues the logic, but the experience of these things also argues that in the most important and deeply connected areas of government activity—that is, the big three of the economy, domestic security, and international security—the public's influence will range from marginal to nonexistent.

Modern economies typically create sharply structured systems of reward, economic well-being, and privilege that are managed and protected by inner government, like the Federal Reserve. All governments arrange their police powers to be able to turn them on their own citizens, in whole or part, should it prove necessary or even just convenient. The choice between war and peace with another country or countries is normally prefigured in the irrevocable diplomatic and military steps that the inner government has already taken long before the public becomes aware of the "crisis."

The multiple problems caused by the phenomenon of inner government cannot all be changed at a stroke. However, my earlier proposals for corporate, police, and worker-related reforms would—should—have material effect, as should some political remobilization among workers. To the extent that something like those proposals could be won, they would go a long way toward effecting major change for the good in our political dynamic. A more representative and democratic corporate governance mechanism, as part and parcel of a more democratically responsible economy, and sharp restrictions on the political role of the police would of themselves reduce the power and the immunities of the inner government to more tolerable levels and to that degree improve both the popular and the feedback characteristics of government. The directly civic effects of wider, direct popular experience with jury panel governance within the corporate firms and on the police boards would serve as a leaven that would revive the role of the voters in the electoral system. A revived labor movement, especially one in which "the lowest of the low" had an appreciable influence, would bring new socially potent assets to the Democracy and, to that extent, correct in part the severe maldistribution of power we now suffer.

Thus, assuming something like those beneficial changes in place or in process of becoming so, what else should be done politically in order to resume the historic advance? My own sense of priorities here is that we ought to be trying to distance the U.S. executive branch, even if only by a little bit, from the imposed imperatives of the international state system. That too would be in aid of a more critically representative, that is to say, beneficially democratic, government mechanism, not only domestically but given the current effect of the United States on others, in the interests of the rest of the peoples of the world.

Government, State, and Divine Right

The recap brings us to the point where we can confront what I feel is the most important remaining institutional obstacle to the continuation of the historical advance. Again we take up the discussion where we left it, in this case, in the previous chapter.

The modern state and international state system are usefully seen as the child of the Peace (or Treaties) of Westphalia of 1648, which ended the Thirty Years' War, fought between two "true faiths," Catholic and Protestant. Both camps had spent the previous decades trying to stamp out the other with God's help, though importantly assisted by sword and gunpowder, with the result that Europe was ravaged from Gibraltar to the Danube and beyond. Eventually the two sides fought each other to a standoff, so that the Peace was in the first instance an undertaking to recognize that very fact. The form the recognition took was that every ruler was to have the right to compel his subjects to adhere to whichever communion he chose. This was revolutionary in the longer historical context. A single European Christendom, the ideal if not quite the reality since the split between Eastern Orthodoxy and Rome some centuries before, was itself now split into two incompatible Christian communions. And further, it was accepted that the authority of the secular ruler would override that of the churches and their leaders even in matters divine. From our present-day standpoint, that further implied that in matters of lesser theological importance, like low worldly things, the will of the sovereign as sovereign in all things in his domain was also confirmed.

Several distinct political legacies have developed from those seeds of three and a half centuries ago.[7] The powers of each state are sovereign, which is to say, unlimited against all others. No state has a legitimate master; it and it alone may judge what is in its interests and pursue those interests to the limit that its power makes possible. Of course, in theory, the modern state system has accepted some limitations on the powers of the individual states in dealing with one another. But compared to the heavy-handed intrusiveness of supranational economic bodies, these are pretty timid. A series of treaties beginning in the last part of the nineteenth century and continuing on through the Kellogg-Briand Pact to the United Nations and beyond has—in theory—reserved certain rights to the organized international community. But for the most powerful states, the United States and the Soviet Union yesterday and the United States and China today, their independence of action in international matters is unchecked—save perhaps by the power of the other. The international state system is such only in the Hobbesian sense of the perennial war of each against all.

At present, the immense military and economic power of the United States roughly matches that of the rest of the developed world combined. The ideological reflex of that power was the doctrine of the Bush II administration that the United States would prevent by military means any other states or groups of people from developing into its power-political rival (J. Mann 2004). Whatever the merits of this position, it exemplifies in its purest form, because conjoined to actual power, the extent of legitimate action that may be undertaken internationally by a state. In this sense, then, as in others that we will explore, we can see that the state form, the dominant political form in the world's relations between countries and peoples, betrays its absolutist origins in the politics of the princes of three and a half centuries ago. From the philosophical standpoint, each state, like a god, has no master and is itself the ultimate judge of what is right and wrong.

The "divine right of kings" is dead, but the "divine right" of the state lives on in the form of many insufferable but hopefully correctable evils. It is a hopeful sign that the smaller, weaker states are often now held accountable to international "law," though they're not the main problem to begin with. The larger, more powerful states act to the limits of their sovereignty, thus guaranteeing a world in which war and chaos, with its rapine and mass killing, are always threats, often present realities. I think the history of Africa since 1945 offers us a model of the outer limits of normalcy in such a world. It is testimony to that international system that much of sub-Saharan Africa is now probably worse off than it was during the wretched era of colonialism, politically anarchic, wracked by internecine wars, sown with land mines, fought over by gangster armies, suffering recurrent famine, and with public health systems collapsed even before the AIDS pandemic. If this is true, as I think it is, it headlines the sheer wickedness of the present international system.

We can get a particularly clear view of the inherent irresponsibility of the system from the memoirs, earlier cited, of the long-time Soviet ambassador to the United States, Anatoly Dobrynin (1996). As he emphasizes, the USSR never defined any important strategic interests in Africa *at all*—none! It intervened there only because important, powerful states exert their power and prestige wherever they can and to whatever limit they can. After it intervened, the USSR had interests—prestige, clients, and markets—but those interests were created by the intervention and did not precede it. Of course, these pointless interventions—in Egypt, Angola, Ethiopia, and Somalia—were not viewed as such by successive U.S.

administrations. True to form, for them all Soviet behavior was evidence of the communist intention to take over the world. Tit-for-tatting, the United States responded with interventions of its own, with, of course, further dire consequences for the continent, the effects of which are still being felt. Worse yet, from the Soviet point of view, their fooling around in Africa helped to convince U.S. officials to take a harder line on issues of nuclear disarmament, détente, antiballistic missiles, and other items that *were* of deepest concern to the Soviet leadership. This is perhaps the most dramatic example of the witless evils that flow from the present international system, but it is surely not the only one. One would like to think that the NATO intervention in the Balkans signaled a fundamental change in this situation, but Europe remains a special case. Elsewhere, there is much disapproval but little state action against even the most brutal national governments, unless, as in Iraq, that moral disapproval provides handy cover for other purposes by powerful countries.

With respect to its own people, every government is both omnipotent and omniscient, meting out lies, discrimination, confiscation, imprisonment, torture, and death to its own subjects to the extent that it wishes—if in doing so it doesn't run afoul of a more powerful country. There is an enormous literature on Hitler's "Final Solution," "the Holocaust," and "the Jewish Catastrophe," to give only a few of the conceptualizations applied to the attempted extermination of European Jewry. And another literature of almost the same scale devoted to the murderous record of, especially, the Stalin period in the history of the Soviet Union. I am reasonably familiar with both literatures and don't recall that this literature points out that those regimes exercised powers over their own subjects that are normally claimed by every regime, namely, the right to punish by its own decision such of its subjects as it chooses and according to its own constitutional framework. Both Nazi Germany and the Stalinist Soviet Union employed conventional state institutions rooted in their national pasts to carry out their mass murders; most German police were grandfathered into their jobs from the previous regime, and the Soviet political police was modeled on, and often its ranks staffed by leftovers from, the Okhrana, the tsar's secret police. It wasn't "obedience to a superior" or political zeal that inspired quite ordinary functionaries to commit repeated atrocities, but merely "obedience to a higher *state official*." I think we now know enough about, especially, the Nazi era, to realize that while German culture and the German past played an enabling role in the Jewish Catastrophe, the really decisive element was that the German state carried it out and was obeyed by its functionaries, as states are wont to be obeyed by their functionaries. Seen in this light, Nazi and Soviet behaviors should be regarded as the outer, limiting cases of the exercise of conventional state authority and legitimacy when dealing with those who fall within its writ.

It is not my intention to paint a night so dark that all cats become black. Granted that the Hitlerite and Stalinist regimes uniquely systematized mass murder—but modern states tend to systematize everything they do, from arts policy to war making. Granted too that the scale of the crimes of each regime was unique—but that should be characterized by saying that they approached the limit on a familiar graded scale of state behavior in these things. Murderous campaigns against national minorities or other officially disfavored people are common, not rare, even nowadays. Physical elimination of real or imagined "enemies of the state" is quite common these days—as it has always been. I think that to be awed by the sheer enormity of the crimes of Nazi Germany and the Soviet Union allows analysts to evade a realistic intellectual and moral confrontation with contemporary state-sponsored atrocities and, at a deeper level, with such a flawed political form as we find in the modern state within the international state system.

For all peoples, this doctrine of sovereignty accompanied by unchecked international power is a major barrier to the historic advance. In the narrow-minded nationalist politics taught in our own media, schools, and universities, and confirmed by so many patriotic symbols and civic exercises, "the United States" has the unconditional abstract right and indeed the duty to "defend its interests." As a practical matter, that means that the current occupant of the White House can position the country for war as and when he chooses. The experience of going to war against Germany in both world wars, of the cold war, of the Vietnam intervention, and of our current wars "against terrorism" and in Iraq amply confirms that presidents have unusual freedom of action to create the conditions under which this country will go to war and can maintain party-political, media, and public assent for that war making for a not inconsiderable period of time. I'll come back to this discussion shortly, but here it is enough to focus on the fact that incumbent presidents have too great a leeway to engage the United States in war or place it on the path to war and can neuter the opposition for too long a time.

In our constitutional tradition, we hedge the theological character of the state by distinguishing *state* from *government,* but only partially so. Pundits and public figures routinely concede to the existing government extraconstitutional authority in matters concerning war, peace, and national security. "The right to self-defense" is the normal, sweeping principle employed here. But that right is not among the powers in the Constitution explicitly granted to Congress or the executive; it is one of those powers reserved to the sovereign people. That matters little since the doctrine of state sovereignty overcomes constitutional writ. Of course, within the international state system it would seem pure folly to restrain the president's war-making powers over a constitutional nicety. But that is the point; in this realm, our thinking and our practice are to confine the Constitution to that realm of nicety and free the incumbent administration to do as it deems fit. The public itself, always prone to panic during real or imagined international crises, is also a major contributor to this state worship.[8]

A Historic Window of Opportunity

Discussion of the power-political link between the American state, the inner government, and the international state system has peculiar importance right now because of a historic window of opportunity. This window is open now, but it will not remain so indefinitely.

This window is the fact that the U.S. state faces no immediate great-power military-political threat. It may be that Europe, China, Japan, India, Brazil, or even Russia, alone or together, will become powerful enough to prevent the United States from throwing its military weight around. But no such prospect is as yet in sight or credible.

The significance of this point is readily understandable. It bears directly on the state's war-making power and war-making initiatives. In our system these rest with the president and, of course, with the inner government of national security. If the United States were under active threat today from another power or powers, proposals to shrink autonomous presidential war-making power would seem and, to an extent, would actually be quixotic. But not at the present time, where no such threat is palpable and where *the near-term policies of U.S. administrations will in part determine whether and when new threats will arise and shape their character.*

There are already stirrings among the national security elite about the threat from China, especially its quest for a "blue water" navy, that is, acquiring long-distance submarines and aircraft carriers. As with the threats posed by the Soviet Union during the cold war, these ascribed threats support the desire of the military industrial complex to have an enemy against whom they can arm with more and more of the most expensive sorts of weapons. Unfortunately, exaggerated fears of enemies have endless credibility among politicians, the media, and the more excitable parts of the public. And, of course, if we arm against China, then China must arm against us, and so on, and so on. As Dobrynin (1996) makes clear, the old Soviet military liked this game as much as ours does, and there is every reason to think the Chinese military will like it too.

But for now we do have a window of opportunity, and it is world historical in its possibilities. No great danger to the security of the United States would now arise as a result of radically limiting the war-making powers of the U.S. president and, via that, of the inner government of national security elites.

At present, the executive branch and our highest elites think and act as if they were still fighting the cold war and thus bend every effort to create for the United States itself, at the expense of others, a more overwhelming military power, a more dominant economy, and a more obsequious set of client states and puppets. Even "the special relationship" claimed by Britain comes mostly to Downing Street doing and thinking what we want it to do and to think. But this is shortsighted. When inevitably U.S. power flags, no matter how far that is over the horizon, we and the rest of the world will then be plunged back into the unreformed international state system that played such a key role in the three great, destructive wars of the twentieth century: the two world wars and the cold war. That is also likely to be a world with a military technology even more threatening than at present.

A farsighted outlook would employ the power we currently have to begin to build international, consensual, political, economic, and legal institutions in which, because of that power, the safety and advantages of the American people could be especially well guarded. Then, when U.S. power weakens in the distant future, its legacy might live on in those beneficent institutions.

This is not a choice between two equal scenarios for the future. Present U.S. power is employed to secure strategic bases, now here and now there, to develop weapons systems like "Star Wars" that are beyond the present economic (but not eventual scientific and technological) capability of future rivals, and to promise to any such aspiring rival that it will be thwarted, possibly by military action, if its rivalry takes palpable form. Our present policy also demands "free trade" policies from others while we protect our agriculture, steel, pharmaceuticals, and even media giants. And, further, while we unilaterally set aside this and that treaty and international agreement, we simultaneously demand of others that they obey them to the letter.

The alternative strategy that I suggest is thus like Pascal's wager. We can bet with the near-term near certainty that the United States will have no great power rivals, followed by the long-term near certainty that when such rivals do eventually emerge, we and the world will be plunged into the old chaos, disorder, and threat. Or we can choose an uncertain, uphill quest to alter that international system over time, to move along the institutional learning curve and to hasten by perhaps only a little bit the arrival of a successor international system that, however far in the future it might be, will alter the undesirable world we have been living with for the past three and a half war-torn centuries.

The "war on terror" is material to this discussion. That pseudo-war is at the center of the illegal, often brutal behavior that we earlier talked of on the part of the several national governments. And that behavior has in turn multiplied the numbers and strengthened the determination of actual terrorists, transforming what was once a modest police problem into a network of movements.

It is and was a patent mistake to think of it as a "war." We accept that for the duration of a war, we have to accept sacrifices of various kinds, including some legal and even constitutional rights. Part of the rationale for that is that wars eventually end. Then, the law and the Constitution can be fully restored. But the so-called war on terror has no end. Destroying Al Qaeda and the Taliban and killing or capturing Osama Bin Laden will not end it. There will always be "terrorist threats" of some kind or other out there. This points up the folly of calling it a *war*, for if it cannot be ended, then neither can the sacrifices that we are called upon to make in order to wage it.

Realistically, the war on terror requires a modest level of police expenditure and police staffing, and not the sort of national emergency and spending it currently enjoys. The genius, if it may be called that, of U.S. aggressiveness against "terrorists" in Afghanistan, Iraq, and possibly now Iran or North Korea is to merge police-level issues with the more dire memories of the two world wars. Like another police problem, the war on drugs, it relies on short-term, quick-fix nostrums. From the standpoint of political realism, both are also wars-on-the-political-cheap in the sense that it is less politically risky for our international and domestic security elites to spend immense sums on police, soldiers, prisons, and weapons than to advocate longer-run strategies to undermine the social, economic, and especially political sources of terrorism.

The present world economic, social, and political failures create motives for terror and recruits for terrorism wholesale, while our police and military responses have at best a retail effectiveness. We are fortunate that only the Islamic world is now generating terrorists and a cause that animates them. Political, social, and economic conditions in sub-Saharan Africa and in South and Central America are at least the equal of those in the Islamic world, often worse. The national humiliation of Palestine and Iraq, which spurs on their terrible defenders, is quite as marked in equatorial Africa as in Colombia, in Haiti, in Peru, and throughout Central and South America and the Caribbean. How long can we expect the more radical advocates of the rights of Liberia or Angola, or of the Dominican Republic, to refrain from the deadly tactics of Islamic terrorists?

A massive police plus military strategy against terror is, of course, politically advantageous to the forces of reaction in the United States and elsewhere. As in the old war on "subversion," the enemy is in our midst, all must be vigilant, better to err on the side of violating civil liberties than to allow the further killing of *our* innocents. All this plays into the hands of the police power, whose failure in the war on drugs was becoming clearer day by day and decade by decade. A "war" on terror also justifies the inflated force levels our military grew accustomed to during the cold war and the lavish and expensive equipment the war-manufacturing sector counts on.

Preemptive U.S. wars against potential rivals, the impoverishing of the majority for the advantage of the few by the IMF/WTO/G-8 consortium, and the police/military strategy of the war on terror are the different dimensions of an approach to the world that is of advantage only to the occupants of inner government and those small private publics they represent. The alternative entails a chancier, more experimental, longer-term effort, better calculated to develop a world system in which all are more likely to live in peace and security and with steady material and spiritual improvements in their lives.

How Do We Reasonably Limit the War-Making Powers of the U.S. President?

One can be quixotic here, but the political locus of the problem is not at all unclear. In the United States, the doctrine of state sovereignty has been taken over into law to give the president extraconstitutional leeway to wage war because he is the commander in chief of the armed forces. While the Bush II administration is seen as the preeminent villain here, every administration since Wilson's has abused this prerogative, and the Obama administration has failed to reject George W. Bush's extraconstitutional actions in principle.

While the elites within the national security apparatus are not politically toothless in their own right, and have powerful means of suasion against even the most determined president, the *institutional* locus of the problem rests in the constitutional and additional, extraconstitutional powers traditionally claimed by the presidency. An important first step, therefore, in limiting the war-making powers of the U.S. state is circumscribing the power of the president to act unilaterally in foreign and international security policy.

It may prove necessary to add to the Constitution itself some explicit reaffirmation that sovereignty always resides in the people, whole and entire, *and* that its delegation is always only limited, situational, and positively covered by law. This should be accompanied by a statement that positively affirms that presidential command of the armed forces asserts only the primacy of civilian over military authority and has no implications for the free use of those armed forces against real or imagined foreign enemies and their alleged domestic collaborators without positive congressional enactment and, especially, as subject to subsequent court review. Here it really is a question of reasserting the authority of the Constitution against its corruption by the system of state sovereignty.

Of itself, this change would be insufficient, but it would be helpful if there were explicit positive constitutional underpinning to the idea that presidential action in foreign policy is never out of reach of the law and the courts. There is a principle at issue here that is too easily swept away when we deal with things like the use both of military and police force. Often the proximate causes of such use of force seem so dire and dangerous that we reasonably grant the benefit of doubt to the attacking president or the shooting cop. Unfortunately, this reasonable benefit of the doubt creates a legal vacuum around the force user. What needs to be asserted is that officers of government are never free, in any of their actions, of the positive, compelling bonds of the law. I think it only prudential, in fact, to argue that absent a positive legislative enactment that controls when and how a president uses the military or a cop shoots someone, the courts should shape a rule, apt to that situation, under which the president or the police officer may be reined in and in particularly flagrant cases perhaps even subject to criminal or related charges. The idea is that that rule should remain valid until such time as the relevant legislature has met to consider it and to make some definite step to confirm it, to reject it or to replace it, but not to ignore it.

What I am proposing has some legal precedent. The idea rests on the development of international standards of conduct prior to the Nuremberg Trials of 1945–46, where it was held that aspects of international law were sufficiently developed, promulgated, and binding, though not always formally written out, that particularly blatant violations could subject the violator to punishment.[9] I don't urge the occasional replacement of a sitting president with a hanged president, but looking ahead, there are lesser sanctions that might be applied; a court recommending or even initiating impeachment, or compelling the resignation of key subordinates, or perhaps just banning the offender from running for or holding office again. The historic window of opportunity that I mentioned makes this sort of finer-grained legal control of presidential action more possible and gives us some time to develop a body of well-considered law that more neatly distinguishes legitimate presidential discretion from ideological willfulness, playing to the patriotic gallery, fronting for this or that firm or industry, or sheer bungling.

To return for a moment to the police, there are many instances of police violence that so breach accepted conceptions of legally responsible behavior that one wants to be able to apply an appropriate punishment even in the absence of a positive statute. If we consider all officers of government as serving only within bounds of behavior that have concrete, specific, positive legal and constitutional sanction, and not merely generalized permission or the fact that something is not explicitly prohibited, then the courts could prescribe that the offender be tried in court-like proceedings and possibly dismissed and direct that further civil or criminal actions be instituted against the offender as well. Again, this is an instance of the operation of that indispensable principle that no agent or officer of government at any level has any powers save those spelled out by the law and the Constitution. Our experience both recent and throughout the span of the twentieth century is that the existence of any legal vacuum around any officer of government creates a far too high probability that illegal and even criminal actions will ensue. Not incidentally, the promulgation of such a principle and the development of a body of precedent rulings should have a deterrent effect on such behavior and, over time, reduce the potential for arbitrariness in applying sanctions against government officers who have technically broken no statute.

There would be another advantage to such a temporary, bounded assumption by the courts of a legislative authority, and it points up the weakness of the War Powers Act approach to limiting presidential discretion. Unfortunately, the problem here ultimately lies in the Congress, the very branch that this approach envisions as a restraint on the executive. But no constitutional prescription can avail against the congressional cowardice and flag-waving that we already know will occur in a pinch. We are only too familiar with elected legislators who shrewdly play it both ways when an international crisis comes on the agenda. In the lead-up to the Mexican War, the Spanish-American War, World Wars I and II, the Korean War, and the Vietnam and the second Iraq wars, the Congress granted sanction in one form or other for the executive to wage war, the unspecified nature of the granted sanction allowing the legislators the weasel room to say later, when the situation had changed, Oh, that's not what we meant! or Oh, we were deceived! That was even true during our Civil War. The use of force by the executive and its officers—or the domestic police—is far too serious a matter to leave within a legal framework that combines a legislative children's playgroup and an executive of adolescent temper.

With respect to the presidency, what this approach really envisions is the development of a new branch of constitutional law, namely, of the gradual creation of a body of court decisions that would over time more closely define the legal nature, limits, timing, triggers, scale, duration, and so on of the operation of the war-making power, the use and the threat of employing the armed forces, and so forth. The difficulties and paradoxes that will have to be resolved in creating this body of law are not a reason to avoid trying to create it. The present and foreseeable military predominance of the United States makes this task both more feasible and more imperative.

But absent additional institutional change, it is unlikely that constitutional restraints on the president's power to make war would either be enacted or, that occurring, have much practical consequence. Again, with the hesitancy with which one must approach any radical alterations in our basic institutions, I would propose the following.

Reconstituting the U.S. Senate—Again

We've already suggested at least in principle the limits on presidential power that ought to be enforceable by the courts. But to make such changes operable, at least one other branch of government has to change too and that appears to be the Congress, most notably the Senate. Several considerations suggest the Senate and not the House. First and foremost is that the Senate already has a uniquely direct and selective constitutional relationship to the office of the president and his conduct of foreign affairs. The House is in theory able to balance the president by its power over spending, but the Senate is already constitutionally charged with having to give prior approval to the appointment of cabinet officers and ambassadors and, by ratifying treaties, to give them the force of law. Most of the powers of the Senate vis-à-vis the president have been eviscerated by the practical imperatives of the international state sovereignty system.

A second, though weaker reason for looking to the Senate is that since the passage of the Seventeenth Amendment, which instituted the direct, popular election of the Senate (1913), replacing the appointment of senators by the state legislatures, there has been a lesser rationale for the Senate as now constituted. In its form of representation it is simply a copy of the House, though with a different apportionment and, usually, from much, much larger voting units—whole states and not just congressional districts.

The legacy of that pre-1913 Senate still makes it too often and too much a club whose membership and rules enable small minorities to act according to their own, sometimes very whimsical, sometimes even peevish lights. Currently, it is not even bound by simple democratic majority rule; it has become the custom for the minority party, especially when Republican, to subject virtually every issue to the threat of a filibuster, that is, to block action on any proposal that cannot muster 60 percent of that body.[10]

Meanwhile, because of the now-stupendous costs of election campaigns, the Senate, slightly more than the House, has become mostly a body of millionaires who enjoy the favor of other millionaires. In theory an elite body less likely to bow to the ill-considered whims of the mob than the more plebeian House, our memories of senators Joe McCarthy, Theodore Bilbo, and, more recently, Ted Stevens of Alaska and James Imhoff of Oklahoma provide decisive evidence to the contrary. It would also take many volumes to describe all the "senatorial privileges" that have no legal or constitutional basis whatsoever but are nonetheless binding on the behavior of the Senate. Their net effect is to hold the Senate hostage too frequently to small factions and even individual caprice. Typically, an individual senator, like Jesse Helms in the recent past, can veto ambassadorial appointments and be routinely supported in this even by colleagues who think his intentions destructive and his preferences at best egomaniacal. The Helms example, and too many others like it, shows us a body that supposedly represents the wisdom of the better classes against the passions of the many but that in reality acts too often like a particularly chummy club for well-off though seldom very talented rich men. In this, the Senate really is the true child of the basic Madisonian-Jeffersonian constitutional prescription that the elite must rein in the mob even at the cost of inflicting elite depredations on the majority.

One shouldn't be entirely carried away in describing the Senate's endemic faults. As against Owen Brewster, Pat McCarran, William F. Knowland, or Strom Thurmond, who were among the grosser senatorial ornaments of and for the McCarthyite era, there have been some truly distinguished senators—Robert La Follette, George Norris, J. William Fulbright, and more recently, Edward Kennedy. The problem is that the Senate is designed to encourage willful individual behavior. In the balance, at least in the present, and most often in the past, the good is outweighed by the bad in that design.

I propose the following in light of that complex historical and constitutional background to the Senate. As before and with I think even greater warrant, senators should be chosen within each state through the same procedures that we name jurors. The current Senate is too small to permit a sufficiently varied membership to emerge from the panel selection method, but a Senate of, say, twice to four times its present size should make that more likely. Under this proposal, each state would send the appropriate, expanded number of senators to the Congress in any one round, their six-year terms staggered as at present. As the reader can see, I'm not settled on the numbers of the Senate, but in any case, the increase in size should of itself ease some of the problems associated with senatorial clubbiness.

With a jury panel method of selection, I think it advisable that senators be limited to one six-year or, perhaps better, one eight-year term. Staggering terms as at present would assure some necessary continuity, and a period of six to eight years provides time for a reasonable amount of seasoning and learning. As before with the police boards, ample, well-funded staff with a strengthened public service ethos are indispensable.

More important than these "housekeeping" questions are the institutional outcomes one is trying to introduce by restraining the war-making powers of the executive. The genius of the jury panel system is that it successfully combines contradictory principles. The jury list from which one chooses a panel has to resemble—"represent"—the citizenry itself: a jury of one's peers. As we recognize at present, the jury system is a profoundly democratic one and one that has over historical time played a, perhaps the, major role in checking government incursions into private life. But the jury itself is not constrained to follow what the citizenry thinks. Instead, it is bound by tradition and its oath to use its most scrupulous judgment in carrying out its tasks. To those political scientists who are enamored of the virtues of elites, one could say that the jury panel system creates temporary elites who then go away without burdening us with their costs for the rest of their days and generations.

The change would also imply a Senate not, as now, of rich men and a few rich women, but one that more closely reflected the political and social experiences, incomes, races, genders, and ethnic groups of the country as a whole. They would be freer of the need to look over their shoulders at campaign donors and excitable constituents when they held their debates and cast their votes. They would accordingly be freer to challenge the president in the midst of patriotic frenzy against this or that real or imagined enemy and, moreover, would be charged by their oaths to do precisely that.

The most powerful objection to choosing the U.S. Senate by lot is that it would place fools and ignoramuses in the Senate chamber, there to decide on the gravest issues of war and peace. But that objection is more rooted in a kind of snobbery peculiar to well-educated people than to a critical examination of the Senate as it is, where fools and ignoramuses have been neither rare nor notably lacking in influence. One salient insight of the jury system is that it is preferable to have neutral jurors, even if ill-educated or lacking in wider social experience, than to have jurors who are or who can become self-interested in the outcome of the case. There is no ignorance and no poorness in judgment worse than the kind that requires one to ignore facts and transgress principles in pursuit of some personal, class, or organizational gain. In the House and the Senate, however, this phenomenon is not common or frequent, it is ubiquitous and constant; whenever an individual member of the House or Senate has no specific goal in mind that might require him or her to ignore facts and transgress principles, he or she will do so on behalf of a colleague, knowing that the favor will be returned. Or, to put it more simply, he or she "goes along into order to get along." Jurors, however, try and for the most part succeed in rising to the occasion when they are confronted with really complex issues of law and evidence. As already suggested, on the recondite issues of war and peace and sliding into crises, what one needs are not people acting as adherents of this or that school or faction in the making of foreign policy or who rise easily to patriotic baits but instead those who, charged with the gravest tasks, are more likely to consider them, however fallibly, in that gravest light.

Criminalizing Some Government Behaviors

I have perhaps repeated too often that the Nazi "Final Solution" and the great Stalinist purges were entirely legal in Germany and the USSR, as are so many continuing crimes by governments. But what I want to follow from this is not self-righteous "finger-pointing at the other fellow"—now too often the response. What has to be grasped is that, because its authority is sovereign, no action whatsoever taken by a national government, no matter how horrendous, need be illegal. Repeating, Hitler's criminal associates were retroactively punished because Germany lost a war, but Stalin's went free because the Soviet Union didn't. Leaders of small countries now sometimes face the court in The Hague; there is no prospect that equally guilty but more dangerous leaders of the larger powers will face that prospect in our lifetimes.

That notwithstanding, if the state system, which allows, even encourages, crime-by-government, is someday to be brought to an end, then we should be looking to criminalize at least some government behaviors now or, if they are already illegal, to restate that illegality more clearly and forcefully and to append mandatory criminal investigation even where there is no likelihood of follow-up punishment.

While this would be a useful, initial project at the international level for the World Democratic Forum, it needs to be complemented by steps here in the United States that clarify in our law the criminality of actions such as "rendition," torture, assassination, kidnappings, indiscriminate use of area weapons like carelessly guided missiles, "iron" (i.e., unguided) bombs, phosphorus bombs, cluster bombs and land mines where civilians are likely to be their victims, other collective punishments, and in general, virtually all governmental actions whereby civilian bystanders are likely to be harmed or *anybody's* rights violated, not just those of U.S. citizens.

It is crucial to a less barbarous future to remove or at least radically weaken the immunity extended to persons when they act as agents of government; as long as that immunity is intact, governments will hide behind it to commit the very acts that have to be effectively criminalized. In an appropriate Statute on Criminal Behavior by Governments (SCBG), we should spell out as closely as possible all of the specific actions that should be illegal, thus leaving less wiggle room for the common second line of defense used to exculpate such criminal behavior, which is to include it within generic categories of crimes whose broadness invites evasion and makes the crime difficult to prosecute. It would indeed be a difficult task to write an effective SCBG now, but as is common in the history of lawmaking, one begins with what appears to be a prudent statute and then amends it by legislation and court interpretation in the light of experience.

One of the features of the SCBG is that it must bear on both the immediate perpetrator *and* his or her policy chiefs "up the line." As we saw in the June 2009 debates over torture and other human rights violations at Guantanamo Bay and Abu Ghraib prison, and earlier during, say, the Vietnam War, not to impose this more inclusive responsibility is in practice to void the ban on the behavior. Typically, as with those who abused prisoners in Abu Ghraib, only lower-level people are criminally prosecuted. Then, because the chain of command goes right up to the president, one cannot fix specific responsibility on the intermediate commanders who were actually on the spot or who also authored or authorized the crimes. In addition, people higher up in the chain of command will routinely cover up for one another, obscure or lose records, and in general form a solid front in their own common defense.[11] But this then weakens the punishment of the actual torturers or, in some cases, murderers who were "acting under orders."

It is a largely empty prescription that in U.S. military law a subordinate is required to disobey an illegal order. A soldier or sailor has to be a bit of a fool not to realize that commanders can "lose the record" of the illegal order and instead charge the disobedient soldier or sailor with some violation of military discipline. "Whistle-blowers" are especially likely to be so singled out. Thus, has it become common and, unfortunately, accepted that only relatively lighter punishments will be levied on the actual perpetrators, even when really horrendous crimes have been committed, as in My Lai or Abu Ghraib, and with the higher-ups getting off either scot-free or with mild reprimands from their equally guilty superiors, along with the government's promise to reform its ways—tomorrow.

Thus, if a ban of this sort of government lawlessness is to be effective, investigation, indictment, prosecution, and trial have to cover all those in the chain of command within which the crime was committed. Assuming that the government's own prosecutors might be loath to pursue embarrassing government behavior, as mostly they have been, the SCBG should also specify the procedures and personnel for bringing actions.

The ideal to aim at is that when a complaint is made of illegal behavior on the part of a government agent, the author of the complaint should enter a special status that prevents punishment, harassment, or retaliation by his or her superiors. The complaint itself should be filed with a court, not a prosecutor, with the court thereby obliged to conduct an inquiry leading to an initial finding of whether or not the complaint is idle. If the complaint is not patently idle, then under the SCBG a fuller investigation would ensue, still directly under the court, with a view to ascertaining the facts and, if called for, bringing an indictment. From the nature of behavior-within-a-hierarchy, the investigation would have as one of its prime aims to discover whether there was complicity in the crime, or even just neglect, by persons higher up the chain of command, who would accordingly be charged in a paired indictment. Here I think the legal presumption must be that a crime by a lower-level agent of government—be it soldier, "spook," or policeman—is likely to be shared up the chain of command. Some burden of proof must rest on the higher-ups to demonstrate that they took positive, competent steps to prevent the sort of crime committed by the person or unit charged with the crime.[12] Obviously this aspect of the SCBG cannot bear on ordinary crimes that government personnel commit that are entirely independent of their official roles and duties. But if a prisoner is tortured, or a civilian raped, wounded, or murdered in a war zone, then the chain of command should be required to show that it took prudential steps to prevent that.

In the short run, it is less important to punish higher-ups for their crimes than to ensure that those crimes are fully documented. That documentation itself will initiate a cultural/legal/political process that will result in effective prosecution of such crimes in some future time. Not to start now because we cannot expect to punish this cabinet official or that police commissioner is to guarantee that the problem will continue unabated.[13]

As in chapter 8, where we argued that every act of every agent of government should require positive legal support and permission, the proposals put forth here under the SCBG pose extremely knotty legal and, obviously, political problems, and it is not likely that much can be done in the near future. But with so much behavior on the part of so many governments descending into barbarism, there is a pressing need to begin laying the intellectual, legal, and political groundwork for a substantial change in the powers of national states both in dealing with their own and other citizens and with foreign governments.

The existing state system is an affront to our Constitution and a threat to the well-being of virtually every person in the world. However confused our insights as to how to change it, however difficult to set in motion the beginnings of change, and however distant the prospect of that change, the effort to conceive of, winnow out, and construct a better system is long overdue.

Empire and Republic

Roman writers worried, as did our "Founding Fathers," whether popular—called then "republican"—institutions could coexist with the imperial impulse. In Rome, the Republic fell before just such a challenge when the forces generated by imperial expansion were turned against it by Caesar, Pompey, and Crassus. History, of course, doesn't repeat itself, but we have seen changes in the United States in which the requirements of the corporate form of business and the society it engenders, along with the international state system, have expanded immensely the powers of the inner, permanent, nonelected government over elected officials, the political and electoral process, and the constitutional stipulation of popular sovereignty itself. As I have tried to emphasize, these pressures have been so powerful that they have really succeeded in nullifying part of constitutional writ, and, no less important, they have also helped to create and maintain a complementary, irresponsible electorate.

The burden of this book has been to argue a variant of the threat of empire to republican institutions. Corporate and Intersection interests, especially those generated by the national security apparatus, have not, as in Rome, overtly toppled the old Republic, but they have extracted a revolutionary accommodation from it. The division of actual authority and political legitimacy between the inner and the elected governments represents in the last analysis a modern form of victory of Empire over Republic. It is, of course, not my claim that the latter is merely a front for the former, or a puppet on its string, but it is clear that the "constitutional" requirements of a private property system that has evolved into modern corporate society have overridden to a startling degree the constitutional prescription of popular sovereignty. In truth, popular sovereignty has been forced to share the constitutional stage with this interest, and not even on an equal basis. The legitimacy of big institutions, camouflaged by their alleged subordination to an impersonal market and the "laws" of private property, have even been introduced into the Constitution by the Supreme Court's odd interpretations of, especially, the amendments that did away with slavery.[14]

In a somewhat similar vein, the popular sovereignty laid out in the Constitution has been forced to accommodate to the exigencies of the international state system, with actual, effective sovereignty passing into the hands of the elites of the inner government. As before, it is not at all clear that the "natural aristocrats" who framed our Constitution would be entirely displeased with the roles played by inner government elites in the property and the national security realms. Their approval of popular government was limited and guarded. What I think explains the anomalous position of the "Founding Fathers" is that they did not anticipate the historical advance, could not readily conceive of a mass electorate, or of the expansion in the sensibilities of the "people" to include political and social rights both unheard of and incongruous in the eighteenth-century world.[14]

But if the die was not cast then, it has been cast since. Constitutional authority has assisted an institutional elite to come to and to retain power outside of and over the principle of popular sovereignty, and that development has converged with the doctrines of the sovereignty of the state itself, which are imposed by the international system. Both developments take concrete form in the inner government elites we have been talking about.

If my analysis in this and the preceding chapters holds, it means that quite serious changes in the property system, in the state system, in the way we govern our major "private" institutions, and in the domestic policing system, along roughly the lines put forward above, are needed to reinaugurate the historic advance. Obviously they can't be preconditions. Nor can they be viewed as long-term goals to be sought in some tomorrow when their prospect looks more realistic than at present. Rather, my understanding is that a renewed historic advance must incorporate within its strategic outlook and philosophy a conscious intent to address and to change those systems and must opportunistically incorporate those particular steps and ideas that at any given time and circumstances appear to move the strategy forward and the goal closer.

It is the paradox of popular movements that they must not only, as it were, lift themselves by their own bootstraps but design and build the bootstraps themselves. "The system" now offers no such aids. The lesson of the termination of the historical advance is that inner government is a system feature of liberal, democratic polities as they have emerged in Intersection society in the past century and that such elite structures constitute a formidable, unyielding barrier to Democratic progress. And as we saw in their reaction to the Sixties, they have even rolled back some of the important political, social, and economic gains of the past. The form that our contemporary paradox takes is that we must somehow engage and defeat the elites who dominate inner government and the other institutions of the Intersection *within the bounds and modalities of that liberal, democratic society* or, to adapt an older idiom, erect a new Democratic Republic within the strictures and structures of Elite Empire. But if the history of the Democracy offers any guide, it is that even that contradiction can, with time, be overcome.

The SFTA embodies a foretaste of the way elites will desirably function in some future, improved form of society. The Roman pontiff, with, one must admit, a degree of distortion, is referred to as "the servant of the servants of God." Contemporary elites in the democratic countries also present themselves as our servants—but then extract immunities and other privileges that befit lords and masters. The papal formulation comes closer to what is most desirable: elites who will serve but as ordinary citizens, without extraordinary recompense and claiming no lingering status or authority. The SFTA is also conceived as a contemporary organization fashioned to best aid the Democracy to sustain a new historic advance. If out of the body of our people there are none who will think, work, and sacrifice anew for that advance, it cannot and will not take place. But such people exist in our society in plenty, and the future is theirs and ours to create.

Notes

Preface

1. I did need the money, and my draft board was after me too. I had managed to hang on until graduating from college, then learned that teaching mathematics qualified me for continued deferment. I remained draft eligible until I turned thirty-five in September 1967 and was actually called down for induction in August of that year—after I had returned from a brief stint as a war correspondent in Vietnam. But that's another story.

2. Long Island University outshone Columbia in the loyalty oath episode. As a part-time, evening philosophy student at Columbia, I ranked just below the kitchen help, but I vaguely knew two professors who had been outspoken on academic freedom issues. However, when I asked for advice on how to fight the oath, neither paused: "Just sign it." Each made it clear that they considered academic freedom important at Columbia but of no great matter at LIU. I rated such snobbery pretty harshly, and my distaste soon led me away from Columbia, ABD and without regret.

There is a happier follow-up. Only a few years later I briefly taught at LIU and, via a shared interest in American history, became friends with the dean, Milton Klein, himself a distinguished historian of New York State. At lunch one day, I asked him about the demise of LIU's loyalty oath. Of course he had seen my letter. There were many like it. There had been so many that the oath had had to be withdrawn. It made me proud to have been part of that anonymous company. Unlike so many who were harmed by the loyalty oath, I wasn't. My academic career was delayed by a few years, but I had learned to trust myself and my own convictions, an infinitely greater thing.

3. This was not Smathers's first contribution to public enlightenment. He is said to have won the 1950 Florida Democratic Senate primary by campaigning through the dimmer regions of the Sunshine State with the charge that his opponent was "a practicing heterosexual."

Introduction

1. The situation in the other Western-style democracies seems to be the same.
2. See Krugman (2009) and Stiglitz (2009).
3. The rationale for the "Democracy" as I have characterized it will be developed in the text, primarily in chapter 1.
4. My choice of term here is tricky. "Middle class" is too analytically soft; "managerial, professional, and technical class" is better but awkward and still insufficiently expressive. It also mutes the point that many, soon most, professions once practiced by free-standing persons are now sited within large, corporately organized institutions. In French and in English, *cadre* aptly, if not quite perfectly, expresses this. Even the infelicity of the term serves to jar us into awareness of its importance.

Chapter 1

1. In an "Americanist" society (Gramsci 1971), the roles and rewards of each class and cognate social formation are tied directly to their functional contributions in a corporatized economy. In a "Bismarckian" society, industrial modernization occurs but without unraveling key premodern social values, institutions, and classes. There is an important literature on the (especially political) implications of Bismarckianism, though not always under that label. See Moore (1966) especially, as well as Craig (1955) and Maier (1988a). Moore emphasizes the importance of how premodern classes exit their modernizing societies. As Callil (2006) illustrates, "modernization" frequently leaves intact premodern classes and values, which, under suitable circumstances, can reenergize to destructive effect. See also Sassoon (1996) and the historical sections of Wedderburn (1972) and Blanpain (1987).

2. Riis (1971) gives us a snapshot of urban worker life in the United States at the early part of the advance; Lynd and Lynd (1929) provide a parallel snapshot at roughly the halfway point.

3. Stone (1975) is a key study on the early evolution of management practices. Note that "employee" is a twentieth-century category. Earlier workers, even in big industry, were under the legal and customary prescriptions of master-servant codes. These conferred an extracontractual authority on the master and obliged obedience and deference on the part of the servant. Supervisors had the right, not infrequently enjoyed, to physically chastise their underlings in, for example, the early modern steel industry; as late as 1920, female schoolteachers in New York City were not allowed to marry. In the United States, the category "employee" did not become legally and practically dominant until the rise of the CIO in 1936–38. For this account, see Lichtenstein (1982).

The current "globalization" of the less developed world is occurring under political conditions that slow the evolution of master-servant relations into the more equitable employer-employee variety.

4. One could not, I think, speak so broadly and assuredly without Sassoon (1996) and that legion of other writers and scholars who provided his sources and, I think, inspiration.

5. See Scott (1967). Marx wrote his *Manifesto* at the request of the German Communist League, a Babeuvist organization, which was linked, through Philippe Buonarotti's League of the Just, to Babeuf's own organization, the Conspiracy of Equals.

6. At a performance of Schiller's *Don Carlos* in Hamburg in the early years of the Third Reich, this very scene received extended applause. The play was immediately banned from the German stage. Klemperer (1999, 91).

7. The Little Blue Books were published by the Haldeman-Julius Company of Girard, Kansas, and Charles H. Kerr Publishing Company of Chicago. I have a 1924 copy of Little Blue Book no. 521, Mike Gold's *Life of John Brown*. The Little Blue Book series included virtually all of Shakespeare's plays, plus the works of Molière, Maeterlinck, Strindberg, Ibsen, Hugo, Aeschylus, and even Schnitzler's exposé *The Anti-Semites*.

8. Sassoon (1996) is an excellent source for the evolution of different organizational and political forms of worker resistance and worker advancement on the Continent. See Brown (1986) and Pelling (1976) for the United Kingdom.

9. Turner's original statement was given as a paper at the 1893 meeting of the American Historical Association. His famous book *The Frontier in American History*, however, did not come out until 1920. Others seized upon his broader views about the American West to argue that the frontier was a "safety valve" that vented social distress westward and thus away from radicalism.

10. In a private communication, Leonard Liggio has argued that the frontier was largely a wheat frontier, generations of the same families moving west to exploit virgin lands where primitive agricultural skills and a very small farming capital could, for a few seasons at least, reap rich harvests. They were successively replaced, in this argument, not by urban worker migrants but by experienced farmer immigrants who had the skills to heal a despoiled landscape.

11. A familiar communist explanation for this flip-flopping is now heard from the South African Communist Party too. "Society must," they argue, "first pass through the bourgeois stage of development." A strange argument indeed, for it appears to translate into "We must strengthen the enemies of socialism in order to achieve socialism!"

12. See Shirer (1971, 292). For Britain, see Hennessy (1993, especially chap. 5).

13. There are almost too many fine accounts of the Homestead Lockout. I'm still partial to Yellen (1976). Serrin (1992) offers a fuller account.

14. The Soviet Union copied American social productive practices in the 1920s; their term, "Fordism," is still reverently employed by mostly Marxist writers who have not kept up with industrial, social-productive changes. The shift from a skilled-worker basis in industry to a managerial basis occurred in Europe and Japan only after World War II. McDermott (1992) goes into considerable detail on the evolution and distinctiveness of the modern system, as well as the archaic quality of "Fordism."

15. The CIO upsurge of the 1930s was peopled but not led by semi-skilled factory workers. These "industrial" (versus "crafts") unions were actually formed and led by crafts workers, who to this day maintain an influence that has typically outweighed that of the semi-skilled. See chapter 10 for more on this subject.

16. Alfred Chandler's 1962 study provides the indispensable foundation for the institutional and, therefore, social analysis of the modern corporation. The reputation of Berle and Means (1933) exceeds its quality. Engler (1961) is an outstanding piece of work that shows that even then the big oil firms acted so powerfully in the setting of energy and related public policies that they were political institutions and not merely goods providers.

17. I coined this term to fill what I consider a gap in the literature.

18. As a colleague has pointed out, monopoly at the producing and selling level also created the corporations as monopsony purchasers, an example of this being the influence exercised by the steel giants over the typically small and mid-sized firms in the bituminous coal industry.

19. The account of Alfred P. Sloan, who was the leading figure in many of these pioneering achievements at GM, is unmatched for its lucidity and intelligence. See Sloan (1964). Given the extraordinary influence of GM in the period just described, its current, perhaps even mortal, problems are an unmistakable sign that we are in a new economic era.

20. For a wider account of the privatization of military functions, see Singer (2003).

21. Though both are useful, I find the institutional conceptualization "the dual economy" in Averitt (1968) more potent than the sociological conception of "labor market segmentation" presented in Edwards, Gordon, and Reich (1975).

22. See Braverman (1974), Edwards (1979), and Taylor (1967). There are other kinds of active participants within the world of the corporate productive structure, including traditional skilled workers and members of the older professions such as law, but they tend either to be declining in number and importance or they are subordinated within producer systems dominated by the corporate triad.

23. This was at the time widely though obscurely understood. Even before 1900 there was wide experimentation in changing the ideas and behavior of workers. Taylor's experiments show this, as do upper-class initiatives in the Settlement House movement; in the Rockefeller Industrial Representation Plan, which came out of the Ludlow Massacre; in the company towns of Pullman, Illinois, and of the textile districts; in the welfare capitalism of U.S. Steel; and in the famous (or infamous) Sociology Department of Ford Motors under (the definitively infamous) Harry Bennett. For U.S. Steel, see Gulick (1968); for Ford Motors, Lacey (1986).

24. Figures from manufacturing index the scale of the wider industrial, hence social change. Nonproduction employees in manufacturing, that is, managers and some technological personnel, were not distinguished in the relevant government statistics until 1889, when they were counted at 348,000, or just under 7 percent of the manufacturing workforce. Their numbers rose dramatically until by 1970 they came to 4,462,000, or just under 25 percent of the manufacturing workforce. See *Historical Statistics of the United States* 1970, series P, 4,

5. The cadre portion of the manufacturing workforce has continued to rise but not so dramatically since 1970. At the same time, even these figures badly understate its growth, for by 1970 they had expanded beyond manufacturing and into virtually every other line of work so that they now make up perhaps 20–25 percent of the entire labor force, with their families roughly the same fraction of the total population.

25. In a Bismarckian society, which we've already met, the social order is dynastically organized by families holding aristocratic rank or other legally and politically formalized *Stände*.

26. See Bowles and Gintis (1976) and Lemann (1999).

27. This is a key point of Stone (1975).

28. On the other hand, when women enter a previously gendered field, such as law or medicine, this is associated with diminishing rewards and prestige. Some of this is related to the continuing vitality of sexism, but some can be accounted for by the absorption of those fields into big law firms and hospitals where lawyers and doctors become supervised "employees," not semi-autonomous "professionals."

29. For an informed discussion of the black middle class, see especially Landry (1987). For some of the knottier legal and philosophical issues raised by racial identities, see Ford (2005).

Early strategies for gender and, especially, racial change pivoted on the creation of a "critical mass," which, it was assumed, would lead over time to the equalization of the minority's place within the larger society. But racial and gender change has not had this *leavening* effect; quite radical advances for a few have nevertheless left the majority of nonwhites and women at the bottom of society. This is consistent with our earlier observation that a reduction of inequality in Intersection society coexists, paradoxically, with a more pronounced stratification.

30. This meant that the necessary modification of the productive characteristics of the workforces, their wider social relationships, and the development of the national productive forces of Bismarckian societies was also slowed. As already indicated, throughout Europe and in Japan, managers and technologists trumped skilled workers only after World War II.

31. In Japan, the mysterious mind of the Orient continued to baffle conservative Westerners by not being mysterious at all. Under the early Occupation, popular elements burgeoned, a feisty free press emerged, militant trade unions grew like weeds, and the Japanese masses acted as rambunctious and demanding as the Parisians of yesteryear. Resolute U.S. force soon restored the oriental stolidity and political inscrutability that General MacArthur and his "old Asia hands" favored and expected. See Gould (1984).

32. A key factor in this U.S. success was its alliance with the Vatican, whereby the old German Catholic Center Party, deeply complicit in Hitler's ascent to absolute power (H. Turner 1996), was rechristened the Christian Democrats and aided to victory and West German dominance. An analogous Washington-Rome axis placed the Vatican-affiliated Italian Christian Democrats (whose past was similarly tainted) in the same leading role there after 1948. The disastrous role of the interwar Catholic parties in Germany and Italy is also analyzed in the excellent Maier (1988a).

Chapter 2

1. See Nixon (1978). Also see Eisenhower Commission (1969) and chapter 3.

2. For more on this distinction, see especially chapter 3. Here it suffices to say that the policies of some of the more important parts of the government apparatus are insulated from election results and their higher-ups especially protected against popular "interference." The three most important of these areas of inner government are international security, monetary and related economics policy, and the domestic police power.

3. In this period a good friend, now sadly passed away or I would not recount the story, came to the house with an air of great secrecy. He insisted that I turn the radio all the way

up before he would open his parcel. It was a weapon "for the armed revolution," an Armalite rifle made by the company that made the U.S. military's ultra-high-velocity, rapid-fire AR-16. I had to explain to him that his AR-15 was different, with a low muzzle velocity, hence pathetically short range, and fired only a single round at a time. He was disappointed to learn that the "enemy ammunition" he expected to capture in the street fighting couldn't be fired from it. In short, his weapon was more suited to stun a squirrel than awe a soldier. But my friend was no fool. He was a veteran of the nonviolent wing of the movement and had previously rendered good service in several capacities. He had become outraged to the point of blindness by our inability to bring about the end of a by then almost universally hated war.

4. As I point out later, many of these same people gravitated into electoral and legislative activity, where they had much to do with Congress's budgetary undermining of the Latin American intervention in the 1970s. This is another topic that needs to be covered in the literature.

5. I experienced this elite-related solidarity. In June 1968, I was asked in the role of gadfly to give a paper before an invitation-only gathering of Vietnam policymakers at the University of Chicago. (The papers and other material from this conference, "The Lessons of Vietnam," were published in Pfeffer 1968.) The conferees were still in shock over the surprise Tet offensive of the previous February and in a mood to reexamine some of their own assumptions. In the paper I argued that in some sense the "Viet Cong" and North Vietnamese constituted among the more representative governments in that part of Asia. One conferee, a serving assistant secretary of state, spoke favorably of my thesis. Immediately, the chair of the meeting, a noted sinologist from Harvard, passed him a note, which he read, crumpled up, and discarded into an ashtray. At the break, I slipped back into the conference room and quite shamelessly retrieved it. "X," the note admonished, "people in your position mustn't say things like that." This was the same period when Attorney General Nicolaus Katzenbach, responsible for civil order in Washington, D.C., had antiwar demonstrators, comrades of his like-minded children, camped in his living room even as he attended Cabinet meetings intended to thwart the demonstrators. He could not, he thought, at threat of his job, give away the presence of the young people to his colleagues, several of whom, like the secretary of state, were actually in similar positions.

A sidebar: Henry Kissinger had just returned from (then) Czechoslovakia, and I was at one time part of a small knot of people he regaled with a contemptuous account of how hopelessly naïve the Czechs and Slovaks were about democracy. He seemed to be a very, very clever man but with an infinitely flawed judgment, a latter-day Viscount Halifax or, taking into account his extraordinary egotism, a less polished version of Lord Louis Mountbatten. I mention Czechoslovakia here, for I felt at the time and still do that these U.S. policymakers, shaken up by Tet, found their feet again after the Russian intervention that fall. "If the Russians can do it, so must we."

6. Again, Marwick (1998) is exceptionally helpful, but even this magisterial volume is marred by the author's dyspeptic view of what he refers to as the "Marxisant" Left. More important, Marwick, in company with the other writers I'll cite, draws a clean distinction between the political and the cultural realms, a distinction which, as I'll show, is simply impossible to maintain generally, much less vis-à-vis the Sixties.

7. Some years ago a friend whom I had known in the political movements of the 1960s was considered for a post within a prestigious graduate social science department. His sponsor, a man of considerable academic accomplishment and repute, warned him against saying anything whatsoever favorable about those movements to the search committee; that alone would void any possibility of appointment. My friend got the job but didn't like sailing under false colors. Currently, he teaches in an institution that is not quite as elite but—to the point—also lacks its intolerance for "the Sixties."

8. Basically, the Bretton Woods system protected domestic wages from international wage competition; the regime of floating rates has just the opposite effect, that is, to subject wage rates everywhere to the competition of the lowest anywhere. Block (1977) and Brown (1986) remain useful on this topic. Guttmann (1994) is encyclopedic and, considering the

age of the book, quite prescient about the fragility of the emerging, unregulated financial system.

9. In New York City in May 1970, in a still cited incident, protesters against the invasion of Cambodia were "spontaneously" attacked by construction workers in lower Manhattan. In fact, the attacks were organized and led by trade union officials. Some attackers were apparently still on the clock as they pummeled the demonstrators. The construction workers were acting in the prowar spirit of the AFL-CIO leadership group, still optimistic of victory in the Vietnam adventure even at that late date. For these events, see Marwick (1998) and Johnson (2003).

10. Marwick (1998) identifies the period from 1958 to 1974 as "the Sixties," further dividing the period into three distinct phases: a preparatory phase until 1964, "the High Sixties" during 1964–68, followed by an ebbing phase from 1968 to 1974. That dating makes sense even and especially when one includes the political developments that Marwick minimizes.

11. See Westmoreland (1976) and, much more useful, Prados (1991, 1995). General Westmoreland's memoirs reveal how utterly at a loss he was to conceive a strategy to win the war. He was content to do what such generals often do—risk the blood of his troops but not his reputation by following a strategy of attrition. Later, still in character, he blamed his superiors for the defeat.

12. See Brown (1986, 159–65).

13. See Barkan (1984) for this interesting discussion.

14. Through *Viet-Report*, I had had from 1965 some distant contact with officials from North Vietnam and the National Liberation Front. However, upon my first face-to-face meeting, in Stockholm in the summer of 1967, the Vietnamese I met were coldly official and standoffish until Philippe Devillers, the eminent French historian of Vietnam, acquainted them with my views about U.S.-Soviet cooperation to end the war short of Vietnam's reunification. The situation unfroze immediately, and there was later opportunity for even a degree of personal exchange with these normally immensely disciplined men. Earlier, within South Vietnam, I had met privately and, of course, secretly with students opposed to their U.S.-sponsored government. I recall their generosity in speaking to an American of "our" international movement.

15. See Gitlin (1987), Marwick (1998), and Daniel Bell (1976). Space limitations prohibit anything more than cursory treatment of the Gitlin volume, which is well known in any case. The Marwick book is uniquely valuable for the scope and detail of his researches but is not as theoretically challenging as Bell's. Accordingly, I'll devote somewhat more space to the latter. I have no hesitation in recommending all three volumes to readers who want to give further thought to the Sixties.

16. People may not even be aware of some of their beliefs until circumstances force or permit a self-recognition. When I read *The Communist Manifesto* and a bit of *Das Kapital* as part of a college assignment in the 1950s, I thought, "Yes, that's basically true and important." But to be a Marxist in my setting then was simply impossible. I went on to other writers whose views didn't pose impossible conflicts between belief and behavior and, of course, didn't threaten to bring hostile authority down on my young head. It was only when the Sixties were over and the political movement and my ideas about it began to dissolve that I went back to read Marx in that new light. I was forty years old at the time.

The late 1950s–early 1960s were a period in which it became possible to think thoughts hitherto hidden by prudence or fear. Often the critical break came when someone who acted on those forbidden beliefs drew one's admiration. I had taken a graduate class with Jacob Lowenberg, a professor who had resisted signing a loyalty oath at Berkeley in 1949 and been accorded a temporary sanctuary at Columbia. As a teacher and philosopher, Lowenberg hadn't at all impressed me, though I do recall thinking well of his stand. Three or four years later, confronted with just such an oath, I found it unthinkable to sign it. One cannot, I think, overestimate the importance of moral example in dissident politics. In my era, the example of people such as Peggy Duff, Bob Moses, Casey Hayden, I. F. Stone, John Lewis, Howard Zinn, A. J. Muste, and many now unsung others was simply irreplaceable.

17. Marwick (1998), otherwise encyclopedic, fails to mention either A. J. Muste or I. F. Stone. To my knowledge, AJ was central to the early growth of the movement in New York City in 1960–65 and, by extension, those many locales which then looked to New York for assistance and example. I admired Izzy Stone, and he was also a friend. My lasting image is of him sitting on the edge of a hotel divan, reading and clipping at supersonic speed, the *New York Times*, the *Washington Post*, the *Los Angeles Times*, the *St. Louis Post-Dispatch*, the *London Times*, and *Le Monde*, all the while carrying on animated conversation. In 1967, I published an article (McDermott 1967) that worked out the story, since confirmed, of the staging of the Tonkin Gulf incident as cover for expanding the war in Vietnam. Izzy was so pleased with it that he proposed that I come in with him in his journal. I turned him down and have had second thoughts ever since.

I've met a small handful of "the great and the good" in my lifetime, including a U.S. president, but none as capable or as dedicated as I. F. Stone, and none who contributed so much to the public life of this country.

18. "Deterrence" is a wonderful example of the misuse of language, as if U.S. nuclear weapons were stored in the back closet, to be taken out only when the country was threatened, and then only very reluctantly. In reality, they were often taken out and brandished to further this or that foreign policy objective in such theaters as Korea in 1953, Indochina in the spring of 1954, Quemoy and Matsu in 1957 and 1958, Berlin in 1961, and Cuba in 1962. Moreover, in each of those cases the then administration publicly declared the conditions under which they would be used. And like Germany, France, and Russia in 1914, each time the United States made itself a hostage to the actions of the other side. It was a fool's game, which the Soviet Union also played when it threatened Britain, France, and Israel with nuclear missiles during the Suez crisis of 1956.

19. For support of this assertion, see Keniston (1965, 1968) and Flacks (1972). I attended one of the many planning meetings for Mississippi Summer 1964, but wasn't able to take part in the actual project. Bob Moses warned the attendees that though every conceivable effort would be made to prevent it, some of those present would likely be killed that summer because, as he explained, that's what happened every summer to civil rights workers in Mississippi. The difference, he said, was that this time some of them would be white and thus the nation would finally have to take notice and act. That, of course, is exactly what happened: one of the people I met at the planning meeting was Mickey Schwerner.

20. The reductio ad absurdum of this worship of economic growth based on technology was given by Herman Kahn, the nuclear war theorist. As he calculated it, even a nuclear war with 80 million Americans dead was an "acceptable" alternative to "Soviet victory" because the GNP could be entirely restored to prewar levels within a generation (Kahn 1961). Now—in 2009—one forgets that Kahn's goofy argument had many supporters among the great and the good. Incidentally, Dr. Strangelove in the film of that name seems to have Von Braun's accent, Henry Kissinger's personality, and Kahn's insanities.

21. Lemann (1999) is indispensable for this discussion.

22. The SDS reporters who broke this story in *New Left Notes* were using press credentials supplied by *Viet-Report* to get access to the Selective Service System. We already "sort of" knew about channeling from our own experiences with our draft boards, but the story needed to be documented. In the event, it was better for *NLN* to break the news because it reached more people sooner. But for all that, it was journalistically maddening to have one's own story scooped by another publication and under the bylines of one's own reporters!

23. I came the same route as did they but a generation later and at a different unit of New York City's then tuition-free higher education system, Brooklyn College, not CCNY. In their excellent book on the New York City fiscal crisis, *The Abuse of Power*, Jack Newfield and Paul Du Brul show that "the bankers" wouldn't put together the financial bailout for the City unless and until it got rid of that free tuition. The reaction against the 1970s took many forms!

24. I think this is why, in elite accounts of the Sixties, a small number of noncharacteristic episodes are so vividly and frequently recalled: the apparently willful destruction of a

professor's notes during the Columbia "occupation" of 1968, the death of a mathematics researcher during a bombing at the University of Wisconsin, the seizure of a building by armed black students at Cornell, and instances of gross student incivility toward university presidents and deans. Even so normally a sagacious figure as the historian C. Vann Woodward was thereby led to call 1960s students worse than the McCarthyites!

25. For the contemporary case against the multiversity, see Ridgway (1968).

26. At Brooklyn College in spring 1954, I studied the Latin texts of Cicero's *Orations*, which charge Catiline with leading the plebes to oppose the Roman Republic. The professor encouraged no discussion of the historical situation Cicero was addressing or of its rights or wrongs. He stuck to grammar and vocabulary. That fall I learned that he had been fired over the summer break (Gideonse, again!) for being a "red," which I found odd, for he certainly hadn't tried to subvert us young Ciceronians. Neither I nor, so far as I know, any significant body of students protested the firing. So he just disappeared. From the story one may gain the flavor of the times at a university within New York City. What it was like for "reds" and alleged fellow travelers out in what we called the "cow colleges" can readily be imagined.

27. In my junior year in 1953, money problems forced me to transfer from a private college to the then free Brooklyn College. I had to take a host of (unbelievably tedious) freshman introductory courses, which lengthened my undergraduate education by a semester and two summers and exposed me even further to the Selective Service System. Worse, Brooklyn College had a very high opinion of itself; all my transferred A's and B's were reduced to C's; I plunged immediately from dean's list to draft bait! My draft board took only weeks to rescind my deferment. I put them off, but the price was to stay draft eligible until I turned thirty-five—that is, fourteen years later. My student generation just jumped through whatever hoop "they" told us to jump through. A few years later people of my sort finally awakened. In retrospect, one can see that student anger at the "University" might be justified.

28. The Weatherpeople were but one of a number of kindred, ultraradical organizations marked by revolutionary posturing; my friend with the rifle, already mentioned, exemplified a wider phenomenon. In any case, the details of the different groups' views and trajectories are not worth tracing out.

Chapter 3

1. See Harz (1955).

2. It is not yet clear as I write this, in June 2009, that the period of conservative ascendancy has fully ended.

3. As a Belgian friend once emphasized to me, in even the most modern societies there persist large and important social groups, ideologies, regions, and intellectuals whose social outlook and moral preferences are relatively unaltered by the processes of modernization.

4. For this discussion, see especially Greider (1987).

5. Again, see Brown (1986, chap. 9, especially 160).

6. I am not alone in being skeptical about the emphasis given to the number and the novelty of "working-class Reagan Democrats" (Bartels 1988). "Working-class Tories," for example, have been a traditional fixture of support for Britain's Conservatives going back to Winston Churchill's first run for Parliament over one hundred years ago (Churchill 1996). What is decisive for workers as voters is not their class or occupational position per se but their organizational links to, especially, trade unions. In collaborating in trade union decline, the New Deal wing of the Democratic Party was self-immolating.

7. There is a rich literature on the economic shifts of the period in question, 1968–79. My own account was especially helped by Block (1977), and by Daniel Bell (1973), Bryan (2001), Greider (1987), Guttmann (1994), Meeropol (1998), Brown (1986), Ross and Trachte (1990), Rothschild (1973), and Sassoon (1996).

8. Large modern firms invest in "market channels," which, as the image suggests, direct their output to the final consumer in the necessary volume and at prices calculated to bring in the desired return. The idea that a big firm will make a product without this previous market engineering is still, unfortunately, assumed in mainstream economic theory, though long belied by empirical studies of firm marketing and pricing behavior. See especially the magisterial Lee (1988). For further, related analysis, see also McDermott (2004, 52–61).

9. See chapter 8.

10. Bryan (2001) points out that the Keynesian economic universe was populated by national economies; the international economy was accordingly depicted only as an offshoot and residue of the different national policies.

11. This particular chicken came home to roost in the credit meltdown of 2008.

12. To introduce "a more competitive environment" into an economy with both small and very large firms is tantamount to decimating the former at the hands of the latter. Small business entrepreneurs commonly see this in the particular case, clamoring for this or that protection from the "unfair" competition of the bigger firms, but typically fail to see that the ideology of competitiveness is itself their deadliest foe. Small to medium firms have an interest in a government-regulated economy, not a free-market one, for they have greater political than economic strength.

13. A South African friend estimates them to number no more than four hundred for the whole world. I've not looked into the exact number, but the economic and political power shift to a finite list of recognizable companies, and away from the classic free market of numberless, anonymous firms, has been a notable feature of modern economic history. These megafirms, created, it was said, to enhance competitiveness, are, at least in the financial sector, now deemed too big and too important to be allowed to fail—no matter how incompetently or dishonestly they have been run by their higher managements. The Washington policy shift from thinking of the economy as a "free market" one to viewing it as "investor-led" by only a few financial institutions dates in the United States from the appointment of Paul Volcker to the chairmanship of the Federal Reserve by President Carter. This is the system of investor oligarchy already commented upon in the introduction.

14. The term was invented and popularized in Galbraith (1952).

15. The *New Yorker* is as always very perceptive about upper-middle-class life and mores. A 2008 cartoon showed a young mother, with child in stroller, chatting with a friend: "We're off to the park," she says, "to check out the competition."

16. Black Americans now make up about one in nine of all Americans.

17. Has the redistribution of income upward, which has been a feature of "privatization," "deregulation," and the rest of the post-Reagan free-market agenda, sharpened social tension in the United States? Until recently that tension had not found dramatic expression in social and political conflict, but its effects can readily be found in medical, mental health, child welfare, crime, and prison statistics, in political cynicism among voters, and so on. It may also provide a clue to the remarkable political mobilization of so many young people for Barack Obama's presidential campaign.

18. Thus the *New Yorker* cartoon, earlier cited. Young middle-class parents in New York City evidently address social mobility issues quite early: there is sharp competition now over places in the right *nursery school*.

19. Some years ago, in mostly teasing mode, I proposed to a racially mixed group of friends that the Irish could not then be considered European, for they had no part in the decisive, defining events of European history. Ireland had not come under the rule of the Roman Empire. The Renaissance, the Reformation, the threat of Islam, the Enlightenment, the Industrial Revolution, and the French Revolution were things that had occurred elsewhere, and Ireland had been for four hundred years a colony of a foreign, European power, suffering political repression, language loss, and economic exploitation on the model subsequently imposed on Africa, Asia, and Latin America. I met not disagreement but bemused bewilderment, even impatience, that I could think such frivolous thoughts. None could wrap his or her mind around the idea that people with European DNA might not be Europeans in

any of the ways in which that concept enters into political and historical analysis. "European," like "African," was, ultimately and decisively, a bioracially defined category. It is this phenomenon that is named in the text.

20. Thus the common use then of the expression "wage slavery."

21. The lower and frontier South was different. Conditions for slaves were more akin to those of ancient Athens. Assigned to open up malarial virgin land and relatively easy to replace, the lives of slaves were literally consumed by their masters.

22. As previously argued, this "critical mass" has not served as leaven for the improvement in the situation of the mass of black people (and women). The previously cited Landry (1987) comprises among other things an assessment of the relative success or failure of this strategy. The very challenging Ford (2005) shows how even recent court decisions have not entirely escaped a logic of black "incorporation."

23. See Kerner Report (1968, 127).

24. But, some years later, on March 17, 1978, President Carter's National Security adviser, Zbigniew Brzezinski, authored a secret, official finding that black militant organizations *might* link up with radical political groups from Africa to the *possible* detriment of the United States. On that finding, Brzezinski directed federal agencies to disrupt the *domestic* activities of a number of black U.S. organizations (the relevant documents can be accessed at http://www.directblackaction.com/MEMO_46.htm).

25. Some lawyer friends have argued that in no major trial against 1960s dissenters, even rioters, were the juries willing to follow prosecutorial lead and vote the desired verdicts. This argues that the popular reaction against the Sixties was not immediate and spontaneous but rather inspired by elite actions and elite propaganda. As Marwick (1998) points out, the peculiar mix of individualistic, expressive values and community solidarity characteristic of the best of the Sixties has had an enduring acceptance among the wider public. Yet the government strategy did largely succeed in blunting the political movements for social change.

26. As I was editing these pages, the press reported that since 1994 the U.S. Defense Department's Reutilization and Marketing Service program has provided, without cost, 1,066 military assault rifles to the police departments of eighty-two different Massachusetts cities and townships, and to the Metropolitan Boston Transit Authority—and at least two M-79 grenade launchers! Until the *Boston Globe* broke the story, the public was not informed, nor indeed was the state's governor! (Slack 2009).

27. It is estimated that George W. Bush was dependent on fundamentalist white Protestants for about 40 percent of his voters. I find many of these voters a puzzle. I recently attended a small-town church funeral service for a friend in which his kindness to the sick and his high sense of community responsibility were recounted in eloquent eulogies. One could not fail to be moved by the social and humane values held in such high regard by the congregation. Yet voters from just such conservative churches and communities seem to have acted in elections as a bottomless source of opposition to a more equitable, humane, and fairer society.

28. The lack of ideological robustness of "1960s youth culture," contra many of its partisans at the time, was shown in the ease with which the modern media redirected the political rebelliousness of some young people on behalf of a more human community into the consumerism, aimless rebelliousness, and antisocial values that Bell rightly found so abhorrent and that too often continues to this day.

29. Medically, heroin addiction per se is apparently less harmful than addiction to either tobacco or alcohol, but the irregular strength of the supply often leads to overdose deaths. The spread of hepatitis, AIDS, and other diseases through the practice of sharing needles is a by-product: hence the desire of many in and outside the medical profession to distribute certifiably clean needles to the user population.

Chronic use of marijuana may create medical problems similar to those associated with tobacco. Cocaine appears to be destructive in all its forms. Even small doses can be fatal to the novice as well as to habitual users. "Meth" and other familiar designer drugs are apparently equally harmful, where not outright deadly. New designer drugs appear fairly regularly, often with dreadful results.

30. Inciardi (1986), just cited, makes a startling admission. Numerous studies have been funded that show that hard drug users typically start off on marijuana and then "graduate" to heroin, cocaine, and so on. These studies are stock-in-trade for drug war supporters. Marijuana use is more or less equivalent to hard drug addiction. QED. But the author also points out that converse studies have not been widespread and are not funded because the few that do exist show that roughly the same proportion of non–marijuana users become addicts as do marijuana users. The difference between "If you are an addict, you started on marijuana" and "Smoking marijuana has no causal relation to later drug addiction" is not subtle. To substitute one for the other is an outright fraud.

31. As a political model, the "war against terror" is the child of earlier crusades against liquor, immigrants, communism, and, more recently, drugs. One pursues hyperxpensive quick-fix, police-heavy strategies that are ineffective, thus keeping the political base in fear, instead of cheaper, slower, more calculated strategies that more likely will erase or at least significantly ease the problem—and decrease budgets.

32. As in Klemperer's wartime Hamburg, so in postwar New York? In 1950, the Metropolitan Opera revived Verdi's opera *Don Carlo*, based on Schiller's play. In both there is an eloquent plea for freedom of thought, directed against the Inquisition. The Met revival was picketed by protesters voicing the same objections to it that Empress Josephine (consort of Napoleon III) had voiced against the original in 1866.

33. As one wag observed, the American Century thus stretched from 1952 to 1956.

34. I earlier mentioned the firing of my Cicero professor. That same semester the college was picketed by a lone student. The background story was that in the 1940s Brooklyn College had had a left-wing student body with a student council filled with noisy "reds" and other colorful types. College president Harry Gideonse, whom I was later to encounter, was brought in "to clean house." He replaced direct election of student representatives with a system based on club representation. Thus the Chess Club, the Flying Club, the Newman Club, the Hillel Association, and so on each had a representative. Never lacking zeal, the lefties colonized club after club in quest of their former majority, but to no avail. They might succeed with, say figuratively, the Piano Club, but think of all those other instruments that had to be mastered: oboes and clarinets, French horns and trumpets, cellos, violas, violins, basses, and so on. And there was the Latin Club, the French Club . . . the Hiking Club, the Swimming Club, Tennis, Badminton, Stamps . . . Zeal was no match for the inventiveness of the house cleaner. The lone picketer publicly accused the Gideonse of copying Mussolini's "corporatist" form of antidemocratic representation and was forthwith *permanently* dismissed from the college. There was a lawsuit, and, in the spirit of the times, judicial wisdom upheld the student's dismissal and the loss of his accumulated credits. I'm sorry to say that, like my contemporaries, though I sympathized with the student, I kept my head down.

35. Contra the conventional view, Baxandall and Ewen (2000) show that in suburbs like Levittown, the newly arriving women quickly replicated the institutions and networks they lost when moving from the city.

36. See Burrin (1996) and Callil (2006). In the very fine Mazower (2008), a substantial part of chapter 13 is devoted to the chameleon-like politics of the French police of that period.

37. There have been police in my immediate family for four generations now, stretching back over one hundred years. By and large it's an exceptionally stressful, socially isolating job that in my direct experience takes a heavy toll on its practitioners' health, mental health, and social attitudes. Radical police reform would be of as much benefit to the police as to the policed.

38. Statistical Abstract of the United States (2006, tables 427, 452, 490, 500, 516, and 604). The discrepancy between growth in the numbers of employees in the police industry and in its budget seems mostly due to prison costs, where non-payroll expenditures predominate.

39. See Burpo, DeLord, and Shannon (1997, xii, 15).

40. The "clearance" rate is not an indicator that there has been an indictment, a trial, and conviction. A crime is "cleared" when there is an arrest or some other step that takes it off the active police register, such as the passage of time. At any rate, as taken from Wikipedia, the FBI's Uniform Crime Reports show that about one homicide in three is never acted upon. This rate is even lower for lesser crimes. These rates rise and fall only slightly from year to year, so the figures given are representative. See http://en.wikipedia.org/wiki/clearance_rate (accessed March 19, 2010).

41. In spring 1996, a federal district court judge in New York City, Harold Baer Jr., ruled against the admission of police testimony and some videotaped evidence in a drug case. He agreed from the bench that an innocent black person might flee from the police when stopped late at night and that of itself police testimony was not of the highest credibility. Immediately he was intemperately criticized by a whole gamut of political and police industry figures and acolytes, including President Clinton himself. There was a call—from which the president did not at first dissociate himself—for Baer to be removed from office. Clinton, however, did join in the clamor for Baer to rescind his decision and apologize to the police. Several federal appellate court judges were sufficiently troubled by this political intervention that they issued a statement in Baer's support, pointing out the dangers which were posed to the court system when it was made subject to such political and media pressures. Judge Baer did bow to the pressure, apologizing for and, more important, reversing his decision about accepting the alleged evidence. See Van Natta (1996, B1).

42. The nation's Catholic bishops have joined here with erstwhile anti-Catholic Protestant evangelicals. On the other hand, those same bishops have been among the strongest partisans of a more humane and democratic social policy. By and large, the Catholic laity supports their bishops on social policy while ignoring them on family planning and abortion.

43. In Eastern Europe then and often in the newly industrializing countries today, the master-servant relationship is still dominant; in cases involving female and child workers, it even approximates to the stark master-slave relationships of yesteryear. Historically, chattel slavery occurred in industrial as well as agricultural settings, as in the silver mines of classical Athens and the merchant marine of classical Rome. In the antebellum South, roughly 10 percent of all slaves worked in industry, not agriculture (Starobin 1970). The famous black abolitionist Frederick Douglass describes his slave assignment in the Baltimore shipyards in his memoirs (Douglass 1983). And there is now an epidemic of sexual slavery of both young girls and boys in many of the tourist locations in the world.

Part 2 Introduction

1. See especially note 2 of chapter 5.

Chapter 4

1. A weakness in the modern class theory that I am familiar with is its reliance on Weberian ideotypical and related Neo-Kantian methods. A Weberian ideal type imposes a prescriptive element into the description process: in defining, say, *social class*, we choose to foreground classification issues more than dynamic ones, and economic relations more than cultural ones, and status dimensions more than ethnic ones, and so forth (see Gerth and Mills 1958, 59–61). As long as one stays within the descriptive, empirical mode, this is sufficiently self-correcting. But embedded in an inferential system, that prescriptiveness tends to "scrub the data." Consider, for example, the influence of the *authoritarian personality* (Adorno et al. 1950) on U.S. political sociology and historiography in the 1950s, particularly its abetting of what some at the time were unkind enough to call "NATO Sociology" and "the American celebration." Or to be more contemporary, consider the *market*, an ideotype

identifying markets as naturally self-regulating, which, of course, they may not be at all. I want to analyze the Neo-Kantian presence in the social sciences more thoroughly and formulate a methodological alternative built around simple, empirically identifiable elements such as, for example, *socially potent assets*.

2. Note, however, that I do not claim for *the general case* how to render the contending historical claims of material culture, great individuals, gender, political structures, culture per se, the class struggle, sheer historical accidents, and so on. For my choice of an *apparently economistic theory of modern society* from this point forward, see the last section of this chapter.

3. For more on "Americanism," see the last section of this chapter.

4. The insight is Marx's; see Marx (1967, 191n). In the first volume of *Capital*, he frequently discusses slavery, as befits an author who was at its writing deeply engaged in the antislavery agitation that prevented the British government from coming to the fraternal rescue of the Confederacy.

5. A friend of mine, active in "the Anthracite" in the 1920s, often mentioned the little "pit ponies" that were used underground. They were valued more by the owners than were the miners themselves. As he explained, replacement coal miners came free; some, literally, were always standing at the mine portals ready to accept a less-than-living wage, but replacing and maintaining ponies "cost money."

6. See also McDermott (2004, 79–103).

7. The primary reference is to Chandler (1962) for the division between strategic and middle to lower management and the familiar Taylor (1967) for that between middle or lower management and the worker. McDermott (1991) brings the work of both Taylor and Chandler together within a wider political economic framework. I cannot help adding that Chandler's failure to win a Nobel in economics, unjust in itself, should also lessen the esteem we owe to that prize.

8. The most vivid example is provided by the West Coast shipyards owned and managed by Henry J. Kaiser during World War II. Kaiser had had no experience in shipbuilding but revolutionized it. The then state-of-the-art technique consisted of laying a keel on a slipway and progressively adding structural members and sheet steel, one piece at a time. The result was one ship per slipway every six to eight months. The basic shipyard worker was a skilled riveter who had learned his skills working as an apprentice and a journeyman. Kaiser had welded sections preassembled elsewhere and brought together on the slipway. His semi-skilled welders could be trained to a high standard in a few days. As a publicity stunt he arranged to complete one of the famous Liberty (cargo) ships in twenty-four hours. The point was made that modern U.S. industrial organization could be married to semi-skilled workers using up-to-date methods and equipment to outproduce the industry of the entire rest of the world.

The legendary "Rosie the Riveter" was likely an aircraft worker riveting cold aluminum, not hot steel. World War II newsreels show British and German aircraft workers stretching and lacquering fabric surfaces on aircraft; the famous Hurricane fighter of the Battle of Britain had fabric, not metal covering. Considerable skill and time was needed to do this job. U.S. firms had pioneered the production of all-metal aircraft in the 1930s that were not only aerodynamically and structurally superior but could be built by briefly trained workers like Rosie.

Interestingly enough, only the then Soviet Union had copied U.S. management arrangements. The extraordinary success of both economies in producing weapons, in the Soviet Union in spite of huge territorial losses, in the United States while maintaining a rising standard of living, led to universal copying of American industrial forms in the postwar years.

9. For an analysis of "administrative relations" not as a form of "bureaucracy" but as interclass relationships, see McDermott (2004, chap. 3).

10. In *Corporate Society: Class, Property, and Contemporary Capitalism* (McDermott 1991), I tried to force class analysis on the material. The Weberian ideotypes I employed then and now consider inadequate obscured the point that the "corporate classes" were actually shaped in decisive ways outside the bounds of and previous to the time of corporate employment. I hope to correct this in a future edition.

11. There is much narrative evidence that the corporate form of organization drew its inspiration from the distinctions between commanders, their staffs, field grade officers, and enlisted personnel in the military. But the system of internal financial reporting and controls, the very essence of the ability of the higher managers to control diverse activities, was pioneered and brought to its present form within, mainly, GM and DuPont. For an especially lucid presentation of the creation of modern corporate management and financial control systems, written by their most important contributor, see Sloan (1964).

12. For Weber, see Gerth and Mills (1958, 181–83); for Marx, Marx (1968).

13. For this discussion, see McDermott (2007).

14. In 1965 or 1966, I attended a civil rights meeting in Georgia that discussed the activities of the local White Citizen's Council. One of the black participants, who could not have been over thirty-five, spoke vividly of the hardships of his life. He had only a minimal, irregular income, lived in an unheated shack without running water, put up with abusive bosses, and lived with the ever present danger that White Citizen's Council hooligans would beat or even kill him. He believed there was little or no prospect that his own life would improve, but he was fiercely determined and even optimistic that his daughter would have a real chance at life. I cannot ever remember being so sobered by someone's words; a man in his mid-thirties accepting that his life prospects were to all intents and purposes closed—but with grace and courage because he both believed in and was willing to fight for his daughter's future. His example is dramatic, but the point is commonplace. Terms of social analysis that don't allow for a time dimension are—in our society at least—not ultimately adequate and should be replaced.

15. Named after Leon Walras (1834–1910), a French economist whose ideas remain widely influential today.

16. For an encyclopedic, annotated, critical review of corporate pricing studies, see again Lee (1998). Edith Penrose's classic study (Penrose 1980) is still invaluable. For the analysis of sale and purchase-in-time, see McDermott (2004, chap. 1).

17. Jacob Riis's photographs of the tenements of lower New York City circa 1890 are in this respect unforgettable. They appear in the Dover edition of his book *How the Other Half Lives*.

18. Both Wright (1984) and Poulantzas (1975) are insightful but ultimately unsatisfactory. Their reliance on spatial metaphor gives away the ultimately classificatory nature of their views and thus does not sufficiently come to grips with time and change, which are integral to the modern system of stratification.

19. This seems plausibly connected to the failure, earlier cited, of a "critical mass" of black and female cadre to act as a leaven for the social prospects of the mass.

20. That legitimacy seems less and less warranted over time, and virtually nonexistent at the present.

Chapter 5

1. Lefebvre (1947) emphasizes this point, as does Moore (1966).

2. I am *not* making an assertion of the form *All things being equal, in a situation of social conflict between two persons one of whose assets are greater or more potent than the other's the resolution of the conflict will reflect that very difference*. My proposition in the text deliberately omits the proviso "all things being equal," frequently Latinized to *ceteris paribus*. For convenience let us refer to the assertion in the text as P and the assertion in the footnote, which is supplemented with *ceteris paribus*, as P*. Propositions of the form P* are common in the social sciences, especially in economics—and, I believe, are almost always illicit.

"P" and "not P*" expresses an empirical tendency, asserted to be generally but not always true and is thus in the indicative mood. But in P* the indicative has given way to the subjunctive. P* is not always and literally true as it stands; in fact the *ceteris paribus* is typically used when a proposition like P* is apparently not true as it stands but *it would be true* (that subjunctive again) within a context provided by some further propositions. Here one tacitly claims that there is a set of further propositions that will either identify the boundaries within which P* is always true or, equivalently, that P*, when combined inferentially with those other propositions, will validly imply true conclusions only. We can say of this that P* is *not descriptively true* but that it is *consequentially true in certain contexts* or, the same thing, that is not descriptively true but is *valid for certain theoretical or inferential uses*.

However, that distinction simply raises the ante. In employing P*, one must be able to formulate those other propositions, for one has asserted, though only tacitly, that the truth conditions for P* are or can be given. But one typically doesn't give those further truth conditions: *ceteris paribus* substitutes for them, and the matter is typically left at that point by authors who wander up this deceptive path.

There is an elementary theorem in (propositional) logic that a false antecedent implies every proposition formulable in a given inferential system, that is, where q is any proposition whatsoever, *true, false, or indeterminate,* and F is a false proposition, [F → q, for every q] is a tautology (in the Hilbert and Ackerman notation for *material implication*). That means that P* when false will (also) validly imply false propositions unless and until the conditions alluded to in *ceteris paribus* are actually formulated. That failing, propositions like P* embody theoretical fraud.

3. Quite fortuitously, as I was composing these very pages the *Boston Globe* of December 16, 2004, carried the obituary of a John LaWare, a prominent banker who, the writer noted, "During his stay in Boston, . . . served a stint as chairman of the Coordinating Committee, commonly known as the Vault, a behind-the-scenes group of about 25 business leaders who serve as unofficial mediators of Boston civic and financial affairs." It is hard to imagine any fair-sized city or county in the United States that doesn't have an equivalent group, formal or informal as the case may be, of leaders who serve "as unofficial mediators of civic and financial affairs."

4. It seems paradoxical, but relations among historical elites tend to be "tolerant," often "democratic." Homosexuality, traditionally punishable by disgrace or even death for nonelites, is often winked at within elite circles. This was even true among the Nazi and SS leadership in the Hitler era both before and after the 1934 murder of Ernst Roehm and his homosexual comrades. Tolerance is also common with respect to financial peculations and other crimes. Intra-elite conflict should be shunned. On the one hand, there is usually "enough to go around"; on the other, elites, unlike nonelites, can hit back.

5. I acknowledge a debt here to the late Robert Engler, who, in his writing and his conversation, first clarified and underlined for me the thesis that corporations are intrinsically, even primarily, political institutions.

6. The tendency to distort or "scrub" the evidence seems endemic to very highly conceptualized, "philosophic" interpretations and deductions regarding historical and social events; it is said that Hegel, when confronted with errors of fact in his *Philosophy of History*, immediately replied, "So much the worse for the facts."

7. Here is one of those instances in which too much circumlocution would be required to express double-edged racial conflict in the language of outcomes, precipitates, and residues. But I hold that the ascription of motive and goal to a putatively elite actor could be entirely eliminated without shifting the substance of the claim I'm making.

8. Individuals and organizations of the political Right, even over to the Far Right, are much more sensitive to the paradoxical status of equality in the United States than their foes and critics. They see the power of "elites" everywhere. It is unfortunate that this perception is squeezed into the form of myths about the preeminence of liberal elites or the virtues of an Arcadian past. The illiberal elites of business, church, and the national security apparatus somehow disappear from view.

9. For example, around the figure of the original John D. Rockefeller were gathered a number of talented associates—Charles Pratt, Henry H. Rodgers, Nelson Aldrich, and Henry Flagler among them—whose families remain linked in business, social, and philanthropic circles more or less down to the present.

10. The lives of Eleanor Roosevelt or, less well known, of Abby Aldrich Rockefeller (1875–1943) provide cases in point. See, for example, Kert (1993).

11. McDermott 1991 conceives of modern *property* and *capital* as "collective" in nature, as contrasted to "private."

12. John McCloy came of middle-class stock but had elite mentors at Amherst and, later, at Harvard Law School. Dean Acheson's family was only modestly prosperous but had a long association with the upper ranks of Yale University through the Anglican ministry. Averell Harriman was the scion of that famous family but felt secure enough to entrust the family business interests to other hands while he set off on a life of public service. In a dramatic way, the careers of each of the three men illustrate different advantages of the institutional or collective form of today's elite over its predecessor, the dynastic form. For biographies of these three, see Bird (1992), Beisner (2006), and Abramson (1992).

13. That fabled "class consciousness" is much more prominent and consequential among elites than among workers. The expression "NOCD" is guaranteed to raise a smile of amused familiarity when someone is described that way in the higher social circles: "Not our class, dear."

14. This was initially written even before the "financial meltdown" of 2008–9. Note the revealing title of a recent *New York Times* article, "Even in a Crisis, Banks Dig in for Battle Against Regulation" (Morgenson and Van Natta 2009). The substance of the piece is that, like the *ancien régime,* the bankers have learned nothing and forgotten everything.

15. The Bush family seems to reflect wider changes among the U.S. elite. Prescott Bush came from an old-line elite Connecticut family: he was, I recall, one of the few outspoken Republican critics of Republican fellow senator Joseph McCarthy. His son, George Herbert Walker Bush, made his fortune in the nouveau riche parts of the Texas oil business, drifting by degrees into Texas's rough-and-tumble state politics and then into government service as a Nixon campaign manager. Rewarded with posts in higher government service, he found his route to the presidency thus opened. George W. Bush, taking advantage of being the son of the father, fell into wealth through some "dicey" Texas real estate schemes for which he served as well-connected front man. His route to the presidency had little to do with the Washington Establishment of which his grandfather and even father were part; he appears in the first instance to have sought the presidency as so many wealthy men seek office today, that is, via access to pots of unregulated money.

16. This point takes on enhanced meaning if we look to the international behavior of U.S. elites, who almost as a rule reach for or threaten military force (or induced military coup) when dealing with other world powers and, especially, the smaller, weaker countries. That that force has failed them in all of its most prominent uses since 1950 does not seem to have sunk in. In Korea, Cuba, Vietnam, Guatemala, and Iran, throughout Central America, in Angola and Somalia, and now in Iraq and Afghanistan, such force has proven a dubious instrument, often creating side effects and consequences worse than the problems it was intended to resolve. John L. Lewis's old observation still makes sense: "You can do almost anything with bayonets except sit on them."

17. For those with short memories, the nuclear "deterrent" was supposed to be just that, a threat hidden in a back closet, never to be used. In fact, U.S. administrations threatened to use nuclear weapons during the Korean truce talks in 1952–53, during the battle of Dien Bien Phu in 1954, during the Quemoy-Matsu crises (against China) in the late 1950s, during a threat to Berlin in 1961, and during the Cuban Missile Crisis of 1962. In addition, ex-president Eisenhower urged the possible use of nuclear weapons on the new Johnson administration to keep the Vietnam War from getting out of hand (Goldstein 2008, 161). For its part, the Soviet Union threatened Britain and France with a nuclear strike with a view to ending the Anglo-French-Israeli attack on Nasser's Egypt in 1956. Nuclear weapons under the regime of "deterrence" were carried on the hip, not left in the back closet.

18. Some years ago an older black student and friend, Joe T., from Roosevelt (Long Island), New York, came to me. There was some local primary opposition to the anointed Republican candidate. The police were going door to door in Roosevelt asking for papers, all

the while maintaining they were just checking on voter registration. Had I ever heard of such a thing before? He reminded me that a policeman on a black doorstep was, all by itself, a threatening thing. He thought the cops were trying to frighten off at least some of the black vote. It seemed to me too that they were reminding those restive voters that they just might be identifying themselves and their families to the police, whose county bosses knew full well the intimidating effect of that.

During the run-up to the national election of 2004, there were a number of reports from closely contested states—Florida comes particularly to mind—that police were being sent around in the black districts to "check the accuracy of voter registrations."

19. Oklahoma's "green corn" rebellion (1917) would provide an instance, as would the history of Winn Parish, in northern Louisiana, home of Huey Long. Or, more widely, the radical wing of the Populist Movement, especially in the South. See Green (1978), Liebling (1961), and Woodward (1963). J. Myrdal (1965) is particularly interesting on this subject.

20. This is my own extrapolation from the very powerful, suggestive analysis of Douglas (1996).

21. The U.S. Roman Catholic hierarchy and clergy, utterly unlike their European colleagues, supported (and still do) democratic changes in the United States and encouraged their laity to participate in them. It's a point of pride in Catholic intellectual circles that their church was a vehicle for the Americanization of the immigrant generations. Trade unions, a font of political alienation in Europe, also served here as a vehicle for the social, political, and cultural Americanization of their members. A close friend, the late Steve Nelson, born in Croatia and formerly a member of the Politburo of the U.S. Communist Party, believed that the Party had been the vehicle for his own Americanization: as he amusedly recalled, he learned English by comparing—word by word, line by line—a Serbo-Croatian copy of the *Communist Manifesto* with an English version, his improving English enabling him to urge other workers to claim their rights as Americans. See also Nelson, Barrett, and Ruck (1981).

Chapter 6

1. I grasped this point long before I was able to analyze why it was true. I've been "political" for fifty years, working at the precinct level in local, state, and national campaigns; as a lobbyist at the state level, locally, and in Washington; and as a journalist writing on issues as diverse as minimum-wage legislation and international security policy. My knowledge about the politics of other countries is neither extensive nor secure, and relies more on just reading than on the interaction of experience with reading.

2. The late I. F. Stone used to say that the importance of "insider" information in government was vastly overrated. If the information was that important, lots of important people had to share it, and some wouldn't agree with it; hence the information pipeline would surely leak if not positively overflow.

3. In the middle 1960s, foreign news sources reported U.S. raids against North Vietnam from secret airbases in Thailand. This was a significant escalation of the war. The *New York Times* and the *Washington Post* cited these sources but added "shirt-tails" in which an anonymous Pentagon "spokesman" denied the story. A "shirt-tail" is a story of only a column inch or so appended at the end of a larger story because it is closely related to it. During this same period, a trade publication of the U.S. Air Force and aerospace industry, *Air Force and Space Digest*, did a cover story about the difficulty of launching from the Thai bases because of their uniquely gritty dust. They even ran a fine picture spread. What one could learn from the *Times* or the *Post* and from the *Air Force and Space Digest* corresponds to the differences between the public public and a private public. "The public" shouldn't have its attention directed to the Thai bases. But people in the industry would have to solve that dust problem; and moreover, they favored expanding the "secret" war.

4. Behind the academic habit of crediting public foolishness to the "millennialism," "chiliastic thinking," and so on of the lower orders, one often finds traces of Adorno's old conception (Adorno et al. 1950) of the "authoritarian personality."

5. Elite figures may also be punished if they break ranks. The conservative press were as a rule hostile to postwar U.S. foreign aid efforts when, in late 1958, a Scripps-Howard newspaper reporter in South Vietnam got wind of a scandal. There had been a warehouse fire in Vietnam in which the receipts for several millions of dollars in foreign aid cash had been destroyed. The reporter leapt into print about "boondoggling," government muddle, incompetent "do-gooders," poor "Uncle Sap," and so on. Almost instantly he and his publisher, Roy Howard, newspaper mogul and close friend of President Eisenhower, were summoned before an outraged congressional committee. They had "blown the cover" on a U.S. intelligence coup. In late 1954, early 1955, several Vietnamese generals in the pay of the French refused to support Ngo Dinh Diem, our candidate for a "reformed, anti-colonial" Vietnamese government. Some shadowy figure was dispatched from Washington with a satchel full of money, and our man Diem was greased into power, the recalcitrant generals departed for lives of ease in France, we "saved South Vietnam from the reds," and the warehouse story was concocted to explain why such a large sum of cash could not be accounted for.

6. In fact, that is the way the New York State Legislature was actually run when I was a lobbyist there.

7. The U.S. Senate is notoriously undemocratic. It takes sixty (of one hundred) votes to bring a measure to a vote, and by its rule of "unanimous consent," any procedure can be blocked by the will of a single senator.

8. Many organizations publish scorecards showing how representatives vote for or against issues, as I used to do at Americans for Democratic Action about the New York State legislature. Such scorecards can be deceptive. One has to know where and when a really key vote is cast. It may be on an obscure amendment or buried in the minutes of a subcommittee meeting. On some issues this obscurity may be designed by the leadership, who can then arrange the public voting to protect or favor, as the case may be, this or that exposed legislator. It would be dangerous for a New York City legislator to vote for high milk price supports even if he or she wanted to. It is common for a legislator in this predicament to pair off with a colleague voting the other way to ensure that their votes cancel out. Later, the favor can be returned when the colleague feels compelled to vote for or against something he or she doesn't like. Educated people underestimate the canniness of politicians. Almost everything they do or say is done or said to have a precise effect on a specific group of voters.

9. The following is familiar to just about everyone who has had personal or other ambitions in a democratic organization. Get a following and split the rest! If someone wants to be president of, say, a hundred-person union local, he or she should get a following of, say, about five other people. Normally, this following is collected not on the issues but by offering each crony the prospect of gaining a special, privileged position in the union, hence on the job itself. There are ninety-four other members, so you now need the support of only forty-five, less than half, to win the union presidency fifty-one to forty-nine and reward your following. Any issues at all that divide the membership will do, for the real priority is for our ambitious person and followers to gain preferment. One can emphasize differences about the contract, pit skilled worker against unskilled, or senior workers against newer ones, or trade on racial, religious, or ethnic differences, or claim vaguely to be more—or less— militant in dealing with the company. In the 1940s just such divisions over communism helped transfer many union leaderships from socially conscious men and women to careerists.

This process by which self-seeking minorities come to control democratic organizations can be prevented. But the prevention and the crime are not symmetrical. Prevention takes political leaders who work endlessly to involve the membership, to keep them informed, and to encourage others to join in the day-to-day work; self-seeking is much easier and thus much more common.

10. In 2004, Texas Republicans excluded the Democrats from voting on reapportionment, and this led to much controversy and a lawsuit or two. The controversy arose from the fact that the Republicans refused to collude with the Democrats *this* time.

11. Up until the 1950s, New York City had a popular, left-wing congressman named Vito Marcantonio. After several redistrictings failed to remove him from office, the Democrats and Republicans jointly nominated and vigorously supported a single candidate, and that, plus the united chorus of the Democratic and Republican newspapers and one more redistricting, finally rid the parties of this nettle. The exclusion of Ralph Nader from the national presidential TV debates in 2000 was jointly imposed by the two major parties.

12. In radio at present, the industry standard is seventeen minutes of advertising to forty-three minutes of programming, which is due to improve slightly because the broadcasters believe that the ads are driving listeners to other media.

13. Before he was New York City's outstanding mayor, Fiorello La Guardia was an outstanding congressman, who, with his colleagues, pioneered much of the legislation that was later to constitute FDR's New Deal. See the very fine Zinn (1959). When he represented Greenwich Village, his district included part of the famous Lower East Side. An opponent, trying to capitalize on this, accused the Little Flower of being an anti-Semite and challenged him to debate the issue. It happened that La Guardia's mother was Jewish and his Yiddish was nearly perfect. He accepted the challenge, but insisted he would only debate in Yiddish, of which, as he knew, his opponent couldn't speak a word!

14. It is proverbially hard to get traditional voters to switch sides, but one may design appeals that tear at the voter's contradictory loyalties. Liberal voters may balk at voting for racist candidates, but if they are sufficiently frightened about racial disorder, indecision will keep them at home on election day.

15. One of the reasons, I surmise, why conservatives have such animus against "activist judges" is that in their eyes the Warren Court betrayed one of the main intended functions of the courts, namely, to check and limit the power of the Democracy. In short, in their eyes, the decisions of the Warren Court weren't just "bad" or even "unconstitutional" but reversals of the Court's ultimate raison d'être.

16. In the United States, treaties are ratified by the Senate and thereby become part of our body of law. For this reason the Bush II violations of the Geneva Conventions on the treatment of war prisoners were also violations of U.S. law, as is the testing of antiballistic missiles.

17. Japan faces an analogous problem today. As in the United States in the time of McKinley, constitutional arrangements that hinder the autonomy of inner national security elites sit ill with a world in which everybody has heavy artillery, soon, it is feared, of the atomic variety. The state system itself intrudes its elite, militarist, antidemocratic values into every country's domestic political system.

18. Mahan, Hay, Root, Stimson, Acheson, McCloy, John Foster Dulles, and his brother Allen were all in their time members of "the Establishment" and served in the influential policy positions of, variously, the McKinley, Theodore Roosevelt, Taft, Franklin Roosevelt, Truman, Eisenhower, and Kennedy administrations. Quite good biographies are available for all of them. Stimson is particularly important. He was Taft's secretary of state and FDR's secretary of war. He was a central figure in the decision to drop the atomic bomb on civilians in Hiroshima and Nagasaki instead of on military targets elsewhere (Malloy 2008).

19. The most important national security document of the postwar era was NSC 47, adopted in 1947 by the Truman administration. The contents of the policy were classified, which made exposing them to the public a crime. In fact, the contents were widely known among those who cared to find out. Thus, the only practical effect of the classification was to ban NSC 47's policies from being debated within the normal political process, that is, it effectively placed the discussion of the single most important U.S. policy outside the legal and electoral pale.

20. It is an unpleasant fact that persons and organizations that oppose elite preferences are quite literally acting as social deviants. The classic case was Martinus van der Lubbe, now thought both to be mentally deficient and a bit deranged. It was he, either acting alone or with the aid of the Nazis themselves, who set fire to the German Reichstag in 1933. Opportunistically blaming the "reds," with whom van der Lubbe had some association, the

Nazi government used the incident to seize total power. In the 1960s, several radical factions of young people conceived that all or most crime was produced by social injustice, accordingly welcomed some criminals into their ranks, and with them went on to commit violent crimes, even murder. The authorities were quick to seize upon this to discredit the wider movement for social change.

Part 3 Introduction

1. For example, after the Civil War there were no unions in the United States in the modern sense of the word; workers did not contend over wages and thought they shouldn't. There were instead group insurance bodies or fraternal lodges and, here and there, revolutionary organizations. Workers accepted economic doctrines, such as John Stuart Mill's concept of the "wages fund," that the relationship between wages, profits, and land rents was immutably fixed, so that if some workers got more, other workers either had to get less or unemployment had to rise. Wage increases were thus "really" bad for the workers. It took many years and much social suffering to change this. See the parallel development of Britain's "New Unionism" in Brown (1986).

Marx's 1849 lecture (and later, pamphlet), *Wages, Price, and Profit*, is perhaps the earliest analysis showing that wage increases could come out of profits without necessarily causing harm to other workers!

Chapter 7

1. In an article about the uses by U.S. banks of the $350 billion authorized by Congress in October 2008 to restore the credit system, the *New York Times* found that "few banks cited lending as a priority. An overwhelming majority saw the bailout program as a no-strings-attached windfall that could be used to pay down debt, acquire other businesses or invest for the future." One banker observed of his own institution that there were no immediate plans to resume lending with the $154 million it had received from the Treasury. "With that capital in hand, he said, 'not only do we feel we can ride out the recession, but we also feel that we'll be in a position to take advantage of opportunities that present themselves once this recession is sorted out.'" McIntire (2009). "I seen my opportunities,' said Boss Tweed, 'and I made the most of 'em!'"

2. The less educated, less cosmopolitan parts of our population were once a fountainhead of trade union, socialist, and populist activities. It is arguable, but little argued, that those tendencies were repressed and made illicit by the government-sponsored Truman "Red Scare/McCarthyism." Their stunted recovery, after a modest 1960s rebound, is similarly explained by government actions following on the Eisenhower Commission's report. Putnam's celebrated "bowling alone" hardly touches on these factors in the decline in political participation, preferring to reach almost entirely for apolitical explanations. See Putnam (2000) and Brzezinski's 1978 memorandum directing federal authorities to disrupt some black organizations.

3. Beijing is still behind London in the installation of surveillance cameras in key public spaces! These "state-of-the-art" surveillance systems are equipped with "face recognition software and even newer behavior recognition software designed to spot the beginnings of a street protest and notify police." The article adds that Wall Street is very excited about this growth market (Bradsher 2007).

4. I was once part of an organization being disrupted by a member who was not willing to take on any organizational responsibilities but insisted on speaking in every setting as if he were speaking for the group. After a great deal of worried discussion in the inner leadership, it occurred to us that all he really cared about was the limelight and to make speeches.

We asked him to serve as our public spokesperson. As we anticipated, he himself cared little about policy choices but did a brilliant job of presenting them to the public.

5. The procedures in *Robert's Rules of Order* enable a willful chairperson to control the outcome of a meeting. A tiny minority can prevent any business from being carried out at all if the chair is weak or secretly allied with that minority. The intricacies of these procedures put off the new person and are a boon to the amateur lawyers found in every group. Their amendment procedure can be and often is used to obscure any issue. It is just about the only book that I would wholeheartedly approve of burning. It would be a useful project if some thoughtful souls devised—or have already devised—a brief handbook of rules of order tailored to fit different sizes and kinds of meetings and organizations.

6. A small group of people must first thrash out what kind of organization is wanted, who its target members are to be, and what sorts of actions (or publications) it intends. They must make a funding plan, raise some seed money, and plan a founding meeting for a larger group. This "ginger group" issues a simple "call" for a public meeting which lays out a rationale for the desired organization. That first public meeting needs a strong chair with a clear sense of what he or she has to accomplish and to avoid. Only one thing is really needed there—a democratic legitimization of the resulting organization. Before the public meeting, the project is only someone's idea: after it, it has public sanction. A draft resolution not terribly different from the "call" should be adopted at the public meeting. It should be ready ahead of time; if there is any disagreement at the public meeting, people should vote to adopt only its "sense" and a "continuations committee" instructed to take into account all the points raised in the public discussion. Its key members should have been designated ahead of time, *and* volunteers should be recruited to it on the spot. The committee should also be asked to draft a constitution or other organic document and to organize a future organizational meeting to formally adopt the organic document, elect officers, and adopt the program. Aside from the legitimization conferred by the public meeting, the crucial function of the public meeting is to recruit new persons into the initial group. One must choreograph everything at the founding public meeting—and be infinitely flexible in carrying it out.

7. For those disputes, and to grasp better the radical individualism and radical communitarian conceptions, the Antifederalist literature is invaluable. See, for example, Strong (1985).

8. The party structure that I experienced looked as follows; I imagine that it is much the same everywhere.

New York State was divided into geographic election districts (EDs), which, in a city, are about neighborhood size and accordingly larger for less populated areas. At least one party, often both, has a parallel party apparatus, that is, a party member elected from or appointed to each ED. I was briefly district captain or some such title for an ED in the Eighth Ward for the Yonkers, New York, Democratic Party. The job of the fifteen to twenty or so captains was to identify the Democrats, and, most important, identify those who could be counted on to support the existing leadership and its candidates. On primary day, we kept lists of who had voted and toward the late afternoon "pulled" "our" voters, that is, telephoned or visited them, often taking them personally to the polls or even watching the kids while they went to vote. We worked hard in the elections themselves, for we understood that a lost election is bad. But a lost primary is a disaster; it's the difference between losing a golden egg and losing the goose that lays it.

The district captains together—in theory—elected the ward leader and then both played a part in electing the city leader, and so on right up to the State Democratic Committee. In practice, the existing party leaders dominated their followers.

This elaborate structure, once common, has been weakened by TV, voter apathy toward the parties, more "big" money in politics, and so on. But just enough of it exists and is rooted in local economic, real estate, and construction interests to make it relatively resistant to change or replacement based on "the issues."

9. There is an older book, too little known, with a treasure of still useful party political information. Fay Calkin's *The CIO and the Democratic Party* (1952) analyzes attempts by CIO

militants to enter and influence candidates and issues in the period after World War II. In some places, the CIO just took over the party apparatus; elsewhere they had to re-create a Democratic Party apparatus in a relative vacuum. Still others aimed at becoming the arbiter between the other power blocs within the party, while in other places the CIO people could aim at no more than parity with the other major players. Where relevant, there were also attempts to set up a third, rival party, and so forth. Also useful is Howard Zinn's 1959 *La Guardia in Congress*. Fiorello La Guardia was a Republican who had to wrest and keep his nomination in the GOP against the opposition of conservative leaders and opportunistic "pols." The skill he showed in this and in the Congress is a model for those interested in electoral politics. The U.S. electoral system yields its rewards only to those who study it closely and are willing to work at it over the long term like my old Yonkers neighbors.

10. The expression "line" has a military origin. Lenin was influenced in his organizational ideas by the Jesuits, whose founder, Saint Ignatius Loyola, was a former soldier. Lenin's polemic *State and Revolution* (1943) can be consulted for more on the rationale and political style of the generic vanguard party.

11. The U.S. Communist Party very early championed the cause of racial equality even when it was unpopular almost everywhere else, as in the 1920s. But what the party proposed was a goofy scheme for the South's "black belt"—areas of black majority—to form a new black soviet socialist republic on the then Russian model!

There is a whole "Left" historiography that exaggerates "the Party's" influence and success in the 1930s, especially in the formation of the CIO unions. In fact, the key strike against GM in Flint, Michigan (1936–37), was brilliantly led by two communists, Wyndham Mortimer and Bob Travis, but the Party *didn't approve of it*. They were antsy about the effect the Flint strike would have on the Party's own relationship to the leader of the CIO, John L. Lewis. They then prevented Mortimer, deservedly liked and respected for his leadership in Flint, from assuming the presidency of the United Auto Workers Union (UAW) as too "controversial." They helped elect a particularly incompetent substitute, Homer Martin, whose ineptness cleared the way for Walter Reuther's anticommunists to seize the union leadership—and oust the "reds." If its 1920s and 1930s racial and labor politics are the criterion, the Party displayed a travesty of misjudgment by consistently second-rate leaders. Mortimer's attractive memoir (1972) is valuable, as is Henry Kraus's (1947) account of Travis's tactical creativity during the Flint strike.

One still influential residue of this historiography is the use of the term "the Left" to identify progressive persons, organizations, and causes. It still carries many of the connotations of a knowing political elite leading the largely passive, easily fooled masses. That muddle should be "consigned to the dustbin of history."

12. When the U.S. Communist Party leadership abruptly "went underground" during the McCarthy period, many progressive organizations and projects that had become dependent on communist leadership immediately collapsed, and there was roughly a ten-year hiatus before progressive political activity regained its former levels. Not incidentally, Putnam (2000) omits this.

13. A friend was recruited into the U.S. Communist Party while at college in the 1940s. The party member who recruited him was an FBI operative who turned his name over to the Bureau immediately. Michael Harrington, with perhaps tongue in cheek, used to argue that the U.S. Communist Party would never have survived the anti-red campaigns of the late 1940s–early 1950s without the dues provided by its numerous FBI members.

14. There is an enormous literature on this subject to which Chandler (1962) and McDermott (1991) may still serve as useful introductions.

15. My own experience here is that lower-class or working-class young persons often feel intellectually starved in their understanding of what makes them different, less esteemed, and less privileged than others in their age cohort. This is a favorable omen for the SFTA.

16. See "Force and the Safety Factor" in chapter 5.

17. For example, Bielenberg (1984).

Chapter 8

1. See, for example, Marwick (1998) on French, Italian, and U.S. police riots during the 1960s. See also the sources mentioned in note 3. Small-town police departments are often different, especially if the town is socially homogeneous. Where there are important class, ethnic, and racial differences, however, all police as a rule support the better-off "us" against the allegedly unruly, disorderly "them."

2. I should mention that my mother's father, my father's brother, and my own brother were New York City cops, that when I lived at home, police relatives, police friends, and police friends of relatives were in and out of the house all of the time, and that the tradition continues into a fourth generation; my brother's daughter is married to a retired cop. Granted, "cop" is out of fashion now, but for me the word carries a ring of knowing sympathy for this unique and really difficult calling.

3. For France, see Burrin (1996) and Callil (2006); for Czechoslovakia, see Mastný (1971); for Poland, Rossino (2003); and for Russia, Browning (1992).

4. In June 1964, the young voting-registration volunteers, Andrew Goodman, James Chaney, and Mickey Schwerner, were arrested by the Mississippi police, held until a lynch mob could be gathered, and then turned over to it by a deputy sheriff. The three were, as planned, beaten almost to death, then shot, and their bodies were hidden in an earthen dam. Closer to home for Northern liberals and civil libertarians were the events in downtown New York City in May 1970, when the police—at best—looked the other way as construction workers attacked antiwar demonstrators and mere passers-by, even invading several office and university buildings to administer their clubbings. Again, see Marwick (1998) for this and other police hostility, here and overseas, against 1960s political demonstrators. See also Johnson (2003, chap. 7).

5. Fogelson (1977) is the standard account of this history. Rare among the genre, this excellent book treats the police under a specifically historical rubric, that is, descriptively and narratively, without awe and with little or no moralizing. But it also depoliticizes an intrinsically political institution. Even so, it is indispensable for study of the modern police.

6. For an account of such behavior in Pittsburgh and elsewhere during the great national railroad strike of 1877, see Yellen (1974, 3–88).

7. The police in New York City even have a term for this—"testilying." It covers the creation or the giving of false evidence when the police feel that the alleged culprit might be let off by the "bleeding hearts" and to protect their fellow cops against charges of undue violence to arrestees, unjustified shootings, thefts of drugs, and worse.

8. Fogelson (1977) traces the history of the main big-city police departments in the United States. The book is indispensable on the history of police "reform," that is, the century-long effort in the United States to professionalize police work by strengthening the authority of professional chiefs of police versus both their own rank and file, elected officials, and, of course, the policed. This is part of the wider movement within modern institutions to centralize authority in their higher elites.

Fogelson's book, as noted, has more or less glossed over the political dimension of police work, that is, the police as an agent of social and political control against the rise of the Democracy. At one point Fogelson was gracious enough to grant me an interview, in which, I hoped, he would explain this whiting out, but he remained as enigmatic as his text. When I now consult his book, I simply read it as if it were in code. His narrative is constructed around the concept of police "corruption," and one can often translate comments about that politically innocent topic into useful insights about police social and political control work. Johnson (2003) is much franker on this aspect of normal police work.

9. The agent of the infamous Ludlow Massacre in southern Colorado in 1912. Again, Yellen (1974) and Auerbach (1964) are useful sources for historical material on private policing. For a modern account, see Johnston (1992).

10. There is an enormous literature on the modern U.S. police. Its quality varies quite widely, and it is endlessly repetitive. However, in addition to those books cited in the text, the

following add something useful to the discussion: Baum (1996); J. Bernstein (1993); Blumenthal (1993); Burpo, DeLord, and Shannon (1997); Epstein (1977); Fosdick (1969); Johnston (1992); Koon (1992); Powers (1987); Skolnick and Fyfe (1993); South (1988); and Winters (1995). the regular press coverage of the police in, especially, New York and New England has been at least equally informative.

11. "International" only to the extent that it covers both the United States and Canada.

12. I discussed clearance rates in chapter 3. With respect to rape, it is now normal for a victim to subject herself to the arduous, emotionally taxing procedure of helping to create a "rape kit" containing DNA, fiber, and other evidence that can be used to identify and subsequently convict the perpetrator. Since many of those arrested for other crimes are screened for DNA, the kits are potentially a major police tool. In New York City, for example, "cold searches" for DNA in conjunction with these kits have increased arrests for rape by about 75 percent. But in other jurisdictions it is common just to file them away. Kristof (2009), drawn from a Human Rights Watch report, is right to see this as a particularly cruel example of shoddy police work. I would be interested to read Kristof's reaction to the policy of charging rape victims for costs of their own kits, which was in effect in Wasilla, Alaska, during the administration of then mayor Sarah Palin. See "New Evidence: Palin Had Direct Role in Charging Rape Victims for Exams!" *Huffington Post*, April 2, 2010, http://www.huffingtonpost.com/jacob-alperinsheriff/sarah-palin-in stituted-ra_b_125833.html/.

13. I was one of several hundred demonstrators arrested in a sit-in in Baltimore County, Maryland, on July 4, 1963. Some of my fellow arrestees, more experienced in these matters, opined that the county jail was the most comfortable they'd ever been in. To the point here, the authorities made every effort, unsuccessfully, to prevent us from infecting the regular inmates with our views about people's rights.

14. As in a well-publicized case in New York City in June 2009.

15. In New York City in November 2006, a group of police fired fifty shots at an unarmed man leaving a bachelor party the night before his wedding. One policeman fired thirty-one of those shots. This was reckless disregard for human life—and mammoth incompetence. He had to reload his weapon at least twice, resuming shooting each time as if in a blind frenzy to blaze away at something. What kind of institution allows such a man—he was a detective, not a lowly cop!—to be a law officer in the first place and then fails subsequently to detect his failings of temperament and of elementary policing skills? For a follow-up story on the weak grand jury indictment, see Baker (2007).

16. We will return to this problem but in a wider context in chapter 12.

17. During the 1940s and 1950s, the federal government waged an enormous police and prosecutorial effort against the U.S. Communist Party in order to minimize its capacity to engage in otherwise legitimate trade union, publication, and political activity. The government was so interested in nullifying the Communist Party's (actually) legal activities that it seemed to have overlooked the Party's role in recruiting spies for the Soviet Union, even serving as a money conduit for espionage activity—which of course *was* a criminal activity. Romerstein and Breindel (2000).

18. See Lindsay (1980, 20).

19. Almost alone among government agencies, the FBI opposed waterboarding and other kinds of torture against suspected terrorists. Many, many lawyers, especially *within* the armed services, have been extraordinarily principled and courageous in their willingness to defend ostensible terrorists by standing up for legal and constitutional safeguards under very, very difficult conditions. One cannot praise these men and women too highly.

Chapter 9

1. Another example of this process is the minimum wage. The federally enacted minimum wage has evolved into a wage standard for whole classes of workers. But because

employers ensure that it stays low and never catches up with inflation, that standard functions more as a ceiling to prevent wages from rising than a floor to prevent them from falling. See McDermott (1995).

2. This is the core argument of McDermott (1991).

3. See, for example, Becker (1949).

4. The New Deal's National Recovery Administration (NRA) and, especially, the Tennessee Valley Authority (TVA) were far more ambitious schemes of government planning than *anything* actually proposed or enacted by any of the Western European socialist or labor parties during their entire twentieth-century history. Nationalization of the British steel and coal industries was intended only to modernize hopelessly backward industries, not introduce socialist principles into their management. The NRA looked to a major role for government in the day-to-day business of each industry, and the TVA carried out a region-wide project animated by the idea that a government agency was to be the center of economic, social, and even cultural planning. For socialist timidity, see the magisterial Sassoon (1996); on the British Labour Party in particular, Hennessy (1993).

5. Two headlines from the *New York Times* tell that story all by themselves: "Bail-Out Is a No-Strings Windfall to Bankers, If Not to Borrowers" (McIntire 2009), and "What Red Ink? Wall St. Paid Hefty Bonuses" (White 2009).

6. Well . . . more or less. Industry conducted a several-month "strike" against the rearmament program in 1940 until FDR gave in and appointed a GM executive to head it. Even then, until the Pearl Harbor attack, many companies, including Lockheed and GM, prioritized commercial production.

7. On corporate "divine right," the coal and iron magnate George F. Baer Jr. is often cited; Baer was the industry leader and spokesperson during the 1902 Anthracite Strike in Pennsylvania. As he declared to the *New York Times* in August of that year, "The rights and interests of the laboring man will be protected and cared for, not by the labor agitators, but by the Christian men to whom God in His infinite wisdom has given control of the property interests of the country." Quoted in Yellen (1974, 160).

8. This was written before the financial debacle of late 2008.

9. Public distrust also entered into the equation. Rockefeller's Standard Oil Trust was soon to be broken up by the government. In addition, the navy worked closely with Bethlehem Steel to develop specialized, higher-quality (and higher-profit) steels for armor plate and gun barrels. For Bethlehem Steel, see Hessen (1975).

10. See McDermott (1991). I have collapsed bonuses, stock options, even promotion to higher-paying, more responsible posts into the simple "profits." This reflects the fact that the classic GM system tied managerial rewards and perquisites to the individual's contribution to company growth and profitability.

11. Often, but not always, in collusion with a few big, favored investors.

12. See McDermott (2004, 177n16).

13. Popper and Hayek actually have the Constitution on their side. In a series of decisions whose effects we still suffer, the post–Civil War Supreme Court determined that a corporation was a person whose property was protected under the due process clause of the Fourteenth Amendment. Clearly, some persons are more equal than others.

14. The argument in the text is also an argument against the concept of "human capital." As a metaphor, that expression is often useful, but analytically it is as great a muddle as one can find in the social science literature for precisely the reasons given in the text.

15. A colleague has taken exception to this formulation on legal grounds, but whatever the *de jure* balance between the rights and obligations of the corporations, it is largely (staying with the Latin) *pro forma*. The firms actually enjoy a wide range of rights and privileges even while they have been able to constrict the scope and nature of the obligations, legal and otherwise, that others can impose upon them.

16. Proposals for popular action are little understood by outsiders. Persons in authority have to do little more than say to one another and their underlings, Reform the SEC! Move our facilities to the lowest-wage area you can find! I exaggerate, but not that much. A popular

movement must convince potential members that something presently somewhat utopian in appearance is possible, that is, convince them to act realistically today on behalf of a goal that seems at best on the very horizon of achievability. Meanwhile, Peggy's Law is operative; those who come in at the utopian beginning of such a movement are apt to walk out as it becomes more "realistic." At the same time, "the other side" is learning how to frustrate or defeat the movement. The point is that virtually every attempt at major social change will have a utopian cast at the beginning; hence those who wish to start such movements need a relatively clear idea not just of the goal of any such movement but of how to motivate good people to take it from conception through birth to development, maturity, and eventual success.

17. At present, each of the items listed is illegal under federal law. A wildcat is a strike in violation of an existing contract; it is a federal offense if the firm is in interstate commerce. A secondary strike, also illegal, is a strike by the employees of one company in support of striking employees of a different company. Historically, these were what distinguished mere labor unions from genuine labor movements. "Cooling off" periods allow the employer to prepare for the strike. Strikes typically hurt the employer more at first, but managers can adjust if given the time. But neither workers nor their unions usually have the financial resources to see them through a lengthy strike. Job actions like "working to rule" (a form of slowdown), deliberate increases in absenteeism, misplacing supplies or tools, and so forth, like any violation of a superior's orders, are violations of law and usually give the employer the right to fire the transgressor.

18. Singer (2003) is important on the current state of privatized military and international security activities. See also Seahill (2007), the study of the private military firm Blackwater, headquartered in North Carolina. For a review of the British edition of Seahill (2007), see Meek (2007).

19. It might be good to bar trade associations from any and all roles in the political process. They don't usually act only in support of this or that specific piece of perhaps-needed legislation but instead tend to ideologize the industry's "needs," that is, to generalize them and, by doing so, to exaggerate low greed into high principle. Corporations are big enough to have powerful voices all by themselves; there is no good reason to permit them to gang up on the public. I confess, however, that I as yet don't see how to maintain the diverse and needed political voices of small business while muting those of the giants.

20. In the 1940s and 1950s, U.S. unions, rejecting socialized medicine as un-American, insisted on a health insurance system tied to one's job. That actually left a majority of citizens and even workers without health insurance and, as we see now, created a system whose finances were inexcusably shaky in the long run.

21. From the moment a worker files a discrimination complaint or a health hazard complaint, he or she is by law protected against retaliation by the employer. If, for example, he or she is transferred to a less desirable site, the burden of proof falls on the employer to show that the transfer was unrelated to the complaint. Granting special legal protection to ostensibly aggrieved employees and shifting the burden of proof to the employer has had very, very substantial positive effect. It is that effect that one wants to create for the whistle-blower.

22. As longtime chair of a labor studies department that offered a university degree, I was familiar with the business curriculum offered by my institution. Some courses were planned and offered jointly by the two faculties, and perhaps half of my students came from the business school. It was apparent that some of my business colleagues taught that whatever was in the interest of the firm was right and good and that social interference with business leadership was unthinkable. My institution was not particularly regressive in this. Some of the most prestigious university business degree programs are the worst contributors to a socially amoral business leadership and cadre. Economics departments are particular offenders on this point. It would violate collegiality to single out this or that person for blame, but it would be unfair not to record that the accounting faculty had the most insight into the economic importance of a socially responsible business philosophy, and the greatest concern about the probable effects of not having such a philosophy. I count myself among their grateful students.

23. My description in the text fits almost exactly the government's role now with respect to the financial industry.

24. The Federal Reserve is a good example of the need for all three proposals for a reformed corporate governance system. In his recent memoirs, its recent chair, Allen Greenspan, tried to effect damage control on his reputation by distancing himself from some of the deficit-creating Bush tax cuts that he—then—enthusiastically supported (Andrews and Sanger 2007).

Although it is a federal agency and its main officials nominally public servants, the reality is that it is a private institution acting with governmental authority. Under Greenspan, it not only sacrificed employees, consumers, and modest investors, it even became, in the eyes of some observers, an integral part of the right wing of the Republican Party. Here one would point to the absence of a majority of independently chosen public members as the missing ingredient in an otherwise well-fashioned institution.

There is no single key to civilizing the corporate system. One needs the legal framework provided by the charter *and* the public's dominating presence within economic institutions *and* a reprofessionalization of every aspect of the management profession. Perhaps more will prove to be needed, but the progressive and the social-democratic experiences argue that nothing less will do.

Chapter 10

1. I was for over two decades a labor scholar, author, and educator and, in later years, an officer in my own union, a sponsor of worker-oriented union workshops, and a volunteer teacher in two different labor studies institutes. I helped manage a continuing education program jointly sponsored by my university and an area-wide health-care union. I hope that I can repay here the kindnesses and the teaching extended to me by my labor friends and colleagues.

Along the way I learned that the trade union world is uniquely insular; age and experience are much more influential in it than in, say, political or academic circles. New ideas, especially if they arise from outside labor's ranks, are coolly received. Unions are at the margins of legitimacy in our society and fearfully keep others out of their affairs. Unfortunately, that also means that learning and innovation are given small latitude. Moreover, those who write about workers and unions are often too ideological and left-wing to be accepted by an essentially conservative institution. Much more important, outsiders rarely understand the dictatorial nature of the modern workplace.

2. Only 12.5 percent of U.S. workers are now represented by unions, down from 20.1 percent in 1983 and 35 percent in 1955. The situation is actually worse than those figures indicate because while 36.8 percent of public-sector workers now have unions, only 7.6 percent of workers in the private sector do. This long-term decline in the private sector is approaching the 1900 figure, when only 5.2 percent of workers had union representation! See http://bls.gov/news.release/union2.TOC.htm.

3. Skilled workers took the lead in founding most of the unions for nonskilled industrial workers (Mortimer 1972). One legacy is that the skilled crafts workers often have their own branch or "department" of the union with its own rules and procedures. They may vote separately on a contract from the rest of the members and thus have, in effect, a veto over it. There are also amalgamated unions, like the Teamsters, whose diverse members range from teachers, to seasonal agricultural workers, to truck drivers. Their mode of representing their members is similar to that of an industrial union.

4. Weiler 1983 is indispensable to this discussion. See also Tomlins 1985.

5. Only in the late 1950s did Congress pass the Landrum-Griffith Act, which expanded workers rights vis-à-vis their own unions. The provisions of this act are mainly procedural in nature and do not modify the worker-employer relationship discussed in the text.

6. In a classic IWW cartoon, an older worker and his younger assistant are shown working on different sides of some imposing machine. The older worker asks his assistant, "Young fellow, if you learn and work hard, do you know where you'll be in twenty years?" The younger one answers, "Yes, on the other side of this @#$%#& machine!"

7. Workers who want a union sign National Labor Relations Board cards asking for a vote on the union. If the union wins a majority in that vote, the NLRB will "certify" it and the employer has to bargain "in good faith" with it. Employers delay those elections to provide time to persuade, threaten, and even blackmail the workers not to vote for the union. Some law and labor relations firms specialize in this often shady work, and they are very successful. Even if the union wins the election, employers delay the onset of collective bargaining, leading to further worker coolness to an "ineffective union." Legislation now before the Congress assumes that this is the major reason for union decline. It would limit the employers' ability to interfere in the election process and to delay collective bargaining. It is thought that these changes, plus an NLRB that is friendlier to labor, will set the unions on the path to growth again. I would like to believe that but am not persuaded.

8. See Brown (1986, fig. 1).

9. Filippelli and McColloch (1995) and Matles and Higgens (1974—a first-person account) focus on the conflicts between the Left and the Right within the unions during especially the 1940s and 1950s but support my point about the need for union leaderships to control the behavior of their members.

10. Wagner's opera *The Mastersingers of Nuremberg*, in its English title, gives an idealized picture of these guilds for the period around 1550. Hans Sachs, its leading figure, makes shoes.

11. Traditional female industrial and vocational skills, many extremely difficult to acquire, such as fine sewing, crocheting, and such, have not historically been recognized as unionizable "crafts." In a private communication, a colleague pointed out that there were medieval guilds of women workers, but they did not survive the transition to factory-based production.

12. Many years ago, my then father-in-law, affiliated with a local of the Carpenters' Union, was in declining health and really needed to retire. But his business agent had expected a "kickback" for assigning work, and my father-in-law had refused to pay. As a result, for several years he didn't get enough work to qualify for his pension. Mr. G. was a revelation to the pretty snotty graduate student who was his son-in-law; a worker intellectual of the old school, he studied his newspapers and listened to the Sunday opinion programs with the attentiveness and insight of a distinguished professor in a university library. Inevitably, he raised the pension problem with me, and after we looked at it from every angle, I am ashamed to say that I advised him to pay up. The bitter taste of that stays with me a full half century later.

13. My account is drawn from Blanpain (1987), as supplemented by Wrigley (1997); Brown (1986); Barkan (1984); and Wedderburn (1972), as supplemented by some memorable discussions with British union members.

14. The persons I represented in grievance procedures were professionals with advanced degrees employed by a university system. In all cases, they had resisted management orders that they believed were inconsistent with their status as professionals. In every case, the university claimed that the "rights of management" entitled them to treat professional workers as simple employees who had to obey their supervisors, come what may. In almost every case, the parent, state-wide union passively accepted management's claim to discipline the employee. Happily, the president of our local and the rest of the officers were unstinting in their support for those I was representing. Management shrewdly didn't want to go to arbitration, which of course we always threatened. That's not unusual; they would have won each time but at the cost of codifying their rights over the issue at hand. They preferred having a blanket "rights of management" rather being limited by precedents and other codified conditions. That helped each time to persuade a very decent personnel office to rescind the discipline, provided we gave them some gesture in the way of face-saving. Clearly, ours was not a typical situation.

15. For a brief but excellent account of the Haymarket affair, see Yellen (1974, chap. 2).

16. Gunn and Gunn (1991) shows that franchised retailers steer too much of their sales income out of the region, thus, if not impoverishing it, making it less economically robust. Higher local wages wouldn't erase this effect entirely but could substantially limit it, to the benefit of the whole community.

17. See Marx (1967, 215–20).

18. For a theoretical argument that a "free market," such as that of Adam Smith or our contemporary economists, cannot *in principle* uniquely determine each wage and price, and thus fails on its own terms, see McDermott (2004, especially chap. 1).

19. A private communication from a colleague points out that my analysis here is incomplete. The figure 10 million is undoubtedly an underestimate of the employment transformation brought about by the war. Many thousands of other people, particularly women and minorities in very low-wage occupations, moved over into higher-paid war work.

20. There is a brief discussion of this important bit of industrial history in McDermott (2004, 179n2). See also McDermott (1992).

21. Present-day minimum-wage laws are poorly enforced. Given the reigning economic orthodoxy on wages, nonenforcement is too often accompanied by official winks and nods. As we have argued, in the natural rights tradition, wage levels have *civic* significance. This point cannot be emphasized too much.

22. The time is more than ripe to aim at a violence-free work experience for women, on the job and going to the job. Three elements are needed, all possible now. These elements could readily be extended for all women, at home, at school, while traveling, in the evening, and so on. Simply to equip every women with an electronic device no larger nor expensive than a cheap cell phone in which simply pressing a button sends an alarm that gives her GPS location to special twenty-four-hour police teams trained and equipped to respond with the highest priority to just such alarms. In a small city or built-up area, the police team could reach the woman almost immediately. A third element is more difficult but not impossible: to prioritize socialization programs for adolescents, in which any use of male physical or even verbal aggression against females is especially, thoroughly, and thoughtfully rejected—by both boys and girls. That ethos needs to be strengthened throughout society. Looking into any schoolyard, one can see the need of it. In fact, some survey evidence shows that nearly 50 percent of teenagers accept violence against girls as normal in "a relationship" (Valencia and Nierstedt 2009). This formative behavior is still insufficiently intercepted by parents and by school and other officials. The problem will be hard to root out, but a radically less threatening society for women (and for men of particularly slight stature) is achievable in the short run.

23. My current views on racial questions have been much influenced by Landry (1987) and Ford (2005). On the other hand, black and other "minority" people stand to gain extra benefit from the proposals advanced in this book precisely because they favor those lower on the scale in the economy.

24. In a front-page story in the *Boston Globe* (Sacchetti 2009), the sheriff of a local county is reported as aggressively lobbying the federal government for the fees that come from holding immigrants in his jail. As Sheriff Hodgson declared, "We aggressively try to market ourselves to get as many of the inmates into our doors as we can."

25. I am grateful to David Barkin of Mexico's Metropolitan Autonomous University for mentoring me on these issues.

26. For further discussion of the problems of international labor migration generally, see United Nations (2003) and ILO (2006). These documents show that there is at present insufficient international support for a humane immigrant labor policy that recognizes (1) a generalized human right for persons to migrate to another nation should they choose to do so; (2) a corresponding obligation on each country to accept immigration but within limitations keyed to the ability to absorb them into its economy, society, polity, and culture in a timely manner and without hardship on them or on its own population; and (3) efficacious enforcement of existing international agreements about legal protections and social rights for alien residents and alien workers.

27. For a wider discussion of the inequities suffered by convicts, ex-convicts, their families, and even their neighborhoods, see DeParle (2007).

One speaks of a "correctional system," though in truth U.S. prisons are more often warehouses where prisoners are stored out of sight and out of mind until released. Worse even than the scarcity of rehabilitation programs is the official indifference to the victimization of prisoners in their prisons. The 2009 National Prison Rape Elimination Commission found over sixty thousand cases of sexual assault in U.S. prisons, most by inmates, some by prison officials (S. Moore 2009b). The commission's chairman added that prison rapes were so common they were almost a cliché in public discourse, as we've seen in films like *The Shawshank Redemption*. It is not hard to imagine that neglect and consequent ill-treatment of inmates, unjust in itself, also contributes to our high rates of recidivism.

28. Again, the nation's antimarijuana laws are a positive evil. Some substantial part of the population, not solely African Americans, believe that the enforcement of antimarijuana laws is intended to victimize black people specifically and poor people generally. Where such a chasm exists between the popular opinion and the courts, the police and the prisons can only function by aggravating lawlessness, both on the part of the unwilling population and within their own ranks. Like Prohibition, criminalization of marijuana is a major source of social and legal breakdown and should be repealed.

Tobacco is at least as medically harmful as marijuana. If on that basis we criminalized tobacco, we would see vast increases in tobacco addiction and tobacco-related diseases and not, as is actually the case, significant declines. We would also see the rise of a major industry in illegal tobacco trafficking, replete with associated crimes of violence, official bribery, and so forth. With respect to marijuana, as in no other area of public policy, the collusion between self-interested parties, like the police power and the ultraconservatives, is simply catastrophic—to the law, to health conditions, and to political dysfunction across the board.

29. To remind the reader, in antidiscrimination law and practice the burden of proof that there has been discrimination falls on the discriminator, not the one discriminated against. Without that provision, the discriminator merely needs to be a good liar to get away with it.

Chapter 11

1. The eight are the United States, Britain, Germany, France, Italy, Japan, Canada, and, with appreciably less influence, Russia.

2. In February 2009, after a three-year inquiry that heard testimony from witnesses from forty countries, the International Commission of Jurists, an NGO active in international human rights matters, reported that the U.S. war on terror "has done immense damage in the last seven years to a previously shared international consensus on the framework underlying both human rights and humanitarian laws. This consensus needs to be recreated and reasserted." International Commission of Jurists (2009).

3. *Nacht und Nebel* is a term used by the Gestapo to describe a secret arrest. No information at all about the person arrested, even the fact that he or she had been arrested, was to reach attorneys, the press, or the arrestee's family. The victim was said to have simply disappeared "into the night and fog."

4. The archetype was the Anglo-U.S. intervention in Iran in 1953. It overthrew the moderately left-wing and secular government of Mohammed Mossadegh and restored the unwanted Pahlevi dynasty.

Neither Western intervention in Greece in 1947–48 nor the U.S. intervention in Guatemala in 1954 rivals the Iranian coup. The Greek people, aided by the European Social Democrats and EU membership requirements, finally managed to put the era of king and jackboot behind them. Guatemala, like so much of Central and South America, still teeters politically from the U.S. overthrow of the Arbenz government in 1954. Iran stands out because in the resistance to the shah a popular, authoritarian movement of the Right emerged dominant. It is reactionary traditionalists of this ilk who are the primary opposition to the globalizers of the IMF, the WTO, and the G-8.

The shah was a secularist, but the rulers in Saudi Arabia, the Gulf States, and Indonesia (after 1965) combine economic modernization for the privileged with encouraging religious reaction among the disfavored masses. Developed country policies toward that world, led by the United States, induce radical economic change while holding back political change, leaving intact the social bases of the more backward tendencies of not only Islam but also of Christianity both Catholic and Protestant, of Judaism, and of the Hindu chauvinists of India.

5. This discussion is drawn from Bryan (2001). I strongly recommend this article to the reader.

6. In this patently inferior, even embarrassing, book by a normally better writer, Friedman's arguments against the antiglobalizing movement mix ad hominem superciliousness (they should "grow up": see Friedman 2005, 389) with the most transparent sort of debater's tricks (see 384–86).

7. The annual World Economic Forum is a small gathering of the very highest, best-connected elites. It is thus more or less a political mirror of the G-8/IMF/WTO consortium. One reporter, especially invited not merely to observe but to participate in the Davos, Switzerland, meeting of 2003, wrote with insight and humor about these oligarchs. The following is excerpted from her unpublished communication: "The world isn't run by a clever cabal. It's run by about 5,000 bickering, sometimes charming, usually arrogant, mostly male people who are accustomed to living in either phenomenal wealth, or great personal power. A few have both. Many of them turn out to be remarkably naive especially about science and technology. All of them are financially wise, though their ranks have thinned due to unwise techstock investing. They pay close heed to politics, though most would be happy if the global political system behaved far more rationally—better for the bottom line. They work very hard, attending sessions from dawn to nearly midnight, but expect the standards of intelligence and analysis to be the best available in the entire world. They are impatient. They have a hard time reconciling long-term issues (global warming, AIDS pandemic, resource scarcity) with their daily bottom line foci. They are comfortable working across languages, cultures and gender, though white caucasian males still outnumber all other categories. They adore hi-tech gadgets and are glued to their cell phones. . . . Welcome to Earth: meet the leaders!"

8. To usher in the year 2000, a TV network started at the International Date Line and broadcast the birth of the millennium as it circled the globe. Music accompanied these festivities: here "traditional" New Zealand music and there "traditional" Javan and then "traditional" Thai, . . . Russian, . . . and then all the way around to, "traditional" Hawaiian. The commentators talked of the national music of this or that country, but most of it was the same generic rock, with Pakistanis playing it on sitars, Scots playing it on bagpipes, the Irish playing it on fiddles, and the Americans on electric guitars. But it was the same stuff! The experience would surely fix in one's mind the suffusiveness of an international music culture.

9. After World War II, national cultural impulses most frequently took secular form, as in the Indonesian, Palestinian, Zionist, and Vietnamese national movements, and were thus connected to a Western or at least Enlightenment model of social, economic, and political development. But at present, the identification of the modernizing impulse with a socially irresponsible, cosmopolitan, and materialist-oriented elite and cadre has created an opening for political opposition taking a highly reactionary religious form. The failure of modernization to benefit anyone outside a very few at the expense of the many provides the material base for the fundamentalists. There is nothing inevitable in this "war between cultures"; as I'll argue in the text, it is directly the product of the contradiction between rapid economic development and repressed political development.

10. See Guttmann (1994) for a discussion of the troubling U.S. role in the international financial system. The author's modest apprehensions about the stability of that financial system have been more than borne out.

11. I am referring here to income, not wealth. In the United States, as in the EU countries, wealth is much more unequally distributed than income.

12. Only in 2008 and by special act of Congress was Nelson Mandela's name removed from the list of "terrorists" not permitted to enter the United States.

13. See Woolf (1969).

14. The first, dramatic international terrorist action in the present era appears to have been the blowing up of a Cuban airliner flying from Mexico to Havana in 1968. There is irony here, since the Cuban exiles responsible for murdering this mixed group of Cuban officials and ordinary travelers had intimate ties with the U.S. intelligence services, as they still do. The irony comes of the fact that that would make U.S. intelligence services the godfather of modern airline and other terrorism.

15. Afghanistan fundamentalists, organized and armed by the United States to fight the Russians, predictably turned their guns on us afterward. It goes without saying that Brzezinski and Kissinger, godfathers of this policy, retain their standing as foreign policy experts.

16. One must mark the late Raoul Hilberg's singular contribution here. It was not until the publication of his book *The Destruction of the European Jews* that the coherent, deliberate program of the Nazi leaders to identify, transport, and destroy all of Europe's Jews was fully described and documented. Hilberg eventually favored the term "the Jewish Catastrophe" in place of the bizarrely theological term "Holocaust" and the Nazi's cover name for genocide, "the Final Solution."

17. Japanese war criminals were tried by an International Far Eastern War Crimes tribunal. Its deliberations never achieved the moral force attached to the Nuremberg proceedings. While the court treated Japanese imperialism as a crime, it included judges from France, the Netherlands, and Great Britain, each of which was at that very moment warring against native insurgents in defense of its own empire. General MacArthur's interventions also compromised the integrity of its proceedings.

18. A friend, a long-time ANC activist, first imprisoned, later exiled to Britain, argues that the end of apartheid came of three indispensable efforts: a civic revolt within South Africa that the government proved powerless to check, the defeat of the South African army in Angola by Cuban-Angolan forces, and the international campaign to divest South African investments and boycott South African goods.

19. The arm of the antiglobalization movement is an organization known as the World Social Forum. The World Democratic Forum proposed in the text would be substantially different, less dedicated to political advocacy, and more embedded in ongoing social welfare, health, civil liberties, and related programs. There would surely be some overlap of groups in both, but one wants a WDF to take advantage of the high prestige and on-the-ground contributions of the humanitarian and libertarian NGOs, using that as a lever to moderate by action, not solely by advocacy, the more dire aspects of current international developments. The WDF should not be "Left," at least in the more formal meanings of that charged political term.

Chapter 12

1. For examples of such foolishness, consider some of Henry Kissinger's actions. He kept the Vietnam War going from 1968 to 1973, only to get a result in 1975 less favorable than was his for the taking in 1968. He urged the disastrous Laotian and, especially, Cambodian invasions in the early 1970s, pressed upon the shah such a plenitude of weaponry that it destabilized Iran, and was one of the early voices for mobilizing fundamentalist Muslim "jihadists." Without getting a quid pro quo from the Israelis, Kissinger announced in the early 1970s that the United States would not even talk with the Palestine Liberation Organization. Save for his (uniquely) praiseworthy efforts to control nuclear arms (Dobrynin 1995), Kissinger has been associated with major foreign policy blunders throughout his career. His, unfortunately, is not an isolated case.

2. On March 17, 1978, Zbigniew Brzezinski, then national security adviser, directed federal police disruption of a broad range of black protest organizations. See http://www.finalcall.com/MEMORANDUM-46.htm. The widely discussed phenomenon of "bowling

alone" (Putnam 2000), that is, declining citizen participation in civic and social activities, undermines its own relevance by failing to incorporate the government's role in demobilizing popular political activism through illegal or questionably legal measures.

3. The possible exception is the Civil Rights Bill of 1957. A weak, compromised bill, it was the first sign that more aggressive legislative steps by the Senate would be possible in the future.

4. My own parents were better than typical; they didn't oppose my involvement in the civil rights movement. Such as they knew of it, that is. My comrades and I typically had to keep a low political profile to avoid family "stress."

5. During this period, the Executive Committee of the liberal organization Americans for Democratic Action voted to condemn the Greenville, N.C., and other sit-ins. It was, they argued, always wrong to break the law. I was present as an observing staff employee and, like most of the other staffers present, was left speechless. The Committee directed that a press release be released on the condemnation. Joseph Rauh, the dominant figure in ADA at the time, had supported the decision but happily must have had second thoughts. I subsequently learned that he had blocked the press release and thus buried the event. Recall that ADA was far to the left of conventional politics then; if they disapproved of the sit-ins (the discussion in the Committee had not been long, hot, and heavy but brief, one-sided, and congenial), imagine what people to the center and right might have felt. The point of the story is that all across the spectrum of political views and institutions the deeper implications of what was developing in the South were simply not understood.

6. Anatoly Dobrynin was Soviet ambassador to the United States from 1962 to 1986. His 1996 memoir, *In Confidence: Moscow's Ambassador to America's Six Cold War Presidents*, details incident after incident in which steps to lessen cold war tensions were not perceived or simply refused. What is striking about the memoir is its even-handedness, for Dobrynin is as critical of his own government's failures here as he is of the U.S. foreign policy elite.

7. The discussion in the text is inspired by A. Mayer (1981) and by discussions with a colleague, Winston Langley.

8. In the days before automated telephone systems, one dialed "411" and got an actual telephone operator. In New York City then, the operators tended to be female graduates of the Catholic high school system, reputed to be eminently trainable and wholesomely docile in the performance of their duties. They always answered with "Number please!" as they had been trained to do and, after a pause to look up the number, ritually responded with, "The number is . . ." In spring 1961, during the Bay of Pigs invasion of Cuba, my wife, Kaye, was doing volunteer work for the anti-interventionist Fair Play for Cuba Committee. One day I dialed Information. "Number please?" "May I have the number of the Fair Play for Cuba Committee." "Fair play for Cuba! They ought to murder the bunch! [*brief pause*] The number is . . ."

9. Part of the legal basis for the Nuremberg Trials was provided by the Kellogg-Briand Pact of 1928. Recall that in the United States, treaties that have been ratified by the procedures called for by the Constitution have the force of law.

10. And, on procedural changes, a single member can veto action.

11. Thus the many military lawyers who have protested abuses at, especially, Guantanamo Bay merit the very highest esteem and gratitude from their fellow citizens.

12. This shifting of the burden of proof will be familiar to the reader from antidiscrimination law. Here, the presence of the law on the books forewarns the potential violator, say a higher intelligence official, that he or she can be brought to justice for what, via the preexisting law, now become culpable crimes of *omission*.

13. The genius of the South African Truth and Reconciliation Commission was that if a perpetrator truly confessed to his or her crimes, no prosecution would be permitted. This led to the crimes of the apartheid regime being documented and discredited by its own agents. This of itself precluded later denials about its crimes and, as important, attempts to revive either its reputation or its sway.

14. Justice Scalia is right to argue that the authors of the Constitution did not believe in modern versions of civil rights or other constitutional entitlements. They believed in a

Republic of the Few who didn't need such things, not a Democracy of the Many who do. The Bill of Rights, not part of the original Constitution, represented a compromise with the emerging democratic spirit of the country. Subsequent Supreme Courts, that of Earl Warren particularly, tried to modernize that compromise. The problem is that at bottom the Constitution is now asked to adjudicate pressing issues that were not even on the furthest mental horizons of the men who wrote it.

Paradoxically, on the president's war-making powers, Scalia is a radical "judicial activist," clearly overriding the anti-executive bias of the Constitution and the debates that framed it. The same should be said for his views on contemporary "private property," a property system that developed a full century after the writing of and the adoption of the Constitution.

References

Abraham, David. 1986. *The Collapse of the Weimar Republic: Political Economy and Crisis*. 2nd ed. New York: Holmes and Meier.
Abramson, Rudy. 1992. *Spanning the Century: The Life of W. Averill Harriman, 1891–1986*. New York: William Morrow.
Acheson, Dean. 1969. *Present at the Creation: My Years at the State Department*. New York: W. W. Norton.
Adams, Sherman. 1961. *First Hand Report: The Story of the Eisenhower Administration*. New York: Harper and Brothers.
Adorno, Theodor, Else Frenkel-Brunswik, Daniel Levinson, and Nevitt Sanford. 1950. *The Authoritarian Personality*. New York: Harper and Row.
Andrews, Edmund L., and David E. Sanger. 2007. "Former Fed Chairman Attacks Bush on Fiscal Role." *New York Times*, September 15, A1.
Arendt, Hannah. 1964. *The Origins of Totalitarianism*. New York: Meridian Books.
Aristotle. 1958. *The Politics of Aristotle*. Edited and translated by Ernest Barker. London: Oxford University Press.
Arnold, Kathleen R. 2008. *America's New Working Class: Race, Gender, and Ethnicity in a Biopolitical Age*. University Park: Pennsylvania State University Press.
Auerbach, Jerald S. 1964. "The La Follette Committee: Labor and Civil Liberties in the New Deal." *Journal of American History* 51 (December): 435–59.
Averitt, Robert. 1968. *The Dual Economy: The Dynamics of American Industry Structure*. New York: W. W. Norton.
Bailey, Thomas A. 1979. *Hitler vs. Roosevelt: The Undeclared Naval War*. New York: Free Press.
Baker, A. 2007. "50 Shot Barrage Leads to Charges for 3 Detectives." *New York Times*, March 17, A1.
Barkan, Joanne. 1984. *Visions of Emancipation: The Italian Workers' Movement Since 1945*. New York: Praeger.
Bartels, Larry. 1988. *Presidential Primaries and the Dynamics of Public Choice*. Princeton: Princeton University Press.
Baum, Dan. 1996. *Smoke and Mirrors: The War on Drugs and the Politics of Failure*. Boston: Little, Brown.
Baxandall, Rosalyn, and Elizabeth Ewen. 2000. *Picture Windows: How the Suburbs Happened*. New York: Basic Books.
Becker, Carl. 1949. *Progress and Power*. New York: Alfred A. Knopf.
Beisner, Robert. 2006. *Dean Acheson: A Life in the Cold War*. Oxford: Oxford University Press.
Bell, Daniel. 1973. *The Coming of Post-Industrial Society: A Venture in Social Forecasting*. New York: Basic Books.

———. 1976. *The Cultural Contradictions of Capitalism.* New York: Basic Books.
Bell, Derek. 1993. *Faces at the Bottom of the Well: The Permanence of Racism.* New York: Basic Books.
Berle, Adolf A. 1959. *Power Without Property.* New York: Harcourt, Brace.
———. 1963. *The American Economic Republic.* New York: Harcourt, Brace, and World.
Berle, Adolf A., and Gardiner Means. 1933. *The Modern Corporation and Private Property.* New York: Macmillan.
Bernstein, Eduard. 1961. *Evolutionary Socialism.* Translated by Edith C. Harvey. New York: Schocken Books. Originally published in 1899.
Bernstein, Jeremy. 1993. *Police Brutality: A National Debate.* Hillside, N.J.: Enslow Publications.
Bielenberg, Christabel. 1984. *The Past Is Myself.* London: Corgi Books.
Bird, Kai. 1992. *The Chairman: John J. McCloy and the Making of the American Establishment.* New York: Simon and Schuster.
Blake, Robert. 1970. *The Conservative Party from Peel to Churchill.* Based on the Ford Lectures delivered before the University of Oxford in the Hilary Term of 1968. New York: St. Martin's Press.
Blanpain, Roger, ed. 1987. *Comparative Labour Law and Industrial Relations.* 3rd ed. Deventer, the Netherlands: Kluwer Law and Taxation.
Block, Fred L. 1977. *The Origins of International Economic Disorder: A Study of United States International Monetary Policy from World War II to the Present.* Berkeley and Los Angeles: University of California Press.
Blumenthal, Ralph. 1993. "Private Guards Cooperate in Public Policing." *New York Times,* July 13, B1.
Bowles, Samuel, and Herbert Ginthis. 1976. *Schooling in Capitalist America: Educational Reform and the Contradictions of Economic Life.* New York: Basic Books.
Bradsher, Keith. 2007. "An Opportunity for Wall St. in China's Surveillance Boom." *New York Times,* September 11, A1.
Braverman, Harry. 1974. *Labor and Monopoly Capital.* New York: Monthly Review Press.
Breitman, Richard. 1991. *The Architect of Genocide: Himmler and the Final Solution.* New York: Alfred A. Knopf.
Brown, Henry Phelps. 1986. *The Origins of Trade Union Power.* Oxford: Oxford University Press.
Browning, Christopher. 1992. *Ordinary Men: Reserve Police Battalion 101 and the Final Solution.* With Jürgen Matthaus. New York: Cambridge University Press.
———. 2004. *The Origins of the Final Solution: The Evolution of Nazi Jewish Policy, September 1939—March 1942.* Jerusalem: Yad Vashem; Lincoln: University of Nebraska Press.
Bryan, Dick. 2001. "Global Accumulation and Accounting for National Economic Identity." *Review of Radical Political Economics* 33, no. 1: 57–77.
Bunker, John Gurley. 1972. *Liberty Ships: The Ugly Ducklings of World War II.* Annapolis: Naval Institute Press.
Burns, Michael. 1991. *Dreyfus: A Family Affair, 1789–1945.* New York: HarperCollins.
Burpo, John, Ron DeLord, and Michael Shannon. 1997. *Police Association Power, Politics, and Confrontation: A Guide for the Successful Police Labor Leader.* Springfield, Ill.: Charles C. Thomas.

Burrin, Philippe. 1996. *France Under the Germans: Collaboration and Compromise.* Translated from the French by Janet Lloyd. New York: New Press.
Calkins, Fay. 1952. *The CIO and the Democratic Party.* Chicago: University of Chicago Press.
Callil, Carmen. 2006. *Bad Faith: A Forgotten History of Family, Fatherland, and Vichy France.* New York: Alfred A. Knopf.
Carley, Michael J. 1999. *The Alliance That Never Was and the Coming of World War II.* Chicago: Ivan Dee.
Caro, Robert. 1990. *The Years of Lyndon Johnson.* New York: Alfred A. Knopf.
Chandler, Alfred D. 1962. *Strategy and Structure: Chapters in the History of the American Industrial Enterprise.* Cambridge: MIT Press.
Chandler, Alfred D., and Herman Daems. 1980. *Management Hierarchy: Comparative Perspectives on the Rise of the Modern Industrial Enterprise.* Cambridge: Harvard University Press.
Channon, Derek F. 1973. *The Strategy and Structure of British Enterprise.* London: Macmillan.
Chernow, Ron. 1990. *The House of Morgan: An American Banking Dynasty and the Rise of Modern Finance.* New York: Simon and Schuster.
Churchill, Winston. 1996. *My Early Life, 1874-1904.* New York: Simon and Schuster.
Clifford, Clark. 1991. *Counsel to the President: A Memoir.* With Richard Holbrooke. New York: Random House.
Cochran, Bert. 1977. *Labor and Communism: The Conflict That Shaped American Unionism.* Princeton: Princeton University Press.
Cochran, Thomas. 1974. *Business in American Life: A History.* New York: McGraw-Hill.
Cook, Don. 1989. *Forging the Alliance: NATO, 1945-1950.* New York: William Morrow, Arbor House.
Craig, Gordon A. 1955. *The Politics of the Prussian Army: 1640-1945.* London: Oxford University Press.
Crankshaw, Edward. 1994. *Gestapo: Instrument of Tyranny.* New York: Da Capo Press.
Crawford, Michael. 1993. *The Roman Republic.* 2nd ed. Cambridge: Harvard University Press.
Dahrendorf, Ralf. 1959. *Class and Class Conflict in Industrial Society.* Stanford: Stanford University Press.
Danziger, Sheldon H., Gary Sandefur, and Daniel H. Weinberg. 1994. *Confronting Poverty: Prescriptions for Change.* New York: Russell Sage Foundation; Cambridge: Harvard University Press.
Davidowicz, Lucy S. 1989. *From That Place and Time: A Memoir, 1938-1947.* New York: W. W. Norton.
Davis, Mike. 1986. *Prisoners of the American Dream.* New York: Verso.
Dent, Bob. 2006. *Budapest 1956: Locations of Drama.* Budapest: Európa Könyvkiadó.
DeParle, Jason. 2007. "The American Prison Nightmare." *New York Review of Books,* April 12, 33-36.
Dobrynin, Anatoly. 1995. *In Confidence: Moscow's Ambassador to America's Six Cold War Presidents.* New York: Random House, Times Books.
Dollard, John. 1937. *Caste and Class in a Southern Town.* New Haven: Yale University Press.

Dos Santos, Theotonio. 1970. "The Concept of Social Classes." *Science and Society* 35 (Summer): 166–93.

Douglas, Ann. 1996. *Terrible Honesty: Mongrel Manhattan in the 1920s.* New York: Farrar, Straus and Giroux.

Douglass, Frederick. 1983. *The Life and Times of Frederick Douglass.* Secaucus, N.J.: Citadel Press.

Drucker, Peter. 1968. *The Age of Discontinuity: Guidelines to Our Changing Society.* New York: Harper and Brothers.

Duménil, Gérard, and Dominique Lévy. 1996. *La Dynamique du Capital: Un Siècle d'economie Américaine.* Paris: Presses Universitaires de France.

Duneier, Mitchell. 1992. *Slim's Table: Race, Respectability, and Masculinity.* Chicago: University of Chicago Press.

Durkheim, Émile. 1972. *Selected Writings.* Edited and with an introduction by Anthony Giddens. Cambridge: Cambridge University Press.

Dwyer, Jim. 2006. "Police Memos Say Arrest Tactics Calmed Protest." *New York Times,* March 17, A1.

Edwards, Richard. 1979. *Contested Terrain: The Transformation of the Workplace in the Twentieth Century.* New York: Basic Books.

Edwards, R., Michael Reich, and David Gordon, eds. 1975. *Labor Market Segmentation.* Lexington, Mass.: D. C. Heath.

Eisenhower Commission. See *National Commission on the Causes and Prevention of Violence.*

Ellis, John. 1986. *The Social History of the Machine Gun.* Baltimore: Johns Hopkins University Press.

Engelmann, Bernt. 1986. *In Hitler's Germany: Everyday Life in the Third Reich.* New York: Pantheon Books.

Engler, Robert. 1961. *The Politics of Oil.* New York: Macmillan.

Epstein, Edward J. 1977. *Agency of Fear: Opiates and Political Power in America.* New York: G. P. Putnam and Sons.

Filippelli, Ronald L., and Mark D. McColloch. 1995. *Cold War in the Working Class: The Rise and Decline of the United Electrical Workers.* Albany: State University of New York Press.

Flacks, Richard. 1972. *Youth and Social Change.* Chicago: Markham.

———. 1988. *Making History: The Radical Tradition in American Life.* New York: Columbia University Press.

Fogelson, Robert M. 1977. *Big-City Police.* Cambridge: Harvard University Press, Urban Institute.

Foner, Eric. 1988. *Reconstruction, 1863–1877.* New York: Harper and Row.

Ford, Richard T. 2005. *Racial Culture: A Critique.* Princeton: Princeton University Press.

Fosdick, Raymond. 1969. *American Police Systems.* Montclair, N.J.: Patterson Smith.

Friedman, Milton, and Rose Friedman. 1962. *Capitalism and Freedom.* Chicago: University of Chicago Press.

Friedman, Thomas L. 2005. *The World Is Flat: A Brief History of the Twenty-first Century.* New York: Farrar, Straus and Giroux.

Galbraith, John Kenneth. 1952. *American Capitalism: The Concept of Countervailing Power.* Boston: Houghton Mifflin.

———. 1967. *The New Industrial State.* Boston: Houghton Mifflin.

Gati, Charles. 2006. *Failed Illusions: Moscow, Washington, Budapest, and the 1956 Hungarian Revolt*. Washington, D.C.: Woodrow Wilson Center Press; Stanford: Stanford University Press.
Gerth, H. H., and C. Wright Mills, eds. 1958. *From Max Weber: Essays in Sociology*. New York: Oxford University Press, Galaxy.
Gitlin, Todd. 1987. *The Sixties: Years of Hope, Days of Rage*. New York: Bantam.
Glazer, Nathan. 1961. *The Social Basis of American Communism*. New York: Harcourt, Brace, and World.
Glotz, Gustave. 1967. *Ancient Greece at Work: An Economic History of Greece from the Homeric Period to the Roman Conquest*. New York: W. W. Norton.
Gold, Michael. 1924. *Life of John Brown*. Little Blue Book no. 521. Girard, Kan.: Haldeman-Julius.
Goldstein, Gordon M. 2008. *Lessons in Disaster: McGeorge Bundy and the Path to War in Vietnam*. New York: Henry Holt.
Goodwyn, Lawrence. 1978. *The Populist Revolt: A Short History of the Agrarian Revolt in America*. New York: Oxford University Press.
Gorlitz, Walter. 1953. *The German General Staff: Its History and Structure, 1657–1945*. London: Hollis and Carter.
Gorz, André. 1980. *A Strategy for Labor*. Boston: Beacon Press.
———. 1982. *Farewell to the Working Class: An Essay on Post-industrial Socialism*. London: Pluto Press.
Gould, William B. 1984. *Japan's Reshaping of American Labor Law*. Cambridge: MIT Press.
Gramsci, Antonio. 1971. *Selections from the Prison Notebooks*. Edited and translated by Quintin Hoare and Geoffrey Nowell Smith. New York: International.
Green, James. 1978. *Grass-Roots Socialism: Radical Movements in the Southwest, 1895–1953*. Baton Rouge: Louisiana State University Press.
Greider, William. 1987. *Secrets of the Temple: How the Federal Reserve Runs the Country*. New York: Simon and Schuster.
———. 1992. *Who Will Tell the People? The Betrayal of American Democracy*. New York: Simon and Schuster.
Grossman, Vasily. 1985. *Life and Fate*. Translated and with an introduction by Robert Chandler. London: Collins Harvill.
Gulick, Charles. 1968. *Labor Policy of the United States Steel Corporation*. New York: AMS Press. Originally published in 1924.
Gunn, Christopher, and Hazel Dayton Gunn. 1991. *Reclaiming Capital: Democratic Initiatives and Community Development*. Ithaca: Cornell University Press.
Guttmann, Robert. 1994. *How Credit Money Shapes the Economy: The United States in a Global System*. Armonk, N.Y.: M. E. Sharpe.
Hacker, Andrew. 1995. *Two Nations: Black and White, Separate, Hostile, Unequal*. Expanded and updated edition. New York: Ballantine Books.
Hammer, Oscar J. 1969. *The Red "48ers": Karl Marx and Frederick Engels*. New York: Charles Scribner and Sons.
Harz, Louis. 1955. *The Liberal Tradition in America: An Interpretation of American Political Thought Since the Revolution*. New York: Harcourt, Brace, and World.
Hayek, Friedrich A. 1944. *The Road to Serfdom*. Chicago: University of Chicago Press.
Heineman, Kenneth J. 1992. *Campus Wars: The Peace Movement at American State Universities in the Vietnam Era*. New York: New York University Press.

Hennessy, Peter. 1993. *Never Again: Britain, 1945–1951*. London: Vintage.
Herman, Edward S. 1981. *Corporate Control, Corporate Power: A Twentieth-Century Fund Study*. Cambridge: Cambridge University Press.
Hessen, Robert. 1975. *Steel Titan: The Life of Charles M. Schwab*. Oxford: Oxford University Press.
Hilberg, Raoul. 1961. *The Destruction of the European Jews*. Chicago: Quadrangle Books.
———. 1993. *Perpetrators, Victims, Bystanders: The Jewish Catastrophe, 1933–1945*. New York: Harper Perennial; Aaron Asher Books.
———. 1996. *The Politics of Memory: The Journey of a Holocaust Historian*. Chicago: Ivan R. Dee.
Hilferding, Rudolph. 1981. *Finance Capital: A Study of the Latest Phase of Capitalist Development*. Translated by Morris Watnick and Sam Gordon. London: Routledge and Kegan Paul. Originally published in 1910.
Historical Statistics of the United States: Colonial Times to the Present. 1970. Washington, D.C.: U.S. Government Printing Office.
Hobsbawm, Eric. 1994. *The Age of Extremes: A History of the World, 1914–1991*. New York: Vintage Books.
Hochschild, Adam. 1998. *King Leopold's Ghost: A Story of Greed, Terror, and Heroism in Colonial Africa*. Boston: Houghton Mifflin.
Hofstadter, Richard. 1960. *The Age of Reform: From Bryan to FDR*. New York: Random House.
Horn, Gerd-Rainer. 2007. *The Spirit of '68: Rebellion in Western Europe and North America, 1956–1976*. Oxford: Oxford University Press.
Horwitz, Morton J. 1992. *The Transformation of American Law, 1870–1960*. Oxford: Oxford University Press.
ILO. *See* International Labour Organization.
Inciardi, James A. 1986. *The War on Drugs: Heroin, Cocaine, Crime, and Public Policy*. Palo Alto, Calif.: Mayfield.
International Commission of Jurists. 2009. "Top International Law Experts Call on U.S. Administration to Reject War Paradigm, Reform Counter Terrorism Policies." Press release, February 27. http://ejp.icj.org (accessed March 20, 2010).
International Labour Organization (ILO). 2006: *International Labour Migration and Development: The ILO Perspective*. Geneva: International Labour Office.
Jackson, Stanley. 1983. *J. P. Morgan: A Biography*. New York: Stein and Day.
Jencks, Christopher, and David Riesman. 1969. *The Academic Revolution*. Chicago: University of Chicago Press.
———. 1992. *Rethinking Social Policy; Race, Poverty, and the Underclass*. Cambridge: Harvard University Press.
Jensen, Arthur. 1969. "How Much Can We Boost IQ and Scholastic Achievement?" *Harvard Educational Review* 39:1–123.
Johnson, Marilynn. 2003. *Street Justice: A History of Police Violence in New York City*. Boston: Beacon Press.
Johnston, Les. 1992. *The Rebirth of Private Policing*. London: Routledge.
Jones, A. H. M. 1977. *Athenian Democracy*. Baltimore: Johns Hopkins University Press.
Judt, Tony. 2005. *Post War: A History of Europe Since 1945*. London: Penguin Books.
Jukič, Ilija. 1974. *The Fall of Yugoslavia*. Translated by Dorian Cooke. New York: Harcourt, Brace, Jovanovich.

Kahn, Herman. 1960. *On Thermonuclear War.* Princeton: Princeton University Press.
Kant, Immanuel. 1999. *The Critique of Pure Reason.* Translated by Max Müller. Edited by Paul Guyer and Allen W. Wood. Cambridge: Cambridge University Press. Originally published in 1781.
Katz, Michael B. 1990. *The Undeserving Poor: From the War on Poverty to the War on Welfare.* New York: Pantheon Books.
Kee, Robert. 1984. *1939: In the Shadow of War.* Boston: Little, Brown.
Keller, Suzanne. 1963. *Beyond the Ruling Class.* New York: Random House.
Keniston, Kenneth. 1965. *The Uncommitted.* New York: Dell.
———. 1968. *Young Radicals.* New York: Harcourt, Brace and World.
Kenyon, Cecilia, ed. 1961. *The Antifederalists: Critics of the Constitution, 1781–1788.* Chapel Hill: University of North Carolina Press.
Kerner Report. See *Report of The National Advisory Commission on Civil Disorders.*
Kersten, Rikki. 1995. *Democracy in Post-War Japan: Masao Maruyama and the Search for Autonomy.* Newark, N.J.: Routledge.
Kert, Bernice. 1993. *Abby Aldrich Rockefeller: The Woman in the Family.* New York: Random House.
Keynes, John Maynard. 1920. *The Economic Consequences of the Peace.* New York: Harcourt, Brace and Howe.
———. 1964. *The General Theory of Employment, Interest, and Money.* New York: Harcourt, Brace. Originally published in 1936.
Khrushchev, S. 1970. *Khrushchev Remembers.* Translated and edited by Strobe Talbott. With introductory commentary and notes by Edward Crankshaw. Boston: Little, Brown.
Kiesling, Eugenia C. 1996. *Arming Against Hitler and the Limit of Military Planning.* Lawrence: University of Kansas Press.
Kleinfeld, N. R., and Steven Greenhouse. 2009. "Meatball Justice." Parts 1, 2, and 3. *New York Times,* March 31, A1 ("A World of Hurt"); April 1, A1 ("That's the Game, Baby"); April 2, A1 ("A Costly Legal Swamp").
Klemperer, Victor. 1999. *I Will Bear Witness, 1933–1941: A Diary of the Nazi Years.* Translated by Martin Chalmers. New York: Modern Library.
Kolata, Gina. 2006. "So Big and Healthy Nowadays Grandpa Wouldn't Know You: The New Age, Older and Better." *New York Times,* July 30, A1.
Kolko, Gabriel. 1967. *The Triumph of Conservatism: A Re-Interpretation of American History, 1900–1916.* Chicago: Quadrangle Books.
———. 1968. *The Politics of War: The World and United States Foreign Policy, 1943–45.* New York: Random House.
Koon, Stacey C. 1992. *Presumed Guilty: The Tragedy of the Rodney King Affair.* Washington, D.C.: Regnery Gateway.
Kraus, Henry. 1947. *The Many and the Few.* Los Angeles: Plantin Press.
Kristof, Nicholas D. 2009. "Is Rape Serious?" *New York Times,* April 30, A25.
Krugman, Paul. 2009. "The Market Mystique." *New York Times,* March 27, A23.
Lacey, Robert. 1986. *Ford: The Men and the Machine.* Boston: Little, Brown.
Lafargue, Paul. 1975. *The Right to Be Lazy.* Translation of *Le Droit à la paresse.* Translation originally published in 1907. Chicago: Charles H. Kerr.
Lamb, Richard. 1989. *The Drift to War: 1922–39.* New York: St. Martin's Press.
Lambert, Andrew. 1998. *The Foundations of Naval History: John Knox Laughton, the Royal Navy, and the Historical Profession.* London: Chatham.

Landry, Bart. 1987. *The New Black Middle Class*. Berkeley and Los Angeles: University of California Press.
Laqueur, Walter. 1974. *Weimar: A Cultural History, 1918–1933*. New York: G. P. Putnam and Sons.
Lee, Frederic S. 1988. *Post-Keynesian Price Theory*. Cambridge: Cambridge University Press.
Lefebvre, Georges. 1947. *The Coming of the French Revolution*. Translated by R. R. Palmer. New York: Vintage Books. Originally published in 1939.
Lemann, Nicholas. 1991. *The Promised Land: The Great Black Migration and How It Changed America*. New York: Alfred A. Knopf, Borzoi Books.
———. 1999. *The Big Test: The Secret History of the American Meritocracy*. New York: Farrar, Straus and Giroux.
Lenin, V. I. 1943. *State and Revolution*. New York: International. Originally published in 1917.
Liebling, A. J. 1961. *The Earl of Louisiana*. New York: Simon and Schuster.
Lichtenstein, Nelson. 1982. *Labor's War at Home: The CIO and World War II*. Cambridge: Cambridge University Press.
Lindsay, John J. 1980. "Endangered Liberals." *Newsweek*, June 30, 20.
Lindsey, Almont. 1964. *The Pullman Strike*. Chicago: University of Chicago Press.
Lipset, Seymour Martin. 1960. *Political Man: The Social Bases of Politics*. New York: Doubleday.
Livesay, Harold. 1975. *Andrew Carnegie and the Rise of Big Business*. Boston: Little, Brown.
Locke, John. 1980. *Second Treatise of Government*. Edited with an introduction by C. B. Macpherson. Indianapolis: Hackett. Originally published in 1690.
Lukacs, John. 1976. *The Last European War: September 1939/December 1941*. Garden City: Doubleday, Anchor Press.
Lynd, Robert S., and Helen Merrell Lynd. 1929. *Middletown: A Study in American Culture*. New York: Harcourt, Brace.
———. 1937. *Middletown in Transition: A Study in Cultural Conflicts*. New York: Harcourt, Brace.
Maclean, Fitzroy. 1991. *Eastern Approaches*. Harmondsworth, U.K.: Penguin Books.
Maier, Charles. 1988a. *Recasting Bourgeois Europe: Stabilization in France, Germany, and Italy in the Decade After World War I*. Princeton: Princeton University Press.
———. 1988b. *The Unmasterable Past: History, Holocaust, and German National Identity*. Cambridge: Harvard University Press.
Maisky, Ivan. 1968. *Memoirs of a Soviet Ambassador: The War, 1939–43*. Translated by Andrew Rothstein. New York: Charles Scribner.
Malloy, Sean L. 2008. *Atomic Tragedy: Henry L. Stimson and the Decision to Use the Bomb Against Japan*. Ithaca: Cornell University Press.
Mangold, Tom. 1991. *James Jesus Angleton: The CIA's Master Spy Hunter*. With Jeff Goldberg. New York: Simon and Schuster.
Mann, James. 2004. *The Rise of the Vulcans: The History of Bush's War Cabinet*. New York: Viking.
Mann, Michael. 1986. *The Sources of Social Power*. Vol. 1, *A History of Power from the Beginning to A.D. 1760*. New York: Cambridge University Press.
———. 1993. *The Sources of Social Power*. Vol. 2, *The Rise of Classes and Nation-States, 1760–1914*. New York: Cambridge University Press.

Marwick, Arthur. 1998. *The Sixties: Cultural Revolution in Britain, France, Italy, and the United States, c. 1958–c. 1974.* Oxford: Oxford University Press.
Marx, Karl. 1966. *Capital.* Vol. 3. Moscow: Progress. Originally published in 1894.
———. 1967a. *Capital.* Vol. 1. New York: International. Originally published in 1867.
———. 1967b. *Capital.* Vol. 2. Moscow: Progress. Originally published in 1885.
———. 1968a. *The Communist Manifesto.* In Karl Marx and Frederick Engels, *Selected Works.* New York: International. Originally published in 1847.
———. 1968b. *Wages, Price, and Profit.* In Karl Marx and Frederick Engels, *Selected Works.* New York: International. Originally published in 1849.
———. 1968c. *Class Struggles in France, 1847–50.* In Karl Marx and Frederick Engels, *Selected Works.* New York: International. Originally published in 1850.
———. 1968d. *The Eighteenth Brumaire of Louis Napoleon.* In Marx and Engels, *Selected Works.* New York: International. Originally published in 1852.
———. 1968e. *Preface to a Contribution to the Critique of Political Economy.* In Karl Marx and Frederick Engels, *Selected Works.* New York: International. Originally published in 1859.
———. 1968f. *The Civil War in France.* In Karl Marx and Frederick Engels, *Selected Works.* New York: International. Originally published in 1871.
Massie, Robert K. 1991. *Dreadnought: Britain, Germany, and the Coming of the Great War.* New York: Random House.
Mastný, Vojtěch. 1971. *The Czechs Under Nazi Rule: The Failure of National Resistance, 1939–1942.* New York: Columbia University Press.
Matles, James J., and James Higgins. 1974. *Them and Us: Struggles of a Rank-and-File Unionist.* Boston: Beacon Press.
May, Ernest R. 2000. *Strange Victory: Hitler's Conquest of France.* New York: Hill and Wang.
Mayer, Arno. 1981. *The Persistence of the Old Regime: Europe and the Great War.* New York: Pantheon Books.
———. 1988. *Why Did the Heavens Not Darken? The Final Solution in History.* New York: Pantheon Books.
Mayer, George H. 1964. *The Republican Party, 1854–1964.* New York: Oxford University Press.
Mazower, Mark. 1993. *Inside Hitler's Greece: The Experience of Occupation.* New Haven: Yale University Press.
———. 2008. *Hitler's Empire: How the Nazis Ruled Europe.* New York: Penguin Press.
McDermott, John F. M. 1965. "Does the Goldwater Movement Have a Future?" *Dissent,* Spring.
———. 1967. "The Crisis Managers." Review of Roger Hilsman, *To Move a Nation. New York Review of Books,* September 14.
———. 1969. "Technology: The Opiate of the Intellectuals." Review of *Harvard Program on Technology and Society, 4th Annual Report. New York Review of Books,* August 31.
———. 1988. "Corporate Form: A Unitary Theory of Technology, Property, and Social Class." *Review of Radical Political Economy* 20, no. 1: 21–45.
———. 1991. *Corporate Society: Class, Property, and Contemporary Capitalism.* Boulder, Colo.: Westview Press.

———. 1992. "History in the Present: Contemporary Debates About Capitalism." *Science and Society* 56 (Fall): 291–23.

———. 1995. "Bare Minimum: A Too Low Minimum Wage Keeps All Wages Down." *Dollars and Sense*, July/August, 26–29.

———. 1997. "On the Origin of the Present World in the Defeat of 'the 60s.'" *Socialism and Democracy* 11 (Fall): 71–107.

———. 1999. Review of Robert Guttmann, *How Credit Money Shapes the Economy: The United States in a Global System*. Armonk, N.Y.: M. E. Sharpe.

———. 2001. "One Hundred Years of ???" A review of *One Hundred Years of Socialism: The West European Left in the Twentieth Century*. *Radical Political Economics* 33:99–115.

———. 2004. *Economics in Real Time: A Theoretical Reconstruction*. Ann Arbor: University of Michigan Press.

———. 2007. "Producing Labor-Power." *Science and Society* 71 (Summer): 299–321.

McGovern, George. 1977. *The Autobiography of George McGovern*. New York: Random House.

McIntire, Mike. 2009. "Bail-Out Is a No Strings Windfall to Bankers If Not to Borrowers." *New York Times*, January 18, A1.

Means, Gardiner. 1962. *Pricing Power and the Public Interest: A Study Based in Steel*. New York: Harper and Brothers.

Meek, James. 2007. "Hooyah!!! The Rise of a Private Army." Review of Jeremy Seahill, *Blackwater: The Rise of The World's Most Powerful Mercenary Arm*. *London Review of Books*, August 2, 3–5.

Meeropol, Michael. 1998. *Surrender: How the Clinton Administration Completed the Reagan Revolution*. Ann Arbor: University of Michigan Press.

Michels, Robert. 1958. *Political Parties: A Sociological Study of the Oligarchical Tendencies of Modern Democracy*. Translated by Eden and Cedar Paul. Glencoe, Ill.: Free Press. Originally published in 1915.

Mills, C. Wright. 1956. *The Power Elite*. Oxford: Oxford University Press.

Molotov, Vyacheslav. 1993. *Molotov Remembers: Inside Kremlin Politics*. Chicago: Ivan R. Dee.

Montesquieu, Charles Louis de Secondat, baron de. 2002. *The Spirit of the Laws*. Buffalo: Prometheus Books. Originally published in 1748.

Montgomery, David. 1987. *The Fall of the House of Labor: The Workplace, the State, and American Labor Activism, 1865–1925*. Cambridge: Cambridge University Press.

Moore, Barrington. 1966. *Social Origins of Dictatorship and Democracy: Lord and Peasant in the Making of the Modern World*. Boston: Beacon Press.

Moore, Solomon. 2009a. "Science Found Wanting in Nation's Crime Labs." *New York Times*, February 5, A1.

———. 2009b. "Study of Rape in Prisons Counts 60,500 Attacks." *New York Times*, June 23, A17.

Morgenson, Gretchen, and Don Van Natta Jr. 2009. "Even in Crisis, Banks Dig in for Battle Against Regulation." *New York Times*, June 1, A1.

Morison, Samuel Eliot. 1984. *A History of United States Naval Operations in World War II*. Vol. 1, *The Battle of the Atlantic*. Boston: Little, Brown.

Morn, Frank. 1982. *"The Eye That Never Sleeps": A History of the Pinkerton National Detective Agency*. Bloomington: Indiana University Press.

Mortimer, Wyndham. 1972. *Organize: My Life as a Union Man*. Boston: Beacon Press.
Mosely, Leonard. 1974. *The Reich Marshall: A Biography of Hermann Goering*. Garden City, N.Y.: Doubleday.
———. 1978. *Dulles: A Biography of Eleanor, Allen, and John Foster Dulles and Their Family Network*. New York: Dial Press.
Mueller, Ingo. 1991. *Hitler's Justice: The Courts of the Third Reich*. Translated by Deborah Lucas Schneider with an introduction by Detlev Vagts. Cambridge: Harvard University Press.
Murray, Charles. 1984. *Losing Ground: American Social Policy, 1950–1980*. New York: HarperCollins.
Musicant, Ivan. 1990. *The Banana Wars: A History of United States Military Intervention in Latin America from the Spanish-American War to the Invasion of Panama*. New York: Macmillan.
Myrdal, Gunnar. 1944. *An American Dilemma: The Negro Problem and Modern Democracy*. With the assistance of Richard Sternert and Arnold Rose. New York: Harper Brothers.
Myrdal, Jan. 1965. *Chinese Journey*. New York: Pantheon Books.
Nash, Gerald D. 1968. *United States Oil Policy, 1890–1964*. Pittsburgh: University of Pittsburgh Press.
National Commission on the Causes and Prevention of Violence. 1969. Washington, D.C.: U.S. Government Printing Office.
Nelson, Steve, James Barrett, and Rob Ruck. 1981. *Steve Nelson: American Radical*. Pittsburgh: University of Pittsburgh Press.
Newfield, Jack, and Paul Du Brul. 1977. *The Abuse of Power: The Permanent Government and the Fall of New York*. New York: Viking Press.
Nichols, A. Alden. 1968. *Germany After Bismarck: The Caprivi Era*. New York: W. W. Norton.
Nietzsche, Friedrich. 1990. *Twilight of the Idols*. Translated by R. J. Hollingdale. London: Penguin Books. Originally published in 1889.
Nixon, Richard. 1978. *RN: The Memoirs of Richard Nixon*. New York: Grosset and Dunlap.
Omissi, David E. 1990. *Air Power and Colonial Control: The Royal Air Force, 1919–1939*. Manchester: Manchester University Press.
Parsons, Talcott. 1968. *The Structure of Social Action*. 2 vols. New York: Free Press. Originally published in 1937.
Patterson, Orlando. 1997. *The Ordeal of Integration: Progress and Resentment in America's "Racial Crisis."* Washington, D.C.: Civitas/Counterpoint.
Pelling, Henry. 1976. *A History of British Trade Unionism*. 3rd rev. ed. Harmondsworth, U.K.: Penguin Books.
Penrose, Edith. 1980. *The Theory of the Growth of the Firm*. White Plains, N.Y.: M. E. Sharpe.
Perlman, Selig. 1949. *A Theory of the Labor Movement*. New York: Augustus M. Kelley. Originally published in 1928.
Persico, Joseph. 1990. *Casey: From the OSS to the CIA*. New York: Viking.
Pethybridge, Roger. W. 1966. *A History of Postwar Russia*. New York: New American Library.
Pfeffer, Richard, ed. 1968. *No More Vietnams: The War and the Future of American Foreign Policy*. New York: Harper and Row.

Phillips, Kevin. 1982. *Post-conservative America: People, Politics, and Ideology in a Time of Crisis.* New York: Random House.

———. 1990. *The Politics of Rich and Poor: Wealth and the American Electorate in the Reagan Aftermath.* New York: Random House.

Phillips-Fein, Kim. 2008. *Invisible Hands: The Making of the Conservative Movement from the New Deal to Reagan.* New York: W. W. Norton.

Platt, Anthony, ed. 1971. *The Politics of Riot Commissions, 1917–70: A Collection of Official Reports and Essays.* New York: Collier Books.

Pogue, Forrest. 1963. *George C. Marshall.* With the editorial assistance of Gordon Harrison. New York: Viking Press.

Pollack, Norman. 1962. *The Populist Response to Industrial America: Midwestern Populist Thought.* Cambridge: Harvard University Press.

Popper, Karl. 1967. *The Poverty of Historicism.* New York: Harper and Row. Originally published in 1957.

Poulanztzas, Nicos. 1975. *Classes in Contemporary Capitalism.* London: New Left Books.

Powers, Richard Gid. 1987. *Secrecy and Power: The Life of J. Edgar Hoover.* New York: Free Press.

Prados, John. 1991. *Keepers of the Keys: A History of the National Security Council from Truman to Bush.* New York: William Morrow.

———. 1995. *The Hidden History of the Vietnam War.* Chicago: Ivan R. Dee.

Prange, Gordon W. 1982. *At Dawn We Slept: The Untold Story of Pearl Harbor.* In collaboration with Donald M. Goldstein and Katherine V. Dillon. Harmondsworth, U.K.: Penguin Books.

Preston, Paul. 1994. *Franco: A Biography.* New York: Basic Books.

Putnam, Robert. 2000. *Bowling Alone: The Collapse and Revival of American Community.* New York: Simon and Schuster.

Reich, Robert B. 1991. *The Work of Nations: Preparing Ourselves for 21st Century Capitalism.* New York: Alfred A. Knopf.

Report of the National Advisory Commission on Civil Disorders. 1968. New York: Bantam Books. The Kerner Report.

Ridgway, James. 1968. *The Closed Corporation: American Universities in Crisis.* New York: Random House.

Riis, Jacob. 1890. *How the Other Half Lives.* Repr., New York: Dover Books, 1971.

Rings, Werner. 1982. *Life with the Enemy: Collaboration and Resistance in Hitler's Europe, 1939–1945.* Translated by J. Maxwell Brownjohn. Garden City, N.Y.: Doubleday.

Romerstein, Herbert, and Eric Breindel. 2000. *The Venona Secrets: Exposing Soviet Espionage and America's Traitors.* Washington, D.C.: Regnery Publishers.

Roskill, Stephen. 1968. *Naval Policy Between the Wars.* Vol. 1, *The Period of Anglo-American Antagonism.* London: Walker.

Ross, Robert, and Kent C. Trachte. 1990. *Global Capitalism: The New Leviathan.* Albany: State University of New York Press.

Rossino, Alexander. 2003. *Hitler Strikes Poland: Blitzkrieg, Ideology, and Atrocity.* Lawrence: University of Kansas Press.

Rossiter, Clinton, ed. 1961. *The Federalist Papers.* New York: New American Library.

Rothschild, Emma. 1973. *Paradise Lost: The Decline of the Auto-Industrial Age.* New York: Random House.

Rubinstein, William D. 1997. *The Myth of Rescue: Why the Democracies Could Not Have Saved More Jews from the Nazis*. London: Routledge.
Rudé, George. 1964. *Revolutionary Europe, 1783–1815*. Cleveland: Meridian Books.
Rudoren, Jodi. 2006. "Inquiry Finds Police Abuse, but Says Law Bars Trial: Prosecutors in Chicago Cite Limitations." *New York Times*, July 20, A13.
Sacchetti, Maria. 2009. "Jailed Immigrants Buoy Budgets: U.S. Pays Sheriffs $90 Per Day to Hold Those Awaiting Deportation" *Boston Globe*, February 9, A1.
Santos, Fernanda. 2007. "Free and Uneasy: A Year in the World." *New York Times*, November 25, A1.
Sassoon, Donald. 1996. *One Hundred Years of Socialism: The West European Left in the Twentieth Century*. New York: New Press.
Schlatter, Richard. 1973. *Private Property: The History of an Idea*. New York: Russell and Russell.
Schlesinger, Stephen, and Stephen Kinzer. 1982. *Bitter Fruit: The Untold Story of the American Coup in Guatemala*. With an introduction by Harrison Salisbury. Garden City: Doubleday.
Schorske, Carl. 1980. *Fin-de-Siècle Vienna: Politics and Culture*. New York: Alfred A. Knopf.
Schumpeter, Joseph A. 1962. *Capitalism, Socialism, and Democracy*. 3rd ed. New York: Harper and Row. Originally published in 1942.
Scott, John Anthony, ed. 1967. *The Defense of Gracchus Babeuf Before the High Court of Vendôme*. Translated by John Anthony Scott. Amherst: University of Massachusetts Press.
Seahill, Jeremy. 2007. *Blackwater: The Rise of the World's Most Powerful Mercenary Army*. London: Serpent's Tail.
Serrin, William. 1970. *The Company and the Union: The "Civilized Relationship" of the General Motors Corporation and the United Automobile Workers*. New York: Vintage Books.
———. 1992. *Homestead: The Glory and the Tragedy of an American Steel Town*. New York: Random House, Times Books.
Shannon, David A. 1955. *The Socialist Party in America: A History*. New York: Macmillan.
Shelby, Tommie. 2006. *We Who Are Dark: The Philosophical Foundations of Black Solidarity*. Cambridge: Harvard University Press, Belknap Press.
Shipler, David. 2004. *The Working Poor: Invisible in America*. New York: Alfred A. Knopf.
Shirer, William L. 1960. *The Rise and Fall of the Third Reich: A History of Nazi Germany*. New York: Simon and Schuster.
———. 1971. *The Collapse of the Third Republic: An Inquiry into the Fall of France in 1940*. New York: Pocket Books.
Sinclair, Andrew. 1981. *Corsair: The Life of J. Pierpont Morgan*. Boston: Little, Brown.
Singer, P. W. 2003. *Corporate Warriors: The Rise of the Privatized Military Industry*. Ithaca: Cornell University Press.
Skocpol, Theda. 1987. "Bringing the State Back In: Strategies of Analysis in Current Research." In *Bringing the State Back In*, edited by Peter B. Evans, Dietrich Rueschmayer, and Theda Skocpol. Cambridge: Cambridge University Press.
Skolnick, Jerome H., and James Fyfe. 1993. *Above the Law: Police and the Excessive Use of Force*. New York: Free Press.

Slack, Donovan. 2009. "Even Small Localities Got Big Guns." *Boston Globe*, June 15, A1.

Slack, Donovan, and Suzanne Smalley. 2005. "Penalties Are Light for Police Charged with Misconduct." *Boston Globe*, October 12, A1.

Sloan, Alfred. 1964. *My Years at General Motors*. New York: Doubleday.

Smalley, Suzanne, and Shelley Murphy. 2006. "Officer Arrested in Drug, Theft Ring: Lesser Charges for Two Others on Boston Force." *Boston Globe*, July 21, A1.

Sombart, Werner. 1976. *Why Is There No Socialism in the United States?* White Plains, N.Y.: International Arts and Sciences Press. Originally published in 1906.

South, Nigel. 1988. *Policing for Profit: The Private Security Sector*. London: Sage Publications.

Stafford, David. 2008. *Endgame, 1945: The Missing Final Chapter of World War II*. Boston: Little, Brown.

Starobin, Robert S. 1970. *Industrial Slavery in the Old South*. New York: Oxford University Press.

Statistical Abstract of the United States. 2006. Washington, D.C.: U.S. Government Printing Office.

Stern, Fritz. 1977. *Gold and Iron: Bismarck, Bleichroeder, and the Building of the German Empire*. New York: Alfred A. Knopf.

Stiglitz, Joseph E. 2009. "Obama's Ersatz Capitalism." *New York Times*, April 1, A25.

Stone, Katherine. 1975. "The Origins of Job Structures in the Steel Industry." In *Labor Market Segmentation*, edited by R. Edwards, M. Reich, and D. Gordon. Lexington, Mass.: D. C. Heath.

———. 2004. *From Widgets to Digits: Employment Regulation for the Changing Workplace*. Cambridge: Cambridge University Press.

Strong, Herbert, ed. 1985. *The Anti-Federalists*. Chicago: University of Chicago Press.

Sullivan, Patricia. 2009. Obituary: "Edward Hanrahan: Oversaw Black Panther Raid." *Boston Globe*, June 13, B9.

Tachibanaki, Oshiaki, and Tomohiko Noda. 2000. *The Economic Effects of Trade Unions in Japan*. London: Palgrave Macmillan.

Taubman, William. 2003. *Khrushchev: The Man and His Era*. New York: W. W. Norton.

Taylor, Benjamin J., and Fred Witney. 1987. *Labor Relations Law*. 5th ed. Englewood Cliffs, N.J.: Prentice-Hall.

Taylor, Frederick. 1967. *The Principles of Scientific Management*. New York: W. W. Norton. Originally published in 1911.

Thompson, Edward. 1966. *The Making of the English Working Class*. New York: Vintage.

Todd, Chuck, and Sheldon Gawiser. 2009. *How Barack Obama Won: A State-by-State Guide to the Historic 2008 Presidential Election*. New York: Vintage Books.

Tomlins, Christopher. 1985. *The State and the Unions: Labor Relations, Law, and the Organized Labor Movement in America*. Cambridge: Cambridge University Press.

Turner, Frederick Jackson. 1975. *The Frontier in American History*. Huntington, N.Y.: R. E. Krieger. Originally published in 1920.

Turner, Henry Ashby, Jr. 1996. *Hitler's Thirty Days to Power: January 1933*. Reading, Mass.: Addison-Wesley.
Tusa, Ann, and John Tusa. 1984. *The Nuremberg Trial*. New York: Atheneum.
United Nations. 2003. *International Migration, Health, and Human Rights*. Health and Human Rights Publications Series. December. New York: United Nations.
Urbina, Ian, and Sean D. Hamill. 2009. "Judges Plead Guilty in Payoffs for Jailing Youths." *New York Times*, February 13, A1.
Utley, Jonathan G. 1985. *Going to War with Japan, 1937–1941*. Knoxville: University of Tennessee Press.
Valencia, Milton J., and Jenna Nierstedt. 2009. "Many Hub Teens Surveyed Say Rihanna Is at Fault for Assault." *Boston Globe*, March 13, B2.
Van Natta, Don. 1996. "Judge Baer Takes Himself off Drug Case." *New York Times*, May 17, B1.
Velebit, Vladimir. 1987. *Yugoslavia in the Second World War*. Translated by Kordija Kveder. Belgrade: Jugoslovenska Revija (Belgrade Review).
Waite, Robert. 1952. *Vanguard of Nazism: The Free Corps Movement in Post-War Germany, 1918–1923*. New York: W. W. Norton.
Watt, Donald Cameron. 1989. *How War Came: The Immediate Origins of the Second World War, 1938–1939*. New York: Pantheon Books.
Watt, Richard M. 1979. *Bitter Glory: Poland and Its Fate, 1918–1939*. New York: Simon and Schuster.
Weber, Max. 1968. *Industry and Society: An Outline of Interpretive Sociology*. Edited by Guenther Roth and Claus Wittrich, with various translators. Vol. 1. New York: Bedminster Press. Originally published in German in 1954.
Wedderburn, K. W. 1972. *Industrial Conflict: A Comparative Legal Survey*. New York: Crane and Russak.
Weiler, Paul. 1983. "Promises to Keep: Securing Workers' Rights to Self-Organization Under the NLRA." *Harvard Law Review* 96, no. 8 (June): 1769–1827.
Westmoreland, William C. 1976. *A Soldier Reports*. Garden City, N.Y.: Doubleday.
Wheeler-Bennett, John W. 1964. *The Nemesis of Power: The German Army in Politics, 1918–1945*. 2nd ed. London: Macmillan. Originally published in 1953.
White, Ben. 2009. "What Red Ink? Wall St. Paid Hefty Bonuses." *New York Times*, January 29, A1.
Wiebe, Robert H. 1967. *The Search for Order, 1897–1920*. New York: Hill and Wang.
Wilson, Edmund. 1953. *To the Finland Station: A Study in the Writing and Acting of History*. Garden City, N.Y.: Doubleday. Originally published in 1940.
Wilson, William Julius. 1987. *The Truly Disadvantaged: The Inner City, the Underclass, and Public Policy*. Chicago: University of Chicago Press.
Winters, Paul A., ed. 1995. *Policing the Police*. An Opposing Viewpoint Series. San Diego, Calif.: Greenhaven Press.
Woodward, C. Vann. 1963. *Tom Watson, Agrarian Rebel*. Oxford: Oxford University Press.
Woolf, S. J., ed. 1969. *European Fascism*. New York: Vintage.
Wright, Erik Olin. 1978. *Class, Crisis, and the State*. London: New Left Books.
———. 1984. "A General Framework for the Analysis of Class Structure." *Politics and Society* 13, no. 4: 384–423.
Wrigley, Chris. 1997. *British Trade Unions, 1945–1995*. Manchester: Manchester University Press.

Yellen, Samuel. 1974. *American Labor Struggles, 1877–1934*. New York: Monad Press.

Zakaria, Fareed. 2008. *The Post-American World*. New York: W. W. Norton.

Zimbalist, Andrew, ed. 1979. *Case Studies on the Labor Process*. New York: Monthly Review Press.

Zinn, Howard. 1959. *La Guardia in Congress*. Ithaca: Cornell University Press.

Index

Abrams, Elliott, 209, 211
Abu Ghraib, 411
Acheson, Dean, 175, 211
ADA (Americans for Democratic Action), 449 n. 5
Addams, Jane, 16, 146
Afghanistan
  fundamentalists in, 448 n. 15
  U.S. aggressiveness against, 78, 402–3
AFL (American Federation of Labor), 329
AFL-CIO, 322, 325, 329, 334, 375
Africa
  assistance for, 375
  globalization failure in, 362
  international government power over, 363
  and international system of state rights, 397–98
  military rule in, 369
  U.S.-Soviet rivalry for, 370–71
agency government in democracies
  anti-democratic forces within, 205–7
  by assent, not consent, 119–20, 193–94
  decent people within, 194, 213
  and ineffective democratic process, 387–89
  minority rule of, 195–99
  paradox of, 193–94, 212–13
  versus parliamentary procedure, 383
  party collusion within, 199–201
  state system in, 207–12
  voting issues in, 194–96, 203–5
agglomeration of corporations, 176, 295–96
air-traffic controller union, 84
Al Qaeda
  Saudi relationship with, 369
  Western focus on, 357
Aldermaston Marches, 227–28, 377
Amalgamated Association of Iron and Steel Workers, 22
American Federation of Labor (AFL), 329
Americanist society
  development from, 13–14
  dominance over Bismarckian society, 44–45
  and life courses, 127
  meritocratic character of, 147–49
  as post-war restructuring force, 45–46

Americans for Democratic Action (ADA), 449 n. 5
anarchy, capitalism as font of, 357–58
Angola, 370, 448 n. 18
Annan, Kofi, 379
anti-abortion drive, 110, 112
anticolonial activism, 58
antidiscrimination laws, 350–52, 353–55
apartheid, 371, 377
Argentine Air Force, 369–70
Aristotle, 15–16, 34–35, 127–28
Arrow, Kenneth, 194
assent versus consent among the governed, 194
auction model of mainstream economics, 143–44
authoritarian regimes, 106–7, 372
auto industry, 21, 25–26, 305, 322, 323, 327

Babeuf, Gracchus, 15–16, 18
Baer, George F., Jr., 441 n. 7
Baer, Harold, Jr., 428 n. 41
"balancing" class, 24, 34–35, 127–28
Balkan ethnic cleansing, 376
Balkans, international government power over, 363
Ban Ki-moon, 379
bank industry bailout, 436 n. 1
Barkin, David, 445 n. 25
Bartels, 424 n. 6
Basque ETA, 357
Beaumarchais, Pierre, 17
Bell, Daniel, 65–66, 67, 68, 71, 72
Berle, Adolf A., 293–95, 304
Berle, Peter, 294
Bernanke, Benjamin, 3
Bernstein, Eduard, 28
Bernstein, Leonard, 17
bias, effect on education, 335
Bilbo, Theodore, 407
Bill of Rights, 449 n. 14
Bismarckian society
  dynastic organization of, 420 n. 25
  failure of, 44–45
  and modernization, 372
  restraints on development, 13–14

Black, Hugo, 245–46
black Americans
    activism and police power response, 96–100
    antidiscrimination legislation for, 93–95
    bipartisan policy on, 78
    Black Power activism, 74, 99
    corporate (group) treatment of, 93–95
    elite class neglect of, 106
    in the military, 390
    and political system failure, 389–93
    slavery, effect on, 92–93
    and social mobility, 87–88, 91–96
    votes of, 204
Black Panthers, 99
Blanqui, Louis Auguste, 16
Blum, Leon, 21
Board of Education, Brown v., 390–91, 393
"bowling alone," 448 n. 2
boycotts, 306, 337, 338
Bretton Woods fixed exchange rates, 57, 83–84
Brewster, Owen, 408
Britain
    and Campaign for Nuclear Disarmament, 227–28, 376
    Labour Party in, 56
broadcast advertising, 202, 203
Brogan, Tom, 237
Brown, Henry Phelps, 82
Brown v. Board of Education, 390–91, 393
Brzezinski, Zbigniew, 426 n. 24, 448 nn. 2, 15
Büchner, Georg, 17
Bureau of Corporations, 289
Burke, Edmund, 15, 182, 207
Bush family, 176
Bush (George W.) administration
    and 2008 economic crisis, 3
    fundamentalist voter support of, 426 n. 27
    noneconomic issues of, 206
    and police power, 282
    and social irresponsibility, 176
    social irresponsibility of, 208–9, 212
    war-making power of, 397, 404
business elites, integration of, 174

cadre class of middle-level workers. *See also* middle classes
    consumption discipline imposed on, 368–69
    democracy, changed attitude toward, 374
    elites, alliance with, 371–72
    at international level, 363–66, 366–69, 371–74
    and international polity, 377
    life course of, 49–50, 86–87, 132
    in organizational structure, 30–31, 33–34, 132
    politics of, 366–69, 377
    transnational culture of, 358–59
    welfare state, reversal on, 225
    worker education and socialization formed by, 42
Cady Stanton, Elizabeth, 227
Califano, Joseph A., 98
Callaghan, James, 326
Campaign for Nuclear Disarmament (CND), 227–28, 376
Canada and land mine treaty, 376
capitalism
    as disintegrative force, 23
    as form of government, 357–58
    impoverishment caused by, 368
    integrative effect of, 23
career and life courses, 130–31
Carnegie Steel strike, 22
Carter administration, 426 n. 24
Casey, William, 208–9, 211
Cassirer, Ernst, 67
CCC (Civilian Conservation Corps), 349
censorship, 104
Center for Constitutional Rights, 375
centralized financial control system, 25–26
Chad, 370
Chaney, James, 257, 439 n. 4
Chekhov, Anton, 19
child-rearing, 134–36
Chile, globalization constituency in, 367
China
    authoritarian, ultranationalist regime in, 372
    cold war potential with U.S., 372–73, 400–401
    consumption discipline in, 368
    and U.S. relations, 396
Church committee, 282
CIO (Congress of Industrial Organizations), 322
civic institutions, corporations as, 292–98
civil disobedience, 393
civil rights movement
    activism for, 54
    Brown v. Board of Education, 390–93
    and civil disobedience, 393
    deaths for, 423 n. 19, 439 n. 4
    and incorporation of black Americans, 95–96

Klan outreach, 245–46
Nixon platform of slowing, 50
and worldwide dissident activism, 58
"civil society," 377–78
Civilian Conservation Corps (CCC), 349
civilians, violence against, 381–82, 410–12
class
  analysis of, 141–47
  corporate-directed education effect on, 40–42
  and family, 35–39
  feminism's effect on, 36–37
  institutions' effect on, 37–38
  nineteen-century health differences in, 145–46
  number of in society, 125–30
  and race, 43
  theory, 123
clearance rates for police investigations, 258
Clifford, Clark, 163
Clinton, Bill, 428 n. 41
CND (Campaign for Nuclear Disarmament), 227–28, 376
coarse planning, 316–18
cold war
  bipartisan collusion in, 393
  with China, potential for, 400–401
  foreign policy formulation, 52, 190, 211
  and peace efforts, 376
  Sixties perspective on, 68
  trade union international activities during, 375
"common sense," 33
communism
  communist parties, 74, 239
  consumption discipline imposed by, 368–69
  in France, 21
  loyalty oath against, ix, 422 n. 16
  social services provided by, 368–69
  and trade unions, 375
conflict
  elite class, conflict resolution within, 136–37, 157–58, 163–65, 178
  engine of progress in Democracy, 231
  nonantagonistic, in Staff for the Advance, 244
Congo, Republic of, 58, 370
Congress of Industrial Organizations (CIO), 322
consensus building, 232–34
consent versus assent among the governed, 194
conservative ascendancy, 77

conservative foundations, 79
conservative parties, noneconomic issues of, 205–6, 213
Constitution
  authority of and the international state system, 414
  framing of, 210
  and war-making power, 403–6
consumption discipline, imposition of, 368–69
consumption patterns of transnational cadre class, 364–65
corporate boards, 310–11
corporate charters, 305–10, 311–13, 331–32
corporate elites, 79–81, 139–40
corporations
  agglomeration of, 176, 295–96
  charters for, 305–10
  as civic institutions, 292–98
  corporate boards, 310–11
  cultural effect of, 26
  in economy, 315–18
  and ethics, 313–15
  and investors, 301–2
  and management profession creation, 313–15
  and managerial behavior, 313–15
  manager-operated, 293–98
  modern form of, 225
  power of, 176–77, 292–93
  private property, confiscation of, 300–302
  reforms attempted, 289–92
  reforms proposed, 302–5
  representation problem, 302–4
  self-interest of, 224
  as social and political institutions, 299–302
  and social surplus, 302–3
  social system created by, 29–32, 286–88
countervailing institutions, 289
craft unions, 322, 329–31
crafts workers, 419 n. 15
criminalization of some government actions, 410–13
Cuba, consumption discipline in, 368
Cuban airline hijacking, 448 n. 14
Cuban Missile Crisis, x, 63, 64, 393
Cultural Contradictions of Capitalism (Bell), 64–65
Czechoslovakia, 421 n. 5

day labor, 348–49
De Gia, Ralph, 63
Debs, Eugene V., 16

Defense Department, 29
Dellinger, David, 63
Democracy
  activists in U.S., 16–17
  agency government in, 387–89
  axis of advance of, 18
  and "civil society," 377–78
  culture of, 17–19
  efforts to support in semifabricated society, 226–27
  evolution of, 14–17
  favoritism of institutions built into, 186–87
  federalist forces within, 205–7
  and institutional representation, 215–17
  limits pressed during Sixties, 52–53
  lower class entry into culture, 4
  negative results of, 17
  participatory, 232–34
  representation, paradox of, 191–92
  revolutionary character of, 15–16
  state system in, 207–12
  U.S. overseas policies impeding, 371–74
  vanguard parties in, 238–40
"democratic dilemma," 393–95
Democratic Party
  antidemocratic tendencies of, 208
  Chicago Convention (1968), 99
  divisions within, 101, 234–36, 236–37
  in New York State, 236–37
  Nixon support from, 56
  Wanderable and Golden Age types, 234–36
democratic task organizations
  class divisions in, 242–43
  conventional forms of, 230–31
  creation of, 230
Department of Labor, 289–90
detective forces, private, 256
"deterrence" in U.S. nuclear program, 180
Devillers, Philippe, 422 n. 14
Diem, Ngo Dinh, 434 n. 5
discriminating power in corporations, 139–40
discrimination laws, 350–52, 353–55
district voting, 196–97
"divine right," 395–400
division of labor. *See* triadic division of labor
Dobrynin, Anatoly, 396, 449 n. 6
Doctors Without Borders, 375
domestic security. *See* police power
Don Carlos (Schiller), 18
Douglass, Frederick, 428 n. 43
drugs, war on, 102–5, 446 n. 28

dual economy, 30
Duff, Peggy, 227–29, 422 n. 16
Dulles brothers, 211
DuPont, 26
DuPont, Pierre, 297
dynastic power, 35–39, 172–73, 420 n. 25

economic crisis
  in 1970s, 79–81
  in 1980s, 81–83
  in 2008, 2–3
economic development
  international civil society involvement in, 382–84
  world government influence on, 360–61
economic growth and social mobility, 88–91
Economics in Real Time (McDermott), 125
economist approach to social stratification, 127
economy, cooperative nature of, 316–18
educational system
  and *Brown v. Board of Education*, 390–91
  consumption discipline assisting, 368
  corporate form of, 39–42, 43
  and influence from Intersection society, 171–72
  as "investment," 301
  multiple hierarchies within, 138–39
  nationalistic nature of, 399
  school boards, 273
  and social mobility, 89–90, 91, 136
  transnational homogenization of, 364–65
  university system in U.S., 71–73
  of working class, 19, 332–35
Einstein, Albert, 17
Eisenhower, Milton, 98
Eisenhower administration, 391–92, 393
Eisenhower Report, 98, 100, 106, 109
elder activism, 59
elected government and inner government, 393–95
election process for Senate, 407–8
elite class
  class consciousness of, 432 n. 13
  clustered advantages of, 157–58
  collaboration within, 136–37
  conflict resolution within, 136–37, 157–58, 163–65, 178
  in conflict with nonelite social groupings, 169–71
  and constitutional authority, 414
  discrediting of opposition, 214
  division of labor within, 172–76
  and dynastic power, 35–39, 172–73

essential social action by, 118–19
fight for own interests by, 189–91
foreign policy exclusive prerogative of, 78
grounding in contemporary society, 6
and institutional power, 38
integration of, 172–76
and Intersection society, 171–72
irresponsible use of power by, 154–55, 176–77
middle class alliance with, 371–72
and modernization, 373–74
necessity of, 154–57
and neglect of race issues, 105–6
opposition to historic advance, 50
outcomes dependent on, 165
power wielded by, 166–67
and property ownership, 125–30
in relation to the poor, 35
in Senate, 407–8
social relationships of, 159–60, 162–63, 165–66
social responsibility of, 154–57
socially potent assets of, 157–58
as social-scale group, 151–54
subsocieties within, 158–61, 162–63
and training of working class, 419 n. 23
and Vietnam policy-making, 56
war, ability to get support for, 208
wealth of maintained during economic crisis, 2–3
empire as threat to republic institutions, 413–15
employment at will, 320–21
employment reform
community/regional representation, 336–39
and the corporate charter, 331
elimination of low-wage jobs, 345–48
for ex-convicts, 352–55
and immigrants, treatment of, 350–52
and wider vocational representation, 332–36
work as natural right, 341–45
work on demand, 348–50
END (European Nuclear Disarmament), 376
engineering workforce, 33, 40–42
Enlightenment, 110, 299, 373, 378
Enron, 176
equality in opportunities, 171–72
ETA, 357
ethnic cleansing, 376
European Nuclear Disarmament (END), 376
European Union, 376, 383
exceptionalism, 19–23

ex-convicts, employment of, 352–55
expressive organizations, 229–30, 232
extraparliamentary activism, 53–57
EXXON, 26

Fabian society, 20
fabricated corporate society, 5, 181, 226–27
Falklands War, 369, 370
Fall of the House of Labor, The (Montgomery), 18
false consciousness, 179
family and class, 35–39
Farewell to the Working Class (Gorz), 21
farmer immigrants, 418 n. 10
fascism, 372
fear and social stability, 179, 180–81
Federal Aviation Administration, 29
Federal Bureau of Investigation (FBI), 210, 251, 255, 280, 283
Federal Reserve, 188, 443 n. 24
Federal Reserve System, 210
federalist forces in democracies, 205–7
feminism, 36–37, 59
feudalism
  absence of in U.S., 20
  influence in U.S. work codes, 92–93
  and property ownership, 127
financial policy, 188
Finland, authoritarian regime in, 372
Fisk, Jim, 293
Fogelson, Robert, 257, 439 n. 8
Food and Drug Authority, 29
Fordism, 419 n. 14
formal ideology in social stability, 178–79
Founding Fathers, intentions of, 182, 200, 207
Fox News, 206
France
  communism in, 21
  socialism in, 20
  war crime tribunal participation, 448 n. 17
franchised retailers, wages from, 337–39
free labor, 320–21
"free market," skewed in favor of developed countries, 368
French Revolution, 16, 18, 53, 56, 126
Frick, Henry Clay, 293
Friedman, Milton, 294, 342, 343
frontier, influence of, 20
Fulbright, J. William, 55, 408
fundraising, political, 201–3

G-8 (Group of Eight), 357, 360, 379, 380
Galbraith, John Kenneth, 289, 294
Gates, Bill, 307

gay bashing, 191
gay marriage, 110
gay student activism, 51
Gaza, 382
Geithner, Timothy, 3
gender
 roles shaped by Intersection society, 42–43, 173–74
 in "worker" history, 18–19
General Electric (GE), 27, 31, 328
General Motors (GM), 25–26, 27, 31, 322
George III, 210
Germany
 civil police in, 106
 educational system of, 32, 42
 and failure of Bismarckian society, 44–45
 fascist regime in, 372
 labor force of, 32
 military society in, 126
 socialism in, 20
 state system in, 398–99
 Vatican post-war influence, 420 n. 32
Gideonse, Harry, ix, 427 n. 34
Gitlin, Todd, 61, 62
global warming, 393
globalization. *See also* international inner government
 constituency formed by, 366–69
 counter-movement proposed, 379–84
 and economies of nation-states, 358, 360–61
 failure of in Africa and Latin America, 362
 international government facilitation of, 362
 and master-servant relations, 418 n. 3
 and production dispersion, 81–83, 358, 362
GM (General Motors), 25–26, 27, 31, 322
Goodman, Andrew, 257, 439 n. 4
Gorz, André, 21
Gramsci, Antonio, 168
Great Britain, war crime tribunal participation, 448 n. 17
great rail strike (1877), 254, 255
Greece
 authoritarian, ultranationalist regime in, 372
 historical preservation in, 376
 military rule in, 370
 social democratic party in, 376
 Western intervention in (1947–48), 446 n. 4
Greenspan, Alan, 443 n. 24
Greider, William, 188, 313, 315

group interests formed by social action, 170
Group of Eight (G-8), 357, 360, 379, 380
Guantanamo Bay, 411
Guatemala
 trade unions in, 375
 U.S. intervention in (1954), 446 n. 4
Gulf War, 153

Hampton, Fred, 99
Hardie, Keir, 227
Harriman, Averell, 175, 237
Harrington, Michael, 438 n. 13
Hay, John, 211
Hayden, Casey, 422 n. 16
Hayek, Friedrich, 117, 161, 247, 299, 300, 301–2
Haymarket Massacre, 337
health care, workers in, 333–34, 335
health differences based on class, 145–46
health insurance, 442 n. 20
Hearst, William Randolph, 293
Hearst press, 206
Heath, Edward, 326
Helms, Jesse, 197–98, 407, 408
Helsinki Treaty, 376
Higgins wage, 319, 341–42, 345–48
Hillberg, Raoul, 448 n. 16
hiring
 economic effects on, 344–45
 during WWII, 344
historic advance
 activism for during Sixties, 52–53
 "Americanist" pattern of social development, 13–14
 changes resulting from, 14
 conditions prior to, 13–14
 dominance over Bismarckian society, 44–45
 halting of, 46–47, 78, 116
 modernization, impeded by, 371–74
 rise and decline of, 3–4
 Staff for the Advance proposed for, 241–46
 U.S. overseas policies impeding, 371–74
Holocaust (Jewish Catastrophe), 252, 376, 398
Homestead Lockout, 22, 30
Hopkins, Harry, 213
Horn, Gerd-Rainer, 52
Horton, Miles, 245
House of Representatives, limited balancing power of, 407
Howard, Roy, 434 n. 5
Howe, Irving, 71

Human Rights Watch, 18, 375
humane international change, 374–78
Hungary, authoritarian regime in, 372
Hutcheson, Bill, 330

IACP (International Association of Chiefs of Police), 257
IBEW (International Brotherhood of Electrical Workers), 329
Ibsen, Henrik, 19
ignorance among voters, 203–5
illegal immigrants, 350–52
IMF (International Monetary Fund), 357, 360, 379, 380
Imhoff, James, 407
immigrant labor force, 32–34, 182, 350–52
inalienable employee rights, 355
Inciardi, James A., 427 n. 30
income distribution, 367–68
independent voters, 203–5
industrial unions, 320–25, 419 n. 15
industry, nationalization of, 21–22
inequality of reward system, 171–72
inertia in social stability, 178
inflation
   in 1960s and 1970s, 57, 81
   and unemployment, 342
infrastructure, public investment in, 300
inmates
   employment training for, 352–55
   normal relationships for, 354
   recidivism rates of, 354
inner government. *See* international inner government
"insider information," overrated status of, 433 n. 2
institutional representation and democracy, 215–17
institutions
   and class, 37–38
   disfunctionality of, 214–15
   government assistance for, 198
   insider status of in liberal democracy, 186–87
instrumental organizations, 229–30
integrative social system, 23, 42, 141
International Association of Chiefs of Police (IACP), 257
International Brotherhood of Electrical Workers (IBEW), 329
International Catholic Relief Services, 375
international civil society, 377–78, 381, 382–84

International Far Eastern War Crimes tribunal, 448 n. 17
international inner government
   counter-movement proposed, 379–84
   development of, 360
   domestic security (police power), 188
   economic influence of, 360–61
   and elected government, 212–13, 393–95
   and elite class, 213–14
   globalization, facilitation of, 362
   high financial policy of, 188
   international and national security, 188
   lawlessness of, 357–59
   national sovereignties, power over, 363
   opportunity to reduce power of, 400–403
   political structure of, 362–63
   preferences of, 361
   public public versus private public, 187–91
International Monetary Fund (IMF), 357, 360, 379, 380
international policy, underdevelopment of, 359
international polity, 374–78
international relationships, 366
International Typographical Union, 330
International Union of Electrical Workers (IUE), 328
internships for growth of democracy, 244
interpersonal relationships versus social relationships, 159–60
Intersection society
   and class mobility, 37
   and the elites, 171–72
   and force for social stability, 182–83
   gender roles, shaping of, 42–43
   and life courses, 136–37
   life courses set by, 5, 40–41, 70–71
   multiple hierarchies within, 138–39
   school system, influence on, 171–72
   Sixties resistance to, 53, 69–73
   socially potent asset in, 117–18
   Staff for the Advance approach to, 246–49
   and triadic division of labor, 136–37
   and worker education, 39–42
inter-war period, 371–72
investment choices in transnational culture, 366
Iran, Anglo-U.S. intervention in (1953), 446 n. 4
Iran-Contra Scandal, 208–9
Iraq, 27, 78, 176, 215, 310, 402–3
Islamic terrorism, 403. *See also* terrorism

isolationism, 190
Israel, 382
Italy
　fascist regime in, 372
　socialism in, 20–21
　trade unions in, 375
IUE (International Union of Electrical Workers), 328

Jackson, Jesse, 235
Japan
　"Americanist" pattern of social development in, 13, 14
　authoritarian, ultranationalist regime in, 372
　under early Occupation, 420 n. 31
　and war crime tribunal, 448 n. 17
Jewish Catastrophe (Holocaust), 252, 376, 398
Johnson administration, 97–98, 391
jury panel system
　for corporate board, 311
　for police operations board, 267, 270, 272–77
　for Senate, 408–10

Kahn, Herman, 423 n. 20
Katzenbach, Nicolaus, 421 n. 5
Keller, Helen, 16
Kellog-Briand Pact (1928), 449 n. 9
Kennedy, Edward, 408
Kennedy, John F., 392
Kennedy, Robert, 55
Kenya, 370
Kerner Commission, 97, 257
Kerr, Clark, 72
Keynesian state system, 360–61
King, Rodney, 276
Kirkland, Lane, 57, 375
Kissinger, Henry, 421 n. 5, 448 n. 15
Klein, Milton, 417 n. 2
Knights of Labor, 336–38
Knowland, William F., 408
Kristol, Irving, 71
Ku Klux Klan, 245–46, 389–90, 391

La Follette, Robert, 213, 256, 408
La Guardia, Fiorello, 237 n. 9, 435 n. 13
labor force
　in conflict with elite class, 169–71
　immigrant sources of, 32
　life courses in, 130–34
　managerial class, 32–34
　natural rights of, 329–41
　production of, 134–36
　social structure of, 24–25
　specialization of, 33
　triadic division of, 24, 30–32, 128–37, 172–76, 287–88, 358–59
　Victorian versus contemporary, 142–43
　women in, 287
labor law, 133
Lafargue, Paul, 19, 227
land mine treaty, 376
Landrum-Griffith Act, 443 n. 5
language in transnational culture, 365
Latin America
　and Bismarckian society, 372
　military rule in, 369
　and Sanctuary movement, 375
　U.S. modernization policy in, 369–70
Latin America, globalization failure in, 362
Le Droit à la paresse (*The Right to Be Lazy*, Lafargue), 19
leadership in organizations, 232–34
Left parties
　in 1960s Europe, 56
　small role of in early Sixties, 63
legal norms, international enforcement of, 376
legislation and police power, 277–79
leisure, workers' right to, 19
Leninist ideology, 19, 238–40
less-developed nations, conflict of roles in, 358–59
Lewis, John, 422 n. 16
liberalism and weakening of political system, 388–89
Liberia, 370
life courses
　and career, 117, 130–31
　versus class, 141–47
　cultural revolt stemming from, 70–71
　difficulty of altering, 141–42
　institutional nature of, 136–37
　in Intersection society, 5, 40–41
　and modern division of labor, 130–34
Liggio, Leonard, 418 n. 10
Lindsay, John, 97
line personnel, 33, 240–41
Lipset, Seymour, 21, 54–55
Little Blue Books, 19
Locke, John, 340
Lowenberg, Jacob, 422 n. 16
lower class involvement in democracy, 242–43
low-wage jobs, 345–48

Madison, James, 200
Mahan, Alfred Thayer, 210, 211
Making of the English Working Class (Thompson), 19
management profession, creation of, 313–15
managerial class
  anti-democratic force of, 371–74
  behavior of, 313–15
  constituency of, 366–69
  consumption discipline imposed on, 368–69
  development of, 32–34
  education as means to enlarge, 39–42
  emergence of international level, 363–66
  nineteenth century development of, 146
  rights of management, 320–21, 325–29, 330
  transnational culture of, 358–59, 363–66
manager-operated corporations, 293–98
Mandela, Nelson, 448 n. 12
manufacturing, division of labor in, 133–34
Marcantonio, Vito, 435 n. 11
marijuana, 102–3, 446 n. 28
Marshall, George, 390
Marwick, Arthur, 52, 64
Marxist guerrilla, replacement of, 373
Marxist theory
  on capitalism and society, 247
  of class, 141, 144–45, 170–71
  on history, 372
  impoverishment caused by capitalism, 368
  social responsibility of elites, 156
  on social surplus, 125–27
master-servant labor codes, 33, 92–93, 111, 418 n. 3
McCarran, Pat, 408
McCarthy, Eugene, 55, 190
McCarthy, Joe, 407
McCloy, John, 175, 211
McDermott, John, 125
McGovern, George, 55
McReynolds, David, 63
Meany, George, 57, 375
media
  corporate effect on, 288
  and police, 258, 264
Medicare, 29
medicine, corporate form of, 43
Mellon, Andrew, 175
membership differences in organizations, 227–29, 231
meritocracy, 147–49
middle classes
  as allies of elite class, 35, 128–29
  Aristotelian "balancing" class, 24, 34–35, 127–28
  elites, alliance with, 371–72
  shift in professional composition of, 89
  in solidarity with elite versus laboring, 127–29
  transnational politics of, 366–69
Middle East, U.S. modernizing support of, 369
military force
  modernization, resistance to, 369–71
  navy, development of, 210
  personnel divisions developed in, 241
  present U.S. policy for, 401–3
  and private contractors, 27
  and racial prejudice, 390
  rule of, internationally, 369–71
  and social surplus of elites, 126–27
  spending, 29
Mill, John Stuart, 342
Mills, C. Wright, 6, 152
minimum wage, 440 n. 1
minority rule in democracy, 195–99
Mobutu, Sese Seko, 370
modern corporate firms
  impacts of, 23–25
  omnicapable corporations, development into, 25–28
modern reaction of business elites, 50
modernization
  and Bismarckian society, 372
  and creation of elites, 367
  and elite class, 373–74
  impeding historic advance, 371–74
  international polity in response to, 374–78
  and military forces, 369–71
  and poverty, 362, 368
  U.S. policy of, 369–71
money in politics, 202–3
Montgomery, David, 18
Moore, Barrington, 36
Morgan, J. P., 297
Moses, Bob, 422 n. 16, 423 n. 19
Moses, Robert, 348
motherhood, corporate influence on, 30
multiuniversity, 72
Murphy, Frank, 322, 323
Muste, A. J., 63, 422 n. 16
My Lai, 411
Myrdal, Gunnar, 390

Nader, Ralph, 235
Napoleon, 264

National Advisory Commission on Civil Disorders, 97
National Commission on the Causes and Prevention of Violence, 98
national economies, world government influence on, 360–61
National Labor Relations Board (NLRB), 289, 338
National Recovery Administration (NRA), 441 n. 4
National Rifle Association, 312
national sovereignties and international government, 363
nationalization of industry, 21–22
NATO and Balkan ethnic cleansing, 376
natural rate of unemployment, 342, 343
natural rights tradition, 329–41
natural society, 5, 120, 181, 182
Nazism, 45, 106, 189–90, 376, 398–99, 410
Nelson, Steve, 433 n. 21
Netherlands, judging at war crime tribunal, 448 n. 17
New Deal, 21, 101, 289, 349, 441 n. 4
New Left Notes, 51, 71
New York State politics, 194, 200
news reporting
  deference to inner government, 188
  and police force, 258, 264
  possibility of finding information, 187
  public public versus private public news outlets, 187
NGOs (non-governmental organizations), 375, 380, 381
Nietzsche, Friedrich, 16
nihilism, 373
Nixon, Richard
  commission on violence, 98
  Democratic support for, 56
  drug policy of, 103
  and police force, 107
  and race issues, 50, 100
NLRB (National Labor Relations Board), 289, 338
non-governmental organizations (NGOs), 375, 380, 381
Norris, George, 408
North, Oliver, 209, 211
North America, "Americanist" social development in, 13, 14
North Korea, 252, 357, 368, 402–3
NRA (National Recovery Administration), 441 n. 4
nuclear disarmament campaigns, 227–28, 376–77

nuclear program, U.S., 57, 62, 64, 68, 180, 413 n. 18
Nuremberg trails, 376, 405

Obama administration, 2, 105, 404
Occupied Territories, 382
omnicapable corporations, 25–28
O'Neill, Tip, 238
opportunity, equality of, 171–72
organizational understanding of changing membership, 227–29, 441 n. 16
Orwell, George, 194
outsider status of citizens in liberal democracy, 186–87
outsourcing of production, 358, 362
owner-operated corporations, 293–98

panic during international crises, 400
parasitical employers and jobs, 345–48
Paris, redesigned by Napoleon, 264
parliamentary procedure, 382–83
Parsons, Talcott, 19
participatory democracy, 232–34
party competition and collusion, 199–203
Passanante, Bill, 194, 213
patriarchal structure of power, 36–37
Paulson, Henry, 3
peace movements, 227–29
Peace of Westphalia, 396
peaceful international change, 374–78
Peggy's Law, 227–29, 441 n. 16
PEN, 375
Perkins, Frances, 213, 322, 323
Perlman, Selig, 330
Philippines, U.S. modernization policy in, 369, 370
Philips curve, 80, 82, 342, 343
Pinkerton agency, 256
Pinochet, Augusto, 376
pluralist theory, 54–55
Podhoretz, Norman, 71
Poindexter, John, 209, 211
Poland, authoritarian regime in, 372
police operations board
  and civic obligation, 271–72
  jury panel system for, 267, 270, 272–77
  lay people in, 269, 271–72
  organization of, 261–66
  review board, different from, 270
  selection methods, 272–77
police power
  abuses of, 252–53, 255, 264–65, 279–82, 405–6
  and authoritarian predilection, 106–7
  and black Americans, 96–98, 100

civilian operational control over, 262–63
civilians, alienation from, 255, 257, 259–60
clearance rates, 258, 265
and commissions on violence, 98–99
and crowd control, 263–64
development of in U.S., 253–56
and dissident activity, 278
federal influence over, 78
growth of, 78
and honorable cops, 253, 439 n. 2
illegal behavior, 256–61, 282–83
informants, symbiotic relationship with, 259–61
institutional organization of, 251–52
investigative efforts not expended by, 258
legislative priorities of, 277–79
life and death choices of, 265–66
and media relationship, 258, 264
modern military form of, 255–56
operations board proposed, 261–66
overzealous shooting by, 264–65
police-industrial complex, size and influence of, 107–9
and political dissidence, 251–53
private sector outsourcing of duties, 256
professionalization of, 257–58, 262, 264–66
and race issues, 109, 432 n. 18
reforms proposed, 261–66, 266–71, 283–84
review boards for, 257, 258–59, 262–63
social stability, force for, 180
and social surplus of elites, 126–27
and stability, 177–83
and trade unions, 85
trade unions for police, 273–74
vanguard parties, penetration of, 240
and war on drugs, 102–4
and war on terror, 279–82, 402–3
in Weimar Germany, 106
political institutions, corporations as, 299–302
Political Man (Lipset), 21
political parties
  idealized version hoped for, 234–38
  orthodoxy within, 212–13, 214
political system, weakening of, 388–89
Popper, Karl, 117, 161, 299, 300, 301–2
Portugal, authoritarian regime in, 372
poverty
  capitalism as cause of, 368
  and wealth, relationship between, 15–16, 34–35

power, "raw" and discriminating, 139–40, 166–67
Power Elite, The (Mills), 6, 152
power position shifts of corporate institutions, 176–77
presidential commissions, 97
Price, Cecil, 257
prisons
  and convict employment, 352–55
  filling of, 262–63
  privately run, 256
  violence in, 446 n. 27
private contractors and U.S. military, 27
private firms, government, social and cultural expansion of, 27–28
private property
  changing understanding of, 341
  corporations, reclaiming from, 306–7
  corporations' confiscation of, 300–302
  ownership, 125–30
  social nature of, 302
privatization, 78
product diversification, 25–26
production, outsourcing on, 358, 362
productivity, rate of, 343–45
Progressive Labor Party, 74
progressives and corporations, 289–92
property. *See* private property
proposition logic, 430 n. 2
public moods, blame for, 190–91
public public versus private public, 187–91
public representatives on corporate boards, 310–11
Pullman, George, 293

race. *See also* black Americans
  and class, 43
  crisis in the Sixties, 392–93
  effect on education, 335
  elite class neglect of, 106
  and police power, 109, 432 n. 18
  policies, failures of, 389–93
Rainbow Coalition, 235
rape, 258, 412
Rauh, Joseph, 449 n. 5
"raw" power in corporations, 139–40
Reagan administration, 79, 84, 103, 206, 208–9
recidivism rates, 354
Red Crescent, 375
Red Cross, 375
regional workers' representation, 336–38
regulation
  firm's control over, 28–29
  in support of elite, 85–86

religious organizations
  and democratic participation, 433 n. 21
  humanitarian work of, 375
  potential influence of, 381–82
  and secular authority, 396
religious political influence, 426 n. 27, 428 n. 42, 433 n. 21
religious social influence, 179–80
religious-institutional elite, 127
representation issues in unions, 320–25
representative government, 119–20, 191–92, 389, 393–95
republic institutions, empire as threat to, 413–15
Republican Party
  antidemocratic tendencies of, 208–12
  and war on terror, 282
revolutionary posturing during the Sixties, 53–54
Revolutions of 1848, 15–16, 82, 207
reward system, inequality of, 171–72
right to work, 329–41
rights of management, 320–21, 325–29, 330
Riis, Jacob, 146
Robert's Rules of Order, 229
Robespierre, Maximilien, 16
Rockefeller, Abby Aldrich, 432 n. 10
Rockefeller, John, 297
Rockefeller, John D., Jr., 118, 140, 293
Rockefeller, Nelson, 102
Roman Catholic hierarchy in U.S., 433 n. 21
Romania, authoritarian regime in, 372
Roosevelt, Eleanor, 432 n. 10
Roosevelt, Elliott, 56
Roosevelt, Franklin, 176–77, 190, 289
Roosevelt, Theodore, 210, 211, 289
Root, Elihu, 211
Rustin, Bayard, 63

Sanctuary movement, 375
Sanger, Margaret, 16
Sassoon, Donald, 361
Saudi royals, 369
Savimbi, Jonas, 370
savings and loan looting, 176
Scalia, Antonin, 449 n. 14
Scandinavian governments, 375–76
SCBG (Statute on Criminal Behavior by Governments), 411–12
Schiller, Friedrich, 17, 18
school-trained managers, 22–23, 33
Schwerner, Mickey, 257, 423 n. 20, 439 n. 4
SDS (Students for a Democratic Society), 51–52, 62, 71

Sears, Roebuck, 31
secret government, 209, 211
Securities and Exchange Commission (SEC), 29, 187, 289–90
securities managers, 298
security, international and national, 188
Selective Service System, 71
self-defense, right to, 399–400
semifabricated society
  democracy support attempted in, 226–27
  stability forces in, 181
semiskilled workers, 322
Sen, Amartya, 375
Senate. *See* United States Senate
Senior, Nassau W., 341–42, 344
Settlement House movement, 16, 419 n. 23
SFTA. *See* Staff for the Advance
Sharpeville Massacre, 58
Shaw, George Bernard, 19
Sixties
  criticism of, 65–68, 423 n. 24
  cultural environment of, 62–65
  extraparliamentary activism during the Sixties, 53–57
  failure of, 73–75
  generational interpretation, 60–62
  historical misunderstanding of, 50–57, 60–65
  historical significance of, 58–60
  inflation blamed on, 57
  Intersection, resistance to, 69–73
  issues during, 65–69
  racial crisis during, 390–93
  worldwide dissidence during, 58–60
skilled workers, 22–23
slave societies, 128, 129–30
Sloan, Alfred P., 225, 297, 315
social breakdown, 79–81
social conflict, fear of, 179
social democratic party, 376
social institutions, corporations as, 299–302
social mobility
  downward movement in, 87–88
  and dynastic power, 35–39
  economic growth, confused with, 88–91
  and race, 87–88, 91–96
  upward versus lateral, 88–90
social relationships versus interpersonal relationships, 159–60, 162–63
social services
  substandard wage producing need for, 345
  work on demand as replacement for, 348
social stratification, 123–24, 169
social structure as dynamic system, 167–71

social surplus, 28–29, 125–30, 302–3
social-democratic movement, 14
socialism
  in Europe, 20–21
  socialist parties, 239
  in United Kingdom, 20
  U.S., lack of influence in, 20
socially potent assets
  clustering of, 123–24
  and elite class, 157–58
  in the Intersection society, 117–18
  in liberal democracy, 186–87
social-organizational influence of corporations, 29–32
social-scale group, 151–54
Sombart, Werner, 19–20
South Africa, 58, 371, 448 n. 18
South African Truth and Reconciliation Commission, 449 n. 13
South Korea, military rule in, 370
"Southern strategy," 100–102
Soviet Union
  in Africa, 370, 397–98
  and cold war with U.S., 63, 190, 376–77, 396, 401
  failure of reform in, 156
Spain
  authoritarian regime in, 372
  legal norms enforced by, 376
  social democratic party in, 376
Sparta, 126, 128
specialization of labor, 33
stability, levels of force for, 177–83
Staff for the Advance (SFTA)
  international presence of, 384–85
  organizational structure of, 241–46
  political differences in membership, 244, 245–46
  politics of, 246–49
staff managers, 33
staff personnel, 240–46
Stalinism, 398–99, 410
Standard Oil Trust, 118, 140
state system
  and constitutional authority, 414
  "divine right" of states, 395–400
  opportunity to reduce power of, 400–403
  as threat to republic institutions, 207–12, 413–15
Statute on Criminal Behavior by Governments (SCBG), 411–12
steel industry, 295
Stevens, Ted, 407
Stevenson, Adlai, 393
Stimson, Henry, 211
Stone, I. F., 63, 422 n. 16, 433 n. 2
Students for a Democratic Society (SDS), 51–52, 62, 71
suburban neighborhoods, idealization of, 104–5
Sudan, assistance for, 375
Summers, Lawrence, 3
superstitions in social stability, 179–80, 225–26
symbolic culture, transnational, 363–66

Taft-Hartley Labor Relations Act, 320, 340
TARP process, 175
tax legislation, industry influence on, 29
Taylor, Charles, 370
technical and technological specialists, 33
technostructure, 294
teenagers as social category, 291
Tennessee Valley Authority (TVA), 441 n. 4
terrorism
  international conflict, response to, 363, 373–74
  Islamic, 403
  potential new sources of, 403
  proposed practices regarding, 382
  war on terror, 279–82, 402–3, 427 n. 31
  Western focus on groups, 357
Thatcher, Margaret, 206
Third International, 17, 18–19
third-party civilians, violence against, 381–82, 410–12
Thirty Years' War, 396
Thompson, Edward, 19
three-party system, resistance to, 199–200, 236–38
Thurmond, Strom, 408
Tibet, 127
Time, Inc., 27
To the Finland Station (Wilson), 15
tobacco industry, 294–95
torture, 410–12
trade associations, 311–13
trade unions
  during cold war, 375
  community/regional representation, 336–39
  in conflict with elite class, 169–71
  and corporate charters, 311–13, 331–32
  craft unions, 322, 329–31
  in Europe, 56
  grievance procedures, 323–24
  and hiring, 344–45

trade unions (*continued*)
  humane international change, support for, 375
  industrial unions, 320–25, 419 n. 15
  legal restrictions of, 338
  managers not permitted in, 133
  and new membership, 325
  outcomes of traditional forms of, 326–27
  for police force, 108, 109, 273–74
  police force response to strikes, 85, 254
  policy assault on, 57, 436 n. 2
  Regan administration conflict with, 84–86
  representation issues, 320–25, 329–31
  and right to work, 329–41
  and rights of management, 325–29
  in Sixties activism, 59
  and two-tier system, 326, 328
  and wages, 82, 341–44
  weakening of, 81
  and wider vocational representation, 332–36
transnational culture, language in, 365
transnational economic parliament, proposal for, 382–84
transnational symbolic culture, 363–66
transportation for workers, 350
Treaties of Westphalia, 396
triadic division of labor, 24, 30–32, 128–37, 172–76, 287–88, 358–59
Truman administration, 190, 289, 389
Trusts, 25, 28
Turner thesis, 20
TVA (Tennessee Valley Authority), 441 n. 4
two-party system, 199–201

UE (United Electrical Workers), 328
ultraconservatives
  mobilization of, 110–11
  political force of, 225–26
  "Southern strategy" for, 100–102, 426 n. 27
  and suburban politics, 104–5
ultranationalist regimes, 372
ultraradical movements, 74, 423 n. 24
unemployment and inflation, 342
union chapels, 20
unions. *See* trade unions
United Electrical Workers (UE), 328
United Kingdom, socialism in, 20, 21
United Nations
  in counter-globalization proposal, 380–81
  defense of less powerful, 379–80
  and international polity, 376
  Security Council, 363
United States
  in Africa, 397–98
  and cold war with Soviet Union, 376–77
  defense of interests, 399
  democratic activism in, 16–17
  foreign policy changes, 78–79, 210
  power, eventual decline of, 401–2
  socialism, lack of influence in, 19–20, 21–23
United States House of Representatives, limited balancing power of, 407
United States Senate
  countering presidential war-making power, 406–7
  membership of, 407–10
  selection reforms proposed, 408–10
Universal Declaration of Human Rights, 381
U.S. Steel, 295

van der Lubbe, Martinus, 435 n. 20
vanguard parties, 238–40
Vatican and post-war Germany, 420 n. 32
Vietnam
  consumption restriction in North, 368
  U.S. supporters in South, 366–67
  Vietnam War, 56, 193, 433 n. 3, 434 n. 5
Vietnam-era activism, 51, 53–54, 59, 255
Viet-Report, 422 n. 14
violence, commissions reports on, 96–100
violence against third-party civilians, 381–82, 410–12
violence in prisons, 446 n. 27
violence in workplace, countering, 445 n. 22
Volcker, Paul, 3
voter distraction, 206–7
voting
  district divisions, 196–97, 199
  ignorance among voters, 203–5
  minority rule by, 195–99
  party collusion affected by, 200–202
  party loyalty of voters, 236
  preference, failure at determining, 194–96

wages
  basic minimum, 319
  establishing living, 341–45
  substandard, 345–48
Wallace, Henry, 190, 235
Walrasian markets, 143–44
war, panic leading to support of, 208
war crime tribunals, 376, 410–13
war on drugs, 102–5, 446 n. 28

War on Poverty, 97, 99
war on terror, 279–82, 402–3, 427 n. 31
War Powers Act, 406
Ward, Lester, 17
war-making power
    Congressional sanctions, 406
    limiting through constitutional law, 403–6
    opportunity to reduce, 400–403
    of president, 399, 403–6
    and public panic, 400
WDF (World Democratic Forum), 380–81, 384, 410
wealth
    creation of, 290–91
    dynastic organization of, 35–39, 172–73
    elite restoration of in economic crisis, 2–3
    and poverty, relationship between, 15–16, 34–35
Weatherpeople, 74
Weberian theory of class, 141, 144–45, 166, 170–71
WEF (World Economic Forum), 380–81
Weill, Kurt, 17
Weinberger, Caspar, 209, 211
welfare, 85, 225
Western Europe
    "Americanist" pattern of social development in, 13, 14
    Left parties in, 56
    post-war restructuring, 45–46
    socialism in, 19–20
whistle-blowers, 296, 313, 411
White Citizens' Councils, 391, 392
Who Will Tell the People? (Greider), 313
Why Is There No Socialism in America? (Sombart), 19–20
Wilson, Edmund, 15
women
    elite class, influence within, 174
    resources in workplace for, 349–50
    in Sixties activism, 51
    and skilled crafts work, 444 n. 11
    in worker history, 18–19
    in workforce, 71, 73, 287
Woodward, C. Vann, 423 n. 24
work as natural right, 341–45
work on demand, 348–50
worker history, 18–19, 59
workers' conditions, 14
working class
    involvement in democracy, 242–43
    migration of, 20
workplace conditions, 14
works councils, 331–32
Works Progress Administration (WPA), 349
World Bank, 357, 375
World Democratic Forum (WDF), 380–81, 384, 410
World Economic Forum, 174, 357, 360, 447 n. 7
World Economic Forum (WEF), 380–81
World Social Forum, 448 n. 19
World Trade Organization (WTO), 357, 360, 379, 380
World War II
    and Americanist victory, 44–46
    and black military personnel, 390
    Britain, assistance to, 189–90
    hiring during, 344
    and international polity emergence, 376
WPA (Works Progress Administration), 349
WTO (World Trade Organization), 357, 360, 379, 380

Yonkers, NY, 236–37
Yugoslavia, authoritarian regime in, 372

Zinn, Howard, 422 n. 16

www.ingramcontent.com/pod-product-compliance
Lightning Source LLC
Chambersburg PA
CBHW020300010526
44108CB00037B/172